T5-CVU-593

QUALITATIVE RESEARCH

QUALITATIVE RESEARCH

VOLUME I

EDITED BY
ALAN BRYMAN
&
ROBERT G. BURGESS

SAGE Publications
London • Thousand Oaks • New Delhi

SAGE Publications Ltd
6 Bonhill Street
London EC2A 4PU

SAGE Publications Inc
2455 Teller Road
Thousand Oaks, California 91320

SAGE Publications India Pvt Ltd
32, M-Block Market
Greater Kailash
New Delhi 110 048

British Library Cataloguing in Publication Data

A catalogue record for this book is available
from the British Library

ISBN 0–7619–6243–3 (set of four volumes)

Library of Congress Cataloging in Publication data has been applied for

Typeset in Berthold Baskerville by The Bardwell Press, Oxford, England
Printed in Great Britain at the Cambridge University Press, Cambridge, England

CONTENTS

VOLUME I

The Research Process

Gaining Research Access

Sampling

Using Informants

VOLUME II

PART TWO
METHODS OF QUALITATIVE RESEARCH

Participant Observation

Interviewing

Focus Groups

Life History and Oral History

Documentary Research

Diaries

Photographs, Films and Video

Conversation and Discourse Analysis

VOLUME III

PART THREE
ANALYSIS AND INTERPRETATION OF QUALITATIVE DATA

Fieldwork Notes and Transcripts

Relationship Between Theory and Data in Qualitative Research

Analytic Strategies

Computers in Qualitative Data Analysis

Narrative Analysis

Semiotics

Postmodernism Meets Ethnography

Writing

Validation Issues

Qualitative Data and Archiving

VOLUME IV

PART FOUR
ISSUES IN QUALITATIVE RESEARCH

Ethical Issues and Values

Issues of Gender and Feminism

Cultural Difference

Qualitative Evaluation Research

Qualitative Research and Policy

Action Research

Practitioner Research

Getting Out

Dissemination

Restudies

APPENDIX OF SOURCES

1. "The Fundamental Concepts of Sociology," *Max Weber*
   Max Weber, *The Theory of Social and Economic Organization* (New York: The Free Press, 1964).

2. "What is Wrong with Social Theory?," *Herbert Blumer*
   American Sociological Review, vol. 19, no. 1, 1954, pp. 3–10.

3. "The Debate about Quantitative and Qualitative Research," *Alan Bryman*
   Alan Bryman, *Quantity and Quality in Social Research* (London: Routledge, 1988).

4. "Deconstructing the Qualitative–Quantitative Divide," *Martyn Hammersley*
   Julia Brannen (ed.) *Mixing Methods: Qualitative and Quantitative Research* (Aldershot: Avebury, 1992).

5. "Attitudes Toward Needle 'Sharing' Among Injection Drug Users: Combining Qualitative and Quantitative Research Methods,"
   Robert G. Carlson, Harvey A. Siegal, Jichuan Wang & Russel S. Falck
   Human Organization, vol. 55, no. 3, 1996, pp. 361–369.

6. "Real Men Don't Collect Soft Data," *Silvia Gherardi & Barry Turner*
   Silvia Gherardi & Barry Turner, *Real Men Don't Collect Soft Data* (Trento: Dipartimento di Politica Sociale, Università di Trento, 1987).

7. "Method Talk," *Jaber F. Gubrium & James A. Holstein*
   Jaber F. Gubrium & James A. Holstein, *The New Language of Qualitative Method* (Oxford: Oxford University Press, 1997),

8. "Building Theories from Case Study Research," *Kathleen M. Eisenhardt*
   Academy of Management Review, vol. 14, 1989, pp. 532–550.

9. "What Can Case Studies Do?," *Jennifer Platt*
   Robert Burgess (ed.), *Studies in Qualitative Methodology*, vol. 1 (Greenwich, CT: JAI Press, 1988).

10. "Case and Situation Analysis," *J. Clyde Mitchell*
    Sociological Review, vol. 31, no. 2, 1983, pp. 186–211.

11. "Library Access, Library Use and User Education in Academic Sixth Forms: An Autobiographical Account," *Lawrence Stenhouse*
    Robert G. Burgess (ed.), *The Research Process in Educational Settings* (London: Falmer Press, 1984).

12. "Scholarship and Sponsored Research: Contradiction, Continuum or Complementary Activity?," *Robert G. Burgess*
    David Halpin & Barry Troyna (eds), *Researching Educational Policy: Ethical and Methodological Issues* (London: Falmer Press, 1994).

42. "Data Logging in Observation: Fieldnotes," *John Lofland & Lyn H. Lofland*
John Lofland & Lyn H. Lofland, *Analyzing Social Settings: A Guide to Qualitative Observation and Analysis* (Belmont, CA: Wadsworth, 1995).

43. "Transcription Quality as an Aspect of Rigor in Qualitative Research," *Blake D. Poland*
Qualitative Inquiry, vol. 1, no. 3, 1995, pp. 290–310.

44. "First Days in the Field," *Blanche Geer*
Phillip E. Hammond (ed.), *Sociologists at Work* (New York: Basic Books, 1964).

45. "What's Wrong with Ethnography? The Myth of Theoretical Description," *Martyn Hammersley*
Sociology, vol. 24, 1990, pp. 597–617.

46. "Grounded Theory Methodology: An Overview," *Anselm Strauss & Juliet Corbin*
Norman K. Denzin & Yvonna Lincoln, eds, *Handbook of Qualitative Research* (Thousand Oaks, CA: Sage, 1994).

47. "Temporality and Identity Loss Due to Alzheimer's Disease," *Celia J. Orona*
Anselm Strauss & Juliet Corbin (eds), *Grounded Theory in Practice* (Thousand Oaks, CA: Sage, 1997).

48. "The Logical Structure of Analytic Induction," *W. S. Robinson*
American Sociological Review, vol. 16, 1951, pp. 812–818.

49. "Symbolic Interactionism: The Fusion of Theory and Research?," *Robin Williams*
David C. Thorns (ed.), *New Directions in Sociology* (Newton Abbott: David & Charles, 1976).

50. "Some Guidelines for the Phenomenological Analysis of Interview Data," *Richard H. Hycner*
Human Studies, vol. 8, 1985, pp. 279–303.

51. "Qualitative Data Analysis: Technologies and Representations," *Amanda Coffey, Beverley Holbrook & Paul Atkinson*
Sociological Research Online, vol. 1, no. 1, <http://www.socresonline.org.uk/socresonline/1/1/4.html>.

52. "NUD*IST in Action: Its Use and its Usefulness in a Study of Chronic Illness in Young People," *K. Buston*
Sociological Research Online, vol. 2, no. 3, <http://www.socresonline.org.uk/socresonline/2/3/6.html>

53. "Sociological and Sociolinguistic Models of Narrative," *Martin Cortazzi*
Martin Cortazzi, *Narrative Analysis* (London: Falmer Press, 1993).

54. "Sounds of Still Voices: Issues in the Use of Narrative Methods with People who have Learning Difficulties," *Tim Booth*
Len Barton (ed.), *Disability and Society: Emerging Issues and Insights* (London: Longman, 1996).

Qualitative Research Methodology – A Review

Alan Bryman & Robert G. Burgess

1. The Nature of Qualitative Research

a) What is Qualitative Research?

Qualitative research is by no means a new strategy or framework for doing social research (Hamilton, 1994; Vidich and Lyman, 1994). None the less, there has been a very considerable growth in the use and popularity of qualitative research since the early 1960s which can easily convey the impression that it is of more recent origin than is in fact the case. Despite the proliferation of writings on qualitative research, defining what it is and what it excludes is no easy matter. There are several reasons for this.

1. The term 'qualitative research' seems to imply any approach which does not entail the collection and analysis of quantitative data. This view is generally regarded as unhelpful, though it does have some currency, largely because for most writers and practitioners it is viewed as being more than the mere absence of quantitative data. This implies that a study which contains little or no qualitative data cannot and should not be regarded as *ipso facto* an example of qualitative research. Gherardi and Turner in Volume I, *Defining Qualitative Research*, are particularly scathing about the suggestion that qualitative research is quantitative research without the quantification.

2. Many writers point to different traditions within the category 'qualitative research' (e.g. Hamilton, 1994; Silverman, 1993), so that there is the risk that the term masks quite substantial differences in approach. The selection from Gubrium and Holstein in Volume I, *Defining Qualitative Research*, represents an attempt to outline some of the more prominent forms of qualitative research.

3. Very often accounts of qualitative research are set up in terms of its difference from, and often opposition to, quantitative research. This strategy is not intrinsically problematic but runs the risk of qualitative research being formulated in terms of what quantitative research is *not*.

Most definitions of qualitative research draw attention to certain features of the approach and these can be taken to draw attention to its core characteristics. These characteristics suggest that qualitative research is a strategy of social research which deploys several methods (often in conjunction in specific studies) and displays a preference for: the interpretation of social phenomena from the point of view of the meanings employed by the people being studied; the deployment of natural rather than artificial settings for the collection of data; and generating rather than testing theory. While not all writers on qualitative research would agree with this definition (e.g. Silverman, 1993), it reflects a widespread view of the approach, such as that offered by the editors of the *Handbook of Qualitative Research* (Denzin and Lincoln, 1994: 2).

b) A Brief History

The early history of qualitative research is diffuse. Its origins can be discerned in the research of social anthropologists who undertook detailed observational studies of non-industrialised settings and in the work of the Chicago School. The Chicago researchers became renowned for their detailed and largely qualitative studies of urban life as revealed through studies of regions of the city and of specific social settings and groups (such as gangs and skid row inhabitants). While the amount of quantitative research at Chicago should not be underestimated (Bulmer, 1984) and the degree to which many of the qualitative studies coming out of Chicago conform to the characteristics of what qualitative research is taken to mean nowadays has been questioned (Platt, 1983, 1996), there can be little doubt that most writers view the Chicago School as a major wellspring for modern qualitative research. Platt (1996) provides a formidable critique of the notion that the Chicago School was a hotbed of qualitative research, referring to this as one of a number of 'origin myths' that she has uncovered in the history of social research methods. However, the fact that the Chicago School is frequently *believed* to have had an important role in the origins of qualitative research is just as significant in this context as whether it was or was not influential.

Also significant in the history of qualitative research is the presence of notable 'exemplars' which relied either exclusively or significantly on the use of the various qualitative methods examined in section 3. Examples of such notable output are studies like the Middletown books by Lynd and Lynd (1929, 1937), which entailed the intensive study of a small American community, and Whyte's *Street Corner Society* (Whyte, 1993 [1944]), which involved a similarly intensive examination of the lives of young men in an Italian-American community in Boston.

After the second world war, the use of qualitative methods declined as the social survey became increasingly prominent in sociology. This development was reflected in many research methods textbooks in the USA and the UK which were written to cater for the growing student body and for prospective researchers. Qualitative methods like participant observation were depicted as 'fringe' methods which resulted in 'quaint but quirky' data. This is not to say that qualitative research went into abeyance: several notable researchers and writers on method, such as Herbert Blumer, Anselm Strauss, and Everett Hughes, employed and developed this approach in their own studies and in work with their postgraduate students.

Around the early 1960s, this picture of decline began to change and the use of qualitative research gathered pace. Not only did a growing number of researchers employ qualitative methods, but also more and more textbooks designed more or less exclusively as introductions to the approach emerged. It is not easy to identify definitive causes of the change of receptiveness, but the following factors may have been influential:

1. The emergence of a certain amount of disillusionment with the output of quantitative research and in particular with its ability to deliver an authoritative account of the social world. This concern was bound up with the pretensions of much quantitative research to adopt the characteristics of the natural sciences and in particular with the positivist assumptions that were seen as characteristic of it.
2. There was also a growing awareness of alternative epistemological viewpoints about how social reality should be studied. These alternatives offered the prospect of a different basis for conducting social research from the one offered by the natural sciences. The growing awareness and use of phenomenological ideas was especially significant in this context, as can be seen in the work of writers like Cicourel (1964).
3. The emergence of strident critiques of the output of quantitative research by writers like Blumer (1956), Cicourel (1964), Phillips (1973), and Willer and Willer (1973). These critiques drew attention to various limitations of research methods like social survey techniques while in many cases drawing attention to the fact that social meanings are constructed and transmitted; an area that quantitative research has typically failed to capture adequately.
4. The emergence of key methodological texts, such as Glaser and Strauss's (1967) explication of grounded theory, which provided the prospect of a viable methodological framework for the process of qualitative research and the analysis of data.

c) Philosophical Issues

Many qualitative researchers have railed against the imposition of a natural science approach on the study of society, as seen in the widespread use of social surveys in sociology and of experimental studies in social psychology (e.g. Filmer et al., 1971; the selection by Blumer in Volume I, *Philosophical Issues*). Such research was seen as excessively imbued with the view of positivists that the principles of the natural sciences have a universal applicability. The two selections in Volume I, *Philosophical Issues*, provide illustrations of prominent anti-positivist streams of thought. Max Weber's notion of *Verstehen* implies the need to take account of people's subjective interpretations in the understanding of social behaviour. The selection by Herbert Blumer, which draws on the sociological perspective known as symbolic interactionism, similarly draws attention to the significance of 'the natural social world of our experience', but goes further in using his reflections as a springboard for making a case for naturalistic research that has been favoured by qualitative researchers. The connections between qualitative research and symbolic interactionism can also be discerned in the selection by Rock in Volume II, *Participant Observation*, which shows the strong affinity between participant observation and symbolic interactionism. The writings of Alfred Schutz (e.g. 1962), which were influenced by both Weber and phenomenology but were not well known until their translation into English in the 1960s, similarly emphasised the importance of developing an interpretative understanding of the social world. In a famous passage that represents both a critique of the application of a natural science approach to social life and a statement about the importance of a focus on individual meaning, he wrote:

> The world of nature as explored by the natural scientist does not 'mean' anything to molecules, atoms and electrons. But the observational field of the social scientist – social reality – has a specific meaning and relevance structure for the beings living, acting, and thinking within it....The thought objects constructed by the social scientist, in order to grasp this social reality, have to be founded upon the thought objects constructed by the common-sense thinking of men, living their daily life within the social world. (Schutz, 1962: 59)

This emphasis on the construction of social meanings can be readily discerned in the selections by Weber and Blumer and also in many of the other selections in the four volumes.

d) The Contrast with Quantitative Research

Implicit in our discussion is that a great deal of what is written about qualitative research entails a contrast with quantitative research. This is the main thrust of the selections by Bryman and Hammersley in Volume I, *Relationships Between Quantitative and Qualitative Research*. Hammersley identifies rather more general points of difference between the two, though both writers identify two common distinguishing features: the tendency for theory to come prior to data collection in quantitative research (deductive) and to be an emergent property of qualitative research (inductive); and the tendency for quantitative researchers to seek generalisable findings (scientific laws) and for qualitative researchers to emphasise contextual understanding, which Hammersley refers to as 'identifying cultural patterns'. However, Hammersley is highly critical of some of the differentiating features, arguing that the polarities are misleading. For example, in relation to the deductive/inductive pairing, he observes that quantitative research does not always involve hypothesis-testing which is conventionally supposed to be typical of a deductive approach, while some qualitative researchers advocate or employ a theory-impregnated approach to data collection.

It is not surprising, therefore, that some writers have described the quantitative-qualitative contrast as 'false' or as no longer having much credibility (e.g. Layder, 1993). To a certain extent, this view represents a drift in recent years towards a *rapprochement* between the two approaches. It also reflects a tendency to conceive of the distinction between quantitative and qualitative research in terms of complementarity rather than opposition (Oakley, 1998). One way in which this *rapprochement* manifests itself is in actual research practice, whereby increasingly researchers are prepared or indeed prefer to employ both approaches within the context of a single research study. There are many ways in which such a mixed methodology approach can occur. Hammersley (1996) identifies three forms: methodological triangulation (employing one to verify or validate the findings of the other); facilitation (where one is used as groundwork for the other); and complementarity (whereby they are used together to explore different aspects of a research question). Bryman (1988, chapter 6) identifies several different forms of the complementarity. The study in Volume I, *Relationships Between Quantitative and Qualitative Research*, by Carlson et al. is primarily an exercise in triangulation in that the authors present both qualitative and quantitative evidence concerning needle sharing among injection drug users in order to determine how far the two sets of data are compatible. There is also an element of facilitation because the authors' questionnaire items that formed the basis for the quantitative research strategy were derived from their qualitative evidence. However, as Deacon et al. (1998) argue, triangulation can be planned or unplanned. The needle users study is a case of planned triangulation, but even when quantitative and qualitative research are combined as complementary approaches, the researcher may well find that he or she is able to compare the two sets of findings in order to see how far they are consistent.

2. Designing Qualitative Research

a) The Case for the Case Study

The case study represents one of the most common frameworks or research designs for the conduct of qualitative research. This is not to suggest, however, that the two should be regarded as more or less synonymous. Many field experiments and studies based on social survey evidence collected in just one or two schools or firms or regions are in fact examples of quantitative research based on a case study research design (Platt, 1992). As a category of research design, the case study is difficult to specify with much accuracy and writers vary quite considerably in what they mean by the term. For example, some writers view cases as existing bounded units which are available for selection by the researcher; others see it as a theoretical construct whose status as a distinctive case is fashioned in the course of doing research (Ragin, 1992).

Over the years, the case study has been controversial. The bulk of the controversy surrounding it has been concerned with the question of generalisation: how can the study of a single case (or even two or three cases) be representative of other cases so that it is possible to generalise findings to those other cases? The answer, of course, is that it cannot. What the case study can provide is the opportunity to develop rich contextual data from which *generalisation to theory* becomes possible. This is one of the chief messages of the article in Volume I, *Research Design*, by Mitchell in which he argues that it is 'the cogency of the theoretical reasoning' that is the crucial feature of a case study, not the ability to generalise to a wider universe of cases. Following the findings deriving from a study, researchers may wish to examine further the cogency of the theoretical reasoning or to extend the case's theoretical ramifications, a process which Yin (1984) has dubbed a *replication logic*. Case studies are also preferred by many qualitative researchers because they can be used to provide in-depth insight into social processes.

The article in Volume I, *Research Design*, by Eisenhardt extends the kind of arguments proffered by Mitchell and Yin by outlining a framework for the generation of theory from case study evidence. Her framework draws heavily on grounded theory, an approach to the analysis of qualitative data discussed in section 4 (c) and in two of the selections in Volume III, *Relationship Between Theory and Data in Qualitative Research*. It is striking that many of the examples Eisenhardt cites from the empirical literature are in fact multiple-case studies. This raises further issues about what constitutes case study research. Platt's article in Volume I, *Research Design*, pays particular attention to the issue of how a case or cases should be selected. She argues that one reason for the limited utility of many case studies is that the grounds on which cases were selected is unclear, resulting in a lack of clarity about the significance of the case studies. She outlines several criteria on which cases can be selected in order to overcome these difficulties.

It should also be borne in mind that not all qualitative research is based on the case study, though it is probably true to say that most research deriving from participant observation and the life history method are based on it. However, when qualitative interviewing is the main research method, the investigation is not necessarily characterised by a case study approach.

b) Problems of Access

When qualitative research is being conducted in connection with a case which is relatively closed to outsiders, access to the setting has to be secured. While Platt (in Volume I, *Research Design*) is undeniably right in drawing attention to the importance and desirability of specifying the criteria on which a case is chosen, gaining access to many settings is fraught with difficulty. Access to closed settings like factories, schools and the police are invariably preceded by protracted negotiations with gatekeepers. This is hardly surprising as the qualitative researcher is likely to be (from the organisation's point of view) an irritant who will take up valuable time and who may even reveal to the outside world aspects of the organisation that it would prefer to keep under wraps. As a result, refusal is likely to be a fairly common experience, so that it may be difficult to conform to Platt's insistence upon clear criteria for case selection. Stenhouse in Volume I, *The Research Process*, demonstrates the way in which multi-site case study is sponsored, designed and conducted in this instance in relation to libraries and sixth form study.

Gaining access can also be problematic in what appear to be open settings, like communities or informal groups, which do not have formal boundaries in the way in which organisations invariably do. Whyte revealed this difficulty in his classic case study *Street Corner Society* when trying to make contacts during his early days in the field in Boston's North End. The following incident occurred in a hotel bar:

> I looked around me again and now noticed a threesome: one man and two women. It occurred to me that here was a maldistribution of females which I might be able to rectify. I approached the group and opened with something like this: "Pardon me. Would you mind if I join you?" There was a moment of silence while the man stared at me. He then offered to throw me downstairs. I assured him that this would not be necessary and demonstrated as much by walking right out of there without any assistance. (Whyte, 1993: 289)

Although Whyte's near escape occurred in an open setting, there is an implication for research in relatively closed settings: even when fieldworkers gain access to relatively closed settings, the issue of access does not stop there because they invariably need access to people. The researcher may be given a *carte blanche* by senior managers or by a headteacher, but such gatekeepers cannot compel others to co-operate fully. Van Maanen's account in Volume I, *Gaining Research Access*, of field relationships in his ethnographic research on the US police points to the ongoing access problems that are likely to beset the researcher. He shows how he had to pass a number of informal tests in order to gain and maintain a modicum of acceptability and probity among the officers he was observing. The selection by Roy in Volume I, *Gaining*

Research Access, demonstrates the role of good fortune and sheer tenacity in gaining access to many organisations. His work also demonstrates that access is an ongoing process, as the researcher is continuously seeking entry to new situations once access has been negotiated and accomplished.

c) Issues of Sampling and Selection

A further aspect of ongoing field relationships is exactly whom to observe and/ or interview. This issue, of course, is to do with sampling, a term that has tended to be associated over the years with the social survey rather than participant observation or informant interviewing. Indeed, the criteria for selecting a sample in survey research are statistical ones – that is, they are based upon well-established and formal statistical grounds for selecting people, documents, organisations or whatever from the population. This approach to sampling and selection is not usually employed by qualitative researchers who typically argue that such criteria are inappropriate (for an example of an exception see, Lupton and Noble, 1997). One of the most systematic approaches to sampling put forward in relation to qualitative research is the notion of *theoretical sampling*. This term was first formulated by Glaser and Strauss (1967) in connection with their account of grounded theory (see 4 (c) below and the selections by Strauss and Corbin and by Orona in Volume III, *Relationship Between Theory and Data in Qualitative Research*). Theoretical sampling is an approach to selecting people which places a priority on theoretical grounds for their inclusion rather than statistical ones. Thus, rather than specifying in advance that a researcher needs to interview or observe *n* people in order to meet the objectives of the research, which is essentially the strategy found in statistical sampling, with theoretical sampling the researcher will interview or observe only enough people for a certain issue or question to be thoroughly investigated and will then move on to a related issue. This process is outlined by Finch and Mason in Volume I, *Sampling*, in connection with their research into family obligations. Also in Volume I, *Sampling*, is a selection by Schatzman and Strauss which outlines a strategy for sampling in qualitative research which draws upon similar ideas to those developed under the grounded theory umbrella. Their distinction between sampling people and sampling events is an important one to bear in mind in the context of qualitative research since the in-depth understanding that is an ingredient of a case study is likely to entail observation in relation to a wide variety of situations as well as observing and interviewing a range of people.

3. Methods of Qualitative Data Collection

Over the years, qualitative research has been associated with many methods of data collection. Participant observation has often been regarded as the quintessential method associated with the collection of qualitative data (e.g. Becker and Geer, 1957). Gradually, the portfolio of research methods available to the qualitative researcher has expanded considerably. The discussion that follows and the selections in Volume II seek to capture the major methods.

a) Participant Observation

Participant observation is generally described as a research method in which a researcher immerses him- or herself in a social context with the aim of uncovering through an empathetic understanding the meaning systems of participants in that social context and hence to see the world from their point of view. It has been the primary method in such classic sociological investigations as Gans (1958), Liebow (1967), and Whyte (1993 [1943]) and in many of the classic studies in social anthropology, including Malinowski (1922) and Mead (1928).

As a research method, participant observation is difficult to define. Three factors are relevant to the method's elusiveness. Firstly, the meaning of the term has changed somewhat over the years. The account of the method offered at the start of this section is very much a modern conception of what it entails. Platt (1983) has shown that in its early years the term betokened a somewhat different set of procedures and meanings. For example, one of the earliest uses of the term was meant to denote 'a natural insider recruited by the investigator as an informant, not the investigator himself' (Platt, 1983 : 386). Secondly, the term is rather ambiguous: the participant observer is rarely 'just' an observer, if we mean by this watching and listening in the social situations in which the researcher is located. Participant observers invariably also interview people, particularly key informants, and examine documents.

Even if we follow the account of participant observation at the start of this section, the practices associated with the method vary widely in two senses. Firstly, participant observers vary widely in terms of such features as their closeness to the people they are studying and the setting itself: they vary from complete immersion at one end of the spectrum in which the observer becomes almost indistinguishable from the subjects of the research, to instances in which the observer is more distant — much more of an observer than a participant. The selections by Roy in Volume I, *Gaining Research Access*, and by Gans in Volume II, *Participant Observation*, bring out some of the ways in which participant observers can vary in terms of the nature of their relationships within the field. Secondly, they vary in their reliance on participant observation as such, in that some participant observers will place a greater emphasis on, for example, interviewing informants, than on watching and listening.

Participant observation may appear to be a method which lacks a sense of structure or perhaps more specifically of guidelines. How after all does one start and finish something as open-ended as entering the social lives of a group of people in order to grasp their culture? A classic article by Becker in Volume II, *Participant Observation*, provides an early attempt to provide some guidelines. However, Becker's approach might be viewed as too inclined to impose a structure on participant observation and some researchers would prefer to retain a greater openness. Such a preference can be discerned in the selection by Rock in Volume II, *Participant Observation*, which, in addition to outlining the nature of participant observation and its links with symbolic interactionism, notes that understanding 'cannot be engendered by fixed schemes and carefully manufactured hypotheses'.

b) Interviewing

The interview is one of the most intensively used methods of data collection in the social sciences and is heavily used in other familiar kinds of investigation, including opinion polls and market research. However, the style of interview that is employed in most qualitative research is different from the kind of interviewing that usually takes place in quantitative research. The key difference revolves around the fact that qualitative researchers rarely employ the kind of structured or standardised interview approach that is typical of quantitative research. Qualitative researchers have typically been very critical of this style of interviewing, viewing it as too structured to provide access to interviewees' meanings and hence to the way in which they apprehend their social world (Mishler, 1986).

However, there is considerable variation in the ways in which qualitative researchers conduct interviews. There is no typical approach to interviewing in qualitative research. At one extreme is the more or less totally unstructured interview, which has the appearance of a lengthy conversation with few prompts on the part of the researcher. The selection by Paget in Volume II, *Interviewing*, reflects this kind of orientation to the interview. It reflects the author's quest 'to explore in-depth interviewing as a science of subjective experience'. At the other extreme is qualitative interviewing in which each respondent is asked the same series of questions, but they are given considerable latitude in how they answer and in the sequence of asking questions. This kind of 'semi-structured' interview is one of the most common approaches to interviewing in qualitative research. The selection by Finch in Volume II, *Interviewing*, is close to this end of the spectrum. Finch also raises broader issues about the nature of interviewing, in particular about the potential for exploitation of the informant interviewee. This ethical sensitivity has been especially evident in the work of feminist social scientists in connection with their interviewing practices in relation to other women (e.g. Oakley, 1981; Ribbens, 1989). This theme can also be discerned in the selections in Volume IV, *Issues of Gender and Feminism*. The other selection in Volume II, *Interviewing*, is an account by Holstein and Gubrium of what they term 'active interviewing'. Like most other forms of interviewing in qualitative research, this style is concerned with uncovering interviewees' meanings, but the authors place a further emphasis on the way in which the meanings that are extracted are part of an active joint collaboration between interviewers and respondents.

c) Focus Groups and Group Interviewing

The focus group is a kind of group interview in the sense that several people have their views elicited by what is variously called an interviewer, moderator or facilitator. However, a distinction is sometimes forged between a focus group and a group interview in that in the former the session usually revolves around a very specific core issue and emphasises and capitalises upon interaction within the group to a greater degree than in the group interview. In the case of the selection by Kitzinger in Volume II, *Focus Groups*, the core issue is the ways in which group members process media accounts of AIDS and how they construct their own meanings of AIDS. Kitzinger's article is particularly concerned with the ways in which meanings are jointly produced through interaction and conversation in the course of the focus group sessions.

Since the publication of a short text on focus group research written specifically for qualitative researchers in the social sciences (Morgan, 1988), the method has grown in popularity. This is not to say that it is new as it has been used intensively in such fields as market research for many years. The selection by Merton in Volume II, *Focus Groups*, is of considerable historical interest in this context. It acts as a useful bridge with the previous section because the idea of a focus group grew to a very large extent out of Merton's research using what he called the 'focused interview', which has many of the characteristics of a semi-structured interview but where 'the persons interviewed are known to have been involved in a particular situation' (Merton, Fiske and Kendall, 1956: 3). Merton's investigations with this technique were gradually extended from interviews with individuals to groups. It is not surprising, therefore, that he is frequently credited with being the inventor of focus groups, a view which, as the article in Volume II, *Focus Groups*, makes clear, he is keen to disavow. It is clear from what Merton writes that he is concerned about the growing proliferation of the focus group method and in particular about the way in which it has been severed from quantitative research, because in his own work the two were linked very strongly.

d) Life History and Oral History

Much qualitative research focuses on the observed present and relies upon data derived from first hand accounts by researchers or their informants who are most often engaged in interviews. Such work focuses on contemporary events and neglects the historical dimension of the situations, events and people that are studied. Yet these deficiencies may be overcome through the collection of historical materials and by the conduct of interviews that focus on the biography and life course of the individual.

As Liz Stanley indicates in Volume II, *Life History and Oral History*, there is much interest in life history, oral history, biography and autobiography as forms of data. Here, Stanley demonstrates that the approaches taken bring together issues about biography, autobiography, and reflection as well as feminist debates that are taken up elsewhere (see sections Volume I, *The Research Process* and Volume IV, *Cultural Difference*). Life history materials bring together written and oral evidence – the classic study in sociology being Thomas and Znaniecki's account of Wladek in *The Polish Peasant in Europe and America* (1918–20). A further classic study is drawn from the Chicago School of Sociology through the publication of Clifford Shaw's *The Jack Roller* (Shaw, 1930). Such studies draw on informant interviews and also on letters, diaries, newspaper accounts and so on (see Volume II, *Documentary Research* and Volume II, *Diaries*).

While these accounts provide numerous sociological insights and understandings about subjective views of institutions they also raise questions about reliability, validity, representativeness and accuracy (see Grele, Volume II, *Life History and Oral History*). Similar issues have also been raised about the use of oral evidence, especially when compared with written evidence. Nevertheless, Paul Thompson (1978) argues that oral history interviews can provide unique insights into historical circumstances that would otherwise not be possible if the researcher relied on written evidence. Oral history provides access to everyday life, to social relationships of people in the past who did not rely on a written tradition. It brings forward a different perspective of the past (Ewart Evans, 1970, Chamberlain, 1975). The focus is often on the autobiographical which raises the question as to whether such accounts are no more than auto/biography (see Bornat, Volume II, *Life History and Oral History*). Yet many oral histories rely on much more than oral evidence and are carefully constructed using a range of documentary materials that are employed in qualitative research.

e) Documentary Research

The institutions, events and people that are studied by qualitative researchers utilise a variety of written documents. The range of material is vast and as Plummer (1983) indicates includes letters, newspaper articles, diaries, memoirs and so on. But how might these be classified? Various distinctions have been drawn by social researchers, including primary sources; that is, material produced first hand by the people studied which consists of: minutes, contracts, memoranda, autobiographies and reports. Alongside these documents are secondary sources that provide commentaries or summaries of original sources. A further distinction that has been suggested by Denzin (1970) is between public and private documents, with the former including newspaper articles and records held by schools, hospitals, factories and so on, while the latter includes letters and diaries. Cross-cutting this classification is Scott's analysis of authorship that may be personal or public and which indicates the purpose of the document (Scott, 1990). In turn, he classifies access to documents as closed, restricted, open-archival and open-published.

But what are the criteria used to evaluate written documents? A checklist established for use in history, anthropology and sociology by Gottschalk et al. (1945) focuses on the accuracy of documents when they ask:

(1) Was the ultimate source of the detail (the primary witness) able to tell the truth?
(2) Was the primary witness willing to tell the truth?
(3) Is the primary witness accurately reported with regard to the detail under examination?
(4) Is there any external corroboration of the details under examination?
(Gottschalk et al., 1945, p 35).

These are some of the key questions that can be used to evaluate documentary evidence that are focused on by Platt in Volume II, *Documentary Research*, in terms of authenticity, selection, sampling and presentation issues. In a recent text, Denscombe (1998) suggests a series of questions that researchers need to use on authenticity (is it the genuine article rather than a fake or a forgery?); credibility (is it accurate?); representativeness (is the document typical and does it represent a typical instance of what it portrays?); meanings (what is said and unsaid?). As such these suggestions direct the researcher towards strategies and styles that can be used to analyse documentary material. Altheide in Volume II, *Documentary Research*, discusses qualitative media analysis. He sees this approach as one that involves asking relatively open-ended questions about texts and in which theoretical categories emerge out of the data. The analyst's role is one of continually reflecting on the emerging categories and their links with the data. This general approach stands in quite considerable contrast to traditional content analysis which adopts a quantitative approach. For example, in traditional, quantitative content analysis theoretical categories are specified in advance by the investigator who searches for their incidence in a set of documents. Qualitative content analysis, by contrast, entails a continuous back and forth movement between concepts and data.

However, it is always essential for qualitative researchers to bear in mind that the data available for analysis are only as good as the data that are recorded.

f) Diaries

The diary takes many forms in social research. First, it is used by the researcher as a means of recording data. Second, it can be a source of material that constitutes research evidence. In Volume II, *Diaries*, examples are given of both uses of a diary: that is, the researcher's diary and the informant's diary. In addition, much use has been made of diaries by practitioners engaged in reflective practice when researching their own work place (see Volume IV, *Dissemination*, in which Griffiths provides his account as a teacher–researcher).

In many accounts a distinction is drawn between logs, diaries and journals as follows:

— The log is a record of information on a particular social situation. It is an *aide mémoire.*
— The diary is a less structured document that contains a record of the experiences of the writer.
— The journal is structured, descriptive and contains objective notes.

While these distinctions may be analytically useful, Burgess (1994a) has argued that 'diaries' contain all these elements of writing: a log of activities and decisions; a free-flowing account; and a record of a situation or event in which the researcher has been involved. The diary is, therefore, a further example of a personal document that can be used to record data or as a source of data on which the researcher can draw.

g) Photographs, Films and Video

Any list of documentary sources in the contemporary world would be deficient if it did not include photographs, films and videos. These materials constitute essential evidence for the social researcher. Rather like the diary, these materials can constitute research evidence as well as being part of the researcher's repertoire of approaches to social investigation. Furthermore, they are used alongside other methods of social investigation. In Volume II, *Photographs, Films and Video*, Rob Walker highlights the ways in which the still photograph can be used as a research tool to generate discussion with informants in the course of a research or evaluation study. In these circumstances, the visual image can be used to stimulate a description of a situation or event. However, the image is static. It is taken from a particular perspective and involves selection in space and time.

One area of debate in the literature on visual representation has been between the use of still photography and film. Hastrup (1992) argues that the photograph is limiting as it offers one fixed perspective, while film allows the picture to move rather than the audience. However, there is little agreement on the use of photographs and films as Pinney (1992) argues that photographs offer too many opportunities to interpret and construct meanings rather than too few.

The debate, which in part shadows those debates on the merits and demerits of participant observation as an approach to research, will continue. However, many authors are able to offer some insights available from film making in ethnographic research (see Henley in Volume II, *Photographs, Films and Video*). No matter what form the debate takes about selection, sampling and editing material, it demonstrates the potential of visual material in the study of anthropology and sociology. Indeed, Macfarlane (1992) shows the potential of the videodisc to blend together photographs, film sequences and text. Certainly this source of data has huge potential to record social behaviour in a way that overcomes the deficiencies associated with the fieldworker's notebook and pencil (Hockings 1975). In this respect, the technology associated with photographs, film and video is an important addition to the research repertoire of the qualitative researcher.

h) Conversation and Discourse Analysis

One significant development in qualitative research has been the rise of language as a focus of social inquiry. This trend has taken a number of different forms of which two stand out as especially noteworthy and which are represented in Volume II, *Conversation and Discourse Analysis*. One is conversation analysis, an approach to the analysis of language use that has its roots in ethnomethodology that was developed in the 1960s by Harold Garfinkel (1967). This strand of qualitative research is mentioned as one of four different varieties of qualitative research outlined by Gubrium and Holstein in the selection in Volume I, *Defining Qualitative Research*. As these authors observe, 'the ethnomethodologist listens to naturally occurring conversation in order to discover how a sense of social order is created through talk and interaction'. Not all researchers who describe themselves as ethnomethodologists would describe their work in this way, although conversation analysis has been one of the most significant developments in ethnomethodology.

The late Harvey Sacks, a student of Garfinkel's, is usually credited with being the originator of conversation analysis and one of his programmatic statements can be found in Volume II, *Conversation and Discourse Analysis*. The selection by Silverman in the same section represents a useful summary of the main components of conversation analysis. It can be seen from these two selections that conversation analysis entails the recording of conversation, which is then transcribed and submitted to a detailed microscopic examination. In this way, apparently taken-for-granted features of everyday conversation such as pauses and the taking of turns in conversations become objects for detailed scrutiny in their own right.

Conversation is also an object of inquiry for practitioners of discourse analysis, who share with conversation analysts a concern for the ways in which social reality is constructed out of language use. Discourse analysts also examine language use in texts as well as in conversation, although the selection by Potter in Volume II, *Conversation and Discourse Analysis*, emphasises the use that can be made of discourse analysis in the study of naturally occurring talk. In fact, there is no single discourse analysis approach in that the term is employed to describe a number of different ways of analysing language (Potter identifies four forms). As Potter makes clear, his account of discourse analysis is one that is rooted in sociology and communication studies. Unlike the other forms of discourse analysis, the approach Potter espouses emphasises the significance of language for the ways in which an understanding of events, social categories and so on are constituted in and through discourse.

4. Analysis and Interpretation of Qualitative Data

a) The Nature of Qualitative Data

Qualitative data can take many different forms, but the main types are field notes, transcripts and texts. Field notes are likely to be the product of a participant observer's record in the field of what he or she sees and hears. The selection by Lofland and Lofland in Volume III, *Fieldwork Notes and Transcripts*, provides an outline of the different types of field notes, the various contexts in which they are likely to arise and some of the difficulties that might be encountered in their production. Transcripts are likely to be the outcome of transcriptions of recorded interviews (including focus groups) or of recorded natural conversations. Texts can come in a variety of forms, including historical materials and organisational records.

The selection by Geer in Volume III, *Fieldwork Notes and Transcripts*, provides a very helpful inside account of what field notes, especially in the initial stages of a qualitative investigation, are like. The fieldwork that she discusses formed the basis for a classic ethnographic study of student life, *Making the Grade* (Becker, Geer and Hughes, 1968), which was heavily influenced by a symbolic interactionist perspective. Geer's account usefully reveals the ways in which the participant observer is not a passive recorder of what is going on but is continually responding to what is heard and observed and is formulating ideas which are meant to assist in the interpretation of what is going on. She also shows that even the early days in the field exert considerable influence over the subsequent progress of research.

In view of the importance of transcripts to interviewing in qualitative research and to such approaches as conversation and discourse analysis, it is surprising that to a very large extent the quality of a transcript has been regarded as almost unproblematic. The article by Poland in Volume III, *Fieldwork Notes and Transcripts*, outlines some of the errors that can occur during transcription and some steps to enhance the quality of transcripts. While his discussion and advice are primarily directed at interview transcripts, there are clearly implications for conversation and discourse analysis as well.

b) Theory and Qualitative Data

One of the most frequently cited contrasts between quantitative and qualitative research is that whereas for the former, theory comes before data, for qualitative research it is an outcome of an investigation (see, for example, the selection by Bryman in Volume I, *Relationships Between Quantitative and Qualitative Research*). However, the article by Hammersley in Volume III, *Relationship Between Theory and Data in Qualitative Research*, problematises this notion by arguing that much qualitative research is insufficiently theoretical in that too often the researcher does little more than transmit what he or she sees and hears with little or no theoretical elaboration beyond that.

Hammersley calls this a 'representational model' of ethnography. In many ways, the identification of this problem draws attention to a tension in much qualitative research: the commitment of many qualitative researchers to naturalism (see Gubrium and Holstein in Volume III, *Fieldwork Notes and Transcripts*) and to taking the view of those being studied can easily result in a strategy in which the researcher becomes uneasy about theorising in relation to his or her data for fear of contaminating its naturalistic base. Rock refers to this tendency towards phenomenalism in the selection in Volume II, *Participant Observation.*

c) Grounded Theory

One of the main frameworks for the generation of theory out of data is grounded theory, which was originally formulated by Glaser and Strauss (1967). Grounded theory is meant to be an iterative process in which the researcher begins to collect data guided by a rather general view of the research issue, theorises about his or her data (for example, by noting interesting general categories and their connections), examines these initial theoretical reflections by carrying out further data collection, theorises further, collects more data and so on. The idea is progressively to elaborate a more general theoretical statement about the data. What is crucial is that the theory is grounded in and a product of the data. There is an important link with the idea of 'theoretical sampling' which has appeared elsewhere (see the discussion in 2(c) above and the selection by Finch and Mason in Volume I, *Sampling*). The notion of theoretical sampling was first formulated specifically in the context of grounded theory and is meant to denote a process whereby the researcher samples people, contexts or whatever on theoretical rather than statistical grounds. Once a theoretical category has been 'saturated' (in the language of grounded theory), further data are collected in terms of emerging theoretical ideas. It is the relevance of prospective people, groups or context to the emerging theoretical ideas that forms the basis for the theoretical sampling strategy.

The selection by Strauss and Corbin in Volume III, *Relationship Between Theory and Data in Qualitative Research*, provides a helpful outline of the main ingredients of grounded theory. The selection by Orona in the same section provides an illustration of the grounded theory approach by one of Strauss's students. Orona's article shows how she gradually came up with an empirically-grounded theoretical account of how those who care for sufferers of Alzheimer's Disease make decisions about placing loved ones in a nursing home and how they accommodate to the different stages of the disease. Having access to such a good example of the application of grounded theory is particularly important in the light of the suggestion by some writers that frequently the approach is paid lipservice to rather than used in a thoroughgoing manner (Bryman, 1988: 85; Locke, 1996).

d) Analytic Strategies

While qualitative methods are capable of generating a great deal of rich data, the large amount of information generated presents the researcher with the difficulty of knowing how best to analyse the largely unstructured information that is typically generated. Grounded theory can be viewed as an approach to analysing such data. The three selections in Volume III, *Analytic Strategies*, represent further strategies for interpreting and analysing qualitative data. These may be thought of as alternative strategies to qualitative data but in certain respects they are compatible with it. Indeed, grounded theory draws upon certain ideas in *analytic induction*, which is outlined in a classic article by Robinson. The process of analytic induction invites the researcher to formulate a hypothesis about a research problem and then to search out cases to test the hypothesis. As soon as a case is encountered which does not fit the hypothesis, a reformulation of the hypothesis has to take place which in turn propels a further search for cases which in turn may result in a further reformulation of the hypothesis if a negative case is encountered. As such, analytic induction is a strategy which entails a search for necessary rather than sufficient conditions for a phenomenon to occur. It is this highly uncompromising nature of the process, requiring a continuous round of hypothesis reformulation and further data collection as soon as a single negative case is encountered, that is responsible for the limited use of the approach over the years. None the less, the article by Bloor in Volume III, *Validation Issues*, provides an interesting application of analytic induction.

The two other selections in Volume III, *Analytic Strategies*, provide further highly contrasting approaches to qualitative data. Williams presents a 'pattern model' which draws upon symbolic interactionist thinking to give greater priority to preserving the nature of social phenomena than is typically found in either grounded theory or analytic induction. Williams argues that 'the act of describing the relation between one action and others in a context is equivalent to interpreting or explaining the meaning of that action'. This stance enables him to exhibit a commitment to naturalism without succumbing to the tendency towards a representational model that Hammersley criticises. Whereas Williams's point of departure in developing an analytic strategy is symbolic interactionism, Hycner's is phenomenology. Hycner outlines a series of stages which allow a phenomenological analysis of interview data to be undertaken. A particularly significant step in Hycner's procedure is 'bracketing and the phenomenological reduction' which entails 'suspending (bracketing) as much as possible the researcher's meanings and interpretations and entering into the world of the unique individual who was interviewed'. This emphasis on bracketing is one of the main motifs of a phenomenological approach and was central to the writings of one of its early proponents, Edmund Husserl. In this phase of the phenomenological procedure we can see the predilection for seeing through the eyes of others that is so central to the work of many qualitative researchers, but it is the additional element of suspension that adds a more specifically phenomenological theme.

e) Narrative Analysis

There are a wide range of narrative styles and the section in Volume III, *Narrative Analysis*, focuses on a series of models (Cortazzi) and the use of narrative methods in a particular social setting (Booth). But what constitutes narrative? Denzin (1989) suggests that:

> a narrative as a story has a plot, a beginning, a middle and an end. It has internal logic that makes sense to the narrator. A narrative relates events in a temporal, causal sequence. Every narrative describes a sequence of events that have happened. Hence narratives are temporal productions. (Denzin, 1989, p. 37)

Accordingly, the focus is upon the story but the question that arises is: what form does formal narrative analysis take? Many writers, including Cortazzi (1993) and Coffey and Atkinson (1996), draw on Labov's approach to narratives that is discussed in Volume III, *Narrative Analysis*. In particular, Coffey and Atkinson note that this approach can help social scientists think about their data and in turn their analysis. They illustrate how Labov's categories allow them to reflect on the story provided in an interview extract and to see how it is structured. In turn, Coffey and Atkinson also give examples of narrative forms including: success stories and moral tales and also the narrative as chronicle. Overall, thinking of data in terms of the ways accounts and stories are developed and constructed helps to provide an analysis of individuals and events in a range of social circumstances.

Narrative analysis is loosely formulated but Manning and Cullum-Swan (1994) state:

> If one defines narrative as a story with a beginning, middle and end that reveals someone's experiences, narratives take many forms, are told in many settings, before many audiences and with various degrees of connection to actual events or persons. (Manning and Cullum-Swan, 1994, p. 465)

It is on this basis that themes, metaphors, structures of stories and conclusions are established. The emphasis on narrative has the advantage over conventional approaches for the analysis of qualitative data as it can help to offset the tendency towards fragmentation of data that tends to occur through the process of coding and categorising qualitative data (Coffey and Atkinson, 1996).

f) Semiotics

Semiotics is frequently referred to as 'the science of signs' and it is scarcely surprising, therefore, that in his brief introduction to this approach in Volume

III, *Semiotics*, Gottdiener places the sign at centre stage. Central to semiotics is the notion that signs have connotations, that is, have meanings. Thus, words, behaviour, objects, and so on can have a meaning and significance beyond their ostensible functions. Semiotic analysis can be performed on all kinds of material, such as promotional material and observations of the built environment, as in Gottdiener's examination of an American hotel, or on data from fieldwork involving non-participant observation and interviews, as in the article on funeral work by Barley which is also in Volume III, *Semiotics*. Both writers show how the apparent minutiae of different settings – the Tiffany lamps in the Hotel Boulderado or the furnishings in a funeral home – are replete with meaning. In both of these instances, such accoutrements are manipulated because of their intended sign value; they are meant to have certain connotations. As both authors make clear, quite why such objects have certain connotations is also of considerable importance within a semiotic analysis.

g) Archiving Qualitative Data

The archiving of qualitative data has come onto the agenda in the 1990s. However, the secondary analysis of quantitative data has been a significant area of activity among quantitative researchers since the late 1960s (Dale, Arber and Procter, 1988) and the establishment of the British Survey Archive (now the Data Archive) in this period was a sign of a significant development supported by the Research Council. In Volume III, *Qualitative Data and Archiving*, Corti, Foster and Thompson describe the setting up of Qualidata at the University of Essex and its approach to archiving such data. The Centre is not a repository for qualitative data; its staff evaluate the data they are sent and if it is considered suitable they then arrange for it to be deposited in a suitable repository. As Hammersley points out in the selection in Volume III, *Qualitative Data and Archiving*, the depositing of qualitative data allows researchers' analyses to be checked and for researchers to conduct their own secondary analyses, perhaps in order to supplement their own investigations. Corti et al. outline some of the chief concerns in the social science community about the depositing of such materials, such as the difficulty of making informants and settings anonymous. Concerns remain, in spite of the authors' attempts to assuage various worries. Hammersley voices a concern over whether secondary analysis of qualitative data can be meaningful when the analyst has been deprived of direct access to the cultural background that lies between the lines of field notes and transcripts. Mauthner, Parry and Backett-Milburn (1998) underscore these kinds of reservations by observing that when each of the authors revisited their own data after several years, they were struck by the way in which their own individual biographies and positions at the time of conducting the research played an important part in the construction of the data and posed problems when those data were revisited. They counsel against a naive realism which treats such data as neutral. This kind of controversy raises important issues, then, about the nature of qualitative data which have strong points of affinity with the issues of representation raised by postmodernist writers (see 5(a) below).

h) The Use of Computers in Qualitative Data Analysis

It was in the early 1980s when the role of computers in qualitative data analysis began to be discussed. The arrival of computer programs designed expressly for qualitative data analysis, such as the ETHNOGRAPH, created the opportunity for greater use of computers for this purpose. Since then, a variety of new programs have come onto the market. One of these, NUD*IST, is described by Richards and Richards (1994). Many of the program's operations have been designed to be compatible with grounded theory. Such computer programs do not take away the hard interpretative work that is a feature of qualitative data analysis. Instead, they obviate much of the manual work involved in cutting and pasting, indexing, and so on. However, the creative and most difficult part is not removed!

In Volume III, *Computers in Qualitative Data Analysis*, Buston has provided a first-hand account of the use of NUD*IST. In the context of data deriving from research into young people's experience of chronic illness, he explores the possibility that far from being a neutral tool CAQDAS changes the way qualitative data analysis is carried out. Buston confirms that such software is labour saving but notes the possibility that it inadvertently promotes 'coding fetishism', whereby more and more codes are generated because of the ease of applying them and of retrieving coded chunks of text. Buston's suggestion that CAQDAS transforms the activity of qualitative data analysis is consistent with research on users of such software (Lee and Fielding, 1995). The selection by Coffey, Holbrook and Atkinson in Volume III, *Computers in Qualitative Data Analysis*, sounds a cautionary note, however, in that the authors argue that in stark contrast to many of the issues raised by the post-modern turn and recent considerations of ethnographic writing (see sections 5(a) and 5(b) below), which point to diversity, CAQDAS points in the direction of a homogeneity of approach, particularly one revolving around grounded theory (section 4(c) above). Lee and Fielding (1996) have taken issue with these suggestions, but the points raised by Coffey et al. have implications for users of CAQDAS at a time when the process of qualitative data analysis is itself a subject of some controversy.

5. Recent Developments in the Analysis and Interpretation of Qualitative Data

a) The Post-Modern Turn in Ethnography

The rise of postmodernism is one of the most significant developments in the social sciences in recent years. Its impact on ethnography has been particularly keenly felt. However, trying to capture succinctly postmodernism's implications for qualitative research, or indeed for social research of any kind, is no easy matter.

The article by Clifford in Volume III, *Postmodernism Meets Ethnography*, provides what is in many ways an early and classic working through of certain postmodernist themes in the context of ethnography. For Clifford the central issue is: 'how is unruly experience transformed into an authoritative written account?' This question, which has several links with the concerns of the next section and with the selections in Volume III, *Writing*, leads Clifford to suggest that what is central to any written ethnography is that it 'enacts a specific strategy of authority'. In other words, the account that we read in a written ethnography is just one of several representations of the culture that has been researched, but the ethnographer has to persuade us of the credibility and the persuasiveness of his or her account. This relates to a prominent theme in postmodernist writing: there can be no truly 'valid' account of any aspect of social reality. Instead, what we are confronted with is a plausible account. The notion that 'this is the way it is' has to be surrendered and in its place we must acknowledge that there can only be versions of that social reality. Clifford's article also points at least implicitly to another motif in postmodernist writing when he raises the issue of 'radical polyphony'. This notion invites us to question the salience of the ethnographer's rendition of social reality. Clifford argues that even when they quote extensively from the people they study, ethnographers are keen to get across a singular chronicle of what is going on. In other words, the variety of voices becomes subordinate to the ethnographer's account, so that even though people are quoted, it is always in the context of the account that the ethnographer is seeking to get across. Their voices have no independence of the ethnographer. We see in such critical consideration the disdain for metanarratives that is a feature of postmodernist writing, and a preference for polyphony and micronarratives. Clifford and many of those who have followed in his wake have sought to find ways of liberating these alternative voices in and through ethnography.

Denzin in the selection in Volume III, *Postmodernism Meets Ethnography*, argues that the rise of postmodernism has created a crisis of representation and legitimacy. As he points out, what is left if 'qualitative researchers can no longer capture lived experience' and if traditional criteria for evaluating qualitative research are challenged? Drawing on the literary works of James Joyce he proposes a way out of the current impasse. His proposals imply a far greater reflexivity than is normally countenanced or encountered and provide a fascinating challenge as ethnographers encounter postmodernism. The selection by Manning in Volume III, *Postmodernism Meets Ethnography*, also reflects upon these concerns. For Manning, the key issue is how to capture the experiential aspects of ethnographic fieldwork while simultaneously recognising the significance of issues of representation. He draws helpfully on some exemplars to shed some light on this dilemma.

b) Ethnographic Writing as a Topic

One of the most striking aspects of the postmodernist turn outlined in the previous section, and to a very large extent prefigured there, is the growth of the writing of qualitative research as a focus of both concern and inquiry. Clifford's selection in Volume III, *Postmodernism Meets Ethnography*, is particularly typical of this development which can also be seen in books like those written by Van Maanen (1988) and Atkinson (1990). One of its main dimensions is a concern with the ways in which qualitative researchers write in order to convince readers of the credibility of their accounts. Geertz's seminal essay 'Thick Description', which is in Volume III, *Writing*, is for many writers a crucial starting point. In this essay, he acknowledges that in much qualitative research, the investigator seeks to capture social reality from the 'native's' point of view, but notes that the researcher has to go further than this: 'we begin with our own interpretations of what our informants are up to, or think they are up to, and then systematise those'. Writing is part of the process of systematisation and his essay contains important reflections on the whole process which have been very influential in the context of many of the current debates about the nature of ethnography. The influence of these writings can also be seen in the selection in Volume III, *Writing*, by Golden-Biddle and Locke. They draw on several qualitative studies of organisations to show the strategies that researchers employ to convince their readers of the validity of their accounts. One of these – conveying a sense of authenticity (a sense of the researcher really being in the field and of having grasped organisational members' understandings) – exhibits a clear affinity with the work of Clifford (in Volume III, *Postmodernism Meets Ethnography*) and Geertz (in Volume III, *Writing*).

c) Validation Issues

LeCompte and Goetz (1982) have taken up issues of validity in qualitative research. They consider issues that have long been important in quantitative research, by asking questions about several areas of activity, such as: measurement validity (does a measure really reflect the underlying concept it is supposed to measure?); internal validity (do the results of a study lead to robust inferences about causality?); and external validity (can the results be generalised beyond the people and context involved in an investigation?). However, many other writers have argued that criteria for the evaluation of quantitative research should not be applied unquestioningly to qualitative research. The selection by Lincoln and Guba in Volume III, *Validation Issues*, is an important statement which not only directly reflects this position but also seeks to outline alternative criteria for evaluating qualitative studies. In place of validity, they propose *trustworthiness* as a criterion of good qualitative research: 'How can an inquirer persuade his or her audiences (including self) that the findings of an inquiry are worth paying attention to ...?'.

The selection suggests many criteria for establishing trustworthiness. This issue is, of course, related to the issue of how the findings from qualitative research are conveyed when they are written up (see 5(c)). One check on trustworthiness proposed by Lincoln and Guba is 'member checks', which involves asking the people on whom research was carried out to check the interpretations that are being proffered about their lives or their views of social reality. An illustration of this technique is provided in the selection by Bloor in Volume III, *Validation Issues*. Bloor's study shows that this kind of exercise, which he calls 'respondent validation' and which entails asking informants to check the credibility of one's interpretations, is by no means unproblematic when researchers encounter alternative renditions to their own. A fascinating insight into the potential for lack of trustworthiness in research involving 'hired hands' is provided in the selection by Roth in Volume I, *The Research Process*, where he argues that a reliance on hired in-terviewers or observers can often result in findings that cannot be relied upon. Roth argues that hired hands in research are more prone to making mistakes and taking short cuts than are researchers conducting their own investigations.

6. Ethical Issues and Values

The research process is permeated by a series of social, ethical and politi-cal problems that have now been well documented; especially by qualitative researchers in a range of reflexive accounts (Burgess, 1989; 1992). Many of these problems relate to classic issues and debates including overt and cov-ert research (an issue examined by Bulmer in Volume IV, *Ethical Issues and Values*), deception and lying (focused on by Goode in Volume IV, *Ethical Issues and Values*) and the value position of the investigator (discussed by Becker in Volume IV, *Ethical Issues and Values*, that was subsequently the subject of a debate with Gouldner who argued that Becker's position amounted to 'taking sides' in social research). Many of the debates are now surrounded by illustrations that have become classic examples of ethical issues in qualitative research.

A key issue in the literature is between overt and covert research which it is argued represent opposite ends of a research continuum. Yet in reality re-searchers have demonstrated that it is rare to find research that is either completely overt or completely covert but instead is often simultaneously overt and covert. The debate about overt and covert research rests upon principles concerned with the responsibilities of the researcher to the researched and to the profession. Indeed, Erikson has argued that:

(1) it is unethical for a sociologist to deliberately misrepresent his iden-
      tity for the purpose of entering a private domain to which he is
      not eligible; and

(2)   it is unethical for a sociologist to deliberately misrepresent the character of the research upon which he is engaged.
(Erikson, 1967, p. 373)

These issues have warranted a response as they assume a distinction can be drawn between public and private settings and that open roles are easier to handle than those that are covert. Indeed, qualitative researchers have chosen a covert role to study a range of organisations including the police (Holdaway, 1983), old-time Pentecostalists (Homan, 1980) and homosexuals (Humphreys, 1970).

It is the study of homosexual encounters in public toilets that has attracted much attention as the researcher, Laud Humphreys, passing as a homosexual by acting as a 'watch queen', disguised the fact that he was recording the situations he observed and deceived his respondents by claiming they were part of a 'health survey'. In these respects, it is argued that the studies infringe privacy and result in deception.

As a consequence of such studies, professional bodies have devised statements of ethical principles and 'codes' of ethics in which they have attempted to codify the way in which researchers might operate by obtaining informed consent from participants in studies where the research will be open to all concerned. Such 'codes' tend to oversimplify the conduct of social research where principles may be easy to establish but research practice involves researchers taking a value position in relation to the circumstances in which they are located.

7. The Significance of Difference in Qualitative Research

a) Gender and Feminism

Within the last twenty years feminism has had a massive impact on the social sciences where it has been responsible for shaping and reshaping some disciplines. In turn, this has also had a considerable impact on the conduct of social research where researchers have considered the way in which feminism has shaped the questions that researchers have posed, the research strategies that have been adopted and the techniques of research that have been adapted (Stanley and Wise, 1993). These perspectives are represented in the accounts provided by Oakley, Mies and Devault in Volume IV, *Issues of Gender and Feminism*.

In particular Oakley, like Finch in Volume II, *Interviewing*, uses her research experience of interviewing women to provide a critique of conventional approaches to interviewing. Such work has allowed researchers to focus on the relationship between the researcher and the researched, and the ways in which the interview takes on the characteristics of conversation (Burgess, 1988a). Such critiques also raise the question whether research on women should only be conducted by women and issues concerning the need to reflect on the different ways in which sex and gender influence the collection of data when engaged in participant observation. Accordingly, many feminist researchers have become advocates for qualitative research arguing for reflexivity, the development of relationships between researcher and researched, and advocating practices that empower women in their studies. Certainly Morgan (1981) has suggested that gender may influence the choice of research topic and the perspective that is taken by the researcher in raising questions in a field of study. Gender therefore has the potential to include as well as exclude researchers from fields of study.

b) Cultural Difference

Many sociologists have commented on the ways in which social divisions based on gender, class and ethnicity permeate society. Yet in considering approaches to research, cultural difference has often been taken for granted. Accordingly, it has become appropriate for researchers, especially those engaged in qualitative research, to consider ways in which the differences between researcher and researched may influence the choice of research field or research project, the use of methods and the kinds of data that are obtained. These issues are examined by Song and Parker and by Anderson in section Volume IV, *Cultural Difference.*

The choice of field for many researchers is influenced by personal experience. Rizvi (1993) indicates how personal incidents between himself and white students helped shape his study of 'racism' in education. Similarly, Troyna (1993) indicates that his involvement in the study of 'race' and education was not the result of 'a disinterested chronicler of trends and patterns' (p. viii) but the direct result of growing up in an area where fellow black students experienced racist abuse and how as a Jewish boy he witnessed racist and anti-semitic activities.

As in feminist research so in research on 'race' and ethnicity, questions have been raised about the role of the white researcher. First, can white researchers elicit data from black respondents given the possibility of differences in power and status? Second, to what extent can white researchers provide adequate analyses of black respondents given they have no experience of what it is to be black? Thirdly, by what right do white researchers take on the self appointed role of 'ombudsman'? However, as Troyna (1993) has indicated, researchers need to find strategies that are sensitive to cultural difference so that data in this field on 'race' and 'ethnicity' can be collected.

The role of the white researcher in an ethnic community is poignantly summarised by Eliot Liebow (1967) in relation to his classic study *Tally's Corner* – an analysis of black street corner men – when he states that the:

> brute fact of color, as they understood it in their experience and as I
> understood it in mine irrevocably and absolutely relegated me to the

status of outsider. I am not certain but I have a hunch that they were more continuously aware of the color difference than I was. When four of us sat around a kitchen table, for example, I saw three Negroes; each of them saw two Negroes and a white man. (Liebow, 1967, pp. 248–9)

However, Liebow argues that this outsider role facilitated observational work. Yet the role of outsider, whilst rendering situations culturally strange, may also act as a barrier to the researcher. For example, language may convey social and cultural meanings that it is essential for researchers to understand if they are to unlock the social situations which they study and comprehend them from the insider's point of view.

8. Qualitative Research in Practice

a) Qualitative Evaluation Research

In the last twenty years, ethnographers and other researchers who utilise qualitative methods of investigation have engaged in evaluation studies. In Volume IV, *Qualitative Evaluation Research*, we turn to a consideration of the characteristics of this approach (Patton) and provide an example of ethnographic evaluation research in action in the field of education (Knapp). But what are the distinctive features of qualitative evaluation? In what ways does it overlap with qualitative research? How does it contribute to policy and practice?

A brief glance at evaluation studies conducted from a qualitative perspective reveals that this approach involves the process of applying ethnographic techniques to evaluation. Among the characteristics of this approach is the use of fieldwork to focus on the cultural attributes of a setting based on the perceptions and perspectives of those who are studied and where the findings are reported in a non-judgemental way. The methods that are used to conduct such studies are very similar to those used in traditional ethnographic studies: participant observation; unstructured and conversational interviews; the use of key informants; and documentary evidence (for an account of these approaches see Volume II). However, it is essential to examine some of the distinguishing characteristics of evaluation research. First, the researcher is often sponsored by a policy maker who needs to understand the effectiveness of a particular programme, especially in fields such as health and education. In turn, the evaluator as fieldworker has to deal with a range of participants (as in any traditional study) but in these circumstances the participants may take on the role of stakeholders whose views need to be represented within the study. Furthermore, the evaluator needs to ensure that the perceptions of the different stakeholders are portrayed in a language that is recognised by the participants. Accordingly, the evaluator needs to consider the different audiences, concepts and languages that are appropriate for reporting. The way in which evaluation reports are written and disseminated is a crucial part of the evaluation process as it is essential to reflect the perceptions of the different stakeholders while adopting a non-judgemental approach. In turn, the evidence, conclusions and recommendations need to be prepared with the different audiences in mind whereby different aspects of the text are appropriate for those who sponsored the study, the programme participants and policy makers.

b) Qualitative Research and Policy

While evaluators using quantitative methods have had to address policy makers who have sponsored their studies, this has not always been the case for qualitative researchers. Indeed, Finch (1988) highlights the absence of policy related work in ethnography by issuing the challenge:

> Can anyone show me a report, book or article, based upon ethnographic work which ends with a section called 'Policy Recommendations' where prescriptions for action are listed? (Finch, 1988, p. 185)

She continues by stating that such conventional policy oriented work has not been a characteristic of ethnographic studies (in this case in the field of education). However, she continues, as in Volume IV, *Qualitative Research and Policy*, to argue for the use of ethnographic and qualitative approaches and illustrates the way this can be done drawing on examples from vocational education and training (Pollard, Purvis and Walford, 1988) as Rojiani does using long term care as an example.

It is fields such as education, social work and health that have witnessed researchers choosing to conduct studies which provide an opportunity to assess the impact of policies at 'local level'. The way in which qualitative researchers focus upon subjective experiences in social life allows them uniquely to offer accounts on the consequences of particular social and educational policies.

The importance of ethnographic and qualitative work in social policy research was noted by Bulmer (1986) and subsequently we have witnessed researchers who had previously worked in fields such as health and education applying methods and techniques derived from qualitative research to questions that are most appropriately addressed by techniques which will provide insights into processes and interactions. As Finch has argued, this allows qualitative researchers to document the effects of policy (Burgess, 1988b), the consequences of policy (Shilling, 1988, Hustler, 1988) and contradictions in policy (Buswell, 1988).

The shift in emphasis from studying policy decisions to policy debates using ethnographic studies is well illustrated in the collection of essays edited by Halpin and Troyna (1994). However, their focus on methodological concerns demonstrates that policy focused research highlights some of the traditional issues: sponsorship (Burgess, 1994b); neutrality (Skeggs, 1994); and political commitment (Walford, 1994). In turn, policy oriented qualitative studies can simultaneously contribute to the development of social theory and further our understanding of policy and practice.

c) Action Research

Action research focuses on practice. It stems from the work of Kurt Lewin (1946) who argued for a research approach which involved closer links between social theory and social problems. Much of the methodological writing on action research has been concerned with its characteristics and is exemplified in Kelly's article in Volume IV, *Action Research*.

The defining characteristics of action research have been identified in a range of different ways as shown below:

Kemmis and Wilkinson (1998)	Denscombe (1998)	Robson (1993) based on Lewin
1. Planning change	1. Practical with a focus on organisational problems	1. Planning
2. Acting and observing the processes and consequences of change	2. Change as an integral part of the research	2. Acting by carrying out the plan
3. Reflection on process and consequences	3. A cyclical process involving a feedback loop so that change is subject to evaluation and further investigation	3. Observing based on planning and fact finding
4. Replanning	4. Participation by practitioners	4. Reflecting and modifying the plan

The result is that many of the attributes of action research can be distilled into a series of spirals (see overleaf).

Furthermore, Kemmis and Wilkinson (1998) argue that action research is a collaborative process and so as well as the spiral of self reflection they argue that it is also characterised by being a social process that is participatory, practical, collaborative, emancipatory, critical and reflexive.

The key question is how such an approach can be used to influence practice which is illustrated by a study of work place health conducted by Hugentobler, Israel and Schurman that is in Volume IV, *Action Research*. Such

Source: Based on Kemmis and Wilkinson (1998), p. 22.

studies illustrate how the focus of action research is upon improvement and involvement for as Carr and Kemmis (1986) indicate, action research is associated with:

> firstly the improvement of a *practice* of some kind; secondly, the improvement of the *understanding* of a practice by its practitioners; and thirdly the improvement of the *situation* in which the practice takes place.... Those involved in the practice being considered are to be involved in the action research process in all its aspects of planning, acting, observing and reflecting. (Carr and Kemmis, 1986, p. 156)

The focus of action research on practice in a particular setting puts it in the tradition of qualitative research. However, it also involves collaborations between researchers and practitioners.

d) Practitioner Research

Most of the research that is reported in these volumes has been conducted by professional researchers. Indeed, some qualitative researchers have argued that 'outsiders' to the setting under study have distinct advantages. In this respect, Blanche Geer (1970) argued in her paper on studying an American College that the ideal researcher will be:

> a rather rare person in research on education – someone so aware of the need for independence, so alert to the possibility of bias that he chooses to study a college campus where he does not teach or study. He is a stranger to the College without obligations.

This model has been adopted in much educational research, but an alternative model has also been presented whereby the practitioner engages in research. Indeed, Stenhouse (1975) argued that teachers could add a research dimension to their role and act as classroom researchers who could evaluate and understand their teaching situation. Such roles are not unproblematic given the availability of time, the nature of the 'insider' role and the potential conflict of a dual role (Robson, 1993, Smetherham, 1978). Nevertheless, it is argued that investigation, enquiry and evaluation becomes part of the role of the 'extended professional' and the 'reflective practitioner' (Schon, 1983).

But how might such an approach work in practice? In Volume IV, *Practitioner Research*, Griffiths, himself a school teacher, demonstrates how the diary keeping method could be adapted to avoid taking too much time while working in the classroom, yet provide insights into the patterns and processes associated with classroom activities. In this respect, his essay demonstrates the role of reflexivity as he points up the problems involved in using a diary to study his own position in the classroom.

Such an approach can be used by practitioners in a range of occupations: teaching; social work; nursing and so on to obtain insights into the situations in which they are located. In these circumstances, as Bloor and McKeganey in Volume IV, *Practitioner Research*, illustrate, ethnography does address the world of the practitioner but does leave problems to be resolved. Practitioner based enquiries draw on traditional qualitative research and highlight issues that still need to be resolved, including negotiating time to do the investigation, working in a team and having some support for the research project (Robson, 1993).

9. Further Issues

a) Getting Out

Perhaps because gaining entry to many social contexts represents a considerable hurdle for many researchers, the issue of possible problems of leaving such contexts has tended to be given less attention by many writers and re-searchers. In Volume IV, *Getting Out*, Altheide discusses the difficulties he experienced in extricating himself from the news organisations in which he conducted his investigations. He shows that the process of getting out varied along a number of dimensions, such as: the nature of the organisations, the nature of the research relationships established, and the kind of investigation being carried out. Moreover, this process is not just to do with the researcher's final withdrawal from the field but also with temporary withdrawals due to other commitments. The selection by Taylor in Volume IV, *Getting Out*, draws on the author's disengagement from researching the mentally retarded to show that withdrawal may be from the investigation but not necessarily from the people concerned, with whom an ongoing relationship may be maintained, at least for a while. Indeed, there is another aspect to this issue, to which Buchanan, Boddy and McCalman (1988) draw attention: when withdrawal is from an organisation, even though the researcher may not continue a rela-tionship with members of the organisation, the process has to be managed and promises kept in order not to make it difficult for future researchers to secure access.

b) Dissemination

The dissemination of one's findings is a step that all researchers face. There are several potential audiences: the academic community, potentially interested practitioners, and the wider public. Moreover, the methods of reaching these audiences are also likely to differ. It might be thought that, like the process of getting out addressed in the previous section, dissemination is a relatively unproblematic activity. This may in fact be the case for much of the time, but the two selections in Volume IV, *Dissemination*, demonstrate in highly contrast-ing ways that dissemination considerations should not be regarded as necessarily free of difficulty. Although his experience is by no means typical, the selection by Morgan provides a cautionary tale. Drawing on his ethnographic research on female workers in two factories, Morgan gave a conference paper which came to the attention of some newspapers. Some of the journalists managed to find out the names of the factories and printed this information in their article. Some of the workers in the firms were extremely distressed by the reports, in particu-lar the older ones, whereas the younger ones were more favourably inclined to the reports. Adler provides a contrasting account of how in the course of doing participant observation research on a US university basketball team, the me-dia magnified his role so that he became something of a celebrity. This aggrandisement amplified what people within and outside the team expected of him, which in turn had implications for the progress of his research. Neither of the selections in Volume IV, *Dissemination*, could or should be seen as typi-cal of qualitative researchers' experiences of dissemination, but they provide insights into what Adler refers to as the 'complex effects of the media upon social scientists and their work'.

c) Restudies

The selections in Volume IV, *Restudies*, deal with the question of the problems and prospects of what happens when a researcher returns to study a social setting in which he or she has previously conducted research (Burgess) and when a researcher returns to study a setting previously studied by someone else (Whyte and Boelen). There is considerable overlap here with the issues raised by writers in connection with the archiving and secondary analysis of qualitative data (see 4(g) above), since the process invariably includes going back to the original study, regardless of whether it is one's own or someone else's. As Burgess shows in his restudy of a Roman Catholic comprehensive secondary school in the UK, the very fact that many research participants knew the book that grew out of his study had an effect on how he was perceived and on the course of the restudy. Moreover, anyone contemplating a restudy has to recognise the significance of several factors to which Burgess draws attention: changes in the social setting and its members; changes in the wider context (in this case, educational); changes in the researcher in terms of interests and theoretical inclinations; and changes in the discipline which drives the researcher's concerns (in Burgess's case, sociology). The second restudy case derives from a critique of a sociological classic, *Street Corner Society* (Whyte, 1993 [1944]), by Boelen. Drawing on her fieldwork in the same community as Whyte, Boelen argues on the basis of fieldwork conducted three to four decades after the original study (her research spanned the 1970–89 period), that the original study was substantially flawed. Whyte is accused of misinterpreting his findings and even of misrepresenting certain aspects of what he saw. There have been several similar accusations over the years of other classic studies in the social sciences. Whyte has written a robust rebuttal which is included in Volume IV, *Restudies*. The obvious question of 'who is right?' cannot be easily resolved by reading these contributions which raise fascinating questions about whether a restudy is possible after so long and hence about the nature of what is a restudy (Bryman, 1994). However, from a postmodernist perspective, the 'who is right?' question is meaningless because it presumes that there can be a definitively correct account of a sphere of social reality (Denzin, 1992; Richardson, 1992).

10. Some Reflections

In this review we have sought to outline some of the essential features of qualitative research and to provide a springboard for an appreciation of the selections in the four volumes. Qualitative research has clearly come a long way since the early 1960s when its coverage in research methods texts was frequently cursory and it was still largely associated more or less exclusively with participant observation and unstructured interviewing. Since those days, it has spawned a variety of specialist methodological texts and journals. Furthermore, it is now associated with a variety of methods that are outlined in these volumes. The case of qualitative research demonstrates that social research is not a static activity but one that is constantly evolving.

What of the future? The following thoughts represent some considerations that we anticipate will be on the qualitative researcher's agenda for several years:

- Qualitative researchers need to ensure that they continue to address concerns in the social science community surrounding validity, reliability and reprentativeness. Whether these notions need to be adapted to the specific nature of qualitative research, as suggested by Lincoln and Guba in Volume III, *Validation Issues*, or are part of a more general set of methodological issues and principles will need to be considered.

- What will be the role of technology for qualitative researchers in the future? It is clear from our selections that photography and film have considerable potential, but an area of some controversy has been the role of computer software in qualitative data analysis. It is clear that such technology can be a useful tool but it is not capable of replacing the analytic skills of the researcher. When the field is reviewed in the future, it will be possible to draw on many years' experience among a wide constituency of researchers. It will then be possible to assess in a more detailed way the significance of the computer for qualitative research.

- In the past, there was a tendency for quantitative and qualitative research to be depicted as incompatible paradigms, but that view has softened a great deal in recent years. More and more researchers are employing both approaches in their investigations. How far this tendency will become more pronounced will be an interesting issue to examine in the future as it may mean that the very distinction between quantitative and qualitative research will be undermined. At the same time, we would caution against any suggestion that such combined research is necessarily superior to research based on either quantitative or qualitative research. As with any research, combined research must be appropriate to the research problem and must be soundly executed.

- Investigators may also want to consider how far qualitative research needs to be adapted for evaluation and policy research. For example, the fact that such research is often issue-focused may be construed as inconsistent with the preference among many qualitative researchers for investigations which do not specify the research problem too tightly in advance.

- Postmodernism has had a considerable impact on the social sciences and on qualitative research in particular. Its influence can be seen in Volume III, *Postmodernism Meets Ethnography* and *Writing*, in particular. However, the implications of postmodernism for established practices in qualitative research, especially the conduct of such research rather than analysis and writing which have been the main foci of attention, needs to be spelled out in a more detailed way in the future.

This is simply a brief short-list of issues that we believe will become increasingly significant for qualitative researchers in the future. In the meantime, as the selections in the four volumes show, qualitative research is a burgeoning field that has already come a long way in the last thirty years.

Bibliography

Atkinson, P. (1990) *The Ethnographic Imagination: Textual Constructions of Society*, London: Routledge.

Becker, H. S. and Geer, B. (1957) 'Participant observation and interviewing: a comparison', *Human Organization*, 16: 28–32.

Becker, H. S., Geer, B., and Hughes, E. C. (1968) *Making the Grade*, New York: Wiley.

Blumer, H. (1956) 'Sociological analysis and the "variable"', *American Sociological Review*, 21: 683–90.

Bryman, A. (1988) *Quantity and Quality in Social Research*, London: Routledge.

—— (1994) 'The Mead/Freeman controversy: some implications for qualitative researchers', in R. G. Burgess (ed.), *Studies in Qualitative Methodology*, 4: 1–27.

Buchanan, D., Boddy, D., and McCalman, J. (1988) 'Getting in, getting on, getting out, getting back', in A. Bryman (ed.), *Doing Research in Organizations*, London: Routledge.

Bulmer, M. (1986) *Social Science and Social Policy*, London: Allen & Unwin.

—— (1984) *The Chicago School of Sociology*, Chicago: University of Chicago Press.

Burgess, R. G. (1988a) 'Conversations with a purpose' in R. G. Burgess (ed.), *Studies in Qualitative Methodology*, Vol I, London: JAI Press.

—— (1988b) 'Whatever happened to the Newsom course?' in A. Pollard, J. Purvis and G. Walford (eds), *Education, Training and the New Vocationalism*, Buckingham: Open University Press.

—— (1989) (ed.) *The Ethics of Educational Research*, London: Falmer Press.

—— (1992) (ed.) *Learning from the Field*, London: JAI Press.

—— (1994a) 'On diaries and diary keeping' in N. Bennett, R. Glatter, R. Levacic (eds) *Improving Educational Management*, London: Paul Chapman Publishing.

—— (1994b) 'Scholarship and sponsored research: contradictory continuum or complementary activity?' in D. Halpin and B. Troyna (1994) (eds), *Researching Education Policy*, London: Falmer Press.

Buswell, C. (1988) 'Flexible workers for flexible firms?' in A. Pollard, J. Purvis and G. Walford (eds), *Education, Training and the New Vocationalism*, Buckingham: Open University Press.

Carr, W. and Kemmis, S. (1986) *Becoming Critical*, London: Falmer Press.

Chamberlain, M (1975) *Fenwomen*, London: Virago.

Cicourel, A.V. (1964) *Method and Measurement in Sociology*, New York: Free Press.

Coffey, A. and Atkinson, P. (1996) *Making Sense of Qualitative Data*, London: Sage.

Cortazzi, M. (1993) *Narrative Analysis*, London: Falmer Press.

Dale, A., Arber, S., and Proctor, M. (1988) *Doing Secondary Analysis*, London: Unwin Hyman.

Deacon, D., Bryman, A. and Fenton, N. (1998) 'Collision or collusion? A discussion and case study of the unplanned triangulation of quantitative and qualitative research', *International Journal of Social Research Methodology*, 1: 47–63.

Denscombe, M. (1998) *The Good Research Guide*, Buckingham: Open University Press.

Denzin, N. (1989) *Interpretive Interactionism*, Newbury Park, California: Sage.

Denzin, N. K. (1992) 'Whose Cornerville is it, anyway', *Journal of Contemporary Ethnography*, 21: 120–32.

Denzin, N. K. and Lincoln, Y. S. (1994) 'Introduction: entering the field of qualitative research', in N. K. Denzin and Y. S. Lincoln (eds), *Handbook of Qualitative Research*, Thousand Oaks, CA: Sage.

Erikson, K. T. (1967) 'A comment on disguised observation in sociology', *Social Problems*, vol. 14, No 4, pp 366–73.

Ewart Evans, G. (1970) *Where Beards Wag All: The Relevance of the Oral Tradition*, London, Faber.

Filmer, P., Phillipson, M., Silverman, D., and Walsh, D. (1971) *New Directions in Sociological Theory*, London: Collier-MacMillan.

Finch, J. (1988) 'Ethnography and public policy' in A. Pollard, J. Purvis and G. Walford (eds), *Education, Training and the New Vocationalism*, Buckingham: Open University Press.

Gans, H. J. (1958) *The Urban Villagers*, New York: Free Press.

Garfinkel, H. (1967) *Studies in Ethnomethodology*, Englewood Cliffs, NJ: Prentice-Hall.

Geer, B. (1970) 'Studying a college' in R. Habenstein (ed.), *Pathways to Data*, Chicago: Aldine.

Glaser, B. G. and Strauss, A. L. (1967) *The Discovery of Grounded Theory*, Chicago: Aldine.

Gottschalk, L. et al (1945) *The Use of Personal Documents in History, Anthropology and Sociology*, Bulletin 53, New York: Social Science Research Council.

Halpin, D. and Troyna, B. (1994) (eds) *Researching Education Policy*, London: Falmer Press.

Hamilton, D. (1994) 'Traditions, preferences, and postures in applied qualitative research', in N. K. Denzin and Y. S. Lincoln (eds), *Handbook of Qualitative Research*, Thousand Oaks, CA: Sage.

Hammersley, M. (1992) 'Deconstructing the qualitative–quantitative divide', in M. Hammersley, *What's Wrong with Ethnography?* London: Routledge.

Hammersley, M. (1996) 'The relationship between qualitative and quantitative research: paradigm loyalty versus methodological eclecticism', in J. T. E. Richardson (ed.), *Handbook of Research Methods for Psychology and the Social Sciences*, Leicester: BPS Books.

Hastrup, K. (1992) 'Anthropological visions: some notes on visual and textual authority' in P. I. Crawford and D. Turton (eds), *Film as Ethnography*, Manchester: Manchester University Press.

Hockings, P. (1975) *Principles of Visual Anthropology*, The Hague: Mouton.

Holdaway, S. (1983) *Inside the British Police*, Oxford: Blackwell.

Homan, R. (1980) 'The ethics of covert methods', *British Journal of Sociology*, Vol. 31, No 1, pp. 46–59.

Humphreys, L. (1970) *The Tearoom Trade*, London: Duckworth.

Hustler, D. (1988) 'It's not like normal lessons: you don't have to wag school anymore' in A. Pollard, J. Purvis and G. Walford (eds), *Education, Training and the New Vocationalism*, Buckingham: Open University Press.

Kemmis, S. and Wilkinson, M. (1998) 'Participatory action research and the study of practice' in B. Atwel, S. Kemmis and P. Weeks (eds), *Action Research in Practice*, London: Routledge.

Layder, D. (1993) *New Strategies in Social Research*, Cambridge: Polity.

LeCompte, M. D. and Goetz, J. P. (1982) 'Problems of reliability and validity in ethnographic research', *Review of Educational Research*, 52: 31–60.

Lee, R. M. and Fielding, N. G. (1995) 'Users' experiences of qualitative data analysis software', in U. Kelle (ed.), *Computer-Aided Qualitative Data Analysis: Theory, Methods and Practice*, London: Sage.

—— (1996) 'Qualitative data analysis: representations of a technology: A comment on Coffey, Holbrook and Atkinson', *Sociological Research Online*, vol. 1, no. 4 (http://www.socresonline.org.uk/socresonline/2/4/lf.html).

Liebow, E. (1967) *Tally's Corner*, Boston, Mass: Little, Brown.

Locke, K. (1996) 'Rewriting *The Discovery of Grounded Theory* after 25 years?', *Journal of Management Inquiry*, 5: 239–45.

Lupton, D. and Noble, G. (1997) 'Just a machine? Dehumanizing strategies in personal computer use', *Body and Society*, 3: 83–101.

Lynd, R. S. and Lynd, H. M. (1929) *Middletown: A Study in American Culture*, New York: Harcourt and Brace.

—— (1937) *Middletown in Transition: A Study in Cultural Conflicts*, New York: Harcourt and Brace.

Macfarlane, A. (1992) 'The potentials of videodisc in visual anthropology: some examples', in P. I. Crawford and D. Turton (eds), *Film as Ethnography*, Manchester: Manchester University Press.

Malinowski, M. (1922) *Argonauts of the Western Pacific*, London: Routledge & Kegan Paul.

Manning, P. K. and Cullum-Swan, B. (1994) 'Narrative, content and semiotic analysis' in N. K. Denzin and Y. S. Lincoln (eds), *Handbook of Qualitative Research*, London: Sage.

Mauthner, N. S., Parry, O., and Backett-Milburn, K. (1998) 'The data are out there, or are they? Implications for archiving and revisiting qualitative data', *Sociology*, 32: 733–45.

Mead, M. (1928) *Coming of Age in Samoa*, New York: William Morrow.

Merton, R. K., Fiske, M., and Kendall, P. L. (1956) *The Focused Interview: A Manual of Problems and Procedures*, New York: Free Press.

Mishler, E. G. (1986) *Research Interviewing: Context and Narrative*, Cambridge, Mass.: Harvard University Press.

Morgan, D. H. J. (1981) 'Men, masculinity and the process of sociological enquiry', in H. Roberts (ed.) *Feminist Research*, London: Routledge.

Morgan, D. L. (1988) *Focus Groups as Qualitative Research*, (Sage University Paper Series on Qualitative Research Methods, Vol. 16. Beverly Hills, CA: Sage.

Oakley, A. (1981) 'Interviewing women: a contradiction in terms', in H. Roberts (ed.), *Doing Feminist Research*, London: Routledge.

—— (1998) 'Gender, methodology and people's ways of knowing: some problems with feminism and the paradigm debate in social science', *Sociology*, 32: 707–31.

Phillips, D. L. (1973) *Abandoning Method*, San Francisco: Jossey-Bass.

Pinney, C. (1992) 'The lexical spaces of eye-spy', in P. I. Crawford and D. Turton (eds), *Film as Ethnography*, Manchester: Manchester University Press.

Platt, J. (1983) 'The development of the "participant observation" method in sociology: origin myth and history', *Journal of the History of the Behavioral Sciences*, 19: 379–93.

—— (1992) 'Cases of cases ... of cases', in C. C. Ragin and H. S. Becker (eds), *What is a Case? Exploring the Foundations of Social Inquiry*, Cambridge: Cambridge University Press.

—— (1996) *A History of Sociological Research Methods in America, 1920–1960*, Cambridge: Cambridge University Press.

Plummer, K. (1983) *Documents of Life*, London: Allen & Unwin.

Ragin, C. C. (1992) 'Introduction: Cases of "What is a case?"' in C. C. Ragin and H. S. Becker (eds), *What is a Case? Exploring the Foundations of Social Inquiry*, Cambridge: Cambridge University Press.

Ribbens, J. (1989) 'Interviewing – an "unnatural" situation?', *Women's Studies International Forum*, 12: 579–92.

Richards, L. and Richards, T. (1994) 'From filing cabinet to computer', in A. Bryman and R. G. Burgess (eds), *Analyzing Qualitative Data*, London: Routledge.

Richardson, L. (1992) 'Trash on the corner: ethics and technography', *Journal of Contemporary Ethnography*, 21: 103–19.

Rizvi, F. (1993) 'Critical introduction: researching racism and education' in B. Troyna, *Racism and Education*, Buckingham: Open University Press.

Robson, C. (1993) *Real World Research*, Oxford: Blackwell.

Schon, D. (1983) *The Reflective Practitioner*, New York: Basic Books.

Schutz, A. (1962) *Collected Papers I: The Problem of Social Reality*, The Hague: Martinus Nijhof.

Scott, J. (1990) *A Matter of Record*, Cambridge: Polity Press.

Shaw, C. (1930) *The Jack Roller*, Chicago: University of Chicago Press.

Shilling, C. (1988) 'The schools vocational programme' in A. Pollard, J. Purvis and G. Walford (eds), *Education, Training and the New Vocationalism*, Buckingham: Open University Press.

Silverman, D. (1993) *Interpreting Qualitative Data: Methods for Analysing Talk, Text and Interaction*, London: Sage.

Skeggs, B. (1994) 'The constraints of neutrality: the 1998 Education Reform Act and Feminist Research' in D. Halpin and B. Troyna (1994) (eds) *Researching Education Policy*, London: Falmer Press.

Smetherham, D. (1978) 'Insider research' in *British Educational Research Journal*, Vol 4, pp. 97–107.

Stanley, L. and Wise S. (1993) *Breaking Out*, London: Routledge.

Stenhouse, L. (1975) *An Introduction to Curriculum Research and Development*, London: Heinemann.

Thomas, W. I. and Znaniecki, F. (1918–20) *The Polish Peasant in Europe and America*, Chicago, University of Chicago Press.

Thompson, P. (1978) *The Voice of the Past: Oral History*, Oxford: Oxford University Press.

Troyna, B. (1993) *Racism and Education*, Buckingham: Open University Press.

Van Maanen, J. (1988) *Tales of the Field: On Writing Ethnography*, Chicago: University of Chicago Press.

Vidich, A. J. and Lyman, S. M. (1994) 'Qualitative methods: their history in sociology and anthropology', in N. K. Denzin and Y. S. Lincoln (eds), *Handbook of Qualitative Research*, Thousand Oaks, CA: Sage.

Walford, G. (1994) 'Political commitment in the study of the City Technology College, Kingshurst' in D. Halpin and B. Troyna (1994) (eds), *Researching Education Policy*, London: Falmer Press.

Whyte, W. F. (1993 [1943]) *Street Corner Society*, third edition, Chicago: University of Chicago Press.

Willer, D. and Willer, J. (1973) *Systematic Empiricism: A Critique of a Pseudoscience*, Englewood Cliffs, NJ: Prentice-Hall.

Yin, R. K. (1984) *Case Study Research: Design and Methods*, Beverly Hills, CA: Sage.

FUNDAMENTAL ISSUES IN
QUALITATIVE RESEARCH

1

The Fundamental Concepts of Sociology

Max Weber

Prefatory Note

An introductory discussion of concepts can hardly be dispensed with, in spite of the fact that it is unavoidably abstract and hence gives the impression of remoteness from reality. Its method, however, makes no claim to any kind of novelty. On the contrary it attempts only to formulate what all empirical sociology really means when it deals with the same problems, in what it is hoped is a more convenient and somewhat more exact terminology, even though on that account it may seem pedantic. This is true even where terms are used which are apparently new or unfamiliar. As compared to the author's essay in *Logos*,[1] the terminology has been simplified as far as possible and hence considerably changed in order to render it more easily understandable. Unfortunately the most precise formulation cannot always be reconciled with a form which can readily be popularized. In such cases the latter aim has had to be sacrificed.

On the concept of 'understanding'[2] compare the *Allgemeine Psychopathologie* of Karl Jaspers, also a few observations by Heinrich Rickert in the second edition of the *Grenzen der Naturwissenschaftlichen Begriffsbildung* and particularly some of Simmel's discussions in the *Probleme der Geschichtsphilosophie*. For certain methodological considerations the reader may here be referred, as often before in the author's writings, to the procedure of Friedrich Gottl in his work *Die Herrschaft des Wortes*. This book, to be sure, is written in a somewhat difficult style and its argument does not appear everywhere to have been thoroughly thought through. As regards content, reference may be made especially to the fine work of Ferdinand Tönnies, *Gemeinschaft und Gesellschaft*, and also to the gravely misleading book of Rudolph Stammler, *Wirtschaft und Recht*, which may be compared with my criticism in the *Archiv für Sozialwissenschaft* (vol. xxiv, 1907). This critical essay contains many of the fundamental ideas of the following exposition. The present work departs from

Source: Max Weber, *The Theory of Social and Economic Organization* (New York: The Free Press, 1964).

Simmel's method (in the *Soziologie* and the *Philosophie des Geldes*) in drawing a sharp distinction between subjectively intended and objectively valid 'meanings'; two different things which Simmel not only fails to distinguish but often deliberately treats as belonging together.

1: The Definitions of Sociology and of Social Action

1. Sociology (in the sense in which this highly ambiguous word is used here) is a science which attempts the interpretive understanding of social action in order thereby to arrive at a causal explanation of its course and effects. In 'action' is included all human behaviour when and in so far as the acting individual attaches a subjective meaning to it. Action in this sense may be either overt or purely inward or subjective; it may consist of positive intervention in a situation, or of deliberately refraining from such intervention or passively acquiescing in the situation. Action is social in so far as, by virtue of the subjective meaning attached to it by the acting individual (or individuals), it takes account of the behaviour of others and is thereby oriented in its course.[3]

(a) The Methodological Foundations of Sociology[4]

1. 'Meaning' may be of two kinds. The term may refer first to the actual existing meaning in the given concrete case of a particular actor, or to the average or approximate meaning attributable to a given plurality of actors; or secondly to the theoretically conceived *pure type*[5] of subjective meaning attributed to the hypothetical actor or actors in a given type of action. In no case does it refer to an objectively 'correct' meaning or one which is 'true' in some metaphysical sense. It is this which distinguishes the empirical sciences of action, such as sociology and history, from the dogmatic disciplines in that area, such as jurisprudence, logic, ethics, and esthetics, which seek to ascertain the 'true' and 'valid' meanings associated with the objects of their investigation.

2. The line between meaningful action and merely reactive behaviour to which no subjective meaning is attached, cannot be sharply drawn empirically. A very considerable part of all sociologically relevant behaviour, especially purely traditional behaviour, is marginal between the two. In the case of many psychophysical processes, meaningful, i.e. subjectively understandable, action is not to be found at all; in others it is discernible only by the expert psychologist. Many mystical experiences which cannot be adequately communicated in words are, for a person who is not susceptible to such experiences, not fully understandable. At the same time the ability to imagine one's self performing a similar action is not a necessary prerequisite to understanding; 'one need not have been Caesar in order to understand Caesar.' For the verifiable accuracy[6] of interpretation of the meaning of a phenomenon, it is a great help to be able to put one's self imaginatively in the place of the actor and thus sympathetically to participate

in his experiences, but this is not an essential condition of meaningful interpretation. Understandable and non-understandable components of a process are often intermingled and bound up together.

3. All interpretation of meaning, like all scientific observation, strives for clarity and verifiable accuracy of insight and comprehension (*Evidenz*). The basis for certainty in understanding can be either rational, which can be further subdivided into logical and mathematical, or it can be of an emotionally empathic or artistically appreciative quality. In the sphere of action things are rationally evident chiefly when we attain a completely clear intellectual grasp of the action-elements in their intended context of meaning. Empathic or appreciative accuracy is attained when, through sympathetic participation, we can adequately grasp the emotional context in which the action took place. The highest degree of rational understanding is attained in cases involving the meanings of logically or mathematically related propositions; their meaning may be immediately and unambiguously intelligible. We have a perfectly clear understanding of what it means when somebody employs the proposition 2 × 2 = 4 or the Pythagorean theorem in reasoning or argument, or when someone correctly carries out a logical train of reasoning according to our accepted modes of thinking. In the same way we also understand what a person is doing when he tries to achieve certain ends by choosing appropriate means on the basis of the facts of the situation as experience has accustomed us to interpret them. Such an interpretation of this type of rationally purposeful action possesses, for the understanding of the choice of means, the highest degree of verifiable certainty. With a lower degree of certainty, which is, however, adequate for most purposes of explanation, we are able to understand errors, including confusion of problems of the sort that we ourselves are liable to, or the origin of which we can detect by sympathetic self-analysis.

On the other hand, many ultimate ends or values toward which experience shows that human action may be oriented, often cannot be understood completely, though sometimes we are able to grasp them intellectually. The more radically they differ from our own ultimate values, however, the more difficult it is for us to make them understandable by imaginatively participating in them. Depending upon the circumstances of the particular case we must be content either with a purely intellectual understanding of such values or when even that fails, sometimes we must simply accept them as given data. Then we can try to understand the action motivated by them on the basis of whatever opportunities for approximate emotional and intellectual interpretation seem to be available at different points in its course. These difficulties apply, for instance, for people not susceptible to the relevant values, to many unusual acts of religious and charitable zeal; also certain kinds of extreme rationalistic fanaticism of the type involved in some forms of the ideology of the 'rights of men' are in a similar position for people who radically repudiate such points of view.

The more we ourselves are susceptible to them the more readily can we imaginatively participate in such emotional reactions as anxiety, anger, ambition, envy, jealousy, love, enthusiasm, pride, vengefulness, loyalty, devotion, and appetites of all sorts, and thereby understand the irrational conduct which grows out of them. Such conduct is 'irrational,' that is, from the point of view of the rational pursuit of a given end. Even when such emotions are found in a degree of intensity of which the observer himself is completely incapable, he can still have a significant degree of emotional understanding of their meaning and can interpret intellectually their influence on the course of action and the selection of means.

For the purposes of a typological scientific analysis it is convenient to treat all irrational, affectually determined elements of behaviour as factors of deviation from a conceptually pure type of rational action. For example a panic on the stock exchange can be most conveniently analysed by attempting to determine first what the course of action would have been if it had not been influenced by irrational affects; it is then possible to introduce the irrational components as accounting for the observed deviations from this hypothetical course. Similarly, in analysing a political or military campaign it is convenient to determine in the first place what would have been a rational course, given the ends of the participants and adequate knowledge of all the circumstances. Only in this way is it possible to assess the causal significance of irrational factors as accounting for the deviations from this type. The construction of a purely rational course of action in such cases serves the sociologist as a type ('ideal type') which has the merit of clear understandability and lack of ambiguity. By comparison with this it is possible to understand the ways in which actual action is influenced by irrational factors of all sorts, such as affects[7] and errors, in that they account for the deviation from the line of conduct which would be expected on the hypothesis that the action were purely rational.

Only in this respect and for these reasons of methodological convenience, is the method of sociology 'rationalistic.' It is naturally not legitimate to interpret this procedure as involving a 'rationalistic bias' of sociology, but only as a methodological device. It certainly does not involve a belief in the actual predominance of rational elements in human life, for on the question of how far this predominance does or does not exist, nothing whatever has been said. That there is, however, a danger of rationalistic interpretations where they are out of place naturally cannot be denied. All experience unfortunately confirms the existence of this danger.

4. In all the sciences of human action, account must be taken of processes and phenomena which are devoid of subjective meaning,[8] in the role of stimuli, results, favouring or hindering circumstances. To be devoid of meaning is not identical with being lifeless or non-human; every artifact, such as for example a machine, can be understood only in terms of the meaning which its production and use have had or will have for human action; a meaning which may derive from a relation to exceedingly various purposes. Without reference to this meaning such an object remains wholly unintelligible.[9] That which is intelligible or understandable about it is thus its relation to human action in the role either of means or of end; a relation of which the actor or actors can be

said to have been aware and to which their action has been oriented. Only in terms of such categories is it possible to 'understand' objects of this kind. On the other hand processes or conditions, whether they are animate or inanimate, human or non-human, are in the present sense devoid of meaning in so far as they cannot be related to an intended purpose. That is to say they are devoid of meaning if they cannot be related to action in the role of means or ends but constitute only the stimulus, the favouring or hindering circumstances.[10] It may be that the incursion of the Dollart at the beginning of the twelfth century[11] had historical significance as a stimulus to the beginning of certain migrations of considerable importance. Human mortality, indeed the organic life cycle generally from the helplessness of infancy to that of old age, is naturally of the very greatest sociological importance through the various ways in which human action has been oriented to these facts. To still another category of facts devoid of meaning belong certain psychic or psychophysical phenomena such as fatigue, habituation, memory, etc.; also certain typical states of euphoria under some conditions of ascetic mortification; finally, typical variations in the reactions of individuals according to reaction-time, precision, and other modes. But in the last analysis the same principle applies to these as to other phenomena which are devoid of meaning. Both the actor and the sociologist must accept them as data to be taken into account.

It is altogether possible that future research may be able to discover non-understandable uniformities underlying what has appeared to be specifically meaningful action, though little has been accomplished in this direction thus far. Thus, for example, differences in hereditary biological constitution, as of 'races,' would have to be treated by sociology as given data in the same way as the physiological facts of the need of nutrition or the effect of senescence on action. This would be the case if, and in so far as, we had statistically conclusive proof of their influence on sociologically relevant behaviour. The recognition of the causal significance of such factors would naturally not in the least alter the specific task of sociological analysis or of that of the other sciences of action, which is the interpretation of action in terms of its subjective meaning. The effect would be only to introduce certain non-understandable data of the same order as others which, it has been noted above, are already present, into the complex of subjectively understandable motivation at certain points. Thus it may come to be known that there are typical relations between the frequency of certain types of teleological orientation of action or of the degree of certain kinds of rationality and the cephalic index or skin colour or any other biologically inherited characteristic.

5. Understanding may be of two kinds: the first is the direct observational understanding[12] of the subjective meaning of a given act as such, including verbal utterances. We thus understand by direct observation, in this sense, the meaning of the proposition $2 \times 2 = 4$ when we hear or read it. This is a case of the direct rational understanding of ideas. We also understand an outbreak of anger as manifested by facial expression, exclamations or irrational movements. This is direct observational understanding of irrational emotional reactions. We

can understand in a similar observational way the action of a woodcutter or of somebody who reaches for the knob to shut a door or who aims a gun at an animal. This is rational observational understanding of actions.

Understanding may, however, be of another sort, namely explanatory understanding. Thus we understand in terms of *motive* the meaning an actor attaches to the proposition twice two equals four, when he states it or writes it down, in that we understand what makes him do this at precisely this moment and in these circumstances. Understanding in this sense is attained if we know that he is engaged in balancing a ledger or in making a scientific demonstration, or is engaged in some other task of which this particular act would be an appropriate part. This is rational understanding of motivation, which consists in placing the act in an intelligible and more inclusive context of meaning.[13] Thus we understand the chopping of wood or aiming of a gun in terms of motive in addition to direct observation if we know that the woodchopper is working for a wage or is chopping a supply of firewood for his own use or possibly is doing it for recreation. But he might also be 'working off' a fit of rage, an irrational case. Similarly we understand the motive of a person aiming a gun if we know that he has been commanded to shoot as a member of a firing squad, that he is fighting against an enemy, or that he is doing it for revenge. The last is affectually determined and thus in a certain sense irrational. Finally we have a motivational understanding of the outburst of anger if we know that it has been provoked by jealousy, injured pride, or an insult. The last examples are all affectually determined and hence derived from irrational motives. In all the above cases the particular act has been placed in an understandable sequence of motivation, the understanding of which myn be treated as an explanation of the actual course of behaviour. Thus for a science which is concerned with the subjective meaning of action, explanation requires a grasp of the complex of meaning in which an actual course of understandable action thus interpreted belongs.[14] In all such cases, even where the processes are largely affectual, the subjective meaning of the action, including that also of the relevant meaning complexes, will be called the 'intended' meaning.[15] This involves a departure from ordinary usage, which speaks of intention in this sense only in the case of rationally purposive action.

6. In all these cases understanding involves the interpretive grasp of the meaning present in one of the following contexts: (a) as in the historical approach, the actually intended meaning for concrete individual action; or (b) as in cases of sociological mass phenomena the average of, or an approximation to, the actually intended meaning; or (c) the meaning appropriate to a scientifically formulated pure type (an ideal type) of a common phenomenon. The concepts and 'laws' of pure economic theory are examples of this kind of ideal type. They state what course a given type of human action would take if it were strictly rational, unaffected by errors or emotional factors and if, furthermore, it were completely and unequivocally directed to a single end, the maximization of economic advantage. In reality, action takes exactly this

course only in unusual cases, as sometimes on the stock exchange; and even then there is usually only an approximation to the ideal type.[16]

Every interpretation attempts to attain clarity and certainty, but no matter how clear an interpretation as such appears to be from the point of view of meaning, it cannot on this account alone claim to be the causally valid interpretation. On this level it must remain only a peculiarly plausible hypothesis. In the first place the 'conscious motives' may well, even to the actor himself, conceal the various 'motives' and 'repressions' which constitute the real driving force of his action. Thus in such cases even subjectively honest self-analysis has only a relative value. Then it is the task of the sociologist to be aware of this motivational situation and to describe and analyse it, even though it has not actually been concretely part of the conscious 'intention' of the actor; possibly not at all, at least not fully. This is a borderline case of the interpretation of meaning. Secondly, processes of action which seem to an observer to be the same or similar may fit into exceedingly various complexes of motive in the case of the actual actor. Then even though the situations appear superficially to be very similar we must actually understand them or interpret them as very different, perhaps, in terms of meaning, directly opposed.[17] Third, the actors in any given situation are often subject to opposing and conflicting impulses, all of which we are able to understand. In a large number of cases we know from experience it is not possible to arrive at even an approximate estimate of the relative strength of conflicting motives and very often we cannot be certain of our interpretation. Only the actual outcome of the conflict gives a solid basis of judgment.

More generally, verification of subjective interpretation by comparison with the concrete course of events is, as in the case of all hypotheses, indispensable. Unfortunately this type of verification is feasible with relative accuracy only in the few very special cases susceptible of psychological experimentation. The approach to a satisfactory degree of accuracy is exceedingly various, even in the limited number of cases of mass phenomena which can be statistically described and unambiguously interpreted. For the rest there remains only the possibility of comparing the largest possible number of historical or contemporary processes which, while otherwise similar, differ in the one decisive point of their relation to the particular motive or factor the role of which is being investigated. This is a fundamental task of comparative sociology. Often, unfortunately, there is available only the dangerous and uncertain procedure of the 'imaginary experiment' which consists in thinking away certain elements of a chain of motivation and working out the course of action which would then probably ensue, thus arriving at a causal judgment.[18]

For example, the generalization called Gresham's Law is a rationally clear interpretation of human action under certain conditions and under the assumption that it will follow a purely rational course. How far any actual course of action corresponds to this can be verified only by the available statistical evidence for the actual disappearance of under-valued monetary units from circulation. In this case our information serves to demonstrate a high degree of accuracy. The facts of experience were known before the generalization, which was formulated afterwards; but without this successful interpretation our need for causal understanding would evidently be left unsatisfied. On the other hand, without the demonstration that what can here be assumed to be a theoretically adequate interpretation also is in some degree relevant to an actual course of action, a 'law,' no matter how fully demonstrated theoretically, would be worthless for the understanding of action in the real world. In this case the correspondence between the theoretical interpretation of motivation and its empirical verification is entirely satisfactory and the cases are numerous enough so that verification can be considered established. But to take another example, Eduard Meyer has advanced an ingenious theory of the causal significance of the battles of Marathon, Salamis, and Platea for the development of the cultural peculiarities of Greek, and hence, more generally, Western, civilization.[19] This is derived from a meaningful interpretation of certain symptomatic facts having to do with the attitudes of the Greek oracles and prophets towards the Persians. It can only be directly verified by reference to the examples of the conduct of the Persians in cases where they were victorious, as in Jerusalem, Egypt, and Asia Minor, and even this verification must necessarily remain unsatisfactory in certain respects. The striking rational plausibility of the hypothesis must here necessarily be relied on as a support. In very many cases of historical interpretation which seem highly plausible, however, there is not even a possibility of the order of verification which was feasible in this case. Where this is true the interpretation must necessarily remain a hypothesis.

7. A motive is a complex of subjective meaning which seems to the actor himself or to the observer an adequate ground for the conduct in question. We apply the term 'adequacy on the level of meaning'[20] to the subjective interpretation of a coherent course of conduct when and in so far as, according to our habitual modes of thought and feeling, its component parts taken in their mutual relation are recognized to constitute a 'typical' complex of meaning. It is more common to say 'correct.' The interpretation of a sequence of events will on the other hand be called *causally* adequate in so far as, according to established generalizations from experience, there is a probability that it will always actually occur in the same way. An example of adequacy on the level of meaning in this sense is what is, according to our current norms of calculation or thinking, the correct solution of an arithmetical problem. On the other hand, a causally adequate interpretation of the same phenomenon would concern the statistical probability that, according to verified generalizations from experience, there would be a correct or an erroneous solution of the same problem. This also refers to currently accepted norms but includes taking account of typical errors or of typical confusions. Thus causal explanation depends on being able to determine that there is a probability, which in the rare ideal case can be numerically stated, but is always in some sense calculable, that a given observable event (overt or subjective) will be followed or accompanied by another event.

A correct causal interpretation of a concrete course of action is arrived at when the overt action and the motives have both been correctly apprehended and at the same time their relation has become meaningfully comprehensible. A correct causal interpretation of typical action means that the process which is claimed to be typical is shown to be both adequately grasped on the level of meaning and at the same time the interpretation is to some degree causally adequate. If adequacy in respect to meaning is lacking, then no matter how high the degree of uniformity and how precisely its probability can be numerically determined, it is still an incomprehensible statistical probability, whether dealing with overt or subjective processes. On the other hand, even the most perfect adequacy on the level of meaning has causal significance from a sociological point of view only in so far as there is some kind of proof for the existence of a probability[21] that action in fact normally takes the course which has been held to be meaningful. For this there must be some degree of determinable frequency of approximation to an average or a pure type.

Statistical uniformities constitute understandable types of action in the sense of this discussion, and thus constitute 'sociological generalizations,' only when they can be regarded as manifestations of the understandable subjective meaning of a course of social action. Conversely, formulations of a rational course of subjectively understandable action constitute sociological types of empirical process only when they can be empirically observed with a significant degree of approximation. It is unfortunately by no means the case that the actual likelihood of the occurrence of a given course of overt action is always directly proportional to the clarity of subjective interpretation. There are statistics of processes devoid of meaning such as death rates, phenomena of fatigue, the production rate of machines, the amount of rainfall, in exactly the same sense as there are statistics of meaningful phenomena. But only when the phenomena are meaningful is it convenient to speak of sociological statistics. Examples are such cases as crime rates, occupational distributions, price statistics, and statistics of crop acreage. Naturally there are many cases where both components are involved, as in crop statistics.

8. Processes and uniformities which it has here seemed convenient not to designate as (in the present case) sociological phenomena or uniformities because they are not 'understandable,' are naturally not on that account any the less important. This is true even for sociology in the present sense which restricts it to subjectively understandable phenomena – a usage which there is no intention of attempting to impose on anyone else. Such phenomena, however important, are simply treated by a different method from the others; they become conditions, stimuli, furthering or hindering circumstances of action.

9. Action in the sense of a subjectively understandable orientation of behaviour exists only as the behaviour of one or more *individual* human beings. For other cognitive purposes it may be convenient or necessary to consider the individual, for instance, as a collection of cells, as a complex of biochemical reactions, or to conceive his 'psychic' life as made up of a variety of different elements, however these may be defined. Undoubtedly such proce-

dures yield valuable knowledge of causal relationships. But the behaviour of these elements, as expressed in such uniformities, is not subjectively understandable. This is true even of psychic elements because the more precisely they are formulated from a point of view of natural science, the less they are accessible to subjective understanding. This is never the road to interpretation in terms of subjective meaning. On the contrary, both for sociology in the present sense, and for history, the object of cognition is the subjective meaning-complex of action. The behaviour of physiological entities such as cells, or of any sort of psychic elements may at least in principle be observed and an attempt made to derive uniformities from such observations. It is further possible to attempt, with their help, to obtain a causal explanation of individual phenomena, that is, to subsume them under uniformities. But the subjective understanding of action takes the same account of this type of fact and uniformity as of any others not capable of subjective interpretation. This is true, for example, of physical, astronomical, geological, meteorological, geographical, botanical, zoological, and anatomical facts and of such facts as those aspects of psycho-pathology which are devoid of subjective meaning or the facts of the natural conditions of technological processes.

For still other cognitive purposes as, for instance, juristic, or for practical ends, it may on the other hand be convenient or even indispensable to treat social collectivities, such as states, associations, business corporations, foundations, as if they were individual persons. Thus they may be treated as the subjects of rights and duties or as the performers of legally significant actions. But for the subjective interpretation of action in sociological work these collectivities must be treated as *solely* the resultants and modes of organization of the particular acts of individual persons, since these alone can be treated as agents in a course of subjectively understandable action. Nevertheless, the sociologist cannot for his purposes afford to ignore these collective concepts derived from other disciplines. For the subjective interpretation of action has at least two important relations to these concepts. In the first place it is often necessary to employ very similar collective concepts, indeed often using the same terms, in order to obtain an understandable terminology. Thus both in legal terminology and in everyday speech the term 'state' is used both for the legal concept of the state and for the phenomena of social action to which its legal rules are relevant. For sociological purposes, however, the phenomenon 'the state' does not consist necessarily or even primarily of the elements which are relevant to legal analysis; and for sociological purposes there is no such thing as a collective personality which 'acts.' When reference is made in a sociological context to a 'state,' a 'nation,' a 'corporation,' a 'family,' or an 'army corps,' or to similar collectivities, what is meant is, on the contrary, *only* a certain kind of development of actual or possible social actions of individual persons. Both because of its precision and because it is established in general usage the juristic concept is taken over, but is used in an entirely different meaning.

Secondly, the subjective interpretation of action must take account of a fundamentally important fact. These concepts of collective entities which are found both in common sense and in juristic and other technical forms of thought, have a meaning in the minds of individual persons, partly as of something actually existing, partly as something with normative authority. This is true not only of judges and officials, but of ordinary private individuals as well. Actors thus in part orient their action to them, and in this role such ideas have a powerful, often a decisive, causal influence on the course of action of real individuals. This is above all true where the ideas concern a recognized positive or negative normative pattern.[22] Thus, for instance, one of the important aspects of the 'existence' of a modern state, precisely as a complex of social interaction of individual persons, consists in the fact that the action of various individuals is oriented to the belief that it exists or should exist, thus that its acts and laws are valid in the legal sense. This will be further discussed below. Though extremely pedantic and cumbersome it would be possible, if purposes of sociological terminology alone were involved, to eliminate such terms entirely, and substitute newly-coined words. This would be possible even though the word 'state' is used ordinarily not only to designate the legal concept but also the real process of action. But in the above important connexion, at least, this would naturally be impossible.

Thirdly, it is the method of the so-called 'organic' school of sociology[23] to attempt to understand social interaction by using as a point of departure the 'whole' within which the individual acts. His action and behaviour are then interpreted somewhat in the way that a physiologist would treat the role of an organ of the body in the 'economy' of the organism, that is from the point of view of the survival of the latter.[24] How far in other disciplines this type of functional analysis of the relation of 'parts' to a 'whole' can be regarded as definitive, cannot be discussed here; but it is well known that the bio-chemical and bio-physical modes of analysis of the organism are on principle opposed to stopping there. For purposes of sociological analysis two things can be said. First this functional frame of reference is convenient for purposes of practical illustration and for provisional orientation. In these respects it is not only useful but indispensable. But at the same time if its cognitive value is overestimated and its concepts illegitimately 'reified,'[25] it can be highly dangerous. Secondly, in certain circumstances this is the only available way of determining just what processes of social action it is important to understand in order to explain a given phenomenon.[26] But this is only the beginning of sociological analysis as here understood. In the case of social collectivities, precisely as distinguished from organisms, we are in a position to go beyond merely demonstrating functional relationships and uniformities. We can accomplish something which is never attainable in the natural sciences, namely the subjective understanding of the action of the component individuals. The natural sciences on the other hand cannot do this, being limited to the formulation of causal uniformities in objects and events and the explanation of individual facts by applying them. We do not 'understand' the behaviour of cells, but can only observe the relevant functional relationships and generalize on the basis of these observations. This additional achievement of explanation by interpretive understanding, as distinguished from external observation, is of course attained only at a price – the more hypothetical and fragmentary character of its results. Nevertheless, subjective understanding is the specific characteristic of sociological knowledge.

It would lead too far afield even to attempt to discuss how far the behaviour of animals is subjectively understandable to us and vice versa; in both cases the meaning of the term understanding and its extent of application would be highly problematical. But in so far as such understanding existed it would be theoretically possible to formulate a sociology of the relations of men to animals, both domestic and wild. Thus many animals 'understand' commands, anger, love, hostility, and react to them in ways which are evidently often by no means purely instinctive and mechanical and in some sense both consciously meaningful and affected by experience. There is no *a priori* reason to suppose that our ability to share the feelings of primitive men is very much greater.[27] Unfortunately we either do not have any reliable means of determining the subjective state of mind of an animal or what we have is at best very unsatisfactory. It is well known that the problems of animal psychology, however interesting, are very thorny ones. There are in particular various forms of social organization among animals: 'monogamous and polygamous families,' herds, flocks, and finally 'state,' with a functional division of labour. The extent of functional differentiation found in these animal societies is by no means, however, entirely a matter of the degree of organic or morphological differentiation of the individual members of the species. Thus, the functional differentiation found among the termites, and in consequence that of the products of their social activities, is much more advanced than in the case of the bees and ants. In this field it goes without saying that a purely functional point of view is often the best that can, at least for the present, be attained, and the investigator must be content with it. Thus it is possible to study the ways in which the species provides for its survival; that is, for nutrition, defence, reproduction, and reconstruction of the social units. As the principal bearers of these functions, differentiated types of individuals can be identified: 'kings,' 'queens,' 'workers,' 'soldiers,' 'drones,' 'propagators,' 'queen's substitutes,' and so on. Anything more than that was for a long time merely a matter of speculation or of an attempt to determine the extent to which heredity on the one hand and environment on the other would be involved in the development of these 'social' proclivities. This was particularly true of the controversies between Götte and Weisman. The latter's conception of the omnipotence of natural selection was largely based on wholly non-empirical deductions. But all serious authorities are naturally fully agreed that the limitation of analysis to the functional level is only a necessity imposed by our present ignorance which it is hoped will only be temporary.[28]

It is relatively easy to grasp the significance of the functions of these various differentiated types for survival. It is also not difficult to work out the bearing of the hypothesis of the inheritance of acquired characteristics or its reverse on the problem of explaining how these differentiations have come about and further what is the bearing of different variants of the theory of heredity. But this is not enough. We would like especially to know first what factors account for the original differentiation of specialized types from the still neutral undifferentiated species-type. Secondly, it would be important to know what leads the differentiated individual in the typical case to behave in a way which actually serves the survival value of the organized group. Wherever research has made any progress in the solution of these problems it has been through the experimental demonstration of the probability or possibility of the role of chemical stimuli or physiological processes, such as nutritional states, the effects of parasitic castration, etc., in the case of the individual organism. How far there is even a hope that the existence of 'subjective' or 'meaningful' orientation could be made experimentally probable, even the specialist to-day would hardly be in a position to say. A verifiable conception of the state of mind of these social animals accessible to meaningful understanding, would seem to be attainable even as an ideal goal only within narrow limits. However that may be, a contribution to the understanding of human social action is hardly to be expected from this quarter. On the contrary, in the field of animal psychology, human analogies are and must be continually employed. The most that can be hoped for is, then, that these biological analogies may some day be useful in suggesting significant problems. For instance they may throw light on the question of the relative role in the early stages of human social differentiation of mechanical and instinctive factors, as compared with that of the factors which are accessible to subjective interpretation generally, and more particularly to the role of consciously rational action. It is necessary for the sociologist to be thoroughly aware of the fact that in the early stages even of human development, the first set of factors is completely predominant. Even in the later stages he must take account of their continual interaction with the others in a role which is often of decisive importance. This is particularly true of all 'traditional' action[29] and of many aspects of charisma.[30] In the latter field of phenomena lie the seeds of certain types of psychic 'contagion' and it is thus the bearer of many dynamic tendencies of social processes. These types of action are very closely related to phenonema which are understandable either only in biological terms or are subject to interpretation in terms of subjective motives only in fragments and with an almost imperceptible transition to the biological. But all these facts do not discharge sociology from the obligation, in full awareness of the narrow limits to which it is confined, to accomplish what it alone can do.

The various works of Othmar Spann are often full of suggestive ideas though at the same time he is guilty of occasional misunderstandings and above all of arguing on the basis of pure value judgments which have no place in an empirical investigation. But he is undoubtedly correct in doing something to which, however, no one seriously objects, namely, emphasizing the sociological significance of the functional point of view for preliminary orientation to problems. This is what he calls the 'universalistic method.' We certainly need to know what kind of action is functionally necessary for 'survival,' but further and above all for the maintenance of a cultural type and the continuity of the corresponding modes of social action, before it is possible even to inquire how this action has come about and what motives determine it. It is necessary to know what a 'king,' an 'official,' an 'entrepreneur,' a 'procurer,' or a 'magician' does; that is, what kind of typical action, which justifies classifying an individual in one of these categories, is important and relevant for an analysis, before it is possible to undertake the analysis itself.[31] But it is only this analysis itself which can achieve the sociological understanding of the actions of typically differentiated human (and only human) individuals, and which hence constitutes the specific function of sociology. It is a monstrous misunderstanding to think that an 'individualistic' *method* should involve what is in any conceivable sense an individualistic system of *values*. It is as important to avoid this error as the related one which confuses the unavoidable tendency of sociological concepts to assume a rationalistic character with a belief in the predominance of rational motives, or even a positive valuation of 'rationalism.' Even a socialistic economy would have to be understood sociologically in exactly the same kind of 'individualistic' terms; that is, in terms of the action of individuals, the types of 'officials' found in it, as would be the case with a system of free exchange analysed in terms of the theory of marginal utility. It might be possible to find a better method, but in this respect it would be similar. The real empirical sociological investigation begins with the question: What motives determine and lead the individual members and participants in this socialistic community to behave in such a way that the community came into being in the first place and that it continues to exist? Any form of functional analysis which proceeds from the whole to the parts can accomplish only a preliminary preparation for this investigation – a preparation, the utility and indispensability of which, if properly carried out, is naturally beyond question.

10. It is customary to designate various sociological generalizations, as for example 'Gresham's Law,' as scientific 'laws.' These are in fact typical probabilities confirmed by observation to the effect that under certain given conditions an expected course of social action will occur, which is understandable in terms of the typical motives and typical subjective intentions of the actors.[32] These generalizations are both understandable and definite in the highest degree in so far as the typically observed course of action can be understood in terms of the purely rational pursuit of an end, or where for reasons of methodological convenience such a theoretical type can be heuristically employed. In such cases the relations of means and end will be clearly understandable on grounds of experience, particularly where the choice of means was 'inevitable.' In such cases it is legitimate to assert that in so far as the action was rigorously rational it could not have taken any other course because for technical reasons, given their clearly defined ends, no other means were available to the actors. This very case demonstrates how erroneous it is to regard any kind of 'psychology' as the ultimate foundation of the sociological interpretation of action. The term 'psychology,' to be sure, is to-day

understood in a wide variety of senses. For certain quite specific methodological purposes the type of treatment which attempts to follow the procedures
of the natural sciences employs a distinction between 'physical' and 'psychic'
phenomena which is entirely foreign to the disciplines concerned with human
action, at least in the present sense. The results of a type of psychological
investigation which employs the methods of the natural sciences in any one
of various possible ways may naturally, like the results of any other science,
have, in specific contexts, outstanding significance for sociological problems;
indeed this has often happened. But this use of the results of psychology is
something quite different from the investigation of human behaviour in terms
of its subjective meaning. Hence sociology has no closer logical relationship
on a general analytical level to this type of psychology than to any other science. The source of error lies in the concept of the 'psychic.' It is held that
everything which is not physical is *ipso facto* psychic, but that the *meaning* of a
train of mathematical reasoning which a person carries out is not in the relevant sense 'psychic.' Similarly the rational deliberation of an actor as to
whether the results of a given proposed course of action will or will not promote certain specific interests, and the corresponding decision, do not become
one bit more understandable by taking 'psychological' considerations into
account. But it is precisely on the basis of such rational assumptions that most
of the laws of sociology, including those of economics, are built up. On the
other hand, in explaining the irrationalities of action sociologically, that form
of psychology which employs the method of subjective understanding undoubtedly can make decisively important contributions. But this does not alter
the fundamental methodological situation.

11. It has continually been assumed as obvious that the science of sociology seeks to formulate type concepts and generalized uniformities of empirical
process. This distinguishes it from history, which is oriented to the causal analysis and explanation of individual actions, structures, and personalities
possessing cultural significance. The empirical material which underlies the
concepts of sociology consists to a very large extent, though by no means
exclusively, of the same concrete processes of action which are dealt with by
historians. Among the various bases on which its concepts are formulated and
its generalizations worked out, is an attempt to justify its important claim to
be able to make a contribution to the causal explanation of some historically
and culturally important phenomenon.[33] As in the case of every generalizing
science the abstract character of the concepts of sociology is responsible for
the fact that, compared with actual historical reality, they are relatively lacking in fullness of concrete content. To compensate for this disadvantage,
sociological analysis can offer a greater precision of concepts. This precision
is obtained by striving for the highest possible degree of adequacy on the level
of meaning in accordance with the definition of that concept put forward
above. It has already been repeatedly stressed that this aim can be realized
in a particularly high degree in the case of concepts and generalizations which
formulate rational processes. But sociological investigation attempts to include

in its scope various irrational phenomena, as well as prophetic, mystic, and affectual modes of action, formulated in terms of theoretical concepts which are adequate on the level of meaning. In *all* cases, rational or irrational, sociological analysis both abstracts from reality and at the same time helps us to understand it, in that it shows with what degree of approximation a concrete historical phenomenon can be subsumed under one or more of these concepts. For example, the same historical phenomenon may be in one aspect 'feudal,' in another 'patrimonial,' in another 'bureaucratic,' and in still another 'charismatic.' In order to give a precise meaning to these terms, it is necessary for the sociologist to formulate pure ideal types of the corresponding forms of action which in each case involve the highest possible degree of logical integration by virtue of their complete adequacy on the level of meaning. But precisely because this is true, it is probably seldom if ever that a real phenomenon can be found which corresponds exactly to one of these ideally constructed pure types. The case is similar to a physical reaction which has been calculated on the assumption of an absolute vacuum. Theoretical analysis in the field of sociology is possible only in terms of such pure types.[34] It goes without saying that in addition it is convenient for the sociologist from time to time to employ average types of an empirical statistical character. There are concepts which do not require methodological discussion at this point. But when reference is made to 'typical' cases, the term should always be understood, unless otherwise stated, as meaning *ideal* types, which may in turn be rational or irrational as the case may be (thus in economic theory they are always rational), but in any case are always constructed with a view to adequacy on the level of meaning.

It is important to realize that in the sociological field as elsewhere, averages, and hence average types, can be formulated with a relative degree of precision only where they are concerned with differences of degree in respect to action which remains qualitatively the same. Such cases do occur, but in the majority of cases of action important to history or sociology the motives which determine it are qualitatively heterogeneous. Then it is quite impossible to speak of an 'average' in the true sense. The ideal types of social action which for instance are used in economic theory are thus 'unrealistic' or abstract in that they always ask what course of action would take place if it were purely rational and oriented to economic ends alone. But this construction can be used to aid in the understanding of action not purely economically determined but which involves deviations arising from traditional restraints, affects, errors, and the intrusion of other than economic purposes or considerations. This can take place in two ways. First, in analysing the extent to which in the concrete case, or on the average for a class of cases, the action was in part economically determined along with the other factors. Secondly, by throwing the discrepancy between the actual course of events and the ideal type into relief, the analysis of the non-economic motives actually involved is facilitated. The procedure would be very similar in employing an ideal type of mystical orientation with its appropriate attitude of indifference to worldly things, as a tool for analysing its consequences for the actor's relation to ordinary life; for instance, to political or economic affairs. The more sharply and precisely the ideal type has been constructed, thus the more abstract and unrealistic in this sense it is, the better it is able to perform its methodological functions in formulating the clarification of terminology, and in the formulation of classifications, and of hypotheses. In working out a concrete causal explanation of individual events, the procedure of the historian is essentially the same. Thus in attempting to explain the campaign of 1866, it is indispensable both in the case of Moltke and of Benedek to attempt to construct imaginatively how each, given fully adequate knowledge both of his own situation and of that of his opponent, would have acted. Then it is possible to compare with this the actual course of action and to arrive at a causal explanation of the observed deviations, which will be attributed to such factors as misinformation, strategical errors, logical fallacies, personal temperament, or considerations outside the realm of strategy. Here, too, an ideal-typical construction of rational action is actually employed even though it is not made explicit.

The theoretical concepts of sociology are ideal types not only from the objective point of view, but also in their application to subjective processes. In the great majority of cases actual action goes on in a state of inarticulate half-consciousness or actual unconsciousness of its subjective meaning. The actor is more likely to 'be aware' of it in a vague sense than he is to 'know' what he is doing or be explicitly self-conscious about it. In most cases his action is governed by impulse or habit. Only occasionally and, in the uniform action of large numbers often only in the case of a few individuals, is the subjective meaning of the action, whether rational or irrational, brought clearly into consciousness. The ideal type of meaningful action where the meaning is fully conscious and explicit is a marginal case. Every sociological or historical investigation, in applying its analysis to the empirical facts, must take this fact into account. But the difficulty need not prevent the sociologist from systematizing his concepts by the classification of possible types of subjective meaning. That is, he may reason as if action actually proceeded on the basis of clearly self-conscious meaning. The resulting deviation from the concrete facts must continually be kept in mind whenever it is a question of this level of concreteness, and must be carefully studied with reference both to degree and kind. It is often necessary to choose between terms which are either clear or unclear. Those which are clear will, to be sure, have the abstractness of ideal types, but they are none the less preferable for scientific purposes.[35]

Notes

1. Vol. iv (1913, pp. 253 ff.); reprinted in *Gesammelte Aufsätze zur Wissenschaftslehre*, pp. 403–450.

2. The German term is *Verstehen.* As Weber uses it this is a technical term with a distinctly narrower meaning than either the German or the English in everyday usage.

Its primary reference in this work is to the observation and theoretical interpretation of the subjective 'states of mind' of actors. But it also extends to the grasp of the meaning of logical and other systems of symbols, a meaning which is usually thought of as in some sense 'intended' by a mind or intelligent being of some sort. The most important point about this concept seems to the editor to be the fact that in so far as phenomena are 'understood' in this technical sense, the relevant facts are stated and analysed within a certain frame of reference, that of 'action.' For present purposes the most important feature of this frame of reference is its use of 'subjective categories.' The essential thing is the operational applicability of such categories, not the common sense empirical question of whether the actor is conscious of the meanings imputed to him or in the ordinary sense 'intended' a given course of action. For a further discussion of these problems, see Talcott Parsons, *The Structure of Social Action*, especially chaps. ii and xix.

It has not seemed advisable to attempt a rigorous use of a single English term whenever Weber employs *Verstehen*. 'Understanding' has been most commonly used. Other expressions such as 'subjectively understandable,' 'interpretation in subjective terms,' 'comprehension,' etc., have been used from time to time as the context seemed to demand. – ED.

3. In this series of definitions Weber employs several important terms which need discussion. In addition to *Verstehen*, which has already been commented upon, there are four important ones: *Deuten, Sinn, Handeln*, and *Verhalten. Deuten* has generally been translated as 'interpret., As used by Weber in this context it refers to the interpretation of subjective states of mind and the meanings which can be imputed as intended by an actor. Any other meaning of the word 'interpretation' is irrelevant to Weber's discussion. The term *Sinn* has generally been translated as 'meaning'; and its variations, particularly the corresponding adjectives, *sinnhaft, sinnvoll, sinnfremd*, have been dealt with by appropriately modifying the term meaning. The reference here again is always to features of the content of subjective states of mind or of symbolic systems which are ultimately referable to such states of mind.

The terms *Handeln* and *Verhalten* are directly related. *Verhalten* is the broader term referring to any mode of behaviour of human individuals, regardless of the frame of reference in terms of which it is analysed. 'Behaviour' has seemed to be the most appropriate English equivalent. *Handeln*, on the other hand, refers to the concrete phenomenon of human behaviour only in so far as it is capable of 'understanding,' in Weber's technical sense, in terms of subjective categories. The most appropriate English equivalent has seemed to be 'action.' This corresponds to the editor's usage in *The Structure of Social Action* and would seem to be fairly well established. 'Conduct' is also closely similar and has sometimes been used. *Deuten, Verstehen*, and *Sinn* are thus applicable to human behaviour only in so far as it constitutes action or conduct in this specific sense. – ED.

4. Weber's text is organized in a somewhat unusual manner. He lays down certain fundamental definitions and then proceeds to comment upon them. The definitions themselves are in the original printed in large type, the subsidiary comments in smaller type. For the purposes of this translation it has not seemed best to make a distinction in type form, but the reader should be aware that the numbered paragraphs which follow a definition or group of them are in the nature of comments, rather than the continuous development of a general line of argument. This fact accounts for what is sometimes a relatively fragmentary character of the development and for the abrupt transition from one subject to another. Weber apparently did not intend this material

to be 'read' in the ordinary sense, but rather to serve as a reference work for the clarification and systematization of theoretical concepts and their implications. While the comments under most of the definitions are relatively brief, under the definitions of Sociology and of Social Action, Weber wrote what is essentially a methodological essay. This makes sec. 1 out of proportion to the other sections of this and the following chapters. It has, however, seemed best to retain Weber's own plan for the subdivision of the material. – ED.

5. Weber means by 'pure type' what he himself generally called and what has come to be known in the literature about his methodology as the 'ideal type.' The reader may be referred for general orientation to Weber's own Essay (to which he himself refers below), *Die Objektivität sozialwissenschaftlicher Erkenntnis*, to two works of Dr. Alexander von Schelting, 'Die logische Theorie der historischen Kulturwissenschaften von Max Weber' (*Archiv fuer Sozialwissenschaft*, vol. xlix), and *Max Webers Wissenschaftslehre*, and to the editor's *Structure of Social Action*, chap. xvi. A somewhat different interpretation is given in Theodore Abel, *Systematic Sociology in Germany*, chap. iv. – ED.

6. This is an imperfect rendering of the German term *Evidenz*, for which, unfortunately, there is no good English equivalent. It has hence been rendered in a number of different ways, varying with the particular context in which it occurs. The primary meaning refers to the basis on which a scientist or thinker becomes satisfied of the certainty or acceptability of a proposition. As Weber himself points out, there are two primary aspects of this. On the one hand a conclusion can be 'seen' to follow from given premises by virtue of logical, mathematical, or possibly other modes of meaningful relation. In this sense one 'sees' the solution of an arithmetical problem or the correctness of the proof of a geometrical theorem. The other aspect is concerned with empirical observation. If an act of observation is competently performed, in a similar sense one 'sees' the truth of the relevant descriptive proposition. The term *Evidenz* does not refer to the process of observing, but to the quality of its result, by virtue of which the observer feels justified in affirming a given statement. Hence 'certainty' has seemed a suitable translation in some contexts, 'clarity' in others, 'accuracy' in still others. The term 'intuition' is not usable because it refers to the process rather than to the result. – ED.

7. A term now much used in psychological literature, especially that of Psychoanalysis. It is roughly equivalent to 'emotion' but more precise. – ED.

8. The German term is *sinnfremd*. This should not be translated by 'meaningless,' but interpreted in the technical context of Weber's use of *Verstehen* and *Sinndeutung*. The essential criterion is the impossibility of placing the object in question in a complex of relations on the meaningful level. – ED.

9. *Unverstehbar*.

10. Surely this passage states too narrow a conception of the scope of meaningful interpretation. It is certainly not only in terms such as those of the rational means–end schema, that it is possible to make action understandable in terms of subjective categories. This probably can actually be called a source of rationalistic bias in Weber's work. In practice he does not adhere at all rigorously to this methodological position. For certain possibilities in this broader field, see the editor's *Structure of Social Action*, chaps. vi and xi. – ED.

11. A gulf of the North Sea which broke through the Netherlands coast, flooding an area. – ED.

12. Weber here uses the term *aktuelles Verstehen*, which he contrasts with *erklärendes Verstehen*. The latter he also refers to as *motivationsmaessig*. 'Aktuell' in this context has

been translated as 'observational.' It is clear from Weber's discussion that the primary criterion is the possibility of deriving the meaning of an act or symbolic expression from immediate observation without reference to any broader context. In *erklärendes Verstehen*, on the other hand, the particular act must be placed in a broader context of meaning involving facts which cannot be derived from immediate observation of a particular act or expression. – ED.

13. The German term is *Sinnzusammenhang*. It refers to a plurality of elements which form a coherent whole on the level of meaning. There are several possible modes of meaningful relation between such elements, such as logical consistency, the esthetic harmony of a style, or the appropriateness of means to an end. In any case, however, a *Sinnzusammenhang* must be distinguished from a system of elements which are causally interdependent. There seems to be no single English term or phrase which is always adequate. According to variations in the context, 'context of meaning,' 'complex of meaning,' and sometimes 'meaningful system' have been employed. – ED.

14. On the significance of this type of explanation for causal relationship, see para. 6, pp. 96 ff. below in the present section.

15. The German is *gemeinter Sinn*. Weber departs from ordinary usage not only in broadening the meaning of this conception. As he states at the end of the present methodological discussion, he does not restrict the use of this concept to cases where a clear self-conscious awareness of such meaning can be reasonably attributed to every individual actor. Essentially, what Weber is doing is to formulate an operational concept. The question is not whether in a sense obvious to the ordinary person such an intended meaning 'really exists,' but whether the concept is capable of providing a logical framework within which scientifically important observations can be made. The test of validity of the observations is not whether their object is immediately clear to common sense, but whether the results of these technical observations can be satisfactorily organized and related to those of others in a systematic body of knowledge. – ED.

16. The scientific functions of such construction have been discussed in the author's article in the *Archiv für Sozialwissenschaft*, vol. xix, pp. 64 ff.

17. Simmel, in his *Probleme der Geschichtsphilosophie*, gives a number of examples.

18. The above passage is an exceedingly compact statement of Weber's theory of the logical conditions of proof of causal relationship. He developed this most fully in his essay *Die Objektivität sozialwissenschaftlicher Erkenntnis*, op. cit. It is also discussed in certain of the other essays which have been collected in the volume, *Gesammelte Aufsätze zur Wissenschaftslehre*. The best and fullest secondary discussion is to be found in Von Schelting's book, *Max Webers Wissenschaftslehre*. There is a briefer discussion in chap. xvi of the editor's *Structure of Social Action*. – ED.

19. See Edvard Meyer, *Geschichte des Altertums*, Stuttgart, 1901, vol. iii, pp. 420, 444 ff.

20. The expression *sinnhafte Adäquanz* is one of the most difficult of Weber's technical terms to translate. In most places the cumbrous phrase 'adequacy on the level of meaning' has had to be employed. It should be clear from the progress of the discussion that what Weber refers to is a satisfying level of knowledge for the particular purposes of the subjective state of mind of the actor or actors. He is, however, careful to point out that *causal* adequacy involves in addition to this a satisfactory correspondence between the results of observations from the subjective point of view and from the objective; that is, observations of the overt course of action which can be described without reference to the state of mind of the actor. For a discussion of the methodological problem involved here, see *Structure of Social Action*, chaps. ii and v. – ED.

21. This is the first occurrence in Weber's text of the term *Chance* which he uses very frequently. It is here translated by 'probability,' because he uses it as interchangeable with *Wahrscheinlichkeit.* As the term 'probability' is used in a technical mathematical and statistical sense, however, it implies the possibility of numerical statement. In most of the cases where Weber uses *Chance* this is out of the question. It is, however, possible to speak in terms of higher and lower degrees of probability. To avoid confusion with the technical mathematical concept, the term 'likelihood' will often be used in the translation. It is by means of this concept that Weber, in a highly ingenious way, has bridged the gap between the interpretation of meaning and the inevitably more complex facts of overt action. – ED.

22. By a negative normative pattern, Weber means one which prohibits certain possible modes of action. – ED.

23. A classical example is Schäffle's brilliant work, *Bau und Leben des sozialen Körpers.*

24. One of the most illuminating treatments of physiological problems from such a functional point of view, which is readily understandable to the layman, is W. B. Cannon: *The Wisdom of the Body*, second edition, 1938. The point of reference on this physiological level is not primarily survival value to the species in the sense of the Darwinian theory of evolution, but rather the maintenance of the individual organism as a 'going concern' in carrying through its typical life cycle. What is the life cycle, is to the physiologist essentially a mattes of empirical observation. – ED.

25. The term 'reification' as used by Professor Morris Cohen in his book, *Reason and Nature*, seems to fit Weber's meaning exactly. A concept or system of concepts, which critical analysis can show to be abstract, is 'reified' when it is used naively as though it provided an adequate total description of the concrete phenomenon in question. The fallacy of 'reification' is virtually another name for what Professor Whitehead has called 'the fallacy of misplaced concreteness.' See his *Science and the Modern World.* – ED.

26. Compare the famous dictum of a well-known physiologist: 'sec. 10. The spleen. Of the spleen, gentlemen, we know nothing. So much for the spleen.' Actually, of course, he 'knew' a good deal about the spleen – its position, size, shape, etc.; but he could say nothing about its function, and it was his inability to do this that he called 'ignorance.'

27. The present state of anthropological research, which has advanced enormously since Weber wrote, would seem to throw considerable doubt on the validity of this statement. In making it, Weber apparently does not adequately take account of the fundamental fact that no non-human species has even a primitive form of language; whereas no human group is known without a 'fully-developed' one. The ability to use language is on the one hand a fundamental index of the state of development of the individual himself, so far as it is relevant to the theory of action. On the other hand, language is perhaps the most crucially important source of evidence for subjective phenomena. What has seemed to so many 'civilized' men to be the strangeness and incomprehensibility of the behaviour and thought of primitive peoples, is apparently primarily a matter of the former's failure to submit the latter to an adequately thorough and rigorous investigation. It can be said with considerable confidence that a competently trained anthropological field worker is in a position to obtain a level of insight into the states of mind of a people whom he has carefully studied, which is quite comparable, if not superior, to that of the historian of a civilization at all widely different from his own. – ED.

28. See, for example, for an account of the state of knowledge of the termites, the study of Karl Escherich, *Die Ameise*, 1906.

29. See sec. 2.

30. Since the term 'charisma' was, in its sociological usage, introduced by Weber himself from a different field, no attempt has been made to find an English equivalent and it will be used directly throughout. Weber took it from the corresponding Greek which was used in the literature of early Christianity and means 'the gift of grace.' For further discussion of the concept, see below, chap. iii, especially secs. 2 and 10. – ED.

31. This is what Rickert means by *Wertbezogenheit.*

32. It is desirable at this point to call attention to Weber's usage of the term 'law' in a scientific sense. In conformity with his strong emphasis upon the role of ideal types among possible kinds of generalized concepts in the social sciences, by 'law,' or a German expression he frequently uses, *generelle Erfahrungsregel,* he usually means what is perhaps most conveniently called a 'type generalization.' It is not an empirical generalization in the ordinary sense in that it does not adequately describe any particular concrete course of events but is abstract in the same sense as the ideal type. Where it is possible on the basis of ideal type analysis to construct not merely a structural form, but, under certain conditions, a course of events which can be predicted if certain conditions are given, it is possible to formulate such generalizations. These generalizations are, however, not methodologically equivalent to most of the laws of physics, especially of analytical mechanics. The latter do not generally formulate a concrete course of events, but rather a uniform relationship between the values of two or more variables. Weber does not even consider the possibility of formulating laws of this latter type, essentially because he does not develop social theory explicitly in the direction of setting up a system of inter-dependent variables, but confines it to the ideal type level. – ED.

33. This is one of the most important problems with which Weber was concerned in his methodological studies. He insisted on the very great importance of the cultural significance of a problem for the values of the time in determining the direction of interest of the investigator. He formulated this relation in his important concept of the *Wertbeziehung* of social science concepts. But he went so far as to deny the legitimacy of the formulation of a generalized theoretical system as an aim of theoretical analysis in social science. This denial seems to rest on a failure on Weber's part to carry his criticism of certain aspects of German idealistic social thought through to its logical conclusion. For Weber's position, see *Die Objektivität sozialwissenschaftlicher Erkenntnis,* op. cit., and Von Schelting, *Max Webers Wissenschaftslehre.* For a criticism of Weber's position, see *Structure of Social Action,* chap. xvi. – ED.

34. The difficulty of maintaining the position Weber here takes has been discussed in the Introduction. See pp. 12 ff. – ED.

35. On all these questions see the author's article in *Archiv für Sozialwissenschaft,* vol. xix, op. cit. Reprinted in *Gesammelte Aufsätze zur Wissenschaftslehre,* pp. 176–214.

2

What is Wrong with Social Theory?*

Herbert Blumer

My concern is limited to that form of social theory which stands or presumes to stand as a part of empirical science.[1]

The aim of theory in empirical science is to develop analytical schemes of the empirical world with which the given science is concerned. This is done by conceiving the world abstractly, that is in terms of classes of objects and of relations between such classes. Theoretical schemes are essentially proposals as to the nature of such classes and of their relations where this nature is problematic or unknown. Such proposals become guides to investigation to see whether they or their implications are true. Thus, theory exercises compelling influence on research – setting problems, staking out objects and leading inquiry into asserted relations. In turn, findings of fact test theories, and in suggesting new problems invite the formulation of new proposals. Theory, inquiry and empirical fact are interwoven in a texture of operation with theory guiding inquiry, inquiry seeking and isolating facts, and facts affecting theory. The fruitfulness of their interplay is the means by which an empirical science develops.

Compared with this brief sketch of theory in empirical science, social theory in general shows grave shortcomings. Its divorcement from the empirical world is glaring. To a preponderant extent it is compartmentalized into a world of its own, inside of which it feeds on itself. We usually localize it in separate courses and separate fields. For the most part it has its own literature. Its lifeline is primarily exegesis – a critical examination of prior theoretical schemes, the compounding of portions of them into new arrangements, the translation of old ideas into a new vocabulary, and the occasional addition of a new notion as a result of reflection on other theories. It is remarkably susceptible to the importation of schemes from outside its own empirical field, as in the case of the organic analogy, the evolutionary doctrine, physicalism, the instinct doctrine, behaviorism, psychoanalysis, and the doctrine of the conditioned reflex. Further, when applied to the empirical world social theory

Source: *American Sociological Review*, vol. 19, no. 1, 1954, pp. 3–10.

is primarily an interpretation which orders the world into its mold, not a studious cultivation of empirical facts to see if the theory fits. In terms of both origin and use social theory seems in general not to be geared into its empirical world.

Next, social theory is conspicuously defective in its guidance of research inquiry. It is rarely couched in such form as to facilitate or allow directed investigation to see whether it or its implications are true. Thus, it is gravely restricted in setting research problems, in suggesting kinds of empirical data to be sought, and in connecting these data to one another. Its divorcement from research is as great as its divorcement from its empirical world.

Finally, it benefits little from the vast and ever growing accumulation of "facts" that come from empirical observation and research inquiry. While this may be due to an intrinsic uselessness of such facts for theoretic purposes, it also may be due to deficiency in theory.

These three lines of deficiency in social theory suggest that all that is needed is to correct improper preoccupations and bad working practices in theorizing. We hear repeatedly recommendations and injunctions to this effect. Get social theorists to reduce drastically their preoccupation with the literature of social theory and instead get in touch with the empirical social world. Let them renounce their practice of taking in each other's washing and instead work with empirical data. Let them develop their own conceptual capital through the cultivation of their own empirical field instead of importing spurious currency from alien realms. Get them to abandon the practice of merely interpreting things to fit their theories and instead test their theories. Above all, get them to cast their theory into forms which are testable. Have them orient their theory to the vast bodies of accumulated research findings and develop theory in the light of such findings.

These are nice injunctions to which all of us would subscribe. They do have a limited order of merit. But they neither isolate the problem of what is basically wrong with social theory nor do they provide means of correcting the difficulties. The problem continues to remain in the wake of studies made with due respect to the injunctions. There have been and there are many able and conscientious people in our field, alone, who have sought and are seeking to develop social theory through careful, sometimes meticulous preoccupation with empirical data – Robert E. Park, W. I. Thomas, Florian Znaniecki, Edwin Sutherland, Stuart Dodd, E. W. Burgess, Samuel Stouffer, Paul Lazarsfeld, Robert Merton, Louis Wirth, Robin Williams, Robert Bales and dozens of others who equally merit mention. All of these people are empirically minded. All have sought in their respective ways to guide research by theory and to assess their theoretical propositions in the light of empirical data. Practically all of them are familiar with the textbook canons of empirical research. We cannot correctly accuse such people of indifference to the empirical world, or of procedural naivete, or of professional incompetence. Yet their theories and their work are held suspect and found wanting, some theories by some, other theories by others. Indeed, the criticisms and counter-criticisms directed to their respective work are severe and box the compass. It is obvious that we have to probe deeper than the level of the above injunctions.

In my judgment the appropriate line of probing is with regard to the concept. Theory is of value in empirical science only to the extent to which it connects fruitfully with the empirical world. Concepts are the means, and the only means of establishing such connection, for it is the concept that points to the empirical instances about which a theoretical proposal is made. If the concept is clear as to what it refers, then sure identification of the empirical instances may be made. With their identification, they can be studied carefully, used to test theoretical proposals and exploited for suggestions as to new proposals. Thus, with clear concepts theoretical statements can be brought into close and self-correcting relations with the empirical world. Contrariwise, vague concepts deter the identification of appropriate empirical instances, and obscure the detection of what is relevant in the empirical instances that are chosen. Thus, they block connection between theory and its empirical world and prevent their effective interplay.

A recognition of the crucial position of concepts in theory in empirical science does not mean that other matters are of no importance. Obviously, the significance of intellectual abilities in theorizing, such as originality and disciplined imagination, requires no highlighting. Similarly, techniques of study are of clear importance. Also, bodies of fact are necessary. Yet, profound and brilliant thought, an arsenal of the most precise and ingenious instruments, and an extensive array of facts are meaningless in empirical science without the empirical relevance, guidance and analytical order that can come only through concepts. Since in empirical science everything depends on how fruitfully and faithfully thinking intertwines with the empirical world of study, and since concepts are the gateway to that world, the effective functioning of concepts is a matter of decisive importance.

Now, it should be evident that concepts in social theory are distressingly vague. Representative terms like mores, social institutions, attitudes, social class, value, cultural norm, personality, reference group, social structure, primary group, social process, social system, urbanization, accommodation, differential discrimination and social control do not discriminate cleanly their empirical instances. At best they allow only rough identification, and in what is so roughly identified they do not permit a determination of what is covered by the concept and what is not. Definitions which are provided to such terms are usually no clearer than the concepts which they seek to define. Careful scrutinizing of our concepts forces one to recognize that they rest on vague sense and not on precise specification of attributes. We see this in our common experience in explaining concepts to our students or outsiders. Formal definitions are of little use. Instead, if we are good teachers we seek to give the sense of the concept by the use of a few apt illustrations. This initial sense, in time, becomes entrenched through the sheer experience of sharing in a common universe of discourse. Our concepts come to be taken for granted on the basis of such a sense. It is such a sense and not precise specifications that guides us in our discipline in transactions with our empirical world.

This ambiguous nature of concepts is the basic deficiency in social theory. It hinders us in coming to close grips with our empirical world, for we are not sure what to grip. Our uncertainty as to what we are referring obstructs us from asking pertinent questions and setting relevant problems for research. The vague sense dulls our perception and thus vitiates directed empirical observation. It subjects our reflection on possible relations between concepts to wide bands of error. It encourages our theorizing to revolve in a separate world of its own with only a tenuous connection with the empirical world. It limits severely the clarification and growth that concepts may derive from the findings of research. It leads to the undisciplined theorizing that is bad theorizing.

If the crucial deficiency of social theory, and for that matter of our discipline, is the ambiguous nature of our concepts, why not proceed to make our concepts clear and definite? This is the nub of the problem. The question is how to do this. The possible lines of answer can be reduced a lot by recognizing that a great deal of endeavor, otherwise conscientious and zealous, does not touch the problem. The clarification of concepts is not achieved by introducing a new vocabulary of terms or substituting new terms – the task is not one of lexicography. It is not achieved by extensive reflection on theories to show their logical weaknesses and pitfalls. It is not accomplished by forming or importing new theories. It is not achieved by inventing new technical instruments or by improving the reliability of old techniques – such instruments and techniques are neutral to the concepts on behalf of which they may be used. The clarification of concepts does not come from piling up mountains of research findings. As just one illustration I would point to the hundreds of studies of attitudes and the thousands of items they have yielded; these thousands of items of finding have not contributed one iota of clarification to the concept of attitudes. By the same token, the mere extension of research in scope and direction does not offer in itself assurance of leading to clarification of concepts. These various lines of endeavor, as the results themselves seem abundantly to testify, do not meet the problem of the ambiguous concept.

The most serious attempts to grapple with this problem in our field take the form of developing fixed and specific procedures designed to isolate a stable and definitive empirical content, with this content constituting the definition or the reference of the concept. The better known of these attempts are the formation of operational definitions, the experimental construction of concepts, factoral analysis, the formation of deductive mathematical systems and, although slightly different, the construction of reliable quantitative indexes. Although these attempts vary as to the kind of specific procedure that is used, they are alike in that the procedure is designed to yield through repeated performances a stable and definitive finding. A definition of intelligence as being the intelligence quotient is a convenient illustration of what is common to these approaches. The intelligence quotient is a stable and discriminating finding that can be checked through a repetition of clearly specified procedures. Ignoring questions as to the differential merit and the differential level of penetration between these approaches, it would seem that in yielding a specific and discriminating content they are the answer to the problem of the ambiguous concept in social theory. Many hold that resolute employment of one or the other of these methods will yield definitive concepts with the consequence that theory can be applied decisively to the empirical world and tested effectively in research inquiry.

So far, the suitability of these precision endeavors to solving the problem of the ambiguous concept remains in the realm of claim and promise. They encounter three pronounced difficulties in striving to produce genuine concepts related to our empirical world.

First, insofar as the definitive empirical content that is isolated is regarded as constituting by itself the concept (as in the statement that, "X is the intelligence quotient") it is lacking in theoretic possibilities and cannot be regarded as yielding a genuine concept. It does not have the abstract character of a class with specifiable attributes. What is "intelligence quotient" as a class and what are its properties? While one can say that "intelligence quotient" is a class made up of a series of specific intelligence quotients, can one or does one point out common features of this series – features which, of course, would characterize the class? Until the specific instances of empirical content isolated by a given procedure are brought together in a class with common distinguishing features of content, no concept with theoretic character is formed. One cannot make proposals about the class or abstraction or relate it to other abstractions.

Second, insofar as the definitive empirical content that is isolated is regarded as qualifying something beyond itself (as in the statement that, "Intelligence is the intelligence quotient" wherein intelligence would now be conceived as including a variety of common sense references such as ability to solve business problems, plan campaigns, invent, exercise diplomatic ingenuity, etc.), the concept is constituted by this something which is beyond the definitive empirical content. But since this "something beyond" is not dealt with by the procedure yielding the definitive empirical content, the concept remains in the ambiguous position that originally set the problem. In other words, the concept continues to be constituted by general sense or understanding and not by specification.

Third, a pertinent question has to be faced as to the relation of the definitive empirical content that is isolated, to the empirical world that is the concern of the discipline. One has to have the possibilities of establishing the place and role of the specific content, in the empirical world in order for the empirical content to enter into theory about the world. A specific procedure may yield a stable finding, sometimes necessarily so by the internal mechanics of the procedure. Unless this finding is shown to have a relevant place in the empirical world under study, it has no value for theory. The showing of such relevancy is a critical difficulty confronting efforts to establish definitive concepts by isolating stable empirical contents through precise procedures. Incidentally, the establishment of such relevancy is not accomplished by making correlations. While classes of objects or items covered by concepts may be correlated, the mere establishment of correlations between items does not form concepts or, in other words, does not give an item as an instance of a class, a place or a function. Further, the relevance of an isolated empirical content to the empirical world is not established merely by using the concept to label given occurrences in that empirical world. This is a semantic pit into which scores of workers fall, particularly those working with operational definitions of concepts or with experimental construction of concepts. For example, a careful study of "morale" made in a restricted experiment may yield a stable finding; however, the mere fact that we customarily label many instances in our empirical world with the term, "morale," gives no assurance, whatsoever, that such an experimental construct of "morale" fits them. Such a relation has to be established and not presumed.

Perhaps these three difficulties I have mentioned may be successfully solved so that genuine definitive concepts of theoretic use can be formed out of the type of efforts I have been considering. There still remains what I am forced to recognize as the most important question of all, namely whether definitive concepts are suited to the study of our empirical social world. To pose such a question at this point seems to move in a reverse direction, to contradict all that I have said above about the logical need for definitive concepts to overcome the basic source of deficiency in social theory. Even though the question be heretical I do not see how it can be avoided. I wish to explain why the question is very much in order.

I think that thoughtful study shows conclusively that the concepts of our discipline are fundamentally sensitizing instruments. Hence, I call them "sensitizing concepts" and put them in contrast with definitive concepts such as I have been referring to in the foregoing discussion. A definitive concept refers precisely to what is common to a class of objects, by the aid of a clear definition in terms of attributes or fixed bench marks. This definition, or the bench marks, serve as a means of clearly identifying the individual instance of the class and the make-up of that instance that is covered by the concept. A sensitizing concept lacks such specification of attributes or bench marks and consequently it does not enable the user to move directly to the instance and its relevant content. Instead, it gives the user a general sense of reference and guidance in approaching empirical instances. Whereas definitive concepts provide prescriptions of what to see, sensitizing concepts merely suggest directions along which to look. The hundreds of our concepts – like culture, institutions, social structure, mores, and personality – are not definitive concepts but are sensitizing in nature. They lack precise reference and have no bench marks which allow a clean-cut identification of a specific instance and of its content. Instead, they rest on a general sense of what is relevant. There can scarcely be any dispute over this characterization.

Now, we should not assume too readily that our concepts are sensitizing and not definitive merely because of immaturity and lack of scientific sophistication. We should consider whether there are other reasons for this condition and ask particularly whether it is due to the nature of the empirical world which we are seeking to study and analyze.

I take it that the empirical world of our discipline is the natural social world of every-day experience. In this natural world every object of our consideration – whether a person, group, institution, practice or what not – has a distinctive, particular or unique character and lies in a context of a similar distinctive character. I think that it is this distinctive character of the empirical instance and of its setting which explains why our concepts are sensitizing and not definitive. In handling an empirical instance of a concept for purposes of study or analysis we do not, and apparently cannot meaningfully, confine our consideration of it strictly to what is covered by the abstract reference of the concept. We do not cleave aside what gives each instance its peculiar character and restrict ourselves to what it has in common with the other instances in the class covered by the concept. To the contrary, we seem forced to reach what is common by accepting and using what is distinctive to the given empirical instance. In other words, what is common (i.e. what the concept refers to) is expressed in a distinctive manner in each empirical instance and can be got at only by accepting and working through the distinctive expression. All of us recognize this when we commonly ask, for instance, what form does social structure take in a Chinese peasant community or in an American labor union, or how does assimilation take place in a Jewish rabbi from Poland or a peasant from Mexico. I believe that you will find that this is true in applying any of our concepts to our natural empirical world, whether it be social structure, assimilation, custom, institution, anomie, value, role, stratification or any of the other hundreds of our concepts. We recognize that what we are referring to by any given concept shapes up in a different way in each empirical instance. We have to accept, develop and use the distinctive expression in order to detect and study the common.

This apparent need of having to make one's study of what the concept refers to, by working with and through the distinctive or unique nature of the empirical instance, instead of casting this unique nature aside calls, seemingly by necessity, for a sensitizing concept. Since the immediate data of observation in the form of the distinctive expression in the separate instances of study are different, in approaching the empirical instances one cannot rely on bench marks or fixed, objective traits of expression. Instead, the concept must guide one in developing a picture of the distinctive expression, as in studying the assimilation of the Jewish rabbi. One moves out from the concept to the concrete distinctiveness of the instance instead of embracing the instance in the abstract framework of the concept. This is a matter of filling out a new situation or of picking one's way in an unknown terrain. The concept sensitizes one to this task, providing clues and suggestions. If our empirical world presents itself in the form of distinctive and unique happenings or situations and if we seek through the direct study of this world to establish classes of objects and relations between classes, we are, I think, forced to work with sensitizing concepts.

The point that I am considering may be put in another way, by stating that seemingly we have to *infer* that any given instance in our natural empirical world and its content are covered by one of our concepts. We have to make the inference from the concrete expression of the instance. Because of the varying nature of the concrete expression from instance to instance we have to rely, apparently, on general guides and not on fixed objective traits or modes of expression. To invert the matter, since what we infer does not express itself in the same fixed way, we are not able to rely on fixed objective expressions to make the inference.

Given current fashions of thought, a conclusion that concepts of social theory are intrinsically sensitizing and not definitive will be summarily dismissed as sheer nonsense by most people in our field. Others who are led to pause and give consideration to such a conclusion may be appropriately disquieted by what it implies. Does it mean that our field is to remain forever in its present state of vagueness and to forego the possibilities of improving its concepts, its propositions, its theory and its knowledge? This is not implied. Sensitizing concepts can be tested, improved and refined. Their validity can be assayed through careful study of empirical instances which they are presumed to cover. Relevant features of such instances, which one finds not to be covered adequately by what the concept asserts and implies, become the means of revising the concept. To be true, this is more difficult with sensitizing concepts than with definitive concepts precisely because one must work with variable instead of fixed forms of expression. Such greater difficulty does not preclude progressive refinement of sensitizing concepts through careful and imaginative study of the stubborn world to which such concepts are addressed. The concepts of assimilation and social disorganization, for instance, have gained more fitting abstraction and keener discrimination through insightful and realistic studies, such as those of W. I. Thomas and Robert E. Park. Actually, all that I am saying here is that careful and probing study of occurrences in our natural social world provide the means of bringing sensitizing concepts more and more in line with what such study reveals. In short, there is nothing esoteric or basically unusual in correcting and refining sensitizing concepts in the light of stubborn empirical findings.

It should be pointed out, also, that sensitizing concepts, even though they are grounded on sense instead of on explicit objective traits, can be formulated and communicated. This is done little by formal definition and certainly not by setting bench marks. It is accomplished instead by exposition which yields a meaningful picture, abetted by apt illustrations which enable one to grasp the reference in terms of one's own experience. This is how we come to see meaning and sense in our concepts. Such exposition, it should be added, may be good or poor – and by the same token it may be improved.

Deficiency in sensitizing concepts, then, is not inevitable nor irremediable. Indeed, the admitted deficiency in our concepts, which certainly are used these days as sensitizing concepts, is to be ascribed to inadequacy of study of the empirical instances to which they refer, and to inadequacy of their exposition.

Inadequate study and poor exposition usually go together. The great vice, and the enormously widespread vice, in the use of sensitizing concepts is to take them for granted – to rest content with whatever element of plausibility they possess. Under such circumstances, the concept takes the form of a vague stereo-type and it becomes only a device for ordering or arranging empirical instances. As such it is not tested and assayed against the empirical instances and thus forfeits the only means of its improvement as an analytical tool. But this merely indicates inadequate, slovenly or lazy work and need not be. If varied empirical instances are chosen for study, and if that study is careful, probing and imaginative, with an ever alert eye on whether, or how far, the concept fits, full means are provided for the progressive refinement of sensi-tizing concepts.

Enough has been said to set the problem of what is wrong with social theory. I have ignored a host of minor deficiencies or touched them only lightly. I have sought to pin-point the basic source of deficiency. This consists in the difficulty of bringing social theory into a close and self-correcting rela-tion with its empirical world so that its proposals about that world can be tested, refined and enriched by the data of that world. This difficulty, in turn, centers in the concepts of theory, since the concept is the pivot of reference, or the gateway, to that world. Ambiguity in concepts blocks or frustrates con-tact with the empirical world and keeps theory apart in a corresponding unrealistic realm. Such a condition of ambiguity seems in general to be true of concepts of social theory.

How to correct this condition is the most important problem of our disci-pline insofar as we seek to develop it into an empirical science. A great part, if not most, of what we do these days does not touch the problem. Reflective cogitation on existing theory, the formulation of new theory, the execution of research without conceptual guidance or of research in which concepts are accepted uncritically, the amassing of quantities of disparate findings, and the devising and use of new technical instruments – all these detour around the problem.

It seems clear that there are two fundamental lines of attack on the prob-lem. The first seeks to develop precise and fixed procedures that will yield a stable and definitive empirical content. It relies on neat and standardized tech-niques, on experimental arrangements, on mathematical categories. Its immediate world of data is not the natural social world of our experience but specialized abstractions out of it or substitutes for it. The aim is to return to the natural social world with definitive concepts based on precisely specified procedures. While such procedures may be useful and valuable in many ways, their ability to establish genuine concepts related to the natural world is con-fronted by three serious difficulties which so far have not been met successfully.

The other line of attack accepts our concepts as being intrinsically sensi-tizing and not definitive. It is spared the logical difficulties confronting the first line of attack but at the expense of forfeiting the achievement of definitive concepts with specific, objective bench marks. It seeks to improve concepts by naturalistic research,[2] that is by direct study of our natural social world wherein empirical instances are accepted in their concrete and distinctive form. It depends on faithful reportorial depiction of the instances and on analytical probing into their character. As such its procedure is markedly different from that employed in the effort to develop definitive concepts. Its success depends on patient, careful and imaginative life study, not on quick shortcuts or technical instruments. While its progress may be slow and tedious, it has the virtue of remaining in close and continuing relations with the natural social world.

The opposition which I have sketched between these two modes of attack sets, I believe, the problem of how the basic deficiency of social theory is to be addressed. It also poses, I suspect, the primary line of issue in our discipline with regard to becoming an empirical science of our natural social world.

Notes

* Paper read at the annual meeting of the American Sociological Society, August, 1953.

1. There are two other legitimate and important kinds of social theory which I do not propose to assess. One of them seeks to develop a meaningful interpretation of the social world or of some significant part of it. Its aim is not to form scientific propositions but to outline and define life situations so that people may have a clearer understanding of their world, its possibilities of development, and the directions along which it may move. In every society, particularly in a changing society, there is a need for meaningful clarification of basic social values, social institutions, modes of living and social relations. This need cannot be met by empirical science, even though some help may be gained from analysis made by empirical science. Its effective fulfillment requires a sensitivity to new dispositions and an appreciation of new lines along which social life may take shape. Most social theory of the past and a great deal in the present is wittingly or unwittingly of this interpretative type. This type of social theory is important and stands in its own right.

A second type of theory might be termed "policy" theory. It is concerned with analyzing a given social situation, or social structure, or social action as a basis for policy or action. It might be an analysis of communist strategy and tactics, or of the conditions that sustain racial segregation in an American city, or of the power play in labor relations in mass production industry, or of the morale potential of an enemy country. Such theoretical analysis is not made in the interests of empirical science. Nor is it a mere application of scientific knowledge. Nor is it research inquiry in accordance with the canons of empirical science. The elements of its analysis and their relations have a nature given by the concrete situation and not by the methods or abstractions of empirical science. This form of social theorizing is of obvious importance.

2. I have not sought in this paper to deal with the logic of naturalistic research.

3

The Debate about Quantitative and Qualitative Research

Alan Bryman

In this chapter, the main contrasting features of quantitative and qualitative research will be etched out. Much of the discussion in the literature on these two research traditions has created a somewhat exaggerated picture of their differences. These discussions reflect a tendency to treat quantitative and qualitative research as though they are mutually antagonistic ideal types of the research process. This tendency can be clearly discerned in some of the programmatic statements relating to qualitative research (e.g. J. Lofland, 1971; Bogdan and Taylor, 1975). While there *are* differences between the two research traditions, as the first section of this chapter will explicate, there are also a number of points at which the differences are not as rigid as the programmatic statements often imply. Consequently, in addressing some of the contrasting features in quantitative and qualitative research, some areas of similarity will also be appraised. The discussion will then proceed to an assessment of the degree to which epistemological issues lie at the heart of the contrast, or whether it is more a matter of different styles of data collection and analysis *tout court.* This issue has implications for the extent to which quantitative and qualitative research are deemed to be capable of integration (the focus of Bryman (1988b), Chapter 6). It also has implications for the question of the extent to which quantitative and qualitative research constitute divergent models of the research process, since it has been the suggestion that they represent distinct epistemologies that has played a major role in the exaggeration of their differences. Finally, the question of whether these two research traditions share some common problems is examined.

Contrasting Features in Quantitative and Qualitative Research

Some of the main contrasting dimensions of quantitative and qualitative research have been either explicitly or implicitly explored in the previous

Source: Alan Bryman, *Quantity and Quality in Social Research* (London: Routledge, 1988).

chapters. This section will draw out these differences more directly. Table 1 lists eight important dimensions on which the two research traditions diverge. The subsequent discussion explores these themes in some greater detail.

Table 1 Some Differences Between Quantitative and Qualitative Research

		Quantitative	*Qualitative*
(1)	Role of qualitative research	preparatory	means to exploration of actors' interpretations
(2)	Relationship between researcher and subject	distant	close
(3)	Researcher's stance in relation to subject	outsider	insider
(4)	Relationship between theory/concepts and research	confirmation	emergent
(5)	Research strategy	structured	unstructured
(6)	Scope of findings	nomothetic	ideographic
(7)	Image of social reality	static and external to actor	processual and socially con-struced by actor
(8)	Nature of data	hard, reliable	rich, deep

View of the Role of Qualitative Research

Quantitative researchers rarely totally deny the utility of qualitative research, but have tended to view it as an essentially exploratory way of conducting social investigations. Consequently, they have typically seen it as useful at the preparatory stage of a research project, a view which is clearly discernible in Blalock's (1970) attitude to participant observation which was quoted in Chapter 1 (Bryman, 1988b). Precisely because of its exploratory and unstructured approach, qualitative research is often depicted as useful as a means of throwing up hunches and hypotheses which can be tested more rigorously by quantitative research. Such a view treats qualitative research as a somewhat second rate activity in implying that qualitative data cannot stand in their own right because they need to be verified. The proponents of qualitative research see it as an end in itself, in particular because of its capacity to expose actors' meanings and interpretations, which is a central requirement of the approach and of its presumptive intellectual underpinnings which were discussed in Chapter 3 (Bryman, 1988). However, it is possible to detect a degree of unease among some qualitative researchers about the extent to which their findings can stand alone. Gans (1962, p. 350), at the end of his participant observation study of an Italian–American slum, exemplified this diffidence in proclaiming that his research 'is a *reconnaissance* – an initial exploration of a community to provide an overview', and went on to say: 'Many of the hypotheses reported here can eventually be tested against the results of more systematic social science research.' Interestingly, in the second edition of the book which derived from this research, Gans (1982, p. 414) has indicated that he would get rid of this 'apologetic conclusion' if he were able to rewrite the book. He argues that the reason for this apologetic style was that at the time social scientists were strongly influenced by a belief in the appropriateness of the scientific method. By implication, Gans seems to be suggesting that the assertiveness of qualitative researchers coupled with the growing disillusionment with quantitative research have created a different climate, whereby investigations of the kind he undertook are increasingly regarded as ends in themselves.

Relationship between Researcher and Subject

In quantitative research the researcher's contact with the people being studied is fairly fleeting or even non-existent. While the data collection phase often extends over many months, the contact with each individual is usually brief. In longitudinal surveys or in before-and-after experiments, the investigator returns to his or her subjects, but the degree of contact is still fairly short-lived. Indeed, the use of some methods associated with quantitative research may require no contact with subjects at all, except in an indirect sense; postal questionnaire surveys, laboratory experiments in which the researcher simply observes while others conduct the experiment (e.g. Milgram, 1963), and many forms of unobtrusive, structured observation (Webb *et al.*, 1966) involve virtually no contact between researcher and subject. Even in interview surveys, the main investigator may have little or no contact with respondents since hired staff frequently carry out many (and sometimes all) of the interviews.

By contrast, qualitative research entails much more sustained contact, especially when participant observation is the central method. The degree to which there is sustained contact within a particular study will vary a good deal; Gans (1962) had some contact with 100 to 150 West Enders but only twenty of these were intense. The need for the fostering of such relationships is a product of the qualitative researcher's need to see the world through his or her subjects' eyes, since the researcher would be unable to gain any leverage on this level of analysis from a distance. Unstructured interviewing typically entails less sustained researcher–subject relationships than participant observation, but is invariably longer than survey interviews. In any case, the wide-ranging nature of the unstructured interview invariably necessitates a fairly close relationship between researcher and subject, which re-visits (which are relatively rare in survey interviewing) may intensify.

This contrast between the two research traditions can be illustrated through the work of Hirschi (1969) and Adler (1985). In the former case, self-administered questionnaires were the chief source of data. The questionnaires were administered to the children by their schools, so that Hirschi's contact with his subjects was minimal. By contrast, Adler had contact over a period of six years with some of the drug dealers she was investigating.

The Researcher's Stance in Relation to the Subject

The quantitative researcher adopts the posture of an outsider looking in on the social world. He or she applies a pre-ordained framework on the subjects being investigated and is involved as little as possible in that world. This posture is the analogue of the detached scientific observer. Hirschi was chiefly concerned to test a theory of delinquency, and adopted a stance towards his subjects which entailed limited contact with them. They were merely fodder for the examination of his concerns, and not people with their own views and perspectives in relation to delinquent behaviour, school, and the other elements of Hirschi's research.

Among qualitative researchers there is a strong urge to 'get close' to the subjects being investigated – to be an insider. For qualitative researchers, it is only by getting close to their subjects and becoming an insider that they can view the world as a participant in that setting. Thus, Hirschi's outsider stance can be contrasted with Adler's view: 'the only way I could get close enough to [upper-level drug dealers and smugglers] to discover what they were doing and to understand the world from their perspectives (Blumer, 1969) was to take a membership role in the setting' (Adler, 1985, p.11). The insider standpoint may have its costs, the most frequently mentioned of which is the problem of 'going native', whereby the researcher loses his or her awareness of being a researcher and is seduced by the participants' perspective. Oakley (1984, p.128), drawing on her research on becoming a mother describes the experience of going native as follows:

> at three forty-five after two hours of a busy antenatal clinic I too would sigh with the doctors as we jointly peeped into the corridor and saw, still waiting, another row of abdomens … Or at two in the morning I wanted someone to get in there quickly and do a forceps delivery so I could (like them) go home to bed.

The experience of going native was not entirely negative in that it enabled her to understand the pressures obstetricians are under. In any event, qualitative researchers are likely to see such drawbacks (if indeed they acknowledge them as such) as unavoidable consequences of a standpoint which is needed to gain access to their subjects' views. It is also apparent that the possibility of going native, with its implication of a loss of detachment, is to a significant degree incongruent with the image of impartial scientist which many quantitative researchers espouse.

Relationship between Theory/Concepts and Research

The model of quantitative research presented in Figure 2.1 (Bryman, 1988b) implies that theories and concepts are the starting point for investigations carried out within its framework. Thus Hirschi in the Preface to *Causes of Delinquency* wrote: 'In this book I attempt to state and test a theory of delinquency.' By contrast, qualitative researchers often reject the idea of using theory as a precursor to an investigation (except perhaps as a means of providing an initial orientation to the situation as in 'grounded theory') since it may not reflect subjects' views about what is going on and what is important. Consequently, as one advocate of qualitative research has put it, 'It is marked by a concern with the discovery of theory rather than the verification of theory' (Filstead, 1979, p. 38). Thus Adler's (1985) chief theoretical contribution – the notion of upper-level drug dealing as a component of a hedonistic life-style rather than an occupation – was an outcome of her research rather than a precursor to it.

In fact, the extent to which quantitative research is explicitly guided by theory has been questioned of many commentators. Instead, theoretical reasoning often occurs towards the end of the research process (Cicourel, 1982, pp.19–20). Indeed, quantitative research is often much more exploratory and unpredictable in outcome than its description by the advocates of qualitative research seems to imply. An example of the misleading nature of the view that quantitive research is devoid of surprise is the study of the International Typographical Union in the USA by Lipset, Trow, and Coleman (1956), which involved a mixture of qualitative research and survey data. The latter were compiled in order to examine *inter alia* the relationship between union shop size and members' political involvement. However,

> This analysis did not merely test hypotheses already held before the survey was conducted. Rather, the earlier hypotheses pointed to a fruitful line of enquiry, but many of the ideas and insights regarding the bearing of shop size on union politics emerged only in the course of the analysis of the survey data. (Lipset, 1964, pp. 116–17)

Lipset (1964, pp. 111–12) also provides a number of other examples of the way in which his survey data were a source of surprise. Similarly, Pugh (1988), writing about the Aston research which was discussed in Chapter 2 (Bryman,

1988b), has commented on his disappointment that the effect of organization size on structure was so pervasive, an observation which can be interpreted as indicative of a certain element of surprise.

Quantitative research is often depicted as a routine practice whereby theories and their integral concepts are simply operationalized with a view to verifying their validity (see, for example, Filstead's remark on this issue in the passage cited on p. 39). Ironically, some qualitative research is showing an explicit concern with theory, not solely as something which emerges from the data, but also as a phase in the research process which is formulated at the outset (Woods, 1986, pp. 156–61). Some of the school ethnographies cited in Chapters 3 and 4 (Bryman, 1988b) show signs of a movement in this direction. Consequently, the contrast between quantitative and qualitative research in terms of verification of theory against preferring theory to emerge from the data is not as clear-cut as is sometimes implied.

Research Strategy

Quantitative research tends to adopt a structured approach to the study of society. To a large extent, this tendency is a product of the methods with which it is associated; both surveys and experiments require that the issues to be focused upon be decided at the outset. In the previous section, the point was made that there is the possibility of an element of surprise in survey research which is frequently underestimated. However, it is evident that such investigations require that the variables be mapped out and introduced into the survey instruments. Survey research is structured in the sense that sampling and questionnaire construction are conducted prior to the start of data collection and then imposed on the sample members. Similarly, in experimental designs, independent and dependent variables, experimental and control groups are all part of the preparatory stage. In both cases, once the research has been designed the broad shape of the findings can be discerned, that is, before one person has been interviewed or one experimental subject has received a treatment. An examination of Hirschi's (1969) questionnaire reveals that he was fully aware of the material that needed to be collected in order to test the theories of delinquency which were to be examined.

By contrast, qualitative research tends to be more open. Many ethnographers advocate that the delineation of a research focus be deferred as long as possible (e.g. Cohen, 1978). Consequently, many qualitative researchers refer to a sensation of being overwhelmed during their early days in the field, since everything they observe is potentially 'data'. Whyte (1984), for example, sees ethnographic research as deriving much of its strength from its flexibility, which allows new leads to be followed up or additional data to be gathered in response to changes in ideas. But he also notes a limitation of such flexibility since 'you may find so many interesting things to study that you are at a loss to delimit the scope of your project and focus on specific problems' (Whyte, 1984, p. 225). Barrett (1976) has shown how his use of a prior theoretical framework (and a structured research strategy which derived from this framework), which was used to guide his anthropological research on the factors associated with the economic success of a village in Nigeria, caused him to misconstrue his data. Initially, his theoretical focus had led him to believe that his data implied that the communal economic organization of the village, rather than religion, was the main contributor to its success. Almost two years after the completion of his thesis which was based on this fieldwork, Barrett felt impelled to accord religion a stronger role, following some critical comments he had received on his explanation. However, Barrett has since revised his explanation yet again to provide what he believes to be the most accurate explanation of the village's success. This explanation differs radically from its predecessors in that it goes far beyond the simple juxtaposition of religion and communal organization and emphasizes the emergence of development as a paramount goal within the village. But Barrett's main point is that he was able to arrive at this more accurate account only when he had cast off the shackles of his prior theoretical framework. Such an experience underscores the strength of the qualitative researcher's preference for postponing theoretical reflection, albeit at the possible cost (noted by Whyte) of being overwhelmed by data. It also suggests that it may be disadvantageous to ethnographers to structure their strategies in advance.

Also, the role of luck may be more apparent in such research, where being in the right place at the right time may significantly affect the direction of the research (Bryman, 1988a), or alternatively may give access to a potential research site (Buchanan, Boddy, and McCalman, 1988). For example, Bresnen (1988) refers to a lucky encounter in the pub soon after he had started his research on a construction project. Most of the site management team were present, but two senior managers had gone home. It became apparent that there was a considerable gap in attitudes between senior and junior management, which prompted Bresnen to develop a new line of questioning following on from this unexpected lead. One of the undoubted strengths which qualitative research affords the practitioner, by virtue of its unstructured nature, is precisely this capacity to encounter the unexpected and possibly to change direction.

Scope of Findings

It is common to conceive of the quantitative/qualitative dichotomy in terms of respective commitments to *nomothetic* and *ideographic* modes of reasoning (Halfpenny, 1979). This distinction effectively refers to the scope of the findings which derive from a piece of research. A nomothetic approach seeks to establish general law-like findings which can be deemed to hold irrespective of time and place; an ideographic approach locates its findings in specific time periods and locales. The former mode is taken to be indicative of the scientific approach, whereas ideographic reasoning is often more closely associated with the historian's method. By taking random, and hence representative, samples, survey research is taken to exhibit a nomothetic approach because of the investigator's ability to infer findings to larger populations. Thus, Hirschi (1969) took great pains to ensure that the data on the children he studied would be representative of the wider population of school children through a stratified random sampling procedure which took account of such population characteristics as race, sex, and school attended.

By contrast, the qualitative researcher frequently conducts research in a specific milieu (a case study) whose representativeness is unknown and probably unknowable, so that the generalizability of such findings is also unknown. Adler's (1985) subjects were acquired in an apparently much less rigorous manner than Hirschi's children. Her initial contacts were accidental and were her source of further contacts. Moreover, these subjects were mainly located in a limited geographical area, so that their broader representativeness may be questioned. Qualitative researchers often exhibit some unease over this point. Liebow (1967) conducted participant observation in relation to 'two dozen Negro men who share a corner in Washington's Second Precinct' (p. 11) and goes on to note:

> To what extent this descriptive and interpretive material is applicable to Negro street corner men elsewhere in the city or in other cities, or to lower-class men generally in this or any other society, is a matter for further and later study. (Liebow, 1967, p. 14)

The discussion about generalization in quantitative research in Chapter 2 (Bryman, 1988b) suggests that the extent to which investigations within this tradition are nomothetic is often exaggerated. Surveys are often not based on random samples and, even when they are, they refer to highly restricted populations. For example, writing about the field of organization studies, Freeman (1986, p. 300) has observed: 'They rarely work with samples that are representative of even the restricted types of organizations they choose to study.' The fact that Hirschi's sample derives from a geographically restricted area – a county in the San Francisco – Oakland metropolitan area – is given much less attention in his book than his attempts to select a random sample of that region's population of school children. Further, the consistency of findings over time is rarely given much attention. Experimental research also suffers from a number of deficiencies in regard to the generalizability of findings stemming from such designs. Moreover, as the discussion in Chapter 4 (Bryman, 1988b) on case study research implies, qualitative researchers are building up strategies for enhancing the generalizability of their research. Consequently, caution is necessary in treating the two research traditions as being strictly associated with nomothetic and ideographic findings.

Image of Social Reality

Quantitative research conveys a view of social reality which is static in that it tends to neglect the impact and role of change in social life. Surveys examine co-variation among variables at a particular juncture; experimental research usually entails the exploration of a restricted range of variables within a restricted time period. While both styles of research examine connections between variables, the proponents of qualitative research argue that quantitative research rarely examines the processes which link them (e.g. Blumer, 1956). They also charge that the 'independent' and 'dependent' variables fail to take into account the flow of events in which these variables are located. Quantitative researchers might argue that they do take such factors into account. For example, the notion of an 'intervening' variable, which is both a product of the independent variable and an influence on the dependent variable, might be interpreted as a device which examines intervening processes (Rosenberg, 1968). However, the suggestion is still open to the accusation that intervening processes are ignored (e.g. between the independent and intervening variables) and that the nexus of factors within which such chains of causality are grounded is rarely examined. For example, the causal chain in Hirschi (1969), quoted in the Introduction, suggests that academic incompetence is causally related to delinquency via a sequential series of intervening variables (poor school performance, dislike of school and rejection of school's authority). It might legitimately be argued that the processes which account for the intermediate connections (e.g. rejection of school's authority and delinquent acts) are unexplored.

The qualitative researcher is in a better position to view the linkages between events and activities and to explore people's interpretations of the factors which produce such connections. This stance affords the qualitative researcher a much greater opportunity to study processes in social life. Adler's (1985) ethnographic research was concerned to demonstrate the nature of the 'career progressions' of the dealers and smugglers with whom she was in contact. She shows how dealers enter and climb to the top of these 'occupations' and how they and their experiences change with their ascendancy into upper-level activities. Similarly, Adler and Adler (1985) used participant observation and unstructured interviewing to study basketball players at an American university in order to examine the relationship between athletic participation and academic performance among college athletes. They note that the bulk of the literature implies that participation in college sports is associated with poor academic performance, although some studies are not consistent with this finding. Adler and Adler confirmed the negative relationship between athletic participation and school performance but show that most athletes come to college with a commitment to doing well in their academic studies. However, they encounter a number of experiences which conspire to deflate their academic motivation: athletic experiences (e.g. the time spent in training, playing and recovering), social experiences (e.g. the domination of their lives by interaction with other athletes) and classroom experiences (e.g. adverse attitudes towards them indicated by their professors) have a deleterious effect on their interest in academic work. Both of these studies inject a sense of process and transformation in social life which quantitative research can rarely address.

In addition to their respective tendencies to convey static and processual views of social life, quantitative and qualitative research differ in their view of the mutual relationship between the individual and social reality. There is a tendency for quantitative researchers to view social reality as external to actors and as a constraint on them, which can be attributed to the preference for treating the social order as though it were the same as the objects of the natural scientist. By contrast, the influence of perspectives like phenomenology, symbolic interactionism, and naturalism led qualitative researchers to suggest that 'we cannot take for granted, as the natural scientist does, the availability of a preconstituted world of phenomena for investigation' but must 'examine the processes by which the social world is constructed' (Walsh, 1972, p. 19). Thus whereas quantitative research tends to invoke a perspective which implies that social reality is static and beyond the actor, the image deriving from qualitative research gives a sense of that same reality in processual terms and as socially constructed. This point can be illustrated by reference to the study of organization structure. Quantitative research on this topic, like the Aston Studies (Pugh and Hickson, 1976; Pugh, 1988), depicted organization structure as something which is determined by forces such as an organization's size or its technology. In turn, organization structure was seen as affecting the behaviour and orientations of its members (Pugh and Payne, 1977; Pugh, 1988). This approach seems to view organization structure as external and as a constraint on the actor, and differs from the qualitative research on a psychiatric hospital by Strauss *et al.* (1963) which suggests that the organization's structure was a 'negotiated order'. This latter study suggests that the behaviour of the hospital's members was largely unaffected by a formal structure of rules and role prescriptions; instead, the various groupings within the hospital produced their own structure, which they negotiated and which was in a constant state of renegotiation.

Nature of the Data

The data emanating from quantitative studies are often depicted as hard, rigorous, and reliable. These adjectives suggest that such data exhibit considerable precision, have been collected by systematic procedures and may be readily checked by another investigator. These positive attributes are often taken to mean that quantitative data are more persuasive and hence more likely to gain the support of policymakers. Okely (1987), for example, has described how she was under great pressure from her employers at a research centre, in which she was to conduct research on gypsies, to use survey methods, because they believed that such research provided the only means of influencing policymakers. She writes: 'At the outset the declared ideal was to be a report "with a statistical table on every page"' (p. 62). Such a view is indicative of the very considerable power of quantitative data, possibly because of their association with 'science', to impress by virtue of their apparent rigour.

Qualitative researchers routinely describe the data deriving from ethnographic work as 'rich' and 'deep', often drawing a contrast with quantitative data, which tend to be depicted as superficial. The denotation 'rich' is generally indicative of the attention to often intricate detail which many qualitative researchers provide. Their sustained contact with the people they study permits a penetrating account, which can explore incidents in great detail and can illuminate the full extent of their subjects' accounts of a variety of phenomena. Further, the predilection of ethnographers for conveying social life in the language and style of their subjects adds to this sense of richness. In terms of conventional sampling, Liebow's (1967) streetcorner men constitute an unacceptably small, non-random sample of unknown representativeness. But they provide, as in much qualitative research, the route to a vivid, detailed portrayal of a small sector of social life. Further, the potential of the attention to rich detail in qualitative research to policy-making and other 'applied' contexts is gaining increasing recognition (Finch, 1986). An interesting anecdote in this respect has been supplied by Okely (1987, p. 58):

> in the 1983 general election [in the UK], the Conservative party geared its campaign to the daily reactions of the floating voter in marginal seats, mainly in southern England. These potential supporters were the subject of in-depth qualitative interviews several times a week. Feedback from these data was used within days to adjust the emphasis in campaign issues.

To many qualitative researchers, quantitative research produces superficial data. They tend to view survey research, for example, as a source of surface information which relates to the social scientist's abstract categories. By contrast, the quantitative researcher may be suspicious of the limited generality of a study of two dozen men in one area of one city (Liebow, 1967) from which data were collected that may have been heavily influenced by the particular emphases and predispositions of the researcher.

A Question of Epistemology or Technique?

What *are* quantitative and qualitative research, as outlined in the preceding section? In the book thus far, there has been a strong suggestion that epistemological issues underpin the divide between them. By an 'epistemological issue' is meant a matter which has to do with the question of what is to pass as warrantable, and hence acceptable, knowledge. In suggesting that quantitative researchers are committed to a positivist approach to the study of society (Filmer *et al.*, 1972), the view is being taken that they subscribe to a distinctive epistemological position, since the implication is that only research which conforms to the canons of scientific method can be treated as contributing to the stock of knowledge. Similarly, by subscribing to positions, such as phenomenology, *verstehen*, and naturalism, which reject the imitation of the natural scientist's procedures and which advocate that greater attention be paid to actors' interpretations, qualitative research can also be depicted as being underpinned by an epistemological standpoint.[1] The tendency among some writers (e.g. Filstead, 1979) to refer to quantitative and qualitative research as 'paradigms' (following T. S. Kuhn, 1970) underscores the fact that they are frequently conceived of as different epistemological positions. The tendency to view the two research traditions as reflecting different epistemological positions, and hence divergent paradigms, has led to an exaggeration of the differences between them. As a consequence of such thinking, quantitative and qualitative research are frequently depicted as mutually exclusive models of the research process.

The following is a representative version of the view that quantitative and qualitative research reflect different epistemological positions:

> Quantitative and qualitative methods are more than just differences between research strategies and data collection procedures. These approaches represent fundamentally different epistemological frameworks for conceptualizing the nature of knowing, social reality, and procedures for comprehending these phenomena. (Filstead, 1979, p. 45)

Similarly, Rist (1977, p. 62) suggests that each of the two research traditions rests on 'an interrelated set of assumptions about the social world'. The view that quantitative and qualitative research constitute different epistemological positions would seem to imply that researchers formulate their views about the proper foundation for the study of social reality and choose their methods of investigation in the light of that decision. This would imply that a researcher's personal commitment to the view that the natural sciences provide the only acceptable basis for generating knowledge would mean that his or her approach to conducting an investigation, as well as the methods of data collection, will be chosen in this light. Likewise, a view that the scientific method provides a poor basis for the study of people, coupled with a commensurate endorsement of a position like phenomenology, will propel an investigator in the direction of a qualitative approach. Alternatively, it might be suggested that a researcher who chooses to carry out a survey, for example, has to recognize that his or her decision to use that method carries with it a train of epistemological implications which need to be recognized at the outset, in case the selection does not fit with the researcher's broader intellectual proclivities.

One might question whether research is conducted in these ways, but the suggestion that the two research traditions are rooted in divergent epistemological implications seems to carry with it connotations of these kinds. However, the view that quantitative and qualitative research represent different epistemological implications is not held by all writers, even though they view the two approaches as distinctive. The alternative standpoint is to suggest that quantitative and qualitative research are each appropriate to different kinds of research problem, implying that the research issue determines (or should determine) which style of research is employed. For example, Walker (1985, p. 16) has proposed: 'Certain questions cannot be answered by quantitative methods, while others cannot be answered by qualitative ones.' This view implies that the decision over whether to use a quantitative or qualitative approach should be based on 'technical' issues regarding the suitability of a particular method in relation to a particular research problem. Accordingly, the different characteristics of quantitative and qualitative research which were summarized in Table 1 can be interpreted as pointing to the respective strengths and weaknesses of these two research traditions. Consider the following rationale for the procedures employed in a study of entrepreneurs in Britain:

> As with all social research, the methods adopted in this enquiry were largely dictated by the nature of the research problem. We set out to study the *dynamics* of small-scale capital accumulation and the *social processes* which account for the reproduction of the entrepreneurial middle class. In addition, it was our intention to define more precisely the *nature* and *interrelationships* of the constituent groupings within this class. The complexity of these issues did not favour quantitative investigation; in our view a qualitative approach was more appropriate. [The authors provide three considerations which determined this view] … Consequently, we undertook an intensive study of a limited number of proprietors using semi-structured interviews which were, to a considerable extent, shaped by the personal experiences of the respondents. (Scase and Goffee, 1982, p. 198)

In this account, there is a recognition of the strengths and weaknesses of quantitative and qualitative research, coupled with a technical decision that the latter will suit their needs better; epistemological issues are not in evidence. By inference, writers who perceive the distinction between the two styles of research in terms of their relative suitability for a particular research topic are effectively suggesting that the differences between them boil down to little more than 'differences between research strategies and data collection procedures' (see quotation from Filstead, 1979, cited on p. 46). This position is not new; it can be discerned in a celebrated exchange between Becker and Geer (1957) and Trow (1957) in which the former argued that participant observation provides 'the most complete form of sociological datum' (p. 28). In reply, it was suggested that 'the problem under investigation properly dictates the methods of investigation' (Trow, 1957, p. 33).

There seem, then, to be two fairly distinct versions of the nature of the differences between quantitative and qualitative research which might usefully be referred to as the 'epistemological' and 'technical' accounts. However, there is a tendency for many writers to oscillate between these two versions. This is particularly evident in some of the discussions about whether it is possible to integrate quantitative and qualitative research within a single study. The ways in which they might be combined constitute the focus of the Chapter 6

(Bryman, 1988b); in the meantime, the broader question of whether in prin-ciple they might be combined is addressed here. The technical version of the differences between quantitative and qualitative research seems to provide few impediments to the possibility of a research strategy that integrates them. While a researcher may prefer to use one to the relative exclusion of the other (as with Scase and Goffee, 1982), if the research problem invites a combined approach there is little to prevent such a strategy, other than the usual rea-sons of time, money, and possibly inclination. The researcher may choose to conduct a predominantly ethnographic study, but decide to add some survey evidence relating to people who are not accessible through the focal method. Woods (1979) buttressed his ethnographic research on a school with a survey of parents for precisely this reason.

The epistemological account would seem to pose more problems in regard to the possibility of combining the two approaches. If quantitative and qualita-tive research are taken to represent divergent epistemological packages (or paradigms), they are likely to exhibit incompatible views about the way in which social reality ought to be studied, and hence what should be regarded as proper knowledge thereof. This incongruence is particularly evident in the implicit critique of the application of the scientific method to the study of society which phenomenology contains. It is not obvious how a marriage of such divergent epistemological positions as positivism and phenomenology (even in the meta-phorical use of the term) can be entertained. Guba (1985) has argued vehemently against the suggestion that the two research traditions might be reconciled. In his view, attempts to combine the two approaches fail to recognize the distinc-tion between a paradigm and a method. He argues that the idea that quantitative and qualitative research can be dovetailed rests on a view that they represent only different methods of investigation; instead, 'we *are* dealing with an either-or proposition, in which one must pledge allegiance to one paradigm or the other' (Guba, 1985, p. 80). Thus in the same way that Kuhn regards paradigms as incommensurable, Guba is suggesting that the collection of assumptions and beliefs about the study of the social order that underpin quantitative and quali-tative research should be treated in the same manner.

Not all writers subscribe to this view. Reichardt and Cook (1979) suggest that the tendency to view the two styles of research as paradigms stands in the way of their joint use within a single project, and prefer to see them as 'method-types'. What is somewhat more surprising is that some writers who subscribe to the epistemological view of the differences between quantitative and qualitative research simultaneously suggest that they might be integrated. Filstead (1979), who was quoted above for his view that they represent 'dif-ferent epistemological frameworks', suggests that 'great advantages can be obtained by creatively combining qualitative and quantitative methods' (p. 42). Bogdan and Biklen (1982), after a discussion of the intellectual foundations of qualitative research (in phenomenology, etc.), ask whether it can be used in tandem with a quantitative approach. They acknowledge that it can, but dis-play a lack of enthusiasm for the idea, not because of any kind of epistemological incompatibility, but for practical reasons. They suggest that research which combines the two approaches 'is likely to produce a big headache' (p. 39), because of the practical problems of producing both a good quantitative and a good qualitative design. Delamont and Hamilton (1984) oscillate in the other direction. In contrasting structured and ethnographic observation in classrooms, they argue against the view that these two styles of observation are 'the equivalent of self-contained epistemological and theoretical paradigms', but then go on to argue that the two methods reflect 'the tension between positivism and interactionism' which 'cannot be done away with by calling for interdisciplinary *rapprochements*' (pp. 5, 6).

There seems, then, to be a tendency for many writers to shuttle uneasily back and forth between epistemological and technical levels of discourse. While much of the exposition of the epistemological debts of qualitative research helped to afford it some credibility, a great many decisions about whether and when to use qualitative methods seem to have little, if any, recourse to these broader intellectual issues.

The Strengths and Weaknesses of Quantitative and Qualitative Research

Underlying much of the preceding discussion is the suggestion that the distinction between quantitative and qualitative research is really a technical matter whereby the choice between them is to do with their suitability in answering particular research questions. Such a view draws attention to the different strengths and weaknesses of the methods of data collection with which the two research traditions are typically associated. It is not uncommon for textbooks on research methods to draw attention to such issues:

> The sample survey is an appropriate and useful means of gathering information under three conditions: when the goals of the research call for quantitative data, when the information sought is reasonably specific and familiar to the respondents, and when the researcher himself has considerable prior knowledge of particular problems and the range of responses likely to emerge …
>
> Participant observation is usually more appropriate when the study requires an examination of complex social relationships or intricate patterns of interaction; … when the investigator desires first-hand behavioural information on certain social processes … ; when a major goal of the study is to construct a qualitative contextual picture of a certain situation or flow of events; and when it is necessary to infer latent value patterns or belief systems from such behaviour as ceremonial postures, gestures, dances, facial expressions or subtle inflections of the voice. (Warwick and Lininger, 1975, pp. 9–10)

As they then go on to say, 'Each is useful for some purposes and useless for others' (p. 12).

This passage illustrates well the suggestion that the decision about which method to employ is essentially a technical issue. As such, the decision about whether to employ quantitative or qualitative research stands cheek by jowl with other familiar technical issues on which students of social research methods are reared, such as when it is appropriate to use a postal questionnaire or to construct a stratified random sample. Warwick and Lininger's list of respective strengths and weaknesses can usefully be expanded. Social surveys are likely to be particularly appropriate where larger scale issues are concerned. The study of social mobility is a case in point (e.g. Goldthorpe, 1980). Of course, it might be argued that much of the recent ethnographic research on schools is concerned with social mobility too (e.g. Lacey, 1970; Woods, 1979; Ball, 1981). However, such research is typically concerned with the processes through which social class is perpetuated by the structure of the school, teachers' practices, and the class based sub-cultures within the school. Studies of social mobility like Goldthorpe's are essentially concerned with the *extent* of social mobility and changes in patterns. Thus, the technical version of the debate would imply that the critical issue about whether a method fits a research problem is not a matter of the area of social life being investigated, but the nature of the issues being raised in relation to it. Similarly, juvenile delinquency may be studied by both survey methods (e.g. Hirschi, 1969) or participant observation (e.g. Patrick, 1973), but the nature of the questions being asked about juvenile delinquency differ. Hirschi was concerned to test the validity of three theories of the causes of delinquency. This preoccupation with the causes of variation in delinquency led him to carry out a survey of over 5,000 school children in California in order to collect sufficient data to separate out the variables which impinged on his dependent variable, delinquency. By contrast, Patrick joined a particularly violent gang in Glasgow as a covert participant observer 'to comprehend and to illuminate their view and to interpret the world as it appears to them' (Matza, 1969, p. 25, cited in Patrick, 1973, p. 9).

Social surveys are also likely to be preferred when, as in the case of Hirschi's study, there is a concern to establish cause-and-effect relationships. Experiments are even stronger in this department, but are likely to be appropriate only to situations in which the independent variable is capable of manipulation and in which random assignment (or at least some form of matching) is feasible. Qualitative researchers are not uninterested in causes, in that they are frequently concerned to establish how flows of events connect and mesh with each other in the social contexts they investigate, or how their subjects perceive the connections between facets of their environment. However, survey and experimental researchers tend to be much more concerned with the precise delineation of a causal factor, relative to other potential causes.

As Warwick and Lininger suggest in the extended quotation above, participant observation has its own strengths. The absence of a highly structured research design means that the investigator can change direction if he or she is lucky enough to hit upon an unexpected but interesting facet of the social setting. The participant observer is better able than the survey researcher to understand social processes.

A further, and neglected, strength of ethnographic studies is their capacity to reveal covert, hidden, even illegal activities. Studies of informal groups in large organizations (Dalton, 1959), output regulation in industrial work groups (Roy, 1960), and pilferage at work (Ditton, 1977) all demonstrate the capacity of ethnographers to look behind the scenes and bring to the centre of the stage aspects of these milieux which would otherwise either be inaccessible or possibly not even uncovered in the first place. The same point can be made about the study of deviant behaviour, a more probing study of which requires sensitivity and a capacity to provide reassurance to the subjects that a survey researcher is unlikely to be able to inculcate. It is difficult to see how Adler's (1985) research on drug dealers could have been conducted with a more formal approach. Indeed, the capacity of ethnographers to gain access to hidden arenas can occasionally cause them difficulties. Serber (1981) sought to conduct an ethnographic study of a government bureaucracy responsible for the state regulation of the insurance industry in California. He rapidly discerned a range of informal practices (e.g. off-the-record meetings) which he chose to make the focus of his investigations, but found his access to people and documents sharply curtailed by senior managers as his awareness of the significance of such undercover processes grew.

The purpose of this discussion was to provide a flavour of the sorts of considerations that are relevant to the technical version of the distinction between quantitative and qualitative research. It is also the case that the choice between the two may derive from reasons other than the epistemological and technical reasons which have been encountered thus far. For example, many women social scientists have drawn attention to the affinity between qualitative research and a feminist perspective (Stanley and Wise, 1983). Oakley (1981) has argued that the typical survey interview, in which the researcher appropriates information from a respondent for the former's use, is incompatible with feminism. A feminist researcher conducting research on women would be setting up an asymmetrical relationship which exploits the already exploited interviewee. In order to mitigate this perpetuation of exploitation she advocates an approach to feminist research whereby the research situation is treated much more as an exchange in which the feminist researcher gives something back – of her own views, experiences and the like – to those being interviewed. Such an approach implies a much more unstructured interview (and hence one closely associated with the qualitative approach) than that associated with the survey. It is striking that research on women's subordination in the workplace, as well as the interface between the workplace and the home, has tended to be the product of qualitative investigations in which participant observation and unstructured interviews figure strongly (Pollert, 1981; Cavendish, 1982; Griffin, 1985a). The underlying issues to the discussion about the appropriateness of particular methods to feminist research imply that considerations other than those which have figured thus far in this book may impinge on choices of method, e.g. ethical, political, ideological considerations.

Similarities in the Technical Problems Associated with Quantitative and Qualitative Research

One reason for giving greater recognition to the technical aspects of decisions relating to the use of quantitative or qualitative research is that it may result in a appreciation of the common technical problems faced by practitioners working within the two traditions. The emphasis on their epistemological sepa-rateness runs the risk of failing to give due attention to these common problems. The recognition of mutual technical problems may also invite a questioning of whether the quantitative and qualitative research traditions are as far apart from each other as the epistemological argument may be taken to imply.[2]

Perhaps the most striking problem which besets both groups of practitioners is that of 'reactivity' – the reaction on the part of those being investigated to the investigator and his or her research instruments. Surveys and experiments create an awareness on the part of subjects that they are being investigated; the problem of reactivity draws attention to the possibility that this awareness creates a variety of undesirable consequences in that people's behaviour or responses may not be indicative of their normal behaviour or views (e.g. Rosenthal, 1966). In experiments subjects may be influenced by what they perceive to be the underlying aims of the investigation, or in interviews re-spondents may be influenced by characteristics of the interviewer, such as the latter's age, race, gender, or whatever. The recognition of such problems led Webb et al. (1966) to propose the greater use of 'non-reactive' methods of gleaning data, such as field experiments in which people do not know that they are under investigation. An example of the latter is Daniel's (1968) study of racial discrimination in England in which actors of different races were hired to seek employment, accommodation, car insurance, and the like in order to determine the extent of such discrimination.

Problems of reactivity confront the ethnographer as well. An obvious so-lution is to engage in covert observation which simultaneously deals with the problem of access. The study by Festinger, Riecken and Schachter (1956) of a religious cult is an example of this strategy, in that the investigators feigned conversion to a group which was predicting the imminent end of the world. Even here the problem of reactivity was not fully overcome, since the research-ers' conversion was treated by the cult's adherents as confirmation of the validity of their beliefs and hardened their resolve to prepare for the fateful day. But the strategy of covert observation is usually frowned upon by social scientists, because it transgresses a number of ethical conventions (Bulmer, 1982), though many of the non-reactive methods suggested by Webb et al. (1966) are suspect in this way as well. By and large, ethnographers prefer to be open about their participation, but frequently display a concern about the effect of their presence on the people they observe. While recognizing the potentially contaminating effects of their presence, ethnographers frequently play down this problem suggesting that their familiarity to the people they study militates against this reactive effect. Gans's (1967) statement about the impact of this presence in a middle class American suburb is indicative of this position: 'After a while, I became a fixture in the community; people forgot I was there and went on with their business, even at private political gatherings' (p. xxiii). Likewise, Atkinson (1981, p. 129), writing about his experience of a participant observation study of clinical education in a medical school, comments:

> Although my presence on the wards had originally taken a fair amount of negotiation, once access had been granted, I was generally taken very much for granted on the wards, and by the students as they went about the hospital ... Indeed, for some doctors I became so much a part of the normal scene that they forgot who I was.

The suggestion here is that the participant observer becomes part of the scenery and hence largely invisible. This process of absorption can be enhanced by not taking copious notes in front of subjects.

However, there is some evidence to suggest that reactive effects may occur. For example, Atkinson's assertion that he became unobtrusive jars somewhat with his admission that both clinicians and students often thought that he was engaged in an evaluation exercise (p. 125), which may have had ramifications for the behaviour of these groups in his presence. An interesting insight on the reactive effect in participant observation can be derived from an anecdote relating to research which was not conducted for the purposes of academic social science. During the 1971–2 football season, a journalist, Hunter Davies, was effectively a participant observer with Tottenham Hotspur Football Club, an experience which spawned a book, *The Glory Game* (1972). Writing in his autobiography about one particular game, the then manager of the club, Bill Nicholson (1984, p. 141), remarked:

> Hunter Davies, a Spurs fan, followed us around that season ... He had been given permission to become virtually one of the players and was allowed in the dressing room which in my view must always be a private place. Permission was not given by me but by someone else at the club. In hindsight I should have overruled the decision.
>
> I know Davies' work was highly acclaimed, but after this particular match I was forced to keep quiet when I wanted to say a lot of things straight away.

It is not apparent whether this was the only incident whereby Davies's presence influenced Nicholson, but the suggestion that he would have overruled the decision indicates that this is at least a possibility. Nor do we know how

representative Nicholson's experience is – but then the subjects of participant observation do not normally write books in which they can refer to
their experience.

There is, then, at least a possibility that the participant observer's presence
may have an effect on what is observed. It is surprising that the widespread
acceptance of interviewing in qualitative research has not been given greater
critical attention as regards the problem of reactivity. Even unstructured interviewing is an obtrusive method and would seem to share some of the
limitations of the familiar survey interview in this regard. Researchers using
unstructured interviews, even though such instruments are longer and much
more likely to produce repeat visits than those of the survey kind, are unlikely
to have the participant observer's capacity for becoming part of the scenery.
The potential for reactive effects in the unstructured interview, though arguably less than in survey interviews, would still seem to be more likely than in
participant observation.

Indeed, the extensive use of interviews in qualitative research points to
another area in which the two research traditions share a common technical
problem. The pervasive acceptance of the unstructured interview as a legitimate tool of qualitative research – either in conjunction with participant
observation or more especially on its own – is occasionally surprising on at
least five further accounts. First, writers like Cicourel (1982, p. 15) have criticized interviews for their lack of 'ecological validity': 'Do our instruments
capture the daily life, conditions, opinions, values, attitudes, and knowledge
base of those we study as expressed in their natural habitat?' Cicourel points
to a lack of ecological validity in interviews in a number of ways; for example, they are very sensitive to slight changes in wording, and the availability
of the necessary knowledge to answer a question on the part of the respondent is rarely addressed. Although survey research is certainly more culpable
in these respects than unstructured interviews, it is possible that they do not
totally escape this criticism. The respondent in an unstructured interview study
is questioned in a much more probing manner than in the conventional interview, but the issue of whether this means that ecological validity is obtained
tends to be unexplored. This issue again suggests a common thread to the technical problems faced by quantitative and qualitative researchers.

Secondly, it is not always clear how well the unstructured interview fits
with the suggestion that qualitative research exhibits a concern for process.
Participant observers would seem to be in a much stronger position to impute the interconnections of events over time than researchers who rely
exclusively on unstructured interviews. The relative absence of a sense of process in research which relies wholly on unstructured interviews can be mitigated
to a certain degree by building in a longitudinal element. In their study of
individuals in arrears with their mortgages, Took and Ford (1987) conducted
unstructured interviews on three occasions with many of their respondents
in order to chart changes in the experience and perception of debt. Thirdly,
survey interviews have long been criticized for their tendency to rely on

attitudes and people's reports of their behaviour, both of which may bear little relation to actual behaviour (LaPiere, 1934; Deutscher, 1966); participant observation displays a technical advantage in this respect by virtue of the researcher's ability to observe behaviour directly (as recognized in the Warwick and Lininger quotation above). There is little reason to believe that unstructured interviews are substantially superior to survey interviews in this connection which also indicates another similarity in technical problems faced. Fourthly, the qualitative researcher may experience some difficulty in establishing the appropriate climate for an unstructured interview on some occasions. For example, in her qualitative research on grandparenthood, Cunningham-Burley (1985) found that some of her unstructured interviews with grandparents took a more formal, ordered character and departed very little from her schedule. Such interviews seem to have had an adverse effect on the qualitative depth of the data. Finally, the unstructured interview is not obviously consistent with the commitment of much qualitative research to naturalism. The interview is an obtrusive interruption of the natural flow of events, so that it is slightly surprising to find writers like Blumer (1969), who are committed to the naturalistic viewpoint, suggesting that it is a legitimate tool for such research. Cunningham-Burley (1985), for example, found that even her most informal interviews conformed to a question–answer format. Together, these features point to a possible need to question the extent to which unstructured interviewing is entirely consistent with the qualitative approach and to more areas in which the two approaches exhibit similar technical problems.

There has been some re-appraisal of the role of interviews in qualitative research, which may have been motivated slightly by such considerations. Paget's (1983) discussion of interviewing artists in New York is indicative of such a re-orientation. She views the in-depth interview as a scientific means of developing systematic knowledge about subjective experience. She sees the in-depth interview as a medium through which the interviewer and interviewee jointly create this knowledge; the former is fully implicated in the process of gaining knowledge about the interviewee's subjective experience. Paget implicated herself in this process by making clear her own interest in the art world and allowed this personal concern to be reflected in the questions she formulated and her own responses to the interviewees' replies. Her interviews, transcripts from which are quoted at length, include numerous switches of both content and direction which are fully followed up in the course of the sessions. The content of replies is fully explored to discern their meaning and significance. Thus a simple question about the nature of an artist's paintings (e.g. whether they were fun to do) rapidly turns into a statement by the interviewee about her commitments to art and some of the financial problems she encountered during the early years (Paget, 1983, pp. 70–1). These points are then followed up and addressed during the interview. Further, the meaning of replies is embedded in the context of the interview situation itself; thus a particular reply is examined by the interviewer in the context of the interviewee's other replies and is possibly returned to when, for example, later exchanges produce information which is puzzling, when viewed in relation to the earlier reply. It is the contextual understanding of respondents' replies that sharply distinguishes this emerging conception of the role of the unstructured interview from the survey interview (Mishler, 1986). The unstructured interview is viewed by writers like Paget as a dynamic process whereby the researcher seeks to gain knowledge – by which she means 'illuminating human experience' (p. 88) – about what art work or whatever entails. This perspective on interviewing seems to harmonize somewhat better with the qualitative research tradition than much unstructured interviewing, by virtue of its explicit concern with respondents' subjective experiences. Further, the tendency to invite interviewees to speak at length possibly renders such interviewing less obtrusive than much unstructured interviewing. The problem of ecological validity may also be reduced since the focus is very explicitly upon what is important to the interviewee rather than to the researcher.

A further technical problem shared by both research traditions relates to the selection of people who are the focus of the research. Quantitative research is concerned to establish that respondents are representative of a wider population, so that the generalizability of findings can be enhanced. In fact, much research departs significantly from this ideal in a number of ways. However, there is a case for suggesting that the issue of representativeness confronts the qualitative researcher too. The avowal to see through the eyes of one's subjects can be interpreted to imply that the ethnographer needs to attend to the question of the typicality of the eyes through which he or she is seeing. This kind of concern may be regarded as indicative of the application of an inappropriate criterion (that is, one deriving from the framework of quantitative research) to the ethnographer's mode of research. For example, in their exposition of grounded theory, Glaser and Strauss (1967) advocate that the qualitative researcher should give less attention to the need to meet statistical sampling criteria in assessing the adequacy of a 'sample'; rather, the researcher should be much more concerned with the issue of whether the sample conforms to the investigator's emerging theoretical framework. For example, in an ethnographic study of power in a medical school in the USA, Bucher (1970, p. 5) proposed that, following a preliminary analysis of her initial observations, 'data are being sought from areas of the organization which should provide test cases, so to speak, for emerging propositions'. According to the principles of 'theoretical sampling' (the term coined by Glaser and Strauss), the researcher observes only as many activities, or interviews as many people, as are needed in order to 'saturate' the categories being developed, and then turns to the next theoretical issue and carries out the same process over again. Thus the question of the adequacy of a sample is determined by the degree to which it permits the qualitative researcher to develop and confirm one or more categories; as soon as the researcher feels satisfied that the theoretical point has been established, he or she can move on to the next issue. This procedure allows the constant interplay between theory and research that Glaser and Strauss are keen to develop.

While Glaser and Strauss's view of sampling serves well to exemplify the disinclination of qualitative researchers to accept the quantitative researcher's preoccupation with representativeness, like other aspects of grounded theory, their particular view of the sampling process is probably cited far more frequently than it is used. Of course, qualitative researchers (especially ethnographers) may not simply sample people, but also activities, time periods, and locations (Burgess, 1984). None the less, if the aim of the exercise is to see as one's subjects see, there is still a problem of the representativeness of the eyes. For example, qualitative researchers sometimes display a concern that the people with whom they come into contact may be marginal to the social setting. Blau (1964) found that during the early period of his field-work in a federal agency, his early contacts and suppliers of information were marginal officials who were keen to voice their criticisms of the agency and their colleagues. As Blau acknowledged, had he not recognized this problem, a distorted picture of the agency would have been generated. Interestingly, Blau (1964, p. 30) argues that the field researcher's own marginality may render him attractive to those who are marginal to the settings in which research is carried out. Similarly, Ball (1984, p. 81), drawing on his ethnographic study of a comprehensive school, has remarked on the untypicality and, in the case of two teachers, marginality of his main informants. Other writers (e.g. Hammersley, 1984, pp. 51–3) have drawn attention to biases which stem from the problem of establishing a picture drawn from a representative spread of contacts and informants.

The purpose of drawing attention to some common technical problems faced by quantitative and qualitative researchers has been to highlight the possibility that discussions of the differences between the two traditions purely in terms of epistemological issues run the risk of exaggerating their distinctiveness. This is not to imply that the differences between quantitative and qualitative research are insignificant, but that they may not be as far apart as is sometimes implied by the epistemological version of the debate about the two research traditions.

The Link between Epistemology and Technique

Quantitative and qualitative research are each associated with distinctive methods of data collection and research strategy, although their differences are not as clear cut as some of the more programmatic statements imply. In particular, it has been suggested in this chapter that the differences between the two research traditions are less precise than writers who emphasize epistemological issues suggest. According to the epistemological version of the debate about the two research traditions, the choice of research method flows from an allegiance to a distinctive position in relation to how social reality ought to be studied. This view suggests that, for example, it would be wholly inappropriate to use a survey in order to conduct research which is grounded in the cluster of intellectual predilections associated with qualitative research. It is not simply that the survey is likely to generate quantitative data; rather, it is seen as better suited to a natural science conception of how social reality ought to be studied, while a technique like participant observation is better attuned to the epistemological commitments of qualitative research.

In other words, the epistemological version of the debate assumes a correspondence between epistemological position and research method. Is this an acceptable view of the way social research is conducted? This question can be tackled in a number of ways, but in the rest of this section some problems with assuming a clear correspondence between epistemology and research technique will be examined.

Ethnography and Positivism

Not all commentators on the nature of social research have accepted the bond between ethnographic research and a nonpositivist approach to the study of social research. In particular, the view has been expressed that ethnographic investigations may also engender a form of empiricism. Willer and Willer (1973) argue that, although participant observation differs from what they call 'systematic empiricism' (as exemplified by the experiment and the social survey), it is none the less empiricist in that it establishes the connections between observed categories. According to this view the empiricism of participant observation resides in the researcher's distrust of categories which are not directly amenable to the senses. This point is highly congruent with Rock's (1973) view that much research in the sociology of deviance (a great deal of which stems from ethnographic investigations) is phenomenalist by virtue of a disinclination among many researchers to dig themselves out of the data on the social world in which they bury themselves. This phenomenalism can be discerned in the following passage from a text on field research by a proponent of qualitative research in the sociology of deviance:

> We begin with direct experience and all else builds on that ... [W]e begin with and continually return to direct experience as the most reliable form of knowledge about the social world. (Douglas, 1976, p. 7)

In like fashion, Willis (1980), the author of a celebrated ethnographic study of working class youth (1977), has referred to a 'covert positivism' in participant observation. By this phrase Willis means that the researcher sees the subject of his or her research as an object who can provide data; further, he argues, the preference of participant observers to postpone the generation of theory in relation to their data enhances a positivist hue by virtue of deferring to what is directly observable. Finally, Delamont and Atkinson (1980) have argued that the tendency towards atheoretical investigations in much school ethnography is conspiring to produce a form of empiricism.

In each of these comments is a view that participant observation does not depart radically from a positivist epistemology. In the view of these authors, the empiricism in much ethnographic research is exaggerated by the widespread tendency to postpone theoretical reflection, if indeed theory comes into the reckoning at all. In Glaser and Strauss's (1967) grounded theory, the view of theory as an emergent product of an investigation is systematized. However, the positioning of theory at the outset of an investigation can also be regarded as retaining positivist elements, by virtue of 'theory' being envisioned as something which needs to be tested by recourse to an examination of the real world. The problem here is that, irrespective of whether theory is seen as something which precedes or succeeds the collection of ethnographic data, a basically positivist precept is being adhered to, since the world of the senses is the ultimate arbiter of whether a theory is acceptable or not. Thus the quest for a more explicit grounding of qualitative research in theory (which some writers have expressed – see Chapter 4 (Bryman, 1988b)) supplants the more obvious empiricism of waiting for the theory to emerge, with the positivist preference for being 'entitled to record only that which is actually manifested in experience' (Kolakowski, 1972, p. 11). It is the manner in which theory is conceptualized in relation to the collection of data that points to an affinity with positivism, and not simply whether theory comes before, during, or after the data collection phase.

Qualitative research may also allow the investigator to impute causal processes which bear a strong resemblance to the kinds of causal statements that are the hallmark of quantitative research (although without the precise delineation of cause and effect which quantitative researchers seek to generate). McCleary (1977) conducted participant observation and interviews with parole officers in a division of a state parole agency in Chicago. He notes that officers should report parole violations known to have been committed by their parolees, but frequently they do not. Through his research, he was able to identify five factors which result in officers' disinclination to report their parolees: full reporting cuts into the officer's time; it may reflect badly on the officer and result in a negative evaluation by his or her superior; the officer's options may be restricted as a result of reporting a violation; and so on. Thus, McCleary was able to identify causes of failure to report parolees, whilst retaining fidelity to the perspectives of parole officers themselves.

Quantitative Research and Meaning

The recurring theme within qualitative research of viewing attributes of the social world through the eyes of the people being studied has led to a convention that only methods like participant observation and intensive interviewing are acceptable in this light. But quantitative researchers also make frequent claims to addressing issues relating to the meaning of aspects of the social world to the people being studied. Social science research on work provides a number of examples of such investigations. The classic study of a sample of adults in the USA by Morse and Weiss (1955) used a survey to discern the range of reasons why people work and what meaning work has for them. The authors found that work does not simply mean the ability to earn money, but has a number of other meanings for people. Goldthorpe *et al.* (1968) conducted a survey in Luton to examine industrial attitudes and behaviour. One of the study's central notions – the idea of 'orientation to work' – draws attention to the variety of meanings which work may have for industrial workers. Finally, in their monograph on social stratification which reports a large scale survey of white-collar employees, Stewart, Prandy and Blackburn (1980) draw attention to the tendency to treat clerks as an undifferentiated category in many discussions of their position in the class structure. By contrast, the purpose of their research was to show that 'the *meaning* of clerical work will not be the same for all engaged in it' (Stewart, Prandy and Blackburn, 1980, p. 112 – emphasis added).

Marsh (1982) has also drawn attention to the capacity of social surveys to provide insights into questions of meaning. For example, the widespread tendency among social researchers to solicit their respondents' reasons for their actions, views, and the like, provides the researcher with people's interpretations of a variety of phenomena. She also points to the research by Brown and Harris (1978), which examined the connection between critical life events (e.g. loss of job, death of husband, childbirth) and depression. Marsh observes that the researchers went to great pains to establish the meaning of each life event to each respondent. For example: 'Childbirth was not normally rated severe unless it happened in the context of bad housing and shortage of money' (Marsh, 1982, p. 117).

The field of cognitive social psychology provides a contrasting example of a subject which is explicitly concerned with meaning but which relies heavily upon quantitative experimental research as a prominent data gathering procedure. Cognitive social psychologists are concerned with 'how people make sense of other people and themselves' and 'people's everyday understanding both as the phenomenon of interest and as a basis for theory about people's everyday understanding' (Fiske and Taylor, 1984, p. 17). For example, in the field of leadership research, a prominent interest has been leaders' perceptions of the causes of their subordinates' success or failure (Bryman, 1986). This level of analysis is concerned with everyday understandings of the meanings of success and failure. Such research has proceeded by experimentally manipulating subordinate behaviour and then gauging leaders' perceptions of the causes of particular levels of that behaviour. Investigators have been particularly concerned to establish the circumstances in which good or poor subordinate performance is deemed by leaders to be a consequence of internal factors (e.g. subordinates' levels of ability or effort), or of external factors (e.g. task difficulty or luck). Thus such research is concerned with the meanings people ascribe to events and to others' behaviour.

It seems, then, that quantitative researchers also make the claim that their methods can gain access to people's interpretations and to the ways in which they view the world.

Participant Observation and Theory Testing

Quantitative research tends to be depicted as well suited to the task of testing explicitly formulated theories, whereas qualitative research is typically associated with the generation of theories. However, there is nothing intrinsic to participant observation, for example, that renders it inappropriate for the testing of preformulated theories. Becker (1958) provided a framework which would facilitate the examination of previously formulated theories by participant observation. He anticipated that his proposed approach would allow qualitative research to assume a more scientific character than that with which it is most closely associated. Other writers, like McCall (1969) and Campbell (1979), have argued along similar lines that the association of qualitative research solely with theory-creation does less than justice to its potential.

Indeed, one of the most celebrated studies using participant observation – Festinger, Riecken and Schachter's (1956) investigation of a religious cult – was designed to test a theory about how people are likely to respond to the disconfirmation of a belief to which they are fervently wedded. The authors suggested that a number of conditions can be envisaged which would allow the belief to be held with greater zeal even when it has been proved to be wrong. Festinger *et al.* learned of a millenarian group that was prophesying the imminent end of the world and felt that it would provide an ideal case for the examination of their theoretical concerns. As mentioned on p. 52, along with some hired observers, they joined the group as participants and 'gathered data about the conviction, commitment and proselytizing activity' (p. 31) of its adherents. More recently, as observed above, some writers have argued for a more explicit approach to the testing of theory by qualitative researchers (e.g. Hammersley, 1985; Hammersley, Scarth and Webb, 1985). Further, the view that qualitative research is compatible with a theory testing approach is implicit in the more recent treatments of the issue of case study generalization which were mentioned in Chapter 4 (Bryman, 1988b). It will be recalled that Mitchell (1983) and Yin (1984) have both suggested that the question of the generalizability of case studies (and thereby much qualitative research) misses the central point of such investigations, in that the critical issue is 'the cogency of the theoretical reasoning' (Mitchell, 1983, p. 207). The Festinger, Riecken and Schachter study is a case in point: the representativeness of the cult is not particularly important; it is its relevance to the theoretical framework which constitutes the most important criterion for assessing the study. Accordingly, the view of qualitative research which plays down its role in relation to the testing of theory may be missing an important strength that qualitative investigations possess. In other words, there is nothing intrinsic to the techniques of data collection with which qualitative research is connected that renders them unacceptable as a means of testing theory.

Conclusion

It has been suggested that there are a number of ways in which the posited connection between epistemology and data collection can be questioned: participant observation (and indeed unstructured interviewing) is not without positivist leanings; survey researchers frequently claim to be looking at the social world from their respondents' perspectives; and participant observation can be deployed within a theory testing framework with which the epistemological basis of quantitative research is conventionally associated. None the less, a recurring theme of this book thus far is that a prominent view of the debate about quantitative and qualitative research is that they are competing epistemological positions, each of which is associated with particular approaches to data collection and research strategy. How should we understand the apparent clash between the suggestion presented here that the link between epistemology and method is not clear-cut and the epistemological account of the debate about quantitative and qualitative research?

One of the most unsatisfactory aspects of the epistemological version of the debate is that it is unclear whether its proponents are arguing that there is a link between epistemology and method of data collection or whether there *ought* to be such a bond. If the argument is that there is such a link, the epistemological argument runs into difficulties. In addition to the points made in the previous section, which suggest that the bond between epistemology and method may be exaggerated, it is also clear that methods like participant observation and unstructured interviewing have been used by various practitioners who have not had an epistemological axe to grind. Writers like Lupton (1963), Gans (1962), and Skolnick (1966), all of whom have written much admired monographs deriving from the use of such methods, seem to have exhibited few, if any, philosophical pretensions in their justifications for the use of qualitative research. These researchers were able to produce highly regarded ethnographic studies without recourse to the programmatic statements surrounding qualitative research. This very fact invites a questioning of the role of programmatic statements in relation to the pursuit of good social research. Rather, these researchers were concerned to get close to the people they were studying, to allow for the possibility of novel findings, and to elucidate their findings from the perspective of the people they studied. While the last of these three concerns is invariably taken as a keynote of the epistemological substructure of qualitative research, a preoccupation with meaning and subjects' perspectives is not exclusive to the qualitative tradition. Further, the methods with which qualitative research is associated have often been chosen on technical grounds rather than epistemological grounds.

The lack of a definitive link between broad epistemological positions and methods has also been suggested by Snizek (1976), who analysed 1,434 articles in sociological journals covering the period 1950 to 1970. Snizek was concerned to find out whether there was a connection between the three paradigms which Ritzer (1975) had suggested underpin sociology and the methods with which they are associated. If these three basic approaches to sociology really are paradigms (T. S. Kuhn, 1970), one would anticipate a link between the endorsement of the epistemology with which each is associated and the methods of research used. Two of the paradigms – the 'social factist' and 'social definitionist' orientations – correspond to quantitative and qualitative research respectively to a fair degree. However, Snizek was unable to discern a clear pattern which linked the general orientation of each paradigm with the methods of investigation employed.

The alternative position is to suggest that there *ought* to be a connection between epistemological positions and methods of data collection. This view would imply that researchers should be much more sensitive to the wider epistemological context of methods of data collection and that they are not neutral technical devices to be deployed under a variety of auspices. Choosing to conduct a survey or an ethnographic study would mean accepting a package of views about social reality and how it ought to be studied. Accordingly, it might be argued that researchers who claim to study subjects' views of the world with a survey (e.g. Goldthorpe *et al.*, 1968) are misguided, since they should have chosen a method more suited to this perspective, like unstructured interviewing. It is not at all clear from the various writings on the debate about quantitative and qualitative research that the view exists that there ought to be a recognition of a mutual interdependence of epistemology and method (as against a view that there is such a connection). The problem with the 'ought' view is that it fails to recognize that a whole cluster of considerations are likely to impinge on decisions about methods of data collection. In particular, the investigator's judgements regarding the technical viability of a method in relation to a particular problem will be important, as the technical version of the debate about the two research traditions implies.

Methods are probably much more autonomous than many commentators (particularly those who espouse the epistemological versions of the debate) acknowledge. They can be used in a variety of contexts and with an assortment of purposes in mind. Indeed, the very fact that many qualitative researchers instil an element of quantitative data collection into their investigations underlines this point to a certain degree. Similar points can be made in relation to the connection between broad theories and methods. As pointed out in Chapter 2 (Bryman, 1988b), Platt (1986) has strongly questioned the supposed link between functionalism and the survey. Similarly, while some writers have found an affinity between a Marxist perspective and qualitative research (e.g. Sharp and Green, 1975; Willis, 1977), others have preferred the methods of quantitative research for the empirical elucidation of concepts associated with this theoretical perspective (e.g. Wright and Perrone, 1977). Symbolic interactionism, while typically associated with participant observation (Rock, 1979), is not universally identified with qualitative research and an anti-positivist epistemology: M. H. Kuhn (1964) used the techniques and research strategies of quantitative research in his attempt to use symbolic interactionist notions; many studies conducted within this theoretical tradition make substantial use of standard survey techniques alongside participant observation; and there is even a questioning of whether G. H. Mead's (1934) writings lead in a direction which is antithetical to the application of the methods of the natural sciences (McPhail and Rexroat, 1979). The tendency to associate particular methods with particular epistemological positions is little more than a convention (which took root in the 1960s), but which has little to recommend it, either as a description of the research process or as a prescriptive view of how research ought to be done.

In comparison with the rather stark contrasts between quantitative and qualitative research which have permeated the pages thus far, the next chapter examines some of the ways in which the two traditions may be used in tandem. The epistemological version of the debate does not readily admit a blending of quantitative and qualitative research since the two traditions are deemed to represent highly contrasting views about how social reality should be studied. The technical version of the debate much more readily accommodates a marriage of the two since it acknowledges the respective strengths and weaknesses of the two approaches as methods of data collection. Many writers shuttle uneasily back and forth between the two ways of thinking about the two traditions. It is little wonder that confusion ensues when there is a lack of clarity about what quantitative and qualitative research are. In this context, the view of a leading writer on the ethnography of schooling is instructive:

> It is not surprising that some work called 'ethnography' is marked by obscurity of purpose, lax relationships between concepts and observation, indifferent or absent conceptual structure and theory, weak implementation of research method, confusion about whether there should be hypotheses and, if so, how they should be tested, confusion over whether quantitative methods can be relevant ... and so forth. (Spindler, 1982, p. 2)

Precisely because many qualitative researchers have failed to sort out whether the style of research to which they adhere is an epistemological or a technical position, it is possible for such confusion to reign. However, when quantitative and qualitative research are jointly pursued, much more complete accounts of social reality can ensue, as many of the examples cited in Bryman, (1988b), Chapter 6.

Notes

1. Symbolic interactionism, by contrast, is a theoretical position developed largely within the social sciences, but which has its roots in an epistemological position, namely, pragmatism.
2. Frequently, discussion in the literature of such issues takes the form of evaluating qualitative research in terms of its validity and reliability (e.g. LeCompte and Goetz,

1982). I have resisted such an approach in this book, because I feel that it imposes a cluster of standards upon qualitative research which to a large extent are more relevant to the quantitative tradition, within which such terms were originally developed.

Bibliography and Author Index

Adler, P. A. (1985), *Wheeling and Dealing: An Ethnography of an Upper Level Drug Dealing and Smuggling Community*, New York: Columbia University Press.

Adler, P., and Adler, P. A. (1985), 'From idealism to pragmatic detachment: the academic performance of college athletes', *Sociology of Education*, vol. 58, no. 4, pp. 241–50.

Atkinson, P. A. (1981), *The Clinical Experience*, Farnborough: Gower.

Ball, S. J. (1981), *Beachside Comprehensive: A Case-Study of Secondary Schooling*, Cambridge: CUP.

Ball, S. J. (1984), 'Beachside reconsidered: reflections on a methodological apprenticeship', in R. G. Burgess (ed.) *The Research Process in Educational Settings: Ten Case Studies*, London: Falmer, pp. 69–96.

Barrett, S. R. (1976), 'The use of models in anthropological fieldwork', *Journal of Anthropological Research*, vol. 32, pp. 161–81.

Becker, H. S. (1958), 'Problems of inference and proof in participant observation', *American Sociological Review*, vol. 23, no. 6, pp. 652–60.

Becker, H. S., and Geer, B. (1957), 'Participant observation and interviewing: a comparison', *Human Organization*, vol. 16, no. 3, pp. 28–32.

Blalock, H. M. (1970), *An Introduction to Social Research*, Englewood Cliffs, NJ: Prentice-Hall.

Blau, P. M. (1964), 'The research process in the study of *The Dynamics of Bureaucracy*', in P. E. Hammond (ed.), *Sociologists at Work*, New York: Basic Books, pp. 16–49.

Blumer, H. (1956), 'Sociological analysis and the "variable"', *American Sociological Review*, vol. 21, no. 6, pp. 683–90.

—— (1969), *Symbolic Interactionism*, Englewood Cliffs, NJ: Prentice-Hall.

Bogdan, R., and Biklen, S. K. (1982), *Qualitative Research for Education: An Introduction to Theory and Methods*, Boston: Allyn & Bacon.

Bogdan, R., and Taylor, S. J. (1975), *Introduction to Qualitative Research Methods: A Phenomenological Approach to the Social Sciences*, New York: Wiley.

Bresnen, M. (1988), 'Insights on site: research into construction project organizations', in A. Bryman (ed.), *Doing Research in Organizations*, London: Routledge & Kegan Paul, pp. 34–52.

Brown, G. W., and Harris, T. W. (1978), *The Social Origins of Depression: A Study of Psychiatric Disorder in Women*, London: Tavistock.

Bryman, A. (1986), *Leadership and Organizations*, London: Routledge & Kegan Paul.

—— (1988a), 'Introduction: "inside accounts" and social research in organizations', in A. Bryman (ed.), *Doing Research in Organizations*, London: Routledge & Kegan Paul, pp. 1–20.

—— (1988b), *Quantity and Quality in Social Researchm*, London: Routledge & Kegan Paul.

Buchanan, D., Boddy, D., and McCalman, J. (1988), 'Getting in, getting on, getting out, getting back', in A. Bryman (ed.), *Doing Research in Organizations*, London: Routledge & Kegan Paul, pp. 53–67.

Bucher, R. (1970), 'Social process and power in a medical school', in M. N. Zald (ed.), *Power in Organizations*, Nashville: Vanderbilt University Press, pp. 3–48.

Bulmer, M. (1982) (ed.), *Social Research Ethics*, London: Macmillan.

Burgess, R. G. (1984), *In the Field: An Introduction to Field Research*, London: Allen & Unwin.

Campbell, D. T. (1979), '"Degrees of freedom" and the case study', in T. D. Cook and C. R. Reichardt (eds) *Qualitative and Quantitative Methods in Evaluation Research*, Beverly Hills, Calif.: Sage, pp. 49–67.

Cavendish, R. (1982), *Women on the Line*, London: Routledge & Kegan Paul.

Cicourel, A. V. (1982), 'Interviews, surveys, and the problem of ecological validity', *American Sociologist*, vol. 17, no. 1, pp. 11–20.

Cohen, A. P. (1978), 'Ethnographic method in the real community' *Sociologia Ruralis*, vol. 18, no. 1, pp. 1–22.

Cunningham-Burley, S. (1985), 'Rules, roles and communicative performance in qualitative research interviews', *International Journal of Sociology and Social Policy*, vol. 5, no. 3, pp. 67–77.

Dalton, M. (1959), *Men Who Manage*, New York: Wiley.

Daniel, W. W. (1968), *Racial Discrimination in England*, Harmondsworth, Middx: Penguin.

Davies, H. (1972), *The Glory Game*, London: Weidenfeld & Nicholson.

Delamont, S., and Atkinson, P. (1980), 'The two traditions in educational ethnography: sociology and anthropology compared', *British Journal of Sociology of Education*, vol. 1, no. 2, pp. 139–52.

Delamont, S., and Hamilton, D. (1984), 'Revisiting classroom research: a continuing cautionary tale', in S. Delamont (ed.), *Readings on Interaction in the Classroom*, London: Methuen, pp. 3–24.

Deutscher, I. (1966), 'Words and deeds: social science and social policy', *Social Problems*, vol. 13, pp. 235–54.

Ditton, J. (1977), *Part-Time Crime: An Ethnography of Fiddling and Pilferage*, London: Macmillan.

Douglas, J. D. (1976), *Investigative Social Research*, Beverly Hills, Calif.: Sage.

Festinger, L., Riecken, H. W., and Schachter, S. (1956), *When Prophecy Fails*, New York: Harper & Row.

Filmer, P., Phillipson, M., Silverman, D., and Walsh, D. (1972), *New Directions in Sociological Theory*, London, Collier-Macmillan.

Filstead, W. J. (1979), 'Qualitative methods: a needed perspective in evaluation research', in T. D. Cook and C. S. Reichardt (eds), *Qualitative and Quantitative Methods in Evaluation Research*, Beverly Hills, Calif.: Sage, pp. 33–48.

Finch, J. (1986), *Research and Policy: The Uses of Qualitative Methods in Social and Educational Research*, London: Falmer Press.

Fiske, S. T., and Taylor, S. E. (1984), *Social Cognition*, New York: Random House.

Freeman, J. (1986), 'Data quality and the development of organizational social science: an editorial essay', *Administrative Science Quarterly*, vol. 31, no. 2, pp. 298–303.

Gans, H. J. (1962), *The Urban Villagers*, New York: Free Press.

—— (1967), *The Levittowners*, London: Allen Lane.

—— (1982), *The Urban Villagers*, 2nd edn, New York: Free Press.

Glaser, B. G., and Strauss, A. L. (1967), *The Discovery of Grounded Theory*, Chicago: Aldine. 3

Goldthorpe, J. H. (with C. Llewellyn and C. Payne) (1980), *Social Mobility and Class Structure in Modern Britain*, Oxford: Clarendon Press.

Goldthorpe, J. H., Lockwood, D., Bechhofer, F., and Platt, J. (1968), *The Affluent Worker: Industrial Attitudes and Behaviour*, Cambridge: CUP.

Griffin, C. (1985a), *Typical Girls? Young Women from School to the Job Market*, London: Routledge & Kegan Paul.

Guba, E. G. (1985), 'The context of emergent paradigm research', in Y. S. Lincoln (ed.), *Organizational Theory and Inquiry: The Paradigm Revolution*, Beverly Hills, Calif.: Sage, pp. 79–104.

Halfpenny, P. (1979), 'The analysis of qualitative data', *Sociological Review*, vol. 27, no. 4, pp. 799–825.

Hammersley, M. (1984), 'The researcher exposed: a natural history', in R. G. Burgess (ed.), *The Research Process in Educational Settings: Ten Case Studies*, London: Falmer Press, pp. 39–67.

—— (1985), 'From ethnography to theory: a programme and paradigm in the sociology of education', *Sociology*, vol. 19, no. 2, pp. 244–59.

Hammersley, M., Scarth, J., and Webb, S. (1985), 'Developing and testing theory: the case of research on pupil learning and examinations', in R. G. Burgess (ed.), *Issues in Educational Research: Qualitative Methods*, London: Falmer Press, pp. 48–66.

Hirschi, T. (1969), *Causes of Delinquency*, Berkeley: University of California Press.

Kolakowski, L. (1972), *Positivist Philosophy: From Hume to the Vienna Circle*, Harmondsworth: Penguin.

Kuhn, M. H. (1964), 'Major trends in symbolic interaction theory in the past twenty-five years', *Sociological Quarterly*, vol. 5, no. 1, pp. 61–84.

Kuhn, T. S. (1970), *The Structure of Scientific Revolutions*, 2nd edn, Chicago: University of Chicago Press (originally published in 1962).

Lacey, C. (1970), *Hightown Grammar: The School as a Social System*, Manchester: Manchester University Press.

LaPiere, R. T. (1934), 'Attitudes vs. actions', *Social Forces*, vol. 13, pp. 230–7.

LeCompte, M. D., and Goetz, J. P. (1982), 'Problems of reliability and validity in ethnographic research', *Review of Educational Research*, vol. 52, no. 1, pp. 31–60.

Liebow, E. (1967), *Tally's Corner*, Boston, Mass.: Little, Brown.

Lipset, S. M. (1964), 'The biography of a research project: *Union Democracy*', in P. E. Hammond (ed.), *Sociologists at Work: Essays in the Craft of Social Research*, New York: Basic Books, pp. 96–120.

Lipset, S. M., Trow, M., and Coleman, J. S. (1956), *Union Democracy*, Glencoe: Free Press.

Lofland, J. (1971), *Analyzing Social Settings: A Guide to Qualitative Observation and Analysis*, Belmont, Calif.: Wadsworth.

Lupton, T. (1963), *On the Shop Floor*, Oxford: Pergamon.

McCall, G. J. (1969), 'The problem of indicators in participant observation research', in G. J. McCall and J. L. Simmons (eds), *Issues in Participant Observation: A Text and Reader*, Reading, Mass.: Addison-Wesley, pp. 230–7.

McCleary, R. (1977), 'How parole officers use records', *Social Problems*, vol. 24, no. 5, pp. 576–89.

McPhail, C., and Rexroat, C. (1979), 'Mead vs. Blumer: the divergent methodological perspectives of social behaviorism and symbolic interactionism', vol. 44, no. 3, pp. 449–67.

Marsh, C. (1982), *The Survey Method: The Contribution of Surveys to Sociological Explanation*, London: Allen & Unwin.

Matza, D. (1969), *Becoming Deviant*, Englewood Cliffs, NJ: Prentice-Hall.

Mead, G. H. (1934), *Mind, Self and Society*, Chicago: University of Chicago Press.

Milgram, S. (1963), 'Behavioral study of obedience', *Journal of Abnormal and Social Psychology*, vol. 67, pp. 371–8.

Mishler, E. G. (1986), *Research Interviewing: Context and Narrative*, Cambridge, Mass.: Harvard University Press.

Mitchell, J. C. (1983), 'Case and situation analysis', *Sociological Review*, vol. 31, no. 2, pp. 186–211.

Morse, N. C., and Weiss, R. S. (1955), 'The function and meaning of work and the job', *American Sociological Review*, vol. 20, no. 2, pp. 191–8.

Nicholson, B. (1984), *Glory Glory: My Life with Spurs*, London: Macmillan.

Oakley, A. (1981), 'Interviewing women: a contradiction in terms', in H. Roberts (ed.), *Doing Feminist Research*, London: Routledge & Kegan Paul, pp. 30–61.

—— (1984), *Taking It Like a Woman*, London: Cape.

Okely, J. (1987), 'Fieldwork up the M1: policy and political aspects', in A. Jackson (ed.), *Anthropology at Home*, London: Tavistock, pp. 55–73.

Paget, M. A. (1983), 'Experience and knowledge', *Human Studies*, vol. 6, no. 1, pp. 67–90.

Patrick, J. (1973), *A Glasgow Gang Observed*, London: Eyre-Methuen.

Platt, J. (1986), 'Functionalism and the survey: the relation of theory and method', *Sociological Review*, vol. 34, no. 3, pp. 501–36.

Pollert, A. (1981), *Girls, Wives, Factory Lives*, London: Macmillan.

Pugh, D. S. (1988), 'The Aston research programme', in A. Bryman (ed.), *Doing Research in Organizations*, London: Routledge & Kegan Paul, pp. 123–35.

Pugh, D. S., and Hickson, D. J. (1976), *Organizational Structure in its Context: The Aston Programme I*, Aldershot: Gower.

Pugh, D. S., and Payne, R. L. (1977) (eds), *Organizational Behaviour in its Context: The Aston Programme III*, Aldershot: Gower.

Reichardt, C. S., and Cook, T. D. (1979), 'Beyond qualitative *versus* quantitative methods', in T. D. Cook and C. S. Reichardt (eds), *Qualitative and Quantitative Methods in Evaluation Research*, Beverly Hills, Calif.: Sage, pp. 7–32.

Rist, R. C. (1977), 'On the relations among educational research paradigms: from disdain to detente', *Anthropology and Education Quarterly*, vol. 8, no. 2, pp. 42–9.

Ritzer, G. (1975), 'Sociology: a multiple paradigm science', *American Sociologist*, vol. 10, no. 3, pp. 156–67.

Rock, P. (1973), 'Phenomenalism and essentialism in the sociology of deviance', *Sociology*, vol. 7, no. 1, pp. 17–29.

—— (1979), *The Making of Symbolic Interactionism*, London: Macmillan.

Rosenberg, M. (1968), *The Logic of Survey Analysis*, New York: Basic Books.

Rosenthal, R. (1966), *Experimenter Effects in Behavioral Research*, New York: Appleton-Century-Crofts.

Roy, D. (1960), 'Banana time: job satisfaction and informal interaction', *Human Organization*, vol. 18, no. 4, pp. 158–68.

Scase, R., and Goffee, R. (1982), *The Entrepreneurial Middle Class*, London: Croom Helm.

Serber, D. (1981), 'The masking of social reality: ethnographic fieldwork in a bureaucracy', in D. A. Messerschmidt (ed.), *Anthropologists at Home in North America: Methods and Issues in the Study of One's Own Society*, Cambridge: CUP, pp. 77–87.

Sharp, R. and Green, A. (1975), *Education and Social Control: A Study in Progressive Primary Education*, London: Routledge & Kegan Paul.

Skolnick, J. H. (1966), *Justice without Trial: Law Enforcement in Democratic Society*, New York: Wiley.

Snizek, W. E. (1976), 'An empirical assessment of "Sociology: a multiple paradigm science"', *American Sociologist*, vol. 11, no. 4, pp. 217–19.

Spindler, G. (1982), 'General introduction', in G. Spindler (ed.), *Doing the Ethnography of Schooling: Educational Anthropology in Action*, New York: Holt, Rinehart & Winston, pp. 1–13.

Stanley, L., and Wise, S. (1983), *Breaking Out: Feminist Consciousness and Feminist Research*, London: Routledge & Kegan Paul.

Stewart, A., Prandy, K., and Blackburn, R. M. (1980), *Social Stratification and Occupations*, London: Macmillan.

Strauss, A., Schatzman, L., Ehrlich, D., Bucher, R., and Sabshin, M. (1963), 'The hospital and its negotiated order', in E. Freidson (ed.), *The Hospital in Modern Society*, New York: Macmillan, pp. 147–9.

Took, L., and Ford, J. (1987), 'The impact of mortgage arrears on the housing careers of home owners', in A. Bryman, B. Bytheway, P. Allatt, and T. Keil (eds), *Rethinking the Life Cycle*, London: Macmillan, pp. 207–29.

Trow, M. (1957), 'Comment on "Participant observation and interviewing: a comparison"', *Human Organization*, vol. 16, no. 3, pp. 33–5.

Walker, R. (1985), 'An introduction to applied qualitative research', in R. Walker (ed.), *Applied Qualitative Research*, Aldershot: Gower, pp. 3–26.

Walsh, D. (1972), 'Sociology and the social world', in P. Filmer, M. Phillipson, D. Silverman, and D. Walsh, *New Directions in Sociological Theory*, London: Collier-Macmillan.

Warwick, D. P., and Lininger, C. A. (1975), *The Sample Survey: Theory and Practice*, New York: McGraw-Hill.

Webb, E. J., Campbell, D. T., Schwartz, R. D., and Sechrest, L. (1966), *Unobtrusive Measures: Nonreactive Research in the Social Sciences*, Chicago: Rand McNally.

Whyte, W. F. (1984), *Learning from the Field: A Guide from Experience*, Beverly Hills, Calif.: Sage.

Willer, D., and Willer, J. (1973), *Systematic Empiricism: A Critique of a Pseudoscience*, Englewood Cliffs, NJ: Prentice-Hall.

Willis, P. (1977), *Learning to Labour*, Farnborough: Saxon House.

—— (1980), 'Notes on method', in S. Hall, D. Hobson, A. Lowe, and P. Willis (eds), *Culture, Media, Language*, London: Hutchinson, pp. 88–95.

Woods, P. (1979), *The Divided School*, London: Routledge & Kegan Paul.

—— (1986), *Inside Schools: Ethnography in Educational Research*, London: Routledge & Kegan Paul. Wright, E. O., and Perrone, L. (1977), 'Marxist class categories and income inequality', *American Sociological Review*, vol. 42, no. 1, pp. 32–55.

Yin, R. K. (1984), *Case Study Research: Design and Methods*, Beverly Hills, Calif.: Sage.

4

Deconstructing the Qualitative–Quantitative Divide[1]

Martyn Hammersley

Introduction

In this chapter I want to challenge the widely held idea that there are two methodological paradigms in social research: the quantitative and the qualitative. This idea seems to have become a matter of consensus over the past few years among many who see themselves on one side of this divide or the other (and even among some who wish to sit astride it). I shall argue, however, that the distinction between qualitative and quantitative is of limited use and, indeed, carries some danger.

It is striking how prone we are to the use of dichotomies, and how these often come to represent distillations of all that is good and bad. Certainly, 'qualitative' and 'quantitative' are sometimes used to represent fundamentally opposed approaches to the study of the social world, one representing the true way, the other the work of the devil. But even where the evaluative overtones are absent and the two approaches are given parity, the distinction is still misleading in my view because it obscures the breadth of issues and arguments involved in the methodology of social research.

In one form or another, the debate about quantitative and qualitative research has been taking place since at least the mid-nineteenth century. At that time there was much argument about the scientific status of history and the social sciences, with quantification often being seen as one of the key features of natural science.[2] Similarly, in US sociology in the 1920s and 30s there was a dispute between advocates of case study and of statistical method. Many of the claims made about quantitative and qualitative method today have their origins in these earlier debates (see Hammersley, 1989a). By the 1940s and 50s in sociology, psychology and some other fields, quantitative method (in the form of survey and experimental research) had become the dominant approach. But since the 1960s there has been a revival in the fortunes of

Source: Julia Brannen (ed.), *Mixing Methods: Qualitative and Quantitative Research* (Aldershot: Avebury, 1992).

qualitative types of research in these disciplines, to the point where their legitimacy is widely accepted.[3] In some areas this has led to a détente (Rist, 1977; Smith and Heshusius, 1986) and to increased interest in the combination or even integration of quantitative and qualitative. But such talk still preserves the dichotomy. And it seems to me that in some respects détente is worse than cold war. In learning to live and let live there is the danger that we will all quietly forget the methodological disagreements that we should be tackling.[4]

What I am recommending, then, is not that we should revert from two paradigms to one, in such a way as to deny the variety of ideas, strategies and techniques to be found in social research. Quite the reverse. My aim is to show that this diversity cannot be encapsulated within two (or, for that matter, three, four or more) paradigms. Nor should the variety of approach be regarded as stemming simply from fundamental philosophical or political commitments. Arguments about the latter are, and should be, important in methodology. However, they are not the only considerations that are significant; the particular purposes of the research and the practicality of various strategies given the circumstances in which the inquiry is to be carried out are others. Nor do philosophical and political assumptions have the sort of determinate implications for method that they are sometimes assumed to have.[5]

What I want to do in this chapter is to identify the various component meanings of the qualitative/quantitative distinction, particularly as used by advocates of qualitative research. I shall argue that these issues are not as simple or as closely related as is sometimes believed. I have identified seven such issues here. There may be others, but these are probably the main ones:

1. Qualitative versus quantitative data.
2. The investigation of natural versus artificial settings.
3. A focus on meanings rather than behaviour.
4. Adoption or rejection of natural science as a model.
5. An inductive versus a deductive approach.
6. The identification of cultural patterns as against seeking scientific laws.
7. Idealism versus realism.

Qualitative Versus Quantitative Data

In their book on qualitative data analysis, Miles and Huberman characterize the distinction between qualitative and quantitative research in terms of the use of words rather than numbers (Miles and Huberman, 1984, p. 15). While it is rare to find such an interpretation spelled out so clearly, it seems to underlie much talk of qualitative methods. And it is true that research reports do differ sharply in the extent to which tables and statistical analysis, on the one hand, and verbal presentations, on the other, predominate. At the same time, a large proportion of research reports (including many that are regarded as qualitative) combine the two, to varying degrees. More importantly, though, the fact that this is not a very satisfactory basis for the distinction between qualitative and quantitative is illustrated by an exchange that took place in US sociology in the 1930s, between Znaniecki (an advocate of case study) and George Lundberg (a positivistic supporter of statistical method). Znaniecki had written a book in which he largely dismissed the use of statistical techniques in sociology. Here is how Lundberg replies to him:

> The current idea seems to be that if one uses pencil and paper, espe-cially squared paper, and if one uses numerical symbols, especially Arabic notation, one is using quantitative methods. If, however, one discusses masses of data with concepts of 'more' or 'less' instead of formal num-bers, and if one indulges in the most complicated correlations but without algebraic symbols, then one is not using quantitative methods.
>
> A striking illustration from a recent book by a prominent sociolo-gist will make the point clear. After a discussion of the lamentable limitations of statistical methods, the author appends this remarkable footnote: 'Wherever the statistical method definitely gains ascendancy, the number of students of a high intellectual level who are attracted to sociology tends to fall off considerably' (Znaniecki, 1934, p. 235). In short, this author finally reverts to a statistical proof of the deplorable effects of statistics. (Lundberg, 1964, pp. 59–60).

It has frequently been pointed out that ethnographers regularly make quan-titative claims in verbal form, using formulations like 'regularly', 'frequently', 'often', 'sometimes', 'generally', 'in the main', 'typically', 'not atypically' etc. And it is fairly obvious, I think, that (as Lundberg indicates) the form in which such claims are made makes no difference to their character.

The contrast between words and numbers does not get us very far, then. But there is an important sort of variation in the nature of data that is not unrelated to the word/number contrast. When quantitative researchers criti-cise ethnographers' use of words rather than numbers what is usually at issue is precision. They are arguing that ethnographers are insufficiently precise in their claims, and that the necessary precision requires quantification.

However, we must ask what precision is, and whether the most precise formulations are always the best; or, indeed, whether they are always neces-sary. And I think it is clear that precision does not necessarily mean numbers. For example, where we are concerned with the presence or absence of a par-ticular type of phenomenon in a situation, this can be described quite precisely without the use of numbers. It is also important to remember that precision is not the only virtue in description and measurement. Accuracy is usually even more important. And it is widely recognized that we should not express our findings in terms that imply a greater degree of precision than their likely accuracy warrants. For instance, to report findings to six figures of decimals is rarely if ever justified in social research. It follows from this that sometimes it may not be legitimate to use terms that are more precise then 'sometimes', 'often', 'generally' etc.[6] Handlin (1979, pp. 11–12) provides an illustration of this from history:

> I cannot wholly agree that historical problems that hinge on the question 'how many?' are always better solved by numerical answers. The more precise statement is not always the more accurate one. In 1813 John Adams tried to estimate how many colonists were for independence and hazarded various guesses – nearly equally divided; a third; five to two. It would no doubt be more precise to be able to say 39 per cent were for, 31 per cent against, and 30 per cent neutral, or to plant a good solid decimal point with a long series of digits behind it. But it would be less accurate to do so, for the data does not support that degree of refinement.

Furthermore, while increased precision may often be of value, it is not always so. It may not be of value because the level of precision already achieved is sufficient for our purposes, or because the likely costs of achieving greater precision are greater than the probable benefits. The latter is an especially important point in the context of case study research, where a relatively wide focus is adopted. Given fixed resources, the attempt to make any part of the picture more precise will necessarily tend to reduce the width of focus that is possible. The researcher must judge whether the benefits of this outweigh the costs, and sometimes they will not. Equally, though, on other occasions they will; and more precise, even numerical, descriptions will be appropriate.[7]

We are not faced, then, with a stark choice between words and numbers, or even between precise and imprecise data. Furthermore, our decisions about what level of precision is appropriate in relation to any particular claim should depend on the nature of what we are trying to describe, on the likely accuracy of our descriptions, on our purposes, and on the resources available to us; not on ideological commitment to one methodological paradigm or another.

Investigation of 'Natural' Versus 'Artificial' Settings

A second interpretation of the qualitative/quantitative distinction focuses on the nature of the phenomenon investigated: whether it is 'naturally occurring' or has been created by the researcher. The sharpest contrast here is between experiments and ethnographic research. The former involves study of a situation especially established by the researchers, probably using volunteer subjects, and designed to capture different values of some theoretical variables while controlling relevant extraneous variables. Ethnographic research, on the other hand, requires the study of situations that would have occurred without the ethnographer's presence, and the adoption of a role in that situation designed to minimise the researcher's impact on what occurs. In common parlance, experimenters study 'artificial' settings, while ethnographers study 'natural' settings; and the implication is that only the latter is worthwhile because it is 'natural' behaviour we are concerned to understand.

The charge of artificiality may also be directed at formal, structured interviews of the kind used by survey researchers. These may be contrasted with unstructured and/or informal interviews, where the interviewer plays a less dominant role. While the latter do not represent an entirely 'natural' setting, it is often argued that their closeness to ordinary conversation renders them approximations to the natural.

In my view this distinction between natural and artificial settings is spurious. What happens in a school class or in a court of law, for example, is no more natural (or artificial) than what goes on in a social psychological laboratory. To treat classrooms or courtrooms as natural and experiments as artificial is to forget that social research is itself part of the social world, something that should never be forgotten.

Once again, though, there is an important issue implicit in this distinction. What is involved is variation in the degree to which the researcher shapes the data. There is a trade-off between, on the one hand, trying to make sure that one gets the relevant data (in the most efficient manner possible) and, on the other hand, the danger of reactivity, of influencing the people studied in such a way that error is introduced into the data. It has long been a criticism of experiments that their findings do not generalize to the 'real world' (that is to non-experimental situations) because people's behaviour is shaped by their awareness of the experimental situation, and by the personal characteristics of the experimenter (or her/his assistants). Similarly, structured interviews have been criticized because we cannot generalize from what is said in them to what is said and done elsewhere.[8] However, while there is some truth in these arguments, they by no means render the results of research using 'artificial' methods of no value. Much depends on whether the reactivity affects the results in ways that are relevant to the research topic and in ways that cannot be allowed for. All research is subject to potential error of one kind or another. Indeed, even ethnographic research in 'natural' settings is not immune to reactivity. While the ethnographer may strive to minimize her or his effects on the situation studied, no one can guarantee this; and sometimes the effects can be significant despite the researcher's best efforts. Also, we must remember what the significance of reactivity is: it makes the setting investigated unrepresentative of those about which the researcher wishes to generalize, an issue sometimes referred to as ecological invalidity. But reactivity is not the only source of ecological invalidity. Even without reactivity, a natural setting can be unrepresentative because it differs in important ways from most other cases in the same category. Simply choosing to investigate natural settings, and seeking to adopt a low profile in them, does not ensure ecological validity.[9]

For these reasons the distinction between natural and artificial settings does not provide a sound basis for the qualitative/quantitative distinction. The terms 'natural' and 'artificial' have misleading connotations. And while the issue of ecological validity is important, it is not the only important methodological issue. Nor does research in 'natural' settings guarantee ecological validity, any more than research in 'artificial' settings automatically debars us from it.

A Focus on Meanings Versus a Focus on Behaviour

This component of the qualitative–quantitative distinction emphasizes the interpretive or hermeneutic character of qualitative research. Of all the issues discussed in this chapter, this one links most obviously back to nineteenth century debates about the difference between natural science and history, as well as to twentieth century disputes such as that surrounding behaviourism.

It is sometimes suggested that the central goal of qualitative research is to document the world from the point of view of the people studied (from the native point of view, in Malinowski's terms), rather than presenting it from the perspective of the researcher. And it is true that qualitative research does seek to understand the perspectives of the people studied, on the grounds that this is essential if we are to describe and explain their behaviour effectively. However, it is very rare for qualitative research to restrict itself to documenting the native point of view. And there are good reasons for not doing this; not the least of which is that the people studied can often do this for themselves! Even those approaches that restrict the research focus to participants' perspectives do not simply reproduce these, but seek to analyse their structure and/or production in ways that are likely to be alien to the people studied. This is true, for example, of both ethnosemantics and ethnomethodology. But, as I have said, most qualitative research does not restrict its focus this narrowly. It seeks to describe and explain both perspectives and behaviour, recognizing that the latter does not merely flow from the former, and may even be discrepant with it. Indeed, such ironic discrepancies have been a major focus for qualitative research (see, for example, Keddie, 1971; Sharp and Green, 1975; and Willis, 1977).

Conversely, much quantitative research is concerned with attitudes rather than simply with behaviour. Advocates of an interpretive approach may argue that attitude research effectively studies attitudes as behaviour displayed in response to interview questions. Yet, critiques of behaviourism emphasise that it is not possible to study human behaviour without attributing meanings, and that behaviourists routinely do this despite themselves. Given this fact, it seems that attitude researchers cannot but be studying 'meanings'. At the very least, this shifts the criticism elsewhere. Moreover, most attitude researchers do not operate on the basis of a strict behaviourism.

It is still true, of course, that there are differences between attitude researchers and qualitative sociologists, both in how they conceptualize the meanings held to underlie behaviour, and in how they seek to identify those meanings. Even here, though, the differences are not as great as is sometimes suggested.

It is common for ethnographers to ascribe perspectives or definitions of the situation to the people they study, and it is not clear how these differ in character from attitudes. Ethnographers may stress that they do not assume a mechanical relationship between attitude and behaviour. However, the more contingent is the relationship between perspective and behaviour, the less value perspectives have as explanatory factors. So this is not an argument that ethnographers can pursue very far without undercutting the basis of their own hermeneutic approach.

As regards differences in the approach that attitude researchers and ethnographers employ in identifying attitudes/perspectives, the contrast is between the use of attitude scales and more unstructured approaches. As such, it reduces to the previous two distinctions I have already discussed, and to the distinction between inductive and deductive approaches that I shall deal with below. Here again, though, we do not have a clear-cut distinction between two contrasting approaches.

Natural Science as a Model

It is common for quantitative method to be criticised for taking natural science as its model. It is worth noting, however, that advocates of qualitative method have sometimes themselves regarded the natural sciences as exemplary. Thomas and Znaniecki, two of the most influential advocates of case study and life history methods in the 1920s and 30s, make the following comment at the beginning of their study of *The Polish Peasant in Poland and America*:

> The marvellous results attained by rational technique (that is, by science) in the sphere of material reality invite us to apply some analogous procedure to social reality. Our success in controlling nature gives us confidence that we shall eventually be able to control the social world in the same measure (Thomas and Znaniecki, 1927, p. 1).

Nor were Thomas and Znaniecki unusual in holding this view. While he was uncertain about the chances of its achievement, Herbert Blumer was also committed, at least in the 1920s and early 30s, to the pursuit of a science of society modelled on the natural sciences. Much the same was true in social anthropology. Boas, Malinowski and Radcliffe-Brown all took the natural sciences as a paradigm for their approach to the study of primitive society; though, as in the case of Blumer and the Chicago sociologists, this was tempered with ideas about the distinctiveness of social phenomena (Hammersley, 1989a).

From a historical point of view, then, differences in attitude to natural science do not seem to map on to the distinction between quantitative and qualitative research in a straightforward way. And, even today, there are advocates of qualitative method who justify their approach precisely on the basis of its similarity to that of natural scientists.[10]

What this points to is that the issue of whether natural science is an appropriate model for social research is not a simple one. There are at least three complications.

First, we must consider which natural science we are taking as the model, and during which period of its development? There are significant differences, for example, between physics and biology; and, indeed, within each natural science discipline over time.

Second, which interpretation of the methods of natural science is to be adopted? Keat and Urry (1975) identify positivist, conventionalist, or realistic interpretations of physics; and even these distinctions do not exhaust the variety of views to be found among philosophers of science.

Third, what aspects of natural science method are to be treated as generic? Not even the most extreme positivist would argue that the methods of physics should be applied lock, stock and barrel to the study of the social world. And there are few supporters of qualitative research who would insist that there is no aspect of natural science method that is relevant to social research. What is involved here is a matter of degree. Once again, we have a complex set of considerations that resist reduction to a simple contrast.

Inductive Versus Deductive Approaches

It is common for qualitative researchers to contrast their own inductive approach with the deductive, or hypothetico-deductive, method of quantitative research. Here too, though, we have an over-simplification. Not all quantitative research is concerned with hypothesis-testing. Many surveys are straightforwardly descriptive, and some quantitative research is explicitly concerned with theory generation. Equally, by no means all ethnographers reject the hypothetico-deductive method.[11] Indeed, it seems to me that all research involves both deduction and induction in the broad sense of those terms; in all research we move from ideas to data as well as from data to ideas. What is true is that one can distinguish between studies that are primarily exploratory, being concerned with generating theoretical ideas, and those which are more concerned with testing hypotheses. But these types of research are not alternatives; we need both. Nor need the former be quantitative and the latter qualitative in other senses of those terms.

A common version of the inductive versus deductive contrast is built into advocacy Verstehen or understanding, as opposed to forms of explanation that rely on observation of the external features of human behaviour.[12] In its most extreme formulation, Verstehen involves some kind of direct contact with the experience of others, or a reliving of it on the basis of one's own experience. Some versions place great importance on the nature of the relationship between researcher and researched, perhaps regarding equality as essential if understanding is to occur. But while there is no doubt that it is important in research to take account of one's own cultural assumptions and to open them up to possible disconfirmation, the idea that Verstehen involves direct contact with social reality or with other people must be rejected. We can never entirely escape our own assumptions about the world.[13] And even in face-to-face contact with people with whom we share a lot, we are not given knowledge that is necessarily beyond reasonable doubt. As has often been stressed in the ethnographic literature, there are advantages and disadvantages to closeness. On the one hand, it may provide us with inside information that we would otherwise not gain, both about what happens and about people's experiences of events. On the other hand, through a process of over-rapport we may come to take over false assumptions held by the people we are studying, and become unable to see the world in any other way than that in which it appears to them. Only if we assume that the perspectives of those we are studying necessarily embody genuine knowledge about the world is over-rapport not a danger. And in my view no individual or group has such a monopoly on truth.

From this point of view, then, we cannot but rely on constructing hypotheses, assessing them against experience and modifying them where necessary. This is true whether we engage in hypothesis testing in a formal, explicit and narrow way that involves subjecting hypotheses to crucial tests; or whether we adopt a more informal approach in which we sacrifice some of the sharpness of the test for a more wide-ranging approach in which we allow more of our assumptions to be thrown open to challenge. Furthermore, which of these approaches is most appropriate depends on our purposes, and the stage that our research has reached, not on paradigmatic commitments.

Identifying Cultural Patterns Versus Pursuing Scientific Laws

Following on from the contrast between qualitative and quantitative approaches in terms of a commitment to the model of natural science is the idea that these approaches differ in their goals. Quantitative research is often believed to be committed to the discovery of scientific laws; whereas qualitative research is concerned with identifying cultural patterns. However, as I pointed out in the previous section, much quantitative research is concerned with description rather than with theory development and testing. And, indeed, rather more survey research may appear to be concerned with discovering theoretical laws than is actually the case because survey researchers sometimes fail to distinguish between this goal and that of explaining particular events or relationships.[14]

Similarly, while it is common these days for qualitative researchers to deny the possibility of scientific laws, this was not always so. In the early decades of this century case-study researchers often justified their approach on the grounds that it could produce laws, whereas statistical method could only produce probabilistic generalizations (Blumer, 1928; Znaniecki, 1934). Even today qualitative researchers often claim that their goal is theory rather than the mere description of cultural patterns. And sometimes the concept of theory involved seems to be not far removed from that characteristic of survey research; though it should be said that there is considerable uncertainty about the precise nature of ethnographic theory (Hammersley, 1992, Chapters 1 and 2). Furthermore, both analytic induction and grounded theorising seem to depend on the assumption of laws. For instance, analytic induction involves reconstructing theories when counter examples are discovered. However, this is only sensible if we assume that theories consist of deterministic laws that apply to all cases. Thus the distinction between identifying patterns and pursuing laws seems to provide little clear basis for the division between quantitative and qualitative methods.

Idealism Versus Realism

At the most abstract philosophical level it has been claimed that qualitative and quantitative researchers are committed to different epistemological positions. A clear example of this argument is to be found in the writings of John K. Smith. He argues that quantitative research is wedded to a realist epistemology in the sense of assuming that true accounts correspond to how things really are and that competing accounts must be judged in terms of whether the procedures adopted ensure accurate representation of reality. By contrast, qualitative method is idealist, he claims, in that it rejects any possibility of representing reality. It recognizes that there may be 'as many realities as there are persons' (Smith, 1984, p. 386).

I think it can be shown with little difficulty that this characterisation is inaccurate empirically. First, not all quantitative researchers are realists. Take the following quotation:

> In any valid epistemological or scientific sense we must say that the substitution of a Copernican for the Ptolemaic theory of the universe represented a major change in the universe. To say that it was not the universe but our conception of it which changed is merely a verbal trick designed to lead the unwary into the philosophical quagmires of Platonic realism, for obviously the only universe with which science can deal is our 'conception' of it.

What we have here is an idealist account of natural science knowledge in which there is a denial that it can represent some independent reality. But it does not come from a qualitative researcher. It comes from George Lundberg again, positivist advocate of quantitative method in the 1930s, 40s and 50s (Lundberg, 1933, p. 309). There was a strong element of phenomenalism in late nineteenth and twentieth century positivism, and Lundberg's anti-realism reflects this. By contrast, Herbert Blumer's influential concept of naturalistic method is quite clearly realist in character: he talks of research being concerned with discovering the nature of social reality, of tearing away the veil of our preconceptions so that we may see it (Hammersley, 1989a). In more recent times, Harré has based his advocacy and practice of qualitative research in social psychology on an explicit realism.[15] And, indeed, the reliance of ethnography on realism has come under increasing criticism, for example from those who stress the creative character of ethnographic writing (see Tyler, 1985 and Clifford, 1988).

More important than the empirical question of whether it is true that quantitative researchers are realists and qualitative researchers idealists, though, is the philosophical issue of whether there is any necessary connection between qualitative method and a particular epistemological position. As I have shown, history suggests that there is little reason to believe that there is such a connection. And we must remember that there are many more than two epistemological positions available within philosophy, nor can these be reduced to a single dichotomy without great distortion.[16]

Conclusion

In this chapter I have looked at some of the components of the conventional distinction between qualitative and quantitative method. In each case I have argued that what is involved is not a simple contrast between two opposed standpoints, but a range of positions sometimes located on more than one dimension. It should also be clear, I think, that there is no necessary relationship between adopting a particular position on one issue and specific positions on the others. Many combinations are quite reasonable. Furthermore, I emphasized that selection among these positions ought often to depend on the purposes and circumstances of the research, rather than being derived from methodological or philosophical commitments. This is because there are trade-offs involved. For instance, if we seek greater precision we are likely to sacrifice some breadth of description; and vice versa. And the costs and benefits of various trade-off positions will vary according to the particular goals and circumstances of the research being pursued.

What all this implies is that the distinction between quantitative and qualitative approaches does not capture the full range of options that we face; and that it misrepresents the basis on which decisions should be made. What is involved is not a crossroads where we have to go left or right. A better analogy is a complex maze where we are repeatedly faced with decisions, and where paths wind back on one another. The prevalence of the distinction between qualitative and quantitative method tends to obscure the complexity of the problems that face us and threatens to render our decisions less effective than they might otherwise be.

Notes

1. My use of the term 'deconstructing' in the title of this chapter is no more than a rhetorical flourish: my philosophical assumptions are very different from those of deconstructionists. However, given their views about meaning, they can have no justifiable complaint against my theft of this term! For an excellent critique of deconstructionism, see Ellis 1989. See also Dews, 1987.

2. This debate has persisted within history, indeed it has intensified in recent years as a result of the growth of 'cliometrics'. For contrasting perspectives on this development see Fogel and Elton, 1983.

3. For a useful discussion of the current state of this debate, see Bryman, 1988.

4. To this extent I am in agreement with Smith and Heshusius, but I disagree with much of the rest of what they say. In my view the commitment to paradigms, in whatever form, tends to close down the debate rather than keep it open (Hammersley, 1989b).

5. This is illustrated by the debates about methodology among Marxists and feminists. See, for example, the debate about Marxism and method in the *Berkeley Journal of Sociology*, 35, 1989, especially the articles by Wright and Burawoy. On feminism and method, see the very different views expressed by Mies, Jayaratne, Reinharz, and Stanley and Wise in Bowles and Klein (1983).

6. My own use of imprecise formulations will not be lost on the reader!

7. There is also the practical question of how much precision is possible. While I would not want to suggest any insuperable barriers to increased precision of measurement of social phenomena, there is no doubt that as things presently stand there are severe practical limits to the level of combined precision and accuracy that can be achieved.

8. In some respects this is a misleading argument since it fails to draw the necessary distinction between, on the one hand, inferring from what people do in interviews to what they do elsewhere, and, on the other, the question of the truth of what people say in interviews about what they and others do elsewhere.

9. Equally, it is worth noting that some quantitative researchers carry out their research in natural settings, notably in the form of systematic observational research.

10. See, for example, the work of Harré: Harré, 1970; Harré and Secord, 1972.

11. On exploratory quantitative analysis, see Baldamus, 1979 for an example; Erickson and Nosanchuk, 1979 for techniques. Some practitioners of analytic induction (such as Lindesmith, 1937) and of grounded theorizing (Strauss, 1987) explicitly equate their approach with the hypothetico-deductive method.

12. Platt (1985) points out that Weber's discussion of Verstehen seems to have had little influence on early qualitative researchers. However, Weber drew the concept from earlier nineteenth century discussions, notably those of Dilthey, and these did have an influence on Chicago sociologists; both directly, and indirectly, through Windelband, Rickert and Simmel, for example. It also seems likely that Cooley, who was quite influential on the Chicagoans, drew his concept of sympathetic introspection from the German Romantics.

13. This is the conclusion of more sophisticated versions of hermeneutics, notably that of Gadamer.

14. On this distinction, see Hammersley, 1992, Chapter 2.

15. See Note 7.

16. For a development of the argument in this section dealing specifically with Smith's position, see Hammersley, 1989b.

References

Baldamus, W. (1979) 'Alienation, anomie and industrial accidents.' In M. Wilson (ed.) *Social and Educational Research in Action.* London: Longman.

Blumer, H. (1928) Method in social psychology. Unpublished PhD dissertation, University of Chicago.

Bowles, G. and Klein, R.D. (1983) *Theories of Women's Studies.* London: Routledge and Kegan Paul.

Bryman, A. (1988) *Quality and Quantity in Social Research.* London: Unwin Hyman.

Clifford, J. (1988) *The Predicament of Culture.* Cambridge, Massachussetts: Harvard University Press.

Dews. P. (1987) *Logics of Disintegration: post-structuralist thought and the claims of critical theory.* London: Verso.

Ellis, J. (1989) *Against Deconstruction.* Princeton: Princeton University Press.

Erickson, B. and Nosanchuk, T. (1979) *Understanding Data: an introduction to exploratory and confirmatory data analysis for students in the social sciences.* Milton Keynes: Open University Press.

Fogel, R.W. and Elton, G.R. (1983) *Which Road to the Past.* New Haven: Yale University Press.

Hammersley, M. (1989a) *The Dilemma of Qualitative Method: Herbert Blumer and the Chicago tradition.* London: Routledge.

Hammersley, M. (1989b) 'The methodology of ethnomethodology', unpublished paper.

Hammersley, M. (1990) Keeping the conversation open: a response to Smith and Heshusius. Unpublished paper.

Hammersley, M. (1992) *What's Wrong with Ethnography? Methodological explorations.* London: Routledge.

Handlin, O. (1979) *Truth in History.* Cambridge, Massachussetts: Harvard University Press.

Harré, R. (1970) *The Principles of Scientific Thinking.* London: Macmillan.

Harré, R. and Secord, P. (1972) *The Explanation of Social Behaviour.* Oxford: Blackwell.

Keat, R. and Urry, J. (1975) *Social Theory as Science.* London: Routledge and Kegan Paul.

Keddie, N. (1971) 'Classroom knowledge.' In M.F.D. Young (ed.) *Knowledge and Control.* New York: Collier Macmillan.

Lindesmith, A. (1937) *The Nature of Opiate Addiction.* Chicago: University of Chicago Libraries.

Lundberg, G. (1933) 'Is sociology too scientific?' *Sociologus,* 9, 298–322.

Lundberg, G. (1964) *Foundations of Sociology.* New York: McKay.

Miles, M.B. and Huberman, M. (1984) *Qualitative Data Analysis.* Beverly Hills: Sage.

Platt, J. (1985) 'Weber's Verstehen and the history of qualitative research: the missing link.' *British Journal of Sociology,* 36, 3, 448–466.

Rist, R. (1977) 'On the relations among educational research paradigms: from disdain to détente.' *Anthropology and Education Quarterly,* 8, 2, 42–49.

Sharp, R. and Green, A. (1975) *Education and Social Control.* London: Routledge and Kegan Paul.

Smith, J.K. (1984) 'The problem of criteria for judging interpretive inquiry.' *Educational Evaluation and Policy Analysis,* 6, 4, 379–391.

Smith, J.K. and Heshusius, L (1986) 'Closing down the conversation: the end of the quantitative–qualitative debate among educational inquirers.' *Educational Researcher,* 15, 1, 4–12.

Strauss, A. (1987) *Qualitative Analysis for Social Scientists.* Cambridge: Cambridge University Press.

Thomas, W.I. and Znaniecki, F. (1927) *The Polish Peasant in Europe and America,* five volumes. Chicago: University of Chicago Press/Boston: Badger Press.

Tyler, S.A. (1985) 'Ethnography, intertextuality, and the end of description.' *American Journal of Semiotics,* 3, 4, 83–98.

Willis, P. (1977) *Learning to Labour.* Farnborough: Saxon House.

Znaniecki, F. (1934) *The Method of Sociology.* New York: Farrar and Rinehart.

5

Attitudes Toward Needle "Sharing" Among Injection Drug Users: Combining Qualitative and Quantitative Research Methods

Robert G. Carlson, Harvey A. Siegal, Jichuan Wang & Russel S. Falck

Across the United States, ethnographers conducting acquired immune deficiency syndrome (AIDS) prevention research among injection drug users have experienced what Michael Agar (1982, 1986) refers to as "breakdowns" – a sense of surprise when one's expectations regarding the values, beliefs, or behaviors of the people with whom one is conducting research are unmet or contradicted. One of the most common "breakdowns" in expectations has been the discovery that injection drug users do not generally value the "sharing" of needles and syringes.[1] As Michael Clatts (1994:94) remarked in reference to 10 years of expedience in AIDS research, "I have never talked to a drug injector who wanted to share needles."

Perhaps like myself (Carlson), many ethnographers in the field came to develop an initial conceptualization, through reading public health literature disseminated early in the AIDS epidemic, that injection drug users desire to "share" needles and that the practice functions as a ritual form of social bonding, a mechanism to create friendship ties, and a symbol of group identity (e.g., Des Jarlais *et al.* 1986; Conviser and Rutledge 1989). Before undertaking ethnographic research among injection drug users in Dayton and Columbus, Ohio, I developed a vision of the needle's role among these drug users as an almost sacred object, as something akin to the Native American peace pipe that had to be passed from individual to individual, thereby increasing the probability of human immunodeficiency virus (HIV) transmission. Moreover, I came to understand that one of the principal goals of AIDS prevention was

Source: *Human Organization*, vol. 55, no. 3, 1996, pp. 361–369.

to change the *values* injection drug users place in the social functions of needle "sharing" to reduce HIV transmission.

Shocked, indeed, I was early in the course of two years (1989–1991) of
ethnographic research on the Dayton/Columbus National AIDS Demonstration Research (NADR) Project, when I learned that injection drug users do
not generally value the "sharing" of needles to serve the functions mentioned
above.[2] When confronted with a breakdown such as this, Agar (1986) suggests that a key part of the process of ethnography is to resolve the
inconsistency and regain a sense of coherence. In Agar's (1986:22) words:

> A coherent resolution will (1) show why it is better than other resolu-
> tions that can be imagined; (2) tie a particular resolution in with broader
> knowledge that constitutes a tradition, and (3) clarify and enlighten, elic-
> iting an "aha" reaction from the members of different traditions that
> make up the ethnographic encounter.

I attempted to investigate and perhaps resolve the "breakdown" by further assessing injection drug users' values regarding needle "sharing" through
participant observation research as well as 65 audiotaped interviews with a
sample of male and female injection drug users from the two major ethnic
groups in the region (African Americans and whites).[3] The results of this research overwhelmingly suggested that injection drug users do not positively
value shooting up with previously used needles and do not recognize the transfer of used needles as a ritual form of social bonding or a symbol of identity
(Carlson 1991; Carlson *et al.* 1994). On the basis of our study, we suggested
that the term "needle sharing" should be replaced with the term "needle transfer" in public health research.

Over time, the scope of our findings appeared to enlarge as we spoke with
ethnographers conducting similar research in New York City (Clatts *et al.*
1994), Denver (Koester 1994a), and San Antonio (Zule 1992), and reviewed
previous literature (e.g., Murphy 1987; Waldorf *et al.* 1990). A similar questioning of the role of needle transferring among injection drug users was
apparently occurring among ethnographers in diverse locations of the country.

Bereft of adequate understanding regarding why some injection drug users do transfer needles, ethnographers enlarged the context of their search for
explanations. Several different explanations for the practice of transferring used
needles have been presented. First, ethnographers have emphasized the importance of the distinction between the relatively immediate transfer of used
needles and the delayed, "random" circulation of used needles that are pooled
in some "shooting galleries" – places in which a drug user pays a fee to inject
his/her drugs and where used needles may be rented (e.g., Page 1990; Page
et al. 1990). In the case of immediate needle transfer, ethnographers discovered that injection drug users generally exchange used needles because new
needles are unavailable. New needles may be unavailable for several reasons,
including the laws in various locations that prohibit the purchase of needles

in pharmacies without a prescription, a lack of money to purchase new needles, and/or simply the serendipitous context of the injection situation (Carlson, Siegal, and Falck 1994; Clatts *et al.* 1994; Koester 1994b; Singer, Irizarry, and Schensul 1991). In addition, the perceived threat of incarceration from laws prohibiting the possession of injection paraphernalia (without medical reason) may inhibit some injection drug users from carrying their own needles and syringes, thereby increasing the likelihood of needle transfer (e.g., Koester 1994a).

Other reasons injection drug users offer for not valuing injecting with previously used needles include: 1) needles become dull and barbed with each use making it more difficult to puncture a vein; 2) waiting for someone else to use a needle is an anguishing experience, given the intense desire to feel the effects of the drug immediately (particularly in the case of opiate withdrawal or cocaine shooting binges); 3) as a corollary to number two, waiting to use a needle and syringe is an expression of subordination; and 4) using someone else's needle is often perceived as an intimate form of exposure to another person (Carlson *et al.* 1994; Connors 1994). It is perhaps because of this last reason that much of the immediate needle transfer that does occur tends to be among individuals involved in intimate relationships: spouses, sex partners, and "running buddies" (drug injectors who hustle to obtain money to purchase drugs). The objectives of this article are twofold. The first is to reevaluate our initial qualitative evidence regarding injection drug users' values toward needle transfer, and some of the possible explanations for this behavior, using quantitative methods. Qualitative findings, as summarized above and discussed in detail elsewhere (Carlson, Siegal, and Falck 1994), were operationalized into a series of questions that were administered as part of a structured questionnaire to 276 injection drug users participating in the Dayton/Columbus AIDS Prevention Research Project. As such, this study is in part an attempt to further assess and refine the generalizability of – and confidence in – our earlier qualitative research regarding needle transfer by using alternative methods, a process Denzin (1970:308) refers to as *methodological triangulation* (see also Agar 1980:137–173). The second objective is to compare drug injectors' attitudes toward needle transfer, perceived needle access, the perceived threat of drug paraphernalia laws, and selected sociodemographic characteristics with their reported needle transferring behavior in the 30 days prior to interview.

Methods

The sample consisted of 276 injection drug users recruited in 1993 through a targeted sampling plan (Carlson *et al.* 1994) for the Dayton/Columbus, Ohio Cooperative Agreement for AIDS Community-Based Outreach/Intervention Project, part of a national effort funded by the National Institute on Drug Abuse (NIDA). Eligibility as an injection drug user was based on positive urine

Table 1: Sociodemographic Characteristics

Variable	No.	%
Gender		
male	215	77.9
female	61	22.1
Ethnicity		
African American	197	71.4
white	79	28.6
Education		
< high school	97	35.1
high school	104	37.7
post high school	75	27.2
Age		
< 30	24	8.7
30–40	125	45.3
> 40	127	46.0
Marital Status		
single	81	29.3
married/common law/		
living with sex partner	89	32.2
separated/divorced	97	35.1
widowed	9	3.3
Employment		
unemployed	149	53.9
full/part-time	50	18.1
disabled	56	20.3
other	21	7.6
Income last 30 days		
< $500	113	41.9
$500–$999	81	30.0
$1,000–$1,999	48	17.8
$2,000–$3,999	19	7.0
> $4,000	9	3.3

screening for cocaine and/or opiates, and/or the observation of recent injection site marks. Each participant completed NIDA's standardized Risk Bhavior Assessment (RBA) questionnaire which focuses on risk behaviors in the previous 30 days. In addition, each participant completed a trailer questionnaire, the Dayton/Columbus RBA Addendum. Among the items included in the addendum were several questions designed to further assess the qualitative findings resulting from our previous NADR Project focusing on attitudes toward needle transfer, perceived needle accessibility, and the perceived threat of drug paraphernalia laws. The addendum was pilot tested with 30 injection drug users; modifications were made based on interviewer comments as well as observations of the interview process.[4]

The data were initially examined with descriptive statistics. Chi-square tests were used to assess binary relations between the use of previously used needles, attitudes toward this behavior, perceived access to new needles, and the perceived threat of legal sanctions due to injection paraphernalia laws. Stepwise logistic regression was then used to analyze the relationships among sociodemographic characteristics, drug use, attitudes, perceptions, and needle transferring behavior while controlling for confounding effects.

Table 2. Drug Use in the Previous 30 Days

Variable	Yes (#)	No (#)	Mean Days Yes	Mean Days No	Percent of Total (%)
Cocaine Injection	144	132	52.2	47.8	7.9
Heroin Injection	216	60	78.3	21.7	19.4
Speedball Injection	120	156	43.5	56.5	10.6
Crack (Smoking)	152	124	55.0	45.0	8.3
Crack (Injection) Frequency*					
Daily	133		48.2		
Non-Daily	143		51.8		

* The categorization of this variable is a rough estimate computed in the following way. The number of days a participant injected seven different drugs (heroin, cocaine, speedball, etc.) in the last 30 days were summed. If the sum was 3 0, the person was classified as a "daily" injector

Results

The mean age of the sample was 39.9 years. Almost 78% (215) of the injection drug users were male, 71.4% were African American, and approximately equal proportions had a high school (37.7%) or less than high school education (35.1%). The most common marital status was being separated or divorced (35.1%); 32.2% were married (legally, living as married, or living with a sex partner). More than half (53.9%) of the injection drug users were unemployed, 18.1% were employed full- or part-time, and 20.3% were disabled. About 42% of the injection drug users earned less than $500 in the previous 30 days, 30.0% made $500–$999, and 17.8% earned between $ 1,000 and $2,000 (see Table 1).

About 78% of the participants injected heroin at least one day in the last 30, 52.2% injected cocaine, and 43.5% injected speedball (heroin and cocaine mixed). The mean number of years of injection was 15.7, and 48.2% were daily

injectors. In addition, 55.0% of the participants reported smoking crack cocaine at least one day in the previous 30 (see Table 2).

Table 3. Attitudes Toward Needle Transfer*

	No.	%
A. When shooting up with other people, I feel like I have to use the same outfit every-one else uses.		
Agree	8	2.9
Neutral	3	1.1
Disagree	265	96.0
B. If a friend wanted me to shoot up with a needle he/she just used, I would find it hard to say no.		
Agree	53	19.2
Neutral	29	10.5
Disagree	194	70.3
C. If a friend refused to lend me an outfit, I would get angry.		
Agree	60	21.8
Neutral	19	6.9
Disagree	196	71.3
D. Sex partners who both shoot dope like to use the same outfit without even cleaning it with water		
Agree	75	27.2
Neutral	23	8.3
Disagree	178	64.5

* All attitudinal statements were recoded in Tables 3 and 4 as follows: very strongly
disagree, strongly disagree, and disagree = disagree; neutral = neutral; and very strongly
agree, strongly agree, and agree = agree.

Attitudes Toward Needle Transfer

As shown in Table 3, an overwhelming majority (96.0%) of the respondents
disagreed with statement A: "When shooting up with other people, I feel like
I have to use the same outfit (needle and syringe or works) everyone else uses."
In addition, 70.3% of the drug injectors disagreed with statement B: "If a friend
wanted me to shoot up with a needle he/she just used, I would find it hard to
say no," 19.2% agreed, and 10.5% were neutral. A similar response pattern
was found in reference to statement C: "If a friend refused to lend me an outfit,
I would get angry" (21.8% – agree; 6.9% – neutral; 71.3% – disagree). Similarly, 27.2% of the sample agreed with statement D: "Sex partners who both
shoot dope like to use the same outfit without even cleaning it with water,"
8.3% were undecided, and 64.5% disagreed.

Perceptions Toward Needle Access and Aids Risk

A majority (72.8%) of the participants agreed with statement E: "I don't carry outfits with me, because I'm afraid I'll get busted," thereby suggesting that injection drug users are fearful to carry their personal syringes and consequently may increase their probability of needing to inject with previously used needles (see Table 4). By contrast, only 16.3% of the sample agreed with statement F: "It's difficult for me to get new/sterile needles," and 79.0% disagreed. Responses to statement G: "Carrying bleach and water is too much of a hassle" were bimodal; 42% agreed, 49.6% disagreed, and 8.4% were neutral. In addition, a majority (62.5%) of the participants perceived they were at risk for getting AIDS through their injection behavior.

Table 4. Perceptions Regarding Needle Access, Drug Paraphernalia, Laws, and AIDS Risk

	No.	%
E. I don't carry outfits with me, because I'm afraid I'll get busted.		
Agree	201	72.8
Neutral	14	5.1
Disagree	61	22.1
F. It's difficult for me to get new/sterile needles.		
Agree	45	16.3
Neutral	13	4.7
Disagree	218	79.0
G. Carrying bleach and water is too much of a hassle.		
Agree	116	42.0
Neutral	23	8.4
Disagree	137	49.6
H. I am at risk for getting AIDS through my needle-using behavior		
Agree	172	62.5
Neutral	23	8.4
Disagree	80	29.1

Needle Transfer Behavior in the Previous 30 Days

About 45% (125) of the injection drug users recalled giving or loaning a previously used needle and syringe to someone else one or more times in the previous 30 days (see Table 5). Similarly, 41.4% (114) said that they had injected with an outfit they know had been used at least once in the previous month. Of the 114 participants who did use previously used needles, a majority (61.6%) did so one or more times without using bleach and water to clean them.

Table 5. Needle Transfer Behavior in the Previous 30 Days

Variable	No.	%
Times gave or loaned used works to others		
0	151	54.7
1–5	80	29.0
6 or more	45	16.3
Times injected with previously used works		
0	161	58.6
1–5	71	25.8
6 or more	43	15.6
Times injected with used works without cleaning with bleach and water*		
0	43	38.4
1–5	34	30.4
6 or more	35	31.2

* n=112 due to missing values.

Assessing the Relationship Between Attitudes and Behavior

Overall, the response pattern to statement A ("When shooting up with other people, I feel like I have to use the same outfit (needle and syringe or works) everyone else uses") suggests that injection drug users in this sample do not positively value the transfer of used needles. Although a majority of the injection drug users also disagreed with statement B ("If a friend wanted me to shoot up with a needle he/she just used, I would find it hard to say no"), statement C ("If a friend refused to lend me an outfit, I would get angry"), and statement D ("Sex partners who both shoot dope like to use the same outfit without even cleaning it with water") focusing on the positive value of needle transfer between themselves and friends or sex partners, a comparatively larger percentage (19%–27%) agreed with these statements.

Bivariate comparison of these attitudes and needle transfer behavior suggest there is considerable consistency between the two. As shown in Table 6, statements B and C are significantly ($x^2 = 26.39$; $p = .000$; $x^2 = 32.52$; $p = .000$, respectively) related to needle transfer behavior; that is, injection drug users who reported transferring needles also tended to agree with statements regarding the value of transferring needles among friends. Significantly, the converse is also indicated. No relationship, however, was found between needle transfer behavior and statement D ("Sex partners who both shoot dope like to use the same outfit without even cleaning it with water").

Needle transfer behavior and perceived difficulty obtaining new/sterile needles (statement E) were also significantly $x^2 = 13.61$; $p = .000$) related, suggesting

Table 6. Binary Relations Between Attitudes Toward Needle Transfer, Perceived Needle Access, Perceived Threat of Paraphernalia Laws, and Behavior[†]

Needle Transfer Variable	No. (#)	Yes (%)	No (%)	x^2	p Value
STATEMENT B[1]					
Agree	53	69.8	30.2		
Disagree	194	30.9	69.1	26.39	.000
STATEMENT C[2]					
Agree	60	71.7	28.3		
Disagree	197	30.5	69.5	32.5	.000
STATEMENT D[3]					
Agree	75	49.3	50.7		
Disagree	178	40.5	59.5	1.69	.193
STATEMENT E[4]					
Agree	201	39.3	60.7		
Disagree	61	44.3	55.7	.48	.489
STATEMENT F[5]					
Agree	116	44.0	56.0		
Disagree	137	39.4	60.6	.54	.464
STATEMENT G[6]					
Agree	45	64.4	35.6		
Disagree	218	34.9	65.1	13.61	.000

[†] Injection drug users who responded neutrally to the statements were excluded from the analyses.
[1] If a friend wanted me to shoot up with a needle he/she just used, l would find it hard to say no.
[2] If a friend refused to lend me an outfit, I would get angry.
[3] Sex partners who both shoot dope like to use the same outfit without even cleaning it with water.
[4] I don't carry outfits with me, because I'm afraid I'll get busted.
[5] It's difficult for me to get new/sterile needles.
[6] Carrying bleach and water is too much of a hassle.

that those injection drug users who have difficulty obtaining new needles also tend to use previously used outfits. By contrast, neither fear of being arrested for paraphernalia laws (statement G) nor perceiving the carrying of bleach and water as a hassle (statement F) were related to needle transfer behavior.

To examine further the correlates of using previously used needles, we conducted a forward stepwise logistic regression, using needle transfer (1 = yes, 0 = no) as the dependent variable. Fourteen independent variables were included: 1) age (treated as a continuous variable); 2) gender (1 = male, 0 =

Table 7. Logistic Regression Results on Needle Transfer

Independent Variable	b	Odds Ratio	95% C.I. of Odds Ratio
Ethnicity			
White	–	–	–
African American	–1.21*	0.30	(0.15, 0.58)
*Marital Status***			
Not married	–	–	–
Married	1.03*	2.79	(1.52, 5.15)
Statement B[†]			
Disagree	–	–	–
Agree	0.25*	1.28	(1.07, 1.54)
Statement C[‡]			
Disagree	–	–	–
Agree	0.26*	1.29	(1.07, 1.56)
Statement F[‡‡]			
Disagree	–	–	–
Agree	0.22*	1.25	(1.02, 1.52)
Log crack[§]	0.27–	1.31	(1.04, 1.66)

Model x^2 72.67 ($p = 0.000$), d.f. = 6. n = 276

[§] The log transformation of crack cocaine use frequency.
–: Reference group.
* Statistically significant at 0.05 level.
** "Married" = legal, living as married, or living with a sex partner.
[†] If a friend wanted me to shoot up with a needle he/she just used. I would find it hard to say no.
[‡] If a friend refused to lend me an outfit, I would act angry.
[‡‡] It's difficult for me to get new/sterile needles.

female); 3) self-assessed ethnicity (1 = African American, 0 = white); 4) marital status (1 = married, common law, or living with a sex partner, 0 = otherwise); 5) income in the previous 30 days (ordinal variable with 8 levels); 6) injection frequency (1 = daily, 0 = non-daily); 7) education (three-level categorical variable with the lowest level omitted in the model), 8) crack use (the log of the number of days used in the previous 30); 9) statement B ("If a friend wanted me to shoot up with a needle he/she just used, I would find it hard to say no;" all attitudinal questions were measured with a seven-point scale and treated as continuous variables: 1 = very strongly disagree through 7 = very strongly agree); 10) statement C ("If a friend refused to lend me an outfit, I would get angry"); 11) statement D ("Sex partners who both shoot dope like to use the same outfit without even cleaning it with water"); 12) statement E ("I don't carry outfits with me, because I'm afraid I'll get busted"); 13) statement F ("It's difficult for me to get new/sterile needles"); and 14) statement G ("Carrying bleach and water is too much of a hassle").

Six of the variables were finally included in the model with a significance level of .05 after forward stepwise selection (see Table 7). The negative and significant coefficient for ethnicity indicates that white injection drug users are significantly more likely than African Americans to inject with previously used needles. Although injection frequency was not selected in the model, frequency of crack-cocaine use was significantly associated with needle transfer; daily crack users were more likely to inject other drugs with used needles. Interestingly, being "married" (legally, living as married, or living with a sex partner) had a positive effect on the transfer of used needles as well. Three attitudinal variables entered the model: statements B and C on needle transfer among friends were positively associated with needle transfer. Finally, the perception of difficulty in acquiring new needles (a positive response to statement F) also had a positive effect on injecting with used needles.

Discussion

Primarily on the basis of qualitative evidence, ethnographers conducting AIDS prevention research throughout the United States have reported that needle transfer among injection drug users is not positively valued; nor is it a mechanism of social bonding, a ritual form of establishing or creating friendship ties, or a symbol of group membership and identity (e.g., Carlson, Siegal, and Falck 1994; Clatts 1994; Koester 1994b; Kane and Mason 1992; Mason 1989; Murphy 1987). Although the value of combining qualitative and quantitative methods has been advocated in ethnographic research on drug abuse and AIDS (e.g., Carlson, Siegal, and Falck 1995), such studies have been the exception (e.g., Booth et al. 1993), rather than the rule.[5] In this study, we operationalized qualitative findings regarding injection drug users' attitudes toward needle transfer as well as their perceptions regarding needle accessibility and the legal consequences of carrying needles through a series of survey questions administered to 276 active injectors. The results overwhelmingly indicate that the vast majority of injection drug users do not positively value using each others' needles in a general sense; nor does needle transfer serve the social functions commonly attributed to a monolithic injection drug user subculture in the field of AIDS prevention research.

These findings contrast sharply with the "fetishizing" of the needle and the creation of a myth that injection drug users positively value needle transfer for its own sake, a representation that constitutes *the* principal point of attack for HIV risk reduction among drug injectors in the field of public health (Grund et al. 1992). In short, the received public health vision has created a monolithic subculture of injection drug users and their values regarding needle transfer that ethnographers have shown is inconsistent with the way these drug users behave and conceptualize their lives (Page 1990; Singer 1991). As others (e.g., Fee and Krieger 1993:1481) have emphasized, AIDS prevention efforts too often follow the logic of biomedical individualism and victim blaming (Ryan 1971), rather than examining the larger social context of disease and risk production and the available options for behavior change.

Rather than being attributable to a monolithic subcultural prescription for normative behavior, needle transfer has been shown to be a complex function of the micro-contexts of injection situations (Page 1990), political-economic conditions, and the laws affecting needle accessibility and portability that is highly variable with respect to age, gender, ethnicity, drug use patterns, and geographical location (e.g., Carlson, Siegal, and Falck 1994; Clatts *et al.* 1994; Koester 1994b; Siegal *et al.* 1994; Singer 1991,1994; Singer, Irizarry, and Schensul 1991). In addition, ethnographers have demonstrated that the process of injecting drugs is extremely complex and entails multiple, potential pathways for HIV transmission through what has become known as "indirect sharing" – risks for HIV transmission that include the sharing of injection paraphernalia other than a needle and syringe and the sharing of drugs (Jose *et al.* 1993; Koester and Hoffer 1994).

The results of our detailed examination of the correlates of needle transfer behavior are similar to some previous research (e.g., Mandell *et al.* 1994). Even though a small percentage (16.3%) of the participants indicated difficulty obtaining new needles, the regression results suggest that these individuals are more likely to inject with previously used needles. As such, even in locations like Dayton and Columbus, Ohio, where needles may be purchased without a prescription, some injection drug users have difficulty in accessing new needles and syringes. This may be a function of a lack of money (although income was not significantly related to needle transfer in the regression), a lack of familiarity with the skills necessary to purchase needles and syringes in pharmacies (perhaps as a result of being a new injector), a lack of diabetic friends (who often serve as a source of new needles), or a combination of these and other factors still to be discovered through future ethnographic research.

Although a minority (about 20%) of the injection drug users responded favorably to survey statements B ("If a friend wanted me to shoot up with a needle he/she just used, I would find it hard to say no") and C ("If a friend refused to lend me an outfit, I would get angry"), such attitudes had significant effects in the regression analysis. We do not interpret these results as indicating that some value needle transfer among friends to serve a social function of establishing friendship ties, but require additional data to further explore this issue. Most likely, we suspect on the basis of previous research that used needle transfer among friends, running buddies, spouses, or sex partners reflects a response to the level of intimacy these relationships entail (in the absence of a supply of new needles that would enable each individual to use a new needle for every injection), rather than the key mechanism available to create intimacy in relationships or a symbol of their identity.

By contrast, although a majority (72.8%) of the injection drug users per-ceived a threat from paraphernalia laws that inhibited them from carrying their own needles and syringes, this variable was not significantly associated with needle transfer behavior. We interpret this finding to suggest that although the perceived fear of paraphernalia laws inhibits carrying needles and is wide-spread, most injection drug users in this location find other means to avoid transferring used needles – perhaps by leaving needles at home and inject-ing there. The direct impact of needle possession paraphernalia laws on needle transfer may differ widely in various locations of the country and is a com-plex issue requiring further research (cf. Koester 1994a).

The significant relationship between crack-cocaine use and needle trans-fer remains unexplained and is another important topic for future ethnographic research. However, the finding that whites tend to transfer needles more than African Americans and have comparatively unsafe injection practices is simi-lar to research conducted in different parts of the country (e.g., Friedman, Des Jarlais, and Sterk 1990; Schilling et al. 1989; Siegal et al. 1994).

The relationships among ethnicity, needle transfer behavior, and HIV se-ropositivity are extremely complex (e.g., Singer, Irizarry, and Schensul 1991:144). In an early national-level study, one explanation that Rogers and Williams (1987:91) offered for the disproportionately high HIV seroprevalence rates among African American and Latino injection drug users compared to whites was that "Sterile needles may be more available to whiles, and whites may be more able to afford them." Such generalizations may be unwarranted. Subsequent research has shown that white injection drug users may gener-ally have safer injection practices compared to drug injectors of other ethnicity in one locale and yet have comparatively unsafe injection practices in another location – such as the case presented here (see also Siegal et al. 1994).[6] Be-cause the dynamics of HIV transmission differ from one geographic location to another – particularly with respect to the background HIV seroprevalence rates and the consequent probability of coming into contact with the virus, the variable natural histories of the subepidemics, the laws affecting needle accessibility, and so on (see e.g., Carlson, Siegal, and Falck 1994; Grund et al. 1992) – the value of national-level generalizations must be questioned. Obviously, this is an area in which a great dead of further research remains to be conducted.

Finally, the finding that injection drug users who are "married" (legally, living as married, or living with a sex partner) tend to exchange used needles is very interesting. Of the 114 drug injectors who did use previously used nee-dles, 30.7% received outfits at least once from a spouse, lover, or sex partner, 61.4% received used outfits from a running buddy or friend, and only 14.9% received needles and syringes from a drug seller, acquaintance or stranger. Chi-square tests revealed significant positive associations between using pre-viously used needles at home and: 1) getting used outfits from a spouse or lover; and 2) getting used outfits from a running buddy or friend (data not shown). Similar to Williams and colleague's (1995) social network research in Dayton/Columbus, Houston, Texas, and Rio Piedras, Puerto Rico, our results also suggest the existence of small networks of injection drug users in the research location; those injection drug users who do transfer used needles tend to do so in their own homes with friends and spouses/sex partners. At the same time, the dynamics underlying needle transfer among individuals in various kinds of relationships involving sex are as yet incompletely understood and deserve future attention (see Bernard 1993; Clatts *et* al. 1994:221).

Implications

As recently as 1993, we still find statements in public health literature substantiating the victim-blaming myth that injection drug users positively value using each other's needles to serve social functions in a monolithic subculture. For example, Krepcho *et al.* (1993: 135–136) state:

> Among IDUs, the act of sharing needles has both a social bonding and economic function. Allegiance to the values of the IDU subculture means that to encourage behavior change, interventions must focus on the perceived values of the subculture, as well as individual behavior change.

The manner in which the researchers substantiate the "perceived values" is unspecified; most likely, the portrayal of perceived values emanates from the received view of public health and not the perceptions of injection drug users themselves. The "economic function" is also unspecified; as noted above, several researchers have pointed to the practical necessity of needle transfer as a result of needle scarcity and to alleviate drug withdrawal symptoms.

One major implication of our study is that the common representation of injection drug users' values, attitudes, and behaviors should be reconsidered. Clearly, additional research is needed in different parts of the country, but we emphasize that the term "needle sharing" should be replaced with the term "needle transfer" (or some other suitable term) that does not implicitly entail the message that injection drug users positively value this behavior or employ it to effect specific social functions. As such, the prevention message, "Don't Share Needles" should also be reconsidered, because it does not reflect accurately an understanding of values among injection drug users, the nature of an addictive illness and the tremendous power of withdrawal in affecting behavior, or the larger context of injection behavior; that is, the problem of needle accessibility. In short, telling injection drug users who generally don't desire to use previously used needles, but sometimes do because a new one is unavailable or because they are suffering the anguish of withdrawal, "Don't Share Needles," disregards the fact that a varying proportion of injection drug users in different locations do not engage in the immediate transfer of used needles, that these drug users generally do not positively value needle transfer, and that new needles may be inaccessible for various reasons (Koester 1994a; Singer, Irizarry, and Schensul 1991). Moreover, the message reflects a general tendency in contemporary Western biomedicine to offer health promoting or disease preventing prescriptions that are incompatible with the contextual circumstances of patients' daily lives. For example, in a study of bus drivers in San Francisco, 60% of the drivers with diagnosed hypertension were unable to comply with antihypertensive diuretic treatment because of the inaccessibility of bathrooms during their strictly scheduled bus routes (Adler *et al.* 1993:3144). If we are to reach a coherent resolution to the "breakdown" in expectations discussed in the Introduction, reconceptualization and modification of our understanding and representation of injection drug users in the field of public health is needed.

The closer examination of those participants who did transfer needles also has general implications for AIDS prevention. As previously noted by others (Celentano *et al.* 1991), triaging injection drug users to select those at greatest risk through needle practices would enable the focusing of scarce resources to effect change and, perhaps, mitigate further transmission of HIV. Our results point toward a means of identifying the characteristics of those at substantial risk of HIV infection through their needle practices.

Finally, we acknowledge the limitations of the study. Although the sample was recruited through a specific targeted sampling plan, it is not random, and it represents a sample of a larger sample still being recruited. Younger or newer drug injectors may have different attitudes toward needle transfer. Therefore, our results are preliminary and must be interpreted cautiously. In addition, we recognize in hindsight that the operationalization of injection drug users' values could be elaborated and improved. It is our hope that other ethnographers in different settings of the United States, and even abroad, will reevaluate and improve on this study in future research.

Afterword: A Note on Methodology

In addition to the substantive focus of this article on attitudes toward needle transfer and the correlates of transferring behavior, we have attempted to demonstrate one of the ways that quantitative methods can be applied in ethnographic research. This is not to suggest that qualitative data and analyses are less rigorous or systematic than quantitative data and analyses; quite the opposite (see Agar 1980; Carlson, Siegal, and Falck 1995). At the same time, qualitative research, including participant observation and various interviewing techniques, is most often a prerequisite to the appropriate application of quantitative methods, if they are to be employed in ethnographic research. As Agar (1980:173) comments, "If you do not make a public attempt to falsify key ethnographic statements, the skeptical outsider will forever dismiss your statements as 'untested.'" Our earlier qualitative findings on injection drug users' values toward needle transfer resulted in "key ethnographic statements" (Carlson *et al.* 1994). This additional check of the findings on injection drug users' attitudes toward needle transfer and some of the underlying reasons why drug injectors do transfer used needles (which we chose to take the form of quantitative assessment) is directed toward anthropologists as well as individuals outside the discipline, particularly those who play key roles in setting public health policy.

Notes

1. See Agar (1986:20ff) for a discussion of the historical roots of the concept of "breakdown." Singer (1991:270ff) discusses the relevance of the concept of "breakdowns" in AIDS prevention education among drug users of different ethnicity. For early research on the meaning of needle sharing, see Howard and Borges (1972) and Mason (1989).

2. See Brown and Beschner (1993) for more details on the National Institute on Drug Abuse's NADR program.

3. Further methodological details and results are presented in Carlson, Siegal, and Falck (1994).

4. Modifications of the instrument consisted primarily of rephrasing and shortening statements to clarify meaning and shorten the length of the interview.

5. See Ashery and Lambert (1995) for additional examples discussing the combination of qualitative and quantitative methods in drug use and AIDS research.

6. In addition, although African American and Latino injection drug users have disproportionately high HIV seroprevalence rates compared to white drug injectors at the national level, this is not always the case in specific geographic locations. For example, in our NADR study of 855 injection drug users in a low HIV seroprevalence area in west-central Ohio, 13 injection drug users were HIV positive – 1.5% of the African-American participants and 1.6% of the whites (Siegal *et al.* 1991: 1643).

References Cited

Adler, Nancy E., W. Thomas Boyce, Margaret A. Chesney, Susan Folkman, and S. Leonard Syme. 1993 Socioeconomic Inequalities in Health: No Easy Solution. *Journal of the American Medical Association* 269:3140–3145.

Agar, Michael H. 1980 *The Professional Stranger: An Informal Introduction to Ethnography.* New York: Academic Press.

—— 1982 Toward an Ethnographic Language. *American Anthropologist* 84:779–795.

—— 1986 *Speaking of Ethnography. Qualitative Research Methods*, Vol. 2. Beverly Hills, CA: Sage Publications.

Ashery, Rebecca Sager, and Elizabeth Lambert, eds. 1995 *Qualitative Research and the Prevention of Drug Use and HIV.* National Institute on Drug Abuse Research Monograph 152.

Barnard, Marina A. 1993 Needle Sharing in Context: Patterns of Needle Sharing among Men and Women Injectors and HIV Risks. *Addiction* 88:805–812.

Booth, Robert E., Stephen K. Koester, Charles S. Reichardt, and J. Thomas Brewster. 1993 *Quantitative and Qualitative Methods to Assess Behavioral Change Among Injection*

Drug Users. In AIDS and Community-Based Drug Intervention Programs: Evaluation and Outreach. Dennis Fisher and Richard Needle, eds. Pp. 161–183. New York: The Haworth Press.

Brown, Barry S. and George M. Beschner, eds. 1993 *Handbook on Risk of AIDS: Injection Drug Users and Sexual Partners.* Westport, CT: Greenwood Press.

Carlson, Robert G. 1991 *HIV Needle Risk Behavior among Injection Drug Users in West-Central Ohio: An Ethnographic Overview.* Presented at the Conference on AIDS and Anthropology in the United States sponsored by The Centers for Disease Control and Prevention. Atlanta, Georgia; October 16–17.

Carlson, Robert G., Harvey A. Siegal, and Russel S. Falck. 1994 Ethnography, Epidemiology, and Public Policy: Needle-Use Practices and HIV-1 Risk Reduction among Injecting Drug Users in the Midwest. In *Global AIDS Policy.* Douglas A. Feldman, ed. Pp. 185–214. Westport, CT: Bergin & Garvey.

—— 1995 Qualitative Research Methods in Drug Abuse and AIDS Prevention Research: An Overview. In *Qualitative Research and the Prevention of Drug Use and HIV.* Rebecca Sager Ashery, and Elizabeth Lambert, eds. Pp. 6–26. National Institute on Drug Abuse Research Monograph 152.

Carlson, Robert G., Jichuan Wang, Harvey A. Siegal, Russel S. Falck, and Jie Guo. 1994 An Ethnographic Approach to Targeted Sampling: Problems and Solutions in AIDS Prevention Research among Injection Drug and Crack-Cocaine Users. *Human Organization* 53:279–286.

Celentano, David D., David Vlahov, Sylvia Cohn, James C. Anthony, Liza Solomon, and Kenrad E. Nelson. 1991 Risk Factors for Shooting Gallery Use and Cessation Among Intravenous Drug Users. *American Journal of Public Health* 81:1291–1295.

Clatts, Michael C. 1994 All the King's Horses and all the King's Men: Some Personal Reflections on Ten Years of AIDS Ethnography. *Human Organization* 53:93–95.

Clatts, Michael C., W. R. Davis, Sherry Deren, Douglas S. Goldsmith, and Stephanie Tortu. 1994 AIDS Risk Behavior among Drug Injectors in New York City: Critical Gaps in Prevention Policy. In *Global AIDS Policy.* Douglas A. Feldman, ed. Pp. 215–235. Westport, CT: Bergin & Garvey.

Connors, Margaret M. 1994 Stories of Pain and the Problem of AIDS Prevention: Injection Drug Withdrawal and Its Effects on Risk Behavior. *Medical Anthropology Quarterly* 8:47–68.

Conviser, Richard and John H. Rutledge. 1989 Can Public Policies Limit the Spread of HIV among IV Drug Users. *The Journal of Drug Issues* 19:113–128.

Denzin, Norman. 1970 The Research Act. Chicago: Aldine.

Des Jarlais, Don C., Samuel R. Friedman, and David Strug. 1986 AIDS and Needle Sharing Within the IV-Drug Use Subculture. In *The Social Dimensions of AIDS: Method and Theory.* Douglas A. Feldman and Thomas M. Johnson, eds. Pp. 111–125. New York: Praeger.

Fee, Elizabeth and Nancy Krieger. 1993 Understanding AIDS: Historical Interpretations and the Limits of Biomedical Individualism. *American Journal of Public Health* 83:1477–1486.

Friedman, Samuel R., Don C. Des Jarlais, and Claire Sterk. 1990 AIDS and the Social Relations of Intravenous Drug Users. *Milbank Quarterly* 68(suppl. 1):85–110.

Grund, John-Paul C., L. Synn Stern, Charles D. Kaplan, Nico F. P. Adriaans, and Ernest Drucker. 1992 Drug Use Contexts and HIV-Consequences: The Effect of Drug Policy on Patterns of Everyday Drug Use in Rotterdam and the Bronx. *British Journal of Addiction* 87:381–392.

Howard, Jan and Phillip Borges. 1972 Needle Sharing in the Haight: Some Social and Psychological Functions. In *"It's So Good, Don't Even Try It Once."* David E. Smith and George R. Gay, eds. Pp. 125–136. Englewood Cliffs, NJ: Prentice Hall, Inc.

Jose, Benny, Samuel R. Friedman, Alan Neaigus, Richard Curtis, Jean-Paul C. Grund, Marjorie F. Goldstein, Thomas P. Ward, and Don C. Des Jarlais. 1993 Syringe-Mediated Drug-Sharing (Backloading): A New Risk Factor for HIV among Injecting Drug Users. *AIDS* 7:1653–1660.

Kane, Stephanie and Theresa Mason. 1992 "IV Drug Users" and "Sex Partners": The Limits of Epidemiological Categories and the Ethnography of Risk. In *The Time of AIDS: Social Analysis, Theory, and Method.* Gilbert Herdt and Shirley Lindenbaum, eds. Pp. 199–224. Newbury Park, CA: Sage Publications.

Koester, Stephen K. 1994a Copping, Running and Paraphernalia Laws: Contextual Variables and Needle Risk Behavior among Injection Drug Users in Denver. *Human Organization* 53:287–295.

1994b The Context of Risk: Ethnographic Contributions to the Study of Drug Use and HIV. *In* The Context of HIV Risk Among Drug Users and Their Sexual Partners. Robert J. Battjes and William C. Grace, eds. Pp. 202–217. *National Institute on Drug Abuse Research Monograph* 143. Rockville, Maryland: National Institute on Drug Abuse.

Koester, Stephen K. and Lee Hoffer. 1994 The Mechanics of Drug Injection: Additional HIV Risks. *AIDS and Public Policy Journal* 9:100–105.

Krepcho, Martin A., Maria Eugenia Fernandez-Esquer, Anne C. Freeman, Elvin Magee, and Alfred McAlister. 1993 Predictors of Bleach Use among Current African-American Injecting Drug Users: *A Community Study. Journal of Psychoactive Drugs* 25:135–141.

Mandell, Wallace, David Vlahov, Carl Latkin, Maria Ozienkowska, and Sylvia Cohn. 1994 Correlates of Needle Sharing among Injection Drug Users. *American Journal of Public Health* 84:920–923.

Mason, Theresa. 1989 *The Politics of Culture: Drug Users, Professionals, and the Meaning of Needle Sharing.* Presented at the Annual Meeting of the Society for Applied Anthropology, Santa Fe, April.

Murphy, Sheigla. 1987 Intravenous Drug Use and AIDS: Notes on the Social Economy of Needle Sharing. *Contemporary Drug Problems* 3:373–396.

Page, J. Bryan. 1990 Shooting Scenarios and Risk of HIV-1 Infection. *American Behavioral Scientist* 33:478–490.

Page, J. Bryan, Dale D. Chitwood, Prince C. Smith, Normie Kane, and Duane C. McBride. 1990 Intravenous Drug Use and HIV Infection in Miami. *Medical Anthropology Quarterly* 4:56–71.

Rogers, Martha F. and Walter W. Williams. 1987 AIDS in Blacks and Hispanics: Implications for Prevention. *Issues in Science and Technology* 3:89–96.

Ryan, William. 1971 *Blaming the Victim.* New York: Random House.

Schilling, Robert, Steven Schinke, Stuart Nichols, Luis Zayas, Samuel Miller, Mario Orlando, and Gilbert Botvin. 1989 Developing Strategies for AIDS Prevention Research with Black and Hispanic Drug Users. *Public Health Reports* 104:211.

Siegal, Harvey A., Robert G. Carlson, Russel Falck, Ling Li, Mary Ann Forney, Richard C. Rapp, Kathy Baumgartner, William Myers, and Morton Nelson. 1991 HIV Infection and Risk Behaviors among Intravenous Drug Users in Low Seroprevalence Areas in the Midwest. *American Journal of Public Health* 81:1642–1644.

Siegal, Harvey A., Robert G. Carlson, Jichuan Wang, Russel S. Falck, Richard C. Stephens, and E. Don Nelson. 1994 Injection Drug Users in the Midwest: An Epidemiologic Comparison of Drug Use Patterns in Four Ohio Cities. *Journal of Psychoactive Drugs* 26:265–275.

Singer, Merrill. 1991 Confronting the AIDS Epidemic among IV Drug Users: Does Ethnic Culture Matter? *AIDS Education and Prevention* 3:258–283.

—— 1994 AIDS and the Health Crisis of the U.S. Urban Poor: The Perspective of Critical Medical Anthropology. *Social Science and Medicine* 39:931–948.

Singer, Merrill, Ray Inzarry, and Jean J. Schensul. 1991 Needle Access as an AIDS Prevention Strategy for IV Drug Users: A Research Perspective. *Human Organization* 50:142–153.

Waldorf, Dan, Sheigla Murphy, David Lauderback, Craig Reinerman, and Toby Marotta. 1990 Needle Sharing among Male Prostitutes: Preliminary Findings of the Prospero Project. *The Journal of Drug Issues* 20:309–334.

Williams, Mark, Z. Zhuo, Harvey A. Siegal, R. Robles, Robert Trotter II, and Adelbert Jones. 1995 A Comparison of Drug Use Networks Across Three Cities. In *Drug Abuse and HIV Transmission*. Richard Needle, ed. Pp. 109–130. Rockville, Maryland: National Institute on Drug Abuse.

Zule, William A. 1992 Risk and Reciprocity: HIV and the Injection Drug User. *Journal of Psychoactive Drugs* 24:243–249.

6

Real Men Don't Collect Soft Data

Silvia Gherardi & Barry Turner

A common usage in discussion of social science links quantitative styles of inquiry and data collection with a 'hard' view of the world, and qualitative approaches with a 'soft' view. As with many unexamined language patterns, these distinctions serve to convey tacit attitudes about the topic under discussion: the connotations of these terms are such as to suggest that 'hard' social science is masculine and to be respected, whilst 'soft' social science is feminine and of a lower order of activity. The message conveyed in these tacit usages is that quantitative work is courageous, hard biting, hard work.

Collecting hard data means making hard decision, taking no nonsense, hardening one's heart to weaklings, building on a hard core of material, using hard words to press on to hard won results which often carry with them promises of hard cash for future research and career prospects. By contrast, soft data is weak, unstable, impressible, squashy and sensual. The softies, weaklings, or ninnys who carry it out have too much of a soft-spot for counter-argument for them to be taken seriously, they reveal the soft underbelly of the social science enterprise, are likely to soft-soap those who listen to them. They are too soft hearted, pitying and maybe even foolish to be taken seriously so that it is only right that they should be employed on soft money.

These contrasts are sufficiently firmly established for journal editors to refuse to accept the phrase 'hard qualitative data' on the grounds that it would be 'confusing to readers', and they deserve discussion because the current usage serves to bias assessments of current new directions in social science research. They are used as code words for a cluster of issues relating not only to the *style of inquiry*, to the *style of questions asked* and the *style of answers* sought, but also to the association of quantitative investigations with major institutionalised patterns of research, and the consequent access to machinery, to research aides and to control over concentrations of resources. The 'hard', macho image is also likely to be associated with the distancing of senior researchers from

Source: Silvia Gherardi & Barry Turner, *Real Men Don't Collect Soft Data* (Trento: Dipartimento di Politica Sociale, Università di Trento, 1987).

'subjects' or 'objects' of inquiry; with the reduction of threats to the self by the use of anxiety-reducing research rituals of execution and research presentation; and with a reduced willingness to tolerate ambiguity in procedures and findings. (Silverman, 1985)

The recent growth of interest in qualitative research makes it important to challenge these clusters of assumptions which get smuggled into discussion of research – and also of research funding – and to question the extent to which such views can automatically be held to be correct. A parallel argument has recently been advanced in the field of management theory, where Basoux (1987) has noted that management was originally formulated as a rational-deductive task to be tackled by men:

"The good manager is aggressive, competitive, firm, just. He is not feminine; he is not soft or yielding or dependent or intuitive in the womanly sense. The very expression of emotion is viewed as a feminine weakness that would interfere with effective business processes."

(McGregor, 1967; 23)

But with the recognition of the central importance of cultural issues in management (Peters and Watermann, 1982) and the need to cope with incursions into the West from Japanese firms, management virtues are now seen to include consensus, involvement, patience, compromise and moderation. The new view promotes a modified role model of the manager as "intuitive, nurturing and accessible – a job description which women are well-placed to fulfil". (Basoux, 1987)

In the complex world of contemporary social science, similar shifts are taking place, and the issues to be confronted are too subtle and too important to be handled by means of a crude and over-simplified dichotomy, especially when this presumed opposition is accompanied by properties derived from sexist stereotypes. In the remainder of this paper, we wish to explore some of the complexities of the current changes which are being handled within social science research, and to relate them especially to the developing trends of investigations within the field of organisational sociology.

The Process of Research

The bureaucratisation of scientific research proceeds on the assumption that the task of research is one which is amenable to the same kind of hierarchical division of labour as are tasks in manufacturing industry or in official administration. This view of research is reinforced by much of the abstract and elaborate edifice of 'research methodology' which the social sciences have generated, (Willer & Willer, 1974; Zetterberg, 1954; Hage, 1972) and which has generated its own momentum and its own autonomy as an area of abstract learning. But there is an obscurity about how the detailed and rule-bound practices advocated for the definition of concepts and for the construction of theory relate to the actual process of ongoing research. Such writings, while pursuing theoretical and logical rigour, produce systems of abstraction with normative undertones – this is how research should be done – whilst retaining a problematic relationship to the processes which they claim to explicate. In a similar manner, as we shall see, attempts to absorb the new emphasis upon qualitative research into existing orthodoxies of research methodology produce an illusory clarity, for they do not look closely enough at the research process.

As always, we find that social reality confounds our simple armchair theorising: it is more messy, more convoluted and more surprising than we thought it would be. Fortunately this realisation, prompted by the growth in the sociology of natural science, has now given us some accounts of how research is pursued in fact, rather than in research methodology. Hammond's pioneering collection *Sociologists at Work* (1964) has been supplemented by other accounts (Bell & Newby, 1984; Bryman, 1988).

There is, then, another opposition, between the structures advocated by the methodologists and the 'theorologists' on the one hand, and the accounts of research as it is done, and theory generation as it occurs, which have been produced by Hammond and his successors. To resolve this opposition, we need to look for an emerging middle ground which presents guides to research procedure and theory generation which accord more with the nature of research practice. And, when we look for this middle ground, we find also that we must tackle issues which blur the simple qualitative/quantitative, hard/soft contrasts with which we began.

We are helped in our task by the way in which investigations into the sociology and the philosophy of natural science have shown it not to be the gleaming aseptic edifice promoted in developments after World War II, but to be a human enterprise, fraught with all of the personal, emotional and political difficulties displayed by any human undertaking. Natural science is, as Ravetz (1971) has demonstrated, a craft process: judgement, craft skills and intuitive knowledge are deployed by natural scientists in the assessment of the satisfactory operation of equipment; in descriptive and other scientific reporting skills; in the intuitive adoption of appropriate preliminary theories about a given context; in judgements about the appropriate use and the appropriate fit of mathematical models; in evaluations of the reliability of data collected, making the transition from collected data to usable information; in the elaboration of argument; (Feyerabend, 1975) in the appropriate use of pre-existing information gathered by other researchers; in the development of tools and techniques and in the acquisition of skills in using them; in the avoidance of pitfalls characteristic of the field of inquiry; and, throughout, in the style of research pursued:

"The investigation of a scientific problem is creative work, in which personal choices as well as personal judgements are involved at every stage up to the last ... Even though (the scientist) is concerned with properties of the external world the work he (sic) produces will be characterised by a certain style unique to himself ... There is no conflict between a highly individual style in the investigation of problems and the production of results which meet the socially imposed criteria of adequacy for the field."

(Ravetz, Ch. 2, 1971)

It is clear that all of the craft elements which Ravetz identifies with the procedures of natural science, and which account for the distinctive development of 'schools' of natural science associated with 'master-pupil' pedigrees stretching over centuries (H.T. Pledge, *Science since 1500*, HMSO, 1939) will be evident within even the most quantitative of social sciences. Judgements about equipment, procedures, abstracting and typifying activities, theorising, modelling and so on pervade any quantitative social science investigation. Baldamus (1976) has drawn attention to the way in which fundamental approaches to theorising and abstraction are embedded in such commonplace social science activities as cross-classification and the construction of two-by-two tables, and has pointed out the manner in which the practical procedures of survey research are saturated with theoretical and value-judgements. Survey research is almost entirely conceived of as a rule-bound methodology, but its operations depend upon the tacit knowledge, developed by researchers in the process of use, which underpins the process of cross-classification, of elaboration analysis, the handling of variables in a statistical manner and so on (Rosenberg, 1968). Without such implicit theoretical techniques, the rules of survey research would enable us to build, as Ravetz phrases it, a plane which would not fly.

And, again, the strictures of the research handbooks have to be reconciled with accounts of how research is actually carried out. Lowe's (1971) analysis of the accounts in Hammond demonstrate that, with one exception the projects embarked upon by these distinguished researchers all reached a point of disruption, where the original plan, the original project, the original rationale for the research suffered a breakdown, precipitating a crisis and requiring activities of what Lowe calls theoretical 'patchworking' or theoretical 'bricolage' in order to repair the breakdown and to present an appearance of coherence in the work. Of course, if research is recognised to be a journey into the unknown rather than a task which can be fully specified and planned in advance, then such breakdowns look less surprising, and we can look (Lowe suggests) at the patchworking as the injection of a creative element into the process.

All of the above is intended merely to make the point that the process of research, even natural science research, is one which involves the use of judgement, craft skills and what Polanyi (1959) calls tacit knowledge, that it frequently does not follow a preordained path and that the intelligence needed to pursue research is not wholly rational-deductive. Witkin (1971) has argued that all creative developments, in the field of both arts and science, involve the use not only of cognitive intelligence but also an affective intelligence, an 'intelligence of feeling': the objective which a scientist pursues is likely to have sensuous properties, and to be affectively or emotionally charged. The personal manner in which this objective is symbolised will direct the process of interaction between the investigator and the particular medium or context which is being investigated. Such a process is not a completely random one, or one without rules, but the rules will relate to the particular combination of [objective] and [investigatory context]. The rules will not be a universally applicable array, but will be context specific, and generated in the process of interaction between investigator and investigatory field, as part of the process of the exercise of the cognitive *and* the affective intelligence. As the American physicist Bridgeman commented, 'science is doing your damndest to understand with no holds barred'.

The rules of scientific investigation to which we have been referring are not those common to research methodology, nor are they the rules for the socially approved presentation of research findings to the scholarly community. They are the rules generated in interaction to guide further investigation in a manner likely to be scientifically fruitful. As the rules of a painting by numbers kit relate to artistic creation, so do sets of research procedures relate to successful scientific investigation.

Let us turn our attention, then, to the related question of number and counting. We would not wish to take up the obscurantist position sometimes encountered among qualitative researchers, that qualitative researchers are not permitted to count. If we are to understand the natural or the social world 'with no holds barred' then we need to deploy whatever appropriate means come to hand. As we suggested at the start, such simple oppositions as 'numbers *versus* no numbers' are inadequate for discussing and understanding the full complexity of the research process. We need, instead, to look a little more closely at what is meant by number and how number might be appropriately deployed in different research contexts.

But number is a metaphor. In counting and quantification, number is employed to draw similarities. Mathematics provides us with accounts of systems of logical operations and interconnections. In the use of mathematics we place sections of the world which we are interested in alongside portions of mathematical reasoning and assert that the two bear some resemblance to each other. This process is as true for the juxtaposition of a row of sheep and the numbers 'one, two, three' as it is for the explorations of parallels between the behaviour of a national economy and the properties of a complex econometric model. We should, therefore, be clear about which of the metaphorical properties of number we wish to use to assist our understanding of the social and organisational world. Is the case to be made that there are no relevant properties? That mathematical counting and related operations cannot possibly help us because we are interested in processes and properties which are inherently uncountable. Or, in a related position, one suggested by William Blake in his famous picture of a godlike figure leaning down from the heavens with a pair of calipers, do we wish to make the case that the process of measurement, of quantification in itself is damaging to the stature, to the quality and to the dignity of humankind? Or are the relevant distinctions not between 'counting' and 'not counting', but between 'counting to one' (unity) and 'counting to more than one', or between 'counting to one, two and three' and 'counting many' (as in several language forms).

Again, to resolve such questions in a research context, we need to think clearly about what we are intending to do when we are suggesting that properties of the systems and activities we are interested in are usefully close to the properties of abstract number systems. When the parallels are close ones, properly constituted, we are able to assist our enquiries because transformations which can be carried out powerfully and with great facility through manipulations of numbers tell us about properties of the social world, but in order to use these we need to ensure that the operations which we apply to our numbers are appropriate ones. The weakest kind of numbering is simply using numbers to identify and label phenomena (as in Mark I, Mark II, etc. James I, James II). These numbers identify unambiguously, but we can do nothing useful if we try operations such as 'James I + James II =' or still less if we ask questions about the square root of James II. At the opposite extreme, we have numbers which reflect all of the properties of natural numbers, so that we can add, subtract, multiply, divide and so on with impunity, confident that the operations carried out on the numbers also mean something for our data. Coleman's *Introduction to Mathematical Sociology*, particularly in the earlier chapters, provides an excellent discussion of these issues. It is important to spend time on these topics because of the peculiar standing of numbers in our civilisation. On the one hand we are mesmerised by numbers, even when they are pseudo-numbers, those who deal with them frequently no less than those who are thrown into a panic by them. On the other hand, the general standard of teaching about mathematical issues is so poor that few people understand fully the nature of the properties of the numbers and number systems which they are advocating or excoriating.

A new and useful notation has recently been developed to draw attention to properties of numbers which are frequently ignored. Ravetz and Funtowicz (1986), alarmed by the misuse of numbers in debates about nuclear safety levels, constructed the NUSAP notation which, though intended for application to natural science and engineering in the first instance, can also helpfully clarify thought in the social science area. The essence of their system is simple: that a single number standing alone is misleading. To evaluate its meaning, we need an additional four pieces of information. Ravetz and Funtowicz express this as N:U:S:A:P – Number: Units: Spread: Assessment: Pedigree. When presenting others with a number to try to elucidate a portion of our research, we will mislead them if we allow this *number* to stand alone. Our audience will need to know the *units* of our measurement, and some measure of the *spread* or distribution around the point specified. And then perhaps even more importantly they need to know where the number has come from, its *pedigree* – is it based upon an exhaustive and detailed measurement process covering every possible variable which might influence the outcome, or upon a snap judgement from someone over the telephone? Associated with the pedigree, the audience would be assisted by an *assessment* of the standing of this number in the eyes of those well placed to make a judgement. Do those in the field think that this is a sensible guess, or a shoddy estimate, is it the best possible attempt at measurement, or a figure over which commentators disagree?

In qualitative analyses, there are no reasons why numbers should not be appropriately deployed: Suttles' use of small tables showing how many gang fights took place in a given period of time in a Chicago slum, or how many members of one ethnic group visited a shop owned by a member of another ethnic group in an afternoon (Suttles, 1978) help to inform us about his territory and add an element to a study otherwise based upon qualitative data gathered through participant observation. When Suttles specifies five fights in a month, we know that he is counting in units of one, that the number could rise above or fall below that in the preceding or following months, that he got the figure by talking to people around the neighbourhood, and that the trust that we can place in the figure is about the same as the trust which we can place upon Suttles' general account, as a competent but human individual observer spending some time in the vicinity. This kind of background information is needed, these kinds of judgements are made, tacitly or explicitly whenever *any* number is presented in a research context.

When is it difficult or inappropriate to count at all? Here it seems to be useful to introduce a distinction between standardised and non-standardised data. To count, the items or the features to be counted need to be available in a standardised form. And, since the world is rarely standardised in itself, we need to have strong rules to declare certain variations in the data as 'error' which can be safely disregarded; when we are happy to do this, we generate data which can be usefully tallied up, in conditions where we judge that anything that is not standard can be safely ignored. By contrast when we are reluctant to specify units, or when we are reluctant to declare the variety in quality between units to be unimportant, or to disregard it, we find ourselves dealing with non-standardised data. We have weak rules for classifying portions of the data as 'error' and we have to find ways to cope with the resulting variations in our analysis which do not make use of the analogous properties of number systems.

To these distinctions we need to add others concerned with broader and deeper philosophical and epistemological issues: with whether our organisational research is to be concerned with prediction, with the generation of theory, with the acquisition of interpretative meanings, or with the informing of political action. Reason and Rowe (1981) offer a distinction, in discussing new approaches to organisational research, between those who are seeking theory as prediction and those who want theory as pattern. Broadly this distinction coincides with that between positivistic inquiry and what Lincoln and Guba (1985) somewhat controversially call 'naturalistic' inquiry. The distinction here is not merely between the uses of theory but also between the different canons which may appropriately be applied to the judgement of the research.

Lincoln and Guba (1985) suggest that, whereas positivistic inquiries are judged according to their rigour, naturalistic inquiries should be assessed on the basis of trustworthiness and authenticity. Rigour conventionally looks at the truth value of propositions, at their validity or generalisability, at their reliability and at their objectivity. Research which fails to meet these criteria is confounded, atypical, unstable or biassed. By contrast, they suggest that appropriate criteria for assessing naturalistic research, appropriate criteria of trustworthiness would be that the research should be credible, its findings should be transferable, dependable and confirmable, and they suggest techniques for the improvement of all of these qualities of 'naturalistic' research[1].

A further distinction in research which can usefully be added to our considerations is that made by Glaser and Strauss (1967) between research which is concerned with verification and research which is concerned with discovery. In the former type, theory serves as a framework to guide verification. In the latter, theory is the 'jottings in the margins of ongoing research', a kind of research in which order is not very immediately attained, a messy, puzzling and intriguing kind of research in which the conclusions are not known before the investigations are carried out. This does not mean that the researcher is unprepared for investigation – "fortune favours the prepared mind". A domain of inquiry needs to be identified, and much preparation can be carried out by becoming familiar with the empirical and theoretical literature concerned with the given domain, several different literatures possibly being relevant to different facets of the research domain.

Against this background, empirical research can commence, with a sharpened perception and an array of questions, uncertainties and doubts. In 'discovery oriented' research, the extent to which the researcher acts as the research instrument is likely to be maximised. An openness of mind requires a faithful attention to the sensations offered in the field situation, but at the same time the essentially active part played by the investigator may be symbolised by the use of the term 'capta' rather than data (Miles and Huberman, 1984) to stress the extent to which information is captured from rather than given by the social setting. Non-standardised information, 'capta' acquired as a result of close attention to a portion of the social world relevant to the research domain will provide the fidelity, trustworthiness and authenticity which Lincoln and Guba have advocated, giving such data an authority which is difficult to overturn in relation to the context in which it was gathered, but which then poses immediately the question of the extent to which the findings are transferable to other contexts.

Theory Generation from Qualitative Data

We are labouring these basic points about painstaking fieldwork because they seem to us to be essential preparation for the work of theory generation in qualitative research.

Good fieldwork can be helped by guides currently available to researchers which explore the problems of data gathering, access and so on (Burgess, 1982; Burgess, 1984) and which alert us to the importance of being appropriately prepared and equipped, of being suitably attentive and sensitive, of assessing the quality of our observations (Turner, 1988) and of being able to negotiate entry to the domain of inquiry. A more difficult process however, and one which is little discussed, is that which follows on the acquisition of a full set of field notes or interview transcripts – the process of typification and categorisation of the data in the initial steps of analysis.

We have learned enough over the past century about cognition and understanding and about the nature of social reality to realise that good research is not simply a matter of reportage, of listing events and encounters to show where we have been. The account of 'reality' which is being sought in the research process is a little different from that which might be offered in a chatty essay or in a short article for a colour supplement. What is wanted is not a social 'shopping list' which records what has been noticed, but an account of a series of interactions with the social world in a form which plausibly alerts us to the possibility of a new order not previously seen – a theoretical account.

This theoretical account of reality has to be one in which we, again, are active contributors. We are active in attending to various facets of the encounters which we experience, we are active in the early stages of analysis when we divide up our experiences into fragments, dimension, characteristics and features which we make noteworthy and we are active in the new syntheses which we start to make as we structure our own past experiences and future expectations. As a young writer, V.S. Naipaul spent much time searching for real 'writer's material' and worrying because he could not find it. He did not, as he later realised, see the richness of the material which surrounded him all the time when he had arrived in his boarding house in post-war London, and only now, thirty years on, is he finding himself able actively to re-evaluate and reinterpret his experiences at that time, seeing or creating their meaning. (Naipaul, 1987) The ordinary encounters which a new researcher is involved with in the field may not look very exciting. He or she may well need reassuring that they are real 'sociologist's material' and further, may need to be convinced that they are accessible in some way to theoretical interpretation.

Of course, as we are structuring our own expectations, we are also trying to structure the expectations of others. To perceive, we typify: there is no alternative. Without structure, perception is chaotic and any account of the world must typify. One of the most difficult tasks in qualitative social science research is deciding just what kind or level of typification is useful in the appraising of field notes and interview transcripts in order to allow the material to release its sociological messages (Martin & Turner, 1987; Strauss, 1987; Turner, 1988).

In the approach known as 'grounded theory' (Glaser & Strauss, 1967; Turner 1981) a crucial but little discussed stage involves precisely this matter of the appropriate level of typification which will serve to articulate a theoretical understanding of a given set of non-standardised data. Both Glaser (1978) and Strauss (1987) recognise this difficulty and suggest that this step can best be learned by example, in research meetings or in collaborative research workshops. This is good advice, and it is even possible to make use of such sessions to train engineering researchers concerned with analysing non-standardised data collected about engineering practice. (Turner, 1987)

But what is happening in such encounters? What tacit research skills are being passed on? One such skill is the ability to judge what level of generality it is helpful to work with (Strauss, 1987) and another is the reassurance that the researcher has to contribute some elements to the data in order to generate a meaningful or an insightful pattern of typification. Only by coming to feel comfortable about 'putting meaning in' can the researcher structure the situation, initially for him or herself and subsequently for the readers of the research account.

A parallel can perhaps be drawn with the painter's contribution to the process of Chinese *hseih-i* watercolour painting. Although in this style, the paintings of plants, animals and landscapes may be based upon many detailed studies and sketches from nature, these form no more than a preparatory stage in the work. The final painting is made from memory, in the studio.

> "We would search in vain for the concrete scenery of Huang's pictures. Instead we would recognise how he unravelled the core of that immense confusion of natural miracles and caprices to create a dignified yet simple landscape core which does not confuse our vision. Huang created a picture of the Yellow Mountains in their sensual and spiritual character out of thousands of views and thousands of experiences."
>
> (Hejzlar, 1987; p. 52)

Or, again, in relation to Wang Ch'ing-Fang's studies of fish:

> "His pictures of the ink carps and small fishes, or golden acquarium fishes in bright red were made with an understanding of the creatures' rhythm of movement and the resistance of the invisible element, water. Boldness and elegance of expression are the result of Wang's immense patience as an observer." [2]
>
> (Hejzlar, 1987; p. 57)

The ideal type, as Weber recognised, bears a similar relationship to a particular set of empirical data as these paintings do to the nature sketches which preceded them. In making sense of our experience we need to produce from a set of qualitative data a theoretical account which summarises our understanding of possible regularities associated with the set. These regularities will have the potential of unifying not only the empirical data which we have already dissected, but also other material which we have not yet seen. Without this potential neither science nor human life would be possible.

The theory will not list our experiences, but will offer an arrangement of elements of those experiences which we find useful and which might be useful to others. We are engaged in the generation of theory not primarily as a predictor of variables, but as a pattern which we will recognise when it recurs (Reason & Rowe, 1981). If the theoretical pattern is sufficiently recognisable, useful and sensitively constructed; and if our segment of the world is not too unrepresentative of aspects of that pattern, it may turn out to be recognisable, appealing and useful to others as well.

Research Communication Over Theory

One of the benefits from trying to make more explicit the processes of qualitative research is to make formerly hidden procedures and practices which have had to be discovered and rediscovered with varying degrees of success by each generation of researchers more accessible and open to discussion and improvement. We are concerned with universal processes of data transformation and the explicit discussion of them is likely to allow for collective improvements to be effected in the manner in which they are tackled.

In consequence of the explicitness, it is possible for communication about the intermediate stages of qualitative analysis to take place, between research principal and research assistants, between research collaborators, between research students and supervisors. Communication may occur by several means: through making explicit the 'low-level theoretical labels' which are generated in the early stages of data analysis as initial coding categories are invented; through discussion of the definitions of the most important and central of these concepts; through theoretical memoranda generated alongside the processes of detailed data analysis; through the use of sections of a research journal if one is being kept by the researchers in question; through communication of those occasional moments of high energy creative synthesis which is one of the rare delights of research and which Glaser has called the 'drugless trip' (1978). It is assumed in each of these possible strands of communication about research that writing is a research skill. We wish to urge a clear separation between writing as a means of organising and presenting final results to an audience and writing as a research skill. The goal of writing every day not only helps to avoid writing blocks, but gives regular practice to the qualitative researcher in externalising thoughts about the issues and evidence of the research in hand. Regular writing for oneself avoids the anxiety associated with having to write a paper for a seminar or a journal. Also, it demonstrates practically that writing is a skill which can be acquired and improved by practice.

Writing externalises thought and in doing so makes it less personal, more durable and more specific. Even without external intervention, writers are likely to learn from feedback from their own externalised thoughts, and this process can be augmented by comments from colleagues, critics and helpers who are able to read the written output (Barzun & Graaf, part III, 1977; Strunk

& White, 1979; Mullins, 1977; Elbow, 1981). I am sure that we all know people with rooms full of research material which they have never been able to publish because they have never been able to write about it. The researcher who makes a habit of writing regularly will find it easier to prepare drafts, discussion papers and outlines to be analysed in discussion session, and will find fewer problems in making the transition from the use of writing as a research skill to the use of writing for the presentation of accounts of research to a professional audience.

Links With Existing Theory

In the nature of the process outlined above the final theoretical stage will involve the building of bridges between the analysis of the field observations and theoretical aspects of existing studies. One would expect that some of these links will reflect the themes explored in initial literature searches, as the analysis picks up, amplifies, questions or modifies previous theoretical views. However, linked with the element of discovery which we have discussed above, we would also expect to be making use of other, more unexpected sets of theoretical writing.

We can trace several sequences in the preceding accounts of the pursuit of soft data. Given that one of the defining characteristics of such research is its stress upon interpretation and upon negotiation. Agar (1986) suggests, following Gadamer, a sequence of interpretations as follows: Encounter; leading to surprise and breakdown; then to resolution and finally to the production of a coherent account. As Lowe's inquiries have suggested, following breakdown the qualitative investigator has also, however, to strive to achieve some degree of coherence, or to move towards some mode of operation which does not in practice cause too much personal distress, between his/her relationships with the observed, and his/her relationships with the scientific community. Ways of seeking coherence may include the following:

* searching for observed actions to locate typical motives, typical ends, typical means in typical situations so that they can be placed in a frame or plan for communication *back* to those observed or *onward* to the scientific community. (Goffman, 1975; Burke, 1969)

* searching for inferences derived from the observations for onward transmission to the scientific community, and in doing so, recognising that there may be a need to use varied forms of logic – logic which is 'fuzzy', or 'plausible', or statements which are only acceptable if they are hedged: 'not exactly …', or 'sort of …'.

* searching for ways of accomodating to the difficulties provoked by competing accounts which are offered – Castenada's works pose these difficulties nicely. (Castenada, 1973) Transformation may be seen as an aspect of context, the elements which comprise a context and the relationship between the elements (information, objects, actions, symbols, identities). A context is a

framework of memory, a set of related elements which gives sense to elements brought into relationship with it.

Transformation then, is a process, although not all processes are transformations. We may change elements or relationships within a context, or we may shift the same element to another context without transformation. (Bateson, 1972)

However merging of contexts frequently generates inconsistency and thus transformation. Transformation requires some shift in the interdependency between context and content.

Transformation may occur when ambiguity or uncertainty appears – there is a strain to consistency in our handling of data, and in resolving inconsistencies at certain levels we may produce transformation. Position and dominance are important in these processes, as are aesthetics and play, and some symbols have transformation inherent within them.

In transforming data we are likely to cluster them or to link them by chronological sequence, or by spatial contiguity, or more generally, by the characteristics of the data gathering operations. In re-sorting and writing up, we rearrange according to criteria of interest, fitness for argument, relevance to certain issues or topics or propositions. In a sense, too, the transforming operation is a problem solving operation, where the starting point poses questions or problems and the task is to answer those questions or to solve the problems.. This parallel makes all of the problem-solving literature potentially relevant to these processes, it also throws into importance the difference between information in a channel of communication and information in a channel of observation. Related to this is the distinction between research in a context of verification and research in a context of discovery. Inquiries designed to solve a given problem, to *verify* can be regarded as treating information as if in a channel of communication. The data located can be assessed according to how far they fill in the gaps in a known puzzle.

Each additional piece automatically has the property of reducing uncertainty, and learning, knowledge acquisition is synonymous with information acquisition. (Turner, 1977)

By contrast, however, inquiries designed to solve an unstated or an ambiguously stated problem, to *discover*, have to treat information as if in a channel of observation. The data located have to be assessed for relevance according to criteria of relevance generated by the observer. While a provisional puzzle may be delineated, and progress made towards solving it, the observer will also monitor this progress and may use judgement to jettison this goal and substitute another, particularly after *surprising* information has been acquired. This mode of progress is consistent with all of those accounts of puzzle-solving which require a reframing or a respecifying of the problem-assumption built into the original problem, transforming or understanding of it.

It is very helpful in this context the observations by the natural scientist Hans Selye about the manner in which he saw natural science ideas and theories coming into existence:

"The human brain is so constructed that it refuses to handle thoughts
unless they can be wrapped up more or less neatly in individual IDEA-
PACKAGES. It is astonishing how much confusion has been caused
by the failure to understand the following three simple facts:
(a) Thoughts, like fluids, can be adequately handled (isolated, meas-
     ured, mixed, sold) only when put up in individual containers;
(b) The thought packages contain previous experiences; only the se-
     lection within the wrapping can be new. We have no thoughts of
     things whose likeness we have never perceived before.
(c) The thought-packages, the idea units, are very loosely bound to-
     gether and their contents are not homogeneous".

                                                         (Selye, 1964, p. 268)

As Selye says, we put into packages those things which we have seen before,
but rearranged, and metaphor may be thought of as a way of rearranging them.
We see that this part of the world is like another entirely different part of the
world, and we use this vision as a guide to our reordering. How can we for-
malise this? Choose a metaphor. Then rearrange incoming data to resemble
the metaphor. That of course is absurdly over-simple, but how must we complicate it to make it more realistic? We would want to bear in mind the
complex, pervasive, connotative symbolic qualities of metaphor rather than
looking upon them solely as an information processing device. Miles and
Huberman refer to metaphor, but they seem to have a very impoverished idea
of what metaphor is or does, and not to realise that virtually all language and
thought is metaphoric.

Notes

  1.   Note that this usage is intended to refer to studies of social phenomena in their
'natural' settings, but it should be distinguished clearly from the long established philosophical use of the term 'naturalism', a position close to positivism and far removed
from naturalistic inquiry.
  2.   We are indebted to Nedira Yakir for the information that Gauguin, too, commented that the only things worth painting are those which are remembered.

References

Agar M., 1986, *Speaking of Ethnography*, Qualitative Method Series, 2, 1985, Beverly
     Hills, CA: Sage.
Baldamus W., 1976, *Inference and Substance in Sociology*, London: Martin Robertson.
Barzun J. & Graff H.F., 1977, *The Modern Researcher*, 3rd ed., New York: Harcourt Brace
     Jovanovich.
Basoux J., 1987, 'Women's contribution and the new vogue', *Times Higher Educational Supp.*
Bateson G., 1972, *Steps to an ecology of mind*, San Francisco: Chandler.

Bell C. & Newby R., eds, 1977, *Doing Sociological Research*, London: George Allen & Unwin.

Bryman A., ed., 1988, 'Connoisseurship in the study of organisational culture', *Doing Research in Organisations*, London: Routledge & Kegan Paul.

Burgess R.G., ed., 1982, *Field Research*, London: Allen and Unwin.

Burgess R., 1984, *In the Field*, London: Allen and Unwin.

Burke K., 1969, *A grammar of motives*, Berkeley: University of California Press.

Castaneda C., 1973, *Journey to Ixtlan: the lessons of Don Juan*, London: Bodley Head.

Coleman, J.S., 1965, *Introduction to Mathmatical Sociology*, New York: Basic Books.

Elbow P., 1981, *Writing with Power*, New York: Oxford Univ. Press.

Feyerabend P., 1975, *Against Method: outline of an anarchistic theory of knowledge*, London: N.L.B.

Glaser B., 1978, *Theoretical Sensitivity: Advances in the methodology of grounded theory*, Mill Valley, CA: Sociology Press.

Glaser B. & Strauss A., 1967, *The Discovery of Grounded Theory*, New York: Aldine.

Goffman I., 1975, *Frame Analysis*, Harmondsworth: Penguin Books.

Hage J., 1972, *Techniques and Problems of Theory Construction in Sociology*, New York: Wiley.

Hammond P., ed., 1964, *Sociologists at Work*, New York: Basic Books.

Hejzlar J., 1987, *Chinese Watercolours*, London: Galley Press.

Lincoln Y. & Guba E.G., 1985, *Naturalistic Inquiry*, Beverly Hill: Sage.

McGregor D., 1967, *The Professional Manager*, New York: McGraw Hill.

Martin P. & Turner B.A., 1987, 'Grounded theory and organisational research', *J. Applied Behavioral Science*, 22 (2), 141–157.

Miles M.B. & Huberman A.M., 1984, *Qualitative Data Analysis*, Beverly Hills: Sage.

Morgan G., 1983, *Beyond Method*, Beverly Hills: Sage.

Mullins C.J., 1977, *A Guide to Writing and Publishing in the Social and Behavioural Sciences*, New York: Wiley.

Naipaul, V.S., 1987, 'The enigma of arrival', *New Yorker*, 11 (Aug.) 26–62.

Peters T. & Waterman R., 1982, *In Search of Excellence*, New York: Harper & Row.

Pledge H.T., 1939, *Science since 1500*, London, H.M.S.O.

Polanyi M., 1959, *Personal Knowledge: towards a post-critical philosophy*, London: Routledge, Kegan Paul.

Ravetz J.R., 1971, *Scientific Knowledge and its Social Problems*, Oxford: Clarendon Press.

Ravetz J.R. & Funtowicz S.O., 1986, 'Policy-related research, a notational scheme for the expression of qualitative technical information', *J. Operational Research Soc.*, 37 (3), 243–247.

Reason P. & Rowen J., 1981, *Human Inquiry: a sourcebook of new paradigm research*, Chichester: Wiley.

Rosenberg M., 1968, *The Logic of Survey Analysis*, New York: Basic Books.

Selye H., 1964, *From Dream to Discovery: on being a scientist*, New York: McGraw Hill.

Silverman D., 1985, *Qualitative Methodology and Sociology*, Aldershot: Gower.

Strauss A., 1987, *Qualitative Analysis for Social Scientists*, Cambridge: C.U.P.

Strunk W. & White E.B., 1979, *The Elements of Style*, 3rd ed., New York: Collier Macmillan.

Suttles G.D., 1978, *The Social Order of the Slum: ethnicity and terror in the inner city*, Chicago: Univ. of Chicago Press.

Turner B.A., 1977, 'Research note: a comment on the nature of information in channels of observation', *Cybernetica* XX (1), 39–42.

—— 1981, 'Some practical aspects of qualitative data analysis: one way of organising some of the cognitive processes associated with the generation of grounded theory', *Quality and Quantity*, 15, 225–247.

—— 1987, 'Grounded theory and knowledge elicitation', Seminar presented at the Department of Civil Engineering, Bristol University, November, 1987.

—— 1988, 'Connoisseurship in the study of organisational culture', in A. Bryman, ed., *op. cit.*

Willer D.E. & Willer J., 1973, *Pseudo-empiricism: a critique of a pseudo-science*, Englewood Cliffs, N.J.: Preston-Hall.

Witkin R.W., 1971, *The Intelligence of Feeling*, London: Heinemann.

Zetterberg H., 1954, *On Theory and Verification in Sociology*, Stockholm: Almqvist & Wisksell.

7

Method Talk

Jaber F. Gubrium & James A. Holstein

The strange idea that reality has an idiom in which it prefers to be described, that its very nature demands we talk about it without fuss ... leads on to the even stranger idea that, if literalism is lost, so is fact.

Clifford Geertz, *Works and Lives: The Anthropologist as Author* (1988, p. 140)

The language of the social sciences shapes how researchers view the world. *Method talk* virtually leads them by the hand into the empiri cal realm. It is the working vocabulary of research procedure. One familiar idiom directs researchers to a real world of facts and figures. A second urges them to focus on how the real world is conceptualized or formed. Other research vocabularies stake out different empirical terrain.

If we accept the tenet that knowledge is humanly produced, it's not hard to conceive of sites of method talk as knowledge factories – places where the work of knowledge construction takes place. Extending the metaphor, colleges and universities stand out as production sites, since nearly all social researchers have professional ties to these institutions. A good way to hear method talk, then, might be to visit a production site, to drop in on a first-rate, if make-believe, department of sociology where research is the order of the day. We're certain to hear people discussing objectives and procedures, even "strange" ideas about reality.

Entering the department on the third floor of a weathered building near the center of campus, it's initially difficult to sort out exactly what's going on. There's not much to see, not a lot of action. But there's plenty of talk. Maybe it's important. Perhaps it's idle chatter. Let's listen.[1]

From offices and seminar rooms, in gatherings at mailboxes and computer terminals, we hear a distinctive vernacular, familiar, yet somehow arcane in its technical idiom. These sociologists are talking about our world, a reality

Source: Jaber F. Gubrium & James A. Holstein, *The New Language of Qualitative Method* (Oxford: Oxford University Press, 1997),

we know in our commonsense fashion, yet the way they talk gives it an almost unrecognizable substance and force. "Structural variables and causal models." "Units of analysis and sampling frames." "Operationalization and measurement." "Cluster analysis and multidimensional scaling." "Stochastic processes, multicolinearity, and autocorrelation." The highly technical vocabulary of quantitative positivism rings down the corridors, virtually permeating the walls. It's just what we'd expect from folks committed to treating social facts as things, then measuring them, with the aim of describing and explaining their relationships.

Around the corner, down the hallway and off to the side, we hear different conversations. From one office comes the earnest exhortation to "go and find out what's really happening!" There's lots of talk about *meaning*, especially what things mean to the people being studied. This is decidedly not talk about predictive models. *Lived* experience is on stage here. Rich description is the name of the game. There's little mention of standardized measurement. Instead we hear the trials and tribulations of "entrée and engagement," "access and rapport." In contrast to descriptions of social facts and variable relations from an "objective" distance – held at arm's length, so to speak – we hear the admonition to get close to people, be involved. "You've got to get out there, into the nitty-gritty, real world. Get your hands dirty. See it up close, for yourself." This must be the qualitative contingent of the department.

A rather small group, this bunch, surrounded by the typical motley collection of skeptical graduate students and other souls who never mastered the nuances of linear regression. The group is easily identified by talk that seems more experientially poignant. If we listen closely, we can even detect distinct dialects, overlapping only slightly with the language of their quantitative cousins.

Here's someone saying that research has become "too damned behavioral, overly cognitive. We have to pay more attention to what really distinguishes human nature." We soon learn that this means paying attention to the truly subjective. "How do emotions *feel?*" "We can't be too scientific because human experience doesn't fit a completely rational model." "Deep down, we are more than cogs on social gears or actors in society's little dramas."

Next door, the discussion centers on human agency and the need to appreciate the richly layered skills, assumptions, and practices through which persons construct the very realities of their everyday lives. We hear that the researcher must always "be careful not to confuse the subjects' categories and concepts with her own analytic constructs." The point, the speaker reminds her listeners, is to see how members of social settings *accomplish* a sense of social order that they experience as real. And we hear words of caution: "Society members' constructions and categories are what we study, so we mustn't slip up by using members' categories as our own explanatory concepts. Remember, they are our topics, not our resources. And above all, *never argue with the members!*"

Across the hall, we hear a voice sounding unsettlingly like that of a literary critic. We haven't wandered into the English Department, have we? But as we listen, we're reassured that we are still in the right place. "Our own sociological work, qualitative work, is inscribed in realist terms that derive from our own authoritative voice." It seems like we're hearing that there's no possibility of unmediated, unfussy description, and that what we know is an artifact of our authority as researchers and writers. It's a matter of "displaced or projected desires." Nearby, we hear other, almost foreign, voices concerned with "image and simulacra," "decenteredness and polysemy," "electronic mediation," and "hyperreality." To what *are* we listening? What does this have to do with qualitative research? What's going on here?

Varieties of Method Talk

At one level, everyone we've heard is talking sociology. But the diversity of lexicons strikes us as significant, the variety of messages crucial. We've overheard some not-so-idle chatter about research procedure and how that relates to empirical reality. The talk deals with how the researcher orients to and interprets facts. Broadly speaking, these are the concerns of any workplace. If we were seeking insight anywhere into how procedural knowledge relates to what is produced, we would certainly take this form of talk into account. Why not consider what method talk can tell us about social research and social reality?

That's what this book aims to accomplish. In its way, it is a sociology of knowledge. It's about what Clifford Geertz, in the opening epigram, refers to as "idioms" of reality. It considers the way the language of qualitative method relates to how researchers view and describe social life. We intentionally use the term *method* (rather than the plural, *methods*) to signal a primary interest in the knowledge-producing dimensions of the various research idioms comprising qualitative inquiry. We noted earlier that method implies a way of knowing as much as techniques for gathering information. In practice, it is, in Ludwig Wittgenstein's (1958) words, "a language game" or "way of life" in the sense that the manner in which one proceeds to do social research organizes the empirical contours of what is under investigation. Method connotes a manner of viewing and talking about reality as much as it specifies technique and procedure.

Qualitative research is a diverse enterprise (see Denzin and Lincoln 1994). Perhaps because it is typically counterposed with the contemporary monolith of quantitative sociology, qualitative method is often portrayed in broad strokes that blur differences. We believe it's important to recognize and appreciate these differences in order to evaluate their separate contributions as well as their overall direction. More importantly, we need to be more aware of the way the language of qualitative method shapes knowledge of social reality. This is impossible if we fail to distinguish working assumptions about the world, conceptualizations of everyday life, and, in particular, vocabularies of research procedure. Our strategy for understanding the diversity of qualitative research is to treat each variant as an enterprise that develops, and is conducted in, a language or idiom of its own. Accordingly, each idiom presents a distinctive reality, virtually constituting its empirical horizons. This chapter highlights just how revealing language is in this regard, setting the stage for the more detailed discussion that follows.

The sociology of work and occupations teaches us that a good way of understanding a profession or occupation is through everyday shoptalk, and we assume that the work of social researchers is no different (see Hughes 1971; Garfinkel 1986, 1995; Miller 1981). The language of quantitative, positivist sociology, for example, owes a profound debt to the natural sciences for both its empirical vision and its orientation to research procedure (Lepenies 1988; Filmer et al., 1973). It pervasively reflects the foundational presumption of an objective world of concrete components that can be represented in terms of "hard data." This world is obdurate and tangible enough in some cases, to put one's finger on, both metaphorically and literally. The research enterprise revolves around measurement and analysis, typically ordering numerically represented variables into explanatory models. The substantiality and coherence of the world so conveyed are impressive. But it is also an artifact of the procedural vocabulary itself. Method talk in the quantitative workplace conveys a deep commitment to systematically and rigorously representing a separate and distinct order of things without disturbing or distorting that order in the process. The talk provides communicative directives for just what the world might be; details are described and problems are solved against this linguistic backdrop.

The language of qualitative research is equally compelling, presenting its own distinctive reality-constituting endeavors, with different interests, goals, and strategies. Let us briefly describe four approaches whose procedural idioms have made their mark on contemporary qualitative research: naturalism, ethnomethodology, emotionalism, and postmodernism. While these are not the only, nor necessarily the "best," of qualitative approaches, viewed comparatively they help us demonstrate how differently method talk can convey the "facts" of the social world.[2]

Describing What Comes Naturally

Naturalism is the original and, arguably, the predominant language of qualitative research. The naturalistic impulse resonates at some level throughout the other idioms. Its goal is to understand social reality on its own terms "as it really is," to describe what comes naturally, so to speak. Taken in its simplest form, naturalism seeks rich descriptions of people and interaction as they exist and unfold in their native habitats. The people have ranged from prisoners and felons (Giallombardo 1966; Irwin 1970; Jones and Schmid 1997), the mentally ill or disturbed (Perrucci 1974; Estroff 1981), and the mentally handicapped (Edgerton 1967) to medical students (Becker et al., 1961; Haas and Shaffir 1987), surgeons (Bosk 1979), seminarians (Kleinman 1984), fantasy gamers (Fine 1983), the homeless (Snow and Anderson 1993), and the elderly (Hochschild 1973). Some of the distinct habitats have been nursing homes (Gubrium 1975; Diamond 1992), hospitals (Glaser and Strauss 1965, 1968), restaurants (Paules 1991), schools and playgrounds (Adler and Adler, 1991; Thorne 1993), households (Hochschild 1989; Rubin 1976), communities (Gans 1962; Suttles 1968), taverns (Spradley and Mann 1975), and street corners (Whyte 1943; Liebow 1967; Anderson 1976). The range of experiences and locales is breathtaking and the interpretations have been remarkably insightful.

Naturalistic method talk is replete with prescriptions and injunctions for capturing social reality on its home turf. Among the earliest and most colorful pleas came from Robert Park, one of the founders of the Chicago School of field research. Reacting to what he saw as "armchair sociology," Park insisted that social researchers become more involved in the real world (Bulmer 1984). Researchers had to get close to the sources of their data; data had to emanate directly from real life. Insisting that his students get "their hands dirty in real research," Park eschewed the research library and official statistics, preferring firsthand observation of city streets, dance halls, hotels, and the like. He virtually implored his students to find data in the natural settings that captured their interest:

> Go and sit in the lounges of the luxury hotels and on the doorsteps of the flophouses; sit on the Gold Coast settees and on the slum shakedowns; sit in Orchestra Hall and in the Star and Garter Burlesque. In short, gentlemen, go get the seat of your pants dirty in real research. (McKinney 1966, p. 71)

It was not enough for Park to simply exhort participant observation. He also insisted that "what sociologists most need to know is what goes on behind the faces of men" (1950, pp. vi–vii). Years later, Erving Goffman (1961) elaborated this appreciation for natively meaningful worlds:

> My immediate objective in doing fieldwork at St. Elizabeth's [psychiatric hospital] was to try to learn about the world of the hospital inmate, as this world is subjectively experienced by him.... It was then and still is my belief that any group of persons – prisoners, primitives, pilots, or patients – develop a life of their own that becomes meaningful, reasonable, and normal once you get close to it, and that a good way to learn about any of these worlds is to submit oneself in the company of the members to the daily round of petty contingencies to which they are subject. (Pp. ix–x)

From this language, we begin to see a working epistemology, a way of knowing that locates meaningful reality in the immediate settings of people's daily affairs. It is the settings' sheer naturalness that makes them authentic. Empirical inquiry must first of all respect the boundaries of real life, but at

the same time penetrate them to reveal what is held in store. The added caution typically is to get close enough to people to recognize and describe the
exquisite details of their social world, but without "going native."

Hearing How It's Done

If naturalism attempts to look inside the social worlds of real people as they
experience those worlds, *ethnomethodology* and several related constructionist
approaches want to look at, and listen to, the social activities through which
everyday actors produce the recognizable features of those social worlds.
Whereas the naturalistic researcher attends to what his or her informants say
in order to understand what things mean to them, the ethnomethodologist
listens to naturally occurring conversation in order to discover how a sense
of social order is created through talk and interaction. At the heart of the research is a deep concern for the ordinary, everyday procedures and practices
that society's members use to make their social experiences sensible, understandable, accountable, and orderly (Garfinkel 1967).

Rather than treating social facts or social structure as objectively natural
parameters, ethnomethodologists approach structure and organization as
achievements in their own right. They are interested in the interpretive activities that persons undertake, moment by moment, to construct, manage, and
sustain the sense that their social worlds exist as factual and objectively "there."
While its focus is more on the construction of social worlds than on experiential meaning, ethnomethodology still maintains a naturalistic orientation in the
sense that it wants to describe in detail the everyday knowledge and interpretive procedures that are used to accomplish social reality (Heritage 1984b).

Given its concern with reality-constituting practices, ethnomethodological
method talk must accommodate active, dynamic social process. Rather than
focusing naturalistically on the more or less stable yet developing, experiential
contours of everyday life, it examines how these contours are continuously
"talked into being" in the first place (Heritage 1984b). The commonplace phenomena that interest the naturalist are temporarily set aside in order to examine
the interactional processes through which those phenomena are constructed.
This requires the ethnomethodological vocabulary to be one of actions more
than things, of social practices more than social settings or social forces.

Ethnomethodology is especially attuned to communicative activity. From
this perspective, conversation is the machinery of reality construction. Ethnomethodological method talk, then, is largely "talk about talk." Its mandate
is for the researcher not only to watch, but also and especially to *listen*, in order
to discern how reality is produced. Taking reality as an interactional activity
(Mehan and Wood 1975) thus requires a vocabulary that can adequately convey what is learned when researchers "hear how reality is done."

As simple as this sounds, ethnomethodological method talk is often quite
esoteric. Less patient or sympathetic observers might describe it as impenetra-
bly complex. One must keep in mind, however, that ethnomethodology wants

to make the taken-for-granted into its research problem. In a sense, it takes social structure – sociology's stock in trade – and turns it upside down. Structure is not viewed as a force compelling and constraining actors; instead it is taken to be a product of social action itself. Listen closely as the pioneer of ethnomethodology, Harold Garfinkel (1967), tells us how describing the "accomplishment" of the taken-for-granted is ethnomethodology's research mission:

> In doing sociology, lay and professional, every reference to the "real world" ... is a reference to the organized public activities of everyday life. Thereby, in contrast to certain versions of Durkheim that teach that the objective reality of social facts is sociology's fundamental principle, the lesson is taken instead, and used as a study policy, that the objective reality of social facts as an ongoing accomplishment of the concerted activities of daily life, with the ordinary, artful ways of that accomplishment being known, used, and taken for granted, is, for members doing sociology, a fundamental phenomenon. Because, and in the ways it is practical sociology's fundamental phenomenon, it is the prevailing topic for ethnomethodological study. Ethnomethodological studies analyze everyday activities as members' methods for making those same activities visibly-rational-and-reportable-for-all practical-purposes. (P. vii)

This extract is typical of what some might call Garfinkel's convoluted method talk, yet it also reveals the signal and unconventional aim of the ethnomethodological project. While the prose is uncommonly dense, it nonetheless provides the patient and careful reader with a sense of ethnomethodology's goal of analyzing and making visible the interactional practices that give taken-for-granted social facts their apparent reality.

Exploring Emotionality

As some qualitative researchers plunge headlong into the subjective, their method talk suggests that being "up close and on the scene" is not enough. For these researchers, subjectivity is truly understood only by delving "inside" experience, usually figuratively, but sometimes literally. Jack Douglas (1977), for example, argues that nearly all versions of sociology overrationalize lived experience, and, in qualitative research, he thinks this is most characteristic of ethnomethodology (see Douglas and Johnson 1977). For Douglas, "*brute being* is that core of feeling and perception that is our innermost selves, our being" (p. 3, emphasis in the original). According to Douglas, this is hardly captured by the methodical analysis of talk and interaction that is limited to the transcripts of audiotapes. To comprehend the depths of social life and lived experience, the researcher must "understand the total man in his total natural environment" (p. 4). Significantly, this extends researchers' interest to *emotionality.* Partly echoing the voice of conventional naturalism, yet now distinctly romanticist, Douglas highlights an inner dimension of reality. Calling for "deep-deep probes into the human soul," he tells us (1985, p. 51) that access to the truths of experience is not gained by mere proximity. It requires open sharing and intimacy, affective sensitivity, even the surrender of "soul" necessary to developing true empathy and understanding. The goal is to capture, even *reenact,* the subject's experience and to describe that in full emotional color.

There is a conspicuous absence here of scientific sounding jargon. This emotionalist idiom is humanistic, even existential. While focusing on naturally occurring settings and interaction, method talk turns from what research subjects do and how they accomplish it, to what they feel. If Park's injunctions played up the need to get one's hands and pants dirty by observing on the scene, the talk of those investigating subjectivity calls for even more intimate contact. This typically is conveyed in the vocabulary of immersion and introspection:

> We do not stand outside experience.... We do not put society on a rack and try to torture the truth out of it.... We seek truth in the ways we find necessary in the natural social world. We create truth from within by finding what works, what enables us to understand, explain, piece together, and partially predict our social world. (Douglas 1977, p. 5)

The range of affective experiences studied by the emotionalists is broad and deep, from heart wrenching child custody hearings (Johnson 1975), emotionally draining abortion decisions (Ellis and Bochner 1992), and the experience of chronic pain (Kotarba 1977), to the seductions of crime (Katz 1988). Because the depths of experience are often considered to be outside the scope of traditional forms of documentation, these qualitative researchers have increasingly experimented with unconventional representational strategies (Richardson 1990). Some express emotional experience through poetry (Richardson 1992), while others turn to dramatic techniques (Ellis and Bochner 1992; Paget 1995) and introspective field notes (Ronai 1992).

For many, the final arbiter of authenticity is the subject. He or she alone knows what the experience under consideration is really like, especially how it feels. Use your own emotional experience, the researcher is told. Delve into personal biography and take the subject's point of view. Give voice to your own feelings (Ellis 1991b). This is not Park's exhortation to show up on reality's doorstep. It is a challenge to go inside, to the heart and soul of the matter.

Postmodernist Self-consciousness

Qualitative researchers have become more and more self-conscious, especially about the relation between method talk and the nature of social reality. There is a growing awareness that the relation is reflexive, that research procedure constructs reality as much as it produces descriptions of it. Listen as Joseph Schneider (1993) simulates a conversation about how sociologists use their analytic texts to bring themselves "into being" as descriptive authorities set apart from their subjects:

> We are the analysts; the experts; the scientists. Our project – our man-date – is to divide the world into them and us, and then to study them and explain why and how they do what they do. You've got to get that clear or you're in for serious personal problems. *They* don't analyze what they do – they don't think about it the way we do; they just do it. We analyze, sociologically, what they do and tell them (and each other) why they behave that way. That's our game (and "it is played").
>   But what about us? What about what we do?
>   You don't get it, do you? Our job is to analyze social *life*, not us.
>   Oh. Yeah. (p 103, emphasis in the original)

As qualitative research has become sensitive to the constructed nature of the social world – to the multiplicity of experiential realities that might be created, including the reality of method as a way of knowing – a crisis has developed concerning the relation between the researcher, representational practice, and those studied. The crisis provokes the question of how, if realities are accomplishments, those realities reported by researchers can be anything but accomplishments themselves. What is the basis for treating research reports as authoritative? How can they be authentic if they, too, are merely representations of experience, themselves grounded in particular places and perspectives?

Method talk becomes problematic in its own right as analysts begin to scrutinize the ways we "write culture" (Clifford and Marcus 1986) or write "against" it (Abu-Lughod 1991), read ethnography (Hammersley 1990; Atkinson 1992), or represent science and its findings (Lynch and Woolgar 1988). Sociological texts, and the practices and circumstances that produce them, become objects for analysis. We examine how qualitative researchers observe, listen, and write, asking, for example, how the exercise of "ethnographic imagination" or the ethnographer's craft constitutes ethnography. In the process, textual explication becomes a research method (Atkinson 1990).

The "crisis of representation" has inspired a host of attempts to "deconstruct" research to reveal its reality-constituting practices. This has produced its own brand of self-consciousness, embodied in *postmodernist* method talk designed to characterize a world whose "free-floating" signs and meanings are set loose from distinct social moorings. Some view this self-consciousness as self-indulgent (Best 1995), as it privileges the act of representation over the represented, sometimes completely upstaging reality. Nonetheless, the language of this so-called postmodern moment reveals an important formulation of what method can mean for the facts produced by researchers.

Common Threads

This brief survey points out some key differences between idioms of qualitative inquiry. Before we are inundated by difference, however, we must remember that the approaches have a great deal in common regarding the research enterprise as a whole. These similarities become more apparent if we consider those concerns that have traditionally animated qualitative research. With common threads firmly established, we can then turn to a more extended discussion of differences in the following chapters of Part I. Part II will then attempt to show how the differences and the common threads might be woven into an analytic fabric that we call a renewed language of qualitative method.

Working Skepticism

Skepticism about what everyone ostensibly knows motivates much qualitative research. The skepticism derives from an uneasiness with the wisdom of received description. While this has been said to characterize the sociological imagination generally (see Mills 1959), it is the everyday calling card of qualitative researchers, who have traditionally tried to describe social life in ways that challenge popular understandings. The underlying presumption is that conventional appraisals, especially systematic quantitative assessments, fail to appreciate the nuances of the social world.

The skepticism prompts various strategies of inquiry, from "debunking" what is commonly thought to be true (that is, exposing the falsities of everyday understandings), to empathizing as completely as possible with those being studied and appreciating their articulations, feelings, and circumstances as they, themselves, do. At either extreme, there is the presupposition that what is conventionally known is somehow lacking. Indeed, as ethnomethodologists express it, the commonly known itself is subject to study for the way it is socially organized and taken for granted.

Commitment to Close Scrutiny

The orienting skepticism prompts qualitative researchers to scrutinize at close range, to place themselves in direct contact with, or in immediate proximity to, the lived world of those being studied. This is not done for the purpose of intervention or social reform, although such goals might indirectly motivate the research. Rather, researchers engage in close scrutiny in order to understand and document the organization of social life as it is practiced. The goal has been to look closely at social phenomena to see that which other kinds of inquiry may have missed.

Close scrutiny may involve a variety of techniques, from trying to document the naturally occurring details of talk and interaction to attempts to reenact subjects' feelings. While methods of close scrutiny vary, the goals are

basically the same: to see the unseen in its own right, to represent the unknown in living color. Qualitative researchers are typically committed to
viewing the details of experience, deferring if not eschewing the broad strokes
of generalization in favor of describing particulars. Sweeping claims about the
influence of social forces that often characterize sociological research are likely
to be softened, qualified, set aside, or replaced by more painstaking accounts
of the complex minutiae of everyday life. But the detail is not trivial; qualitative researchers characteristically maintain that only close scrutiny can give
voice to the eloquence of the commonplace.

Search for the "Qualities" of Social Life

Concern for detail allows qualitative research to pay special attention to the
"qualities" of experience, aspects of life that quantitative approaches typically
gloss over. Indeed, this may be a defining distinction between the two. Rather
than simply enumerating categories of social structure or interaction, qualitative researchers seek to understand and describe the categories as problematic
in their own right. What quantitative researchers take for granted, their qualitative kindred study for meaningful substance, working boundaries, and
everyday usage. For qualitative researchers, categories of social life are not
so much given as they are subject to careful and systematic scrutiny in themselves.

   Those seeking predictive or explanatory models of social behavior often
decry qualitative studies as "merely descriptive," but qualitative researchers
have staunchly resisted the pejorative connotation. Instead, they insist that we
must have a good, clear picture of the qualities of the world before we can
attempt to explain it, let alone predict or modify it. Thus, description justifies
itself, as researchers aim to apprehend and comprehend the diversity, intri-
cacy, subtlety, and complications that compose the social.

Focus on Process

Qualitative research also is distinguished by a commitment to studying social
life in process, as it unfolds. Researchers extend their analyses of the qualities
of the social to the ways its processes both enter into, and reflexively constitute, everyday life. Because the various idioms share an understanding of the
social world as fluid and elastic, they direct their attention to the working definitions and procedures by which that world is given meaning. Seeing people
as active agents of their affairs, qualitative inquiry has traditionally focused
on how purposeful actors participate in, construct, deeply experience, or imagine their lives.

   The various approaches may differ on just what role process plays, however. For some, it is a configuration of meaningful responses to the
circumstances and contingencies of an obdurate, yet manageable reality. For
others, social process constitutes the very circumstances, contingencies, and

meanings of everyday life. Yet, while it differs from one idiom to the next, there is an enduring appreciation for the working subject who actively injects life into, and shapes, her or his world.

Appreciation for Subjectivity

For better or worse, qualitative inquiry has long been associated with subjectivity. One misinformed criticism alleges that qualitative research is little more than a set of subjective impressions, unsubstantiated by rigorous research procedure or "hard" data. This ignores the subject and the subjective as integral features of social life, and neglects the fact that the researcher is a subject in his or her own right, present in the same world as those studied. As we will see in Chapter 5, some qualitative researchers have taken this to heart and it has led to a crisis of representation. At the same time, both the focus on subjectivity and the crisis have enhanced the appreciation for subjectivity. This is now tied to the key question of how to represent matters that cannot be literally described by an objective observer.

Qualitative researchers have long insisted that they are not lax, imprecise, or unsystematic, and have now assembled a massive technical literature attesting to this (see Denzin and Lincoln 1994). Still, they can never completely distance themselves from subjectivity, inasmuch as subjectivity, broadly speaking, is their domain. Reluctance to standardize data collection and unwillingness to sacrifice depth for generality are matters of analytic necessity, not technical inadequacies. A world comprised of meanings, interpretations, feelings, talk, and interaction must be scrutinized on its own terms. Qualitative inquiry has always maintained this commitment, now more than ever.

Striving for rigor, qualitative research also honors perspective. For some researchers, this means documenting versions of subjectivity, such as describing how something looks or feels from various subjects' viewpoints. Indeed, portraying the world from alternate vantage points has been a goal of qualitative research from the earliest ventures of the Chicago School, all the way to the imperatives of contemporary, poststructuralist feminists (Reinharz 1992; Harding 1987; Smith 1987). As different as qualitative researchers' descriptions might (indeed, must) be, the common thread here is the recognition that subjectivity is perspectival. While some qualitative researchers are not so much interested in subjects' inner experiences as they are in the possibility of subjectivity and subjects' mundane belief in the perspectival nature of experience and personal knowledge (see Pollner 1987), the topic of subjectivity nonetheless is paramount.

Tolerance for Complexity

Finally, qualitative researchers maintain an abiding interest in interactional complexity. While this is sometimes mistaken for analytic fuzziness or a reluctance to generalize, it more accurately reflects the researchers' orientation to the working intricacies of human agency and circumstance. A skeptical orientation to the commonplace, a commitment to the close scrutiny of social action, the recognition of variety and detail, the focus on process, and the appreciation of subjectivity, all, in one form or another, suggest that everyday life is not straightforwardly describable. This could hardly be captured by the operational designation of variables, social forces, and the like. A subsequent tolerance for complexity militates against the impulse to gloss over troublesome uncertainties, anomalies, irregularities, and inconsistencies in the interest of comprehensive, totalizing explanation. As a matter of principle, qualitative inquiry accommodates and pursues the problematic finding or the unanticipated occurrence. The research in many ways mirrors, and is mirrored by, its findings, offering the world as fine-grained, variegated, and to some extent, always resistant to comprehensive explanation.

The common threads combine to underscore the complexity of meaning. Writing of the methodological position of symbolic interactionism, but speaking in terms congenial to most qualitative approaches, Herbert Blumer (1969) articulated the following principle:

> The meanings that things have for human beings are central in their own right. To ignore the meaning of the things toward which people act is seen as falsifying the behavior under study. To bypass the meaning in favor of factors alleged to produce the behavior is seen as a grievous neglect of the role of meaning in the formation of behavior. (P. 3)

The methodological implications are clear, as Blumer once again notes:

> We can and, I think, must look upon human group life as chiefly a vast interpretive process in which people singly and collectively guide themselves by defining objects, events, and situations which they encounter.... Any scheme designed to analyze human group life in its general character has to fit this process of interpretation ... interpretation is a formative or creative process in its own right. It constructs meanings which, as I have said, are not predetermined. (Pp. 132–35)

The pursuit of meaning plunges qualitative inquiry into the complexities of social context. On the one hand, context is interactive. People develop and use meanings with respect to themselves and others. Because interaction resists analysis in terms of fixed variables (Blumer 1969), qualitative research has taken responsibility for its "thick description" (Geertz 1973). The constitutive theoretical linkage to method is undeniable: if everyday life is construed as ongoingly social, it can be analyzed only by way of flexible, empathetic, qualitative technique. On the other hand, context implies circumscribed configurations of understanding, or culture. Here, we take culture in its broadest sense, as complexes of shared usages that distinguish a community, a setting, or a situation. These are webs of significance, more or less fixed, that variably suffuse and surround everyday life, yet also offer members resources for further interpretation (Geertz 1973). Taken together, interaction and culture both specify and generate meaning, the study of which is necessarily complex.

References

Abu-Lughod, Lila. 1991. "Writing against Culture." Pp. 137–62 in *Recapturing Anthropology*, edited by Richard Fox. Santa Fe, NM: School of American Research Press.

Adler, Patricia A. and Peter Adler. 1991. *Backboards and Blackboards*. New York: Columbia University Press.

Anderson, Elijah. 1976. *A Place on the Corner*. Chicago: University of Chicago Press.

Atkinson, Paul. 1990. *The Ethnographic Imagination*. London: Routledge.

—— 1992. *Understanding Ethnographic Texts*. Thousand Oaks, CA: Sage.

Becker, Howard, Blanch Geer, Everett Hughes, and Anselm Strauss. 1961. *Boys in White*. Chicago: University of Chicago Press.

Best, Joel. 1995. "Lost in the Ozone Again: The Postmodernist Fad and Interactionist Foibles." *Studies in Symbolic Interaction*. 17:125–30.

Blumer, Herbert. 1969. *Symbolic Interactionism*. Englewood Cliffs, NJ: Prentice-Hall.

Bosk, Charles. 1979. *Forgive and Remember*. Chicago: University of Chicago Press.

Bulmer, Martin. 1984. *The Chicago School*. Chicago: University of Chicago Press.

Clifford. James and George E. Marcus (eds.). 1986. *Writing Culture*. Berkeley, CA: University of California Press.

Denzin, Norman K. and Yvonna S. Lincoln (eds.). 1994. *Handbook of Qualitative Research*. Thousand Oaks, CA: Sage.

Diamond, Timothy. 1992. *Making Gray Gold*. Chicago: University of Chicago Press.

Douglas, Jack D. 1977. "Existential Sociology." Pp. 3–73 in *Existential Sociology*, edited by J. D. Douglas and J. M. Johnson. New York: Cambridge University Press.

Douglas, Jack D. 1985. *Creative Interviewing*. Beverly Hills, CA: Sage.

Douglas, Jack D. and John M. Johnson (eds.). 1977. *Existential Sociology*. New York: Cambridge University Press.

Edgerton, Robert B. 1967. *The Cloak of Competence*. Berkeley: University of California Press.

Ellis, Carolyn. 1991b. "Sociological Introspection and Emotional Experience." *Symbolic Interaction* 14:23–50.

Ellis, Carolyn and Arthur P. Bochner. 1992. "Telling and Performing Personal Stories." Pp. 79–101 in *Investigating Subjectivity*, edited by C. Ellis and M. G. Flaherty. Newbury Park, CA: Sage.

Estroff, Sue E. 1981. *Making it Crazy*. Berkeley: University of California Press.

Filmer, Paul, Michael Phillipson, David Silverman, and David Walsh. 1973. *New Directions in Sociological Theory*. Cambridge, MA: MIT Press.

Fine, Gary Alan. 1983. *Shared Fantasy*. Chicago: University of Chicago Press.

Gans, Herbert. 1962. *The Urban Villagers*. New York: Free Press.

Garfinkel, Harold. 1967. *Studies in Ethnomethodology*. Englewood Cliffs, NY: Prentice-Hall.

—— (ed.). 1986. *Ethnomethodological Studies of Work*. London: Routledge and Kegan Paul.

—— 1995. "Shop Floor Achievements and Shop Floor Theorizing in the Work of Designed Enterprises: Constituents of the Shop Floor Problem." Presented at the Annual Meeting of the American Sociological Association, August, Washington, D.C.

Geertz, Clifford. 1973. *The Interpretation of Cultures*. New York: Basic Books.

—— 1988. *Works and Lives: The Anthropologist as Author*. Stanford, CA: Stanford University Press.

Giallombardo, Rose. 1966. *Society of Women*. New York: Wiley.

Glaser, Barney G. and Anselm L. Strauss. 1965. *Awareness of Dying*. Chicago: Aldine.

—— 1968. *Time for Dying*. Chicago: Aldine.

Goffman, Erving. 1961. *Asylums*. Garden City, NY: Doubleday.

Gubrium, Jaber F. 1975. *Living and Dying at Murray Manor*. New York: St. Martin's.

Haas, Jack and William Shaffir. 1987. *Becoming Doctors*. Greenwich, CT: JAI Press.

Hammersley, Martyn. 1990. *Reading Ethnographic Research: A Critical Guide*. London: Longman.

Harding, Sandra (ed.). 1987. *Feminism and Methodology*. Bloomington: Indiana University Press.

Heritage, John. 1984b. *Garfinkel and Ethnomethodology*. Cambridge: Polity.

Hochschild, Arlie R. 1973. *The Unexpected Community*. Berkeley: University of California Press.

—— 1989. *The Second Shift*. New York: Viking.

Hughes, Everett C. 1971. *The Sociological Eye: Selected Papers*. Chicago: Aldine.

Irwin, John. 1970. *The Felon*. Englewood Cliffs, NJ: Prentice-Hall.

Johnson, John M. 1975. *Doing Field Research*. New York: Free Press.

Jones, Richard S. and Thomas Schmid. 1997. *Doing Time: Prison Experience and Identity*. Greenwich, CT: JAI Press.

Katz, Jack. 1988. *Seductions of Crime*. New York: Basic Books.

Kleinman, Sherryl. 1984. *Equals before God*. Chicago: University of Chicago Press.

Kotarba, Joseph A. 1977. "The Chronic Pain Experience." Pp. 257–72 in *Existential Sociology*, edited by J. Douglas and J. Johnson. Cambridge: Cambridge University Press.

Lepenies, Wolf. 1988. *Between Literature and Science: The Rise of Sociology*. New York: Cambridge University Press.

Liebow, Elliot. 1967. *Tally's Corner*. Boston: Little, Brown.

Lynch, Michael and Steven Woolgar. 1988. "Sociological Orientations to Representational Practice in Science." *Human Studies* 11:99–116.

McKinney, John C. 1966. *Constructive Typology and Social Theory*. New York: Appleton-Century Crofts.

Mehan, Hugh and Houston Wood. 1975. *The Reality of Ethnomethodology*. New York: Wiley.

Miller, Gale. 1981. *It's a Living*. New York: St. Martin's.

Mills, C. Wright. 1959. *The Sociological Imagination*. New York: Oxford University Press.

Paget, Marianne A. 1995. "Performing the Text." Pp. 222–44 in *Representation in Ethnography*, edited by J. Van Mannen. Thousand Oaks, CA: Sage.

Park, Robert E. 1950. "An Autobiographical Note." Pp. vi–ix in *Race and Culture*. Glencoe IL: Free Press.

Paules, Gerta. 1991. *Dishing It Out*. Philadephia: Temple University Press.

Perrucci, Robert. 1974. *Circle of Madness*. Englewood Cliffs, NJ: Prentice-Hall.

Pollner, Melvin. 1987. *Mundane Reason*. New York: Cambridge University Press.

Reinharz, Shulamit. 1992. *Feminist Methods in Social Research*. New York: Oxford University Press.

Richardson, Laurel. 1990. *Writing Strategies.* Newbury Park, CA: Sage.

—— 1992. "The Consequences of Poetic Representation." Pp. 125–37 in *Investigating Subjectivity,* edited by C. Ellis and M. Flaherty. Thousand Oaks, CA: Sage.

Ronai, Carol R. 1992. "The Reflexive Self through Narrative." Pp. 102–24 in *Investigating Subjectivity,* edited by C. Ellis and M. Flaherty. Newbury Park, CA: Sage.

Rubin, Lillian B. 1976. *Worlds of Pain: Life in the Working Class Family.* New York: Basic Books.

Schneider, Joseph. 1993. "'Members Only': Reading the Constructionist Text." Pp. 103–116 in *Reconsidering Social Constructionism: Debates in Social Problems Theory,* edited by J. Holstein and G. Miller. Hawthorne, NY: Aldine de Gruyter.

Smith, Dorothy E. 1987. *The Everyday World as Problematic.* Boston: Northeastern University Press.

Snow, David A. and Leon Anderson. 1993. *Down on Their Luck: A Study of Homeless Street People.* Berkeley: University of California Press.

Spradley, James P. and Brenda J. Mann. 1975. *Cocktail Waitress.* New York: Wiley.

Suttles, Gerald. 1968. *The Social Order of the Slum.* Chicago: University of Chicago Press.

Thorne, Barrie. 1993. *Gender Play: Girls and Boys in School.* New Brunswick, NJ: Rutgers University Press.

Wittgenstein, Ludwig. 1958. *Philosophical Investigations.* New York: Macmillan.

Whyte, William Foote. 1943. *Street Corner Society.* Chicago: University of Chicago Press.

8

Building Theories from Case Study Research

Kathleen M. Eisenhardt

D evelopment of theory is a central activity in organizational research. Traditionally, authors have developed theory by combining observations from previous literature, common sense, and experience. However, the tie to actual data has often been tenuous (Perrow, 1986; Pfeffer, 1982). Yet, as Glaser and Strauss (1967) argue, it is the intimate connection with empirical reality that permits the development of a testable, relevant, and valid theory.

This paper describes building theories from case studies. Several aspects of this process are discussed in the literature. For example, Glaser and Strauss (1967) detailed a comparative method for developing grounded theory, Yin (1981, 1984) described the design of case study research, and Miles and Huberman (1984) codified a series of procedures for analyzing qualitative data. However, confusion surrounds the distinctions among qualitative data, inductive logic, and case study research. Also, there is a lack of clarity about the process of actually building theory from cases, especially regarding the central inductive process and the role of literature. Glaser and Strauss (1967) and more recently Strauss (1987) have outlined pieces of the process, but theirs is a prescribed formula, and new ideas have emerged from methodologists (e.g., Yin, 1984; Miles & Huberman, 1984) and researchers conducting this type of research (e.g., Gersick, 1988; Harris & Sutton, 1986; Eisenhardt & Bourgeois, 1988). Also, it appears that no one has explicitly examined when this theory-building approach is likely to be fruitful and what its strengths and weaknesses may be.

This paper attempts to make two contributions to the literature. The first is a roadmap for building theories from case study research. This roadmap synthesizes previous work on qualitative methods (e.g., Miles & Huberman, 1984), the design of case study research (e.g., Yin, 1981, 1984), and grounded theory building (e.g., Glaser & Strauss, 1967) and extends that work in areas such as a priori specification of constructs, triangulation of multiple investigators,

Source: *Academy of Management Review*, vol. 14, 1989, pp. 532–550.

Table 1: Process of Building Theory from Case Study Research

Step	Activity	Reason
Getting Started	Definition of research question	Focuses efforts
	Possibly a priori constructs	Provides better grounding of construct measures
	Neither theory nor hypotheses	Retains theoretical flexibility
Selecting Cases	Specified population	Constrains extraneous variation and sharpens external validity
	Theoretical, not random, sampling	Focuses efforts on theoretically useful cases – i.e., those that replicate or extend theory by filling conceptual categories
Crafting Instruments and Protocols	Multiple data collection methods	Strengthens grounding of theory by triangulation of evidence
	Qualitative and quantitative data combined	Synergistic view of evidence
	Multiple investigators	Fosters divergent perspectives and strengthens grounding
Entering the Field	Overlap data collection and analysis, including field notes	Speeds analyses and reveals helpful adjustments to data collection
	Flexible and opportunistic data collection methods	Allows investigators to take advantage of emergent themes and unique case features
Analyzing Data	Within-case analysis	Gains familiarity with data and preliminary theory generation
	Cross-case pattern search using divergent techniques	Forces investigators to look beyond initial impressions and see evidence thru multiple lenses
Shaping Hypotheses	Iterative tabulation of evidence for each construct	Sharpens construct definition, validity, and measurability
	Replication, not sampling, logic across cases	Confirms, extends, and sharpens theory
	Search evidence for "why" behind relationships	Builds internal validity

Step	Activity	Reason
Enfolding Literature	Comparison with conflicting literature	Builds internal validity, raises theoretical level, and sharpens construct definitions
	Comparison with similar literature	Sharpens generalizability, improves construct definition, and raises theoretical level
Reaching Closure	Theoretical saturation when possible	Ends process when marginal improvement becomes small

within-case and cross-case analyses, and the role of existing literature. The result is a more nearly complete roadmap for executing this type of research than has existed in the past. This framework is summarized in Table 1.

The second contribution is positioning theory building from case studies into the larger context of social science research. For example, the paper explores strengths and weaknesses of theory building from case studies, situations in which it is an attractive research approach, and some guidelines for evaluating this type of research.

Background

Several pieces of the process of building theory from case study research have appeared in the literature. One is the work on grounded theory building by Glaser and Strauss (1967) and, more recently, Strauss (1987). These authors have detailed their comparative method for developing grounded theory. The method relies on continuous comparison of data and theory beginning with data collection. It emphasizes both the emergence of theoretical categories solely from evidence and an incremental approach to case selection and data gathering.

More recently, Yin (1981, 1984) has described the design of case study research. He has defined the case study as a research strategy, developed a typology of case study designs, and described the replication logic which is essential to multiple case analysis. His approach also stresses bringing the concerns of validity and reliability in experimental research design to the design of case study research.

Miles and Huberman (1984) have outlined specific techniques for analyzing qualitative data. Their ideas include a variety of devices such as tabular displays and graphs to manage and present qualitative data, without destroying the meaning of the data through intensive coding.

A number of active researchers also have undertaken their own variations and additions to the earlier methodological work (e.g., Gersick, 1988;

Leonard-Barton, 1988; Harris & Sutton, 1986). Many of these authors acknowledge a debt to previous work, but they have also developed their own "homegrown" techniques for building theory from cases. For example, Sutton and Callahan (1987) pioneered a clever use of a resident devil's advocate, the Warwick group (Pettigrew, 1988) added triangulation of investigators, and my colleague and I (Bourgeois & Eisenhardt, 1988) developed cross-case analysis techniques.

Finally, the work of others such as Van Maanen (1988) on ethnography, Jick (1979) on triangulation of data types, and Mintzberg (1979) on direct research has provided additional pieces for a framework of building theory from case study research.

As a result, many pieces of the theory-building process are evident in the literature. Nevertheless, at the same time, there is substantial confusion about how to combine them, when to conduct this type of study, and how to evaluate it.

The Case Study Approach

The case study is a research strategy which focuses on understanding the dynamics present within single settings. Examples of case study research include Selznick's (1949) description of TVA, Allison's (1971) study of the Cuban missile crisis, and Pettigrew's (1973) research on decision making at a British retailer. Case studies can involve either single or multiple cases, and numerous levels of analysis (Yin, 1984). For example, Harris and Sutton (1986) studied 8 dying organizations, Bettenhausen and Murnighan (1986) focused on the emergence of norms in 19 laboratory groups, and Leonard-Barton (1988) tracked the progress of 10 innovation projects. Moreover, case studies can employ an embedded design, that is, multiple levels of analysis within a single study (Yin, 1984). For example, the Warwick study of competitiveness and strategic change within major U.K. corporations is conducted at two levels of analysis: industry and firm (Pettigrew, 1988), and the Mintzberg and Waters (1982) study of Steinberg's grocery empire examines multiple strategic changes within a single firm.

Case studies typically combine data collection methods such as archives, interviews, questionnaires, and observations. The evidence may be qualitative (e. g., words), quantitative (e.g., numbers), or both. For example, Sutton and Callahan (1987) rely exclusively on qualitative data in their study of bankruptcy in Silicon Valley, Mintzberg and McHugh (1985) use qualitative data supplemented by frequency counts in their work on the National Film Board of Canada, and Eisenhardt and Bourgeois (1988) combine quantitative data from questionnaires with qualitative evidence from interviews and observations.

Finally, case studies can be used to accomplish various aims: to provide description (Kidder, 1982), test theory (Pinfield, 1986; Anderson, 1983), or

Table 2: Recent Examples of Inductive Case Study Research*

Study	Description of Cases	Research Problem	Data Sources	Investigators	Output
Burgelman (1983)	6 internal corporate ventures in 1 major corporation	Management of new ventures	Archives Interviews Some observation	Single investigator	Process model linking multiple organizational levels
Mintzberg & McHugh (1985)	1 National Film Board of Canada, 1939–1975, with 6 periods	Formulation of strategy in an adhocracy	Archives Some interviews	Research team	Strategy-making themes, "grass roots" model of strategy formation
Harris & Sutton (1986)	8 diverse organizations	Parting ceremonies during organizational death	Interviews Archives	Research team	Conceptual framework about the functions of parting ceremonies for displaced members
Eisenhardt & Bourgeois (1988)	8 microcomputer firms	Strategic decision making in high velocity environments	Interviews Questionnaires Archives Some observation	Research team Tandem interviews	Mid-range theory linking power, politics, and firm performance
Gersick (1988)	8 project groups with deadlines	Group development in project-teams	Observation Some interviews	Single investigator	Punctuated equilibrium model of group development
Leonard-Barton (1988)	10 technical innovations	Internal technology transfer	Interviews Experiment Observation	Single investigator	Process model
Pettigrew (1988)	1 high performing & 1 low performing firm in each of 4 industries	Strategic change & competitiveness	Interviews Archives Some observation	Research teams	In progress

* Examples were chosen from recent organizational writing to provide illustrations of the possible range of theory building from case studies.

generate theory (e.g., Gersick, 1988; Harris & Sutton, 1936). The interest here is in this last aim, theory generation from case study evidence. Table 2 summarizes some recent research using theory building from case studies.

Building Theory from Case Study Research

Getting Started

An initial definition of the research question, in at least broad terms, is important in building theory from case studies. Mintzberg (1979, p. 585) noted: "No matter how small our sample or what our interest, we have always tried to go into organizations with a well-defined focus – to collect specific kinds of data systematically." The rationale for defining the research question is the same as it is in hypothesis-testing research. Without a research focus, it is easy to become overwhelmed by the volume of data. For example, Pettigrew and colleagues (1988) defined their research question in terms of strategic change and competitiveness within large British corporations, and Leonard-Barton (1988) focused on technical innovation of feasible technologies. Such definition of a research question within a broad topic permitted these investigators to specify the kind of organization to be approached, and, once there, the kind of data to be gathered.

A priori specification of constructs can also help to shape the initial design of theory-building research. Although this type of specification is not common in theory-building studies to date, it is valuable because it permits researchers to measure constructs more accurately. If these constructs prove important as the study progresses, then researchers have a firmer empirical grounding for the emergent theory. For example, in a study of strategic decision making in top management teams, Bourgeois and Eisenhardt (1988) identified several potentially important constructs (e.g., conflict, power) from the literature on decision making. These constructs were explicitly measured in the interview protocol and questionnaires. When several of these constructs did emerge as related to the decision process, there were strong, triangulated measures on which to ground the emergent theory.

Although early identification of the research question and possible constructs is helpful, it is equally important to recognize that both are tentative in this type of research. No construct is guaranteed a place in the resultant theory, no matter how well it is measured. Also, the research question may shift during the research. At the extreme, some researchers (e. g., Gersick, 1988; Bettenhausen & Murnighan, 1986) have converted theory-testing research into theory-building research by taking advantage of serendipitous findings. In these studies, the research focus emerged after the data collection had begun. As Bettenhausen and Murnighan (1986, p. 352) wrote: "… we observed the outcomes of an experiment on group decision making and coalition formation. Our observations of the groups indicated that the unique character of each of the groups seemed to overwhelm our other manipulations." These authors proceeded to switch their research focus to a theory-building study of group norms.

Finally and most importantly, theory-building research is begun as close as possible to the ideal of no theory under consideration and no hypotheses to test. Admittedly, it is impossible to achieve this ideal of a clean theoretical slate. Nonetheless, attempting to approach this ideal is important because pre-ordained theoretical perspectives or propositions may bias and limit the findings. Thus, investigators should formulate a research problem and possibly specify some potentially important variables, with some reference to extant literature. However, they should avoid thinking about specific relationships between variables and theories as much as possible, especially at the outset of the process.

Selecting Cases

Selection of cases is an important aspect of building theory from case studies. As in hypothesis-testing research, the concept of a population is crucial, because the population defines the set of entities from which the research sample is to be drawn. Also, selection of an appropriate population controls extraneous variation and helps to define the limits for generalizing the findings.

The Warwick study of strategic change and competitiveness illustrates these ideas (Pettigrew, 1988). In this study, the researchers selected cases from a population of large British corporations in four market sectors. The selection of four specific markets allowed the researchers to control environmental variation, while the focus on large corporations constrained variation due to size differences among the firms. Thus, specification of this population reduced extraneous variation and clarified the domain of the findings as large corporations operating in specific types of environments.

However, the sampling of cases from the chosen population is unusual when building theory from case studies. Such research relies on theoretical sampling (i.e., cases are chosen for theoretical, not statistical, reasons, Glaser & Strauss, 1967). The cases may be chosen to replicate previous cases or extend emergent theory, or they may be chosen to fill theoretical categories and provide examples of polar types. While the cases may be chosen randomly, random selection is neither necessary, nor even preferable. As Pettigrew (1988) noted, given the limited number of cases which can usually be studied, it makes sense to choose cases such as extreme situations and polar types in which the process of interest is "transparently observable." Thus, the goal of theoretical sampling is to choose cases which are likely to replicate or extend the emergent theory. In contrast, traditional, within-experiment hypothesis-testing studies rely on statistical sampling, in which researchers randomly select the sample from the population. In this type of study, the goal of the sampling process is to obtain accurate statistical evidence on the distributions of variables within the population.

Several studies illustrate theoretical sampling. Harris and Sutton (1986), for example, were interested in the parting ceremonies of dying organizations. In order to build a model applicable across organization types, these researchers purposefully selected diverse organizations from a population of dying organizations. They chose eight organizations, filling each of four categories: private, dependent; private, independent; public, dependent; and public, independent. The sample was not random, but reflected the selection of specific cases to extend the theory to a broad range of organizations. Multiple cases within each category allowed findings to be replicated within categories. Gersick (1988) followed a similar strategy of diverse sampling in order to enhance the generalizability of her model of group development. In the Warwick study (Pettigrew, 1988), the investigators also followed a deliberate, theoretical sampling plan. Within each of four markets, they chose polar types: one case of clearly successful firm performance and one unsuccessful case. This sampling plan was designed to build theories of success and failure. Finally, the Eisenhardt and Bourgeois (1988) study of the politics of strategic decision making illustrates theoretical sampling during the course of research. A theory linking the centralization of power to the use of politics in top management teams was built and then extended to consider the effects of changing team composition by adding two cases, in which the executive teams changed, to the first six, in which there was no change. This tactic allowed the initial framework to be extended to include dynamic effects of changing team composition.

Crafting Instruments and Protocols

Theory-building researchers typically combine multiple data collection methods. While interviews, observations, and archival sources are particularly common, inductive researchers are not confined to these choices. Some investigators employ only some of these data collection methods (e.g., Gersick, 1988, used only observations for the first half of her study), or they may add others (e.g., Bettenhausen & Murnighan, 1986, used quantitative laboratory data). The rationale is the same as in hypothesis-testing research. That is, the triangulation made possible by multiple data collection methods provides stronger substantiation of constructs and hypotheses.

Of special note is the combining of qualitative with quantitative evidence. Although the terms *qualitative* and *case study* are often used interchangeably (e.g., Yin, 1981), case study research can involve qualitative data only, quantitative only, or both (Yin, 1984). Moreover, the combination of data types can be highly synergistic. Quantitative evidence can indicate relationships which may not be salient to the researcher. It also can keep researchers from being carried away by vivid, but false, impressions in qualitative data, and it can bolster findings when it corroborates those findings from qualitative evidence. The qualitative data are useful for understanding the rationale or theory underlying relationships revealed in the quantitative data or may suggest directly theory which can then be strengthened by quantitative support (Jick, 1979). Mintzberg (1979) described this synergy as follows:

> For while systematic data create the foundation for our theories, it is the anecdotal data that enable us to do the building. Theory building seems to require rich description, the richness that comes from anecdote. We uncover all kinds of relationships in our hard data, but it is only through the use of this soft data that we are able to explain them. (p. 587)

Also, of special note is the use of multiple investigators. Multiple investigators have two key advantages. First, they enhance the creative potential of the study. Team members often have complementary insights which add to the richness of the data, and their different perspectives increase the likelihood of capitalizing on any novel insights which may be in the data. Second, the convergence of observations from multiple investigators enhances confidence in the findings. Convergent perceptions add to the empirical grounding of the hypotheses, while conflicting perceptions keep the group from premature closure. Thus, the use of more investigators builds confidence in the findings and increases the likelihood of surprising findings.

One strategy for employing multiple investigators is to make the visits to case study sites in teams (e.g., Pettigrew, 1988). This allows the case to be viewed from the different perspectives of multiple observers. A variation on this tactic is to give individuals on the team unique roles, which increases the chances that investigators will view case evidence in divergent ways. For example, interviews can be conducted by two person teams, with one researcher handling the interview questions, while the other records notes and observations (e. g., Eisenhardt & Bourgeois, 1988). The interviewer has the perspective of personal interaction with the informant, while the notetaker retains a different, more distant view. Another tactic is to create multiple research teams, with teams being assigned to cover some case sites, but not others (e.g., Pettigrew, 1988). The rationale behind this tactic is that investigators who have not met the informants and have not become immersed in case details may bring a very different and possibly more objective eye to the evidence. An extreme form of this tactic is to keep some member or members of the research team out of the field altogether by exclusively assigning to them the role of resident devil's advocate (e.g., Sutton & Callahan, 1987).

Entering the Field

A striking feature of research to build theory from case studies is the frequent overlap of data analysis with data collection. For example, Glaser and Strauss (1967) argue for joint collection, coding, and analysis of data. While many researchers do not achieve this degree of overlap, most maintain some overlap.

Field notes, a running commentary to oneself and/or research team, are an important means of accomplishing this overlap. As described by Van Maanen (1988), field notes are an ongoing stream-of-consciousness commentary about what is happening in the research, involving both observation and analysis – preferably separated from one another.

One key to useful field notes is to write down whatever impressions occur, that is, to react rather than to sift out what may seem important, because it is often difficult to know what will and will not be useful in the future. A second key to successful field notes is to push thinking in these notes by asking questions such as "What am I learning?" and "How does this case differ from the last?" For example, Burgelman (1983) kept extensive idea booklets to record his ongoing thoughts in a study of internal corporate venturing. These ideas can be cross-case comparisons, hunches about relationships, anecdotes, and informal observations. Team meetings, in which investigators share their thoughts and emergent ideas, are also useful devices for overlapping data collection and analysis.

Overlapping data analysis with data collection not only gives the researcher a head start in analysis but, more importantly, allows researchers to take advantage of flexible data collection. Indeed, a key feature of theory-building case research is the freedom to make adjustments during the data collection process. These adjustments can be the addition of cases to probe particular themes which emerge. Gersick (1988), for example, added several cases to her original set of student teams in order to more closely observe transition point behaviors among project teams. These transition point behaviors had unexpectedly proved interesting, and Gersick added cases in order to focus more closely on the transition period.

Additional adjustments can be made to data collection instruments, such as the addition of questions to an interview protocol or questions to a questionnaire (e.g., Harris & Sutton, 1986). These adjustments allow the researcher to probe emergent themes or to take advantage of special opportunities which may be present in a given situation. In other situations adjustments can include the addition of data sources in selected cases. For example, Sutton and Callahan (1987) added observational evidence for one case when the opportunity to attend creditors' meetings arose, and Burgelman (1983) added interviews with individuals whose importance became clear during data collection. Leonard-Barton (1988) went even further by adding several experiments to probe her emergent theory in a study of the implementation of technical innovations.

These alterations create an important question: Is it legitimate to alter and even add data collection methods during a study? For theory-building research, the answer is "yes," because investigators are trying to understand each case individually and in as much depth as is feasible. The goal is not to produce summary statistics about a set of observations. Thus, if a new data collection opportunity arises or if a new line of thinking emerges during the research, it makes sense to take advantage by altering data collection, if such an alteration is likely to better ground the theory or to provide new theoretical insight. This flexibility is not a license to be unsystematic. Rather, this flexibility is controlled opportunism in which researchers take advantage of the uniqueness of a specific case and the emergence of new themes to improve resultant theory.

Analyzing Within-Case Data

Analyzing data is the heart of building theory from case studies, but it is both the most difficult and the least codified part of the process. Since published studies generally describe research sites and data collection methods, but give little space to discussion of analysis, a huge chasm often separates data from conclusions. As Miles and Huberman (1984, p. 16) wrote: "One cannot ordinarily follow how a researcher got from 3600 pages of field notes to the final conclusions, sprinkled with vivid quotes though they may be." However, several key features of analysis can be identified.

One key step is within-case analysis. The importance of within-case analysis is driven by one of the realities of case study research: a staggering volume of data. As Pettigrew (1988) described, there is an ever-present danger of "death by data asphyxiation." For example, Mintzberg and McHugh (1985) examined over 2500 movies in their study of strategy making at the National Film Board of Canada – and that was only part of their evidence. The volume of data is all the more daunting because the research problem is often open-ended. Within-case analysis can help investigators cope with this deluge of data.

Within-case analysis typically involves detailed case study write-ups for each site. These write-ups are often simply pure descriptions, but they are central to the generation of insight (Gersick, 1988; Pettigrew, 1988) because they help researchers to cope early in the analysis process with the often enormous volume of data. However, there is no standard format for such analysis. Quinn (1980) developed teaching cases for each of the firms in his study of strategic decision making in six major corporations as a prelude to his theoretical work. Mintzberg and McHugh (1985) compiled a 383-page case history of the National Film Board of Canada. These authors coupled narrative description with extensive use of longitudinal graphs tracking revenue, film sponsorship, staffing, film subjects, and so on. Gersick (1988) prepared transcripts of team meetings. Leonard-Barton (1988) used tabular displays and graphs of information about each case. Abbott (1988) suggested using sequence analysis to organize longitudinal data. In fact, there are probably as many approaches as researchers. However, the overall idea is to become intimately familiar with each case as a stand-alone entity. This process allows the unique patterns of each case to emerge before investigators push to generalize patterns across cases. In addition, it gives investigators a rich familiarity with each case which, in turn, accelerates cross-case comparison.

Searching for Cross-Case Patterns

Coupled with within-case analysis is cross-case search for patterns. The tactics here are driven by the reality that people are notoriously poor processors of information. They leap to conclusions based on limited data (Kahneman & Tversky, 1973), they are overly influenced by the vividness (Nisbett & Ross, 1980) or by more elite respondents (Miles & Huberman, 1984), they ignore basic statistical properties (Kahneman & Tversky, 1973), or they sometimes inadvertently drop disconfirming evidence (Nisbett & Ross, 1980). The danger is that investigators reach premature and even false conclusions as a result of these information-processing biases. Thus, the key to good cross-case comparison is counteracting these tendencies by looking at the data in many divergent ways.

One tactic is to select categories or dimensions, and then to look for within-group similarities coupled with intergroup differences. Dimensions can be suggested by the research problem or by existing literature, or the researcher can simply choose some dimensions. For example, in a study of strategic decision making, Bourgeois and Eisenhardt (1988) sifted cases into various categories including founder-run vs. professional management, high vs. low performance, first vs. second generation product, and large vs. small size. Some categories such as size and product generation revealed no clear patterns, but others such as performance led to important patterns of within-group similarity and across-group differences. An extension of this tactic is to use a 2×2 or other cell design to compare several categories at once, or to move to a continuous measurement scale which permits graphing.

A second tactic is to select pairs of cases and then to list the similarities and differences between each pair. This tactic forces researchers to look for the subtle similarities and differences between cases. The juxtaposition of seemingly similar cases by a researcher looking for differences can break simplistic frames. In the same way, the search for similarity in a seemingly different pair also can lead to more sophisticated understanding. The result of these forced comparisons can be new categories and concepts which the investigators did not anticipate. For example, Eisenhardt and Bourgeois (1988) found that CEO power differences dominated initial impressions across firms. However, this paired comparison process led the researchers to see that the speed of the decision process was equally important (Eisenhardt, in press). Finally, an extension of this tactic is to group cases into threes or fours for comparison.

A third strategy is to divide the data by data source. For example, one researcher combs observational data, while another reviews interviews, and still another works with questionnaire evidence. This tactic was used in the separation of the analyses of qualitative and quantitative data in a study of strategic decision making (Bourgeois & Eisenhardt, 1988; Eisenhardt & Bourgeois, 1988). This tactic exploits the unique insights possible from different types of data collection. When a pattern from one data source is corroborated by the evidence from another, the finding is stronger and better grounded. When evidence conflicts, the researcher can sometimes reconcile the evidence through deeper probing of the meaning of the differences. At other times, this conflict exposes a spurious or random pattern, or biased thinking in the analysis. A variation of this tactic is to split the data into groups of cases, focusing on one group of cases initially, while later focusing on the remaining cases. Gersick (1988) used this tactic in separating the analyses of the student group cases from her other cases.

Overall, the idea behind these cross-case searching tactics is to force investigators to go beyond initial impressions, especially through the use of structured and diverse lenses on the data. These tactics improve the likelihood of accurate and reliable theory, that is, a theory with a close fit with the data. Also, cross-case searching tactics enhance the probability that the investigators will capture the novel findings which may exist in the data.

Shaping Hypotheses

From the within-site analysis plus various cross-site tactics and overall impressions, tentative themes, concepts, and possibly even relationships between variables begin to emerge. The next step of this highly iterative process is to compare systematically the emergent frame with the evidence from each case in order to assess how well or poorly it fits with case data. The central idea is that researchers constantly compare theory and data – iterating toward a theory which closely fits the data. A close fit is important to building good theory because it takes advantage of the new insights possible from the data and yields an empirically valid theory.

One step in shaping hypotheses is the sharpening of constructs. This is a two-part process involving (1) refining the definition of the construct and (2) building evidence which measures the construct in each case. This occurs through constant comparison between data and constructs so that accumulating evidence from diverse sources converges on a single, well-defined construct. For example, in their study of stigma management in bankruptcy, Sutton and Callahan (1987) developed constructs which described the reaction of customers and other parties to the declaration of bankruptcy by the focal firms. The iterative process involved data from multiple sources: initial semi-structured telephone conversations; interviews with key informants including the firm's president, other executives, a major creditor, and a lawyer; U.S. Bankruptcy Court records; observation of a creditors' meeting; and secondary source material including newspaper and magazine articles and firm correspondence. The authors iterated between constructs and these data. They eventually developed definitions and measures for several constructs: disengagement, bargaining for a more favorable exchange relationship, denigration via rumor, and reduction in the quality of participation.

This process is similar to developing a single construct measure from multiple indicators in hypothesis-testing research. That is, researchers use multiple

Table 3: Example of Tabulated Evidence for a Power Centralization Construct*

Firm	CEO Decision Description	CEO Power Score	CEO Power Distance[a]	CEO Dominated Functions	Story Decision Style[b]	Examples[c]
First	Strong Volatile Dogmatic	9.6	3.5	Mkt, R&D, Ops, Fin	Authoritarian	Geoff (Chairman) is THE decision maker. He runs the whole show. (VP, Marketing)
Alpha	Impatient Parental Tunes You Out	9.6	3.8	Mkt, R&D, Ops, Fin	Authoritarian	Thou shalt not hire w/o Presidential approval. Thou shalt not promote w/o Presidential approval. Thou shalt not explore new markets w/o Presidential approval. (VP, Operations)
Cowboy	Strong Power Boss Master Strategist	9.1	3.1	Mkt, R&D, Fin	Authoritarian Consensus	The tone of meetings would change depending upon whether he was in the room. If he'd leave the room, discussion would spread out, go off the wall. It got back on focus when he came back. (Director of Marketing)
Neutron	Organized Analytic	9.1	2.3	Mkt, Ops, Fin	Authoritarian	If there is a decision to make, I will make it. (President)
Omicron	Easy Going Easy to Work With	8.4	1.2	Fin	Consensus	Bill (prior CEO) was a suppressor of ideas. Jim is more open. (VP, Mfg.)
Promise	People-Oriented Pragmatic	8.9	1.3	Ops, Fin	Consensus	(My philosophy is) to make quick decisions involving as many people as possible. (President)
Forefront	Aggressive Team Player	8.3	1.2	None	Consensus	Art depends on picking good people and letting them operate. (VP, Sales)
Zap	Consensus-Style People-Oriented	7.5	0.3	Fin	Consultative	It's very open. We're successful most of the time in building consensus. (VP, Engineering)

[a] Difference between CEO power score and score of next most powerful executive.
[b] Authoritarian – Decisions made either by CEO alone or in consultation with only one person.
 Consultative – Decisions made by CEO in consultation with either most of or all of the team.
 Consensus – Decisions made by entire team in a group format.
[c] Individual in parentheses is the source of the quotation.
* Taken from Eisenhardt & Bourgeois, 1988.

sources of evidence to build construct measures, which define the construct and distinguish it from other constructs. In effect, the researcher is attempting to establish construct validity. The difference is that the construct, its definition, and measurement often emerge from the analysis process itself, rather than being specified a priori. A second difference is that no technique like factor analysis is available to collapse multiple indicators into a single construct measure. The reasons are that the indicators may vary across cases (i.e., not all cases may have all measures), and qualitative evidence (which is common in theory-building research) is difficult to collapse. Thus, many researchers rely on tables which summarize and tabulate the evidence underlying the construct (Miles & Huberman, 1984; Sutton & Callahan, 1987). For example, Table 3 is a tabular display of the evidence grounding the CEO power construct used by Eisenhardt and Bourgeois (1988), which included qualitative personality descriptions, quantitative scores from questionnaires, and quotation examples. The reasons for defining and building evidence for a construct apply in theory-building research just as they do in traditional, hypothesis-testing work. That is, careful construction of construct definitions and evidence produces the sharply defined, measurable constructs which are necessary for strong theory.

A second step in shaping hypotheses is verifying that the emergent relationships between constructs fit with the evidence in each case. Sometimes a relationship is confirmed by the case evidence, while other times it is revised, disconfirmed, or thrown out for insufficient evidence. This verification process is similar to that in traditional hypothesis testing research. The key difference is that each hypothesis is examined for each case, not for the aggregate cases. Thus, the underlying logic is replication, that is, the logic of treating a series of cases as a series of experiments with each case serving to confirm or disconfirm the hypotheses (Yin, 1984). Each case is analogous to an experiment, and multiple cases are analogous to multiple experiments. This contrasts with the sampling logic of traditional, within-experiment, hypothesis-testing research in which the aggregate relationships across the data points are tested using summary statistics such as F values (Yin, 1984).

In replication logic, cases which confirm emergent relationships enhance confidence in the validity of the relationships. Cases which disconfirm the relationships often can provide an opportunity to refine and extend the theory. For example, in the study of the politics of strategic decision making, Eisenhardt and Bourgeois (1988) found a case which did not fit with the proposition that political coalitions have stable memberships. Further examination of this disconfirming case indicated that the executive team in this case had been newly formed at the time of the study. This observation plus replication in another case led to a refinement in the emergent theory to indicate that increasing stabilization of coalitions occurs over time.

At this point, the qualitative data are particularly useful for understanding why or why not emergent relationships hold. When a relationship is supported, the qualitative data often provide a good understanding of the dynamics underlying the relationship, that is, the "why" of what is happening. This is crucial to the establishment of internal validity. Just as in hypothesis-testing research an apparent relationship may simply be a spurious correlation or may reflect the impact of some third variable on each of the other two. Therefore, it is important to discover the underlying theoretical reasons for why the relationship exists. This helps to establish the internal validity of the findings. For example, in her study of project groups, Gersick (1988) identified a midpoint transition in the lives of most project groups. She then used extensive qualitative data to understand the cognitive and motivational reasons why such abrupt and precisely timed transitions occur.

Overall, shaping hypotheses in theory-building research involves measuring constructs and verifying relationships. These processes are similar to traditional hypothesis-testing research. However, these processes are more judgmental in theory-building research because researchers cannot apply statistical tests such as an F statistic. The research team must judge the strength and consistency of relationships within and across cases and also fully display the evidence and procedures when the findings are published, so that readers may apply their own standards.

Enfolding Literature

An essential feature of theory building is comparison of the emergent concepts, theory, or hypotheses with the extant literature. This involves asking what is this similar to, what does it contradict, and why. A key to this process is to consider a broad range of literature.

Examining literature which conflicts with the emergent theory is important for two reasons. First, if researchers ignore conflicting findings, then confidence in the findings is reduced. For example, readers may assume that the results are incorrect (a challenge to internal validity), or if correct, are idiosyncratic to the specific cases of the study (a challenge to generalizability). Second and perhaps more importantly, conflicting literature represents an opportunity. The juxtaposition of conflicting results forces researchers into a more creative, framebreaking mode of thinking than they might otherwise be able to achieve. The result can be deeper insight into both the emergent theory and the conflicting literature, as well as sharpening of the limits to generalizability of the focal research. For example, in their study of strategy making at the National Film Board of Canada, Mintzberg and McHugh (1985) noted conflicts between their findings for this highly creative organization and prior results at Volkswagenwerk and other sites. In the earlier studies, they observed differences in the patterns of strategic change whereby periods of convergence were long and periods of divergence were short and very abrupt. In contrast, the National Film Board exhibited a pattern of regular cycles of convergence and divergence, coupled with a long-term trend toward greater diversity. This and other conflicts allowed these researchers to establish the unique features of strategy making in an "adhocracy" in relief against "machine bureaucracies" and "entrepreneurial firms." The result was a sharper theory of strategy formation in all three types of organizations.

Similarly, in a study of politics, Eisenhardt and Bourgeois (1988) contrasted the finding that centralized power leads to politics with the previous finding that *decentralized* power creates politics. These conflicting findings forced the probing of both the evidence and conflicting research to discover the underlying reasons for the conflict. An underlying similarity in the apparently dissimilar situations was found. That is, both power extremes create a climate of frustration, which leads to an emphasis on self-interest and ultimately politics. In these extreme situations, the "structure of the game" becomes an interpersonal competition among the executives. In contrast, the research showed that an intermediate power distribution fosters a sense of personal efficacy among executives and ultimately collaboration, not politics, for the good of the entire group. This reconciliation integrated the conflicting findings into a single theoretical perspective, and raised the theoretical level and generalizability of the results.

Literature discussing similar findings is important as well because it ties together underlying similarities in phenomena normally not associated with each other. The result is often a theory with stronger internal validity, wider generalizability, and higher conceptual level. For example, in her study of technological innovation in a major computer corporation, Leonard-Barton (1988) related her findings on the mutual adaptation of technology and the host organization to similar findings in the education literature. In so doing, Leonard-Barton strengthened the confidence that her findings were valid and generalizable because others had similar findings in a very different context. Also, the tie to mutual adaptation processes in the education setting sharpened and enriched the conceptual level of the study.

Similarly, Gersick (1988) linked the sharp midpoint transition in project group development to the more general punctuated equilibrium phenomenon, to the literature on the adult mid-life transition, and to strategic transitions within organizations. This linkage with a variety of literature in other contexts raises the readers' confidence that Gersick had observed a valid phenomenon within her small number of project teams. It also allowed her to elevate the conceptual level of her findings to the more fundamental level of punctuated equilibrium, and strengthen their likely generalizability to other project teams. Finally, Burgelman (1983) strengthened the theoretical scope and validity of his work by tying his results on the process of new venture development in a large corporation to the selection arguments of population ecology. The result again was a higher conceptual level for his findings and enhanced confidence in their validity.

Overall, tying the emergent theory to existing literature enhances the internal validity, generalizability, and theoretical level of theory building from case study research. While linking results to the literature is important in most research, it is particularly crucial in theory-building research because the findings often rest on a very limited number of cases. In this situation, any further corroboration of internal validity or generalizability is an important improvement.

Reaching Closure

Two issues are important in reaching closure: when to stop adding cases, and when to stop iterating between theory and data. In the first, ideally, researchers should stop adding cases when theoretical saturation is reached. (Theoretical saturation is simply the point at which incremental learning is minimal because the researchers are observing phenomena seen before, Glaser and Strauss, 1967.) This idea is quite similar to ending the revision of a manuscript when the incremental improvement in its quality is minimal. In practice, theoretical saturation often combines with pragmatic considerations such as time and money to dictate when case collection ends. In fact, it is not uncommon for researchers to plan the number of cases in advance. For example, the Warwick group planned their study of strategic change and competitiveness in British firms to include eight firms (Pettigrew, 1988). This kind of planning may be necessary because of the availability of resources and because time constraints force researchers to develop cases in parallel. Finally, while there is no ideal number of cases, a number between 4 and 10 cases usually works well. With fewer than 4 cases, it is often difficult to generate theory with much complexity, and its empirical grounding is likely to be unconvincing, unless the case has several mini-cases within it, as did the Mintzberg and McHugh study of the National Film Board of Canada. With more than 10 cases, it quickly becomes difficult to cope with the complexity and volume of the data.

In the second closure issue, when to stop iterating between theory and data, again, saturation is the key idea. That is, the iteration process stops when the incremental improvement to theory is minimal. The final product of building theory from case studies may be concepts (e. g., the Mintzberg and Waters, 1982, deliberate and emergent strategies), a conceptual framework (e.g., Harris & Sutton's, 1986, framework of bankruptcy), or propositions or possibly midrange theory (e.g., Eisenhardt and Bourgeois's, 1988, midrange theory of politics in high velocity environments). On the downside, the final product may be disappointing. The research may simply replicate prior theory, or there may be no clear patterns within the data. The steps for building theory from case studies are summarized in Table 1.

Comparison with Other Literature

The process described here has similarities with the work of others. For example, I have drawn upon the ideas of theoretical sampling, theoretical saturation, and overlapped coding, data collection, and analysis from Glaser and Strauss (1967). Also, the notions of case study design, replication logic, and concern for internal validity have been incorporated from Yin (1984). The tools of tabular display of evidence from Miles and Huberman (1984) were particularly helpful in the discussion of building evidence for constructs.

However, the process described here has important differences from previous work. First, it is focused on theory building from cases. In contrast, with the exception of Glaser and Strauss (1967), previous work was centered on other topics such as qualitative data analysis (e.g., Miles, 1979; Miles & Huberman, 1984; Kirk & Miller, 1986), case study design (Yin, 1981, 1984; McClintock et al., 1979), and ethnography (Van Maanen, 1988). To a large extent, Glaser and Strauss (1967) focused on defending building theory from cases, rather than on how actually to do it. Thus, while these previous writings provide pieces of the process, they do not provide (nor do they intend to provide) a framework for theory building from cases as developed here.

Second, the process described here contributes new ideas. For example, the process includes a priori specification of constructs, population specification, flexible instrumentation, multiple investigators, cross-case analysis tactics, and several uses of literature. Their inclusion plus their illustration using examples from research studies and comparison with traditional, hypothesis-testing research synthesizes, extends, and adds depth to existing views of theory-building research.

Third, particularly in comparison with Strauss (1987) and Van Maanen (1988), the process described here adopts a positivist view of research. That is, the process is directed toward the development of testable hypotheses and theory which are generalizable across settings. In contrast, authors like Strauss and Van Maanen are more concerned that a rich, complex description of the specific cases under study evolve and they appear less concerned with development of generalizable theory.

Discussion

The process of building theory from case study research is a strikingly iterative one. While an investigator may focus on one part of the process at a time, the process itself involves constant iteration backward and forward between steps. For example, an investigator may move from cross-case comparison, back to redefinition of the research question, and out to the field to gather evidence on an additional case. Also, the process is alive with tension between divergence into new ways of understanding the data and convergence onto a single theoretical framework. For example, the process involves the use of multiple investigators and multiple data collection methods as well as a variety of cross-case searching tactics. Each of these tactics involves viewing evidence from diverse perspectives. However, the process also involves converging on construct definitions, measures, and a framework for structuring the findings. Finally, the process described here is intimately tied with empirical evidence.

Strengths of Theory Building from Cases

One strength of theory building from cases is its likelihood of generating novel theory. Creative insight often arises from the juxtaposition of contradictory or paradoxical evidence (Cameron & Quinn, 1988). As Bartunek (1988) argued, the process of reconciling these contradictions forces individuals to reframe perceptions into a new gestalt. Building theory from case studies centers directly on this kind of juxtaposition. That is, attempts to reconcile evidence across cases, types of data, and different investigators, and between cases and literature increase the likelihood of creative reframing into a new theoretical vision. Although a myth surrounding theory building from case studies is that the process is limited by investigators' preconceptions, in fact, just the opposite is true. This constant juxtaposition of conflicting realities tends to "unfreeze" thinking, and so the process has the potential to generate theory with less researcher bias than theory built from incremental studies or armchair, axiomatic deduction.

A second strength is that the emergent theory is likely to be testable with constructs that can be readily measured and hypotheses that can be proven false. Measurable constructs are likely because they have already been measured during the theory-building process. The resulting hypotheses are likely to be verifiable for the same reason. That is, they have already undergone repeated verification during the theory-building process. In contrast, theory which is generated apart from direct evidence may have testability problems. For example, population ecology researchers borrowed the niche concept from biology. This construct has proven difficult to operationalize for many organizational researchers, other than its originators. One reason may be its obscure definition, which hampers measurability: "... that area in constraint space (the space whose dimensions are levels of resources, etc.) in which the population outcompetes all other local populations" (Hannan & Freeman, 1977, p. 947). One might ask: How do you measure an area in constraint space?

A third strength is that the resultant theory is likely to be empirically valid. The likelihood of valid theory is high because the theory-building process is so intimately tied with evidence that it is very likely that the resultant theory will be consistent with empirical observation. In well executed theory-building research, investigators answer to the data from the beginning of the research. This closeness can lead to an intimate sense of things – "how they feel, smell, seem" (Mintzberg, 1979). This intimate interaction with actual evidence often produces theory which closely mirrors reality.

Weaknesses of Theory Building from Cases

However, some characteristics that lead to strengths in theory building from case studies also lead to weaknesses. For example, the intensive use of empirical evidence can yield theory which is overly complex. A hallmark of good theory is parsimony, but given the typically staggering volume of rich data, there is a temptation to build theory which tries to capture everything. The result can be theory which is very rich in detail, but lacks the simplicity of overall perspective. Theorists working from case data can lose their sense of proportion as they confront vivid, voluminous data. Since they lack quantitative gauges such as regression results or observations across multiple studies, they may be unable to assess which are the most important relationships and which are simply idiosyncratic to a particular case.

Another weakness is that building theory from cases may result in narrow and idiosyncratic theory. Case study theory building is a bottom up approach such that the specifics of data produce the generalizations of theory. The risks are that the theory describes a very idiosyncratic phenomenon or that the theorist is unable to raise the level of generality of the theory. Indeed, many of the grounded case studies mentioned earlier resulted in modest theories. For example, Gersick (1988) developed a model of group development for teams with project deadlines, Eisenhardt and Bourgeois (1988) developed a mid-range theory of politics in high velocity environments, and Burgelman (1983) proposed a model of new product ventures in large corporations. Such theories are likely to be testable, novel, and empirically valid, but they do lack the sweep of theories like resource dependence, population ecology, and transaction cost. They are essentially theories about specific phenomena. To their credit, many of these theorists tie into broader theoretical issues such as adaptation, punctuated equilibrium, and bounded rationality, but ultimately they are not theories about organization in any grand sense. Perhaps "grand" theory requires multiple studies – an accumulation of both theory-building and theory-testing empirical studies.

Applicability

When is it appropriate to conduct theory-building case study research? In normal science, theory is developed through incremental empirical testing and extension (Kuhn, 1970). Thus, the theory-building process relies on past literature and empirical observation or experience as well as on the insight of the theorist to build incrementally more powerful theories. However, there are times when little is known about a phenomenon, current perspectives seem inadequate because they have little empirical substantiation, or they conflict with each other or common sense. Or, sometimes, serendipitous findings in a theory-testing study suggest the need for a new perspective. In these situations, theory building from case study research is particularly appropriate because theory building from case studies does not rely on previous literature or prior empirical evidence. Also, the conflict inherent in the process is likely to generate the kind of novel theory which is desirable when extant theory seems inadequate. For example, Van de Ven and Poole (in press) have argued that such an approach is especially useful for studying the new area of longitudinal change processes. In sum, building theory from case study research is most appropriate in the early stages of research on a topic or to provide freshness in perspective to an already researched topic.

Evaluation

How should theory-building research using case studies be evaluated? To begin, there is no generally accepted set of guidelines for the assessment of this type of research. However, several criteria seem appropriate. Assessment turns on whether the concepts, framework, or propositions that emerge from the process are "good theory." After all, the point of the process is to develop or at least begin to develop theory. Pfeffer (1982) suggested that good theory is parsimonious, testable, and logically coherent, and these criteria seem appropriate here. Thus, a strong theory-building study yields good theory (that is, parsimonious, testable, and logically coherent theory) which emerges at the end, not beginning, of the study.

Second, the assessment of theory-building research also depends upon empirical issues: strength of method and the evidence grounding the theory. Have the investigators followed a careful analytical procedure? Does the evidence support the theory? Have the investigators ruled out rival explanations? Just as in other empirical research, investigators should provide information on the sample, data collection procedures, and analysis. Also, they should display enough evidence for each construct to allow readers to make their own assessment of the fit with theory. While there are no concise measures such as correlation coefficients or F values, nonetheless thorough reporting of information should give confidence that the theory is valid. Overall, as in hypothesis testing, a strong theory-building study has a good, although not necessarily perfect, fit with the data.

Finally, strong theory-building research should result in new insights. Theory building which simply replicates past theory is, at best, a modest contribution. Replication is appropriate in theory-testing research, but in theory-building research, the goal is new theory. Thus, a strong theory-building study presents new, perhaps framebreaking, insights.

Conclusions

The purpose of this article is to describe the process of theory building from case studies. The process, outlined in Table 1, has features which range from selection of the research question to issues in reaching closure. Several conclusions emerge.

Theory developed from case study research is likely to have important strengths like novelty, testability, and empirical validity, which arise from the intimate linkage with empirical evidence. Second, given the strengths of this theory-building approach and its independence from prior literature or past empirical observation, it is particularly well-suited to new research areas or research areas for which existing theory seems inadequate. This type of work is highly complementary to incremental theory building from normal science research. The former is useful in early stages of research on a topic or when a fresh perspective is needed, while the latter is useful in later stages of knowledge. Finally, several guidelines for assessing the quality of theory building from case studies have been suggested. Strong studies are those which present interesting or framebreaking theories which meet the tests of good theory or concept development (e.g., parsimony, testability, logical coherence) and are grounded in convincing evidence.

Most empirical studies lead from theory to data. Yet, the accumulation of knowledge involves a continual cycling between theory and data. Perhaps this article will stimulate some researchers to complete the cycle by conducting research that goes in the less common direction from data to theory, and equally important, perhaps it will help others become informed consumers of the results.

References

Abbott, A. (1988, September) *Workshop on sequence methods*. National Science Foundation Conference on Longitudinal Research Methods in Organizations, Austin.

Allison, G. (1971) *Essence of decision*. Boston: Little, Brown.

Anderson, P. (1983) Decision making by objection and the Cuban missile crisis. *Administrative Science Quarterly*, 28, 201–222.

Bartunek, J. (1988) The dynamics of personal and organizational reframing. In R. Quinn & K. Cameron (Eds.), *Paradox and transformation: Towards a theory of change in organization and management* (pp. 137–162). Cambridge, MA: Ballinger.

Bettenhausen, K., & Murnighan, J. K. (1986) The emergence of norms in competitive decision-making groups. *Administrative Science Quarterly*, 30, 350–372.

Bourgeois, L., & Eisenhardt, K. (1988) Strategic decision processes in high velocity environments: Four cases in the microcomputer industry. *Management Science*, 34, 816–835.

Burgelman, R. (1983) A process model of internal corporate venturing in a major diversified firm. *Administrative Science Quarterly*, 28, 223–244.

Cameron, K., & Quinn, R. (1988) Organizational paradox and transformation. In R. Quinn & K. Cameron (Eds.), *Paradox and transformation* (pp. 1–18). Cambridge, MA: Ballinger.

Eisenhardt, K. (in press) Making fast strategic decisions in high velocity environments. *Academy of Management Journal*.

Eisenhardt, K., & Bourgeois, L. J. (1988) Politics of strategic decision making in high velocity environments: Toward a mid-range theory. *Academy of Management Journal*, 31, 737–770.

Gersick, C. (1988) Time and transition in work teams: Toward a new model of group development. *Academy of Management Journal*, 31, 9–41.

Glaser, B., & Strauss, A. (1967) *The discovery of grounded theory: Strategies of qualitative research*. London: Wiedenfeld and Nicholson.

Hannan, M., & Freeman, J. (1977) The population ecology of organizations. *American Journal of Sociology*, 82, 929–964.

Harris, S., & Sutton, R. (1986) Functions of parting ceremonies in dying organizations. *Academy of Management Journal*, 29, 5–30.

Jick, T. (1979) Mixing qualitative and quantitative methods: Triangulation in action. *Administrative Science Quarterly*, 24, 602–611.

Kahneman, D., & Tversky, A. (1973) On the psychology of prediction. *Psychological Review*, 80, 237–251.

Kidder, T. (1982) *Soul of a new machine*. New York: Avon.

Kimberly, J. (1988) A review of Walter R. Nord and Sharon Tucker: Implementing routine and radical innovations. *Administrative Science Quarterly*, 33, 314–316.

Kirk, J., & Miller, M. (1986) *Reliability and validity in qualitative research*. Beverly Hills, CA: Sage.

Kuhn, T. (1970) *The structure of scientific revolutions* (2nd ed.). Chicago: University of Chicago Press.

Leonard-Barton, D. (1988) Synergistic design for case studies: Longitudinal single-site and replicated multiple-site. Paper presented at the National Science Foundation Conference on Longitudinal Research Methods in Organizations, Austin.

McClintock, C., Brannon, D., & Maynard-Moody, S. (1979) Applying the logic of sample surveys to qualitative case studies: The case cluster method. *Administrative Science Quarterly*, 612–629.

Miles, M. (1979) Qualitative data as an attractive nuisance: The problem of analysis. *Administrative Science Quarterly*, 24, 590–601.

Miles, M., & Huberman, A. M. (1984) *Qualitative data analysis*. Beverly Hills, CA: Sage Publications.

Mintzberg, H. (1979) An emerging strategy of "direct" research. *Administrative Science Quarterly*, 24, 580–589.

Mintzberg, H., & McHugh, A. (1985) Strategy formation in an adhocracy. *Administrative Science Quarterly*, 30, 160–197.

Mintzberg, H., & Waters, J. (1982) Tracking strategy in an entrepreneurial firm. *Academy of Management Journal*, 25, 465–499.

Nisbett, R., & Ross, L. (1980) *Human inference: Strategies and shortcomings of social judgment*. Englewood Cliffs, NJ: Prentice-Hall.

Perrow, C. (1986) *Complex organizations* (3rd ed.). New York: Random House.

Pettigrew, A. (1973) *The politics of organizational decision making*. London: Tavistock.

—— (1988) Longitudinal field research on change: Theory and practice. Paper presented at the National Science Foundation Conference on Longitudinal Research Methods in Organizations, Austin.

Pfeffer, J. (1982) *Organizations and organization theory*. Marshfield, MA: Pitman.

Pinfield, L. (1986) A field evaluation of perspectives on organizational decision making. *Administrative Science Quarterly*, 31, 365–388.

Quinn, J. B. (1980) *Strategies for change*. Homewood, IL: Dow-Jones Irwin.

Selznick, P. (1949) *TVA and the grass roots*. Berkeley, CA: University of California Press.

Strauss, A. (1987) *Qualitative analysis for social scientists*. Cambridge, England: Cambridge University Press.

Sutton, R., & Callahan, A. (1987) The stigma of bankruptcy: Spoiled organizational image and its management. *Academy of Management Journal*, 30, 405–436.

Van De Ven, A., & Poole, M. S. (in press) Methods to develop a grounded theory of innovation processes in the Minnesota Innovation Research Program. *Organization Science*, 1.

Van Maanen, J. (1988) *Tales of the field: On writing ethnography*. Chicago: University of Chicago Press.

Yin, R. (1981) The case study crisis: Some answers. *Administrative Science Quarterly*, 26, 58–65.

—— (1984) *Case study research*. Beverly Hills, CA: Sage Publications.

9

What Can Case Studies Do?

Jennifer Platt

Introduction

'Case study' is a familiar term but, in sociology at least, case studies have in recent years been used more than they have been written about. In the inter-War period 'case study', normally contrasted with 'statistical method', was a key idea in methodological discussion in U.S. sociology; since World War II the textbook contrast has commonly been between 'participant observation' and 'survey', which brings out somewhat different issues, while maintaining the qualitative versus the quantitative theme (Platt 1981). The revival of interest in qualitative method, and the increase in attempts to systematize it, have once again directed attention to case studies, with most emphasis on methods of data collection. This paper is not concerned with data collection, but with design issues and related questions of research strategy.

For our purposes here, a 'case study' is one where more than one case may be used, but if more than one is used the individuality of each case is retained and/or the *number* of cases falling into a given category is not treated as of significance. (Note that this definition subsumes most versions of 'comparative method'. The distinction between designs where comparison is internal to the study and those where it draws on other work is not of logical importance.) The unit case may be a person, a small group, a community, an event or an episode. Historically, 'case study' has carried a heavy burden of connotations going beyond the literal meaning of the words to include ideas such as an emphasis on subjective meanings, and the use of life histories. This has tended to confuse discussion, because it has not been clear to which features consequences were being imputed. We shall attempt not to assume anything which goes beyond the definition given above. In particular, we shall not assume that a case study is necessarily internally non-quantitative; even when the case is an individual, data on the person may be quantified and, quantified or not, it remains a single case. Writers on case studies have tended to

Source: Robert Burgess (ed.), *Studies in Qualitative Methodology*, vol. 1 (Greenwich, CT: JAI Press, 1988).

think of them as providing a complete method. We shall not limit ourselves to this, but shall take anything from fundamental to incidental use as falling within our remit.

The discussion will draw heavily on examples (thus demonstrating some of the uses of cases discussed) both because this helps exposition and because it brings out points about usage in practice. Were I familiar with other examples, further uses might have become evident; the listing may well not be comprehensive, and readers are invited to supplement it. Each use I distinguish is not in practice clearly distinct and, indeed, it is common for them to overlap or for the use to be ambiguous. I attempt, however, to draw out the ideal-typical features of each example to illuminate the general logic of the procedure.

Writers in this field tend to divide into those who see little legitimate role for the case study except *faute de mieux* and those who urge its inherent superiority for all valued goals – though they may have different goals in mind. This paper aims to take seriously the potential of the case study for the whole range of possible goals, without partisan commitment to criteria which guarantee the outcome of evaluation.

Recent Discussions

A brief review needs to be made of what recent general discussion there is of case study method. Much of this has been outside sociology, and it is interesting to note the ways in which different disciplinary traditions skew the definitions used, the possibilities considered and the alternatives envisaged. (Aspects to do with the possibility of generalizing from case studies are reserved until later, pp. 170–175.)

Becker (1968) writes about case studies under a heading which includes 'observation', and thinks primarily of the sociological tradition of participant observation. He takes it for granted that the study will be of a group, and sees it as aiming to understand all of the group's behaviour, though in practice eventually focusing on 'a few problems that appear to be of major importance in the group studied'. No attention is given to how cases are chosen, except in the suggestion that a series of related studies, each of which looks at a different set of conditions, can be useful in building generalizations.

Lijphart (1971, pp. 691–3) writes in the context of a discussion of comparative method in politics. He takes it for granted that a case study is of only one case, since if there were more it would for him become 'comparative'. He has in mind as the typical case a whole polity, with its weight of history, and perhaps it is for this reason, as well as for philosophical ones, that he assumes that one case can in no sense establish a general proposition. He sketches six ideal types of case study, ranging from the completely atheoretical and descriptive to deviant cases which may lead to the modification of theory. It is assumed that general theory is the desirable goal in relation to which alternatives are evaluated.

Eckstein (1975), again writing from within political science, gives a typology very similar to Lijphart's, although he is more sympathetic to the potential of case studies. He addresses the problem of what should count as an individual case (do the voters of one polity count as one case or many?) and resolves it by the decision that 'a "case" can be defined technically as a phenomenon for which we report only a single measure on any pertinent variable' (p. 85); however, nothing subsequent seems to depend on this definition. His one type not corresponding to one of Lijphart's is the 'plausibility probe', whose function is 'to determine whether potential validity may reasonably be considered great enough to warrant the pains and costs of testing' (p. 108). Once again his eye is on the target of generalizing theory, and comparative method (with the polity as its characteristic unit) is the understood alternative.

The authors whose papers are collected in Simons (1980) are not in complete agreement, but there is a fair level of consensus in addition to the homogeneity which comes from their shared interest in educational evaluation For Hamilton the perceived alternative is the survey, for Kemmis the experiment: education draws on more than one disciplinary tradition. There is an agreed definition of a case as a 'bounded system', and an understanding that it will be a single case studied intensively. Stake says that 'the boundaries are kept in focus. What is happening and deemed important within those boundaries are considered vital and determine what the study is about, as contrasted with other kinds of study where hypotheses or issues previously targeted by the investigators determine the content of the study' (p. 71). Research evaluating education is almost invariably done for practical purposes, and is highly likely to be reported to its subjects and to other practitioners, who will not be academic members of the researcher's discipline and will be less interested in general propositions than in the cases on which they have to act. In those circumstances, the attractions of a method likely to speak directly to the concerns of this audience, and to be accessible to them, are evident. Validity, too, is seen as residing in the nature of the direct experience which the case study provides, and the sense of recognition it gives in the light of prior experience (Adelman et al., p. 52; Stake, pp. 69–72; Kemmis, p. 128). The emphasis is, thus, on 'understanding' and 'tacit knowledge' rather than formal method and explicit theorizing.

Runyan (1982) defines case study method as 'the presentation and interpretation of detailed information about a single subject, whether an event, a culture, or ... an individual life' (p. 121). However, his book is called *Life Histories and Psychobiography* and, like most other psychologists writing in this area (cf. Hersen and Barlow 1976; Kratochwill 1978; Bolgar 1965; Kazdin 1982), his real focus is on individual persons, normally considered as objects of treatment. Case study method is justified in terms of its inherently greater suitability for 'tasks such as describing an individual's experience ... developing idiographic interpretations of that experience, and developing context-specific predictions, plans and decisions' (p. 125). His criteria for a good case study (p. 152) are skewed towards insight, empathy and the rhetorical virtues rather than 'explanation'. He contrasts the case study, in the sense in which it concerns him, with single-case experimental designs on the ground that it looks at the whole person in the context of his life history, rather than only the causal relations among specific variables (pp. 146–7); the experiment is clearly the alternative.

Yin (1984) is also a psychologist by training, but has made a career in consultancy, specializing in case studies of organizational processes. It is understandable, therefore, that his approach is eclectic but tends to assume that policy conclusions will be drawn. He offers this definition of a case study: 'an empirical inquiry that: – investigates a contemporary phenomenon within its real-life context; when – the boundaries between phenomenon and context are not clearly evident [cf. Stake]; and in which – multiple sources of evidence are used' (p.23). This definition, curious in its absence of any reference to the idea of a case, is, the context makes clear, intended to distinguish what he has in mind from history, experiment or survey. The cases may be single or multiple, but if they are multiple the logic is of replication rather than sampling.

Mitchell, an anthropologist, defines a case study as 'a detailed examination of an event (or series of related events) which the analyst believes exhibits (or exhibit) the operation of some identified general theoretical principle' (1983, p. 192). It is clear that the case is an *event* which *exemplifies* because it is taken for granted that the real focus of interest is the underlying social structures which generate the event; note, however, that these structures might to other writers constitute the 'case'. His implicit paradigm, at least at some points in the article, is the traditional anthropological one in which the analyst has very intensive knowledge of one society, and a prime interest in making general statements about that society as a unique entity. (Because this is taken for granted, the whole society cannot be the 'case' in any sense which implies that the use of case studies is distinctive.) This makes some problems less salient than they might be, and places him less clearly in the group of those who do not regard cases as of interest in their own right than might initially appear.

These instances show how writers tend to have in mind, even when making apparently quite general statements, the sort of case and the sort of method most salient in their own intellectual setting. Psychologists think first of individuals in treatment, anthropologists of events in whole small societies, and political scientists of polities. Where experiments are normal there is sensitivity about problems of imputing causation, and where surveys are normal it is about sampling and numbers of cases. Where experiments or surveys are normal the holistic and naturalistic potential of case studies is valued; where the making of practical decisions is at stake, relevance to concrete individual cases and the capacity to communicate with decision-makers are issues. No doubt the discussion below will not be immune from such unconscious biases, but it will strive not to be limited by them.

Functions of the Case Study: Rhetorical

What are the possible functions of case-study material? It is convenient to divide these between two general headings, which we shall call the rhetorical and the logical. The logical functions are those which are an essential part of the formal argument of the work; the rhetorical functions are those which are to do with the presentation of that argument, and which could be changed without affecting its essence. In practice, of course, a given instance may perform multiple functions, almost inextricably entangled, and the author's intentions may not be clear. It is also arguable that rhetorical strategies are an aspect of logic, perhaps micro to its macro, while logical structure may itself operate as rhetoric in, for instance, evoking the prestige of 'scientific method'. Nonetheless, the distinction has its uses. We start with the rhetorical functions. (Note that it is not intended to imply that these functions can only be, or always are, performed by case study material, but merely that at least some kinds of case material may legitimately perform them, or are particularly well suited to them.) These include ostensive definition, illustration, mnemonic, empathy, revelation, persuasion and aesthetic appeal.

In ostensive definition, material is presented to show what is meant by an abstract term; this helps the reader without a background of experience in the field to grasp the implications of the discussion, or makes clear the way in which a specialist usage differs from the familiar. Illustration is similar: it aids understanding by offering an example. It is a more problematic process, however, because of its potential for taking on latent logical functions; there can be confusion about whether a particular case is merely illustrating a point made in other ways, or being used as evidence for the point. If it is being used as evidence, questions arise about its adequacy as such. For instance, Young and Willmott (1957, pp. 82–4) exemplify a general point about the density of social relations in Bethnal Green by reporting one woman's comments on her connections with people whom she met on half-an-hour's shopping trip. Is she typical? It is not clear, although other evidence is given to support the general statement which her case illustrates and so, in this instance, the lack of clarity does not matter (cf. Gluckman (1961) on the weaknesses of the 'apt illustration').

It is not by chance that I remember that shopping trip more clearly than many of the more general findings in the book: rich and specific detail sticks in the memory, and is an effective mnemonic device. This may not be unequivocally desirable, since it may be the inessentials which are more clearly retained. But if the case in some way encapsulates a central message, it may be a valuable tool. This is true of Lerner's 'Grocer of Balgat', presented in what he aptly subtitles 'a parable' to show the personal meanings of modernization in underdeveloped countries (Lerner 1958).

In addition the story of the grocer (who dreamed of modernization but died before it came to his village) is moving, and thus involves the reader and so helps to stimulate empathy. Empathy (as distinct from sympathy) enables the reader to grasp the meaning of the data presented and the lives they stand for; this is particularly helpful when those lives are unfamiliar or alien ones. Case material can not only present the subjective meanings of the subjects, but can also give holistic accounts of events or life-patterns which show social supports and constraints, help understanding of how one event is linked to another in a strange setting, and generally give the context of the particular topic. (Obviously the material chosen can be misleading, and empathy may sometimes have drawbacks, especially when it leads to sympathy.)

'Revelation', our next function, is the making visible of phenomena which would otherwise be cut off from the audiences at which the work is aimed. James Bennett (1981), in a fascinating book on the history of the use of oral histories of delinquents, argues that one of the conditions for the production of such oral histories is the existence of a social distance between delinquents and a potentially philanthropic middle-class public which reformers wish to bridge in order to persuade the middle classes to support reforms. The oral history makes the delinquent visible. This is a necessary stage in a strategy of persuasion. Revelation does not seem to have a special logical link with the desire to persuade, although it may have an empirical one. In principle, it is relevant wherever there is something surprising or unjustly ignored to be brought to attention, and the surprise or the injustice might relate to theoretical or historical assumptions. It seems probable that case material becomes more valuable for this purpose as the ignorance or resistance to be overcome becomes greater; a detailed and concrete instance carries more conviction of the tangible reality of what is described (cf. Freud on childhood sexuality, perhaps?).

The relation of such revelation to persuasion is evident when what is revealed is a situation which the writer can be confident will be regarded by the audience as scandalous or avoidably undesirable. When Townsend tries 'to let the facts reported by the respondents speak for themselves' (1979, p. 304) in a chapter of vignettes of families living in poverty, each one of which refers to state benefits received and any inadequacies or underpayments in them, it would be a hard reader indeed who did not draw policy morals – especially when that chapter is succeeded by one with vignettes of the rich. In a sense the same points are made by the quantitative data also presented, but the family case studies put them together in a way which can more easily be identified with and related to personal experience. Bennett argues that the oral histories of delinquents serve to persuade the reader to support positions which see delinquency as a social rather than a biological or a moral issue. This might suggest that different sorts of case material are suited to persuade to different conclusions, or that there are some issues on which case material, and others on which non-case material, would be more persuasive.

Case study material gives aesthetic appeal by providing 'human interest', good stories and a more humanistic mode of presentation than that of the traditional 'scientific'/quantitative style. To the extent that the material must particularize, it is harder to write about it in abstract theoretical jargon, and so it is (at least superficially) simple, even if what is described is complex. This

makes for easy and pleasant reading, and a wide and not exclusively professional appeal. Thus aesthetic appeal may be a means of persuasion in the sense
that it eases access for practice-oriented and non-academic audiences. Clearly
this may be bought at an unacceptable price of sacrifice of systematic presentation of evidence, but it does not have to be. How great the tension is between
aesthetic and scientific criteria probably varies with the character of the case
study and its role in the research as a whole. It is likely to be easier, for instance, to present an individual life history in an attractive literary form than
it is to do the same for a comparative study of communities.

I am not sure whether the provision of 'insight', 'understanding', 'feel for
the situation', insofar as these are not covered by 'empathy', should be classified under the head of rhetoric or of logic. Those who value these things highly
would probably see them as logical, while those who distrust them would see
them as (merely) rhetorical. The problem is that it is by definition impossible
to give an analytical account of how the end state in the reader is arrived at
or to be justified although, equally by definition, it gives a satisfaction which
feels as though it justified itself. Elements of intellectual taste are involved here,
and my personal taste is for that which can be analysed. Sophisticated arguments, analysing the process in terms of the roles of 'tacit knowledge' and
'naturalistic generalization', are possible (e.g. Stake 1980), but for public social science it seems more appropriate for the tacit to be made explicit. It could
also be argued that a sense of *dissatisfaction* is heuristically preferable, even if
it were not too easy to accept interpretations which attract for reasons other
than the adequacy of the evidence supporting them.

The previous paragraph may suggest a conventionally scientistic position
which defines rhetoric as a bad thing and logic as a good thing. But that position can only be held if one conceives it possible to eliminate rhetoric, which
it is not; everything has to be presented somehow, and a purely 'scientific'
style has its own rhetoric (Gusfield 1976). Effective communication of a good
argument is a good thing, of a bad argument a bad thing, insofar as medium
and message can be distinguished. The peculiar rhetorical strengths of case
study material, especially, but not exclusively, for audiences without research
involvement in the same field, make it important that such material be used
carefully in ways which support, rather than override, the logical grounds for
the conclusions reached. The rhetorical functions it can perform are nonetheless of value.

Functions of the Case Study: Logical

We turn now to consider the logical functions which may be performed by
case studies. This is an area which has been more explored by other writers,
particularly Eckstein (1975) and Lijphart (1971), and their work is drawn on.
We start with comparatively tentative and exploratory functions, and work
up to those permitting relatively strong assertions.

First, then, it is universally recognized, even by those who scarcely allow it any other role, that a case study may suggest hypotheses, interpretations, empirical uniformities, for future (quantitative) investigation. It does so by showing that things are so, or that such an interpretation is plausible, in the particular case, so that they might also be so in other cases. Closely related to this, in that the emphasis is on a main study yet to come which will use other methods, is its use as a pilot study, trial or demonstration project: methods, approaches or policies are tried out to see what are the difficulties that need to be dealt with before the main study takes place. Clearly such use must assume that the case studied is representative in at least some ways of some others, or the exercise would be pointless, but the conclusions reached by using it are instrumental rather than terminal. Probably no-one does a case study with the deliberate intention of adding to the stock of those available for analysis by others, but since quite a lot of such secondary analysis is done (whether within an elaborate system, such as that provided by the Yale Cross-Cultural Index, or less formally) the potential contribution here of purely descriptive material, whatever its first intended use, should be noted.

The remaining uses may be classified along two dimensions: how far they are confined to the particular case(s) studied, and whether they purport to demonstrate a point directly or to provide a basis for inference to it. We shall work our way through the cells of the implied table, starting with direct demonstration about the particular case.

It has been a common feature of the literature critical of case studies to assume that generalizing theory is the only worthwhile goal. There can, however, be a legitimate interest in particularization (especially, though not only, among practitioners responsible for policy in particular cases (Stake 1980, p. 70)). It is evident that a case study is the best possible source of description or historical material about a particular case seen as inherently interesting in its own right. Howard Gruber's study of Charles Darwin and the processes by which he eventually arrived at the theory of evolution is an instance of this (1974). Clearly Darwin was an exceptional man, although even here there could be implicitly generalizing ideas about, say, the conditions for intellectual innovation or about Victorian scientific styles. Gruber is a psychologist; many studies by historians of people or episodes have the same character. Weber's account of the role of the Protestant ethic in the development of capitalism could be put in the same category were it not for its comparative logic in the context of his larger *oeuvre*.

One might treat as a subcategory of that type (because it is differentiated mainly by the author's intention or the use made of it by others, rather than by what is actually done in the case) the presentation of the nature of an experience from which the readers may draw their own conclusions. Studs Terkel (1980) provides examples of this. Such presentations are always open to questioning of the author's good faith: how was the material selected? have conclusions really been left open?

A case may also be chosen, not because it is in itself of special interest, but because it shows the effects of a social context which is the object of interest –

a social barium meal, whose progress through the system illuminates it. Some of Townsend's cases (e.g. Townsend 1979, pp. 850–9) clearly perform this function as they show, through the history of an individual family's interaction with state agencies, how the system of social benefits operates in practice. Robert E. Lane's cases of 'common men' and their political ideologies could be taken in the same way, given the emphasis on the system pressures which affect their beliefs (Lane 1962). In principle, studies of 'great men' could also operate in this way: insofar as the great man made a difference, to study his influence is to suggest what things would have been like without him. Obviously the question remains as to how much of a system a single case can illuminate.

Our second cell contains uses of case studies for inference to other aspects of the particular case. Much the most important use under this heading is in the prediction of future developments in the case of interest. The sorts of cases for which this is done are individuals (normally either as subjects of therapeutic intervention or as occupants of positions of power where their actions have important consequences for others), organizations and political or economic systems. The implication of such analyses is that, although there may be general laws which are relevant, there are so many idiosyncratic and historically specific factors involved that it would be impractical to specify the necessary initial conditions for the application of the laws. It is reasonable to ignore such factors when the focus of interest is on general laws for which merely probabilistic confirmation may be quite satisfactory, but not where one will be either right or wrong (Stake 1982, p.70). It is, of course, possible that there are general laws specific to the particular case, but even if there are not the practical reasons for concentrating on the case of interest remain (cf. Diesing 1972, ch. 18). That such concentration can be unwise when a comparative perspective would be beneficial, or can implicitly draw on general propositions which are not acknowledged and/or would be shown by the study of further cases to be erroneous, does not weaken the general point, although it suggests caution. One form such caution may take is the comparative use of more than one case (Cook and Campbell 1979, pp. 96–7), which may be focused on the reasons for the differences between them and hence the distinctiveness of each. An example of this is provided by Duncan Gallie's masterly comparative study, at one level of Britain and France as whole societies, at another level of industrial relations and worker attitudes at two oil refineries in France and two in Britain (1978). By choosing industrial settings which are closely comparable, he is able to show that differences between their workers must be attributable to other, nationally specific, factors. (He also relates this to more general theoretical ideas about technology and class consciousness.)

Also included in this cell should be the possible use of a case study to make inferences as to the nature of its context or social setting, regarded as another case. Such an inference would inevitably be either speculative or rather vague and non-specific unless more general propositions were at least tacitly invoked, and hence questionable. Perhaps it is as well that I cannot recall a specific example.

Our third cell is that where something is demonstrated directly which is taken to be descriptively true or have implications beyond the particular case. Proponents of case studies commonly argue that they can provide material, inaccessible or less easily obtained by other means, which fills in what Cook and Campbell (1979, p.32) call the 'micromediation' of social processes. This includes the process of development over a long time-span, the subjective perspectives of participants on events, the ways in which complex sets of factors interact to produce real-life outcomes, and the nature of the mechanisms or processes by which outcomes are generated. There are some difficulties with this conception. These things may indeed be demonstrated in the particular case(s) studied, but the application of the findings to cases not studied must surely entail inference (however well-grounded) rather than direct demonstration. Attention should also be drawn to the fact that such claims are normally made about 'case studies' which are defined in terms that go beyond the design features on which we are concentrating here, and usually rest on the particularly detailed and intensive nature of the data collected. The reasons why detailed and intensive data are not usually collected on large numbers of cases treated quantitatively are practical not logical, and so give such data no *inherent* association with cases treated non-quantitatively. (The issues raised about the possibility of generalization are treated below.)

Another function, however, remains in this cell and is not open to question. A single case can undoubtedly demonstrate that its features are possible and, hence, may also exist in other cases and, even if they do not, must be taken into account in the formulation of general propositions. Representativeness is of no importance to this function and, indeed, it is more effectively performed by extreme or atypical cases. Similar to this, but without any special role for the unusual case, is the demonstration that factors which are individually specific, or commonly ignored, did indeed make a difference in the particular case(s) studied. From this it may reasonably be taken to follow that analogous types of factor – not necessarily the same ones – may also need to be taken into account in other cases. Mandelbaum, for instance, concludes on the basis of a detailed life-history of Gandhi: 'Each person is both a bound actor and a free agent.... This [life-history] approach enables us to see that an individual has some opportunity for self-direction within the unwritten scenario of his culture and the open-ended drama of his society' (1973, p. 194). Similarly Wallman chooses eight ordinary households living in one area to show how they are 'active subjects who have choices to make within the constraints of the environment they share', and choose differently (1984, p. vii), thus both showing something of the range of possible choices in that setting and implying that there are choices available in other settings.

Finally we come to the cell where the case(s) studied are taken to provide a basis for inference to points not directly demonstrated and with relevance to cases not studied. Many dismissals of case-study method treat this as the only significant cell, and it is certainly the one which raises the most serious intellectual problems and so is considered here at greatest length.

That which is inferred is normally a general proposition, theoretical or empirical. If the uniformity of nature is assumed the problem vanishes: any case will do to demonstrate what can be taken to be true of all other cases of the same class. This is a normal assumption in the natural sciences, though it might be thought to be rare or non-existent in the social sciences. Not so, however, in some areas (cf. Dukes 1965; Kazdin 1982, pp. 3–10). Both Piaget and Freud notoriously developed general theories on the basis of small numbers of unsystematically-selected cases, Piaget's his own children. Piaget is so unselfconscious about this that in *The Origins of Intelligence in the Child* he has no discussion of method, or even description of the cases when first introduced; their names are simply attached to the reported observations, from which general conclusions are reached. It is not only founding fathers who adopt such practices. A recent article makes its assumptions very clear: 'Our analysis of the language used by Helen and by Alice for the coordination of visual attention to things clearly supports Brown's functional characterization of nominations ... [it] also demonstrates important matters concerning early lexical development' (Edwards and Goodwin 1985, p. 490). The study of language seems traditionally to have a cavalier attitude to issues of sampling, also exemplified in, for instance, Atkinson's fascinating work analysing the features of politicians' speeches which evoke applause (Atkinson 1984). Perhaps the uniformity of human language indeed justifies such assumptions. It is highly questionable, however, whether much else in the subject matter of the social sciences does or, if it does, whether the range of uniformity can be judged without empirical study.

There is also a tradition of doing a study in one country and then stating a conclusion about what happens 'in an industrial society', although it has often been shown that industrial societies differ. (It should perhaps be noted that this is not quite the same as the practice, within some relatively recent Marxian paradigms, of reaching conclusions about what happens 'in a capitalist society', because there, although some data may be presented, the conclusion is seen as following by definition from the abstract models of the theory.) In actual practice the classical laboratory experiment, while certainly not normally regarded as a case study, has been one in just this way (as many critics have pointed out, if not always in these terms): the focus has been on a few variables, treated as if they were independent of their bearers or of the context, and concern with representativeness has been focused on the comparability of experimental and control groups rather than on their relation to the wider population.

Where complete uniformity is not assumed, cases may still be treated (with more or less plausibility) as representative of the population to which findings are generalized. (The methods of formal sampling are too familiar to be worth discussion here. They could be applied to the selection of cases which would then be treated non-quantitatively to reach general conclusions, but I cannot recall any instance of this, and there is an obvious tension between the logics of the two procedures.) Occasionally the daring claim is made that extraordinary cases are in some sense especially representative. Mandelbaum, for instance, argued that Gandhi 'evoked ideas and emotions so deeply characteristic of his countrymen that millions of them recognized in him their own deep-rooted feelings' (1973, p. 183), and Erikson says of Luther that his solution to his life crisis 'roughly bridged a political and psychological vacuum which history had created in a significant portion of Western Christendom' (1959, p. 13); this is the representativeness of the epitome or the pure type, rather than of the average case. More often the basis of, and justification for, the claim to representativeness is not very clear. Let us consider an example. Hill has written an excellent study of the local political process in the town of Tiraspol in the Soviet republic of Moldavia (1977). On the cover it is called *Soviet Political Elites*, which certainly suggests generality, although the title page modifies it with the subtitle 'The Case of Tiraspol'. Hill sets the scene for his study by giving a brief description of the town 'showing how typical it is of Soviet urban communities' (p. 9). Even this phrase is ambiguous, though no doubt unintentionally so, since it could mean either showing that it is typical or showing *how far* it is typical. After a few pages of description, he concludes that 'Tiraspol is a fairly typical Soviet town', although almost immediately he raises questions about what this might mean by citing an urban geographer's classification of it as falling into 'the most common type of city in the Soviet Union' and then adding, 'It is perhaps more typically Soviet than ... other towns in the republic' (p. 14). Clearly the author is anxious that the book should not be regarded merely as the study of one case, but as throwing light on the Soviet Union more generally, while aware that the claim could be questioned. It must be taken as part of the implicit logic of the claim, although this is not spelled out, that the Soviet Union is politically a highly centralized society and so much of what goes on in any locality will be a product of the same central forces as affect other localities. Many other studies of particular towns, schools, delinquent gangs make analogous assumptions. Their authors could choose to write up their material in a way which emphasizes the *special* features of their cases, but do not do so. Only such ambiguous and partially tacit claims to representativeness can be made when no procedure has been followed in the choice of case which might justify it. This does not mean that such claims may not be reasonable ones. They become convincing when the interaction between evidently general and probably particular factors is shown, and the general conclusions indicated are not simply generalizations of the precise outcomes in the case(s) studied.

Inevitably, however, one is left uncertain about what to expect in a Soviet town of a different size, a school with a different head, a gang from another ethnic group. Becker (1968) suggests that in each study 'we strip away what is historically unique and concentrate on the generic properties of the group, viewed as an example', but does not spell out how this is to be done, nor when one can tell that it has been done successfully. Note that the discussion above does not refer to instances where only one or a few cases are presented but they represent more which have actually been studied; this can mean that the case focus is more rhetorical than logical.

A quite different strategy for claiming representativeness is followed by Lacey in *Hightown Grammar* (1970). This is a case study of one school, but it is a chapter on the internal dynamics of pupil stratification that we look at here. In this chapter, Lacey presents eight cases of pupils, 'selected to illustrate the nature of the relationship between a number of the major social factors relevant to this book'. The cases are taken one from each cell of a typology defined by the three dichotomized variables of social class, parental interest and encouragement, and achievement (p. 125). Each is presented separately, and they are then compared and general conclusions drawn in terms of the resources which each family brought to the school arena. The case studies of individuals do not constitute the whole of the research, but their presentation does more than merely 'illustrate' points made elsewhere in other ways, although the availability of other data takes some of the weight of necessity off their claims to representativeness. The most interesting aspect is the explicitly systematic principle of choice, designed not to give quantitative representation (Lacey says that there were far more cases of some types than others) but to show the full range of possibilities as defined by the key theoretical variables. In a sense each case is taken to represent its category, and here representativeness can be questioned, although perhaps the predefined homogeneity might be seen as making this unimportant; moreover, the author's very detailed familiarity with the institution – he did participant observation as well as using many other types of data – gives some confidence that his judgment on the typical nature of the processes shown in these cases may be trusted. More important, however, is the qualitative representation of each type, which both implies a different relevant conception of representativeness and demonstrates a useful principle for the selection of cases.

Another excellent example of systematic choice of cases is provided by Hagood (1969). She uses several different strategies, but the most original is to locate every illustrative case being presented in relation to the mode and the extreme values on the variable of concern. As she rightly points out, this 'avoids the featuring of pathological cases as typical', as well as stressing the variation within even a fairly homogeneous group (pp. 228–9). (Pahl has an interesting discussion of the dangers, in presenting vignettes chosen to represent types, of giving a false impression of homogeneity within the type (1984, p. 278). He ends up giving only two case studies to illuminate his quantitative data, showing the process of change over time and the way it responded to circumstances.)

Examples of research where the whole study rests on cases chosen in this way are hard to come by, but explicitly comparative designs may have similar features. Orloff and Skocpol (1984) compare Britain 1900–11 with Massachusetts 1880–1920 in order to discuss theories of the development of welfare state provision. Britain did have certain kinds of provision which the U.S. did not; the comparison is with Massachusetts rather than the U.S. as a whole because it, unlike most other states, was closely similar to Britain on variables which appear in various theories on the welfare state. The cases thus occupy different cells in a typology, which could be expanded, on the dependent variable. If a wider range of cases had been considered, a positive theory could be put forward more confidently, in addition to the dismissal of others' theories. Another example is Powell's *Getting Into Print* (1985), a study of how publishing-house editors make decisions about what gets into print. He presents intensive studies of two contrasted scholarly publishing houses, which are shown to be different in a variety of ways. Two kinds of general conclusion are drawn, however, one about the process of publication and the other about organization theory. The strength of the conclusions about publishing rests on the fact that they are true of both houses despite their differences; the strength of those about the relations between organizations and their environments rests on the observation that factors were relevant to the organizations studied which other theories have not taken into account (but which there is reason to believe also occur in other cases). In each of these studies the logic of the comparison is that it allows some factors to be held constant while others are examined, and differences are imputed to the remaining factors. This is a powerful device for showing the inadequacy of theories which only include the factors held constant, but does not enable one to make empirical generalizations beyond the cases studied except of the kind urging that other factors need to be taken into account. Powell's book, however, also employs another logic, that of diversity of cases rather than representativeness as a basis for generalization. The potential of diversity for this purpose has more often been recognized in passing than elaborated or acted upon as a principle. It seems to rest on the *a fortiori* argument that if such diverse cases can be encompassed by the same general proposition, it must follow that those with other (perhaps less extreme) values on the same variables are also covered by it. For this to work, the other cases must in some relevant sense be of the same kind. If the cases studied are extremes it suggests more confident coverage of the whole field, but raises the problem that extremes may have special characteristics.

But 'diversity' is probably more often thought of as qualitative rather than quantitative. A fascinating example of a rare type of this is provided by Homans's *The Human Group* (1951). He takes five cases, each of them already studied by someone else, and aims to establish abstract general propositions about the behaviour of the human group. It is not absolutely clear how far he sees the propositions as either inductively derived from, or tested by, the data. He says that his case method means that 'general theories are shown to arise out of, and to be supported by, specific, detailed matters of observation' (1951, p. 18), and later that what he is trying to do in the book is merely 'to set up ... a series of hypotheses' (p. 117). The form many of his statements on particular subjects take is more like that of conclusions, and the anxieties he shows about applicability are more to do with which other factors are also relevant than with whether the ones mentioned so far are sufficiently supported. On the issue of diversity, Homans says, 'By taking only five cases, we shall sacrifice wide coverage but we shall gain in intensity of analysis' (Homans

1951, p. 19). Of the five cases, four are drawn from the U.S.A. (and these are all studies done at Harvard!). Despite this, 1 suspect that I am not the only reader who initially read the book as an impressive synthesis of a wide range of material, even if Homans' own statements suggest something more like a uniformity-of-nature approach in which more cases than one are required only in order to help elucidate general principles which interact in their effects on particular cases. At any rate, even if the actual range of diversity is not great, this remains an instance where qualitative diversity is used to reach highly general conclusions. Whether those conclusions are justified, even for the cases used, is another matter, although one reason for doubting this – the use of such abstract concepts that it is not clear what would or would not count as an instance of them – is irrelevant here. The argument would be more persuasive if the cases used were drawn from more varied settings, and had been studied by social scientists from more varied intellectual backgrounds. But what constitutes 'variety'? That will depend on the factors known social-scientifically, or believed commonsensically, to be likely to make a difference; the more surprising the uniformity, the greater the conviction it carries (Polya 1968, p. 9). Davies (1980) uses a large number of case studies, made by others, of personality in relation to politics, and attempts to fit them all into one framework. The choice of cases is more convincing than that of Homans, not because there are more of them, although that helps to increase the variety, but because the original authors have more varied backgrounds.

The *a fortiori* principle may also be used in a much simpler way. Goldthorpe et al. (1969) study a situation of the kind which, in the theorizing of others, is seen as *most* likely to lead to 'embourgeoisement' among affluent manual workers, on the reasonable assumption that if it is not found to be taking place even there (as it was not), then neither can the theory be correct for less favourable cases.

This can have something in common with the study of deviant (or apparently deviant) cases. If a case is truly deviant on closer inspection, it either refutes a generalization or requires that it be modified. If it turns out not to be deviant really, it gives stronger confirmation to the generalization than if it had looked all along like just another instance of a known regularity (Polya 1968, pp. 6–9). Lipset et al. (1956) provide an interesting example of this in their study of the ITU, the New York printers' union. Contrary to Michels' 'iron law of oligarchy' about such organizations, it had a flourishing system of participatory democracy. Does this refute Michels' 'law'? When the union is studied more closely, it emerges that a variety of special circumstances violate all the initial conditions which Michels had assumed. It may thus actually be taken to *support* his reasoning, and even to strengthen his generalization. Other kinds of deviant case may lead to modification of a theory – by, for instance, redefining the limits of its applicability, or suggesting further variables that need to be incorporated, into it.

Clearly there are ways in which case studies can legitimately be used in reaching generalizations, even if they are open to misuse, and this is so even if one is committed to a hypothetico-deductive strategy and a covering-law model of explanation. The question is not whether it can be done at all, but *from* what one can reasonably generalize *to* what. (It is curious how often criticisms of case studies as a basis for 'generalization' use ideas of representative sampling, appropriate only for estimating the prevalence of a characteristic in a population, to dismiss their adequacy for making contributions to theoretical explanation.) No-one disputes that a single case may be a useful source of hypotheses, or refute a universal generalization, or demonstrate the existence of a phenomenon which needs to be taken into account. *A fortiori* and similar arguments, though seldom discussed, create little difficulty. As soon as it is recognized that there are degrees of plausibility or confirmation, not just simple right and wrong, many difficulties vanish, since these are plainly affected by the character of cases: a least-likely case provides a particularly strong confirmation (Eckstein 1975, p. 119); a case very different from those previously studied gives a greater confidence than a similar one (cf. Polya 1968, pp. 4–20); and so on. The problematic areas are the representativeness of cases, and the extent to which they provide a challenge to the fit of theory. We shall consider each of these in turn.

There seems no reason to except case studies from the normal assumption that one can reasonably make generalizations from what one knows already until information inconsistent with this becomes available; whatever is true of one instance should also be true of other instances of the same sort. (This does not mean that generalizations which turn out to be wrong may not too easily be made; for examples where quantitative data changed ethnographic impressions, see Paul (1984, p. 14) and Coulson (1967, p. 14).) The difficulty lies in establishing which instances *are* of the same sort in relevant respects. An accumulation of instances of much the same sort, whether as single cases *or* in a representative sample, is little help here. All a representative sample can add is some assurance that the cases studied have not omitted types occurring often enough to appear in it; the problem of defining the population from which the sample is to be drawn still remains. Mitchell (1983, pp. 198-200) argues that the process of inference to general propositions is always 'logical' rather than 'statistical'. Statistical inference, which requires numbers of cases, is merely about 'the concomitant variation of two characteristics. The analyst must go beyond the sample and resort to theoretical thinking to link those characteristics together.... The inference about the *logical* relation between the two characteristics is.... based.... upon the plausibility or upon the logicality of the nexus between the two characteristics'. Thus case studies are just as good a basis for such inference as other sorts of study, although its justification will also depend upon the adequacy of the theory and the corpus of related knowledge. This argument suggests that a strategic choice of types is likely to be more use than either a single case or a representative sample. How should types be defined? Taxonomy and typology have been curiously neglected in systematic writing on method, unless the more elaborate experimental designs could be counted under this head (cf. Heslop-Harrison

(1960) for a discussion of taxonomy in botany which also raises issues for social scientists). One of the strengths of the last stages of the pre-War case-study tradition was the use made of typological strategies (e.g. Angell 1936), which now might usefully be looked at again. Lazarsfeld's technique of the 'substruction' of the property-space implied by the concepts already in use is a valuable one (Barton 1955, pp. 50–53). In practice, of course, much depends on the work already done, which will define predictions not yet tested etc.

It has often been suggested that a key weakness in the use of single or few cases is that it is too easy to devise an interpretation to fit them. Many interpretations can be devised which are compatible with such limited data; there is no ground for choosing among them, and so the interpretation offered cannot even be treated as valid for the particular case(s) studied. This point applies both to the initial proposal of an interpretation, and to its testing on cases not defined as crucial, extreme and so on. There is an adequate reply to it, which refers not to the number of cases used but to the nature of the data on them. If there is a rich and detailed account of many features of the case(s), it may be a considerable achievement to devise an interpretation which can deal with all of them, and this may pose a greater challenge than the fitting of superficial generalizations to larger numbers. Campbell (1975, pp. 181–2) points out that there is a pattern-matching process in which the theory is in effect tested with the degrees of freedom which come from its multiple implications. Diesing (1972, p. 58) sees the process as one in which a holistic model is developed incorporating a whole network of propositions grounded in evidence; individual propositions may be separately questionable, but 'the larger and more complex the pattern, the more difficult it is to imagine an alternative, and the time comes when no plausible alternative is imaginable'. Eckstein (1975, p. 113) adds to this the argument that case studies can only be seen as useless where comparative (and other) studies are useful for the development of theory on the basis of the inductive fallacy: 'the belief that theories, being contained in phenomena, can be fully derived from observations by simple inspection' (cf. Mitchell 1983). Moreover, if there is a clear theory in advance, making a precise prediction, the fact that a single case falls exactly where it should on the curve is a very strong confirmation, given the unlikelihood that it would do so by chance (p. 117).

Thus it is eminently arguable that case studies can be used to generalize even in some of the ways less often accepted. But generalization is not the only desirable goal, and there are other goals for which cases are not merely adequate, but better than the alternatives. A basic distinction here is that between the search for propositions about variables, and for ones about historical individuals. It is evident when studying historical individuals (persons, events) that many factors affect outcomes which cannot be neglected, but which it would be hard to put in general terms. Diesing (1972, pp. 158–63) argues that case studies do and should use a version of Kaplan's 'pattern' model of explanation, rather than the deductive one. In this, no general laws appear; the whole explains the parts of the system, both are on the same level of generality, and no statement within the explanation need be generalized. Even if a deductivist could succeed in spelling out covering laws implied in such an explanation they would not be of much use, since the tentative generalizations would usually not be as well verified as the model of the particular case, and if the covering laws were well-confirmed they would only specify the probability of alternative outcomes rather than explain the specific outcome in question. He thus gives a philosophical mandate for strategies which may also be justified on practical grounds.

Conclusions

Thus case studies can do a whole variety of things. But some case studies do not do any of them well, and this is often because no particular rationale has dictated the choice of case. It is only too easy to study a case merely because it is convenient, and hope that something of more general interest will come of it, whether the study is an ethnographic one or a sample survey. Valuable secondary studies have been made which draw systematically on case studies done for other purposes (e.g. Frankenberg 1966; Murdock 1949), but ones especially designed for the purpose would have been better. (However, intensive case studies are more likely to be open to reuse by others simply because they offer data on a wide range of variables.) Despite this, there are case studies whose prime rationale is happy accident: data are only available on one case (e.g. Ladurie 1978). It would be a great waste not to exploit such material: serendipity is not to be sniffed at.

In general, *post hoc* rationalizations are not very persuasive. Nonetheless, it is not just through intellectual sloppiness that they are especially likely to be offered for case studies. It is because case studies, especially those which start with the case in its own right rather than as an instance, are more likely to uncover unanticipated findings as the details are explored. This openness to surprise and availability for multiple purposes is a real strength. When the case is only part of the study, or used for rhetorical purposes, there are dangers and, again, need for more self-consciousness and explicitly systematic procedure. The rhetorical appeal of rich data, real people, a story to tell, may make obscure to the reader – and even to the writer – the logic of what is going on. Case students, you have nothing to lose but your claim to be only poets really; why not come out of the closet and confess that you are also social scientists just like the rest?

Just like the rest, but also different. In some areas case studies can make the same sort of contribution as other types of research, while in other areas they can do things better or worse, or equal though different. Whatever the area, case studies have in common with other methods that they are only part of a larger enterprise transcending the individual work, and can only be used or evaluated against that background which, whether or not this is explicitly acknowledged, is a component in the research design.

References

Adelman, C., Jenkins, D. and Kemmis, S. 1980 'Rethinking case study: notes from the second Cambridge Conference' in Simons, q.v., pp. 47–61.

Angell, R. C. 1936 *The Family Encounters the Depression*, New York: Charles Scribner's Sons (reprinted 1965, Gloucester, Mass.: Peter Smith).

Atkinson, M. 1984 *Our Masters' Voices*, London: Methuen.

Barton, A. 1955 'The concept of property-space in social research' in P. F. Lazarsfeld and M. Rosenberg (eds.) *The Language of Social Research*, Glencoe, Ill.: Free Press.

Becker, H. S. 1968 'Observation: social observation and social case studies' in D. L. Sills (ed.) *International Encyclopaedia of the Social Sciences*, vol. II, New York: Macmillan, pp. 232–8.

Bennett, J. 1981 *Oral History and Delinquency*, Chicago: University of Chicago Press.

Bolgar, H. 1965 'The case study method' in B. B. Wolman (ed.) *Handbook of Clinical Psychology*, New York: McGraw-Hill.

Campbell, D. T. 1975 '"Degrees of freedom" and the case study', *Comparative Political Studies*, 8 (July), pp 178–93.

Colson, E. 1967 'The intensive study of small sample communities' in A. L. Epstein (ed.) *The Craft of Social Anthropology*, London: Tavistock.

Cook, T. D. and Campbell, D. T. 1979 *Quasi-Experimentation*, Chicago: Rand McNally.

Davies, A. F. 1980 *Skills, Outlooks and Passions*, Cambridge: Cambridge University Press.

Diesing, P. 1972 *Patterns of Discovery in the Social Sciences*, London: Routledge and Kegan Paul.

Dukes, W. F. 1965 'N = 1', *Psychological Bulletin*, 64 (July), pp. 74–9.

Eckstein, H. 1975 'Case study and theory in political science' in F. E. Greenstein and N. Polsby (eds.) *Handbook of Political Science*, vol. 7, pp. 79–137, Menlo Park, CA: Addison-Wesley.

Edwards, D. and Goodwin, R. 1985 'The language of shared attention and visual experience', *Journal of Pragmatics*, 9, pp. 475–93.

Erikson, E. H. 1959 *Young Man Luther*, London: Faber and Faber.

Frankenberg, R. 1966 *Communities in Britain*, Harmondsworth, Middlesex: Penguin.

Gallie, D. 1978 *In Search of the New Working Class*, Cambridge: Cambridge University Press.

Goldthorpe, J. H., Lockwood, D., Bechhofer, F. and Platt, J. 1969 *The Affluent Worker in the Class Structure*, Cambridge: Cambridge University Press.

Gruber, H. E. 1974 'A psychological study of scientific creativity' in H. E. Gruber and P. H. Barrett, *Darwin on Man*, New York: Dutton.

Gusfield, J. 1976 'The literary rhetoric of science ...', *American Sociological Review*, 41 (February), pp. 16-34.

Hagood, M. J. 1969 *Mothers of the South*, New York: Greenwood Press. (Reprinted from 1939, University of North Carolina Press.)

Hamilton, D. 1980 'Some contrasting assumptions about case study research and survey analysis' in Simons (ed.), q.v., pp. 78–92.

Hersen, M. and Barlow, D. H. 1976 *Single-Case Experimental Designs*, Oxford: Pergamon.

Heslop-Harrison, J. 1960 *New Concepts in Flowering-Plant Taxonomy*, London: Heinemann.

Hill, R. J. 1977 *Soviet Political Elites*, London: Martin Robertson.

Homans, G. C. 1951 *The Human Group*, London: Routledge and Kegan Paul.

Kazdin, A. E. 1982 *Single-Case Research Designs*, New York: Oxford University Press.

Kemmis, S. 1980 'The imagination of the case and the invention of the study' in Simons, q.v., pp. 96–142.

Kratochwill, T. R. 1978 *Single-Subject Research*, New York: Academic Press.

Lacey, C. 1970 *Hightown Grammar*, Manchester: University of Manchester Press.

Ladurie, E. Le R. 1978 *Montaillou*, London: Scholar Press.

Lane, R. E. 1962 *Political Ideology*, New York: Free Press.

Lerner, D. 1958 *The Passing of Traditional Society*, New York: Free Press.

Lijphart, A. 1971 'Comparative politics and the comparative method', *American Political Science Review*, 65 (Sept.), pp. 682–93.

Lipset, S. M., Trow, M. A. and Coleman, J. S. 1956 *Union Democracy*, Glencoe, Ill.: Free Press.

Mandelbaum, D. G. 1973 'The study of life history: Gandhi', *Current Anthropology*, 14 (June), pp. 177–206.

Mitchell, J. C. 1983 'Case and situation analysis', *Sociological Review*, 31(2), pp. 187–211.

Murdock, G. P. 1949 *Social Structure*, New York: Free Press.

Orloff, A. S. and Skocpol, T. 1984 'Why not equal protection? ...', *American Sociological Review*, 49 (December), pp. 726–50.

Pahl, R. E. 1984 *Divisions of Labour*, Oxford: Blackwell.

Piaget, J. 1953 *The Origins of Intelligence in the Child*, London: Routledge and Kegan Paul.

Platt, J. 1981 'Whatever happened to the case study?', University of Sussex, Photocopy.

Polya, G. 1968 *Patterns of Plausible Inference*, New Jersey: Princeton University Press.

Powell, W. W. 1985 *Getting Into Print*, Chicago: University of Chicago Press.

Runyan, W. M. 1982 *Life Histories and Psychobiography*, New York: Oxford University Press.

Simons, H. (ed.) 1980 *Towards a Science of the Singular*, University of East Anglia, Norwich: Centre for Applied Research in Education, Occasional Publications, no. 10.

Stake, R. E. 1980 'The case study method in social inquiry' in Simons, q.v., pp. 64–75.

Terkel, S. 1980 *American Dreams, Lost and Found*, New York: Pantheon.

Townsend, P. 1979 *Poverty in the United Kingdom*, Harmondsworth, Middlesex: Penguin.

Wallman, S. 1984 *Eight London Households*, London: Tavistock.

Yin, R. K. 1984 *Case Study Research*, Beverly Hills, CA: Sage.

Young, M. and Willmott, P. 1957 *Family and Kinship in East London*, London: Routledge and Kegan Paul.

10

Case and Situation Analysis[1]

J. Clyde Mitchell

Clearly one good case can illuminate the working of a social system in a way that a series of morphological statements cannot achieve.

(Gluckman 1961: 9)

Introduction

The current division between those sociologists who prefer to rely on survey techniques and quantitative analysis in the prosecution of their art as against those who prefer to rely on observation and verbal types of analysis has had a long history. Just over fifty years ago – in the late 1930s in fact – the division manifested itself in a lively debate in some of the journals about the validity of statistical methods of enquiry on the one hand as against what were called 'case studies'.[2]

Textbooks on sociological methods of research published before say 1955 such as Young 1939 (226–54) or Goode and Hatt 1952 (313–40) invariably included a chapter on case studies but since then the topic seems to have lost its appeal, since while non-quantitative procedures such as participant observation receive extensive treatment the issue of the role of case studies as such seems to have disappeared. The change in emphasis is dramatically reflected in the general index of the *American Journal of Sociology* which had its origin in Chicago from which the most important case studies first emerged and which carried the account of the debate in its pages. The Cumulative Index at 1950 contained sixteen references to case studies and case histories.[3] The most recent reference is to Oscar Lewis's discussion of the detailed studies of families in 1950. After that the entry for case studies disappears from the index! A paper on case studies appeared in *Social Forces* at about the same time (Foreman 1948). Since then it appears to have faded from sociological discussion but it has survived in education research (see Simons 1980).

Source: *Sociological Review*, vol. 31, no. 2, 1983, pp. 186–211.

This eclipse of interest in case studies as a method of sociological analysis is partly due to the vast expansion of quantitative techniques stimulated by the wide availability of computers which has broken the back of formerly extremely time-consuming processing of large sets of survey data. Hand in hand with the steady strides in the sophistication of statistical techniques a theory of sampling soundly based on probability mathematics has grown up so that the survey analyst has available an extensive armamentarium of procedures and techniques all resting on firm epistemological grounds.

The foundation of statistical inference from samples representative of a wider population has now become commonplace knowledge and most first year students in the social sciences are made familiar with such notions as 'a representative sample', 'sampling error', 'biased and unbiased estimates' and similar ideas developed to express the logic of making inferences about a larger population from a considerably smaller sample.

In the course of this development the epistemology of the case study seems to have been neglected with a corresponding confusion about the degree to which those who either by force of circumstances or by deliberate choice find themselves engaged in case studies. The consequence is that we find criticism of their findings to the effect that these findings are invalid because they are based on only one case.[4] This confusion of procedures of statistical inference with those appropriate to case studies is indexed particularly by the challenge frequently addressed to those who have chosen to pursue the deviant path of case studies: 'How do you know that the case you have chosen is typical?'

I shall argue that this question betrays a confusion between the procedures appropriate to making inferences from statistical data and those appropriate to the study of an idiosyncratic combination of elements or events which constitute a 'case'. It is my purpose to establish what these differences are and thereby one hopes to provide guidelines for the use of case studies in social investigation and theory building.[5]

The Case Study In Social Anthropology

The method of case studies is, of course, general and has been extensively used, for example, in political science and in sociology. But more than in other social sciences, perhaps, each fieldworker who presents a study of some 'people' or another in a social anthropological monograph is in fact doing a case study. Possibly because quantitative techniques do not play so central a role in social anthropology as in sociology there has been more discussion of the method of case study in anthropology. One of the earliest general statements about the role of case studies by Barnes in 1958 drew a contrast between the formal method of institutional analysis and the complexity of the 'Russian novel' approach through case studies (Barnes 1958). In 1960 he described the case-history approach as a 'distinctive feature' of presentday social anthropology (Barnes 1960: 201).

Each people an anthropologist studies may be looked upon as displaying a unique combination of cultural characteristics. But the anthropologist sets out to interpret some aspect of the way of life of this people by using an approach which an anthropologist studying some quite different people may also employ. In short nearly the whole of the respectable body of anthropological theory has been built up over the years from a large number of separate case studies from which the anthropologists have been prepared to draw inferences and to formulate propositions about the nature of social and cultural phenomena in general. What appears not to be so widely discussed in anthropology, however, is the epistemological basis upon which these generalisations have been made and it is to this question that I wish to turn with its implication for the role of case studies in the development of theories in general whether in social anthropology or not.

A more focused statement appeared in 1961 when Max Gluckman discussed the history and use of case material in anthropological analysis (Gluckman 1961). In it he drew the important distinctions among what he called 'apt illustrations', 'social situations' and 'extended case studies', the implications of which I return to later (see p. 185 below). The basic problem in the use of case material in theoretical analysis, however, is that of the extent to which the analyst is justified in generalising from a single instance of an event which may be – and probably is – unique. This problem is normally presented as that of the 'typicality' of the case which is used to support some theoretical analysis. A typical case implies that the particular set of events selected for report is similar in *relevant* characteristics to other cases of the same type.

Gluckman was well aware of this since he raises the question in the following terms: 'I can touch only briefly on the problem of typicality for a society of the area of social life selected for analysis in this way. In the first place the use of the extended case does not do away with the need for the outline of social morphology, on which Malinowski insisted and this may have to be illustrated by apt examples. But here the increasing use of statistics, in more refined form, by anthropologists provides an important safeguard' (Gluckman 1961: 14).

He argues in effect that a specification of the general wider context in which the events of the case are located must be based on other analytical techniques. Typicality, therefore, in his argument pertains to the social morphology rather than to the case, which may only be an apt illustration of it. Similarly the use of statistical analysis as a counter-measure to the untypicality of the case material also implies the use of methods other than the case study as a basis to assure typicality. Gluckman does not develop these points which remain peripheral issues to his argument as a whole so that the crucial issue of the basis upon which the case analyst may extrapolate from his material is left unanswered.

In another important discussion of case analysis van Velsen 1967 once again addressed the problem of the typicality of the case chosen for analysis. His essay is concerned with a variant of case analysis, that is, with situational analysis, and his main purpose is to redress the imbalance he saw in the over-emphasis on structuralist types of analysis in anthropology at that time. He argues instead for a greater emphasis on the optative approach in which the choice-taking of actors is given due weight as against the concentration on the institutional framework within which the actors were operating. Analysis of this kind requires a very detailed and intimate familiarity by the observer of the behaviour and cognitive orientations of the actors in the events being described. The restriction on the coverage such detailed investigation requires necessarily imposes limitations on the extent to which the observer is able to describe the whole 'culture' or whole 'society' of the people being studied. These restrictions, van Velsen argues, raise 'the question of the typicality of the anthropologist's analysis' (1967: 145). Van Velsen resolves this question by arguing that the object of the analysis is not in fact 'culture' or 'society' of which the events studied might be considered samples but rather social processes which may be abstracted from the course of events analysed.

At this point, I feel, van Velsen stops short of making the essential point about the basis of making inferences from case material: that the extrapolation is in fact based on the validity of the analysis rather than the representativeness of the events. This is a point to which we will need to return but before doing so it is necessary to specify more exactly the sort of material implied by the terms 'social situation' or 'case'.

Specification of the Case Study

The term 'case study' may refer to several very different epistemological entities and it is necessary at the outset to specify the particular meaning I am attributing to it here.

In its most basic form a case study may refer to the basic descriptive material an observer has assembled by whatever means available about some particular phenomenon or set of events. The case material here is simply the content of the observer's field notes prior to any deliberate analysis or selection for presentation in some analysis. Similar in character are the case records developed by practitioners in some field of action – physicians, clinical psychologists, psychiatrists, social workers, probation officers and the like. Normally these practitioners are trained in the art of systematically recording information which may be germane for their practical action.

Both of these types of 'case study' may become the basis of the rather more specific means I shall be attributing to the terms here, that is, as material from which some theoretical principles are to be inferred. Some writers like Madge (1953: 100) are mainly concerned with the material of this kind so that the problem then becomes the procedure upon which data may be extracted from material of this kind for theoretical purposes.

But throughout what follows I shall be assuming that the 'case study' refers to an observer's data; i.e. the documentation of some particular phenomenon or set of events which has been assembled with the explicit end in view of drawing theoretical conclusions from it.[6] The focus of the case study may be a single individual as in the life-history approach or it may be a set of actors engaged in a sequence of activities either over a restricted or over an extended period of time. What is important is not the content of the case study as such but the use to which the data are put to support theoretical conclusions.

In what way then does a case study differ from any other way of assembling systematic information about social phenomena for research purposes? Goode and Hatt, the authors of one of the few textbooks on sociological methods which discusses case studies, describe the case study as a 'a way of organizing social data so as to preserve the *unitary character of the social object being studied.*' They go on:

> 'Expressed somewhat differently, it is an approach which views any so-
> cial unit as a whole. Almost always this means of approach includes
> the development of that unit, which may be a person, a family or other
> social group, a set of relationships or processes (such as a family crisis,
> adjustment to disease, friendship formation, ethnic invasion of a neigh-
> bourhood etc.) or even an entire culture.'
> (1952: 331: original italics)

They contrast this with the 'survey' type of analysis in which the person is replaced by the trait as the unit of analysis. The wholeness 'characterising' the case study, they point out, is determined by the extent to which the analyst has assembled enough information about the object of study to provide sufficient specification of the research purpose in mind.[7] As they point out, 'The case study attempting to organize the data around the unit of growth, or group structure, or individual life pattern, does force the researcher to think in these terms rather than fall back on trait analysis alone' (Goode and Hatt 1952: 339).

But Goode and Hatt in this early – and relatively rare – discussion of the use of case studies in sociological research overlook two crucial features of the case study which bear directly on the main topic of this paper, that is, the basis of extrapolation or of inference from case studies. In the first instance Goode and Hatt assume without demur that the *only* way of extrapolating from data is on the basis of a statistically representative sample and they spend a good deal of space pointing to the problems of securing representative cases for subsequent statistical analysis. The second point is that while they emphasise the 'wholeness' of the case they appear to be unaware that each individual case is influenced by circumstances which the researcher may wish to control for in the analysis. All cases, as van Velsen (1967: 146) and Garbett (1970: 217) point out so clearly, are located within some wider context which in turn imposes constraints on the actions of the protagonists in the case study. These contexts constitute a panoply of *ceteris paribus* conditions which the analyst will need to allow for in some way.

With this background in mind we may now turn to a specification of what we imply by the term 'case' or the cognate term 'social situation'. As a working definition we may characterise a case study as a detailed examination of an event (or series of related events) which the analyst believes exhibits (or exhibit) the operation of some identified general theoretical principle.

The important point here is the phrase 'the operation of some general theoretical principle' since a narrative account of some event or a series of related events does not in itself constitute a case study in the sense in which I am using the notion here. A case study is essentially heuristic; it reflects in the events portrayed features which may be construed as a manifestation of some general abstract theoretical principle.

Material derived from cases or from social situations however may be used analytically in different ways and it is to this question that we now turn.

Types of Case Study

It was one of the merits of Gluckman's early (1961) essay in which he discussed case studies that it drew a sharp distinction between 'apt illustrations', 'social situations' and 'case studies', and how they may be used in theoretical analysis. These types of case phenomena may be viewed as falling along a continuum of increasing complexity.

(i) Near one limit – the simple end – would fall what Gluckman called 'the apt illustration' (1961: 7). The apt illustration is normally a description of some fairly simple event or occurrence in which the operation of some general principle is clearly illustrated. An anthropologist may, for example, describe how he had noticed a man step off a path to conceal himself as his mother-in-law approached, and use this account to illustrate the operation in daily life of mother-in-law/son-in-law avoidance. The particular event is sequestrated from all other ongoing events either connected with the behaviour among other in-laws or from other events going on at the same time in the vicinity. The use of case material in this way is, as Gluckman's terminology indicates, merely illustrative. A *sine qua non* is that the observer must be convinced of its typicality to be able to use it as an illustration.

(ii) Considerably more complex is the analysis of a social situation. A social situation is a collocation of events which the analyst is able to construe as connected with one another and which take place in a relatively restricted time span.[8] The classic example of a social situation used as an analytical tool is Gluckman's description and analysis of the official opening of a newly-built bridge in Zululand in 1935 (1958). In the analysis of a social situation some restricted and limited (bounded) set of events is analysed so as to reveal the way in which general principles of social organisation manifest themselves in some particular specified context. The official opening of the bridge brings together representatives of different sectors of the population in Zululand, Blacks and Whites, Christians and pagans, officials and citizens, Zulu nobles and commoners, and Gluckman shows how their behaviour leading up to, during and following the opening of the bridge reflects the structure of South African society with all its alliances and cleavages at the time when the study was done. The analysis of social situations has become a significant example of case analysis and has been discussed particularly by van Velsen (1967) and Garbett (1970).

(iii) At the complex end of the continuum is the extended case study. This is a further elaboration of the basic study of case material for it deals with a sequence of events sometimes over quite a long period, where the same actors are involved in a series of situations in which their structural positions must continually be re-specified and the flow of actors through different social positions specified. The particular significance of the extended case study is that since it traces the events in which the same set of main actors in the case study are involved over a relatively long period, the processual aspect is given particular emphasis. The extended case study enables the analyst to trace how events chain on to one another and how therefore events are necessarily linked to one another through time. I used this procedure in a study of the social structure of a people in Malawi (Mitchell, 1957: 86ff). In the first four chapters of the book I set out the general features of morphology of social life of the people. In this section in order to locate the operation of the general features of morphology, as for example the struggle for status among village headmen, I use case material as apt illustrations.

Subsequently I move to an analysis of the process whereby the villages grow and break up. For this purpose I make use of several case studies, including one which is in fact an extended case. The events described started some eight years before I was in the field and continued while I was in the field – and no doubt continued after I left it. The circumstances revolve around the daily incidents, the squabbles and altercations, the births and deaths, all of which the protagonists relate to their position in the general matrilineal kinship structure of the village, in which witchcraft accusations, marriage arrangements, village moots and even physical assaults are involved. These events in juxtaposition with one another provide us with an analytical prism through which the basic principles of matrilineal kinship located in the context of local politics may be refracted into relatively clearcut terms.

The extended case is similar to, but broader than, the 'social dramas' which Turner (1957) used in his analysis of Ndembu social life. Social dramas are accounts of a series of crises in the daily life of the people during which, as Turner expresses it,

> The social drama is a limited area of transparency on the otherwise opaque surface of regular, uneventful social life. Through it we are enabled to observe the crucial principles of social structure in their operation and their relative dominance at successive points in time. (1957: 93)

The rationale upon which the distinctions among 'apt illustration', 'social situations' and 'extended cases' are differentiated is not immediately explicit in

Gluckman's presentation. While the three types of case material are all used to support theoretical statements as against the distinction between 'clinical' and 'theoretical' case studies referred to earlier, the distinction between 'apt illustration' and 'social situations' is clearly one of the degree of complexity of the events described, the distinction between 'social situations' and 'extended cases' is partly one of even more complexity, but it is also one of the duration of time spanning the events described. Complexity and duration are obviously linked since events covering a longer time period are likely to reflect changes and adjustments as well as simple patterns of relationships.

For this reason the classification of case studies suggested by Eckstein (1975: 94–123) is perhaps more instructive. Eckstein distinguishes five categories of case study which highlight the way in which they may be used as a contribution to theoretical thinking.

These five ways of using case material are as follows:

(i) *Configurative-idiographic studies* in which the material is largely descriptive and reflects the particular concatenation of circumstances surrounding the events in a way which, while they may provide insights into the relationships among the component elements in the case, do not easily lead to direct general theoretical interpretations.

(ii) *Disciplined-configurative studies*, as their name implies are still configurations or patterns of elements but the observer does not look upon these as unique or 'idiographic'. Instead the analyst seeks to interpret the patterns in terms of general theoretical postulates. Eckstein writes:

> The chain of enquiry in disciplined-configurative studies runs from comparatively tested theory to case interpretations and thence, perhaps, via *ad hoc* additions, newly discovered puzzles, and systematised prudence, to new candidate theories. Case study is thus tied to theoretical inquiry – but only partially, where theories apply or can be envisioned; passively, in the main, as a receptacle for putting theories to work; and fortuitously as a catalytic element in the unfolding of theoretical knowledge. (Eckstein 1975: 100)

However, Eckstein goes on to point out that

> The application of theories in case interpretation, although rarely discussed, is not at all a simple process, even leaving aside the question of how valid theory is to be developed. Such applications only yield valid interpretations if the theories permit strict deductions to be made and the interpretations of the case are shown to be logically compelled by the theories. (Eckstein 1975: 103)

He argues that the major utility of attempted disciplined case interpretation is that it 'forces one to state theories more rigorously than might otherwise be done – provided that the application is truly "disciplined" i.e. designed to show that valid theory compels a particular case interpretation and rules out others' (Eckstein 1975: 103).

(iii) *Heuristic case studies* are distinguished from configurative-idiographic and disciplined-configurative studies in that they are deliberately chosen in order to develop theory. As Eckstein phrases it, the heuristic case study is

> deliberately used to stimulate the imagination towards discerning important general problems and possible theoretical solutions.... Such studies, unlike configurative-idiographic ones, tie directly into theory building, and therefore are less concerned with overall concrete configurations than with potentially generalisable relations between aspects of them: they also tie into theory building less passively and fortuitously than does disciplined-configurative study, because the potentially generalisable relations do not just turn up but are deliberately sought out. (Eckstein 1975: 104)

(iv) *Plausibility probes* are case studies used specifically to test interpretative paradigms which have been established either by previous case studies or by other procedures. Eckstein writes:

> In essence plausibility probes involve attempts to determine whether potential validity may reasonably be considered great enough to warrant the pains and costs of testing, which are almost always considerable, but especially so if broad, painstaking comparative studies are undertaken.' (Eckstein 1975: 108)

Plausibility probes may be undertaken after heuristic case studies have been successfully concluded. They may constitute part of a series of case studies devoted to the expansion and development of an interpretative schema or theoretical formulation relative to phenomena represented by the case. As Eckstein points out, 'The essential point for us that as empirical plausibility probes, case studies are often as serviceable, as or more so, than comparative ones – and nearly always a great deal cheaper' (1975: 110). Plausibility probes are used, then, as a preliminary test of theoretical formulations previously established by some other procedures, before a rigorous test by formal procedures.

(v) *Crucial case studies* are, as the name suggests, similar to the crucial experiment in the natural sciences, and offer the circumstances which enable the analyst to reject some theoretical proposition or, which amounts to the same thing, to support it when the circumstances appear to be loaded against it. The selection of the case is clearly difficult: the assumption is that enough will be known about the phenomenon *a priori* to enable the analyst to recognise its particular significance for the way in which the proposition has been formulated. A detailed study of the case will then enable the analyst to relate events to the theoretical proposition.

Throughout this discussion the role of theory and of theorising in the use of case material is of paramount importance and it is this feature which provides the means through which the fundamental problem in case studies may be approached: the basis upon which general inferences may be drawn from them.

Inference And Extrapolation From Case Studies[9]

However clearly the basic principles are reflected in some particular case material the crucial question upon which there is much misgiving is that of the extent to which the analyst is justified in making generalisations from that particular case to all instances of that type. In ordinary English usage there is a strong connotation that the word 'case' implies a chance or haphazard occurrence.[10] This connotation is carried over into more technical and sociological language in the form of implying that a case history or case material refers to one 'case' and is therefore unique or is a particularity. If this is true then how can unique material form the basis of inference about some process in general?

That case material may so be used is apparent since, as previously mentioned, most social anthropological and a good deal of sociological theorising has been founded upon case studies. The difficulty arises, I conjecture, out of the common assumption that the only valid basis of inference is that which has been developed in relation to statistical analysis. In the procedure considerable care is taken to select a sample from some parent population in such a way that no bias is introduced to the sample. The implication of the notion of 'no bias' is that the examples in the sample are not selected in a way which would reflect inaccurately the characteristics of the parent population. The procedures for achieving this are varied, the most straightforward of which is the simple random sample. The assumption behind this procedure is that if the instances for inclusion in the sample are selected in a way which excludes any possibility of biased selection then the characteristics of the sample will reflect those of the parent population within some range of certainty which may be estimated using the assumptions of probability theory. By this procedure the sample is typical of the parent population or in more common terminology it is a 'representative sample'.

The logic in this procedure is that the incidence and in fact the coincidence of characteristics in the sample reflect within the range of sampling error the incidence or coincidence of the characteristics of the parent population. Inferences are made about the parent population from the characteristics in the sample population so that dependence on a 'representative' sample is, of course, vital.

In so far as the descriptive features of the sample (and therefore of the parent population) are concerned the validity of the inference is probably sound. The distribution of age of a representative sample drawn from a parent population probably reflects reasonably accurately – given sampling errors

– the distribution of ages within that population. A difficulty arises however when the relationship *between* characteristics is considered. In the sample analysed a relationship – a correlation – in fact may be noted between say age and the probability of being married. In terms of the canons of statistical inference the analyst may assume that the same relationship exists between the same characteristics in the parent population. Note, however, that the inference from the sample in relation to the parent population is simply about the concomitant variation of two characteristics. The analyst must go beyond the sample and resort to theoretical thinking to link those characteristics together – in terms for example of an appreciation of normal life-cycle processes in the instance of age and marriage. The relationship between the characteristics may be validated by other types of observation and encapsulated in the values of the people concerned. The inference about the *logical* relationship between the two characteristics is not based upon the representatives of the sample and therefore upon its typicality, but rather upon the plausibility or upon the logicality of the nexus between the two characteristics.

The point is well illustrated in another context by Lykken (1970) who, for purposes other than those I have in mind, quotes a finding reported by Sapolsky, who records the responses of respondents with or without dietetic disorders to Rorschach ink-blots. Sapolsky found that among sixty-two respondents some identified the ink-blots as a frog and some did not but that there was an appreciable tendency for those with dietetic disorders to react to the blot in terms of a 'frog' response and for those without these disorders not to do so. In fact some 61 per cent of those with dietetic disorders reacted with the 'frog' response to the ink-blots whereas only 16 per cent of those without dietetic disorders responded with a 'frog' response. If we are able to assume that the sample of respondents is in fact representative of the population at large we would estimate from the chi-square statistic that a sample with a departure of this extent from the state where the frog response is distributed equally among those with and those without dietetic disorders would arise by chance sampling errors in less than one occasion in 1000 samples.

We may be reasonably confident therefore that the relationship between a respondent's interpreting the ink-blot as a frog and also having a dietetic disorder seems unlikely to have arisen purely by chance and we rely on statistical inference to assert this. But the explanation that Sapolsky advanced for this association was according to Lykken 'an unconscious belief in the cloacal theory of birth' which involves notions of oral impregnation and anal parturition. The excretary and reproductive canals of the frog are – they constitute the cloaca – common and this biological fact presumably provides the rationale for the belief. 'Since patients should be inclined to manifest eating disorders: compulsive eating in the case of those who wish to get pregnant and anorexia in those who do not.... such patients should also be inclined to see cloacal animals such as frogs on the Rorschach' (Lykken 1970: 267). Lykken then asked twenty of his colleagues, many of them clinicians, about the hypothesis. As Lykken reports it, their reaction before they were given the experimental results was 'I don't believe it', and after they were given the experimental results it was 'I still don't believe it' (Lykken 1970: 268).

The issue raised here is essentially that of the relationship between the theory linking the interpretation of the Rorschach ink-blots with dietary disorders. While the clinical psychologists may well have accepted that more people with dietary disorders saw the blots as frogs than those without, they could not accept the *explanation* of the relationship between the two characteristics the original author chose to link to one another.

The distinction is that of the commonly accepted distinction between what has been called statistical inference on the one hand or scientific or causal inference on the other (see Henkel and Morrison 1970 *passim*). Statistical inference is the process by which the analyst draws conclusions about the existence of two or more characteristics in some wider population from some sample of that population to which the observer has access. Scientific or causal – or perhaps more appropriately – logical inference, is the process by which the analyst draws conclusions about the essential linkage between two or more characteristics in terms of some systematic explanatory schema – some set of theoretical propositions. In analytical thinking based on quantitative procedures *both* types of inference proceed *pari passu* but there has been some tendency to elide logical inferences with the logic of statistical inference: that the postulated *logical* connection among features in a sample may be assumed to exist in some parent population simply because the features may be inferred to *coexist* in that population. This is the point that Lykken was making about Sapolsky's study of the frog response among people with dietary disorders. By contrast I argue that the process of inference from case studies is only logical or causal and cannot be statistical and that extrapolability from any one case study to like situations in general is based only on logical inference. We infer that the features present in the case study will be related in a wider population not because the case is representative but because our analysis is unassailable. The emphasis on case studies used to relate theoretically relevant characteristics reflected in the case to one another in a logically coherent way. Analytically sound studies using statistical procedures are of course doing the same thing but two very different inferential processes are involved in them: logical inference is epistemologically quite independent of statistical inference.

Enumerative And Analytical Induction

This distinction between logical and statistical inference is related to the notions of enumerative and analytical induction introduced to sociology by Znaniecki as long ago as 1934. Znaniecki, a vehement opponent of the vogue for quantitative studies which were becoming popular at the time of his writing, contrasts the two modes of inference. Enumerative induction in his view exists in the form either of simple enumeration in which the characteristics of a class of phenomena are established simply by listing them, or in the more elaborate form of statistical induction in which probability theory is involved. In the simple form, he argues, enumerative induction has 'continued to be used with very little change, in ethical and political works from antiquity, down to present times, whenever an author not satisfied with deducing rules of conduct from principles accepted *a priori* attempts to base this view on experience and observation' (Znaniecki 1934: 221). He describes its general principles as

> an attempt to discover some final truths about a certain class of empirical data, circumscribed in advance, by studying a number of cases belonging to this class. Originally and fundamentally, the truths sought for are to be characters common to all data of the given class and only to these.' (Znaniecki 1934: 222)

This implies identification of a class of phenomena by some identifiable but not necessarily essential characteristics and then examining a set of instances of this class to identify those features of the instance that define that class. By contrast,

> in analytical induction certain particular objects are determined by intensive study, and the problem is to define the logical classes which they represent. No definition of the class precedes in analytical induction the selection of data to be studied as representatives of this class. The analysis of data is all done before any general formulations; and if well done, there is nothing more of importance to be learned about the class which these data represent by any subsequent investigation of more data of the same class. (Znaniecki 1934: 249)

Znaniecki goes on to say:

> It may be said that analytical induction ends where enumerative induction begins; and if well conducted leaves no really soluble problems for the latter. With such a radical difference in logical problematisation, the logical procedure should naturally differ widely. While both forms of induction tend to reach general and abstract truths concerning particular and concrete data, enumerative induction abstracts by generalisation, whereas analytical induction generalises by abstracting. The former looks in many cases for characters that are similar and abstracts them conceptually because of their generality, presuming that they must be essential to each particular case; the latter abstracts from the given concrete case characters that are essential to it and generalises them, presuming that insofar as essential, they must be similar in many cases.' (Znaniecki 1934: 250–251)

The process of analytical induction proceeds according to Znaniecki not by developing a self-sufficient theory from one instance well analysed for he criticises Durkheim's analysis of religion based on Australian totemism (Znaniecki 1934: 237) but rather by examining cases so selected as to illuminate formerly obscure aspects of the general theory.

Znaniecki's discussion of the significance of exceptions and how they may be made to 'prove the rule' (Znaniecki 1934: 305–6) appears to contradict his austere statement quoted earlier to the effect that 'if well done there is nothing more of importance to be learned about the class which these data represent by any subsequent investigation of more data of the same class'. But we should distinguish here between the *principles* of analytical induction and its *practice*. The intention behind analytical induction is to specify the necessary connections among a set of theoretically significant elements manifested in some body of empirical data. But in practice any one set of data is likely to manifest only some of the elements whose explication would contribute to a cogent theoretical interpretation of the processes involved. An indeterminate number of strategically selected sets of events would need to be examined, therefore, before the state of complete knowledge that Znaniecki refers to can be approached:

This issue was specifically recognised by Znaniecki for after developing the point about the establishment of complete knowledge from only one instance he goes on to say:

> Of course the inductive scientist continuously goes on investigating objects or processes already defined and classified even though he does not doubt the validity of his former definition, for there is always something to learn about individual data: concrete reality as we have said is an inexhaustible source of new knowledge.
> (Znaniecki 1934: 250)

But he goes on to specify that the new knowledge he refers to is not a mere supplement to pre-existing knowledge but rather an extension of *theoretical* knowledge.

Robinson (1951, 1952) subsequently in a criticism of Znaniecki's ideas distinguished between analytic induction as a research procedure, as a method of causal analysis and as a method of proof. Any of these epistemologically disjunct implications might be conveyed by the term. The main burden of Robinson's argument, however, is that there is no essential contradiction between analytical induction and enumerative induction on the grounds that by its procedures analytical induction isolates the *necessary* circumstances for the manifestation of some phenomenon but does not in itself establish *sufficient* conditions. Analytic induction, Robinson argues, enables the analyst to 'establish the conditions without which the phenomenon would not appear' (Robinson 1951: 815), whereas enumerative induction, as exemplified by statistical procedures, establishes sufficient conditions for the phenomenon to occur. His argument is based on the premise that analytical induction as exemplified by case studies examines only instances in which the phenomenon under investigation in fact occurs, whereas statistical procedures ideally would also take into account those occasions when the phenomenon does not ocur. This, he argues, allows the analyst to establish sufficient conditions as distinct from necessary conditions for the phenomenon to occur. He goes on to argue that as a practical as against a logical procedure there is little difference between enumerative and analytical induction since practitioners of the art of analytical induction indirectly study cases in which the phenomenon in which they are interested does not occur. Radcliffe-Brown, it is said, was interested in totemism. In order to understand it more fully therefore he elected to study the Andamanese islanders amongst whom there was no totemism. The point is that if an analyst is working with some conception of the general role of totemism in a social system then an examination of the operation of the social system in which totemism does not occur ought to enable the analyst to some assessment of the *absence* of totemism. The essential point is the one which Robinson makes: 'The success of analytical induction in producing complete explanation is due to its procedure, to its systematisation of the method of the working hypothesis and not to its logical structure' (1951: 816).

In reality no case study can be presented in isolation from the corpus of empirical information and theoretical postulates against which it has significance. The point is well made by Kaplan who quotes Hartmann in relation to clinical observation in psychiatry: 'Every single clinical "case" represents, for research hundreds of data of *observed regularities* and in hundreds of respects' (Kaplan 1964: 117, original italics). The single case becomes significant only when set against the accumulated experience and knowledge that the analyst brings to it. In other words the extent to which generalisation may be made from case studies depends upon the adequacy of the underlying theory and the whole corpus of related knowledge of which the case is analysed rather than on the particular instance itself.

The Significance Of The Atypical Case

This consideration justifies the selection of the case for study (or for exposition) in terms of its explanatory power rather than for its typicality. Formally any set of events deemed to reflect the abstract characteristics that the observer wishes to use in analysis may be used. Since the analyst's purpose is to demonstrate how general explanatory principles manifest themselves in the course of some ongoing set of events the particular set of events is in itself a subsidiary consideration.

There is absolutely no advantage in going to a great deal of trouble to find a 'typical' case: concern with this issue reflects a confusion of enumerative and analytic modes of induction. For general purposes any set of events will serve the purpose of the analyst if the theoretical base is sufficiently well developed to enable the analyst to identify within these events the operation of the general principles incorporated in the theory.

There is, however, a strategic advantage in choosing particular sets of events for study or for exposition. It frequently occurs that the way in which general explanatory principles may be used in practice is most clearly demonstrated in those instances where the concatenation of events is so idiosyncratic as to throw into sharp relief the principles underlying them.[11] The point is analogous to the crucial role that untoward events have played in the elucidation of unexpected connection in the natural sciences. A dramatic example is provided by the veterinary scientist W. I. B. Beveridge who describes how in 1889 a laboratory assistant chanced to notice that flies had congregated around the urine of a dog from which the pancreas had been removed A test showed sugar in the urine thus leading to the establishment of the connection between the pancreas and diabetes.[12] (Beveridge 1950: 28) So in the social sciences an illuminating case may make theoretical connections apparent which were formerly obscure.

It is of course obvious that the significant case is only so because the analyst is able to perceive the illuminating contradictions in the material. But the contradictions only become significant because of the observer's familiarity with current theoretical formulations in terms of which the contradictions are articulated. This highlights the point made earlier that the presentation of a case study is significant only in terms of some body of analytical theory. Pasteur's aphorism is highly apposite: 'Where observation is concerned chance favours only the prepared mind' (Oxford Dictionary of Quotations 1979: 369).

The Case In Its Context

The characteristic uniqueness of each case is largely due to the fact that the particular events described in the case are usually presented in the first instance at a fairly low level of abstraction. The observer provides a detailed account of who the *dramatis personae* were, what they did and how they reacted to the events (and their social relationships) in which they were involved. The particularities of the context, of the situation and of the actors, then, are important features of case studies.

It is this particularity of case studies which has been the basis of what I consider to be ill-founded criticism of the use of case studies as a basis for generalisation. But of course in interpreting the events in any particular case theoretically the analyst must suppress some of the complexity in the events and state the logical connexions among some of the features which are germane to the interpretation. This process of abstraction and the suppression of contextually irrelevant features has led Ralph Turner to a critique of the process of analytical induction. Turner sees analytical induction primarily as a procedure for establishing the necessary and essential features that characterise the phenomenon or class of events under consideration, that is, as a definitional procedure. These necessary and essential features, however, are usually part and parcel of some coherent and cogent theoretical explanatory system so that analytical induction necessarily involves what Turner calls 'causal closure', that is, that the procedure must produce causally self-contained systems. This implies that an explanation of events based on analytical induction relates typically to a limited set of events restricted in the sense that the events must of necessity be explicable in terms of the explanatory rubric that informed the analysis. In these circumstances, Turner argues, the 'causal prime mover' must be outside the set of events being considered, or in his words, 'the system is not capable of activation from within but only by factors coming from outside the system' (1953: 609). It is for this reason that predictions from an analysis based on case study techniques tend to be *theoretical* rather than *empirical*. External factors, or *intrusive* factors as Turner calls them, always influence the events in a case study but can only be included in the theoretical explanation by their incorporation into the case as one of the essential and necessary characteristics.

But it is not essential that events located, from the analyst's point of view, outside the events with which the case is concerned and which need to be taken account of in the explication of the case material, need be treated in the same detail as the events in the case itself. The problem of isolating events intellectually from seamless reality in order to facilitate their analysis in terms of some explanatory system was discussed at some length by Gluckman and his colleagues (Gluckman (Ed.) 1964). One of the points Gluckman makes is that it is perfectly justifiable for the analyst to operate with a simplified account of the context within which the case is located provided that the impact of the features of that context on the events being considered in the analysis are incorporated rigorously into the analysis.

All cases are necessarily contextualised and generalisations made from case studies must therefore be qualified with a *ceteris paribus* condition. It is incumbent on the observer to provide readers with a minimal account of the context to enable them to judge for themselves the validity of treating other things as equal in that instance.

The very particularity of the case study, located as it is in some setting, however, can be turned to good advantages; it can provide the opportunity to demonstrate the positive role of exceptions to generalisation as a means of deepening our understanding of social processes. It is only under specified conditions that a clear and simple formulation of the operative principles underlying a social process can be stated. But the very circumstances of the case study make a strict imposition of a *ceteris paribus* condition impracticable. The analyst may therefore take account of the unique circumstances surrounding the event in the case being analysed in order to show these circumstances obscure the simple and direct way in which the general principles should be operating. Because of the intimate knowledge of the relationships in the particular circumstances which connect the events in the case, the analyst might be able to show how the general principles being examined manifest themselves in changed form.

The contextual features surrounding the case are in effect held constant by a process of logical analysis. It is in this sense that Znaniecki remarks:

Wherever, thus, an exception can be explained, that is, can be proved only apparent, not real, we gain not only a confirmation of our previous knowledge but also new knowledge: we discover the limits within which our causal processes occur or find some other causal process and thus determine the range of validity of our law or validate some other law.... it is not the exception that matters, but our attitude towards it: if we refuse to submit to it, but go on analysing our data, it is a factor of scientific discovery, whereas if we passively accept it, it is a check on further progress.' (Znaniecki 1934: 306)

The case study, because of the observer's intimate knowledge of the connections linking the complex set of circumstances surrounding the events in the case and because of the observer's knowledge of the linkages among the events in the case, provides the optimum conditions in which the general principles may be shown to manifest themselves even when obscured by confounding side effects.

Conclusion

The argument that has been advanced here, then, is that case studies of whatever form are a reliable and respectable procedure of social analysis and that much criticism of their reliability and validity has been based on a misconception of the basis upon which the analyst may justifiably extrapolate from an individual case study to the social process in general. A good deal of the confusion has arisen because of a failure to appreciate that the rationale of extrapolation from a statistical sample to a parent universe involves two very different and even unconnected inferential processes – that of statistical inference which makes a statement about the confidence we may have that the surface relationships observed in our sample will in fact occur in the parent population, and that of logical or scientific inference which makes a statement about the confidence we may have that the theoretically necessary or logical connection among the features observed in the sample pertain also to the parent population.

In case studies statistical inference is not invoked at all. Instead the inferential process turns exclusively on the theoretically necessary linkages among the features in the case study. The validity of the extrapolation depends not on the typicality or representativeness of the case but upon the cogency of the theoretical reasoning.

In terms of this argument case studies may be used analytically – as against ethnographically – only if they are embedded in an appropriate theoretical framework. The rich detail which emerges from the intimate knowledge the analyst must acquire in a case study if it is well conducted provides the optimum conditions for the acquisition of those illuminating insights which make formerly opaque connections suddenly pellucid.

Notes

1. This paper has been in draft form for some time. I am grateful to the following who have provided me with bibliographical references or valuable comments: David Boswell, Robert Burgess, Jean Edwards, Barry Glassner, Les Green, Sheldon Himmelfarb, Elinor Kelly, Chris Pickvance, Dave Reason, Ralph Ruddock, Sue Smith, Rory Williams; seminar groups at Adelaide, Durham and Oxford and two anonymous referees. Unfortunately I have not been able to take all of their suggestions into account.

2. Prior to the development of the social survey in the 1930s case studies seemed to feature regularly in sociological research (see bibliography in Young 1939: 569–72) and there were several useful discussions of the method e.g. Cooley (1930). Znaniecki writing in 1934 (246–8) reflects this division very clearly and lists a number of contemporary works that have used the case approach. Znaniecki points out that at that time the model for sociological case studies were the clinical methods in psychiatry, particularly since the spread of psychoanalysis, but also by social work. He lists several sociological studies which had used case studies analytically most of them part of the 'ethnographic' wing of the Chicago school such as works by Thomas, Cooley, Shaw, Park and Burgess. He also, however, drew attention to the division of opinion between those using case methods and those using survey methods. Articles bearing on the debate are Burgess 1927, 1945, Eldridge 1935, Hotelling and Sorokin 1943, Jocher 1928, Jonassen 1949, Lewis 1950, Queen 1928, Sarbin 1943, Shaw 1927 and Waller 1935.

3. The references to case studies were Waller 1935, Eldridge 1935, Hotelling 1943, Sarbin 1943, Burgess 1945, Komarovsky and Waller 1945 and Lewis 1950.

4. As for example in Ashton's review of Blackburn, R. M. and Mann, M.: *The Working Class in the Labour Market* in *The Sociological Review* (1980) 28: 433–4. Ashton's point, however, that Blackburn and Mann fail effectively to establish the *ceteris paribus* conditions of their generalisation is valid.

5. Recently Hamilton, working in the field of educational studies, has yet again drawn the contrast between case studies and survey analysis and concludes that 'the assumptions of case study research and survey analysis stand in mutual opposition' (1980: 90). My own argument, however, is that in the end the oppositions are more apparent than real.

6. c.f '[the case study] attempts to arrive at a comprehensive understanding of the group under study. At the same time the case study also attempts to develop more general theoretical statements about the regularities in social structure and process' (Becker 1968: 233).

7. Goode and Hatt go on to discuss other features that distinguish case studies from other research procedures such as the breadth of data, the levels of data, the identification of types and profiles and the significance of the developmental aspects of the case.

8. Garbett (1970: 215) defines a social situation as a temporarily and spatially bounded series of events abstracted by the observer from the ongoing flow of social life.

9. Stake (1980) provides one of the few discussions of the nature of generalisations from case studies and from survey findings but his emphasis is on the quality of the generalisations rather than on the basis upon which they are achieved.

10. Captured by the Shorter Oxford English Dictionary phrase 'an event or occurrence, hap or chance'. The word 'hap' is defined in the same dictionary as 'a chance accident or occurrence'.

11. Lindesmith in his comments on Robinson's paper phrases the same point in terms of discovering the case that *disproves* the rule. He writes: 'There is no point to

the random selection of cases when this is obviously not the most efficient manner of seeking evidence' (1952: 492).

12. Beveridge heads the chapter in which he discusses the role of chance in making important theoretical connections in physiology with a quote from Charles Nicolle: 'Chance favours only those who know how to court her.'

References

Barnes, J. A. (1958), Social anthropology: theory and practice: inaugural lecture at Sydney University, in *Arts: the Proceedings of the Sydney University Arts Association.*

—— (1960), 'Intensive studies of small communities', in *Meanjin: A Quarterly of Literative Art Discussion,* 19:201–3.

Becker, H.S. (1968), 'Social observation and case studies', in Sills, David L. (ed) *International Encyclopedia of the Social Sciences,* New York: The Macmillan Company and the Free Press: vol.11: 232–8.

Beveridge, W.I.B. (1950), *The Art of Scientific Investigation,* London: Heinemann.

Burgess, E.W. (1927), 'Statistics and case studies as methods of sociological research', *Sociology and Social Research* 12: 103–20.

Burgess, T.W. (1945), 'Sociological research methods', *American Journal of Sociology* 50: 474–82.

Chassan, J.B. (1960), 'Statistical inference and the single case in clinical design', *Psychiatry* 23: 173–84.

Cooley, C. H. (1930), 'The case study of small institutions as a method of research', in *Sociological Theory and Social Research,* New York, Henry Holt & Co: 313–22.

Eckstein, H. (1970), 'Case study and theory in political science', in Greenstein, F. and Polsby, N. (eds), *The Handbook of Political Science: Strategies of Inquiry,* London: Addison-Wesley: vol.7: 79–137.

Eldridge, S. (1935), 'Textbooks, Teachers and Students', *American Journal of Sociology* 40: 637–45.

Foreman, Paul (1948) 'The theory of case studies', *Social Forces* 26: 408–19.

Garbett, G. Kingsley (1970), 'The analysis of social situations', *Man* 5: 214–27.

Gluckman, M. (1958), *The Analysis of a Social Situation in Modern Zululand,* Rhodes-Livingstone Paper no. 28, Manchester: Manchester University Press for Rhodes-Livingstone Institute.

—— (1961), 'Ethnographic Data in British social anthropology', *Sociological Review* 9: 5–17.

—— (ed.) (1964), *Closed Systems and Open Minds: The Limits of Naivety in Social Anthropology,* London: Oliver & Boyd.

—— (1967), 'Introduction' in Epstein, A.W. (ed.), *The Craft of Social Anthropology,* London: Tavistock: i–xxiv

Goode, William J. and Hatt, Paul K. (1952), *Methods in Social Research,* New York: McGraw-Hill.

Hamilton, David (1980), 'Some contrasting assumptions about case study research and survey analysis', in Simon, H. (ed.), *Towards a Science of the Singular: Essays about Case Study in Educational Research and Evaluation,* Care Occasional Publications no. 10, Norwich, Centre for Applied Research in Education: 78–92.

Henkel, R. E. and Morrison, D. E. (eds) (1970), *The Significance Test Controversy,* London: Butterworth.

Hotelling, H. and Sorokin, P. (1943), 'The prediction of personal adjustment: a symposium', *American Journal of Sociology* 48: 61–86.

Jocher, K. (1928), 'The case study method in social research', *Social Forces* 7: 512–15.

Jonassen, C.T. (1949), 'A re-evaluation and critique of the logic and some methods of Shaw and McKay', *American Sociological Review* 14: 608–14.

Kaplan, A. (1964), *The Conduct of Enquiry: Methodology for Behavioral Science,* San Francisco: Chandler.

Komarovsky, M. and Waller, W. (1945), 'Studies of the family', *American Journal of Sociology* 50: 443–51.

Lewis, Oscar (1950), 'An anthropological approach to family studies', *American Journal of Sociology* 55: 468–75.

Lindesmith, A. R. (1952), 'Comments on W. S. Robinson's "The logical structure of analytical induction"' *American Sociological Review* 17: 492–3.

Lykken, David (1970), 'Statistical significance in psychological research', in Henkel, R. E. and Morrison, D. E. (eds), *The Significance Test Controversy*: 267–279.

Madge, John (1953), *The Tools of Social Science,* London: Longmans, Green & Co.

Mitchell, J. Clyde, (1956), *The Yao Village,* Manchester University Press for the Rhodes-Livingstone Institute. Oxford (1979), *The Oxford Dictionary of Quotations,* 3rd edn, Oxford University Press.

Queen, S. (1928), 'Round table on the case study in sociological research', *Publications of the American Sociological Society*: 22.

Robinson, W.S. (1951), 'The logical structure of Analytical Induction', *American Sociological Review* 16: 812–18.

—— (1952), 'Rejoinder to comments on "The logical structure of Analytical Induction"', *American Sociological Review* 17:494.

Sarbin, T.R. (1943), 'A contribution to the study of actuarial and individual methods of prediction', *American Journal of Sociology* 48: 593–602.

Shaw, Clifford (1927), 'Case study method', *Publications of the American Sociological Society.* 21: 149–57.

Simons, Helen (ed.), (1980), *Towards a Science of the Singular: Essays about Case Study in Education Research and Evaluation,* Care Occasional Publications no. 10, Norwich: Centre for Applied Research in Education.

Stake, Robert E. (1980), 'The case study method in social enquiry', in Simon, H. (ed.), *Towards a Science of the Singular: Essays about Case Study in Educational Research and Evaluation,* Care Occasional Publications no. 10, Norwich, Centre for Applied Research in Education: 64–75.

Turner, Ralph H. (1953), 'The quest for universals in sociological research', *American Sociological Review* 24: 605–11.

Turner, V. W. (1957), *Schism and Continuity in an African Society,* Manchester University Press for the Rhodes–Livingstone Institute.

Van Velson, J. (1967), 'The extended case method and situational analysis', in Epstein, A. L. (ed), *The Craft of Social Anthropology,* London: Tavistock: 129–49.

Waller, Willard (1935), 'Insight and scientific method', *American Journal of Sociology* 285–97.

Weinberg, S. Kirston (1952), 'Comment on W. S. Robinson's 'The logical structure of analytical induction', *American Sociological Review* 17: 493–4.

Young, Pauline (1939), 'The Case Study Method', in *Scientific Social Surveys and Research,* New York: Prentice Hall: ch. X, 226–54.

Znaniecki, Florian (1934), *The Method of Sociology,* New York: Rinehart.

11

Library Access, Library Use and User Education in Academic Sixth Forms: An Autobiographical Account[1]

Lawrence Stenhouse

I take an autobiographical account to be simply a recollection, as opposed to a 'retrospective analysis' in which recollection is verified against documentary evidence and the recollections of others (Wise, Singer, Altschuld and Berk, 1977). The project which is the subject of this autobiographical account was funded under the title which stands at the head of this paper, but we use the short title 'Library Access and Sixth-Form Studies' (LASS). LASS is funded by the British Library Research and Development Department as part of its programme of research in user studies. The proposal was written by me and is dated June 1979. The project runs for two and a quarter years from January 1980, and the budget is £47,850. Members of staff from the following institutions are working on the project: Centre for Applied Research in Education of the University of East Anglia; Centre for Research in User Studies, University of Sheffield; Crewe and Alsager College of Education; and Keswick Hall College of Education (now the School of Education of the University of East Anglia). Five freelance researchers are also involved. I am the 'Head of Project' (BL's term) and the Coordinator of the Project is Beverley Labbett, both of the Centre for Applied Research in Education.

Background to the Proposal

The proposal originated in the following way. I was unaware of the existence of the British Library Research and Development Department until they sent me a proposal to referee. The proposal was 'illuminative' in style (cf. Stenhouse,

Source: Robert G. Burgess (ed.), *The Research Process in Educational Settings* (London: Falmer Press, 1984).

1979a; Parlett and Hamilton, 1972), and it cited my book as the source for its design (cf. Stenhouse, 1975). Another similar proposal followed, and then an invitation to speak at a conference on library research, at which I was, to my surprise, introduced as one whose work in curriculum was 'revolutionizing' research on library user studies!

My previous research project on problems and effects of teaching about race relations was coming to an end (cf. Stenhouse, Verma, Wild and Nixon, 1982), and it seemed reasonable to try and see if there were any coincidence between my research interests and those of the British Library that would make for a profitable partnership. Also I suppose I felt to some extent challenged to show that case study methods would pay off in this area of research.[2]

The primary substantive field in which I have been interested is the problem of emancipation through schooling in the face of the social control problem in the school. This was the theme of the Humanities Curriculum Project,[3] which I earlier directed, and this was followed by the project on race relations teaching, which focused on similar issues. I was attracted by the possibility of looking into the process of emancipation into individual study in the sixth form. And I had always been interested in libraries and in study.

Of course, you might ask why I should be writing proposals at all. The background to that lies in the history of our Centre, at the University of East Anglia, which carries a fair number of valued people on 'soft money', and is continuously concerned with proposal writing. When you finish one proposal, you start the next. So this seemed a good one to write. I submitted it to the British Library, and in due course it was funded.

The Research Proposal

When it comes to research aims, I think I have always worked with double sets of aims – one for the sponsor and one for myself! The proposal sets out the job I hope to do for the sponsor – in this case as follows:

1 to reconceptualize academic sixth-form education in respect to its relation to library access;
2 to draw implications for teaching in the presence of libraries and for user education;
3 to consider the significance of library access for educational opportunity at sixth-form level and draw conclusions for the organization of education and library provision at age 16–18;
4 to consider the concept and possible form of compensatory user education;
5 to document the styles of librarians and teachers as managers of knowledge;
6 to make recommendations for curriculum development in user education at sixth-form level.

The whole art of the business in funded research is to find scope for your own aims within and alongside the sponsor's aims – and without costing the sponsor anything. I saw in the project the possibility of building the theory of schooling on which I have been working for the last twenty years or so. The theme of emancipation, which I have already mentioned, is potentially a matter of conflict in the sixth form, and largely because of the growth of independent study and the student's capacity to appeal against the teacher to the library. As one of our students says in interview, teachers' encouragement of independent study places them in danger of a kind of redundancy. This is fascinating territory. So too is the possibility of making comparisons across the divide between private and state school systems. Finally, I was interested in undertaking the design and management problems of multi-site case study and hopeful of accumulating an archive through this research which would be a resource for other researches and researchers. I was confident both that I would get plenty out of the work for the British Library and that I would be able to follow my own intellectual quests, and so I was able to work in a style comfortable to my bent with comparatively little preordinate planning and plenty of responsive thinking.[4] Look for a rich seam and then dig!

What I suppose might be called the research design is treated in the proposal under the heading, 'Method':

> generalization across twenty-six descriptive case studies based upon condensed fieldwork involving tape recorded interviews, observations and collection of documents, including both qualitative and quantitative data. The fieldworkers will produce indexed case records to form an archive.

The use of the word 'generalization', here, is problematic and I must leave for later discussion: an explanation was clearly not of interest to the sponsors. The central design feature is multi-site case study based on condensed fieldwork.

The Context of the Proposal

Interestingly enough I had proposed a multi-site case study of Scottish comprehensive schools to the Scottish Education Department in about 1965, without of course using that terminology. It had been turned down. Later, as director of the Humanities Project, I had written a proposal for an evaluation which called for the appointment of a Schools Study Officer who was to study classrooms during the experiment as a basis for designing an evaluation of the Project in its dissemination phase. In practice, the evaluation, under Barry MacDonald, extended its study to schools. It could thus be called a multi-site case study, though again the term was in nobody's mind at the time. During that evaluation, two things became clear. In such an exercise you cannot employ traditional ethnographic methods because you must move at the pace of the events you are studying; hence the process which was later named by Rob Walker 'condensed fieldwork'.[5] Secondly, in case study work it is often difficult to get your data into shape for publication, and there is little or no access to that data until it is published.

My next experiences ran side by side. I directed a project on problems and effects of teaching about race relations in which there was a strong teacher–researcher element and in which Bob Wild contributed the case studies.[6] The case study element went alongside a fairly large testing programme with a conventional pre-test post-test design. Case studies were mainly of classrooms, and they were created from classroom tapes with supporting interviews with teachers. At the same time I was contributing a case study to Barry MacDonald's SAFARI Project (Success and Failure and Recent Innovation). This was my first fieldwork experience using condensed methods in schools. Out of all this came the conviction that qualitative case study was not being successfully integrated with the quantitative data based on sampling (cf. Sieber, 1973), that there were critical problems in organizing data in such a way that colleagues could discuss them together and that the problem of working across cases at the writing-up stage had not been satisfactorily tackled.

In a study of the dissemination of the Race Project, Jean Rudduck, who was responsible for executing the study, found herself case studying a series of events such as conferences and committee meetings.[7] Each might be regarded as complete in itself, and one approach would have been to produce case studies of each as she went along. In fact, however, she produced a lightly edited case record – that is, a collection of data – from each event, and used these as the basis of her final write-up. The case records were paper-bound volumes. It was easy for me to read them and to discuss her conclusions with her.

There followed a project funded by the SSRC on educational case records. In this, four or five colleagues undertook condensed case studies concentrating on the record of fieldwork. We produced various different records; I made an attempt to write up a very elementary case, citing records as an historian would. We held a conference on case study and case records in York in 1980.[8]

Meanwhile, over in the United States, Bob Stake and Jack Easley had conducted a multi-site case study, *Case Studies in Science Education* (1978), within the American responsive evaluation tradition. Rob Walker from CARE had contributed two of the case studies.[9] Bob Stake worked from case studies rather than case records, and I came to feel that this was a mistake, both because of what was lost from the good case studies and even more because I had the impression that some of the case studies were not too securely founded.

The message is that I have been interested in case study for a long time: in 1957 I wrote a proposal for a comparative study of Macclesfield Grammar School and Dunfermline High School; since 1968 I have supported and maintained active contact with school case study work, and since 1975 I have been directly involved in fieldwork for case studies. LASS is another course in the wall I have been some time building.

Table 1: The Case Studies and the Fieldworkers

CR*	Present type	Sex	Formerly	Total number of students	Number of students in VI**	Number of books in library***	Fieldworker
1	comprehensive	m	amalgamation of 3	1400	165	4500?	Sue Stone CRUS
2	comprehensive	m	grammar	1050	170	?	Iain Smith C & A Bob Cooper C & A
3	comprehensive	m	sec. mod.	2050	350	?	Karl Openshaw USA
4	comprehensive	m	sec. mod.	1000	76	?	John Cockburn CARE
5	comprehensive	m	grammar	1150	220	10000	Lawrence Stenhouse CARE
6	comprehensive	m	sec. mod.	1100	40	?	Charles Hull CARE
7	comprehensive	m	grammar	1300	200		Bev Labbett CARE
8	comprehensive	m	middle	1050	150	5000?	Bev Labbett CARE
9	comprehensive	m	sec. mod.	650	30	?	Harry Torrance CARE
10	comprehensive	m	grammar	1000	120	5000?	Iain Smith C & A
11	grammar	m	tech. high	750	128	11000+	Jim Butler Australia
12	comprehensive	m	p. built	2200	235	19000	Cherry Harrop CRUS
13	comprehensive	m	p. built	1700	172	5000	Mike Hayhoe KH
14	comprehensive	m	p. built	1650	150	?	Iain Smith C & A Bob Cooper C & A
15	sixth-form college	m	grammar	500	500	12000	Pauline Heather CRUS
16	sixth-form college	m	grammar	700	700	12000	Christine Beal CRUS
17	public boarding	b	–	850	219	20000	Bev Labbett CARE
18	public boarding	m	–	370	149	27000	Lawrence Stenhouse, Beverley Labbett; Charles Hull CARE
19	public boarding	g	–	850	280	30000	Jean Rudduck CARE
20	independent day	b	–	550	160	8000	John Pund KH
21	independent day	g	–	700	160	12000+	Anne Murdoch UEA
23	college of FE	m	–	1700 f.t. 4500 p.t.	–	35000	Ed Parr Australia
25	tertiary college	m	–	1000 f.t. 2500 p.t.	–	32000	Lawrence Stenhouse CARE
26	independent day	b	–	1450	532	25000	Lawrence Stenhouse CARE

Notes:

*   Numbers 22 and 24 were not completed.

**   Number of students in VI include A-level and non-A-level students.

*** Several librarians did not know what the library was holding and would not hazard a guess. Some guessed. The figures listed are only a rough guide: it is not always clear exactly what is included in the figure given (CRI: number is for upper school library only.)

Key:

CARE   Centre for Applied Research in Education, University of East Anglia.
CRUS   Centre for Research in User Education, University of Sheffield.
C & A Crewe and Alsager College of Education.
KH   Keswick Hall College of Education (now School of Education, University of East Anglia).
UEA   University of East Anglia.

The LASS Project

In the LASS Project eighteen fieldworkers have, in the end, contributed twenty-four case records. The contract with each fieldworker is for an indexed case record of an institution agreed with the project. Because no case study is asked for, each participant researcher is free to do a case study negotiated with the institution concerned. We monitor lightly to make sure that nothing is going to blow up in our faces. There is a substantial area of freedom here, which I think is valuable. In addition, all participants have access to the archive on condition that they write no case studies of institutions or individuals where the fieldwork is not their own. There is an open invitation to contribute to the final report or to the book that we hope will follow it.[10]

The fieldworkers received support from the project in the form of travelling expenses and subsistence during fieldwork, and transcription of all their tape-record interviews. In addition they were invited to two conferences at which they had the opportunity of discussing together the problems and opportunities of fieldwork. Fieldwork was limited to twelve days for each school and on that basis it was possible for two experienced secretaries to handle the task of transcription. I should add that few fieldworkers used all twelve days. The shortest contact was three days – which was all the school would allow – but they were three days of undesirably intensive interviewing, brought off rather well, I thought, by one of our doctoral students. Beverley Labbett and I did four case studies, and our two colleagues from Crewe and Alsager did three between them. Other fieldworkers did one case study each. The case studies that were done and the fieldworkers involved are shown in Table 1.

Of course, Beverley and (to a lesser extent) I were available for consultation and fieldworkers, especially those lacking experience, did seek our advice. I cannot speak for him, but though I did talk to the team about what I had in mind for the project, much more time was spent in explaining that what I had in mind was less than they suspected! I also explained that as all of them had some educational or library experience they could draw on this experience in interview and observation. In a way, it is a classic position on fieldwork: you learn by getting your hands dirty. And you have to remember never to submerge your own intelligence and sensitivity in the interest of some set of rules – certainly not on authority; it is not that there are no rules, but rather that you have to see the need for them in the context of experience of fieldwork and its problems.

Beverley, the project coordinator, has been much more closely in touch with the people on the project than I have, perhaps partly through my illness. But he, after all, is the manager. I imagine I'm a bit more remote, whereas he has travelled round more and consulted more and consoled more. Of course, it is crucial that people have a limited and clear contract and know what to do if they have any difficulties in keeping it. Two agreed case studies failed to arrive. One study is really very weak. But my general assessment is that the approach worked and that the risks with experienced professional people or selected doctoral students of the kind we were working with are containable. On the whole we are pleased with the case records and find them usable.

The biggest problem was getting people away from the notion that qualitative data had to be comparable in the sense that quantitative data do. With a background in history I am puzzled by this difficulty. If such comparability were necessary across sources, history could not exist; and I find history more rigorous than social science. It is certainly encouraging to my view to find in *Montaillou* that the records of the Inquisition allow the reconstruction of a vivid and largely convincing portrait of a mediaeval Pyrenean village (Le Roy Ladurie, 1978).

Gaining Access in a Multi-Site Project

So far as access to institutions is concerned, our procedures were variable. The CRUS people in Sheffield and the Crewe and Alsager staff were invited to negotiate access in their own way once we had agreed with them which institutions they would try to bring in. Most entries, however, were negotiated through the project either by Beverley or by myself. Where I accompanied a fieldworker on a first negotiating visit, it was my purpose to suggest that the worker and the institution could come to any agreements they liked within the framework of the minimum obligation to contribute an anonymized case record to the archive.

I can talk in greater detail only about the cases in which I was involved in some way. One case on which I worked with Beverley Labbett, but playing only a minor part, was an independent public boarding school. We started by writing to the head, and when we went to the school, Beverley found that one of the deputy heads had been at university with him: she acted to some extent as a key informant, but so did the librarian. Another case, an independent public day school, was also approached through the head. I saw him on my first and last visits but my interviews were arranged by the librarian, who acted as my host. In two other cases I negotiated access to schools through Chief Education Officers. In the county in which I worked myself, this led to a meeting with two advisers, a rather long discussion of several possible schools, and the final selection of three to our mutual satisfaction. Entrance was then requested by me in letters to the heads that took the following form:

Centre for Applied Research in Education,
University of East Anglia,
Norwich
NR4 7TJ

15 February 1980

Dear [head's name],

As you know, I came over to [place name] for a discussion with [name of LEA advisers] about the possibility of a limited number of schools participating in our British Library Project on Library Access and Sixth Form Studies. I have now heard from [adviser] that you are agreeable to our discussing the possibility of [your school] taking part.

Should you do so, the project would like to assign to the school one of its researchers. From the point of view of the project the research-er's task would be to produce a record or study of library access and sixth-form study in your school which would contribute to a descrip-tive national survey.

From the point of view of the school it is open to you to negotiate with the researcher whatever form of service in the way of report writing or consultancy seems best to repay you for granting us access for the study. All that has to be borne in mind is the background obligation to the project I have already outlined.

The project has only just started, and the study visits to the school will take place in the session 1980–81. It has been decided that I shall be the researcher working in [your] school if participation is agreeable to you, and I should very much like to make a visit on which I can explain the pattern of the project to you, so that you can make a final decision about participation. [There follows a passage about dates of possible meetings.] I am enclosing three copies of a short statement about the project and I can send you more if you should want more. We shall try to keep you in touch with develop-ments as we set up the project, though, since we are assuming that our studies will keep schools anonymous, it is not possible for us to put the group of schools in touch with each other.

We look forward greatly to the possibility of our working with your school.[11]

Yours sincerely,

Lawrence Stenhouse
Professor of Education
Director of Centre

I visited each school to talk to the heads personally. The approach was differ-ent again in relation to a tertiary college: here, my first contact was with the Chief Education Officer, who approved my writing to the principal; the mat-ter was then passed to the vice-principal with whom I negotiated. The librarian was my informant,[12] so far as I had one. I saw the principal in the corridors, but I never met him.

Issues of Selection

I should say something about sampling – I do not think we are engaged in sampling. There is a complicated argument behind that position. So let us cut corners and talk about our collection of cases. Of course, in gathering that collection we are selecting,[13] and I suppose our selection is rather close to what sociologists following Glaser and Strauss would recognize and call a 'theoretical sample' (cf. Glaser and Strauss, 1967). Basically the attempt is to get an extended range of different settings and different problems. We looked for three public boarding schools and got one boys', one girls' and one mixed. Our public day schools differed in size. Two were boys' schools, one girls'. We went for two sixth-form colleges, two tertiary colleges and two colleges of further education. The rest – apart from one local authority grammar school – were comprehensive schools of various kinds. We bore in mind the need to have some access to different social and environmental settings: for example, in rural areas we looked for plains villages as compared to linear valleys and the like. And of course we went for schools with different levels of library provision; indeed, our main reason for taking more than one school from a local authority was to balance a badly provided school with a well provided one in order to protect the Chief Education Officer who would be vulnerable if he allowed us to represent his authority only with a poorly provided school.

We also selected three Advanced level subjects for the centre of our attention: history, French and biology. The idea was to protect us from promising too much, but at the same time to draw into the penumbra of our vision the other subjects which A-level candidates in these subjects were also taking. We could then follow interesting trails that presented themselves. For example, in my state grammar turned comprehensive, it became clear that there were particularly interesting things going on in Russian and chemistry and I followed these up.

One particular case shows how far from experimental controls our selection of cases was. In one independent day school the head, with regret, rejected my first request to study the use of the library – he was dissatisfied with the condition of the library and the way it was being run. Some months later, he 'phoned me up and said that he had taken my first visit as a cue to approach his governors, and the library was now being reformed and revitalized. He was happy that we should study it. Although it was our approach that had changed the situation, we were very happy to get an example of what such an independent school regarded as the provision that should be aimed at, and how they went about their programme of renovation.

Interviewing on the Project

One is naturally sensitive to the effects of sponsorship on interviews. My judgement is that there were virtually no effects of this kind. No-one, I think, disbelieved me when I described the conditions of confidentiality before the interview. I think some felt that I was perhaps being overscrupulous. The most serious possibility was in the one case where I was entertained to coffee and tea daily by the head. However, I think this was scarcely seen by any of the staff. In that school I had an interviewing room off the library and never entered the staffroom until the day of my last visit.

The undesirable aspect of that study was that my fraternization with the head produced an intimacy that led to a taped interview in which the head exercised too little restraint. This led in turn to censorship of the transcript. I thought of the classic advice to fieldworkers: 'Never accept hospitality and always take your own marmalade.' In this case there was little or nothing crossed out which bore on my interests, but what I did was to go back and explain why I thought that the head had had to cross out so much and then I interviewed her again and now I have two interviews, one hacked and one complete.

I ought to say perhaps at this point something about my own interviewing style, though, of course, this is not something of significance across the project, since the view we took was that each was free to develop a style within the critical framework provided by project discussions. I am rather keen not to sit facing the interviewee, but rather side by side or angled towards each other. This allows me to seek or to avoid eye contact. I explain to interviewees that I prefer to sit beside them and look out at the world with them, sharing their view.

As an interviewer I try to be polite, attentive, sensitive, thoughtful, considerate, but not familiar – rather respectful. I feel it is part of my job to give people the feeling not merely that they have my ear, my mind and my thoughts concentrated on them but that they want to give an account of themselves because they see the interview as in some way an opportunity: an opportunity of telling someone how they see the world. I hope that the occasion is slightly flattering to the person being interviewed.[14] Interviewees should recognize that they are more important than they thought they were by reflecting about themselves and their work. I am told by readers of my transcripts that my questions encourage by naiveté, but I really only muse about what is being said and follow my curiosity:

Example 1

LS: If I knew a mathematician – well I'm only saying I'm not a mathematician myself, so don't feel you have to talk for me – but if I knew a mathematician is there any way in which I could describe to him the kind of maths that you are teaching in this school? It might not be comprehensible to me but might be comprehensible if I knew more.

Teacher: Well I suppose you mean whether it's modern or traditional? Is that the kind of crude terminology?

LS: I don't know enough about maths to know whether that's a question I should be asking or whether I should be asking, 'Is it pure or applied'? (Case Record No. 5 B (Teacher Interview) p. 51)[15]

[This exchange was followed by a long response from the teacher.]

Example 2

Teacher: ... the ... edition [of Shakespeare's plays] is now become the one bought in school because the footnotes are on the page that you're reading and not at the back....

LS: I suppose the annotations are the beginning of study skills.

Teacher: I'm sure they are ... all the staff here have had this broader study skills course you know with our felt tip pens and our diagrams, etc. so that creeping into lessons from time to time must be, as you say, study skills – how to plan an essay and all those other things but I don't know if I'm referring to quite what you mean by reference books and books of criticism.

LS: Well, I don't know. I'm trying to –

Teacher: You're just asking me.

LS: Yes. I'm trying to see what's in the word, and feeling that the phrases that I pick up from a conference about libraries and schools, I'm not sure what they mean either.

Teacher: Well study skills to me very often means that they have to rule off at the end of one piece of work and date each piece of work and head it properly so that they know where they're going and so do I. But I suppose that's extremely primitive and has nothing to do with the subject. (Case Record No. 5 B (Teacher Interview) p. 68)

Example 3

LS: If one were to drive that to its furthest point and say, 'Well yes there are a lot of books that aren't used but it's a kind of wall covering that reminds people about books and if it were a bare study room people would perhaps study less and ...' Is there anything in that or is that just a sort of romance ... ?

(Case Record No. 5 B (Teacher Interview) p. 88)

Example 4

LS: I've become interested without really being able to come to any conclusion as to whether the solitary practice of a musical instrument, training in physical education – I mean training means trotting round on your own, working on your own, that kind of thing – actually contribute to the capacity for independent study, to habituate people to the notion of something, some learning entered into through an effort of concentrated application, conducted on your own without supervision. (Case Record No. 5 D (Senior Management Interview) p. 13)

There is then a loose form to my interview. For example, in my interviews with sixth-form pupils I asked them first for a job description of being a pupil in the lower school:

Example 1

LS: Now what about your experience in the lower school. Let me talk about the job of being a pupil. What was the job of being a pupil like in the lower school? (Case Record No. 5 A (Student Interview) p. 95)

Example 2

LS: And you studied those for five years, starting off at the beginning. Did you.... I'm trying to get some notion of what the job of being a pupil in the lower school is like. Did you have to use the library in any of those subjects? (Case Record No. 5 A (Student Interview) p. 2)

I then explored the difference in the sixth-form, then looked at the differentiation of job between subjects ... and so on.

On the whole I feel that if you are not ethnographically inclined, but closer, as I am, to oral history, and if you are not doing evaluation, that is to say, if you are clearly concerned with an educational problem that is of interest to teachers, then the business of getting response is pretty robust. In the end, however, my judgement can only be confirmed by looking at my interview transcripts and making up your own mind about it. My contention is that these matters are much more readily judged on the basis of interview scripts than on the basis of described procedures. But then my position close to historians naturally leads me to believe that documents (including interview transcripts) can be criticized and that well-grounded judgements can be made about them.

Another problem is that in all my case study settings I got at the students through the teachers. I am still unsure how I feel about that. A lot depends on the kind of study you are trying to do. I've got lazy people among the students, academics and also highly utilitarian people who have specific uses for A-levels and no great interest beyond them. I don't think I've got many disruptors, but then it is doubtful how many disruptors you would get in the academic sixth form anyway. I'm just not sure about this factor; and my feeling is that my own view will become clearer as I work through the materials closely.

What I feel pretty sure about is that we were much more concerned with people's perceptions and conceptions – their meanings – than with their behaviour or with events. That is not to say that we never asked people about what they did or what they observed, but rather that we should treat accounts of behaviour or events with scepticism and with a greater interest in the meanings they revealed than their direct evidential status. It is only when particularly stringent critical controls are exercised, and material survives them, that one can use interview data as a source of information about happenings. If a pupil says: 'I don't often go to my local library because it's not much use to me for A-level work – it's really a general library', I'd rather conclude that the library is perceived in that way either because it is true or because of some factor that hides its potential from that pupil than accept the statement as reliable direct evidence. On the other hand, I would accept that he or she doesn't often go, because I can see in context no reason why he or she should be self deceived or intentionally deceiving in saying that.

Interview and Observation in Multi-Site Case Study

So much for the witness gathered from interview. But let's contextualize that. When you are working in multi-site case study, you are working lightly in each case and trying to get out of the comparison among cases something of the force that the classic ethnographer gets from depth in a single case. We bargained for twelve days of fieldwork in each school, and immediately that seems to me to mean that the case studies are predominantly interview-based. You are not getting enough time to do true participant observation, and therefore you are trying to collect, in interview, observation from participants.

Observation by fieldworkers is brief and, mainly non-participant (though not necessarily non-reactive). For my part, I spent some time in the library, sitting and working at taking notes, and I also visited the libraries in the catchment area of the schools, observing in the process something of the area itself. You must, however, beware of false impressions gathered from the observation of what just happens to come your way over a short period of time.

In both interviewing and observation it is important that one has some experience of schools and of libraries – a good second record, to use a phrase of Hexter (1972). I think I feel as an interviewer that I am trying to help the interviewee to give me a skilled interview. A lot of my work is in helping interviewees to structure their statements. Sometimes it will be as simple as reminding them when they have made three points, that they were going to make four; but it isn't easy to describe the pattern and function of one's interventions. It is as if one were helping the interviewee to master an unaccustomed art form. I did a paper on interviewing for the project (1979b), but it's a highly provisional piece which I hope to revise when I have been through all the records.

Styles of Data Recording

Our interviews are always tape-recorded unless the interviewee demurs, which we find rather rare. In that case, however, I take notes, always in two columns, the left column being a running record of the interview in catchword and brief note form, the right column being literal quotation. If the transcription is not possible because of resource constraints, I generally advise note-taking from tape in this form.[16]

I never try to hide or play down the tape recorder. On the whole I find that most subjects forget it or ignore it very quickly indeed. I think that is because I find it easy to ignore myself. If the interviewer is relaxed and natural, then that helps the interviewee. I would not under any circumstances choose to use notes to help me to conduct the interview. I think that really does destroy my rapport with the person I am interviewing. I also find it unacceptably intrusive when people are interviewing me.

CENTRE FOR APPLIED RESEARCH IN EDUCATION
University of East Anglia, Norwich, NR4 7TJ

I am prepared to give authority for the transcript of this interview of myself by (name of fieldworker) to be reproduced in an anonymised form for use in conferences, teaching and research and for lodgement in an archive in print or microfiche which shall be open to researchers.

Signed ....

Date ....

The interviews come back from fieldwork and they are transcribed from tape by our secretaries, who are skilled and experienced in this kind of work. In fact they preserve more in the way of hesitation phenomena than I think is important for our purposes, but that is the way to have it, because that leaves the professional researchers rather than secretaries in control. When the transcriptions come back to me, I'll either go through them listening to the tape if I think there is any difficulty, or I'll read them carefully in the light of my memory of the interview and my 'second record';[17] and I'll make corrections, usually very few. For example, the typist may fail to pick up proper names, titles of textbooks, initials of examination boards and the like. After I've been through the transcripts, I post them back to the people who gave me the interviews, inviting them to correct any errors of fact that may have crept in and to strike out anything which must be off the record. Overall, we have had very few alterations or excisions in most interviews. About one in twenty or one in thirty people want to make fairly extensive alterations, most often to improve the grammar and syntax of the spoken word. I try to dissuade them if I can but accept their alterations if I have to.

Transcripts go back with a cover sheet which the interviewee is asked to sign: in this project this gives clearance for the use of material in anonymized form by researchers in conferences and in teaching. I would not anonymize again if I could avoid it, though I recognize that abandoning anonymization necessitates a gradual progress to greater honesty about schooling that cannot too much be hurried. I feel we should have taken that line in LASS. One of the things that attracts me to the project is that it seems to me relatively rich in research meaning without being very sensitive, and that favours openness.

We are only now (March 1982) beginning to tackle the problem of data analysis and reporting. Thus this account is necessarily truncated. We sit in a room with twenty-four box files along a shelf and various other bundles of documents, and discuss where we hope to get and how we are going to get there.[18]

One hope I have is that participants in the project will find the archive useful both in generating grounded theory and in testing theory, that the sponsors will find the report useful for their formulation of future policy and that teachers and students will find the report, the book and other materials produced useful in developing more emancipatory forms of sixth-form *and* lower school work. I certainly believe that such an emancipatory thrust is possible. Resistance is not the only escape from reproduction of the hegemony at cultural levels.

Notes

1. This paper was revised after the death of the author. The revisions, the notes and some examples have been provided by Robert Burgess, David Jenkins and Jean Rudduck who have, where possible, used the author's work and words. Some material has been taken from a tape recording of the session at which the first draft of this chapter was discussed by Lawrence Stenhouse at the Whitelands College workshop in March 1982.

2. Throughout this chapter the term 'case study methods' is used rather than 'ethnographic methods', for Stenhouse considered that ethnography is not devoted to the people it studies while, in contrast, he was devoted to the teachers and pupils with whom he worked. Stenhouse saw ethnography as tainted with colonialism (cf. Asad, 1973) Furthermore, for him ethnographers were strangers to the situations they studied, while he was no stranger to educational settings as he maintained: 'There is one

place where I feel that I understand the environment and that I am at home and that is in schools' (taped discussion).

3. For discussions of the Humanities Curriculum Project see, for example, Stenhouse (1973; 1975; 1980b; 1983), Rudduck (1976), Verma (1980), MacDonald (1979), Elliott (1983).

4. For discussions of Stenhouse's style of work in this area and his ideas on the approach involved see Stenhouse (1978; 1979a; 1979b; 1980a; 1982a).

5. For an account of this approach see Walker (1974), and for Stenhouse's interpretation of this style of work see Stenhouse (1982a).

6. See Stenhouse et al. (1982), pp. 119–84.

7. An account of this work is given by Jean Rudduck in chapter 8 of Burgess (1984): 'A Study in the Dissemination of Action Research' (see also Rudduck and Stenhouse, 1979).

8. The project proposal, which was called 'Exemplary case studies: Towards a descriptive educational research tradition grounded in evidence', was submitted to the SSRC in December 1977. Exemplary records were produced but remain unpublished:
ECR 1 Hawthorn School: A Case Record
ECR 2 Furzedown Comprehensive: A Case Study
ECR 3 Senior Management at the Jepson School: A Case Record
ECR 4 Towards the History of Risby Church School 1914–1918.

9. See Stake and Easley (1978). The two studies by Rob Walker are collected in volume I of the project publication:
No. 6 Pine City: A Rural Community in Alabama.
No. 11 Greater Boston: An Urban Section in Metropolitan Boston.

10. When Lawrence Stenhouse died Jean Rudduck took responsibility for writing up the project report (Rudduck et al., 1983). Rudduck had to work quickly and therefore did not pursue the idea of the 'open invitation' to fieldworkers to contribute to the final report. Indeed, Rudduck feels that she will be unable to operationalize this idea in the book that may follow, since it will reflect very closely the structure of the report.

11. This was the standard letter that was used in the project, modified according to the circumstances that have been discussed. The letter to independent schools included the following statement: 'We are keen to study three public schools where the sixth-form tradition has deep roots because we think this will place the situation in state schools in a properly broad perspective.'

12. In several settings the librarian acted as internal coordinator of the study and the fieldworker tended to spend more time with the librarian, developing a relationship that led to an easy flow of data, with the result that the librarian became an informant.

13. For discussions of selection in case study work see Stenhouse (1978; 1980a) also see the chapters by Martyn Hammersley and Stephen Ball in this book that discuss this issue.

14. For a discussion of interviewing see Stenhouse (1979b).

15. The twenty-four interview-based case records produced for this project are publicly accessible and are indexed and anonymized. They can be consulted at the Centre for Applied Research in Education, University of East Anglia, Norwich.

16. It was this style of note-taking that Lawrence Stenhouse used when reading through the case record to prepare for writing the report.

Interview with boy

CR4/A/85	Change to less directed work in VIth
CR4/A/86	Use of library & use of common room
CR4/A/87	'We're given textbooks, so l just use those. I find I don't need to use it. If we're told to look at something in the library, we do.'
CR4/A/88	Manner of writing essays. Subjects: maths, combined maths & physics and economics
	'I study most upstairs' (common room) 'Well, physics and maths, it's generally having to consult with people....'
CR4/A/89	Interested in physics, electronics

Interview with two girls

CR4/A/90	Girl students (2) (1) A level Art, English & some O levels, more freedom, not treated as children in VI form
CR4/A/91	Classes smaller
CR4/A/92	Of essays –
	'You've got to be more aware of how you write it and what you put into it – the way you set it out to get better marks....' 'Well, I study most at home – but I do a lot of my studying in free time upstairs in the common room, because I can't work when it's too quiet.'
	Sometimes if it's too noisy comes to library, but lighting isn't good (fluorescent)
CR4/A/93	Picks relevant chapter from contents

KEY: CR4 = Case record 4
          A = Interview with students
         85 = Page reference within student interviews in CR4

17. The idea of the 'second record' comes from Hexter's book, *The History Primer* (1972) (Chapter 4, 'The sown and the waste or the second record'). Stenhouse introduced the idea in a paper written in 1981, 'The Verification of Descriptive Case Studies'. He begins by talking about fiction, suggesting that 'in realistic fictions verification depends upon the reader's judgments about the trustworthiness of a portrayal in terms of verisimilitude: a likeness to factual truth'. He goes on to suggest that the 'organized trace of the reader's experience' to which appeal is made in the verification of a realistic fiction might be called 'a general second record'. If the account offered is not confirmed by the general second record of the reader, 'either the portrayal will be dismissed or it must be upheld by a revision of the record of one's own experience'. Stenhouse then moves the argument across from fiction to history and thence to case study. A later paper (1982b) defines the second record as 'the accumulated experience of the reader'. Here Stenhouse argues that while verification may appeal to the second record of the reader, authentication requires a first record – the documents of the case.

18. Lawrence Stenhouse was working on the case records until ten days before he died in September 1982, trying to immerse himself in the data and making notes for the report. Jean Rudduck, who was one of the eighteen fieldworkers, agreed to take over responsibility for writing the report. She completed it in March 1983 (see Rudduck *et al.*, 1983). She invited two people who had not been involved in the fieldwork to make a contribution to the report: the two outsiders were thus able to test the potential of the archive of twenty-four case records as a source which people who had not taken part in the project could use; they also provided a check on the lineaments of her own interpretation of the situation. Jean Rudduck also took responsibility, but with very limited time and resources, for preparing the archive for use: this involved completing the indexing of the case records and their anonymization. The state of the case records in terms of uniformity of typeface and general presentation is poor: there was no money to have pages retyped after correction by interviewees and after anonymization.

In addition to the report to the British Library Research and Development Department, a number of articles and a book are planned.

References

Altschuld, J. (1977) 'A retrospective analysis of the development of a project monitoring system', paper given at American Educational Research Association (AERA), New York City.

Asad, T. (Ed.) (1973) *Anthropology and the Colonial Encounter*, Ithaca, University of Ithaca Press.

Berk, L. (1977) 'Characteristics of good retrospective analysis', paper given at AERA, New York City.

Burgess, R. G. (ed.) (1986) *The Research Process in Educational Settings,* Lewes: Falmer Press.

Elliott, J. (1983) 'A curriculum for the study of human affairs: The contribution of Lawrence Stenhouse', *Journal of Curriculum Studies*, 15, 2, pp. 105–23.

Glaser, B. and Strauss, A.L. (1967) *The Discovery of Grounded Theory*, Chicago, Aldine.

Hexter, J.H. (1972) *The History Primer*, London, Allen Lane; first published New York, Basic Books, 1971.

Le Roy Ladurie, E. (1978) *Montaillou,* London, Scolar Press.

MacDonald, B. (1979) *The Experience of Innovation*, Norwich, CARE, University of East Anglia.

Parlett, M. and Hamilton, D. (1977) 'Evaluation as illumination, in Hamilton', D. *et al.* (Eds) *Beyond the Numbers Game*, London, Macmillan, originally published in 1972.

Rudduck, J. (1976) *The Dissemination of Innovation: The Humanities Curriculum Project*, Schools Council Working Paper 56, London, Evans/Methuen Educational.

Rudduck, J. and Stenhouse, L. (1979) *A Study in the Dissemination of Action Research*, report to the SSRC, HR 3483/1.

Rudduck, J., Hopkins, D., Groundwater Smith, S. and Labbett, B. (1983) *Library Access and Sixth Form Study*, report to the British Library Research and Development Department.

Sieber, S. (1973), 'The integration of fieldwork and survey methods', reprinted in Burgess, R.G. (Ed.) *Field Research: A Sourcebook and Field Manual*, London, Allen and Unwin.

Singer, N. (1977) 'A retrospective analysis of the development of program criteria', paper given at AERA, New York City.

Stake, R.E. and Easley, J. (1978) *Case Studies in Science Education*, Centre for Instructional Research and Curriculum Evaluation and Committee on Culture and Cognition, University of Illinois School of Education.

Stenhouse, L. (1973) 'The Humanities Curriculum Project', in Butcher, H.J. and Pont, H.B. (Eds) *Educational Research in Britain 3*, London, University of London Press.

Stenhouse, L. (1975) *An Introduction to Curriculum Research and Development*, London, Heinemann.

Stenhouse, L. (1978) 'Case study and case records: Towards a contemporary history of education', *British Educational Research Journal*, 4, 2, pp. 21–39.

Stenhouse, L. (1979a), 'The problem of standards in illuminative research', *Scottish Educational Review*, 11, 1, pp. 5–10.

Stenhouse, L. (1979b) 'Gathering evidence by interview', Norwich, CARE, University of East Anglia, mimeo; later published in Kemmis, S., Bartlett, L. and Gillard, G. (Eds) *Perspectives in Case study 2: The Quasi-Historical Approach – Case Study Methods*, Deakin University Press.

Stenhouse, L. (1980a), 'The study of samples and the study of cases', *British Educational Research Journal*, 6, 1, pp. 1–6.

Stenhouse, L. (Ed.) (1980b) *Curriculum Research and Development in Action*, London, Heinemann.

Stenhouse, L. (1981) 'The verification of descriptive case studies', in Kemmis, S., Bartlett, L. and Gillard, G. (Eds) *Perspectives in Case Study 2: The Quasi-Historical Approach – Case Study Methods*, Deakin University Press.

Stenhouse, L. (1982a) 'The conduct, analysis and reporting of case study in educational research and evaluation', in McCormick, K. (Ed.) *Calling Education to Account*, London, Heinemann.

Stenhouse, L. (1982b) 'Case study in educational research and evaluation', in Fischer, D. (Ed.) *Methodische Traditione und Untersuchungsalltag in Fallstudienterr in der Pädagogik: Aufgaben Methode in Wirkungen*, Konstanz, Fauder.

Stenhouse, L. (1983) *Authority, Education and Emancipation*, London, Heinemann Educational.

Stenhouse, L., Verma, G.K., Wild, R.D., and Nixon, J. (1982) *Teaching about Race Relations*, London, Routledge and Kegan Paul.

Verma, G.K. (Ed.) (1980) *The Impact of Innovation*, Norwich, CARE, University of East Anglia.

Walker, R. (1974), 'The conduct of educational case study: Ethics, theory and procedures', in MacDonald, B. and Walker, R. (Eds) *Innovation, Evaluation, Research and
  the Problem of Control – Some Interim Papers*, Norwich, CARE, University of East
  Anglia, pp. 75–115; reprinted in Dockerell, W.B. and Hamilton, D. (Eds) (1980)
  Rethinking Educational Research, London, Hodder and Stoughton.
Wise, R. (1977) 'A case for the value of retrospective accounts of curriculum development', paper given at AERA, New York City.

12

Scholarship and Sponsored Research: Contradiction, Continuum or Complementary Activity?

Robert G. Burgess

The terms scholarship, research, sponsorship and in turn contract research are all contested concepts. They are the subject of discussion and debate among researchers in higher education. In part, the debate relates to the social and political context in which higher education institutions, not only in the UK, but also worldwide are now located. Furthermore, in Britain debates about research have been fuelled by discussions from the funding councils on research selectivity and the way in which research is to be assessed for the purposes of grant allocations to institutions. In these discussions some distinctions have been drawn between basic, strategic and applied research with a hierarchy being implied through the use of these terms in different contexts. In these circumstances, one question that arises, is the appropriateness of this terminology for social and educational research. In part, the title of this chapter is taken from a series of conversations that I have had with colleagues over the last year or so. One of my colleagues always makes the point 'I'm not a scholar, I'm a researcher'. A statement that signals (at least for him) a distinction between these activities. A further colleague also in conversation with me, outlined a similar distinction when he remarked: 'I have a postgraduate who has few opportunities of getting a job so I suppose she will have to go into contract research. She will be doing contract research during the day and working as a scholar, writing social theory in the evening.' Such comments leave researchers in little doubt that distinctions are made about the activities in which they are involved. This has been highlighted recently in the field of political science where Allison (1993) has suggested that the word research has taken on a talismanic power. In particular, he argues:

Source: David Halpin & Barry Troyna (eds), *Researching Educational Policy: Ethical and Methodological Issues* (London: Falmer Press, 1994).

> Given the financial pressures that academic institutions are under, what counts as research is whatever an outside body is prepared to pay for … So we now have a system of incentives which rewards those who spend the most public money and penalises those who do not spend any. (Allison, 1993)

Indeed, he goes on to state that much funded research in the humanities and the social sciences involves 'Questions of relatively local interest whose answers have relatively short sell by dates'. This overstates the case. All research in higher education is funded by public money. However, it does raise questions about the relationship between funding, scholarship and research.

We can begin by asking: how far do these comments on scholarship, research and contract research apply to social and educational research? In recent years there have been discussions in the field of education about the opportunities that exist for researchers to engage in research and evaluation supported by a range of sponsors including government departments (Taylor, 1985). However, given the scale of change that has occurred consequent upon the passing of the Education Reform Act in 1988, there have been opportunities not only for researchers to pose their own questions, but requests from a variety of national and local organizations for researchers to engage in examining, monitoring and evaluating change consequent upon the legislation. It is some of these issues that will be examined in this chapter with reference to funded research.[1] Such issues can be examined from a range of perspectives: a sponsor, a project steering group, a researcher employed on a funded research project or a project director. In this chapter, I draw on my experience as a project director to comment on some contemporary issues concerning research sponsorship and contract research.

Sponsored Projects

Sponsorship of social and educational research takes many forms. The sponsorship of projects by the Economic and Social Research Council is one where the researcher decides on the area of study, specifies the research questions, the methodology and the approach to be taken, the time period concerned and the funding required. Such projects are subject to peer review. This is basic or fundamental research that will support the development of social science long-term rather than being of direct use to policy makers. Yet in turn, much work in the field of education can inform policy making as well as contributing to the mainstream development of social and educational enquiry. Indeed, the White Paper entitled 'Realising Our Potential' (HMSO, 1993) has suggested that fundamental research needs to be considered in terms of its link with 'wealth creation' and the 'quality of life' – terms that are now included in the mission statement of the Economic and Social Research Council and highlights the importance of fundamental research for users.

In contrast, policy makers may also commission research. Much of this work links with the notion of the customer–contractor principle that was discussed in the Rothschild Report on the *Organisation and Management of Government R and D* (HMSO, 1971). Here a fundamental distinction is drawn between basic and applied research and the way in which applied research should be commissioned. The Report stated:

> This report is based upon the principle that applied R and D, that is R and D with a practical application as its objective, must be done on a contractor–customer basis. The customer says what he wants, the contractor does it (if he can) and the customer pays. Basic, fundamental or pure research ... has no analogous customer–contractor basis. (HMSO, 1971, par. 9)

As I have indicated elsewhere (Burgess, 1993a), this customer–contractor principle can be considered in relation to educational research that is contracted by a government department, or by a local education authority or by a commercial or industrial concern. However, it is important to consider the elements involved in the customer–contractor principle and the assumptions associated with it. First, a distinction is drawn between pure and applied research. Secondly, there is a suggestion that the customer knows what is required. Thirdly, it assumes that the contractor carries out the work on behalf of the customer in order to 'answer' the questions that have been posed. But questions can be raised in relation to each of these principles. First, questions can be asked about the possibility of making distinctions between basic and applied research. In turn, we can enquire whether, as in many sponsored studies, fundamental research may lead to applied research and in turn whether applied activities may result in contributions of a fundamental kind to social theory and to social science methodology. Secondly, questions can be raised about the extent to which customers know the kind of research problems that can be posed. Indeed, customers may have a knowledge and understanding of the area in which they wish an investigation to take place, but have no notion as to how this may be developed into a series of questions linked to the social sciences and education. Finally, there is the question of methodology and the extent to which the contractor rather than the customer needs to be able to specify the methodology not only in terms of research design but also in relation to data collection, styles of data analysis and in turn the ways in which the report can be written and disseminated. Such issues take us away from the notion that contractors are mere technicians. However, when the customer–contractor principle is applied to the social sciences a further dimension is involved. In a subsequent report, Rothschild (1982) indicates that

> the social science 'customer' includes all those who have a part to play in the decision making process. (Rothschild, 1982, par. 3.10)

In these circumstances, customers can commission work that will assist with policy making and decision-making – a situation that seems to have direct applicability to social and educational research. Indeed, in recent years I have worked on projects that have been commissioned by government bodies, local education authorities, industrial companies, commercial organizations and other public bodies. In all these projects, questions arise about the relationship between the customer and the contractor. But there are also other issues that have long-term implications for the social sciences. They include matters relating to the design of research projects, data collection and data analysis (see Burgess, 1993b). In addition, there are also issues concerned with dissemination and reporting (see Burgess, 1990). Such projects and the issues that surround them also raise questions about the independence of the researcher (Simons, 1984; Norris, 1990). Finally, there are also questions about funding, research careers (and in turn intellectual property rights), methodological development, ethical considerations and scholarship which will be examined in this chapter.

Funding and Planning

The sociologist C. Wright Mills writing in *The Sociological Imagination* (1970) commented on the way in which research design was often linked with funding and planning, in as far that he claimed, social scientists only felt a need to write plans when they were going to ask for funding for a specific piece of research. He continued:

> It is as a request for funds that most 'planning' is done, or at least carefully written about. However standard the practice, I think this is very bad; it is bound in some degree to be salesmanship, and, given prevailing expectations very likely to result in painstaking pretensions: the project is likely to be 'presented', rounded out in some arbitrary manner long before it ought to be: it is often a contrived thing, aimed at getting the money for ulterior purposes, however valuable, as well as for the research presented. (Mills, 1970, pp. 217–18)

Here, Mills points to several dilemmas for those engaged in contract research. First, whether the research proposal is merely 'salesmanship' – an attractive proposition, carefully costed that will win the tender. Secondly, whether projects are over simplified and contrived in this context. Finally, whether such plans and proposals attempt to gain money for ulterior purposes. In response, one could argue that all research proposals are to some extent acts of 'salesmanship' in as far that they promote pieces of work the researcher may wish to conduct or in some cases has to conduct in order to remain in employment. Secondly, research proposals should not be rounded out but should demonstrate some of the possibilities and problems that might occur in the project and how these can be handled. A research proposal and indeed a research design is not a static object but a statement at a given point in time from which the researcher orientates an investigation. It is a plan about what might occur rather than what should occur. It is not a blueprint. Finally, there is the question of whether research proposals are an attempt to get funds for ulterior purposes (a statement that several commentators have made). This can be turned to the advantage of the investigator as indicated by Stenhouse (1984) when he remarked:

> When it comes to research aims, I think I have always worked with double sets of aims – one for the sponsor and one for myself! The proposal sets out the job I hope to do for the sponsor ... the whole art of the business in funded research is to find scope for your own aims within and alongside the sponsor's aims – and without costing the sponsor anything. (Stenhouse, 1984, p. 213)

While this may be a way of approaching sponsored research a question is also raised; how might this be done? In this context, I take as an illustration, research that I have conducted for Sheffield Local Education Authority.

In June 1991 the Sheffield LEA indicated that they were interested in commissioning a research project on the resourcing of Sheffield schools. In particular, the local authority was interested in four key questions which were stated as follows:

1   What principles should guide the funding of three to eighteen-year provision?
2   What is the appropriate level of funding for pupils at different stages taking into account appropriate comparisons for other LEAs?
3   What baselines should be set for class size, non contact time, management time, support time, equipment and books and non-statemented special needs support?
4   What should be the aims and funding levels of special needs and positive action? (Sheffield City Council Education Department, 1992).

The proposal continued with an outline of the timetable which it was claimed was such that the full report should be completed by Easter 1992 in order that it could be considered by schools and by the local education authority in setting the budget for that Autumn. In addition, interim findings in relation to the key questions were to be available for discussion at the end of September 1991 so that they could be used in the budgeting for 1992–3. Finally, it was signalled that the project should be commissioned by the end of June in order that work could begin before the Summer vacation.

This project was to have a steering group consisting of officers and advisers together with representatives from nursery, primary, secondary and special schools and colleges. This was the group who would be responsible for receiving the project report and liaise with the research team. They were the group who would establish the remit of the research project, choose a suitable research unit to conduct the research and receive the project reports. At this stage, there was no indication of the funding available or any details about the methodology. These gaps were subsequently filled in by an education officer in a series of telephone conversations prior to a proposal being written. The officer suggested that the authority would be willing to spend somewhere between £40,000 and £50,000 over a six-month period for work on resource-allocation mechanisms in Sheffield and elsewhere, the presentation of an analysis on Sheffield's spending in schools for the 3–18 age range and an analysis of Sheffield's spending by age group and by socio-geographical areas in the city. The study was to be conducted by desk research, survey investigation, and by intensive case-study work.

Table 1: Proposed Project Timetable for the Sheffield Resource Allocation Project

September 1991	•	Policy analysis, analysis of statistical data, comparison with other LEAs and Sheffield. Report on policy.
October 1991	•	Main case studies in nursery, primary, secondary and further education.
November 1991	•	Issue of questionnaire. Analysis of case-study data.
December 1991	•	Interim report to schools and colleges (Return by 15 Dec.).
	•	Reports of case studies.
January 1992	•	Analysis of questionnaire data and report writing.
February 1992	•	Final report; writing thematic report; comparisons between age phases; dissemination meetings.

To assess whether a group can engage in such research activities a number of issues arise. First, does the research that is required fall within the expertise of the individual who is preparing the proposal? Secondly, does the research fit with the portfolio of expertise that the individual or group possess? Thirdly, does the research provide the investigators with an opportunity to explore a range of issues in addition to those which are required by the customer? In this instance, the research fitted with the expertise of the Centre in which I am located. We had been conducting investigations for a number of local authorities across the country (Salford, Hampshire, Coventry, Warwickshire and Solihull among others). Secondly, it fitted in the sense that we had already begun to conduct work on local management of schools and in particular had some experience of monitoring local financial management in the context of nursery schooling. Thirdly, the Centre had conducted research in a range of age phases from nursery through to further education and in addition we had worked regularly with a consultant who had direct experience of policy-focused research in the context of resource allocation. Accordingly, it seemed appropriate to offer a project proposal that could be used to conduct this study. The project specification contained in our initial research proposal indicates that we could cover all age phases represented in the authority using eight staff. In practice, only six members of staff were used and of these only four had been named in the initial proposal. The research was perceived as policy-focused and would result in statistical analysis, policy analysis and also a series of institutional accounts based on case studies. The timetable suggested is outlined in Table 1.

In the proposal, it was argued that the project would generate a policy analysis of resource allocation in Sheffield with comparisons to other LEAs, case studies of resource allocation within all the age phases in the city, a survey based upon an authority-wide study and a thematic report which would include recommendations. In framing the proposal I took each element contained in the specification document and suggested ways in which we would compare Sheffield with other authorities through pupil–teacher ratios, staffing analyses, incentive allowances, staff turnover and so on. Secondly, that we would study school policy and school ethos, as I argued:

> It will be essential to conduct some case studies of resource allocation in each age phase. The number of case studies to be conducted in each phase will depend on the number of schools and colleges in the Sheffield authority together with advice from the steering group members. (Burgess, 1991)

The case studies in each sector would need to provide comparative data and I indicated factors that would be covered in each case study including the deployment of staff, teacher–pupil ratios, contact ratios, teaching-group sizes, and special needs support – again the emphasis was upon areas that had been covered in the research specification with additions of my own. Overall, I stressed that comparable data needed to be collected to develop comparisons within the authority and beyond it.

By the time the authority evaluated the proposals and set up interviews three months had elapsed. I was interviewed (on behalf of our team) alongside three other teams. Although the research study brief had indicated that one team was to be used, the steering group decided to employ a team composed of staff from the universities of Sheffield, York and the Open University to conduct the survey work, while our Centre was invited to conduct the case-study work. Members of the steering group had decided to have teams that would collect different but complementary evidence with a view to links being established between the two teams (Brannen, 1992). However, the timetable had to be readjusted given that the project had been originally timed to start in the late Summer. Accordingly, we were asked to start work immediately in late September in order that reporting could occur in June 1992.

In such projects, a range of issues arise. Firstly, about the formulation and modification of the research specification. Secondly, the extent to which research careers and research teams can be developed in the time available. Thirdly, the way in which methodological development can take place within such projects. It is to some of these issues that we turn in subsequent sections. However, at this stage it is important to emphasize that winning this contract provided not only continuity of employment for some research staff but also allowed them to develop their expertise in areas in which they were already working and on which they had established research records. Nevertheless, it highlights the problem a research director has in building research teams on short-term projects and the problem researchers have in building a research career out of several short-term and seemingly loosely coupled projects.

Building Careers and Building Teams

A number of dilemmas surround personnel matters in funded research. These are well summed up by Wright Mills (1970) when he writes:

> Now I do not like to do empirical work if I can possibly avoid it. If one has no staff it is a great deal of trouble; if one does employ a staff then the staff is often even more trouble. (Mills, 1970, p. 225)

Such a comment points to a problem that is often perceived by many research directors. First, what kind of staff with the appropriate skills and expertise can be effectively hired for a project? Secondly, what kinds of responsibilities does the director have to the project staff? Thirdly, to what extent can staff redefine the project? Fourthly, how can a project team be developed? Fifthly, who owns the data on such projects – the director, the fieldworkers, the team, the institution in which they work, or the research sponsor? Finally, how can comparable data be collected?

Some of these dilemmas have been discussed by a number of individuals who have worked in research teams. Porter (1984) and Brown (1994) have indicated the problems associated in contract research for itinerant researchers who can be marginal to a research project and marginal to the institutions, departments and centres in which they are located. Meanwhile, Wakeford (1985) has indicated some of the dilemmas for the directors of such projects and the extent to which project autonomy may be given to a researcher. Finally, some of the difficulties associated with the relationship between a project director and a researcher are highlighted by Bell (1977) in his discussion of work that was conducted on the Banbury re-study (Stacey, Batstone, Bell and Murcott, 1976). All these issues are present for research teams that engage in contract research. Some of these difficulties were evident in the Sheffield resource-allocation project. First, if we had won the full project I would have had difficulty in staffing it as the project had to begin immediately. The reason for this difficulty was because some of the people who were named in the original application were no longer available by the time the research came to be commissioned. In this respect, time-scales are essential for both the researcher and the research and in such circumstances a group of staff who are adequately trained for a variety of research projects need to be available. Indeed, in a visit to a government department to talk about the possibility of bidding for contract research I was frequently asked the question: 'What size is your field force?' Here, it was assumed that a relatively large group of researchers was permanently on stand-by. This in itself represents a dilemma for a research director engaged in contract research. How do you maintain a sufficiently flexible group of people who have research experience and expertise on the one hand and on the other can be deployed almost at a moment's notice? There is also a further problem of gaining staff with such expertise. Is it that social science groups in general and research groups in higher education institutions in particular have a generic set of skills that can be deployed across any project? Does expertise need to be established in particular areas? In turn, this situation also raises a number of problems for contract research staff concerning the range of their methodological training, the level of expertise required together with issues surrounding their continuity of employment and the extent to which short-term projects can contribute to a research career.

In the area in which we were awarded funding for the resource-allocation project we could build on previous experience and develop research themes. First, we had a group of researchers who had expertise in conducting case studies in a range of educational settings. Secondly, we could provide a team of researchers who had expertise in conducting case studies within particular age phases – for example Christina Hughes had conducted case studies in nursery education (Burgess, Hughes and Moxon 1989) and Christopher Pole had conducted case studies in secondary schooling (Pole, 1993). However, more was called for than those with case-study experience. We also needed expertise in resource allocation, local financial management and policy-related work. As far as local financial management was concerned Burgess and Hughes were working on another study for a local authority which was introducing local financial management into nursery schools. Secondly, as far as local financial management and resource allocation were concerned we had available the expertise of individuals who had worked in the education service and could therefore discuss these issues with the research team from the perspective of the officers and advisers of a local education authority. However, it remained important for the team to be able to translate these issues into a set of research questions that could be used in case-study investigations. Finally, all members of the team had engaged in social science research that informed policy analysis in the field of education.

The team had the necessary expertise but it was important to consolidate and build team membership so that a united and purposive research team would be developed that would share similar perspectives on the project and in turn contribute to a coherent project report (Brown, 1994; Burgess, Hockey, Hughes, Phtiaka, Pole and Sanday, 1992a). In this instance, the strategy that was used was to hold regular meetings to design and specify the research questions and in turn to discuss units of analysis and the writing process in relation to the research design and the fieldwork (see Olesen, Droes, Hatton, Chico and Schatzman 1994). Accordingly, on the basis of their literature searches, members of the team drew up sets of questions that were to be used with headteachers, governors and class teachers in schools throughout the authority in order that the case studies would deal with similar issues and include comparable data that were reliable and valid. Secondly, discussions were held about the field-work process which in turn led to themes being developed across the case studies. Whilst these were not uniform they involved sufficient similarity in order that generalizations could be developed from this multi-site case-study investigation – a style that Burgess and Pole had developed with another research team on an earlier research project (Burgess, Pole, Evans and Priestley, 1994). Thirdly, while the writing of each case study involved the person who had conducted it, the studies were also rewritten by other members of the team so that authorship genuinely belonged not with any individual but with all members of the research team.

This style of writing may give coherence to a research project but presents a dilemma for the contract researcher who may prefer individual authorship rather than collective ownership of a range of reports where individual contributions go unidentified. The potential for doing contract research involved meeting the requirements of the sponsor in terms of evidence on resource allocation, but in turn led to a number of other developments concerning the extension of our understanding of team-based research and methodological developments concerning the relationship between applied research and basic research in the context of multi-site case study (see Burgess, Connor, Galloway, Morrison and Newton 1993c; Burgess and Rudduck 1993; Burgess, Pole, Evans and Priestley, 1994).

Methodological Developments

Some methodologists, including Hammersley (1992) have suggested that social and educational researchers in general and ethnographers in particular have had little impact on policy, partly as a result of their research not being directly related to the policy-making process. Meanwhile, others have indicated the way in which ethnographic research can be shifted to make links with policy making and in that way basic and applied research can take place simultaneously (see for example Woods and Pollard, 1988; Pollard, 1984; Finch, 1985 and 1986; Burgess, 1993a). Indeed, it is often where contract research is conducted that social and educational researchers in general and ethnographers in particular are able to contribute to the policy-making process.

But in turn we might ask, what is their contribution to methodological development? – an issue to which we now turn.

Many researchers have made the false assumption that standard procedures which have been used in basic research can also be utilized in sponsored and contract research, yet this is not always the case. The principle might be the same; that is to collect data that are reliable and valid. However, the means by which this is done may be different. Ethnographic research has often involved investigators working alone for periods of up to eighteen months in any research site. This is a luxury which is rarely possible in contract and sponsored research. Indeed, the Sheffield project is a useful example as the work had to be commissioned, conducted, analysed, reported and disseminated within a ten-month period. Accordingly, a different research strategy was required. Here, the principles associated with ethnography: observation and participation through the use of methods such as participant observation, unstructured interviews and documentary evidence were used but in a concentrated timespan. According to my calculations the project had been funded at a level for all costs concerning staff, travel, consumable materials and related activities that would involve a maximum of 150 days. On the basis of preliminary work, meetings, and my estimates of meetings to come I suggested to the team that the project budget in terms of days might be as follows:

	Days
Preliminary work	20
Meetings (so far)	6
Meetings to come (estimate)	14
Fieldwork (including analysis and writing)	110
Total	150

The field work involved the study of institutions associated with different age phases and the allocation of time was as follows:

	Days
1 Tertiary college	20
2 Secondary schools at 15 days	30
5 Primary schools at 10 days	50
1 Nursery school at 10 days	10
Total	110

I suggested that the time allocations should include data collection, data analysis and writing. In allocating a number of days to sites, I had attempted to take account of the complexity of the organizations that were to be studied. In order to deal with this time-scale it was important that documentary evidence was collected from all the institutions prior to the fieldwork and in turn prior to the detailed planning of that fieldwork. In this way, the documentary evidence could be used to create themes that would be taken up subsequently through interviews and observations within the institutions. Finally, many of the themes would need to be followed up through interviews conducted with headteachers, teachers and governors so that they could be used in the data analysis and writing which were all to be conducted within this time-scale.

A second issue to emerge from the case-study investigation was the use of multi-site case-study data. This is a topic that was not specified by the sponsor. Instead, it was an issue in which we were interested in exploring across a variety of projects and had already done some work in investigating in-service education and training (Burgess, Connor, Galloway, Morrison and Newton, 1993). First, we were interested to investigate ways in which multi-site case study could be conducted within one project with a research team. Secondly, we wanted to explore ways in which common sets of data could be collected. Thirdly, we wished to examine strategies for reporting multi-site case studies. Fourthly, we intended to explore ways in which generalizations could be made on the basis of multi-site case-study evidence. Finally, we wanted to develop different ways in which research report writing could be conducted in this context.

This takes us to a further area of methodological development, within this project. There was an opportunity to explore writing styles – a topic which has begun to interest a number of anthropologists and ethnographers (Atkinson, 1990; Becker, 1986). In this project, the style for analysing and writing could not be conducted in the same way as it occurs in other more traditional ethnographies, given the time available to us. Instead, a strategy had to be developed to handle the data and in turn to write about the situation studied. Accordingly, the research team devised a set of themes which were used by the individual researchers to write a first draft of the institutional case study where they had conducted the fieldwork. Among the issues that were explored was whether the project-team members would write in the first person, the extent to which verbatim quotations would be used and the extent to which conclusions and recommendations could be drawn from individual case studies. Some of these issues were resolved in team-based discussions and in turn by other members of the team taking the material that had been drafted by the case-study worker and reworking it. As a consequence, first-person accounts were not possible in this context but verbatim quotations were used and conclusions were drawn from the individual case studies. At this stage I read each of the case studies and reworked some of the data, not to bring a uniformity to them but to highlight some of the common themes that arose across the different case-study sites and which would subsequently be utilized in a thematic project report. The writing was the responsibility of the whole team and not an individual – the case studies were a team product (Burgess, Hockey, Hughes, Phtiaka, Pole and Sanday, 1992b). While this may contribute to the development of case studies, it may also raise problems for individual researchers about publication and the acknowledgment of their contribution in team-based research.

Ethical Issues: Whose Side Are We On?

Within much social and educational research there has been considerable discussion and debate about the ethical dilemmas that confront researchers in general and ethnographers in particular (see Bulmer, 1982; Burgess, 1989). In particular, ethical dilemmas are highlighted in sponsored and contract research. However, the manner in which these dilemmas arise is often different from those that occur in research over longer time periods. First, the short-time scales raise particular problems concerning anonymity and confidentiality. Often those who are receiving the reports have had some involvement in the selection of the research sites (as in the Sheffield study) or even where they have not it is possible for recognition of institutions and individuals to take place given that the research location is carefully specified. Secondly, the question 'whose side are we on?' (Becker, 1967; Gouldner, 1968) is well placed here. In particular, many contract-research projects involve the researcher in presenting draft material to those who have sponsored the investigation. In some instances, agreements are reached whereby those who have been interviewed can comment on the draft material.

The politics of the Sheffield resource-allocation project were such that an agreement had been reached whereby case studies would be returned to the schools in which they were conducted for comment. Often this meant studies being looked at by headteachers and in some cases members of senior-management teams rather than by a whole staff or by all those who had been interviewed. In the majority of cases we found that minor points of detail were picked up. There was no objection to the form case studies took, apart from in one school. Here, the headteacher questioned some of the statements we made. In one instance, we indicated that parents had been involved in painting the school – a statement which was part of a quotation we had used. However, it triggered a response from the head 'we have never had parents painting the outside windows! What some staff will say!' Secondly, it was argued that our comments that sixth-formers were used in supervisory roles in the school could not be sustained even though we had evidence to the contrary. Thirdly, it was argued that a quotation that portrayed pastoral care as 'chatting with kids in corridors' was not how things occurred in the school. Indeed, the head commented:

> It is quite outrageous and should be deleted *it is absolutely not a staff consensus* and I think it quite disgraceful that your researcher could make such an unfounded statement.

In all these instances we had evidence of the statements we had made and we also had quotations to support them. However, for the head many of the statements were just 'idiotic chit-chat at the level of the garden fence, and any researcher with some understanding would surely have simply ignored it'. Yet this is to miss the point. As far as researchers are concerned and especially all ethnographers; all comments are potential data. There is no ultimate truth and indeed the truth about a situation does not reside with one individual; especially a headteacher or a headteacher and a senior-management team. Yet the head of this particular school found difficulty in accepting this situation. He argued that some of our statements should be deleted from the report as the senior-management team could not agree with them.

This presented problems for me. As soon as a researcher operates beyond the correction of minor errors, difficulties arise. If we had taken the perspective of the head and his senior management team the report would have been different and arguments could be made that a different project had been done from the study that was commissioned. Furthermore, we would be perceived by the teachers who had been interviewed as taking sides by portraying the view of the senior-management team rather than the views that had been expressed by teachers during interviews. Accordingly, we attempted to steer a middle path by adding statements which suggested that the senior staff did not share the particular perspective that was portrayed by a particular quotation. While the head accepted the changes we had made, he still maintained that the staff views were confused. Indeed, in a letter he remarked:

> The major benefit I have derived from reading this report is the realization of how confused much staff thinking is hence the determination I have formed to provide more information this year in the hope of clarifying to them many aspects of the current management situation. The school's ability to solve its problems, improve and progress depends first and foremost on an understanding by all staff teaching and non-teaching of the situation in which the school currently finds itself. Strategies for change cannot be adequately formulated until we all understand and agree where we are now.

Such a statement indicates a misunderstanding of what a case study can do. The head thought it would portray one single view of the school and the way it operated. Indeed, it is apparent that for this headteacher the notion that a school involves members with a number of competing views and interpretations is not something that he could perceive. The result is that researchers are bound to be at odds with such headteachers who have an expectation that a case study will represent one view. Yet to represent one view would involve betraying those with whom the case-study workers have been involved. In this respect, researchers need to maintain integrity and standards of scholarship in handling such issues in contract research.

Conclusion

At this point we have come full circle to our starting point where we discussed scholarship, research and sponsorship. This chapter has focused on contract research and some of the dilemmas which arise for the research director (and in some cases the researcher) out of sponsorship. But where does such research articulate with scholarship (if at all)? At this point we might return to the work of C. Wright Mills, writing in *The Sociological Imagination* where he attempted to discuss issues pertaining to scholarly activity when he wrote:

> It is best to begin, I think, by reminding you, the beginning student, that the most admirable thinkers within the scholarly community you have chosen to join do not split their work from their lives. They seem to take both too seriously to allow such dissociation, and they want to use each for the enrichment of the other. Of course, such a split is the prevailing convention among men in general, deriving, I suppose, from the hollowness of the work which men in general now do. But you will have recognised that as a scholar you have the exceptional opportunity of designing a way of living which will encourage the habits of good workmanship. Scholarship is a choice of how to live as well as a choice of career; whether he knows it or not, the intellectual workman forms his own self as he works towards the perfection of his craft; to realise his own potentialities, and any opportunities that come his way, he constructs a character which has as its core the qualities of the good workman. (Mills, 1970, pp. 215–16)

In this sense, if the contract researcher develops the qualities of the good worker that person will have also started to develop the attributes of the scholar in the research community. Yet that community needs to consider how to develop the career of the contract researcher who has the potential to make a significant contribution to fundamental and applied work in social research and educational studies.

Note

1. I would like to thank David Halpin and Barry Troyna for inviting me to write this paper for their seminar entitled 'Commissioned Research for Contemporary Educational Policy' in the series sponsored by the ESRC. In revising this paper for publication in this volume, I have drawn on comments I have received from the seminar participants, from CEDAR staff and from Rosemary Deem and Stan Green to whom I am most grateful.

References

Allison, L. (1993) 'Sorry I just teach …', *Daily Telegraph*, 18 March.
Atkinson, P. (1990) *The Ethnographic Imagination*, London, Routledge.
Becker, H.S. (1967) 'Whose side are we on?', *Social Problems*, 14, pp. 239–47.
—— (1986) *Writing for Social Scientists*, Chicago, University of Chicago Press.

Bell, C. (1977) 'Reflections on the Banbury restudy', in Bell, C. and Newby, H. (Eds) *Doing Sociological Research*, London, Allen and Unwin.

Brannen, J. (Ed) (1992) *Mixing Methods: Qualitative and Qualitative Research*, Aldershot, Avebury.

Brown, A. (1994) 'Being a researcher', in Burgess, R.G. (Ed) *Issues in Qualitative Research*, London, JAI Press.

Bulmer, M. (Ed) (1982) *Social Research Ethics*, London, Macmillan.

Burgess, R.G. (Ed) (1989) *The Ethics of Educational Research*, London, Falmer Press.

—— (1990) 'Shooting the Messenger? A study on the Politics of Dissemination', CEDAR Conference, September.

—— (1991) 'Resourcing 3–18 year education services in Sheffield', Unpublished research proposal submitted to Sheffield LEA.

—— (1993a) 'Customers and Contractors: a research relationship?', in Burgess, R.G. (Ed) *Educational Research and Evaluation: For Policy and Practice?* London, Falmer Press.

—— (1993b) 'Biting the hand that feeds you?', in Burgess, R.G. (Ed) *Educational Research and Evaluation: For Policy and Practice?* London, Falmer Press.

Burgess, R.G., Connor, J., Galloway, S., Morrison, M. and Newton, M. (1993) *Implementing In-service Education and Training*, London, Falmer Press.

Burgess, R.G., Hockey, J., Hughes, C., Phitiaka, H., Pole, C. and Sanday, A. (1992a) 'Case Studies: A Thematic Look at Issues and Problems', in Sheffield City Council Education Department, *Resourcing Sheffield Schools*, Sheffield, Sheffield City Council.

—— (1992b) *Resourcing Sheffield Schools: Part II The Case Studies*, Sheffield, Sheffield City Council.

Burgess, R.G., Hughes, C. and Moxon, S. (1989) *Educating the Under Fives in Salford*, CEDAR, University of Warwick.

Burgess, R.G., Pole, CJ., Evans, K. and Priestley, C. (1994) Four studies from one or one study from four? Multi-site case study research', in Bryman, A. and Burgess, R.G. (Eds) *Analysing Qualitative Data*, London, Routledge.

Burgess, R.G. and Rudduck, J. (Eds) (1993) *A Perspective on Educational Case Study: A Collection of Papers by Lawrence Stenhouse*, CEDAR Occasional Paper No 5, CEDAR, University of Warwick.

Finch, J. (1985) 'Social policy and education: Problems and possibilities of using qualitative research', in Burgess, R.G. (Ed) *Issues in Educational Research: Qualitative Methods* Lewes, Falmer Press.

—— (1986) *Research and Policy*, Lewes, Falmer Press.

Gouldner, A. (1968) 'The sociologist as partisan: Sociology and the welfare state', *American Sociologist*, 3, pp. 103–16.

Hammersley, M. (1992) 'Ethnography, Policy Making and Practice in Education', Paper prepared for ESRC Seminar on Methodological and Ethical Issues associated with research into the 1988 Education Reform Act, University of Warwick, July 1992.

HMSO (1971) *A Framework for Government Research and Development*, London, HMSO.

—— (1993) '*Realising Our Potential*', (White Paper on Science Technology and Engineering), London, HMSO.

Mills, C.W. (1970) *The Sociological Imagination*, Harmondsworth, Penguin.

Norris, N. (1990) *Understanding Educational Evaluation*, London, Kogan Page.

Olesen, V., Droes, N., Hatton, D., Chico, N. and Schatzman, L. (1994) 'Analysing together: Recollections of a team approach', in Bryman, A. and Burgess, R.G. (Eds) *Analysing Qualitative Data*, London, Routledge.

Pole, C.J. (1993) *Assessing and Recording Achievement*, Milton Keynes, Open University Press.

Pollard, A. (1984) 'Ethnography and social policy for classroom practice', in Barton, L. and Walker, S. (Eds) *Social Crisis and Educational Research*, London, Croom Helm.

Porter, M. (1984) 'The modification of method in researching postgraduate education', in Burgess, R.G. (Ed) *The Research Process in Educational Settings: Ten Case Studies*, Lewes, Falmer Press.

Rothschild Lord (1982) *An Enquiry into the Social Science Research Council*, London, HMSO.

Sheffield City Council Department (1992) *Resourcing Sheffield Schools*, Sheffield, Sheffield City Council.

Simons, H. (1984) 'Principles and procedures in the conduct of an educational evaluation', in Adelman, C. (Ed) *The Politics and Ethics of Evaluation*, London, Croom Helm.

Stacey, M., Batstone, E., Bell, C. and Murcott, A. (1976) *Power, Persistance and Change: A Second Study of Banbury*, London, Routledge and Kegan Paul.

Stenhouse, L. (1984) 'Library access, library use and user education in academic sixth forms: An autobiographical account', in Burgess, R.G. (Ed) *The Research Process in Educational Settings: Ten Case Studies*, Lewes, Falmer Press.

Taylor, W. (1985) 'The organisation and funding of educational research in England and Wales', in Nisbett, J. (Ed) *World Yearbook of Education 1985 Research Policy and Practice* London, Kogan Page.

Wakeford, J. (1985) 'A director's dilemma, in Burgess, R.G. (Ed) *Field Methods in the Study of Education*, Lewes, Falmer Press.

Woods, P., and Pollard, A. (Eds) (1988) *Sociology and the Teacher*, London, Croom Helm.

13

Hired Hand Research*

Julius A. Roth

Case I

After it became obvious how tedious it was to write down numbers on pieces of paper which didn't even fulfill one's own sense of reality and which did not remind one of the goals of the project, we all in little ways started avoiding our work and cheating on the project. It began for example when we were supposed to be observing for hour and a half periods, an hour and a half on the ward and then an hour and a half afterwards to write up or dictate what we had observed, in terms of the category system which the project was supposed to be testing and in terms of a ward diary. We began cutting corners in time. We would arrive a little bit late and leave a little bit early. It began innocently enough, but soon boomeranged into a full cheating syndrome, where we would fake observations for some time slot which never observed on the ward. Sam, for example, in one case, came onto the ward while I was still finishing up an assignment on a study patient and told me that he was supposed to observe for an hour and a half but that he wasn't going to stay because he couldn't stand it anymore. He said he wasn't going to tell anyone that he missed an assignment, but that he would simply write up a report on the basis of what he knew already about the ward and the patients. I was somewhat appalled by Sam's chicanery, and in this sense I was the last one to go. It was three or four weeks after this before I actually cheated in the same manner.

It was also frequent for us to miss observation periods, especially the 8 to 9:30 a.m. ones. We all had a long drive for one thing, and we were all chronic over-sleepers for another. For a while we used to make up the times we missed by coming in the next morning at the same time and submitting our reports with the previous day's date. As time went on, however, we didn't bother to make up the times we'd missed. When we were questioned by our supervisor about the missing reports, we would claim that there had been an error in scheduling and that we did not know that those time slots were supposed to be covered.

Source: *American Sociologist*, vol. 1, no. 4, 1966, pp. 190–196.

There were other ways we would cheat, sometimes inadvertently. For example, one can decide that one can't hear enough of a conversation to record it. People need to think fairly highly of themselves and when you think that you're a cheat and a liar and that you're not doing your job for which you are receiving high wages, you are likely to find little subconscious ways of getting out of having to accuse yourself of these things. One of the ways is to not be able to hear well. We had a special category in our coding system, a question mark, which we noted by its symbol on our code sheets whenever we could not hear what was going on between two patients. As the purgatory of writing numbers on pieces of paper lengthened, more and more transcripts were passed in with question marks on them, so that even though we had probably actually heard most of the conversations between patients, we were still actually avoiding the work of transcription by deceiving ourselves into believing that we could not hear what was being said. This became a good way of saving yourself work. If you couldn't hear a conversation, it just got one mark in one column of one code sheet, and if you wrote down an elaborate conversation lasting even ten minutes, it might take you up to an hour to code it, one hour of putting numbers in little blocks. In the long run, all of our data became much skimpier. Conversations were incomplete; their duration was strangely diminishing to two or three minutes in length instead of the half-hour talks the patients usually had with each other. We were all defining our own cutting off points, saying to ourselves "Well, that's enough of that conversation." According to the coding rules, however, a communication can't be considered as ended until the sequence of interaction has been completed and a certain time lapse of silence has ensued.

In order to ensure the reliability of our coding, the research design called for an "Inter-Rater Reliability Check" once every two months, in which each of the four of us would pair up with every other member of the team and be rated on our ability to code jointly the same interaction in terms of the same categories and dimensions. We learned to loathe these checks; we knew that the coding system was inadequate in terms of reliability and that our choice of categories was optional, subjective, and largely according to our own sense of what an interaction is really about, rather than according to the rigid, stylized, and preconceived design into which we were supposed to make reality fit. We also knew, however, that our principal investigators insisted on an inter-rater reliability coefficient of 70 in order for the research to proceed. When the time came for another check, we met together to discuss and make certain agreements on how to bring our coding habits into conformity for the sake of achieving reliability. In these meetings we would confess our preferences for coding certain things in certain ways and agree on certain concessions to each other for the duration of the check. Depending on what other individual I was to be paired with. for example, I had a very good idea of how I could code in order to achieve nearly the same transcriptions. We didn't end it there. After each phase of a check each pair of us would meet again to go over our transcriptions and compare our coding, and if there were any gross discrepancies, we corrected them before sending them to the statistician for analysis. Needless to say, as soon as the reliability checks were over with, we each returned to a coding rationale which we as individuals required in order to do any coding at all – in order to maintain sanity.

Case II

There didn't appear to be too much concern with the possibility of inconsistency among the coders. Various coders used various methods to determine the code of an open-end question. Toward the end of the coding process, expediency became the key-note, leading to gross inconsistency. The most expedient method of coding a few of the trickier questions was to simply put down a "4" (This was the middle-of-the-road response on the one question that had the most variation.). If the responses were not clear or comprehensible, the coder had two alternatives: on the one hand, he could puzzle over it and ask for other opinions or, on the other hand, he could assign it an arbitrary number or forget the response entirely.

In the beginning, many of us, when in doubt about a response, would ask the supervisor or his assistant. After a while, I noted that quite often the supervisor's opinion would differ when asked twice about the same response and he would often give two different answers in response to the same question. One way the supervisor and his assistant would determine the correct coding for an answer would be to look at the respondent's previous answers and deduce what they should have answered – thereby coding on *what they thought the respondent should have answered*, not on the basis of what he *did* answer. One example that I distinctly remember is the use of magazines regularly read as reported by the respondent being used as a basis on which to judge and code their political views. This, in my opinion, would be a factor in some of the cases, such as the reading of an extreme leftist or extreme rightist magazine, but to use magazines such as *Time* or *Reader's Digest* to form any conclusions about the type of person and his views, I feel is quite arbitrary. Furthermore, I feel questionnaires should be used to see *if* consistent patterns of views exist among respondents and it is not the coder's job to put them in if the respondents fail to!

Some of the coders expected a fixed pattern of response. I, not being sure of what responses meant in a total political profile, treated each response separately – which I feel is the correct way of coding a questionnaire. Others, as I learned through their incessant jabbering, took what they thought was a more sophisticated method of treating an interview. A few would discuss the respondent's answers as if they took one political or social standpoint as an indicator of what all the responses should be. They would laugh over an inconsistency in the respondent's replies, feeling that one answer did not fit the previous pattern of responses.

The final problem leading to gross inconsistency was the factor of time. The supervisor made it clear that the code sheets had to be in to the computation center by Saturday. This meant that on Saturday morning and early afternoon the aim of the coders was to code the questionnaires as quickly as possible, and the crucial factor was speed, even at the expense of accuracy. The underlying thought was that there were so many questionnaires coded already (that were *assumed* to be coded consistently and correctly) that the inconsistencies in the remainder would balance themselves out and be of no great importance. I found myself adapting to this way of thinking, and after spending two or three hours there on Saturday morning, I joined in the game of "let's get these damn things out already." It did indeed become a game, with the shibboleth, for one particularly vague and troublesome question, "Oh, give it a four."

Case III

One of the questions on the interview schedule asked for five reasons why parents had put their child in an institution. I found most people can't think of five reasons. One or two – sometimes three. At first I tried pumping them for more reasons, but I never got any of them up to five. I didn't want (the director) to think I was goofing off on the probing, so I always filled in all five.

Another tough one was the item about how the child's disability affected the family relationships. We were supposed to probe. Probe what? You get so many different kinds of answers, I was never sure what was worth following up. Sometimes I did if the respondent seemed to have something to say. Otherwise I just put down a short answer and made it look as if that was all I could get out of them. Of course, (the director) *did* list a few areas he wanted covered in the probing. One of them was sex relations of the parents. Most of the time I didn't follow up on that. Once in a while I would get somebody who seemed to be able to talk freely without embarrassment. But most of the time I was afraid to ask, so I made up something to fill that space.

Then there was that wide open question at the end. It's vague. Most people don't know what to say. You've been asking them questions for about an hour already. Usually you get a very short answer, I didn't push them. I'd write up a longer answer later. It's easy to do. You have their answers to a lot of other questions to draw on. You just put parts of some of them together, dress it up a little, and add one or two bits of new information which fits in with the rest.

Any reader with research experience can probably recall one or more cases in which he observed, suspected, or participated in some form of cheating, carelessness, distortion, or cutting of corners in the collection or processing of research data. He probably thought of these instances as exceptions – an unfortunate lapse in ethical behavior or a failure of research directors to maintain proper controls. I would like to put forth the thesis that such behavior on the part of hired data-collectors and processors is not abnormal or exceptional, but rather is exactly the kind of behavior we should expect from people with their position in a production unit.

The cases I have presented do not constitute proof, of course. Even if I presented ten or twenty more, my efforts could be dismissed as merely an unusually industrious effort to record professional dirty linen (or I might be accused of making them up!) and not at all representative of the many thousands of cases of hired researching carried out every year. Rather than multiply examples, I would like to take a different tack and examine the model we have been using in thinking about research operations and to suggest another model which I believe is more appropriate.

The ideal we hold of the researcher is that of a well-educated scholar pursuing information and ideas on problems in which he has an intrinsic interest. Frequently this ideal may be approximated when an individual scholar is working on his own problem or several colleagues are collaborating on a problem of mutual interest. Presumably such a researcher will endeavor to carry out his data-collection and processing in the most accurate and useful way that his skills and time permit.

When a researcher hires others to do the collecting and processing tasks of his research plan, we often assume that these assistants fit the "dedicated scientist" ideal and will lend their efforts to the successful conduct of the overall study by carrying out their assigned tasks to the best of their ability. As suggested by my examples, I doubt that hired assistants usually behave this way even when they are junior grade scholars themselves. It becomes more doubtful yet when they are even further removed from scholarly tradition and from the direct control of the research directors (e.g., part-time survey interviewers).

It seems to me that we can develop a more accurate expectation of the contribution of the hired research worker who is required to work according to somebody else's plan by applying another model which has been worked out in some detail by sociologists – namely, the work behavior of the hired hand in a production organization. First, let us look at one of the more thorough of these studies, Donald Roy's report on machine shop operators.[1]

Roy's workers made the job easier by loafing when the piece rate did not pay well. They were careful not to go over their informal "quotas" on piece rate jobs because the rate would be cut and their work would be harder. They faked time sheets so that their actual productive abilities would not be known to management. They cut corners on prescribed job procedures to make the work easier and/or more lucrative even though this sometimes meant that numerous products had to be scrapped. Roy's calculations show that the workers could have produced on the order of twice as much if it had been in their interest to do so.

But it is *not* in their interest to do so. The product the hired hand turns out is not in any sense his. He does not design it, make any of the decisions about producing it or about the conditions under which it will be produced, or what will be done with it after it is produced. The worker is interested in doing just enough to get by. Why should he concern himself about how well the product works or how much time it takes to make it? That is the company's problem. The company is his adversary and fair game for any trickery he can get away with. The worker's aim is to make his job as easy and congenial as the limited resources allow and to make as much money as possible without posing a threat to his fellow workers or to his own future. The company, in turn, is placed in the position of having to establish an inspection system to try to keep the worst of their products from leaving the factory (an effort often unsuccessful – the inspectors are hired hands, too) and of devising some form of supervision to limit the more extreme forms of gold-bricking and careless workmanship.

Almost all the systematic research on "restriction of output" and deviation from assigned duties has been done on factory workers, office clerks, and other low prestige work groups. This is mostly because such work is easier to observe and measure, but also because much of this research has been controlled in part by those in a position of authority who want research done only on their subordinates. However, there is evidence to indicate that work restrictions and deviations in the form of informal group definitions and expectations are probably universal in our society. They can be found among business executives and in the professions, sports, and the creative arts. They are especially likely to crop up when one is working as a hired hand, and almost all productive activities have their hired hand aspects. A professor may work hard on scholarly tasks of his own choosing and perhaps even on teaching a course which he himself has devised, but he becomes notoriously lax when he is assigned to a departmental service course which he does not like – spending little or no time on preparation, avoiding his students as much as possible, turning all the exams over to a graduate assistant, and so on.

"Restriction of production" and deviation from work instructions is no longer regarded by students of the sociology of work as a moral issue or a form of social delinquency. Rather, it is the expected behavior of workers in a production organization. The only problem for an investigator of work practices is discovering the details of cutting corners, falsifying time sheets, defining work quotas, dodging supervision, and ignoring instructions in a given work setting.

There is no reason to believe that a hired hand in the scientific research business will behave any different from those in other areas of productive activity. It is far more reasonable to assume that their behavior will be similar. They want to make as much money as they can and may pad their account or time sheet if they are paid on that basis, but this type of behavior is a minor problem so far as the present discussion is concerned. They also want to avoid difficult, embarrassing, inconvenient, time-consuming situations as well as those activities which make no sense to them. (Thus, they fail to make some assigned observations or to ask some of the interview questions.) At the same time they want to give the right impression to their superiors – at least right enough so that their material will be accepted and they will be kept on the job. (Thus, they modify or fabricate portions of the reports in order to give the boss what he *seems* to want.) They do not want to "look stupid" by asking too many questions, so they are likely to make a stab at what they think the boss wants – e.g., make a guess at a coding category rather than having it resolved through channels.

Even those who start out with the notion that this is an important piece of work which they must do right will succumb to the hired-hand mentality when they realize that their suggestions and criticisms are ignored, that their assignment does not allow for any imagination or creativity, that they will receive no credit for the final product, in short that they have been hired to do somebody else's dirty work. When this realization has sunk in, they will no longer bother to be careful or accurate or precise. They will cut corners to save time and energy. They will fake parts of their reporting. They will not put themselves out for something in which they have no stake except in so far as extrinsic pressures force them to. Case No. I is an excerpt from the statement of a research worker who started out with enthusiasm and hard work and ended with sloppy work and cheating when she could no longer escape the fact that she was a mere flunky expected to do her duty whether or not it was meaningful. The coders in Case II soon gave up any effort to resolve the ambiguities of their coding operation and followed the easiest path acceptable to their supervisor. In this case, the supervisor himself made little effort to direct the data-processing toward supplying answers to meaningful research issues. We must remember that in many research operations the supervisors and directors themselves are hired hands carrying out the requests of a client or superior as expeditiously as possible.

Many of the actions of hired hand researchers are strikingly analogous to restrictive practices of factory operatives. Interviewers who limit probing and observers who limit interaction recording are behaving like workers applying "quota restriction," and with interacting hired hands informal agreements may be reached on the extent of such restrictions. To fabricate portions of a report is a form of goldbricking. The collusion on the reliability check reported in Case I is strikingly similar to the workers' plot to mislead the time-study department. Such similarities are no accident. The relationship of the hired hand to the product and the process of production is the same in each case. The product is not "his." The production process gives him little or no opportunity to express any intrinsic interest he may have in the product. He will sooner or later fall into a pattern of carrying out his work with a minimum of effort, inconvenience, and embarrassment – doing just enough so that his product will get by. If he is part of a large and complex operation where his immediate superiors are also hired hands with no intrinsic interest in the product and where the final authority may be distant and even amorphous, quality control of the product will be mechanical and the minimal effort that will get by can soon be learned and easily applied. The factory production situation has at least one ultimate limitation on the more extreme deviations of the hired hands: the final product must "work" reasonably well in a substantial proportion of cases. In social science research, on the other hand, the product is usually so ambiguous and the field of study so lacking in standards of performance, that it is difficult for anyone to say whether it "works" or not.

What is more important is the effect of the hired hand mentality on the *nature* of the product. Workmen not only turn out less than they could if it were in their interest to maximize production, but often produce shoddy and even dangerous products.[2] In the case of research, the inefficiency of hired hands not only causes a study to take longer or cost more money, but is likely to introduce much dubious data and interpretations into the process of analysis. Our mass production industrial system has opted to sacrifice individual efficiency and product quality for the advantages of a rationalized division of labor. The same approach has been applied to much of our larger scale scientific research and the results, in my opinion, have been much more disastrous than they are in industrial production with little of the compensating advantages.

When the tasks of a research project are split up into small pieces to be assigned to hired hands, none of these data collectors and processors will ever understand all the complexities and subtleties of the research issues in the same way as the person who conceived of the study. No amount of "training" can take the place of the gradual development of research interests and formulations on the part of the planner. Since the director often cannot be sure what conceptions of the issues the hired hands have as a result of his explanations and "training," he must make dubious guesses about the meaning of much of the data they return to him. If he attempts to deal with this difficulty by narrowly defining the permissible behavior of each hired hand (e.g., demand that all questions on a schedule be asked in a set wording), he merely increases the alienation of the hired hand from his work and thus increases the likelihood of cutting corners and cheating. As he gains in quantity of data, he loses in validity and meaningfulness.[3]

I do not want to give the impression that the hired hand mentality with its attendant difficulties is simply a characteristic of the large-scale on-going research organization. We may find it at all size levels, including the academic man hiring a single student to do his research chores. The argument may be advanced that assignment of specified tasks by the director of a study is essential to getting the job done in the manner that he wants it done. My answer is that such assignments are often not effectively carried out and it is misleading to assume that they are.

Let me illustrate this point. A researcher wants to do a study of the operation of a given institution. He has some definite notion of what aspects of behavior of the institutional personnel he wants information about and he has some ideas about the manner in which he will go about analysing and interpreting these behaviors. He finds it possible and useful to engage four trained and interested assistants. Let me outline two ways the study might be conducted:

A. Through a series of discussions, general agreement is reached about the nature of the study and the manner in which it might be conducted. Some division of labor is agreed upon in these discussions. However, none of the field workers is held to any particular tasks or foci of interest. Each is allowed to pursue his data-collection as he thinks best within the larger framework, although the field workers exchange information frequently and make new agreements so that they can benefit from each other's experience.

B. The director divides up the data-collection and processing in a logical manner and assigns a portion to each of the assistants. Each field worker is instructed to obtain information in all the areas assigned to him and to work in a prescribed manner so that his information will be directly comparable to that of the others. The director may use a procedural check such as having each assistant write a report covering given issues or areas at regular intervals.

Which is the preferred approach? Judging from my reading of social science journals, most research directors would say Method B is to be preferred. Method A, they would maintain, produces information on subjects, issues, or events from one field worker which is not directly comparable to that collected by another field worker. They would also object that if each field worker is permitted to follow his own inclinations even in part, the total study will suffer from large gaps. These accusations are quite true – and, I would add, are an inevitable result of dividing a research project among a number of people. What I disagree with, however, is the assumption that Method B would not suffer from these defects (if indeed, they should be regarded as defects). It is assumed that the assistants in Method B are actually carrying out their assigned tasks in the manner specified. In line with my earlier discussion of the behavior of hired hands, I would consider this highly unlikely. If the information produced by these assistants is indeed closely comparable, it would most likely be because they had reached an agreement on how to restrict production. And, whether the study is carried out by Method A or by Method B, gaps will occur. The difference is that the director of Study A – assuming he had succeeded in making his assistants into collaborating colleagues – would at least know where the gaps are. The director of Study B would have gaps without knowing where they are – or indeed, that they exist – because they have been covered over by the fabrications of his alienated assistants.

It is ironic that established researchers do not ascribe the same motivating forces to their subordinates as they do to themselves. For many years research scientists have been confronting those who pay their salaries and give them their grants with the argument that a scientist can do good research only when he has the freedom to follow his ideas in whatever way seems best. They have been so successful with this argument that university administrations and research organization directorates rarely attempt to dictate – or even suggest – problems or procedures to a researcher on their staff, and the more prominent granting agencies write contracts with almost no strings attached as to the way in which the study will be conducted. Yet research directors fail to apply this same principle to those they hire to carry out data-collection and processing. The hired assistant's desire to participate in the task and the creative contribution he might make is ignored with the result that the assistants' creativity is applied instead to covertly changing the nature of the task.

There has been very little discussion in our journals and our books on research methods on the relationship of the hired hand to the data collected. Whatever discussion there *has* been can be found in the survey interview field where there have been some studies of the effect of such demographic factors as age, sex, and race, sometimes measured personality traits, on "interviewer bias." The nature of the interviewer's status in a research organization is seldom discussed in print. The problem of interviewer cheating, although a common subject of informal gossip, is seldom dealt with openly as a serious problem. When Leo Crespi published an article twenty years ago in which he expressed the worry that cheating was seriously affecting the validity of much survey data,[4] those who responded (mostly survey organization executives) stated reassuringly that few interviewers cheated and that they had pretty effective ways of controlling those who did.[5] If the analysis offered in this paper is correct, the first part of this reassurance is almost certainly wrong. The low-level flunky position which most interviewers occupy in survey organizations[6] should lead us to expect widespread deviations from assigned tasks. The survey executives who responded give no convincing evidence to the contrary. As for the second part of the assertion, their descriptions of their control measures indicate that they can hope to block only the cruder, more obvious, and repeated forms of cheating. The postal card follow-up will catch the interviewer who does not bother to contact his respondents at all. Spot-check follow-up interviewing may eventually catch the interviewer who makes contacts, but fabricates demographic data (to fill a quota sample) or completes only part of the interview and fills in the rest in a stereotyped manner later on. (Even here, many of his interviews may be used before he is detected.) However, from the cases of hired hand interviewing which I am familiar with, I would say such crude cheating is not the most common form of cutting corners on the job. Far more common is the kind found in Case III where the interviewer makes his contact, obtains a fairly complete interview, but leaves partial gaps here and there because he found it time-consuming, embarrassing, or troublesome, felt threatened by the respondent, or simply felt uncertain about how the study director wanted certain lines of questioning developed. With a little imagination, such gaps can be filled in later on in a way that is very unlikely to be detected in a follow-up interview. If, for example, a supervisor in Case III had returned to the respondents and asked them whether the "five reasons" listed on their interview form were accurate reflections of their opinion, probably most would have said yes, and the few who objected to one or two of the reasons could have been dismissed as the degree of change that one expects on re-interview.[7]

Some gimmicks for catching cheaters may even put the finger on the wrong person. Thus, one approach to detecting cheating is to compare the data of each interviewer to the group averages and to assume that if one deviates markedly from the group, he is cheating or doing his work improperly. This reasoning assumes that cheating is exceptional and will stand out from the crowd. I have already suggested that the opposite is often the case. There-fore, if the cheaters are working in the same direction (which is readily possible if they have reached an informal agreement or if the question is of such a nature as to suggest distortion in a given direction), it is the "honest" person who will deviate. In the study alluded to in Case III, for example, one of the interviewers always left spaces open on the "five reasons" item. At one point the director reprimanded him for not obtaining five responses "like the rest of the interviewers." The director preferred to believe that this man was not doing his job right than to believe that all the rest were making up responses.

Large survey organizations have at least made some attempts to control the cruder forms of cheating. In most studies using hired hands, even this limited control is absent. The academic man with one or a few assistants, the research organization study director with one or a few small projects, usually has no routine way of checking on the work of his assistants. If he duplicates much of their work or supervises them very closely, he may as well dispense with their services. If he gives them assignments without checking on them closely, he is in effect assuming that they are conducting their assignment more or less as directed and is accepting their products at face value. This assumption, I as-sert, is a dubious one. And since it is a common practice nowadays to farm out much of one's research work – quite often to accumulate research grants only to hire others to do the bulk of the work – the dubious nature of hired hand research is a widespread problem in small as well as large scale research, in surveys, in direct observation, and in various forms of data processing.

I do not want to suggest, however, that the major failure of hired hand research is the lack of control of cheating. Rather, the very fact that we are placed in a position of having to think up gimmicks to detect cheating is in itself an admission of failure. It means that we are relying for an important part of our research operation on people who have no concern for the out-come of the study. Such persons cannot have the kind of understanding of the data-collection or data-processing procedures which can come only with working out problems in which the researcher has an intrinsic interest and has gone through a process of formulating research questions and relevant ways of collecting and processing data.

I can hear the objection that much social science cannot be done without hired hands. But we should at least be aware of the doubtful nature of some of the information collected in this way and construct our data-collection and processing in such a way as to reduce the encouragement of cheating and re-striction of production as much as possible. (See Crespi's list of "ballot demoralizers."[8]) More important, however, I believe the need for hired hands has been greatly exaggerated. Why, for example, must we so often have large samples? The large sample is frequently a contrivance for controlling various kinds of "errors" (including the "error" introduced by unreliable hired hands). But if the study were done on a much smaller sample by one person or several colleagues who formulated their own study and conducted it entirely by themselves, much of this error would not enter in the first place. Isn't a sample of fifty which yields data in which we can have a high degree of confidence more useful than a sample of five thousand where we must remain doubtful about what it is that we have collected? Often a large-scale study tries to do too much at one time and so ends up as a hodge-podge affair with no integration of ideas or information ever taking place because it is, in effect, *nobody's* study. How often have you read the report of a massive study expending large amounts of money and employing large numbers of people where you were disappointed at the paucity of the results, especially when compared to a far smaller project on a similar issue conducted entirely by one or a few people?

Let me repeat that I am not singling out large-scale operations as the only villains. The current structure of professional careers is such that often small studies are turned over to hired hands. We tend to be rated on how many studies we can carry on at the same time rather than on how thoroughly and carefully we can carry through a given line of research. Soon we find that we do not have time for all of the projects we have become involved in and must turn some over to others of lower professional status. This might not be so bad if we were willing to turn over the research work wholeheartedly. We might simply act as entrepreneurs to funnel funds to others and to provide them with appropriate clearance and an entrée to research settings. We can then leave the specific formulation of the problem and procedure (and the credit for doing the work) to the person we have helped out. Such is often done, of course. However, there are many instances in which the senior researcher believes those he has hired cannot be trusted to formulate their own plans, or professional career competition convinces him that he cannot "afford" to give up any of his studies to others. In such cases he is likely to maintain a semblance of control by mechanically structuring a research plan and making assignments to his assistants. This, as I have indicated, is the way to the hired hand mentality with its attendant distortions of research data.

What is a hired hand? So far I have been talking as if I knew and as if the hired hand could readily be distinguished from one who is not. This, of course, is not true. The issue is a complex one and information on it is, by its very nature, not very accessible. It is a crucial question which deserves study in its own right as part of the more general study of the process of "doing research."

Let me attempt a crude characterization of hired hand research, a characterization which hopefully will be greatly refined and perhaps reformulated with further study. A hired hand is a person who feels that he has no stake in the research that he is working on, that he is simply expected to carry out assigned tasks and turn in results which will "pass inspection." Of course, a hired assistant may not start out with the hired hand mentality, but may develop it if he finds that his talents for creativity are not called upon and that his suggestions and efforts at active participation are ignored.

From specific examples from the research world and by analogy from research on hired hands in other occupational spheres, I am convinced that research tasks carried out by hired hands are characterized, not rarely or occasionally, but *typically*, by restricted production, failure to carry out portions of the task, avoidance of the more unpleasant or difficult aspects of the research, and outright cheating. The results of research done in part or wholly by hired hands should be viewed as a dubious source for information about specific aspects of our social life or for the raw material for developing broader generalizations.

Of course, this leaves open the question of what constitutes a "stake in the research" and how one avoids or reduces the hired hand mentality. Again, I have no specific answers and hope that issue will receive much more attention than it has up to now. A stake may mean different things in various circumstances. For graduate students, a chance to share in planning and in writing and publication may often be important. For interviewers or field workers, the determination of the details of their procedure may be crucial. In an applied setting, the responsibility for the practical consequences of the research findings may be most important.[9]

It would also be worthwhile to examine the conditions which make for hired hand research. Here again, I have little specific to say and this subject, too, needs much more investigation. However, I will suggest a few factors I consider important.

Size: Hired hands can be found in research staffs of all sizes from one on up. However, it is clear that when a very small number of researchers are working together, there is a greater possibility of developing a true colleagueship in which each will be able to formulate some of his own ideas and put them into action. The larger the group, the more difficult this becomes until the point is probably reached where it is virtually impossible, and the organization must be run on the basis of hierarchical staff relations with the lower echelons almost inevitably becoming hired hands.

Subordination: If some members of the research group are distinctly subordinate to others in a given organizational hierarchy or in general social status, it will be more difficult to develop a true colleague working relationship than if their status were more closely equal. The subordinate may hesitate to advance his ideas; the superordinate might be loath to admit that his lower-level co-worker be entitled to inject his ideas into the plans. Formal super–subordinate relationships can of course be muted and sometimes completely overcome in the course of personal contact, but certainly this is an initial, and sometimes permanent, basis for establishing hired hand status.

Adherence to Rigid Plans: If a researcher believes that good research can be done only if a detailed plan of data-collection, processing, and analysis is established in advance and adhered to throughout, he has laid the basis for hired hand research if he makes use of assistance from others who have not participated in the original plan. Sticking to a pre-formed plan means that others cannot openly introduce variations which may make the study more meaningful for them. Any creativity they apply will be of a surreptitious nature.

In their research methods texts, our students are told a great deal about the mechanics of research technique and little about the social process of researching. What little is said on the latter score consists largely of Pollyannaish statements about morale, honesty, and "proper motivation." It should be noted that appeals to morality and patriotism never reduced goldbricking and restriction of production in industry, even during the time of a world war. There is no reason to believe that analogous appeals to interviewers, graduate students, research assistants, and others who serve as hired hands will be any more effective. If we want to avoid the hired hand mentality, we must stop using people as hired hands.

Glaser and Strauss state that we regularly "discount" aspects of many, if not most, of all scientific analyses we read because we consider the research design one-sided, believe that it does not fit the social structure to which it was generalized, or that it does not fit in with our observations in an area where we have had considerable experience.[10]

I would like to suggest another area in which we might consistently apply the "discounting process." When reading a research report, we should pay close attention to the description of how the data was collected, processed, analyzed, interpreted, and written up with an eye to determining what part, if any, was played by hired hands. This will often be a difficult and highly tentative judgement, requiring much reading between the lines with the help of our knowledge of how our colleagues and we ourselves often operate. However, we can get hints from such things as the size of the staff, the nature of the relationship of the staff members, the manner in which the research plans were developed and applied, the organizational setting in which the research was done, mention made of assignment of tasks, and so on. If there is good reason to believe that significant parts of the research had been carried out by hired hands, this would, in my opinion, be a reason for discounting much or all of the results of the study.

Notes

* This paper was initially prepared for The Columbia University Seminar on Content and Method in The Social Sciences, December 14, 1965.

1. Donald Roy, "Quota Restriction and Goldbricking in a Machine Shop," *American Journal of Sociology*, 57 (March 1952), pp. 427–442.

2. I want to emphasize once again that in a business setting, supervisors and executives, as well as production line workmen, participate in aspects of the hired hand mentality. None of them may have an intrinsic interest in the quality of the product. (See, for example, Melville Dalton, *Men Who Manage*, New York: John Wiley and Sons,

Inc., 1959, especially Chapters 7, 8, and 9.) The same is the case in much large-scale research.

3. In this discussion I am assuming there *is* some one (or a small group of colleagues) who has initially formulated the research problem or area of concern because of intrinsic interest and curiosity. In much of our social science research, we do not have even this saving grace and the research is formulated and carried out for various "political" reasons. In such cases, we cannot count on having anyone interested enough to try to turn the accumulations of data into a meaningful explanatory statement.

4. Leo Crespi, "The Cheater Problem in Polling," *Public Opinion Quarterly*, Winter 1945–1946, pp. 431–445.

5. "Survey on Problems of Interviewer Cheating," *International Journal of Opinion and Attitude Research*, 1 (1947), pp. 93–107.

6. Julius A. Roth, "The Status of Interviewing," *The Midwest Sociologist*, 19 (December 1956), pp. 8–11.

7. I have even heard the argument that it makes no difference if perceptive interviewers make up parts of the interview responses with the help of information from other responses because their fabrications will usually closely approximate what the subject would have said if he could have been prompted to answer. But if we accept this argument, a large portion of the interview should have been eliminated to begin with. It means we already claim to know the nature of some of the relationships which the study is purportedly investigating.

8. Leo Crespi, *op. cit.*, pp 437–439.

9. The "human relations in industry" movement has given us some useful suggestions about the circumstances which alienate workers and executives, and also ways in which industrial employees may be given a real stake in their jobs. See for example, Douglas McGregor, *The Human Side of Enterprise*, New York: McGraw-Hill Book Co., 1960, Part 2.

10. Barney Glaser and Anselm L. Strauss, "Discovery of Substantive Theory: A Basic Strategy Underlying Qualitative Research," *American Behavioral Scientist*, 8 (February 1965), pp. 5–12.

14

The Study of Southern Labor Union Organizing Campaigns

Donald Roy

T he thought of my dispensing advice on field-study procedures brings to mind imagery of a grizzled prospector demonstrating the use of his pick and shovel and pan to operators of a modern gold dredge. Modes of inquiry that were already of questionable status when I was taking faltering steps of research apprenticeship appear now to be completely out of fashion. My data-gathering experience has been largely restricted to participant observation, in several of its various forms. Should I, a procedural anachronism, hold up my primitive research tools for inspection?

At the moment, however, as far as research involving union–management conflict in the South is concerned, what else is there but my pick and shovel and pan? The behemoth of inquiry, equipped with grant, computer, interviewers, and technicians, hasn't appeared on the scene of industrial conflict below the Mason–Dixon line. The machinery is in vogue, but the subject matter isn't. The heavy stuff won't roll in until the study of union–management relations becomes respectable. As to an approximate date for the rise of respectability, I wouldn't hazard a guess. In the meantime the war between the two perennial adversaries beckons to the lone researcher with bewitching promise. As the shuffling sourdough might put it, "There's data in them thar hills! And maybe theory, too!" I have poked around a bit, and, urged to talk about my searchings, I'll tell what I've been trying to find out and the trails that I've followed. Perhaps such an account will prove refreshing, if not instructive.

Buford Junker has offered a fourfold classification of subtypes of participant observation, from the "complete observer" to the "complete participant," with the two intermediate categories of "observer-as-participant," and "participant-as-observer."[1] Since acceptance of, or at least reference to, this typology has become fairly general, I shall place my own fieldwork procedures within the Junker scheme. I recognize two of the categories, "complete participant" and "participant-as-observer," as providing bins of comfortable fit for research

Source: Robert W. Habenstein (ed.), *Pathways to Data* (Chicago: Aldine, 1970).

approaches with which I am familiar, with the latter as descriptive of the pathway to data that I have been following in my study of southern labor union organizing campaigns. The main distinction between the two subtypes seems to lie in the matter of research-role concealment. The participant-as-observer not only makes no secret of his investigation; he makes it known that research is his overriding interest. He is there to observe. To mention a second distinction that I regard as important, the participant-as-observer is not tied down; he is free to run around as research interests beckon; he may move as the spirit listeth.

The complete participant, on the other hand, as far as the study of industrial situations is concerned, is stuck with the work. With an emphasis on observation, the participant-as-observer may lend a hand on occasion to push a desk across a room, or a tongue to seal envelopes; the complete participant may find his nose so incessantly pressed to the grindstone of work routines that he has little time or opportunity to observe the social interaction going on around him. A benign nod might be tossed in the direction of a complete participation role as drummer in a hot rock-and-roll combo, as taster in a winery, or as commander of a flagship in peacetime. But there are manifold activities, particularly those of interest to an industrial sociologist, in which participation can be stupefactive. As one who has put in many stultifying hours in concealed dedication to sociology in the lower depths of factory work, let me express frank enthusiasm for the participant-as-observer role. In my experience its advantages outweigh its disadvantages, and I favor it against the third approach listed by Junker, that of observer-as-participant. The chief distinctions here lie in the quality and quantity of contacts with respondents. Whereas "the observer-as-participant role is used in studies involving one-visit interviews,"[2] "numerous brief contacts with many persons,"[3] and "relatively more formal observation than either informal observation or participation of any kind,"[4] the participant-as-observer role calls for informality of relationship with a few key informants or guides over a long period of time, and perhaps more intensive immersion in the minute details of the processes being studied.[5] The first is primarily an "outsider" role,[6] the second an "insider" role.

Junker's fourth category, the complete observer role, I have not had occasion to employ. I do not see how it could be maintained in the study of union organizing campaigns in the South. The larger mass meetings, conducted by union officials for the recruitment and morale-boosting of those eligible for union membership, might be open to those who would observe from the concealment of the mass; but in the general meetings of the size that union leaders of my acquaintance have been able to muster, such concealment would be difficult to sustain without correlative establishment of a complete participation role in the workplace involved. I do recall the case of an enterprising white student of mine who played the complete observer at a gathering of a local chapter of the Black Muslims by crawling under a pile of boards heaped at the back of a rickety meeting hall. However, the likely consequences of detection being what they were, this student limited occupancy of his observation post to a one-night stand.

I had become habituated to the participant-as-observer role long before I knew it by that name. Before reading Junker's work, I had become resigned to the cumbersome designation "continuous observation and interviewing in context," though until this moment there has been no printed announcement of my own awkward terminology. I now make a further distinction, a subclassification, in regard to my preferred research role, in the hope of clarifying as I complicate. I refer to a differentiation of perspective that has, I think, special relevance for the study of social conflict. One perspective entails observation from and participation with both sides of the conflict; the researcher stalks with the Hatfields and ambushes with the McCoys. The other perspective provides a running view of the war with the compliments of one of the two combatants. These distinctions cry for naming, and various designations come to mind. I have settled, for the time being, on "fence-riding" for the dual, or split, affiliation. "Tightrope walking" might do just as well, with "riding a tiger" crudely apt, but too heavily freighted, perhaps, with distracting imagery. I have thought of "above the battle," which carries agreeable connotations of professional elevation, removing all suggestion of precarious, undignified, or otherwise uninviting position. It also carries a gargantuan load of wishful thinking: maintaining effective research communication with conflicting groups over an extended period of time is a ticklish undertaking. If the researcher seeks to hoist himself too far above the battle, he may encounter stratospheric conditions where data run disappointingly thin. If he plunges into the thick of things, hobnobbing in easy camaraderie with both Hatfields and McCoys, he may at any time, particularly during periods of acute hostility, be perceived as too chummy with the opposition; as a consequence he may be drummed out of both clans. I have found that fence-riding can be a nerve-racking experience, even in a northern industrial situation where collective bargaining has been established and where union–management relations go on from day to day in apparent harmony.

The alternative perspective available to the researcher who would essay a participant-as-observer approach to the study of organizing campaigns I have given a provisional label: "Ernie Pyling." Ernie Pyle, it may be remembered, was a news correspondent who followed American troops, including front-line fighting units, during World War II.[7] Like Pyle, I have during recent years followed the troops, representing one side of the union–management conflict that rages in the South. Since the focus of my investigation has been primarily on the organizing campaign, with my interest in the strike incidental to overall organizing efforts, and since unions initiate and conduct the campaigns in the role of attackers, the observational perspective that I have chosen would appear to be the logical one to take. It would be unrealistic, I am sure, to attempt a fence-riding approach in a conflict so permeated with strong passions and gut-deep estrangement, where both sides go all out to win and play for keeps. I have encountered nothing in my reading to induce me to drop the presumption that reciprocal hostilities between union and management were just as intense in times past in the industrial areas of our North and West. Maintaining effective research communication with both sides in situations characterized by a reluctant willingness of management to "live with the union" is difficult enough. Where the two antagonists have not even achieved a stage of incipient accommodation, possibilities of fence-riding would be slim indeed. I am willing to entertain, far back in my mind, the possibility that someone else, someone with the right dual connections carefully developed and maintained, someone recognized by both sides as possessed of impeccable neutrality and trustworthiness, or someone of exalted status or overwhelming charisma, might be able to conduct a study of labor union organizing campaigns in the South with a participant-as-observer approach *and* with the sustained cooperation of both adversaries. Certainly, one who has been Ernie Pyling with the union forces would not be given the opportunity to acquire data accessible only through a management group. As far as possibilities for application of other research procedures are concerned, it would appear likely that some type of polling or interviewing technique would have a better chance of winning dual cooperation. Yet here too I am inclined toward pessimism. The word that I get, indirectly and from a variety of sources, is that the management of southern industry does not look with favor on the study of union organizing regardless of research procedures contemplated. University professors of my acquaintance, who possess detailed familiarity with the mores of both business and academe in the South, have said, "You don't study unions down here." Puzzled students have told me of the refusal of relatives, highly placed in southern industry, to discuss with them the managerial point of view on unions. Some of these students were not members of my classes; nor can I claim blame as a source of their curiosity. One writer, a contributor to national magazines, called on me when she heard that I was studying unions. "I wanted to see what you looked like," she said. "You know, this just isn't done in the South."

At this point I must make two confessions. The first is that my choosing a taboo subject for research was not due to any deliberate boldness on my part. The investigation wasn't planned. I stumbled into it quite by chance. I blush now at my naïveté at my first encounters with union officials and pro-union workers. Secondly, I must admit that conversing with working stiffs is for me a matter of taking the line of least resistance. The union organizers of my acquaintance are for the most part only improved varieties of old-fashioned blue-collar drudges, and having experienced somewhat the same beatitudes and stringencies of condition, I find a pleasing measure of fellow feeling in our otherwise professional relationships and correlatively an ease in informal communication. My academic career has been, in a sense, an appendage to an earlier horizontal progression through a series of miscellaneous low-caste occupations. During my graduate student days, research in a factory gave me an opportunity to escape from my reference group to spend the afternoon observing and interviewing the machine-tending hoi polloi. In the bowels of the factory we were all dropouts; I was the dropout who went on to get a Ph.D.

During recent years there has sprung up in our centers of higher learning and research a group of students who seem to have the inclination, if not the background, to interact informally with the great unwashed. However, their interest in the working class, employed or unemployed, centers on the development of action programs, not field study. Graduate student rosters of southern universities may include a few potential Ernie Pylers; however, under present-day pressures to speed up processes of qualifying for niches in the academic woodwork, candidates for the Ph.D. cannot spare the time for observational procedures that may get them involved for many months in the field with no assurance that their gleanings can be shaped and tidied into dissertation form. For those who find themselves thus cramped for time to follow a possible research interest in union–management conflict in the South, there are alternative sources of data to draw upon, such as the library, the files, and use of more formal techniques of interviewing. Recourse to these and possibly additional options meets with rather severe limitations. During one campaign I employed a fixed-choice questionnaire with results that were not disappointing. However, this undertaking represented but one phase of a larger effort, and it was not carried out in conformity to acceptable standards of survey research.

I see no problem of entrée for the researcher who elects to study union–management conflict from an Ernie Pyle perspective if he is willing to make his observations from the union side of the fence. I have found, at all levels of union officialdom, doors wide open to the study of organizing campaigns. Although my contacts with union organizers and officials have not been widespread, owing to the character of my research, which has been intensive rather than extensive, I am led by the invariably friendly reception that I have received to the presumption that union leaders in general, at least on the southern scene, welcome the spotlight of the sociologist. They feel, I gather, that they have much more to gain than to lose by investigation and its possibilities of consequent publicity. This is not to say that the open-door policy represents a despairing "What have we got to lose?" attitude. It is true that some unions have been taking campaign beatings with almost monotonous regularity and for a long time; but other unions rack up victories in a majority of their campaigns, and they too are likely to give the researcher a friendly reception. In fact, a representative of one union took the initiative in inviting me to have a look at some union victories. The researcher cannot, of course, expect a union to offer a ringside seat to witness the exchange of punches that commonly takes place in labor–management relations after the union has won the right to representation and a contract, and collective bargaining has been instituted. Permission to watch collective bargaining sessions, or other types of infighting that are conducted on company property, would have to come from management as well as from the union. But I discovered to my initial surprise and subsequent embarrassment that under certain circumstances the managerial invitation may be graciously though unenthusiastically extended when gentle pressure is applied by an apparently ascendant union official. I have been ushered into the offices of managers of fairly large business establishments, to their obvious discomfort and mine, along with plant employees and union stewards, to watch the union business agent handle employee grievances, beating company officials into the ground, figuratively speaking, while doing so. Although this sort of approach to observation of in-plant aspects of union–management conflict can indeed be productive of abundant, sometimes astonishing data, its use would appear to be limited to a relatively rare set of circumstances.

Opportunity to observe my first organizing campaign came quite unexpectedly. An organizer for the Textile Workers Union of America, who had heard of my interest in industrial relations from a friend of one of my former associates at the University of Chicago, called at my office at Duke University one spring day to ask me if I knew of any Duke students who might be willing to work a few hours for the union, for pay. He wanted men to help distribute leaflets at the site of a prospective organizing campaign, about ten miles from the university. Our encounter netted no student help for the organizer (this was prior to the development of a New Left movement at Duke), but in the course of our conversation the organizer suggested that I might like to attend a mass meeting that was to be held to kick off a campaign for employees of a textile mill located in the foothills of the Blue Ridge. It sounded like an interesting outing, and I showed up, on a rainy Sunday afternoon. The meeting was brief, held in the soggy out-of-doors on a dirt crossroad near a baseball park. My new acquaintance and members of his workers' organizing committee had been unable to obtain indoor facilities in the mill town or in other towns of the surrounding area. The scene in the rain impressed me – the opening prayer, the earnest speakers, the intently listening mill hands, men and women, and the nearby ball park with a roofed-over grandstand, dedicated to local heroes who had fought for justice and freedom in World War II, but denied to some of those heroes who were standing in the rain.

The campaign lasted the rest of the spring, all summer, and into the autumn. The union got beat, the first of a long, unbroken series of defeats that I was to witness or to hear about. I watched the process, from the April kick-off meeting to a November dismantling of the goal posts, by averaging every other weekend at field headquarters. Since my organizer-sponsor had been laying the groundwork for another campaign for several weeks before taking his final lumps in the first one, I was able to make the switch from one observation post to another with no problems of clearance. I would have experienced no difficulty in establishing myself in the second situation anyhow. During the course of the first campaign I met some visiting dignitaries, officials of the union at the vice-presidential level, who came down from national headquarters in New York or over from regional headquarters in Charlotte to contribute speeches designed to improve morale and to appraise the progress and prospects of the campaign. Also, early in the summer, I had

attended a union conference at regional headquarters, and there, over a period of two days, I made the acquaintance of other union officials and many
of the southern organizers. I learned, from these extended contacts, that my
sponsor was highly esteemed by his superiors in the union hierarchy, but that
he was also regarded with mixed feelings as a man of unconventional organizing ideas. Now, knowing him over a longer period of time, I am inclined to
the belief that my Ernie Pyleship was launched as one of his innovations. At
any rate, if my experience may be considered as indicative of what other
sociologists might reasonably expect, neither establishment nor maintenance
of access to observation posts for close scrutiny of union organizing processes
poses any notable difficulty.

It is my feeling that if major hindrances to a durable and productive field-
study relationship with southern union people are to be encountered, they will
be found in the behavior of the researcher. I suspect that organizers, and workers too, would rather quickly tire of a would-be Pyler who had been
oversocialized to a teaching role, didactic style, to the extent that he would
feel comfortable in human interaction only while lecturing the other fellow.
Such a need to hold the floor would be especially handicapping, I think, if it
were accompanied by mannerisms indicating a self-conception creaking with
status. A prevailing inclination to listen, heightened by genuine interest and
curiosity, and suspended only long enough to ask for further relevant information or to raise pertinent questions, would carry one best, I am sure, over
the long haul.

Besides a tendency to let the other fellow do the talking, I have had one
other important thing going for me in my study of union–management conflict. Early in my first campaign I began to arrange my searchings around a
central question: How can we account for the union's success or failure in
organizing campaigns? This question, of course, was of vital practical concern
to the organizers, and it tended to be sure-fire in eliciting the interest of workers
in my research. How to win was not just a problem to the union officials, it
was *the* problem. For the dedicated it was all-consuming. For those with minimal devotion to the cause – that is, the organizers called "pork-choppers" –
it was at least the heart of a job. No matter how deep or how superficial the
occupational motivation, the question was always good for thoughtful discussion, sometimes animated argument when the experts found themselves in
disagreement. And there was frequently disagreement when the question was
tossed into a group – if not over basic matters, then over the fine points.

Those who remained relatively silent in group disputations would impress
upon me later a point that they had failed to make, one that they had been
reluctant to put forth in the group situation or one that had come to mind
after the discussion had ended. I could also expect to hear again in private
the analyses and expansions thereof of those who had been most loquacious
or argumentative when the discussion was on. The question appears to be a
simple one, but the answer becomes complex. The way for blue-collar and
ex-blue-collar people to present complex matters clearly and convincingly to

their fellows is to bring forth concrete examples, that is, to talk about a specific campaign that they have experienced. And since the success/failure question has a perpetual relevance to the work at hand, it could be introduced, in one form or another, at just about any time, on the job or during off hours. Such shop talk never seemed importunate. It was in season at field headquarters, driving along county roads to the home of some prospective union member, with groups that lingered on after the mass meeting, at mealtime in the Greasy Spoon, in the hotel lobby at regional conferences, or over a beer anywhere.

During recent years the big question has bifurcated to include a twin problem of deep concern: how to win a contract for collective bargaining after winning the certifying election that decides campaign victory or defeat. The additional topic for discussion does nothing to impede or to retard the continuous interviewing and observation in context; it augments it. I feel certain that I would not have received the same gratifying quality of acceptance during the early phases of my study had I seized upon and belabored a question of slight intrinsic interest to the union people. After friendships were developed and trust was established, the nature of the subject matter of inquiry became less important, I feel, for the development and maintenance of my relationships. The situation is becoming one in which I no longer volunteer explanation of my research purpose as I move from one observational post to another; and rarely am I asked, as new faces appear, what I am doing. I seem to move from situation to situation over bridges of organizer interacquaintance. Perhaps the questioning goes on during my absence, with organizers vouching for my trustworthiness to each new group of workers. However, I suspect that my welcome in union circles might have deteriorated rather quickly had I shifted my orientation from topics of vital interest to my respondents to questions of little or no appeal.

In general, the organizing campaign, as I am familiar with it, represents an attempt by a group of international labor union officials to induce the employees of a given industrial or commercial establishment to give an explicit indication of their desire to form a local chapter of the union served by the men who do the urging. This evocation of avowal takes time, from several months to a year or more. Several determinants have a hand in dragging out the process. For one thing, the explicit indicating must follow certain procedures instituted by the National Labor Relations Board. Arrangements are made, in most cases, for conducting a union certification election by secret ballot. This election normally terminates the campaign; its results spell victory or defeat for the union. Also, NLRB officials will insist on seeing, before calling for the vote, evidence that at least 30 percent of the employees involved have expressed their desire, by petition, for an election. The organizer in charge of a campaign usually takes upon himself the responsibility of acquiring the necessary proportion of signatures, and this may take a few weeks. However, the organizer will not pass on to the NLRB the minimal 30 percent of possible signatures that it takes to get the election wheels rolling until he has received some form of assurance that the union has a good chance of winning, that pro-union ballots will be in the majority, preferably by substantial majority. This assurance may be hard to come by, may take many months in the getting, and may never be obtained if the organizer feels that he must have in his possession petition cards signed by 50 percent, 60 percent, or 70 percent of the eligible voters before he extends an election request to the NLRB. It may take less time to come to the decision that a union victory is a good bet if the organizer seeks other signs of good omen, such as the size, morale, and effectiveness of an organizing committee that he has developed among strongly pro-union workers. It takes time, of course, to shape up such a committee and to assess the results of its work. If management, as a counterorganizing tactic, should fire the organizing committee, or a substantial proportion of its membership, then the organizer has to shape up another committee if he is to go on with the campaign. One organizer had two committees shot out from under him before losing his certification election. Finally, the campaign may be prolonged by managerial action that is legalistic as well as legal. Company officials may delay the setting of an election date by requesting a special hearing to reach decisions on matters connected with delineating the electorate. In the view of union organizers, calling for a hearing represents delaying tactics on the part of management, which seeks additional time to allow its employees to reconsider their urge to union membership.

Management, of course, provides the eligible voters with ideational material for their second thoughts. Just as the organizer and his staff encourage workers to sign petition cards and to vote for the installation of a union, company officials exude counteracting discouragement. As the union officials organize, management officials disorganize. In fact, the campaign involves the attempts of both sides to organize relationships with the potential electorate and to disorganize relationships built up by the opposition. Furthermore, the organizing efforts of the two adversaries may reach far beyond the employees of the mill or factory in question. Both attempt to build supportive linkages with other groups and agencies in the community and over a wider canvas in state and nation. Most strikingly, the community gets drawn into the struggle, with management characteristically gaining the most effective help. The campaign thus gets spread out over a network of intergroup relations while it extends over stretches of time.

The election administered by the NLRB is the concluding event of a series that gives the organizing campaign a typical form. Possible and actual variation of doings and happenings within a general context of tactics, occurrences, and conditions engenders uncertainty of outcome. The union may win an election that its officials expected to lose; more often it loses when victory has been predicted. Many campaigns wind up with defeat or triumph by very close margins. As the campaign spins out, as things happen, as conditions develop, as the union employs routine tactics or tries something different, as management counterattacks, each successor in the stream of events is assessed by the organizer and his group at field headquarters as to nature and degree of influence on the progress and outcome of the campaign. These appraisals are grist for my curiosity mill, which grinds away on the question: How may we explain success or failure? They direct my vision, point out to me what I should see and take into account, and supply me with hypotheses for rumination, selections, and reformulation. When I notice something hitherto undiscussed, the experts at hand offer explanation. I come to understand what I see. By watching the campaign roll on in its full development and in its particulars, I get a better grasp of what the experts are talking about when they relate experiences of other times and places. I come to understand what I hear. I get steeped in the lore of campaigning. I acquire an acquaintance knowledge for ease of mentation within the imponderabilia of the occupation of union-organizing. I establish a base in the tacit knowledge of the craft. I get pictures in detail, from which abstractions may be constructed with minimal distortion, so that a union official with decades of experience can say, after reading one of my theoretical efforts, "You've got the picture." Thus I might claim that the participant-as-observer role provides me with both the "act-meanings" of *Verstehen* and the tentative "action-meanings"[8] requisite for the development of theory.

Since my teachers and informants are not passive spectators of campaign processes, but practitioners trying to utilize their skills and various other resources to overcome great obstacles to attain their end in view; since these practitioners apply alternative ideas, sometimes new and highly imaginative ones, in the attempt to solve their problems; and since I observe such activities over the organizer's shoulder and in his very shadow, so to speak, I might also claim an adumbrative "learning by doing" method of inquiry, given strong recommendation by John Dewey[9] and Mao Tse-tung.[10] To call it "incipient experimentation" might be stretching the claim too far, but I do see these observational procedures as efficacious preliminaries to field experiment.

I offer brief depictions of types of situations in which the Ernie Pyling technique can be used for observing characteristic activities of the organizing campaign. In most of these situations the researcher not only sees and hears what is going on within range of his eyes and ears; he gets reports on what is happening beyond the limits of his perception. He gets common-sense interpretations of these events, both near and far, and he can initiate or intervene in conversation for heightened apprehension and comprehension of observation and idea.

Hanging Around Headquarters

Perhaps the most fruitful hours of fieldwork, in regard to the organizing campaign, are spent at field headquarters, usually located in an office in a union hall or in a suite of motel rooms, and not many miles from the factory under organizing attack. If the location is a union hall, it may be the property of a sympathetic labor union that has won its campaign and has settled in the community. If it is a motel room, it will be in an establishment where the proprietor is not so hostile toward unions that he will not tolerate the protracted residence of organizers and the almost continual coming and going of pro-union workers. The organizer in charge of a campaign spends a great proportion of his time in his office, which serves as the center of a web of communication. If the target of the organizing attempt is a large mill, the union may assign several more organizers to assist the man in charge; these assistants drop in from time to time to report the work done in the field, that is, their successes and failures in contacting workers in their homes for petition-card signatures or their progress in developing groups of "actives" as organizing committees to participate in phases of the organizing process. The assisting organizers also engage in exchanges with their chief involving appraisals of the campaign situation and in discussions on tactical problems and possibilities. Pro-union workers drop in, too. There is a day-long stream of callers, arriving singly, in twos, threes, and large groups, fitting visits to their work schedules. They bring the news of the hour from the mill and the community, informing the organizer of ominous, promising, or amusing events and answering his searching questions. These callers serve as extra eyes and ears for the organizer; through them he keeps tabs on what goes on in the mill, department by department. He is ever on the alert for materials that can be shaped into issues to be played up in leaflets or at mass meetings to advance identification with the union and disaffection toward management. So the stretchout has hit the weave room? So the spinners are unable to understand how their piecework pay is computed and think they're being cheated? So the superintendent has been calling the loom fixers to the office for questioning and brainwashing against unionism? So the second hands have been saying that the company would never work with a union, hinting that the mill would be shut down and leased out as a warehouse if the union won the election? So the forelady in sewing has been very nice to the girls lately? So they're starting to hand out the sweet stuff, repainting the rest rooms and installing new toilet bowls? So the company president has sent out a love letter to his blue-collar employees, telling them of his hopes and plans for better days together if everyone continues to pull together for that brighter future? So the food-cart service is getting worse every day, the Brunswick stew isn't fit for the hogs, and Sonny Pickens dug around in his potato salad today until he found a spider, held it up, and shouted triumphantly, "I found it!" thus indicating to everyone that there was sure to be something wrong with the company-dispensed lunch?

The organizer finds out what is going on in the workplace, in all detail of possible relevance to his organizing effort; and, privileged to sit in on the têtes-à-têtes, so does the researcher. If the foreman lets his female employees hold prayer meetings on company time to keep them happy and nonunion, if supervisors are cracking down on employee conversation to reduce possible union talk, the researcher hears about it from the lips of the workers involved. If he wants to discuss these or other matters with the visitors, he may. He'll meet them again, at the office or at meetings, and they'll converse with him freely, having noticed that the organizers speak without constraint in his presence.

If the organizer looks for a high proportion of signed petition cards in relation to the number of eligible voters, he may keep a very careful accounting of the process of card-signing, referring almost daily to his file of contact cards. On each card, headed by employee name, job designation, department, and home address, he may note date of contact, name of person who did the contacting, and a few lines of appraisal of the employee's union orientation, including the yes or no of his petition-card signing. With a select group of trusted actives, representing the various mill departments by work shift, the organizer may go over his contact cards. In private conferences with individuals or small groups the organizer may receive help in casting about for possibilities of inducing the unsigned to come into the fold. From the thoughtful discussions will come a consensus, either that further effort should be expended on the refractory or slippery ones or that further effort would be futile. By listening to these discussions the researcher discerns a variety of pressures, interests, and circumstances that serve as counterinfluences to appeals made by union adherents, and thus may bear on campaign outcome. The following excerpts from my field notes, taken down verbatim during assessments of the unsigned, offer an example of the appraisal process and the type of opportunity given the researcher to observe and record it. In this particular instance, head organizer George Forstal (all names are fictitious) and two of his staff, Mike and Lucille, discuss with a committee of four textile workers some card-signing possibilities in the napping department:

> *George:* We should sit down and go over the names of those who haven't signed. We should talk about what kind of people they are – how to approach them, who their brother or father is, who they ride with. We need one more card from Napping B [second shift of the napping department] and we'll have a majority.

One worker suggested the name Garver, asked George if he had signed. George said no.

"Then he told a lie," said a second worker. He added, "My brother is quitting Thursday. He's going to school, the Hilltop Bible School."

> *1st worker:* Your brother's a minister, isn't he?
> *George:* (referring to names again): Adkins. Doesn't he roll blankets?
> *3rd worker:* He's gone [out of Napping B].
> *George:* The way they move around!
> Other names were discussed – Chester, Graham.
> *3rd worker* (in reaction to the name Graham): I don't believe he'll sign.
> *Lucille:* Yes, I believe he will sign. I talked to him. He just didn't understand what the union is all about.

2nd worker: He's the kind of guy that will find out things from you and tell others.

* * *

George: Sparks? Whitaker's working on him. Somebody said his wife was the key.

4th worker: I don't know.

George: Earl Waddell?

2nd worker: Can't do anything with him. He's got one of those pie-eating jobs.

George then mentioned Jack Scott, a "colored fellow."

3rd worker: If you get Gaither, you get Scott. Scott does what he says.

George: Some of the boys have been deviling Jack, and they've got him scared. They've been sticking union cards in his pocket, so they show, and then asking him where he got them.

During most of my observation situations throughout this campaign, I was able to take notes with pencil and pad as I watched, listened, and conversed. The fact that George did not disapprove of this note-taking made it all right with those who called at union headquarters. Occasionally at some of the larger gatherings and formal meetings questioning eyes would be directed my way; but always George's lack of concern over my activity seemed to allay suspicion of my motives. I would replace pad after pad as they filled up with my own special shorthand and grind down pencil after pencil with the small plastic pencil sharpener that I carried with me.

Observing Mass Meetings

But I did not venture to take notes openly in all campaigns and all situations. In my observation of mass meetings conducted by George Forstal I did not hesitate to bring out pencil and paper for verbatim recording. But during a campaign led by an organizer I shall call Wren I watched and listened with folded arms during the weekly mass meetings held in a hall provided by another union. The following excerpt from my observations, within an hour after the close of one meeting, indicates the type of material gathered at mass meetings when I did not consider it advisable to flash a pencil.

Wren now called on Jones to talk. "I see that the colored workers are well represented tonight. It looks like Brother Jones has been doing a good job. Brother Jones, do you want to say a few words?"

Jones, a large, raw-boned Negro who had served as a organizer for another union in another area, and who now volunteered his services to help with the organizing of the few colored workers of the target mill, stood up from his seat in the rear of the hall. "I just want to say that I agree with what you said a hundred percent. You've all got to get out and sell people on having a union. I've been in union work for twenty-one years, and I know that people stay home and don't attend meetings. And they're going to go and stay home after you have a union here, and only a few of you will go to the meetings. You are the leaders, and you will keep it going."

Jones went on: "There are two stages, the way I look at it, in getting a union. The first stage is the drive, where you get out, as you did, and get enough cards to petition for an election. The second stage is the stage you are going into now, and that is the contest stage. You are in a contest with the company to win the election. It's a contest over who's to decide things in the plant from now on, whether the bosses and their stooges are going to go on deciding everything themselves, or whether you are going to have some say in what happens to you, some say about your wages and hours and working conditions."

Jones's voice, when he started to talk about the "contest," rose in increasing emotionalism, and he was shouting loudly when he spoke of the bosses and their stooges and deciding things. His voice resumed a moderate tone now, as he referred to the Scriptures.

Jones said that there was a passage in the Scriptures that he thought was appropriate here: "As a man thinketh, so is he." He also cited another line, which I am unable to recall. I did not get too clear a connection between this line and what Jones then said, that they were right in what they were trying to get for themselves, and since they were right they could win.

"You can be a success, because you are on the Lord's side in this, and the Lord's side is the side to be on [voice raising again]. Even if they argue that they're not making much money, that there's work enough for only four days a week and this is not the time to organize a union, remember that they're making money whenever they run. They're making money out of our work even if they run three, two, or even one day a week. They don't operate unless they can make money. The bosses make a profit on all that you do, and it's up to you to get your share, just as much as you can get."

Jones was now shouting enough to raise the roof. I noted that the white people in front of me looked a little restive, as if wishing that Jones would finish and sit down. I noticed a sort of restiveness in myself, perhaps an embarrassment for the speaker and an empathy with the audience. I was wishing that Jones would finish and sit down, or at least talk more moderately. It was if he were abusing his invitation to "say a few words" by launching a long, loud speech. (Jones took longer in his talk than I indicate in the telling.) I noted, however, that some of the Negroes were obviously enjoying Jones's harangue. They were grinning and making gestures of strong approval.

Other Observation Situations

Other types of observation situations of the participant-as-observer variety included those afforded by accompanying organizers on house calls at the homes of mill workers for the purpose of obtaining petition-card signatures, making trips to the mill gates at shift-change time to watch organizers hand out union leaflets to homeward-bound workers, and joining worker crowds at picket lines during strikes, with the special excitement at shift change when carloads of nonstriking workers, with the protection of city, county, and state police, would drive through the lines to the accompaniment of shouts and jeers from the strikers. These three types of situations provided, of course, ample opportunity for interviewing in the form of conversation.

In one campaign involving six plants of one company, I attended the special meetings held each week at a central location for the dozen organizers involved. These meetings, conducted by a union vice-president, centered around reports of the organizers on events of the week in their respective campaigns and discussion of tactics to foster the progress of the organizing drive. In this situation I was privileged to sit back from the conference table and take verbatim notes.

My strike-watching opportunities included not only headquarters and picket-line observations in four strikes conducted for the purpose of pressuring company officials to bargain collectively after certification elections had been won; they also included observation in a miscellany of situations connected with a long strike of considerable magnitude, drama, and significance for the southern future of an international union. This strike found me in daily courtroom attendance in a small town. Several union officials of my acquaintance and four active millworkers were given prison sentences for conspiring to dynamite an electric power substation. The problem of note-taking in a courtroom where the judge was lavish with his contempt-of-court citations and sentences was solved by the screening provided by the heads and torsos of several cooperative millworkers.

Interviewing

As I have already noted, my application of the participant-as-observer role to the study of union–management conflict involved continuous interviewing as well as observation. This interviewing, conducted as informal conversation, varied from direct questioning on a great variety of specific topics of timely interest to nondirective exploration of perception and feeling.

In two of the campaigns of the six-plant drive I launched programs of formal interviewing of employees with the use of four-page questionnaires. In the first of these interviewing attempts I approached my respondents without the seal of approval of the organizers. In the second situation an organizer accompanied me to each house to make the introduction and to provide assurances that I was OK, that I was really from Duke, was not a stooge of the company, and would hold confidential what was told me. In the first situation the fearful workers expressed their suspicions by either refusing to talk with me or providing false answers to my questions.

The following offers a sample of responses received from the nonsponsored questioning of one Medford Sprinkle, who was first asked to accept one of five statements that came closest to expressing his feelings about having a labor union in his mill:

(*a*) We are very much in need of a union in our mill.
(*b*) Conditions in the mill aren't too bad, but I think a union would help a lot.
(*c*) I can't see that it makes much difference whether we have a union or not.
(*d*) A union might help us a little on a few things, but generally it would do more harm than good.
(*e*) All that a union would bring us is a lot of trouble.

Sprinkle was unable to pick a position. He handed the five cards back to me, saying, "I haven't any opinion about the union. I haven't been thinking about it. I haven't had time to think about it." He then explained that his mother had "taken sick" a month ago, and that he spent his spare time visiting her. "I go over to my mother's when I get up in the morning, and don't get back till two o'clock, when it's time to go to work."

Sprinkle's answers to some of the succeeding questions were recorded as follows:

Q. 3: Sprinkle was unable to suggest any good things or any bad things that might come of having a union. He repeated his lack of opinion, spoke again of his sick mother.
Q. 4: Sprinkle said that none of the influences listed had any influence on him. Of newspaper articles he said, "I've seen nothing in the paper about the union." Sprinkle didn't know what locally prominent people said about the union, nor did he know what nationally prominent people said. He hadn't talked the subject over with relatives, neighbors, or friends. When I asked him about talks with neighbors, he said "I haven't been anywhere. Just to my mother's." He said, in a sort of summary here, "I haven't heard any talk about the union at all."
Q. 8: He said that an organizer called on him once during the campaign. "A guy was here, but I wasn't home." Sprinkle couldn't give any opinions about the organizers because he hadn't met any of them.
Q. 19: He took (a) position here, indicating he felt that the foreman in his department was well liked by the workers. Sprinkle commented, "He's too good for his own use. Nobody could dislike him. He even worries about the help. I was raised with him and went to school with him."

I discovered, after this survey was abandoned, that Sprinkle was not only in surreptitious communication with the organizers as a strongly pro-union worker, but was regarded as possessing potentialities for leadership.

In contrast, Mattie Reece provided frank answers to the formal questioning when I called at her home a few days after being introduced to her by the organizer in charge of the campaign. After completing the questionnaire, Mrs. Reece went on to talk freely about the stretchout in the weave room:

> If the union falls through, we haven't ever seen such hard times as we'll get. I can't keep my job going now. I can't get looms fixed. I can't get running. The second hands [supervisors] show no interest. A second hand said that it's easy now, but if the seconds [defective weaving] don't come down, it's hard to tell what we'll get later on. I figure he meant after the union is gone.
>
> In a big meeting they asked about the restroom ventilation. Some girls had complained that it was too hot to change clothes in there. They asked me how it was in the restroom. I said I didn't know. I said I don't get to stay long enough to find out. Some days I can't get the time to go in. I punish myself. There's not time to go in there. I go straight in and out and don't take the time to comb my hair.
>
> The other weavers are in the same fix. There's no time to eat. I've worked day in and day out without stopping to eat. The dope wagon [lunch cart] comes in and half the looms are standing. Many times I just take coffee or milk. It's that way with the other weavers, too.
>
> When I first came to work, twenty years ago, I could go to the waterhouse [restroom] and talk or rest five minutes. Now there's no time for anything. Grady Spicer told me that if he goes to the waterhouse the second hand comes in there watching him.
>
> It's killing us all. My health is affected. I'm so nervous some days.... Everybody is on pins and needles. They're afraid to say anything, or do the least thing wrong. It's a continual strain for everybody. They're all afraid they'll lose their jobs, and if anybody needs a job, I do.

John Crawford, loom fixer with fifteen years' seniority, also previously assured of my trustworthiness, had no hesitation in telling of his turning from anti-union to pro-union:

> I changed my mind about the union. I was for the company. I even went to the union hall and talked for the company....
>
> They used to call me in the office. They asked me what I thought about the union ... all such as that. In the first campaign [five years earlier] they wanted me to talk for them.... They wanted to know how I was going to vote. I told them that before this they said it was going to be secret. They said, "Crawford, if you go with the wrong crowd,

you'll suffer with the wrong crowd." That was my second hand and the big boss in the office.

When I came here, weavers had thirty-six looms. Now they've got eighty-eight or ninety. When I came here there was one weave room and three smash hands. Now there are two [smash hands per weave room]. Fixers have a whole lot more looms. They had forty-two or forty-three when I came. Now it's sixty-two looms to keep repaired.... You don't stand around and laugh and talk, not even at dinnertime. You eat your dinner at your workbench.... When you get more than you can do, it's hard on your nerves. I come in at night jittery.

Documentary Materials

Although the participant-as-observer relies, in the main, on watching, listening, and conversing in the gathering of his data, he may have access to a variety of documentary materials that have bearing on his chosen problem. In my own study of labor union organizing I find that each campaign produces a plethora of printed matter, including mimeographed and typed materials. The union disseminates occasional messages to members of the work force in the form of one-sheet leaflets, distributed at the mill gates. It also mails out letters. One could obtain a rough idea of the progress of a campaign by perusal of the union publications as they are issued. Also available is the company campaign literature, offered less frequently in the form of printed booklets and letters from the company president, mailed to a body of employees with the potential electorate obviously in special view. The company literature, always brought to the attention of the organizers by pro-union workers, can readily be obtained by the researcher. Likewise, copies of strongly anti-union periodicals, mailed to workers directly from the publisher during the organizing campaign, are readily available. The researcher can always find a pro-union worker who is willing to give up his copy of *Militant Truth*, a four-pager that seems to appear at irregular intervals when needed. With Bible and American flag riding the upper corners of page 1, this periodical is unwavering in its attack on those fraternizing conspirators: Reds, atheists, race-mixers, carpetbaggers, and labor union bosses. In addition, mimeographed or typed materials intended for a more restricted distribution are sometimes obtainable. A worker may take advantage of a careless supervisor or solve the problem of lock and key to smuggle out sheets of advice or instructions on counterorganizing. Such materials will be photocopied for quick return to the foremen's desk or file, and copies may be reduplicated.

Duplicates of several lengthy documents involving the hearings of fired workers before the Employment Security Commission have come into my possession. One such document, having special relevance to the progress of an organizing campaign, reveals the question-and-answer details of a hearing given a fired millworker before an agent of the ESC. In this instance the terminated employee, a loom fixer with over fifteen years' seniority, was handed a penalty of nine weeks, meaning that he would not be able to draw unemployment compensation until nine weeks had elapsed. The decision of the appeals deputy carried further meaning, as an obvious warning to other employees, that those who received disaffectionate discharges need not hope to cushion their drop from the payroll with the timely support of weekly checks from the government. To accomplish this, a company attorney brought witnesses before the deputy to testify that the fired worker had violated a company rule prohibiting sleeping on the job. The critical question was: Did the discharged employee lose consciousness when he closed his eyes while taking a smoking break in a booth provided for that purpose? In the following excerpt from a copy of the transcript of the hearing, the company attorney presses the question:

Q. Well, will you say now that you did not lose consciousness while you were in the smoking booth?

A. I don't believe I did.

Q. Well, are you sure?

A. Well, I am pretty sure that I didn't, for Henry Settle walked in and said slip over and I slipped over.

Q. Yes, sir, but you could have been out for a little while while you were ...

A. It would have had to been a little bit if I was.

Q. But you say you could have been out for a little while?

A. Well, I'd say that I was nodding. I won't say that I was conscious all the time, and I won't say that I wasn't. That's about the only way I can say it – but ...

Q. Well, then you would have to say that you could have been unconscious for part of the time, isn't that right?

A. Well, I don't ... No, I won't say that.

Q. Well, you said you didn't know whether you were all the time or not, didn't you?

A. I don't know....You asked me there if I was or I wasn't and so I will say that I was conscious, for when Settle walked in and said slip over, I did.

Q. Yeah, but I am talking about before that time.

A. I was conscious I would say all the time I was in there.

* * *

Q. And of course, you admit that you did have your eyes closed and everything?

A. Yeah, my eyes was closed.

Q. Do you know how long they were closed?

A. No, I was gone from my job approximately ten minutes but I don't know how long.

Q. Well, it could have been as long as five minutes?

A. I guess so, I don't know, I wouldn't say that. I wouldn't say exactly how long my eyes was closed.

It was decided that the fired fixer had lost consciousness during his smoking break; so in addition to losing his job, he had to wait nine weeks for his unemployment compensation.

Of supplementary use to observing participants who seek to describe, understand, or analyze the southern labor union organizing campaign are various compilations of data that are readily available to anyone. Found in libraries, these materials may lend themselves to special studies, statistical or historical in nature. The annual reports of the NLRB available in law libraries, offer statistics on cases involving unfair labor practices. Classifications are according to size of establishment involved, industry, geographic area, and outcome of hearing. These reports also provide statistics on representation elections by number, labor union involved, size of bargaining unit, number of employees voting, industry, geographic distribution by states, and election outcome. Additional data available in these reports include number and outcome of decertification elections and results of appeal of Board decisions to the courts. The written decisions of the NLRB and the court judgments made in cases that were appealed from Board decisions are available in bound volumes dating back to the Board's inception in 1935.

A handy guide to all formal decisions handed down by the NLRB in disposing of unfair labor practices issues and union representational matters is the *Labor Law Reporter*, a comprehensive digest found in law libraries. For each case of unfair labor practices the *Reporter* offers quotations from the statement of the trial examiner, the Board's areal representative who investigates and passes judgment. Judgments of the national Board, given when the trial examiner's decision is contested by employer, employee, or union, are also given in the *Reporter*. The following provides an example of the type of material published. The statement presented here is that offered by a three-man board; the judgment was made in recent months after a trial examiner's decision, favorable to a southern local of the Teamsters, was contested by the employer:

> The main issue of this case is the charge that employer violated Section 8 (a) (3) and (1) of the Act by laying off and discharging employees because of their union activity. A more novel issue is whether employer caused to be published a document threatening to close its plant because of union activity, or whether the group publishing that document was an agent of employer.
>
> Employer made no secret of the fact that it was opposed to the union campaign in its plant. Within the first weeks of the campaign, employer made several anti-union speeches to the employees, and then laid off or terminated many of the employees.

About the same time, a meeting of community businessmen was held at a local bank and addressed by employer. In the course of its remarks employer indicated that it was opposed to organization of its employees by a union. After employer left the meeting, several of the businessmen formed an ad hoc committee called the Committee of Interested Citizens for Continued Progress. Within a few days the committee published a "fact sheet" that was distributed through the community and asserted that employer would close its plant unless the employees rejected the union.

Shortly afterwards, employer made a public statement to the effect that every citizen had a right to express his views and that employer was not responsible for the committee's publications and views. However, employer did not deny or repudiate the committee's publication, and in effect suggested that the committee was performing a civic duty when it issued the publication. This was a tacit acknowledgment that the assertion in the fact sheet was true. Therefore, while there is no real evidence to show that employer instigated formation of the committee or publication of the fact sheet – and hence no showing that the committee was employer's agent – employer's response to the publication did convey the impression that the publication was correct and employer would close plant rather than go union. This response undoubtedly had a coercive effect upon the employees, and violated Section 8 (a) (1) of the Act. By the same token, it helps to show that employer's mass layoffs and discharges in the first week of the union drive were discriminatory, and in violation of Section 8 (a) (3) and (1) of the Act.

The committee has also been charged with violating the Act in connection with the publication of the fact sheet. But no agency relationship having been established between employer and the committee, there can be no such finding.[11]

The Bureau of Labor Statistics offers annual summary tables on work stoppages, with data on number of work stoppages by industry group, by state, by metropolitan area, and by major issues involved. Also listed are statistics on average days lost by stoppage, number of workers involved, percent of total employed involved, and percent of total work time of man-days idle.

The Duke University library has a collection of manuscripts donated by a former southern regional director of a textile union. These records, once kept in the files at union regional headquarters, might interest historians of southern labor–management relations. They cover a fourteen-year period, from 1927 to 1941. I have been informed by union officials that local unions keep in their files all materials pertaining to organizing campaigns, including leaflets, letters, NLRB judgments, and court decisions. "Nothing is ever thrown away," said one union business agent. When the files fill up, the more ancient materials are sent to a central collection point for continued preservation.

Unlike materials stored in libraries, however, contents of union files are not offered for public perusal. One may explore the union's archives only at the discretion of union officials. I have been offered access to files in several instances, but as yet have not taken advantage of this opportunity. Company officials undoubtedly preserve their own records of organizing campaigns in similar fashion. It is possible that access to such files might be accorded those who do their Ernie Pyling from the company side of the fence. It is also possible that unaffiliated researchers might be permitted to examine some of the organizing campaign materials stored by the antagonists. Since the police of municipality, county, and state get involved from time to time in matters connected with organizing campaigns, such as strike activity and surveillance of organizers, there may be materials stored in files that would be of value to students of labor–management conflict.

Evaluation of the Participant-as-Observer Role

I can offer only a cursory evaluation of the role of participant-as-observer in field investigation, owing to limitations of space and my own research experience. I find that the observing participant has certain rather obvious advantages in comparison with the complete participant and the participating observer. There are also, I have discovered, certain handicaps or problems connected with my favorite role, some of which may have special connection with the study of social conflict from the minority side of the fence. In addition, I have arrived at the tentative conclusion that my Ernie Pyling approach shares with other kinds of participant observation some necessary functions of social research that are inadequately performed with nonparticipatory procedures of inquiry.

First of all, as I indicated earlier, I would give a high joy-in-work rating to the role of participant-as-observer in comparison with other field-study techniques with which I am familiar. I appreciate the freedom of movement, the ability to go where the action is, lacking in the role of complete participant, as well as the freedom from boring work. It may be possible for the complete participant to overcome the usual problem of limited range of observation by selecting a job that places him at the hub of interaction. In one fortunate job placement in a large expensive restaurant I was assigned duties that kept me close to the chef, at the very center of the web of communication. As kettle-washer for a man who dirtied a lot of cooking paraphernalia, I could unobtrusively take it all in as I scrubbed pots and stoves and refrigerators and mopped floors. The chef was the beloved leader of the kitchen crew, in hostile relationship with white-collar management. In important respects the situation was similar to my activities in union research, when I attached myself to the organizer in charge of a union organizing campaign. Still, there were the long hours at my own tedious work role, my inability to press the chef and members of his staff with out-of-work role questions, and the ever present danger of being caught applying stubby pencil to pocket notebook. Running around with organizers has been far more exciting. The comparison may be a bit unfair here, with research procedures entangled with subject matters. The work of the organizer seems intrinsically more interesting than that of the scullion or the factory hand. Perhaps I would find complete participation as an organizer even more absorbing than participation as an observer in an organizing campaign.

A possible disadvantage of my favorite research role appears to lie in the combination of an Ernie Pyling data-gathering approach with the substantive area of social conflict. This handicap would in all likelihood be shared by any research procedures that involved participation with one of two warring parties; the researcher finds himself persona non grata with the opposition. This kind of consequence should be given serious consideration by the prospective Ernie Pyler, especially in situations such as union–management conflict, where the stakes are high, a heavy line of societal cleavage is maintained, and one side possesses a preponderance of power, with ramifications of the ascendancy extending through many aspects of life. In the South "union" is openly recognized by a majority of the people, including nearly all of those who count, as a dirty word. In other regions of the United States too, I am led to suspect, the influential circles of business, industry, and the professions regard labor unions as unacceptable in both practice and principle. No matter how conservatively they are led, the potential challenge of labor unions to concentrations of power is there. Early in my research on union campaigns I was warned by a managerial representative of one of our large industrial organizations that my association with union organizers might cut me off permanently from rewarding relationships with managerial America; and a University of Chicago Ph.D. failed to acquire a teaching position in a small southern college when he expressed a desire to live near me in order to share my research interests.

In addition to other reputed weaknesses of participant observation, the likelihood of bias in the gathering of data by Ernie Pyling procedures must concern members of the sociological fraternity. Granting that there is danger of bias in all research, because we can't keep the researcher out of his equations, and that the probabilities of distortion are increased when affiliatory feelings are involved, I would suggest that the ultimate goal of scientists, theory that works, will eventually provide its own correctives. Aware of the pragmatic necessities of the logic of science that we all must face eventually, the social researcher who seeks to make contributions that will further the development of his craft and add building material to the house of knowledge will take care to separate his emotional attachments to people and causes from the hypotheses he is testing. It is not likely that the sociologist who has spent years in his investigations would insouciantly risk seeing his work go down the drain by allowing prejudice to sway scientific caution. In my view, perhaps a naïve one, the challenge and excitement of creativity involved in concept and theory construction affords an overwhelming counterforce to any motivation to express a substantive bias.

Relatively minor problems do pop up from time to time during the course of an investigation involving participation. For the most part these special difficulties are mere embarrassments. For instance, as an observing participant trying to preserve the modicum of dignity expected of a university researcher, I have been put to the poise test by male factory workers who call out in loud voices to female workers, "Here he comes, girls! Watch out – don't let him get behind you!" It is also difficult to carry on unruffled in the midst of a picket-line crowd when an organizer announces loudly for the benefit of three or four state policemen who are monitoring the situation, "Professor Roy is with us today to witness this travesty of justice!" When shift change brings arrival and departure of carloads of strikebreakers through the picket line amid the jeers, catcalls, and threatening gestures of the strikers, and an organizer calls out, "You can yell at the scabs too, Professor!" – then I am not only embarrassed by the presence of state troopers, but also made slightly uneasy by the hard stares of some of the strikers, who note for the first time that I have not been yelling at the scabs too. In fact, I am chronically faced with small decisions in regard to degree of participation. It is not difficult to avoid the kind of participation that might have appreciable influence on the outcome of a campaign, but sticky situations involving the appearances of affiliation keep coming up. In labor–management conflict in the South there are no neutrals. People are on one side or the other, and to the pro-union worker, already feeling somewhat paranoid from his perceived persecution, the nonsupportive stranger might well be a company spy. Organizers seem to understand and accept the research function; they are pleased to help the researcher get the facts. It is the occasional mill hand, or group of mill hands, that creates temporary embarrassment. I say temporary, because I have always been able to count on the intervention of an organizer to allay the suspicions of workers.

During the early days of one very bitter strike I looked around while eating a hamburger in a small restaurant near the picket line to find myself hemmed in by a semicircle of staring, angry eyes. Recognizing in the encircling group the faces of several inflexible members of the M Squad, an auxiliary of enforcers for the striker cause, I headed, sensibly, for union headquarters, two blocks away. There I exchanged ol'-buddy greetings with the organizer in charge. He explained my presence to the half-dozen M squaders who had silently escorted me to the hall, and later, with inappropriate cheerfulness, he informed me of the plot to assault me, checked and finally abandoned when I made a beeline for the union stronghold. I have endured anxious moments at mass meetings and at committee meetings when jittery workers have announced "There's a spy in our midst! The bosses know everything that goes on in these meetings!" In most instances, however, no one questions my presence, and the organizer will assure me privately after the meeting that I am not the suspect and that "any time over five people get together, one of them is a spy."

During the past year I have had to put up with a new sort of uneasiness. I have been observing the organizing of a local union composed largely of

Negro women, and since Negro women in the South characteristically do not own automobiles, I am asked by organizers to help with the transportation problem after evening meetings. I am, of course, glad to build up acceptance of my research role with such minor services. However, occasionally my last passenger is an attractive young woman who lives across town from the next-to-last drop, or several miles out in the country. I can imagine what the situation might seem like to passing motorists, or to pedestrians if I acquired motor trouble or a flat tire. At such times I am torn between my desire to get the young lady to her home as quickly as possible and my fear of attracting the attention of the police if I go over the speed limit.

A more serious sort of anxiety swept over me one night last year during my observation of interaction between scabs and strikers at a midnight shift change. The crowd of strikers was small at that hour. The second-shift strike-breakers had driven on past them, through the usual verbal onslaught, but with the ample protection of four armed state patrolmen. One of the strikers, assigned the job of counting the cars, announced to the others that there were a dozen or so automobiles unaccounted for in the night exodus; they must be still in there, waiting for the strikers to leave. The strikers decided to pretend to depart, thus drawing off the state patrolmen, who would be only too glad to conclude a trying day. By circling back after the police had left, the strikers could handle the remaining scabs in more relaxed fashion. The police left, as predicted, and we didn't have long to wait before the first of a line of cars appeared. When the rocks started to fly, I found myself in an awkward situation. What if the police weren't as dumb as the strikers thought they were, saw through the ruse, and returned to pack us off to jail? What was I doing, at my age and with all those diplomas, shoulder to shoulder with a bunch of men throwing rocks at a bunch of other men in the middle of the night? I didn't have time to go to jail. I had to get back to Durham no later than the next day, back to my classes, to my eager students. Should I make a brisk dash for the cover of yon cornfield before the police returned? Could I make it, before getting shot, if they should return immediately? Surely the first car in the caravan of dented bodies and fenders would have reached a telephone by now. But if I streaked for the cornfield, the strikers would see it, and such behavior would mark the end of my study of union–management relations in these parts, perhaps in the entire South. Maybe it would be better if I were to start throwing things myself, before the strikers noticed my inactivity and interpreted it as anti-union behavior; for there was no organizer on the scene to explain sociological research. I made my decision. Sweating freely – it was a warm night – I ran back and forth with the strikers, stooping and swaying and swinging my arms in a balletic imitation of a man throwing rocks. Finally the last car screamed around the bend in the road. With my companions I made a rapid but dignified dash for my own automobile. The cops did not show up.

On the positive side again, the participant-as-observer shares with the complete participant the strong advantage of being able to penetrate the veil of public relations that is such an impediment to the one-shot interviewer, with distortion of response especially characteristic of situations where forthright answers to the questions of the inquisitorial stranger might lead to unpleasant consequences. A bit of dramaturgy may be encountered from time to time, most of all in the early stages of an investigation; but in the ordinary course of events acceptance comes, trust deepens, the guard drops, the researcher can move about freely to interview as he wishes, and he can get honest answers to his direct probing.

The opportunity to build a relationship of trust with the organizer, and with others deeply involved with the organizing process, may lead not only to effective interviewing, but also to effective observation. The organizer, as a skilled practitioner possessed of acquaintance knowledge, knows more than he can tell.[12] By moving over the campaign scene and living through the campaign process with the organizer, trying to see what he sees as he in turn tries to explain it all, the researcher can, to a degree, acquire a vicarious grasp of his mentor's know-how. He can fill in the contextual details in their spatial configurations to get, in Susanne Langer's words, "the picture."[13] And, by maintaining his interviewing and observing relationship over a period of time, he can see a moving picture with its axial strand, the story, which gives the changing contextual configurations of episodes their meaning.[14] The observer of organizing campaigns may thus gain an apprehension of the perceptions, or "act-meanings,"[15] of those who participate in the intersubjective world of labor–management conflict. From his *Verstehen* of the common-sense meanings of everyday life, the fieldworker may be able to offer "comprehensive gross descriptions"[16] of human behavior that ring true when read back to participants of his special world of investigation.

The researcher will also know more than he can tell when he essays verbal description of the campaign; but since he is a scientist, his problem goes beyond that of accurate representation. The researcher's task is to transcend his acquired acquaintance knowledge to establish the inferential linkages, or, as Kaplan would term it, the "action-meanings,"[17] that constitute scientific explanation. While accepting Dewey's counsel that "acquaintance knowledge is frequently *not* knowledge in the sense of being warrantably assertable,"[18] and Kaplan's warning that "familiarity helps us see an explanation, but it does not necessarily help us have one,"[19] I press the claim that the *Verstehen* of acquaintance knowledge, acquired by participant observation, provides the soundest base, as well as the most fruitful source, for the engendering of action-meanings in human affairs. I would stress, with Alfred Schutz, the function of common-sense constructions of the reality of everyday life as "thought objects" in the determination of human behavior,[20] averring that such *a priori* conceptions in perception – or "symbolic pregnancies"[21] – provide salient constituents in the kind of problematic situations[22] that sociology must face. In the closing pages of his *magnum opus, The Philosophy of Symbolic Forms,* Ernst Cassirer notes that "in its beginnings the theoretical concept clings to perception as though to exhaust it, as though to gain possession of all the reality it contains."[23] And in a summary statement he says:

The history of exact science teaches us over and over that only such concepts as have grown out of the very source of thought have ultimately proved equal to experience. We may say, with an image borrowed from the language of chemistry, that sensory intuition acts as a catalyst for the development of scientific theory. It is indispensable for the process of exact concept formation.[24]

Notes

1. Buford Junker, *Field Work: An Introduction to the Social Sciences* (Chicago: University of Chicago Press, 1960).

2. Raymond L. Gold, "Roles in Sociological Field Observations," *Social Forces*, 36 (March 1958): 221.

3. Marion Pearsall, "Participant Observation as Role and Method in Behavioral Research," *Nursing Research*, 14, no. I (Winter 1965): 38.

4. Gold, "Roles in Sociological Field Observations."

5. Pearsall, "Participant Observation as Role and Method."

6. *Ibid.*

7. See Ernie Pyle, *Here Is Your War* (New York: Pocket Books, 1944).

8. Abraham Kaplan, *The Conduct of Inquiry* (San Francisco: Chandler, 1964), pp. 358–63.

9. John Dewey, *The Quest for Certainty* (New York: Minton, Balch, 1929).

10. Mao Tse-tung, *Selected Works* (Peking: Foreign Languages Press, 1965), vol. 1, pp. 295–309.

11. "NLRB Decisions," *Labor Law Reporter 1968-1 CCH*, p. 29857.

12. See Michael Polanyi, *The Tacit Dimension* (New York: Anchor Books, Doubleday, 1967), pp. 4–11.

13. Susanne K. Langer, *Philosophy in a New Key* (New York: Mentor Books, 1948), pp. 87–88.

14. See John Dewey, *Experience and Nature* (Chicago: Open Court Publishing Co., 1925), p. 307.

15. Kaplan, *Conduct of Inquiry*, p. 360.

16. Arthur F. Bentley, *Behavior, Knowledge, Fact* (Bloomington, Ind.: Principia Press, 1935), p. 322.

17. Kaplan, *Conduct of Inquiry*, p. 331.

18. John Dewey, *Logic: The Theory of Inquiry* (New York: Holt, 1938), p. 152.

19. Kaplan, *Conduct of Inquiry*, p. 331.

20. Alfred Schutz, "Common Sense and Scientific Interpretation of Human Action," *Philosophy and Phenomenological Research*, 14, no. I (September 1953): 3.

21. Ernst Cassirer, *The Philosophy of Symbolic Forms*, (New Haven: Yale University Press, 1957), vol. 3, *The Phenomenology of Knowledge*, p. 202.

22. Dewey, *Logic*, pp. 107–108.

23. Cassirer, *Philosophy of Symbolic Forms*, vol. 3, p. 451.

24. *Ibid.*, p. 416.

15

Playing Back the Tape: Early Days in the Field

John Van Maanen

I t is neatly the case that persons under the eye of an avowed researcher may well act in ways knowledgeable of this fact. This principle has been documented so many times that any statement attesting to its presence is now a methodological cliché. What is often overlooked, however, is the implicit reciprocity embedded in the cliché. That is, while researchers attend to the study of other persons and their activities, these others attend to the study of researchers and their activities. An underlying theme of the confessional and cautionary tale I tell here is that the success of any fieldwork endeavor depends inherently on the results of the unofficial study the observed undertake of the observer.

My own research takes place in police agencies, where for the past 20 years I have been in and out of various research roles. Primarily from the bottom up, I have been trying to make sense out of the police life, its consequences for the people who live it and for those subject to it. Like my own, it is a life patterned by the society in which it is located and by the specific organizations that, in imperfect ways, direct it. Significantly, a large body of writing relevant to the police life, policing as an activity, and police organizations in general has been generated through ethnographic fieldwork of the sort I practice. This chapter is about some of my practices as played out in the early days of my work with the police.

Framing my remarks is the view that social researchers are typically aliens in the worlds they study, if only because of their supposed double-edged and academic interests in these worlds. Fieldwork amplifies such strangeness because the researcher comes into the setting as an uninvited, unknown guest, carrying a suitcase, wearing an uncertain smile, and prepared for a long stay (Sanday, 1979). Moreover, the work routines of a field-worker, what Agar (1980) calls a "professional stranger," are rather unnatural or at least unusual ones in most settings – hanging around, snooping, engaging in seemingly idle

Source: William B. Shaffir & Robert A. Stebbins (eds), *Experiencing Fieldwork* (Newbury Park, CA: Sage, 1991).

chitchat, note taking, asking odd (often dumb) questions, pushing for dis-closures on matters that may be a source of embarrassment to some on the scene, and so forth. In image and in fact, the activities that fill out the eth-nographic curiosity represent a most uncommon adult role in virtually any social setting.

In strong form, the role carries with it a social stigma that can potentially discredit the field-worker who embodies the role. Much of a fieldworker's behavior – particularly during the initial stages of a lengthy, live-in project – can be understood as an attempt to manage this stigma so that it does not loom large in everyday interaction and its potential is never fully realized. In weak form, the field-worker is in a betwixt-and-between position, akin to any newcomer on the studied scene who must undergo a shift from outsider to insider, recruit to member, observer to participant. Understanding fieldwork from this angle requires coming to terms with the characteristic problems faced by neophytes everywhere (Jackson, 1990). Both of these perspectives are applied below as I play back some of the actions that marked my initial en-counters in the police world.

Rationalizing Fieldwork

My work began with a nine-month stay in the field. From the beginning, my official interest in police organizations has been presented to others in the form of a most practical logic. In 1969, for example, I wrote in my the-sis proposal:

> The police are quite possibly the most vital of our human service agen-cies. Certainly they are the most visible and active institution of social control, representing the technological and organizational answer to the question of social order. Through their exclusive mandate to intervene directly into the lives of the citizenry, the police are crucial actors in both our everyday and ceremonial affairs. As such, they deserve inten-sive and continual scientific study for their role and function in society is far too important to be taken-for-granted, or worse, ignored.

Such high-sounding sentiment provides a sort of doctrinaire or ideologi-cal canopy to cover my work. Although rooted in an appealing common sense, it is a woefully inadequate sociological explanation for my work on at least two counts. First, because I conveniently ignore what is to be explained or how such explanations might be forthcoming, my research (and fieldwork) is being used only rhetorically, to establish my credibility and moral authority. The logic of the statement is Olympian and can be read as an inverted Pogo-like aphorism: "I have found the solution and the solution is me." It is, in brief, a gate-opening ploy designed to persuade, not to establish purpose. Second, research canopies such as my formal statement carefully play down the fact

that research is both a social and personal act. It is subject to the same bio-
graphically and situationally specific understandings by which any individual
act is made sensible.

In my case, I began thinking of the police for a research topic in the late
1960s. Whether damned or praised, the police were then prominently fixed
in the public imagination as crucial actors in the dramas of the day. I found
the police intriguing in that cultural moment for no doubt the same reasons
that had occurred to other intellectual types – journalists, novelists, and historians (e.g., Mailer, 1968; Rubinstein, 1973; Wambaugh, 1970). Nor were the
police being ignored by my sociological kin (e.g., Bittner, 1970; Manning, 1972;
Reiss, 1971; Skolnick, 1966). The police were, in the vernacular, happening
and hot and, therefore, dramaturgically attractive to me. Closer to home,
however, I also had grown up subject to what I regarded as more than my
share of police attention and hence viewed the police with a little loathing,
some fear, and considerable curiosity. Nor were such feelings devoid of analytic supposition. I did not go to the field out of affection for the police. In
many ways, I had it in for them as I packed my bags.

The general point here is that despite the conversions sure to occur with
field experience, it is important for the would-be (and wanna-be) fieldworker
to recognize as legitimate the personal matters that lead one into a project.
Moreover, I suspect staying with a lengthy project may have more to do with
the emotional pull and attraction of a given setting on the field-worker than
with any abstracted notions of disciplinary aims such as the conventional one
of "making a contribution to the field." There is always a person standing behind the research project, but the standard vocabularies of motive associated
with the social research trades often preclude the public appearance of such
a person.

Also at play during the early phases of fieldwork is the emergence of methodological ideals and a heightened self-consciousness. Method textbooks are
of some comfort, but perhaps the most helpful advice to be found in print
comes from carefully combing the prefaces and personal asides written (occasionally) by those who have field experience in the setting of interest. In
my own work, the words of police researcher William Westley (1970) were
particularly striking:

> There was a terrible tension in the flow of this semi-participant research,
> for to understand, he had to sympathize; but, in attempting to sympa-
> thize, he wanted to be liked. To be liked, he had to play by their rules
> and not ask too many questions. Thus, the work went in waves of care-
> fully building up confidences and inevitably becoming involved in their
> regard, then asking questions, sharp probing questions that soon caused
> rejection. This proved to be personally painful, in the sense that there-
> after he had to push himself on men who he felt disliked and were afraid
> of him and, practically disastrous, since if the men refused to talk to
> him, the research would stop. (p. vii)

The practical significance of such accounts are, I hasten to add, rather slight. Westley's words were riveting only after some of my perhaps overly eager fieldwork gestures failed to open up conversations (or, conversely, worked to close them down). Cautionary tales may alert one to a few of the situational demands of fieldwork, but they hardly offer much guidance as to how one will personally answer and remain alive to such demands. Thus, although Howard Becker's (1965) classic query, "whose side are you on" (p. 239) went with me to the field, what it meant when I arrived there was entirely another matter.

Two concrete and apparently common problems cast shadows over the early stages of fieldwork in organizational settings. First, because fieldworkers typically force themselves through a third party – in my case, the high officials of the studied police agency – into the life situations of others, they must first disassociate themselves as best they can from the interest and control the third party may have over those who are studied. Second, field-workers must recognize that they cannot offer very much of obvious value to those who are studied. As such, there are few, if any, compelling reasons for people to participate in their studies. I could not reasonably claim to be able to cure police problems, teach the police very much, or influence their respective careers. The problem at both levels is to find people for whom one's practiced cover story for the research makes sense and for whom one's presence is not too great a burden.

To move into the flow of events that characterize the work and social situations of those studied requires the assistance of a few reasonably knowledgeable and reliable guides. They run interference for the field-worker, provide testimony as to the field-worker's aims and character, and, in general, offer member interpretations for the passing scene such that the field-worker can assume lines of conduct that are more or less acceptable to others in the setting. Securing such assistance is a delicate and never-ending task. It is not a single, immutable role a field-worker builds, but an emergent and many-sided one. With many patrolmen, for example, I wanted to appear as a humble, helpful sort, the proverbial "good guy" who would not be likely to do anyone harm. I did little favors for people, provided a sympathetic ear, and when they discussed the topics to which the men of the police culture invariably turned when filling up their day – sex, sports, cars – I joined in eagerly with my own two cents worth.

I tried also to display a good deal of circumspection in relation to what I heard and saw. I wanted to learn the ordinary standards of performance, not establish, recite, or mock them. In a sense, I sought to be accepted by others in the role of an appreciative student or worthy apprentice and sought explicitly to disclaim the judgmental prerogatives commonly associated with a research or expert role (Van Maanen & Kolb, 1984). Yet any form of sustained inquiry implies an evaluative framework – even if one is no more than a reluctant witness. Distrust, suspicion, and guarded conduct cannot be dispelled simply by assuming a sort of "good guy" stance.

The obvious point here is that fieldwork turns not on claims, candor, or mutual regard per se, but on trust. Conventional theories of trust locate its origins in the person toward whom it is directed rather than in the particular occasions of its appearance. This view is, I think, quite misleading not only because it glosses over the ebb and flow of trust over time, but also because it reduces the field-worker or confidant to something of a doofus or cipher, an altogether accommodating sort of nonperson, totally embraced by a research role. Trust underlies all social interaction. In the field, it is built slowly and comes forth only in particular situations with particular people as the field-worker displays a practical understanding, a partisan stance, and a visible conformance to the forms of conduct followed by those studied.

To demonstrate competence in the performances appropriate to a specific social setting does not mean that the field-worker must engage in some sort of echolalia, imitating gesture for gesture and thought for thought the actions of others on the scene. Nor does it mean that one should take a servile stance toward others. In the police world, both orientations would be inappropriate. The first would be detected quickly as phony and resented because no one likes to be mimicked. The second would jar the refined sense of propriety among the police, who in general interpret weakness or lack of opinion and judgment on the part of another as a sure sign of moral decay. Competence consists of hanging on to a part of one's own identity and style while staying within the boundaries of tolerable behavior as established by those on the scene. Strategy, however, can go only so far.

Disagreeable and unapproachable people are sure to be among those with whom the field-worker must deal. Not everyone is equally open or receptive to the field-worker's presence. Nor is it the case that relationships in the field should be – even in the ideal – random, representative, or equal. Members of the studied world are hardly equivalent in the knowledge they possess. Field-workers do not want to become close to just anyone, but rather want to count among their associates the more open, knowledgeable, comfortable, good-natured, well-placed, and articulate members of the organization. The fact is, however, that informants probably select the researcher as much as the researcher selects them. There is a rather impenetrable barrier between what a grizzled 58-year old street cop will tell a green pea regardless whether the green pea is a rookie patrolman or a merry field-worker. Glimpses of these boundaries are provided by some snippets of unambiguous rejection recorded in my fieldnotes:

What do you expect to learn from me? I'm another cabbage around here just trying to lay low and keep outta trouble. Go talk to the blue-light-and-siren boys, they've got the corner on the action. Me? I don't do any police work anymore, haven't for twenty years I'd say.

Stay outta my life, Van Maanen. I don't have nothing to say to you and you don't have nothing to say to me. I'm putting in my time…. I don't know what you want and I wouldn't give a shit even if I did. You mind your business and I'll mind mine.

Sociologists? Shit. You're supposed to know what's going on around here. Christ, you come on asking questions like we're the fucking problem. Why don't you go study the goddamn niggers and find out what's wrong with them? They're the fucking problem, not us. I haven't met a sociologist yet who'd make a pimple on a street cop's ass.

Testing the Field-Worker

The field-worker's biographical particulars (both fixed and variable) and the situationally specific suppositions (including the unarticulated sort) carried by those in the setting interact, of course, in uncountable ways. Moreover, the biographical particulars and situationally specific suppositions that matter most to others are precisely what the fieldworker has gone into the field to locate. Understanding why and where one's presence is likely to bring forth an "oh fuck, here he comes again" response on the part of others is not merely a tactical consideration. A good part of fieldwork is simply paying attention to the impressions one's location, words, and activities cast off. Being out of line or, more crudely, making an ass of oneself is an operational indicator of subjecting oneself to the life situation of others. From this perspective, field-workers are concerned not only with what is revealed explicitly by others but also with the conditional properties that appear to lubricate (or jam) such revelations. Sharpening one's character in the field is both a means of inquiry and, when recognized, an end. Consider now some setting-specific features of my fieldwork with the police.

My entrance into the police world was intended to be similar to that of any recruit. I made no effort to conceal my identity or the general purposes behind my work – although the meaning of this work for those who knew me or of me was no doubt highly variable. In the beginning, I was provided a uniform, a reservist badge and number, a departmental-issue .32-caliber revolver, and a slot in the police academy training class. From an insider's perspective, passage through the academy represents the first common and fundamental test of membership. Few fail, although reputations can be earned in the academy that live long lives. For a field-worker as for a recruit, academy life provided an instant set of cohorts, a source and sense of identification with the agency, and a few but precious friends.

Following graduation, I moved to the street and assumed a less participative role, though on my body I still carried a badge and gun. These symbols of membership signified to others my public commitment to share the risks of the police life. Aside from a few special events, parades, and civic ceremonies where uniformed bodies were in short supply, I was, as the police said, out of the bag. I dressed for the street as I thought plainclothes officers might

– heavy and hard-toed shoes, slit or clip-on ties, and loose-fitting jackets that would not make conspicuous the bulge of my revolver. I carried with me chemical Mace, handcuffs, assorted keys, extra bullets, and sometimes a two-way portable radio and a concealed two-inch revolver loaned to me by co-workers who felt that I should be properly prepared.

My plainclothes but altogether coplike appearance created some status confusion for citizens who took me for another officer, perhaps a ranking one. On the streets, citizens would often direct their comments to me. I usually deflected these comments back toward my police companions. On occasion, however, there was no one to deflect such comments back to because my companions were busy elsewhere. At such moments, I more or less bumbled through the encounter by doing what I thought would be approved by my workmates. Mistakes were common.

Crucial to the matter of gaining some acceptance within the agency is what both the police and I have labeled a "balls test" – an assessment made by veteran police officers as to the willingness of a rookie, gender notwithstanding, to support a fellow officer physically. Although all policemen accept colleagues whom they criticize for their odd views, dishonesty, personal habits, or character, they will not tolerate a colleague in their midst whom they consider dangerous to their health and safety.

For a field-worker alongside the police, this test was, without doubt, far less extreme than it was for the fully committed. There were instances, however, where I felt it necessary to assist – in police parlance, to back up – the patrolmen whom I was ostensibly observing. At such moments, I was hardly making the rational, reasoned choice in light of the instrumental research objectives I had set. I was reacting as the police react to the unavoidable contingencies of unfolding events. Whether or not I passed these tests with colors flying or dragging is a matter of retrospective opinion. I can say that after a time, most men seemed to accept my presence in the department and appeared at ease when I worked a shift with them.

It is also worth noting that the height of moral duplicity would be to create this sort of partnership impression among the people one studies and then refuse to act in line with the implicit bargain such an impression conveys. For me to pose as a friend of the police and then not back them up on a potentially risky encounter, an encounter they may well have undertaken only because of the additional safety they believed my presence provided, would be to violate the very premises of field research and the importance that human relationships play in its enactment.

Prudence is another tested aspect of the research role. Virtually all policemen have engaged in activities that, if known to some, could get them fired, or, worse, land them in jail. A field-worker who spends more than a trivial amount of time among the police quickly discovers this. A glib statement attesting to one's confidential intents will not be taken at face value. Polite acceptance or even deep friendship is not sufficient to get one into the back regions of police departments. Only practical tests will demonstrate one's trustworthiness; liking a person is no guarantee that one can also trust them.

I was party to much discrediting information regarding the legality and propriety of police action. On occasion, I was present when illegal acts took place and, as such, I was as culpable legally as any witness to such actions. One tactic of neutralizing the power of observation is to involve the faultless in potentially embarrassing acts, thus making the faultless as vulnerable to sanction as others. Debts and obligations are, therefore, equalized and discretion becomes almost a structural and taken-for-granted matter. On and following these troublesome incidents, the choices I made followed police custom: I kept my mouth shut.

Less crucial perhaps were other rather individually tailored forms of character testing. Early in my police academy days, for example, I was given a series of "gigs" – punitive assignments – for what I took to be fabricated offenses: jogging, not running, from the parking lot to the academy classroom; yawning, stretching, and not paying attention in class; whispering to others; and presenting a dirty weapon at morning inspection. In a short time, I had amassed enough gigs relative to others in the class to convince myself that the academy staff was pushing to find out just how attached I was to my studies. Privately bitching, I plodded through without great clamor and, by so doing, rediscovered the universal irony of direct social control. By serving as the target for discipline administered by one group, I became entrenched more firmly within the protective circle of another group, thus making control, in the end, far more problematic.

As one might surmise, I think neutrality in fieldwork is an illusion. Neutrality is itself a role enactment and the meaning of such a role to people will, most assuredly, not be neutral. Only by entering into the webs of local associations does the field-worker begin to understand the distinctive nature of what lies within and without these webs. The field-worker's initial tasks involve finding out what classes of people are present on the scene and trying to figure out the cleavages that operate within these classes. There is unlikely to be much of a honeymoon period in fieldwork, for in short order the field-worker will have to decide which of the inner circles and classes to accept as his or her own.

By staking out a particular research patch, a field-worker soon learns that much of the concern and information in one segment of the organization is about another segment. Even among my confidants, talk was more readily forthcoming about someone else's patrol unit, squad, shift, or division. People apparently are far more willing to hold forth on the alleged secrets of others than they are their own. By collecting such tales and noting the regions within which they fell, I was, of course, far more worried about marking the boundaries than with assessing the truth of any given story. Truth in fieldwork, as in life, lies in the eyes of the beholder. The beholders of my work have been, by and large, street cops for whom the adage "there ain't that much truth around" represents the human condition.

In sum, the majority of my time in the police field has been spent within the patrol division and, in particular, with specific squads and shifts within the division. Moreover, I have spent far more time with some squad members than others. These officers were my guides in both the sponsorship and informational senses of the term. They positioned me in the department and suggested to others where precisely my loyalties and sentiments lay. The ecological rights to be close to them, in a sense, were gained early on but had to be sustained continually. A good part of this proximity was attributable to a novitiate's willingness to live with all the good and bad things that took place within this distinct work circle. Understanding, from this perspective, is not mysterious or analytic but rather pragmatic and empathetic. It comes largely from being caught up in the same life situation and circumstances as those one studies. One knows how others feel because one feels it, too.

The Field-Worker's Conceit

This last point is, alas, a conceit. Although field-workers attempt to get as close to others as possible and then stay there for awhile, it is the case that they can pick up and go whenever they choose. Though they may act as though this is impossible, such restraint is always an act. This reflects a basic distinction between the member's "native understanding" and the field-worker's "specimen understanding" of the social world they both share for a time (Bittner, 1973). Although I believe I have learned to think like a cop, I still can stand back and critique that particular frame of mind from another – safe – position. This is a curious and privileged state of mind, not at all characteristic of many men and women I know in the police world who, of practical necessity, take for granted as fact much of what I regard as relative matters. To suggest that I have come to understand the police world as the police themselves do would be a grave error. I do not have to live with the results of police action in the same way as those I study must. The result is that field-workers, by moving in and out of distinct social worlds, come to regard the factual validity of the studied worlds as far more subjective and conjured than many members do.

Not all members fit this rather vulgar characterization. Certainly some are tuned as finely, if not more so, to the stranger's perspective as the field-worker. Double agents, immigrants, marginal members, skeptical tourists, spies, missionaries out to make over the organization, inside theorists and critics, court jesters, and even fellow sociologists (in and out of uniform) often are not hard to locate within a studied scene. In many respects, they all share a common project with the field-worker – spoken or not – which is to question and thus underline the reality claims made by other more central, self-satisfied, and powerful organizational members, both high caste and low. Fieldwork as practiced at home in familiar institutions is almost inevitably a subversive and, to a degree, collective project.

There is a final irony worth noting in this respect because I have come to believe that successful fieldwork depends on being able for a time to forget (or, at least, overcome) this standard fieldwork plot. Indeed, one implication to be drawn from the body of this chapter is that field-workers should cut their lives down to the bone on entrance to a field setting by removing themselves from resources – physical, social, and intellectual – outside the studied scene. Every social world provides something of a distinctive life for people and the best way to gain access to such a life is to need it by not importing a life of one's own (Goffman, 1989). Cutting one's self off for a time and looking to build a life with one's new colleagues means that penetration is achieved when the field-worker puts down the subversive project, the notebook and pen, the decentered attitude carried into the scene and begins to anticipate as unremarkable and welcome the daily sights and sounds, to appreciate, if not enjoy, life among the studied, to joke back and forth across the membership, to move at the same tempo as his or her companions, to find comfort in work routines established by others, and to not be sought out by would-be donors of trade secrets or critical tales.

All of this unfolds as a highly personal, contingent, temporal process. If one were to wind the tape back to the early days of my fieldwork and let it play again from an identical starting point, I think the chances are astonishingly low that anything like the same study would grace the replay. Obviously, with the luxury of hindsight, sweet reason and rule can be marshaled out to frame much of my actions in the field. Yet reader beware: Self-justification and surely self-parody lurk just beneath the surface in confessional tales. When called on to scrutinize our past, we quite naturally merge the question of what we did with the question of what we should have done, and the answer to one becomes the answer to the other. There is no way to duck this matter and no way to calibrate just how self-serving we have been until perhaps our written-about natives decide to start writing about us and putting on display some of our own odd and exotic ways. At that point, the subjective and conjured features of our own research world and work can come to be appreciated.

References

Agar, Michael. (1980). *The professional stranger*. New York: Academic Press.

Becker, Howard S. (1965). Whose side are we on? *Social Problems*, 14, 239–247.

Bittner, Egon. (1970). *The functions of the police in modern society*. Washington, DC: U.S. Government Printing Office.

—— (1973). Objectivity and realism in sociology. In G. Psathas (Ed.), *Phenomenological sociology* (pp. 108–125). New York: John Wiley.

Goffman, Erving. (1989). On fieldwork. [Transcribed and edited by Lyn H. Lofland]. *Journal of Contemporary Ethnography*, 18, 123–132.

Jackson, Jean E. (1990). Déjà Entendu: The liminal qualities of anthropological fieldnotes. *Journal of Contemporary Ethnography*, 19, 8–44.

Mailer, Norman. (1968). *The armies of the night*. New York: New American Library.

Manning, Peter K. (1972). Observing the police. In J.D. Douglas (Ed.), *Research on deviance* (pp. 213–268). New York: Random House.

Reiss, Albert J. (1971). *The police and the public*. New Haven, CT: Yale University Press.

Rubinstein, Jonathan. (1973). *City police*. New York: Farrar, Straus & Giroux.

Sanday, Peggy. (1979). The ethnographic paradigm(s). *Administrative Science Quarterly*, 24, 482–493.

Skolnick, Jerome. (1966). *Justice without trial*. New York: John Wiley.

Van Maanen, John, & Kolb, Deborah. (1984). The professional apprentice. In S.B. Bacharach (Ed.), *Perspectives in organizational sociology* (pp. 1–33). Greenwich, CT: JAI.

Wambaugh, Joseph. (1970). *The new centurions*. New York: Norton.

Westley, William A. (1970). *Violence and the police*. Cambridge: MIT Press.

Author's Related Publications

Van Maanen, J. (1973). Observations on the making of policemen. *Human Organization*, 32, 407–418.

—— (1974). Working the street. In H. Jacobs (Ed.), *The potential for reform of criminal justice* (pp. 83–130). Beverly Hills, CA: Sage.

—— (1975). Police socialization. *Administrative Science Quarterly*, 20, 207–228.

—— (1978). The asshole. In P. K. Manning & J. Van Maanen (Eds.), *Policing: A view from the street* (pp. 221–238). New York: Random House.

—— (1978). Watching the watchers. In P. K. Manning & J. Van Maanen (Eds.), *Policing: A view from the street* (pp. 309–351). New York: Random House.

—— (1981). The informant game. *Urban Life*, 9, 469–494.

—— (1983). The boss. In M. Punch (Ed.), *Control in the police organization* (pp. 275–318). Cambridge: MIT Press.

—— (1984). Making rank. *Urban Life*, 13, 155–176.

—— (1986). Power in the bottle. In S. Srivastva (Ed.), *Executive Power* (pp. 204–239). San Francisco: Jossey-Bass.

—— (1988). *Tales of the field*, Chicago: University of Chicago Press.

16

Decision Taking in the Fieldwork Process: Theoretical Sampling and Collaborative Working

Janet Finch & Jennifer Mason

O ne of the key ways in which qualitative or fieldwork methods differ from social surveys is in the sampling or selection of the people and situations that are studied. In surveys, such decisions are made once-and-for-all at the beginning of a project, and follow formalized statistical procedures for sampling. In fieldwork, such decisions are taken at various stages during the course of the project on the basis of contextual information. To outsiders who are not privy to the changing contextual basis of this project, research decisions can look rather ad hoc.

In this chapter we are going to discuss the questions of whether and how decisions about fieldwork sampling can be taken in a systematic way. We will use our experiences of working together on the research study of Family Obligations to provide the contextual information necessary for a discussion of systematic decision taking.[1] At the time of writing we are at the mid-point of this study with most of the data collected but much of the formal analysis still to be done, so we cannot relate our sampling strategies to our final analysis. However, what we have tried to do is to reflect the blend of practical and intellectual considerations that form the basis of decision taking in the field-work process, at a stage when these are fresh in our minds.

We begin by briefly describing the Family Obligations project before out-lining the principle of theoretical sampling, which represents a possible model of systematic selection in qualitative research. In the main part of this paper we discuss how we attempted to develop and apply this principle in our own research and we use our experience to suggest more generally the problems and possibilities of this approach. A further important theme in our discus-sion is the extent to which working collaboratively facilitates systematic qualitative research.

Source: Robert G. Burgess (ed.), *Studies in Qualitative Methodology*, vol. 2 (Greenwich, CT: JAI Press, 1990).

The Family Obligations Project

Our project involves investigating patterns of support, aid and assistance, of both practical and material kinds, between adult kin in a survey population based in the Greater Manchester area. As well as being interested in patterns of support, we are exploring concepts of obligation and responsibility to assist one's relatives, the circumstances in which these come into play, and the processes through which these are related to actions. We have used a conceptual framework for studying family obligations based on a contrast between two different ways of conceptualizing obligations: as moral norms and as negotiated commitments (Finch, 1987). On the one hand, family obligations might be seen as part of a structure of normative rules that operate within a particular society, and which simply get applied in appropriate situations. On the other hand, they might be seen as agreements that operate between specific individuals and are arrived at through a process of negotiation. This negotiation may be explicit, or more likely may be covert. We would argue that a full understanding of what family obligations mean and how they operate almost certainly contains elements of both of these.

Our perspective suggests that these norms are not really like rigid and precise rules that must be followed, or that are imposed on passive individuals. Rather they are general guidelines for "proper" or "correct" behavior toward one's relatives, which "everyone is aware of," but that need to be interpreted or tailored in specific situations. It is at this level of interpretation that the notion of negotiated commitments comes to the fore: if it is the case that norms are not sufficiently detailed or universally applicable to be used straightforwardly in concrete situations among relatives, then in what ways are actual commitments and responsibilities negotiated? This part of our perspective casts "negotiation" in broad terms, allowing not only for "round the table" explicit negotiations, but also for other processes by which particular patterns of obligation become "obvious" to members of kin groups.

We are not going to discuss the substantive issues in the project here, but it is necessary to give some detail so that we can explain the nature of the decisions that we had to take about selection and sampling. The perspectives upon the study of family obligations that we have outlined here guided the overall planning of the project, and led to a research design that included both a large-scale quantitative survey and also a second stage of qualitative fieldwork, mainly based on in-depth interviews. In the survey we were concentrating solely upon data about normative beliefs, and at the second stage we wanted to use qualitative techniques to understand more about the complexity of beliefs, as well as the relationship between beliefs and actions, and how people actually negotiate commitments with their own relatives.

It is this second stage that we discuss in this chapter, as this was where we were trying to put theoretical sampling into practice. We planned to use the survey population as a sampling frame from which to select individuals for

more detailed study. We had a total survey population of 978 randomly selected individuals over the age of eighteen, of whom 85% had agreed at the
time of the survey that they would be willing to be reinterviewed.[2]

We, therefore, had the possibility either of choosing another randomly selected group for more detailed study or of targeting particular subgroups. A
further consideration was that we hoped to be able, in some cases, not only
to reinterview a survey respondent, but also to interview members of his or
her kin group, thus building up a more complete picture of negotiations within
families. In a sense, therefore, we were operating two levels of selection: interviewees from the survey population, then the kin groups of some of those
interviewees. There was a limitation of numbers in that we had budgeted for
120 interviews at this second stage, but other than that we were free to be
guided by theoretical considerations, and by our preliminary analysis of the
survey data, in deciding whom to interview. However, we needed a strategy
that was very flexible so that we could: (1) change direction as we went along
if necessary, (2) leave open the possibility of doing more than one interview
with some respondents, and (3) maintain the possibility of interviewing other
members of the kin group.

We had, therefore, in effect set ourselves the task of being both flexible
and systematic in our selection of interviewees for the qualitative stage. In
practice this seems commonly to be the aim of much fieldwork based research,
and certainly sits comfortably with a strategy of theoretical sampling.

A Guiding Principle: Theoretical Sampling

What are the main themes in the existing literature on fieldwork that can help
to guide our thinking on this process? In addition to the emphasis upon selection as an on-going process, the two important themes seem to be first the
interplay of theory and data, and second that the analysis of data is a process
that continues throughout the project rather than occurring as a discrete phase
after the data collection is complete. Theory should guide data collection and
the on-going analysis of data should feed back into theory, which in turn guides
the next phase of data collection. Most fieldwork researchers would acknowledge that this is the model to which they aspire, but as other commentators
have noted this process is often not put into practice very effectively, leaving
(and there are often) quite serious gaps between theory and data (Hammersley
and Atkinson 1983, p. 174).

The concept of theoretical sampling is probably the most common way
of translating this model of the research process into guidelines about selection of research situations or informants. Certainly this is the concept that
guided our own thinking and it forms a central focus of this chapter. We offer
an account of our own experience of trying to put into practice the notion of
theoretical sampling, and use this to draw out some general principles about
how qualitative research can be done in a systematic way.

The term "theoretical sampling" is generally associated with Glaser and Strauss's treatise on the discovery of grounded theory (1967), but its logic and practice has become part of a tradition of qualitative research (Bertaux 1981; Schwarz and Jacobs 1979; Baldamus 1972; Hammersley and Atkinson 1983). Essentially, theoretical sampling means selecting a study population on theoretical rather than, say, statistical grounds. The underlying logic is one of analytical rather than enumerative induction which were distinguished many years ago by Znaniecki in the following way:

> Enumerative induction abstracts by generalisation, whereas analytic induction generalises by abstracting. The former looks in many cases for characters that are similar and abstracts them conceptually because of their generality, presuming that they must be essential to each particular case; the latter abstracts from the given concrete case characteristics that are essential to it and generalises them, presuming that insofar as they are essential, they must be similar in many cases (Znaniecki 1934, pp. 250–251).

This means that theoretical sampling involves a search for validity of findings, rather than representativeness of study population. However, for some degree of generalization to be made about the consequent research findings, it is vital that the processes of theoretical sampling (as well as data presentation) be *systematically* carried through and documented.

Yet when viewed apart from its context, certain aspects of theoretical sampling can appear ad hoc and unsystematic. In particular, from a positivist standpoint, where research decisions are made in advance of operationalization and tested through hypotheses on a randomly sampled population, the continual making of decisions throughout the course of the research can itself appear very unsystematic. Of course this is partly because the two endeavors are not entirely comparable: qualitative researchers following theoretical sampling are generally looking to build theory from data rather than to test hypotheses on representative populations. At the same time, however, we are not suggesting that qualitative researchers have license to be unsystematic in their decision making simply because it cannot be done in "one go." Rather, we would emphasize that the validity of the qualitative researcher's interpretations depends in part upon the quality and relevance of their in-process decisions.

But what does this actually mean in practice? How is theoretical sampling *done*? Given that such importance is placed upon in-progress decision making in particular research settings, then it is inappropriate to set down in advance a series of general rules about how to make informed and systematic decisions. Instead we describe below what we did, and on what basis we made our decisions. As well as giving a more situated feel for theoretical sampling, this will in a sense provide the data from which to extrapolate some more general observations at the end.

A Guiding Practice: Collaborative Working

A vital part of the way in which we have put theoretical sampling into practice in the Family Obligations project has been through collaborative working. Neither of us had worked in a close collaboration of this kind before, and, therefore, part of our task was to develop ways of working together effectively. Janet Finch had set up the project and organized the survey fieldwork[3] and Jennifer Mason joined her at the stage when that was completed. It had been agreed that we each would take an equal share in planning and conducting the qualitative fieldwork, but we wanted to ensure that our contributions were fully integrated with each others' and that the fieldwork would be a genuine collaboration. We tried to achieve this in a number of ways.

Joint Discussions and Planning

From the beginning we held regular joint discussions about our plans, strategies and practice. Our early discussions centered on ways of working together, how often we should meet and so on. We decided at that time always to take decisions together about overall strategy and practice. This may seem a rather obvious point to make about collaboration, but we know from our own contacts with other researchers, as well as from a few published accounts, that decisions are not always taken openly and explicitly in research teams, leaving the opportunity for misunderstandings and disagreements to arise about what strategy is actually being followed (Platt 1976; Bell 1977; Porter 1984).

Division of Labor

One aspect of our practice that we have always discussed, rather than assumed, is our division of labor. Jennifer Mason was employed for three years full-time on the Family Obligations project, and Janet Finch, who holds a full-time university teaching post, had arranged to have one year seconded to the research project. This meant that our first year of working together could involve collaboration on a full-time basis for both of us. One of the reasons Janet Finch had set up the project timing and staffing in this way was so that she could maintain a full involvement in the fieldwork stage, and the research process that we discuss in this chapter all took place during that time.

Therefore, when discussing our fieldwork division of labor we could take an equal share of the tasks. As a result, we were able to organize ourselves to conduct half of the interviews each, as well as to structure in time to keep up to date with what the other was doing. Some of the procedures we used to maintain an ongoing preliminary analysis of the fieldwork are described later.

Collective Research Diary

One of the mechanisms that we used to achieve this was a collective research diary. We agreed at an early stage that we would record all substantial discussions that we had about the research, and would always give each other a copy of any notes that were made individually. In each of our joint meetings, we would agree that one of us would take notes and produce a record of the meeting, so that our collective research diary is made up of contributions from both of us.

It is this collective research diary that forms the basis of our discussion here. We have decided to include extracts from this diary and we have kept these in their raw state with no editing, so that readers can see the actual process of decision taking at work. When these notes were written, we had no idea that we might publish them in this way, and they were written solely for our own use although we did anticipate reflecting on them and using them in our analysis. We have little idea whether our procedures match other people's since personal research diaries of this kind are seldom made publicly available. Equally, we know little about the actual day-to-day procedures that people use to work collaboratively, and how far ours are distinctive. We have decided to include our raw notes as extracts because of the lack of discussion in the literature about these issues, although the importance of making public the research process in this way has been noted by others (Stenhouse 1980; Burgess 1984).

Initial Selection of Interviewees

We shall deal with issues of selection as they occurred chronologically telling our story in the order in which things actually happened, but also drawing out theoretical points as we go along. Figure 1 provides a "map" of the sequencing of events in the story.

The first set of decisions that we had to make concerned which people in the survey population would be chosen for more detailed study. We also had to decide how many to select. There were a number of interwoven considerations here concerning: principles of selection; the possibility of having subgroups and how many of these we would realistically include; strategies for selection to retain maximum flexibility especially to accommodate successful attempts to move outward to some interviewees' kin. Extract A is taken from the record of the planning meeting in which we talked through all these issues.

Extract A: Notes from the Record of Planning Meeting 5/8/86 (recorded by Janet Finch)

Our final decision was as follows:
    We will begin selecting interviewees from two sub groups: people who have been divorced and/or remarried; young adults (under 25 at the time of the survey).

Figure 1: Decision-Taking Sequence

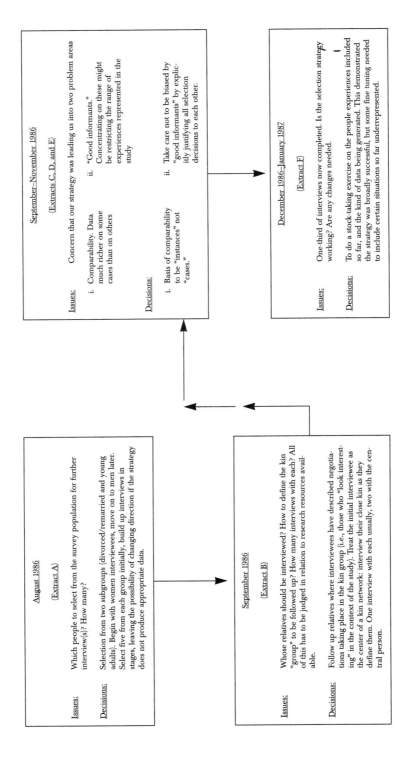

We will begin with women, until we have our selection procedures running smoothly and have decided on the merits of employing a male interviewer.

We will begin with five from each group, randomly selected from our list of people who meet these criteria. If we have a refusal, we will replace it with another name, selected randomly.

We will build up from there, seeing how far we can get with the kin groups of each, and adding more names from our sample. Our final aim will be to have qualitative data not only from people whose current, recent life experience has involved a renegotiation of family relationships (the basis of the above categories) but also people whose experience is close to the stereotypic norm of family life. If we do not pick up such people via kin groups, we may select from a different sub group of our sample, such as people with large kin networks who were once married or "women in the middle" (of a younger and older generation). We also want our final selection to have a reasonably good social class spread, and therefore we may select interviewees at a later stage which enable us to do that. Social Class I may be a case in point.

This strategy also opens the possibility of finding some other sub group, or individuals with particular characteristics who emerge as important during the course of earlier interviews.

The reasoning which lies behind this strategy included the following considerations:

1. A target sample of sixty individuals at the second stage means that four sub groups (i.e., fifteen in each) looks like the absolute maximum. But if we are successful in interviewing kin, then the number selected from the sample will be smaller than sixty. Our strategy of two main sub groups therefore seems realistic.

2. Our two sub groups are selected on the basis of life experience, and we have focused on people where their family relationships are likely to have undergone some renegotiation, which makes issues of obligation more explicit. They are also sub groups which seem to be significant in terms of social change, in that the rules of family obligations are currently probably being written/rewritten – because of divorce/remarriage becoming an increasingly common experience and because of pressures which seem to be creating longer periods of non-independence for young people.

3. We considered principles of selection based upon views expressed in the interview, especially people who gave "standard" answers and people who were in "deviant" minorities. We rejected this because: it seemed less important than the other principles of selection and we didn't want to multiply sub groups; we can probably get a lot out of the interviews themselves in relation to these issues; the second stage interviews are to concentrate upon experience rather than beliefs.

4. We considered adding a third group which would effectively be a control group, composed of people whose experience seems near to the stereotype norm. Although we agreed that it is important to build in the principle of comparison between typical and atypical experience, we decided not to select these initially as a former control group, because: we want to maintain maximum flexibility; to add a third group would mean that we reduce the numbers in the other two at an earlier stage; we may well pick up people whose experience is close to the norm *via* the interviewees initially selected on the other criteria. So we decided instead to treat this as a gap filling exercise at a later stage.

5. Part of the reason for rejecting a formal control group was that this concept derives from an underlying logic which doesn't really fit this stage of the project. We aren't aiming at generalisation based on representativeness, etc. Instead, we think that our agreed strategy is actually quite faithful to the principles of inductive logic. Indeed, we have left our options open to select cases which emerge as key in the course of our interviews.

It can be seen from this extract that we decided to sample initially from two subgroups: people who had been divorced and/or remarried, and the youngest age group in our population, namely people aged eighteen to twenty-four at the time of the survey. The reasons for this are centrally concerned with theoretical sampling. We quickly rejected the idea of a randomly selected subgroup on the grounds that we were not trying to use our qualitative data to make generalizations based on representativeness (although the survey data of course could be used in that way). Since fieldwork was principally to be concerned with understanding the process of negotiation between relatives, we decided that it would be much more useful to focus upon individuals who might currently or recently have been involved in processes of negotiation and renegotiation of family relationships. We hoped that talking to these individuals would give us access to family situations in which those processes would be most visible. The two groups that we chose seemed to fulfill these criteria.

It is important to underline (as we have found that people sometimes misunderstand what we are saying about our selection strategy) that we did not select these two as comparison groups in the orthodox sense. We were not seeking straightforwardly to compare the experience of young adults and divorced people, but were using both groups as a "way in" to the kind of family situations that we did want to study. We were, for example, very interested in the care of elderly people and how responsibilities for that develop over time within families, but we did not select an elderly subgroup because we hoped that our selection strategy would lead us to such situations in the kin group of the young people and the divorced people whom we had selected. In this sense, we were selecting kin groups (or at least situations in kin groups) as the focus of our study, rather than individuals. We recognized, of course, that this strategy might not work, and it can be seen from Extract A that we built in the possibility of re-viewing and revising our strategy during the course of the fieldwork.

The major principle that we used to guide our selection, therefore, was theoretical significance: we chose to focus on those groups that would enable us best to evaluate and develop the theoretical ideas and concepts with which we began the project. However, it can be seen from Extract A that we were also juggling with a number of other considerations that helped to shape our overall strategy. We will comment briefly on these.

1. Although we were not aiming at statistical representativeness in this field-work study, we did want to ensure that we included a range of experiences of family life. We wanted to include some situations (like divorce) which would be a minority experience and others that were more routine and typical. Fur-ther, we could see from our survey data that some subgroups in the population had answered our questionnaire in a distinctive way, and we wanted to en-sure that their personal experiences were reflected in our qualitative study. People in Social Class I were one example mentioned in the Extract. There were other groups – for example, people who have experienced unemploy-ment – whose experience we also wanted to include because of its public importance in contemporary Britain. At this initial stage we decided to wait and see if our selection strategy based on two subgroups would lead us to a good range of situations which included all of these. If not, we left open the possibility of rethinking our strategy at a later stage.

2. The inclusion of the experience of non-white people presented us with particular problems since the survey population had only a small number of respondents from ethnic minorities (the refusal rate having apparently been high among these groups). We were also aware that we might want to change slightly the format of our interview to make it appropriate to distinctive cul-tural experiences, and that we might wish to seek advice on this. At the initial selection stage, while we were strongly committed to not producing an eth-nocentric piece of research, we decided that we would come back to the issue of specifically selecting some non-white interviewees at a later stage in the fieldwork, after we had gotten our procedures operating smoothly.

3. We took a similar decision in respect of interviewing men, although for completely different reasons. We wanted to include both women and men in our study, both in our initial selection of interviewees and as relatives of those selected. However, since we would be conducting interviews in people's own homes, and because we were two female researchers, we were conscious of issues about personal safety and felt that it would be unwise for either of us to go alone into the homes of unknown men (McKee 1983). We considered various possible strategies, including employing a male interviewer, but at this stage in the project we felt dissatisfied with all of the possible solutions. We decided, therefore, that the first group of interviewees selected would be all women, thus buying ourselves time to get our interview procedures running smoothly before we tried to solve the problem of men.

The skeptical reader might accuse us of having put off a great many decisions and conclude that we were unclear about what we wanted to do and unwilling to make firm choices. However, the whole point about trying to achieve an interplay between theory and data, and the logic of analytic induction that underlies fieldwork procedures, is that decisions cannot be taken in a final and irrevocable form before any data are collected. This is because we cannot know in advance of studying some actual cases what are (to put it in Znaniecki's terms) the essentials that we would want to abstract in order to compare them with other cases and to test and refine our generalizations. What we were trying to do at the initial stage of selection was to decide *where to look* for the processes of negotiating obligations in families, rather than to prejudge what we would find. In these decisions about where to look we were trying to be guided in a systematic way by theory, while maintaining the flexibility to look elsewhere at a later stage if we had gotten it wrong, and to be able to build in, at a later stage, the comparisons that would emerge as most significant on the basis of our initial cases.

These principles of selection had to then be translated into practical strategy, and we decided that we would proceed by selecting small numbers of people from each subgroup. We actually selected five at a time from each subgroup, giving ourselves the opportunity to assess how many actual interviews we were achieving, and how many relatives we were following up, before going on to select some more initial contacts. We had a total list of 117 young adults who were willing to be interviewed again and 112 people who had been divorced and/or remarried. Each time we selected from these lists we did so using a table of random numbers, since we did not want to develop more detailed criteria about whom to follow up. This, of course, still left open the possibility that at a later stage we could "search" for people who had a particular combination of characteristics that we might wish to include. For example, we could look for people who were unemployed as well as in the young adult group if this experience was not being included in the cases we had initially selected.

At this initial stage we think that our procedures do demonstrate a fairly successful attempt to be both systematic and flexible. We recognize that the actual detail of what we did could not be straightforwardly translated into a different project. We had, for example, a great deal of prior information about potential interviewees based on the survey questionnaires, probably far more than is usually available at the beginning of a piece of fieldwork. But we think that the underlying logical procedures that we were using can certainly be translated to other contexts.

Selecting Kin Groups

Our procedure for sampling individuals from the survey population proceeded as described. After the first five sampled from each group, we continued sampling in small bunches, substituting refusals by another random selection from the same subgroup. Having set the wheels in motion in this way we had to decide whose relatives we would like to include in our study. Developing criteria for identifying kin to be followed up proved to be the selection task that we found most difficult and we will discuss it in detail in this section.

Extract B shows how our initial thinking on this issue developed.

Extract B: Notes from Record of Planning Meeting 23/9/86 (recorded by Jennifer Mason)

Interviews with Members of the Kin Group – Discussion of Rationale and Strategy

Whose Kin Group Do We Want to Study?
We discussed the pros and cons of either using our respondent as the central person and examining their kin group, or of using them as a way into a variety of kin groups. We decided on the former strategy because:

> we will then have survey data on all the people whose kin groups we are examining, because they will all have been survey respondents.
> there is a logic of selection whereas if we were to get deflected into other kin groups it would all become very haphazard.
> interviews with relatives will thus be used to elucidate our survey respondent's kin group and the negotiations within it.

Which Relatives to Select
After a fairly detailed discussion we decided to use the following selection principles:
> we will try to interview relatives with whom negotiations have taken place (i.e., where our survey respondent has told us about these).
> we will exclude those in "crisis situations" on ethical grounds.
> people with whom there has been close contact at some time in the past, i.e., where there has been some kind of negotiation, but where there is now little or no contact.
> This is a way of selecting people with whom we might expect our survey respondent to be negotiating, but where negotiation appears to be absent, without necessarily limiting ourselves to primary kin.

By following these selection principles we will be being more precise about who we follow up than if we simply interviewed all "significant others" (i.e., significant from our survey respondent's point of view).

How Many Interviews With Each?

As with all the issues we discussed today, we had implicit assumptions and rationales about how many interviews we would want with different types of respondent, and once we had made them explicit we came up with the following:

With our survey respondent we want to know about her/his relationships in all directions, because it is her/his kin group we are studying. With other relatives, although we will have to understand something about their relationships in all directions in order to understand their relationship with our survey respondent and his/her kin, we are interested chiefly in their relationship with her/him. Therefore, *generally we will want*:

one interview only with relatives of our survey respondent, *except*:

> where relatives are clearly "significant others" as far as she/he is concerned, in which case they are likely to have more to say about relationships with her/him. In these cases we will want two interviews.
> where relatives fall into either our divorced/remarried or young adult categories, in which case we will want two interviews to further our understanding of issues relevant to these categories.

As far as interviews with spouses are concerned, we will only want one because we are less interested in the conjugal tie than in other aspects of kinship. Furthermore, it is neat and tidy to finish the third interview with our survey respondent at the same time as finishing the one with the spouse (i.e., where these interviews are conducted simultaneously). Also, the interpersonal point about feeling awkward because we (including Social and Community Planning Research), will have made three visits to the household by this time.

At this stage we had no idea how successful we would be at gaining access to relatives: we thought it quite possible that our interviewees would decline to pass us on, and even if they agreed, that relatives might refuse to be interviewed. Beyond that unknown element, our major concern at this stage was to decide upon the appropriate balance between getting very detailed information from a very small number of kin groups, and including a range of different experiences in our study. Given the practical limitation of having budgeted over 120 interviews, we could not do both.

Looking back on our research diary from that period, we seem to have resolved that issue (although this is not spelled out in the notes) by going back to look at the purpose of studying kin groups, that is, by working through from the logic of our theoretical ideas and the research issues upon which we were focusing. Certainly our notes do record that we clarified that our purpose in studying kin groups was to understand the process involved in negotiations between kin over financial and material support. We, therefore, felt that we needed to include a range of experiences to help us to generalize about these processes. On the other hand, the whole purpose of studying kin groups rather than individuals was to get accounts of the same issues from different parties involved, and we needed to try to interview enough people from each kin group studied to give us a rounded picture.

We decided to try to follow up the kin group of those people where the initial interview had revealed examples of negotiations between relatives over issues concerning financial or material support. In that sense we were select-ing for more intensive study the kin groups of people who "looked interesting" in relation to the issues that we wanted to study. While in the end we stuck to that strategy, it was this particular issue that subsequently gave us cause for concern as we shall explain shortly.

The more practical issues to be resolved at this stage concerned how to define a kin group and how many interviews to have with each person. Our reasoning on both these issues can be seen in Extract B. We decided that in each case we would treat the person who had been in the survey population as the center of a personal kin network, and would focus on that person's sig-nificant or close kin as she or he defined them, rather than trying to be passed ever outward along chains of kin. Having taken that decision to focus on clearly defined kin "groups" centered on an individual who had been in the survey, the question about how many interviews to conduct followed fairly straightforwardly: we would do two more with the key person and one each with his or her relatives since our aim was to generate a detailed set of data on the group which centered on our key person. We anticipated that we might sometimes want two interviews with certain relatives for special reasons, but in the event we did not do this.

The disadvantage of this strategy is that it closed off the possibility of fol-lowing through other relationships that looked relevant to our concerns if they did not involve the key person in the kin group. This did indeed occur. There were several instances where we interviewed a sister or a cousin of our key person who would themselves have made excellent subjects for detailed study. Extract E (see below) shows that we did go on noticing these examples and paused to consider whether our strategy should be changed. However, we continued to reason that we were prepared to sacrifice those possibilities in order to create a systematic selection strategy that would enable us to study a range of different situations. Other researchers might have taken a different decision but we felt any other approach would have led us into a series of ad hoc decisions which, in the end, would be difficult to justify.

Problem 1: Comparability

Equipped with a reasonably coherent selection strategy, we, therefore, began identifying interviewees whose relatives we would like to follow up. However, we felt a continuing concern to formalize and crystalize our thinking on these issues. The first issue that concerned us was comparability. In each case we were making decisions for good reasons, and following the principles that we had articulated, but we were concerned that these might result in a set of interviews that could be difficult to handle as comparable cases. We would have two interviews with some people, and one with others; with some people we would be following through their relatives and with others we would not.

We resolved this by deciding to turn an apparent weakness to good effect. Extract C shows how we reasoned this through.

Extract C: Janet Finch's Research Notes for 27/10/86

The principle of *instances rather than cases* as the basis of comparability seems to be particularly suited to this project, since we are searching for a range of experiences and social phenomena, and we don't know in advance of the first interview which are present for a given interviewee. We concentrate on those which we do find, but that means that the idea of comparability between cases does not fit this study in any event. Because people have different experiences, we have data on different topics from each person. The principle of taking "instances" as the basis of comparability in a way just goes one step beyond saying that we will have to count up how many interviewees have had a given experience, and that this will be less than the total number in the study. To put together instances of an event from each "side" of it, plus accounts given by third parties gives a more rounded picture. We will need to be able to justify third party examples in terms of taking these accounts *as seriously as* accounts of personal experience, but of course *not the same as* them. Third party accounts are important to us precisely because people are distanced somewhat from the circumstances and therefore they reflect a more "public" view of the situations, reflecting something of how the public morality of obligations gets applied in particular instances, I suspect.

This approach is of course *not the only way* in which we should use examples from our data. I would anticipate that we will want to present it in different forms, and that another obvious one is extended discussion of individual cases (which might be individual people, or kin groups). Obviously the people on whom we have got the most data are likely to be the most suitable candidates for this, although that might not always be the case. My idea about comparability of instances is not to close off other methods of analysis, but simply to see a way through the problems created by the need to present some of the data in aggregated form (i.e., not *just* as a series of individual cases) and the particular issues of comparability that we seem to be building in.

Our idea was that much of our analysis should proceed, not on the basis of comparing each individual person or "case" with another but on the basis of comparing "instances" or examples in our data of particular circumstances in which we are interested. To take one example: people who have temporarily moved back into a parent's home after divorce. Instead of simply counting the number of people interviewed who themselves have moved back and comparing their experiences, we could search in our data for all examples of this happening: people who themselves had done it, people who had been the "receiving" parent, examples given of third parties doing it. Of course, for some of the instances we would have much more detailed data than for others, and for some we would have accounted from more than one party to the arrangement. Some would be personal accounts and some would be second hand accounts. That variability obviously would have to be acknowledged in the way we used the data, but in principle we could draw together a range of instances in this way from wherever they occurred in our data.

The principle of instances rather than cases as the basis of comparability seemed to be particularly suited to our project, since we were searching for a range of experiences and social phenomena, and we did not know in advance of the first interview which would be present for a given interviewee. Again, this comes back to analytic rather than enumerative induction, because it is based on the validity of instances or processes, rather than the representativeness of the sample, as a means of generalizing and of making sociological statements. Furthermore, it illustrates ways in which we were linking our strategies at this stage to ideas about how we would use and write up the data in our formal analysis.

Problem 2: Good Informants

We resolved the question of comparability to our own satisfaction but fairly soon after this we began to be concerned about another issue connected with selection criteria for following up kin. The core of the problem here was that we were worried that we were being seduced into following up the kin groups of people whom we found interesting to interview and who made it easy for us to spot situations apparently concerning negotiations in their kin group. Some of our respondents made very "good informants" in the sense that they talked about their families using concepts that were quite close to our own, whereas others presented material in a more bland way that did not highlight issues like reciprocity, conflict, compromise, working things through, talking things out, and so on. However, this latter group might well be involved in negotiations – in the broad sense – about kin support. Were we in danger of missing the full range of experiences open to us by tending to follow up the people who were – on our distinctive definitions – most articulate and interesting?

Although the detail will vary in different projects, this must be an issue commonly faced by field researchers who want both to use "good informants" and also to produce a rounded picture of the situations they are studying that does not systematically exclude certain kinds of informants or experience. Extracts D and E show our attempts to resolve this issue. We discussed it on several occasions without getting very far before we decided that Jennifer Mason (who had originally spotted the significance of this issue) should spell out the nature of the problem on paper (Extract D). Janet Finch then responded (Extract E). As a procedure we found this a helpful way of moving beyond our verbal discussions where, on this issue in particular, we had been tending to go round in circles. In these notes, we had reached the stage where we were able to discuss concrete examples of interviews that had been completed. In the extracts these are referred to by their interview numbers.

Extract D: Jennifer Mason's Research Notes 3/11/86

Further Thoughts on Following Up Kin Groups

I have been concerned lately about the implicit criteria I am using during and after interviews to make decisions about whether people's kin groups are worth following up. After talking with Janet we agreed that I should try to make my worries explicit by writing them down.

My main worry has been that there is a danger of only following up the kin groups of articulate respondents – "good informants" – for example 01 or 110. I think my problem is that respondents like this approach some of the issues we are interested in an analytical way – they are able to reflect and philosophise about their kin relationships – which means that they draw out interesting situations, relationships, etc. to tell us about. In fact, in both of these cases, there are situations which we could presumably identify as interesting even if they were not articulated to us in this way: e g., sharing accommodation. But I suppose I am concerned that conceptual issues might sway us into following up a kin group – e.g., things like reciprocity, independence and dependence, conflict and tension, giving and lending – and that not all of our initial contact respondents will articulate these. However, their behaviour and kin relationships may still be bounded by/governed by these sorts of issues. So, for example, 101 did not make sharing accommodation sound half as interesting as 110, or 106.

These worries were thrown into relief a bit for me in considering 108 because I had just about made the decision during the interview (exactly as I had made the converse decision with 110), that her kin group would not be worth following up. Yet "objectively" there seemed to be some interesting features: e.g., her relationship with her mother, the effective dissolution of the family home when our respondent bought a house with her boyfriend and her mother moved into warden assisted housing at the age of sixty, examples of cohabitation vs. marriage, her mother's role in caring for her parents before their death a couple of years ago, her mother's widowhood at the age of forty and her consequent retraining and employment as a book keeper, our respondent's consequent close relationship with her grandparents, her determination to marry on the same day as her grandparents, using her grandmother's wedding ring, etc! But all of these things were not articulated in a way which made them sound inherently fascinating. Would 01 have made them sound interesting for us?

I think my nagging doubt is that if we are not careful we will systematically exclude certain types of kin groups, or at least the kin groups of certain types of initial contact respondent, i.e., those who do not reflect or are not fascinated by the intricacies and ambiguities, etc. of family relationships and/or those who are unable or unwilling to articulate these.

Extract E: Janet Finch's Research Notes 5/11/86

Following Up Kin Groups: My Response to Jennifer's "Further Thoughts"

We are trying to use 108 as the focus for deciding more clearly our principles for who not to follow up. But when I listened to this tape, I found it rather interesting, and can identify a number of issues which might well make it worth following through her kin group. (Issues listed in detail at this point.)

So for me, 108 doesn't perhaps present quite the perfect example of the dilemma which Jennifer wrote about, because I think I find it intrinsically more interesting. It may be that there is a general lesson to be learned here: she did the interview, but I have only listened to the tape. It may well be that it is easier to listen for and find interesting issues to pursue when you can listen to the tape without having been influenced by the nature of the interaction. If the interview interaction was difficult, or even just not specially exciting, it may well be more difficult to get enthused about it afterwards than it is for someone who comes to it fresh. So that probably means that we should certainly involve each other actively in any decision *not* to follow up a kin group – whichever of us has not done the interview may be able to spot more interesting possibilities.

My conclusion therefore is that we should probably follow up the kin of 108 working on the criteria which we have already established. But Jennifer's note about the danger of not following up less articulate respondents does convince me that there is a potential problem which I had perhaps been a bit slow to recognise.

What worries me now is: if we recognise that some people's kin groups may be more interesting (to us) than they seem at first sight, are we ever going to have a reason for not following up (other than the separate sets of reasons to do with not probing around in crisis situations, etc.)?, i.e., does this effectively amount to a decision to follow up everyone whom we reasonably can? In some ways that would be the easiest strategy to operate and to justify, but I don't feel wholly comfortable about it. I think I am worrying mainly about the best use of our limited resources, in that the more kin we follow up, the fewer kin groups overall we can study. Since material from kin groups (where we do succeed in getting it) is essentially bound to be used as case study material, because we are not attempting to select groups in a way which would make them comparable with each other, then I suppose I have a niggling feeling that I want to get the *best cases* which we can, and which will enable us to understand social interaction and social process but which of course will not in any sense be representative. I don't feel inclined to shift from the strategy of treating our initial contact as the "centre" of a kin group and not to keep snowballing on infinitely with her relatives, and then theirs. To have a cut off of that kind is bound to produce some examples of individuals whom we would have been very happy to see as the contact person themselves (a recent example for me would be 08, who is the cousin of 01, who has a very interesting situation in her own right) but I think I accept that as a consequence of our strategy.

The main way in which we worked through to a solution of the problem of good informants was to capitalize upon having two researchers working collaboratively. Since only one of us was normally present at an interview (and if we were both present, only one of us took an active role and the other was purely an observer) we found that the person who had not conducted the interview was often able to see more clearly the merits of following up a particular case. That person was less likely than the person who had done the interview to be over enthused by a particularly good interviewee, or to dismiss the situation of a more difficult interviewee as being not worth following through. In other words, the other's judgment was unlikely to be clouded by issues connected with having had the responsibility for maintaining the interview as a successful *social* interaction. In this way we were able to take decisions on a case by case basis and to continue to select certain kin groups for detailed study, but not others. It can be seen from Extract E that at this point there was some danger that we should slide back into following through all possible cases, on the grounds that it was just too difficult to distinguish between one and another. But the process of working through the issue with each other and on paper enabled us to confirm that our selection strategy remained appropriate.

From this point onward we adopted a procedure where we always documented the pros and cons of following up the relatives of each interviewee individually. After each interview, but prior to transcription, the person who had conducted it listened to the tape, and produced a family tree, summaries of information given about relatives, and a life story chart. This material, together with the tape, was then passed to the other and formed the basis of a joint discussion about following up kin. This means that in each case both of us listened to the interview tape, and took the next decision collaboratively on the basis of a preliminary analysis. In this way, we felt that we could ensure that we were being as systematic as possible in our choices.

Stock Taking Exercise

Alongside this developed a more cumulative strategy of discussing each case not just on its own merits, but as part of a growing data set. In this way we tried to keep an eye on the range of experiences that we were studying, and to identify obvious gaps. We formalized this, about halfway through the interview stage, in a stock taking exercise. Again, this was premised upon analytic induction, the logic now being that we should both plug the gaps and begin to seek for "negative instances." As Hughes has pointed out, analytic induction involves:

> A strategy which calls for the investigator to search deliberately for instances that negate his (sic) hypothesis and, using these, to refine the hypothesis further ... In practice, the process of analytic induction proceeds by formulating a rather vague generalisation and then revising it in the light of contrary evidence, so that there is a continual process of redefinition, hypothesis testing, and a search for negative cases until a point is reached where a universal relationship can with some confidence be established (Hughes 1976, p. 128).

Our stock taking involved a preliminary but systematic categorization both of characteristics of people and kin groups in the study, and instances of kin support and negotiation in the interviews done so far (41 completed and 17 firmly arranged, out of a target number of 120). On the basis of this, we were able to assess and modify our strategy for the second half of the qualitative stage. Janet Finch did the detailed work of itemizing and categorizing the range of situations already present in our data, and Extract F comes from the record of the meeting where we discussed this stock taking document and used it as the basis for the last major stage in refining our selection strategy.

Extract F: Notes From The Record Of Planning Meeting 14 and 15 January 1987 (recorded by Jennifer Mason)

We used Janet's "taking stock exercise" as a discussion document for our meeting, taking each point in turn. The following are the major points arising:

1. Categories to Include

We decided that, overall, our present strategy for sampling is working fairly well, but that we need to refine it a bit to ensure that certain categories of people are included:

a. Men. We agreed, perhaps a bit reluctantly (!) that we cannot simply continue to rely on being passed on to men via the kin groups of our "key" women. We need to select some men who have also been survey respondents, not least so that we can then gain access to their kin groups, hence not filtering out this possibility at the start by only selecting women. We acknowledged that this would raise again the unresolved problems of personal safety we discussed a few months ago. We decided that the best strategy would be to go together to interview men and, where that was not possible, to approach a male colleague with experience of field research with a view to his being a "minder." We talked about the possibility of employing a man to do the interviews with men, but agreed that this would be an inadequate substitute for us, given our familiarity with the objectives, perspectives, data already collected on the project.

b. We agreed that unemployment was an important enough contemporary issue, with implications for our work, for us to include some unemployed people in our sample. Although we cannot tell who is currently unemployed from the questionnaires, which are now a year old, we agreed that we could select people who were unemployed at the time of the survey, and had been for some time, e.g., over a year. If it transpired that they were no longer unemployed such people would nevertheless have experience of a fairly lengthy, and recent, period of unemployment. We agreed to confine this to the under forties or fifties, to prevent the conceptual difficulties with unemployment in later life.

c. Ethnic Minorities. We agonised over this, feeling that in some ways it would be racist to exclude them, but also to include them on different terms. We agreed that if we were to include people from ethnic minorities they should certainly be people who fitted into our two main sampling categories: young adults and divorced/remarried. Finally we decided that we would get a list of the people involved, and literally take out the questionnaires and examine them to see just exactly what we have got, and what the nature of the situation is. We also agreed that Janet would approach a personal contact with a view to our interviewing him and his wife as a sort of pilot interview. This would enable us to see if our questions made sense, and to discuss with them what sorts of modifications would be appropriate for the different ethnic minorities.

d. Social Class I, IV and V. We reaffirmed that we want to get a range of experience in our study, whilst also not making any claims as to the representativeness of our qualitative study group for the general population. Thus, we agreed there was a need for us to gain more people from classes IV and V, to offset the clustering we have at the moment in the middle (II and III). Weight is added to this when we looked at the housing tenure distribution, and our overwhelming bias towards owner occupation. We felt that a conscious attempt to gain people from classes IV and V would help offset this. We also agreed that our survey data made Social Class I (men especially) look interesting enough to warrant a conscious selection strategy here too. Weight was added to this by Janet's "hypothesis" that the continuance of "friendly and civilised" contact following divorce might be a middle class phenomenon (nicknamed the Posy Simmonds phenomenon).

e. Divorce and Widowhood. Janet's suggestion that widowhood might help to throw some light on our understanding of divorce seemed compelling, and we agreed that we should try to include some widows especially those under fifty years old where this is less common and in a sense more comparable with divorce (does not conflate issues of ageing and widowhood, etc.). We agreed that divorce continued to be a worthy focus and sampling strategy for us, not least because our divorced survey respondents have led us into kin groups displaying a good spread of other "situations" we are interested in. If Janet's "Posy Simmonds" hunch about middle class divorce is right, then our SCI respondents might prove interesting here too. We talked about the possibility of refining our strategy of centering on our "key" respondent as far as divorce was concerned, so that for example if we were to discover a divorced person in their kin group we could possibly follow them up in their own right, that is by treating them as another key person with a kin group. We decided that this would be perfectly valid, and indeed that we could "look out" for some of our other categories and situations in this way too. Now that we are almost halfway through the qualitative bit, and are in a position to reflect on where we are going in the light of where we have been, we felt that there was less danger of losing our focus than there might have been last year in a strategy which allows us to follow up someone who is not necessarily a key figure in our initial contact's kin group, but who is, for example, divorced and of interest in their own right.

f. Elderly. We agreed that we wanted to keep on the look out for elderly, and particularly fit elderly, people in the kin groups, but not to modify our selection strategy in this respect. One of the problems with doing the latter is the danger of our crashing in on a crisis situation which would, in any event, lessen our potential for following up kin given our strategy of non intervention in crises.

g. Step Children and Step Grand Parenting. We agreed that given our interest in divorce and remarriage, this was actually a fairly central issue and we should give it a higher priority. We discussed ways of identifying step parents from the survey questionnaires – i.e., by choosing people who are (divorced or) remarried and who have children listed under "spouse kin." We agreed that we should look out for step parenting situations in the kin groups, but also at the selection stage in the questionnaires.

2. How Many to Sample For Each Category

We agreed, given the fairly heavy commitment of our resources involved, that it would be acceptable to treat men as a "minority group" in our sampling strategy. Partly, we felt this justifiable because our female respondents *are* yielding men in their kin groups. We agreed that we should continue sampling until we have achieved ten men – five divorced/remarried, and five young adults. These ten men can include people in Social Class IV and V, and unemployed (which in fact they do), and we agreed that we should monitor refusals very carefully during this phase, so that where men in these categories refuse we can replace them with other men in these categories.

That would leave us with the following to achieve: ethnic minorities, Social Class I, adult stepchildren/parents, young widowed. We agreed that we would be best to leave until later the sampling decision about young widowed and step children, when we will be in a position to see what we have achieved in these respects from the kin groups. We decided we should target about three or four SCIs, probably men but they could be women (Janet has one potential in her five male divorced/remarried survey candidates). We agreed that we would be lucky to get three ethnic minority initial contacts, at most.

Most of these precise decisions about sampling numbers cannot be made very effectively at this stage, and we agreed that a good strategy would be to allow ourselves a further "taking stock" exercise when we can assess how well "represented" our categories are, and whether there is a case for including other groups/categories/situations. When we are at a stage where we are beginning to feel confident of ideas/theories being generated, we could therefore adjust the sampling a bit in line with the logic of analytic induction.

At this point we were able to be much more focused about selection issues than was possible at an earlier stage. While we were pleased to be able to confirm that the strategy we had been pursuing was generating the kind of data we had hoped for, we were able to engage in some fine tuning. For example, we came back to the categories of respondents whose experiences we wanted to include, but where we had decided at an earlier stage to delay a decision. Thus, we decided actively to seek out examples of people who had been unemployed since we were not picking up examples of these in our existing strategy; but by contrast we concluded that we did not specifically need to seek out elderly interviewees, since we were successfully including their experiences through following them up as relatives within our existing subgroups. We also finally took a decision about men, confirming that we needed to include some as the focal person of a kin group (not just as relatives of women) and resolved the practical problems of security by opting for the labor intensive strategy of accompanying each other to initial interviews with men about whom we had no information beyond the survey interview. We also agreed upon a strategy for selecting people from ethnic minority groups, leaving open the possibility that we might go beyond our two major subgroupings in the case only, to make sure that some non-white experiences were included in our study. This arose solely from the fact that we had a very small number of survey respondents from whom to make a selection; but in principle we were able to confirm that our basic strategy of selecting from the two subgroups of young adults and divorced/remarried was leading us to examples of negotiations within families, and all other selections were made from *within* those two subgroups.

Another slightly different issue that emerged from our stock-taking exercise was that we had so far been interviewing people from a rather narrow social class range, namely, from the middle of the range as defined in orthodox terms. From the point of view of reflecting a range of social experiences in our data, it seemed important to broaden that and we agreed that we should seek out respondents within our main subgroups who fell into classes I, IV, and V. The value of having undertaken a systematic stock-taking exercise at the midway point in the fieldwork is very clear in this instance, since neither of us had realized that our interviewees were bunched in this way. If we had relied upon our informal and intuitive knowledge built up in the course of interviews, we would not have identified this problem until it was too late to do anything about it.

The principle of analytic induction is very explicitly followed in another set of decisions that we took at this time concerning our interest in families that had been reconstituted through divorce and marriage. In the interviews that we had already completed we had plenty of examples of renegotiation of relationships with the person's own relatives, but very few of continuing relationships with relatives of the former spouse. The common pattern seemed to be to cut off contact completely. The "rather vague generalization" with which we began (to put it in Hughes' terms) was that there would be circumstances under which relationships with former in-laws would continue in a renegotiated form. The data that we had collected in the first half of our fieldwork suggested that we should modify our hypothesis to: active relationships with in-laws continue in a renegotiated form after divorce only in unusual circumstances, if at all.

Thus, our data were helping us to modify our theory and that in turn enabled us to test our revised theory further. We decided to do this in two ways. First, we would search for negative instances, which in the context of our modified hypothesis meant that we would seek out those situations where we were most likely to find continuing relationships after divorce. In discussing where to look for these we brought to bear our wider knowledge of social theory and of other studies and decided that the desire to continue "friendly and civilized" relationships after divorce is probably a phenomenon associated with the intellectual middle classes. We christened it the "Posy Simmonds" phenomena in our notes: *Guardian* readers will be familiar with this kind of "civility" in the cartoons of Posy Simmonds. This confirmed that we should specifically select some interviewees from Social Class I.

Second, we decided to try to refine our theory further by testing out whether the process of cutting off from in-laws is a consequence of divorce specifically or whether it is a result of the tie that previously bound the people together having been removed. If it were the latter, people who had been widowed would undergo a similar process to the divorced; if the former, the pattern of relationships with in-laws after divorce or widowhood would be very different. This reasoning led us to a decision to select some "young widows" (of either sex) for interview, to test out this distinction by comparing widows and divorcees whose family circumstances were otherwise quite similar.

Extract F shows that we translated these modifications into a selection strategy for the second part of the fieldwork in which we were able to be quite precise about the numbers we were seeking in each category. In terms of the balance between being systematic and being flexible it is clear that we were able to be systematic in a much more overt sense at this stage than we had been at the beginning of the process. But we were still able to retain a degree of flexibility as our notes indicate, we built in the possibility of further stock taking at a later stage. We did in fact repeat the exercise when we were about three quarters of the way through our interviews – this time Jennifer Mason doing the itemizing and categorizing but we made no significant changes at that point.

Conclusion

In telling the story of our own project we have made a number of points about how the principles involved in theoretical sampling can be applied and we will not repeat them here. We make no special claims to methodological virtue but we think that it is quite possible to produce a selection strategy in field research that is systematic rather than ad hoc, while maintaining a level of flexibility that is essential within this research paradigm. We have shown how we selected cases to study for their theoretical significance, worked through problems associated with comparability, applied the principle of analytic induction, and made systematic appraisals of the data that we were generating as we went along – all of these within the normal practical constraints of money, time, and, in our case, a concern about the personal safety of the researchers.

We shall conclude by highlighting some of the more general principles that can be drawn from this description of our research process.

1. It is clear that analysis of some kind is constantly taking place, and forms the basis for decisions about strategies, within the overall parameters set at the beginning through a particular theoretical perspective. Different levels of analysis can be relevant here, for example, listening to interview tapes, making a preliminary assessment of each case, itemizing and categorizing characteristics and situations. Preliminary forms of analyses such as these are the raw materials from which informed decisions are made. Theoretical sampling, therefore, encompasses a good deal more than processes generally considered to constitute sampling.

2. Leading on from the first point, this means that decisions made on this basis are not ad hoc. Rather they are both situated and informed. Some decisions simply cannot be made at the very beginning of the research enterprise without loss of theoretical and data sensitivity, yet each time a decision is made it is important to be clear about the principles underlying it, the reasons for it, possible alternatives and so on. On the one hand, informed decisions are part of a process of sharpening or modifying – underlying principles leading to theory that is grounded in data. On the other hand, this is only possible because to recognize that informed decisions have to be made continually is to acknowledge that the research process takes the researcher through changing contexts. These result from the data being generated, and from continuing exposure to other researchers' theories and findings in relation to her or his own.

3. The implication of this is that delaying some decisions until a later stage of the research process, rather than taking them all at the beginning, is a positive rather than a negative feature. However, this is not a license for the researcher to be ad hoc, and to make decisions simply off the top of her or his head. In essence, what must be gained from any situated description of informed decisions is a lesson in how to be systematic. This is rather more of a challenge than to be systematic in a positivistic sense, because informed decisions made in-progress can easily appear ad hoc and inconsistent if the researcher cannot be entirely clear about the changing contexts of those decisions, their purposes and consequences, and the principles underlying them. In the absence of this vital contextual information, it is dangerously easy for researchers to telescope decisions made into a positivistic model, by suggesting that they had sorted out most of the issues at the very start.

4. Being systematic in preliminary analyses of one's data in this way represents the beginning of a cumulative development of principles of analysis. Therefore, as well as it being important to record both decisions and contexts for an expose of the practicalities of theoretical sampling, these very records form excellent documents for use in the early stages of the formal analysis of data.

5. Collaborative working methods are, we have found, a positive bonus in all of this. We have been able at each stage to have real discussions about decisions and issues as they occur, and kept records of these discussions as well as our individual endeavors. However, if some of the processes involved in being systematic seem more obvious in a collaborative working context, they do not have to be exclusive to it.

Acknowledgments

We would like to thank Bob Burgess, Caroline Dryden, John Hockey, and Sue Scott for reading and commenting on an earlier version of this chapter. Also thanks to colleagues present at the meeting of the qualitative methods study group in the Department of Social Administration at the University of Lancaster, where we discussed an early version of this paper: Nick Derricourt, Joy Foster, Anne Williams.

Notes

1. This study is supported by a grant from the Economic and Social Research Council, 1985–89. The total grant was £121,000 of which about £50,000 represented the cost of the fieldwork and data processing for the large-scale survey which formed part of the study.

2. The survey was conducted in the Greater Manchester area and was based on the electoral register in forty cluster sampled wards. A response rate of 72% was achieved, making a total of 978 completed interviews. At the end of the questionnaire respondents were asked, "It is possible that a researcher on this project might want to come back in some months' time. Would you be willing to give another interview?" Eighty-five percent said they would be willing.

3. The survey fieldwork was organized and conducted through Social and Community Planning Research, and we would like to gratefully acknowledge Gill Courtenay's contribution and support in this stage of the project.

References

Baldamus, C., 1972 "The Role of Discoveries in Social Science." In T. Shanin (ed.), *The Rules of The Game*. London: Tavistock.

Bell, C., 1977 "Reflections on the Banbury Re-study." In C. Bell and H. Newby (eds.), *Doing Sociological Research*. London: Allen and Unwin.

Bertaux, D., 1981 *Bibliography and Society*. Beverly Hills, CA: Sage.

Burgess, R. G., 1984 "Autobiographical Accounts and Research Experience." In R.G. Burgess (ed.), *The Research Process in Educational Settings: Ten Case Studies*. Lewes: Falmer Press.

Finch, J., 1987 "Family Obligations and the Life Course." In A. Bryman, B. Bytheway, P. Allatt, and T. Keil (eds.), *Perspectives on the Life Cycle*. London: Macmillan.

Glaser, B. and Strauss, A., 1967 *The Discovery of Grounded Theory.* Chicago: Aldine.

Hammersley, M. and Atkinson, P., 1983 *Ethnography: Principles and Practice.* London: Tavistock.

Hughes, 1976 *Sociological Analysis: Methods of Discovery.* London: Nelson.

McKee, L. and O'Brian, M., 1983 "Interviewing Men: 'Taking Gender Seriously.'" In E. Gamarnikow et al. (eds.), *The Public and The Private.* London: Heineman.

Platt, J., 1976 *The Realities of Social Research.* Brighton: Chatto and Windus/Sussex University Press.

Porter, M., 1984 "The Modification of Method in Researching Postgraduate Education." In R.G. Burgess (ed.), *The Research Process in Educational Settings: Ten Case Studies.* Lewes: Falmer Press.

Schwarz, H. and Jacobs, J., 1979 *Qualitative Sociology: A Method to the Madness.* New York: Free Press.

Stenhouse, L., 1980 "The Study of Samples and the Study of Cases." *British Educational Research Journal* 1–6.

Znaniecki, F., 1934 *The Method of Sociology.* New York: Farrar and Reinhart.

17

Strategy for Getting Organized

Leonard Schatzman & Anselm L. Strauss

Mapping

The researcher has now gained formal entry, though he has come only through the front door. Armed with a measure of authority, he can move about the site with relative freedom. Now, also, he can attend to gathering data systematically – but quite possibly he does not yet have a workable and reliable perspective on the whole of his field; not even the more obvious, presenting properties are substantially known to him What he requires is a working conception of the relevant dimensions of the site, including its outer boundaries and inner locales;[1] also, the classes of things, persons, and events which inhabit these locales. For all this, he requires a number of "maps": social, spatial, and temporal. In institutional research, such formal maps are usually available as tables of organization, schedules of routines and special meetings, and drawings of street and building plans. These maps are useful as aids to orientation in the early stages of research. They are data also: they indicate, in special form, some of the reality that the hosts present to themselves and others. In the study of social movements, however, such maps are rare and probably not very reliable because of the more ephemeral nature of members and activities, and their temporal–spatial loci. Entrée may have been permitted in the expectation that the researcher himself will eventually provide the leadership with some reliable maps. In any event, how does the researcher provide himself with a set of maps on which he can depend?

He undertakes a mapping operation, moving among the various locales he knows of, listening for evidence of still others, and visiting most or all of these. This is a tour of limited discovery – a first reliable and extensive (not intensive) look at the things, persons, and activities that constitute the site. An operation of this sort is not mandatory, but if the researcher is to be systematic, he needs a sense of population or universe. Besides, given the complexity of the task before him, what better way is there for establishing the properties

Source: Leonard Schatzman & Anselm L. Strauss, *Field Research: Strategies for a Natural Sociology* (Englewood Cliffs: Prentice Hall, 1973).

to be observed and priorities for dealing with them? In studying institutional phenomena of such complexity – where the parameters of the object exist in outline – this procedure is particularly economical of time and energy. When studying a movement, which has few or no clear lines, the universe may well be the last item discovered; mapping would then be indistinguishable from substantive data gathering, and not be at all a preliminary stage.

A number of tactical moves can help facilitate the mapping operation. The researcher can, of course, perform the task himself; but it is helpful to have the services of an informant or guide – a "man Friday" – to escort and inform him, and introduce him to many persons whom he will later wish to observe and speak with at greater length. A request that the leadership provide such a person offers two tactical advantages: the researcher gets the help he needs, and the leadership is assured that the guest will get to see the "right" things and people – and also be kept out of trouble. The researcher should suggest that the guide be a person of somewhat lesser rank and an "old-timer." Such a person is part of the history as well as the structure of the organization, and as he escorts the guest can indicate important elements of social process, particularly of social and ideological succession. He can introduce the researcher to people whom he knows, giving names, ranks, and relationships. In addition to or instead of a single guide, the researcher can establish the same relationship with certain individuals at the several sub-sites: "old-timers" and secretaries know a great deal about people and places and can be excellent informants; also, they wield special powers. However the mapping tour is arranged – with or without a guide – it is important that the researcher signal his arrival at locations in advance to avoid surprise and embarrassment. He can do this by phone, or have someone call ahead for him, thereby providing a social bridge from one key person and locale to the next.

Mapping serves a number of important research interests: methodological, interactional, and substantive. Of these, the most important is the first mentioned; for shortly the researcher will need to know what to watch and with whom to converse – where, when, how much – and in what order. Hence, in mapping the researcher attends particularly to demographic data. For his "social map," he records numbers and varieties of persons, their hierarchical arrangement, divisions of labor, and other facts pertinent to his own operational decisions. For the same reason the researcher constructs his "spatial map," locating persons, equipment, and specialized centers of work and control. He also notes the corridors along which pass people, goods, and services. His "temporal map" will contain data bearing upon the ebb and flow of people, goods, services and communications. He looks for and asks about schedules which tell of hourly, daily, and weekly rhythms of work and play; also, he locates, in time, the special assemblies, rituals, and routines that characterize the locations. After he does this, he is in an excellent position to adjust his own time and other resources to the research task – or even alter the task, since even a quick "look-see" may uncover properties that alter his perception of the magnitude or complexity of the site and therefore alter the scope and direction of his research. For example, very early in our study of a private psychiatric hospital we found it necessary to look beyond the hospital in order to explain its workings. We discovered that the psychiatrists and residents were intricately associated with outside professional organizations and that these associations significantly shaped their day-to-day operations and professional commitment to the hospital itself.

Visits to the many locations lead the researcher to people who are variously delighted or annoyed with his presence, hungry for recognition, eager for audience, or embarrassed by some immediate state of affairs which would be threatened by exposure. The researcher senses these postures and feelings; he sizes them up for the next tactical stage in his research, for unless he requires starting his systematic observation in one locale rather than another, he might as well take advantage of the varieties of reception given him. He might as well, also, temporarily avoid those locales which make him particularly uncomfortable or anxious by virtue either of the work done there or of the kind of people who work there – or both. It makes sense, then, to begin systematic observation where he is most welcome and feels least anxious. Thereby he both spares those at the site undue anxiety over his presence and gives other sites time to prepare a welcome at some later date. Besides, those who would welcome him now are likely to be more eager to teach and inform him, and this is precisely what he seeks. The skilled observer is not concerned with the bias implicit in the differences in receptivity at locales; as he proceeds, he learns what and what not to discount.

In the same way, the experienced field observer will learn how to deal with the variety of persons who very willingly or insistently cast themselves into helping roles as "research assistant," "confidant," "tipster," "friend" (or enemy) of the establishment. As enthusiasts, apologists, ideologues, or disgruntled detractors of the organization or movement, these persons provide many bits of very useful information. Their "biases" are no less data than that offered by the more "objective" members of organization. In fact, they may alert the observer to matters that probably he would not discover until weeks later. Hence, these persons also must be kept in mind for later work – not only for the help they offer but for the problems they pose, if they turn out to be pests.

Additionally, the mapping tour alerts persons in the many areas or jurisdictions to the presence of the researchers. Key persons may not have been properly informed (or informed at all) of the study, by the leadership or others. Moreover, these persons at the sub-sites must be brought to concur with the earlier granting of entrée by others, or brought to terms with it in a manner that is advantageous to the research. By presenting himself informally, for a brief visit, the researcher achieves some tactical advantages: he is in a position to inform people of the nature of his study, give them a chance to look him over, and allow them to "test" his stated interests as these might affect them. At this time, the researcher seemingly comes to meet people, and not to "work." Actually he is always working, but the thrust of his first visit is a casual one of socially natural introductions and mutual examination. In some respects, the visit "ennobles" the people, constituting an act of some symbolic importance to many sub-groupings who – particularly in the basements and odd corners of an organization – may feel tangential to central operations.

Of course, the mapping operation provides the researcher with substantive data, even though he may have attended to them mainly for their operational or interactional value. Some experiences are quickly recorded as *methodological notes*, some as *theoretical* (or *inferential*) *notes*, and some as *observation notes*. (See the chapter on strategy for recording.) At this stage of operations the researcher subordinates somewhat his substantive experiences to methodological ones, not only to provide himself with material that will help him plan his next stages, but also to avoid being "flooded" by a mass of new, exciting, and highly undifferentiated happenings. Novices waste much time and energy, and often become confused, when they try to attend to and record everything that they are experiencing; later they spend days wondering why they had done so. The experienced observer is not overly concerned about "missing" things; most of what occurs will happen again and again. If a specific event does not get repeated, another which points to the same underlying pattern of occurrences very likely will. Besides, we are dealing with an ongoing process, and the special or untoward event which happened the day before the research began is theoretically no more important than the one which happens during the research. Any field researcher will recognize the plaint: "You should have been here last week (month, year)!" He will only shrug his shoulders regretfully and ask, "Tell me about it. What happened then?" In any event, all recorded happenings are convertible to a variety of purposes; thus, the record of the name and status of a person, used to develop a social map for methodological purposes, is also a note pertaining to substantive purposes.

With some skill in observing, and through careful listening (and the right kinds of questioning), the researcher assembles the data pertinent to his maps. The information garnered to date from the "casing," the negotiation with the leadership, from informants and visits, constitutes not only mapping information but also initial data. Almost immediately the researcher can begin his analysis; he need not wait until "all" or "much" of the data are in to do his thinking. This is not, after all, a final analysis; it is only the beginning.

By now, he has a considerable amount of data, and depending upon his experience with similar phenomena he can begin to coordinate some facts and inferences, and develop some cogent propositions along with plans for checking them out. Propositional statements, hypotheses, or hunches about processes or structural properties may be little more than simple declarative sentences, but they can be linked to each other and to the starting framework of concepts about organization, communication, control, socialization, and so on. Surely, many a historic decision affecting organizational policy is made with less care and in less time; but our researcher has a different kind of job to do. His understanding of the whole is still a bit shaky; it lacks validation if not plausibility, since at this point it is based as much upon his own past experience as upon his present ones.

Selective Sampling

Our field researcher now is in position to conduct selective observations at selected sub-sites. His mapping tour (or tours) has provided him with sets of population or universes – of people, places, events, and any other categories determined to be of some importance. He cannot hope to observe everything, since "everything" – even for a large research team – is only a theoretical possibility, particularly for such complex phenomena as we are dealing with here. Hence, selective sampling is a practical necessity and is theoretically mandatory; it is shaped by the time the researcher has available to him, by his framework, by his starting and developing interests, and by any restrictions placed upon his observation by his hosts.

Considering the stage of the research, and all that has happened to the researcher by way of experience, he may elect to step back – even leave the field for hours or days – to recoup his strength, to sort out what he has learned, and to decide more precisely upon his next sequence of operations. His strategy for the next stage is to move from one selected sub-site to another and sample at each site various "dimensions": time, space, people and events. Although his samples may appear to be numerically inadequate, it should be kept in mind that there is an "overlap" or intersection of these dimensions at all times. Thus, when the researcher samples persons, encounters with them will occur at a given time or over a span of time, at a place, in and around certain events. Even small samples of each dimension yield considerable "mileage" in the others.

Organizing Time

First, a brief word about the sampling of time. The researcher now has a general idea about the temporal activities of the various people at the site. He knows something of the routine, and not so routine, rhythms of the place. Of course, 24 hours per day is a theoretical limit. Whether the organization is a hospital, factory or a police system, he must discover what occurs, say, at 2:00 A.M., just as he must at any other hour. In other organizations or perhaps in a social movement, people do not work around the clock either by shifts or any other way, and this fact will have to be taken into account; still, the researcher may discover later that, despite a presumed eight-hour work pattern, certain persons in almost every social organization may meet regularly in "off hours" to work, plan, or simply fashion ideologies through informal conversation. Then he will have to make his own plans accordingly.

Time can be broken into hours and sampled directly, or sampled through events and activities including routines. Thus, if meetings are held at 9:00 A.M., the researcher covers *both* time and activity. If the researcher elects to observe work around the clock, he can first observe a day shift for several days, then evenings and then nights, for a period of consecutive days until he is reasonably familiar with all three shifts. Or he may cover events at any given sub-site by "overlapping" time on consecutive dates – for example, 7:00 A.M. to 9:00 A.M., 8:00 A.M. to 10.00 A.M., 9:00 A.M. to 11:00 A.M. – and over a period of days cover the organization around the clock. These tactical decisions will be made on any of several grounds: the researcher's other (nonresearch) obligations, sleeping habits, tolerance for dealing with different kinds of phenomena, and so on. Such methodical sampling will continue profitably only to the point of general familiarity; but also – or mainly – until the researcher has developed hypotheses or theoretical propositions whose importance demands increasingly, or from time to time, a reordering of his own schedules.

In situations where staffing patterns provide shift breaks and successions of personnel, however, the researcher will be certain to observe and to listen at these critical moments or events; for the personnel on each shift will be busy representing to each other, as realities, what transpired during the preceding time periods (which the researcher may or may not have observed directly that day). Also, timed observations will "tell" the researcher not only of 24-hour activity, but what occurs on weekends as against weekdays, Saturdays as against Sundays. These may be quite as different as the day is from the night. The researcher's increasing understanding of the time dimension in terms of events will affect his own operational decisions bearing upon the temporal dimension.

Deciding on a Research Location

Now a brief discussion bearing on the sampling of space or place. Of course the researcher must make critical decisions about *where* he should locate himself at any given time. There is a relationship between a location and the kinds of information and events that will come within his line of sight. Therefore, he constantly must ask himself, and others, where he should be; also in any specific location where he should stand or move about – indeed, whether he should follow particular persons who move (whose job it may be to move) from one situation or locale to another. Every decision will affect what kinds of events will come to his attention. The researcher must also consider that informal bits of evidence about the very location he is observing might actually be offered elsewhere, such as in a lounge or dining area.

Inevitably the researcher discovers that while he was observing at one subsite something happened at another that was more "significant" for his research; he may curse inwardly because he missed being at the event. Again, no matter – he made his decision to be where he was, and now must stick by it. At other times, the researcher begins to wonder whether he should not leave his current observation post, even though he may have been at it only an hour or so, because "nothing seems to be happening" that isn't familiar. He asks himself, "Shouldn't I be expending my energies elsewhere?" It is just such decisions over which novices anguish, but actually they need not. They must learn to live with the reality that is research, as is life – while such decisions must be made, proper selective sampling eventually will meet their most stringent research requirements.

All this suggests decisions among *single, multiple* and *mobile* positioning, and alternations among these. Obviously, a single position yields a relatively narrow perspective, even though the researcher is picking up a variety of cues about what is going on elsewhere, particularly as these events impinge upon the single station. There are some advantages, however, to "staying put" for longer periods: the researcher stabilizes time as well as place (eventful time elsewhere may be quite different); also he gains the advantage of having greater familiarity with those who work at this specific site (they may find it easy to explain their work to someone interested enough to tarry).

Multiple positioning has its advantages, too. It provides comparative data of all sorts, and allows the researcher to raise hypotheses about relations among people at different locations; he gets wider perspective. Also, he can move about, particularly in the early stages, using movement as a tactic for giving "relief" to persons in any given location who communicate their unease at being observed. There is also a tactic of *tracing* wherein the researcher attaches himself to a single person (of a class of people) and follows him or them about through the entire course of a single task, or even an entire work shift. (We say more about this tactic in a later chapter.)

In connection with the sampling of locations, the observer also may have in mind sampling *things*, such as instruments or other equipment located in special rooms. These are pertinent to given tasks at the site, and although ultimately related to people and activity, they may constitute a kind of spatial sample because of their location.

The various tactics of spatial observation are by no means mutually exclusive; they complement each other and present an almost infinite variety of opportunities – also some headaches and hard decisions concerning where to be at any given time. Again, randomness has little value; interest and emergent opportunities have priority.

Sampling People

In his sampling of people, the researcher works from a sociologically axiomatic base: that in any human organization, people stand in different relationships to the whole of that organization, in some important respects probably viewing and using it differently; and that these differences can be gleaned from what people say and how they act. While the researcher anticipates meeting certain classes of persons at the site or the sub-site, certain existential properties of people will be "presented" to him, and also he understands that probably he will discover classes of people not initially obvious to him. Certainly he could do the sampling task randomly; but again he has selected samples in mind, and probably in such density as to insure the necessary coverage of all the important or at least obvious ones. He will probably select from among the universe of people according to their functions *for his research*. Thus, if his perspective and interests are predominantly historical, his central selective principle may be seniority in the organization: old-timers and new-comers have entered the stream of organizational history at different points. They have had not only different past experiences but now experience the movement or the organization differently by virtue of their respective differences in time of entry – and probably also because of qualitative differences in their organizational commitments. On the other hand if the researcher's interest bears mainly on the exercise of power, probably he will give higher priority – greater sampling chance – to the category of "echelon." Likewise, other categories (such as age, sex, status, role or function in the organization, or even stated philosophy or ideology) might operate as departures for selective sampling. Our researcher is quite aware that his own activity might, and probably will, lead to discoveries of *new* categories. Hence, those regarded earlier of relative unimportance may become extremely important. For example, *sex differentiation* may appear initially of no importance but later the researcher realizes that important differences exist within the organization by virtue of sex; consequently he develops appropriate hypotheses and so plans more thorough sampling by that particular dimension.

Sampling Events

Another dimension that the researcher finds very important concerns *events or situations*. In truth, this dimension is at the heart of his research insofar as time, place, and even people represent – sociologically speaking – merely a context for situations and activities. There is a universe of situations or events from which the researcher can sample. Generally speaking, events or situations are of three orders: routine, special, and untoward. To the extent the human organization that he is studying is institutionalized, it will undoubtedly have many routine events, but even social movements will have some of these. Routine events are regularly scheduled situations wherein people meet to work or to discuss their activities. These situations include all regular meetings, conferences, and ordinary daily activities or work. Special events include fortuitous but anticipated occurrences, which, though not necessarily routine, are organized for moving the organization through successive stages of its activities. There are special meetings, outings, prearranged visits by outsiders, and the like. Untoward events include those that are entirely unanticipated, of an emergency nature, or to some extent anticipated but untimed. Clearly the situational dimension is highly interrelated with the temporal and spatial dimensions.

The easiest and most obvious procedure is to obtain lists of scheduled events that occur during any given period, such as a week, and selectively sample each event. Situations are, in fact, of such critical importance that the researcher might not even sample; he might take the entire universe – so that he is assured of having observed at least once every routine event which occurs in the organization. Later, he can establish the importance of any of these events, and decide how many successive visits and observations he would need before he could fully understand the implications of each event. In the course of these visits and participations, the researcher will hear of special events

upcoming and will take pains to attend and observe at these, for he can expect that special events have special implications for the participants. To the
extent that either is at any given location within the organization or moving
about, he is in a position to witness untoward events. And if not actually there
in the midst of a unique occurrence, he will have people at hand with whom
he can speak about what had actually occurred – usually picking up a variety of perspectives on any given occurrence. He can maximize this variety
by seeking out persons whom he anticipates might have differential perspectives, including those that represent people low in hierarchy or tending to hold
marginal or "peculiar" views.

The Task and the Resources to Do It

The researcher has just about finished his mapping procedures and now has
an opportunity to look more fully at the task he has set for himself. On a closer
look probably the task has presented him with new properties: technical problems, and intellectual or research opportunities that he had not anticipated.
Any of these possibilities may have altered his original foci of interest – sharpened or shifted them. In fact, this is a critical juncture in his research, for he
will find it necessary to measure the task (as a result either of prior expectation or new revelation) that he wishes to accomplish against his available
resources. These resources include mundane but very important factors such
as his own time, energy, and money – the last mentioned bearing on whether
he can hire research or clerical assistants.

The researcher knows he must make some difficult decisions, but he can
employ a number of alternate tactical plans. Let us imagine first several new
problems in his research. One obvious problem is that "the thing" is bigger
than he had originally thought: the institution is more complex than anticipated. Perhaps the social movement has unanticipated dimensions of ideology
and organizational activity, or the movement once thought distinctive is now
found to be intricately tied to another movement. Also, as the researcher
moved about among locales and among advocates of the social movement,
he had found it too scattered spatially for the kind of work he imagined he
would be doing, or so ephemeral that locations as well as people are very
mobile and therefore elusive. Perhaps he would need far more time than
anticipated to search for events and people, and perhaps many have no phones
nor even stable addresses. In institutional research, an equivalent problem may
be the difficulty of making appointments to see people and even to locate them
within rooms and corridors. Such problems threaten the researcher's entire
timetable. Additional difficulties that may befall any researcher are easily
conjured up.

Of course, these problems are variously difficult or significant as defined
by a researcher in terms of his own personal properties. He must count his
pennies, find an automobile that will give the needed mobility to track down

respondents; also he must assess his own talent, skills and motivations for tracking people down, and for persuading them to talk freely and to accept him as a sort of constant companion. Can he indeed change his sleeping habits and alter his schedule of relations with family and friends? Does he have the patience and the thickness of skin necessary to find people and to persuade them to cooperate? In short, this is a time when the researcher must negotiate with himself.

In handling the above problems, the researcher has a number of options. He can narrow his focus and settle on only one rather than two or three important questions that he might ask about his object of inquiry. After all, a little earlier he may have found that some of his initial ideas were not very clever or profound; even have discovered some new and potentially more fruitful foci of interest. Now is the time to seize the opportunity actually to restructure interests and simultaneously tailor the task more realistically to one's resources and talents. Perhaps now he can sacrifice some breadth for depth of coverage, concentrating on a narrower range – though he may not if he finds good reasons not to do so.

Another option is to increase the number and depth of interviews, but reduce somewhat the time devoted to observation. After all, when one measures the cost-effectiveness of interviewing against observation, the former is more economical. The researcher need not, however, abandon observation; he will still do it but mainly to test what he hears, rather than primarily to discover something new that way. Certainly, for social movements in early development there is relatively little to observe. As for institutional life and work where ideology and operational philosophy are fairly well articulated, the researcher can skillfully pit one interview against another and only sparingly observe his respondents in action to insure the validity of their remarks. Also, following his mapping tour and initial assessment of the task, he may have become sufficiently savvy to develop a brief but incisive questionnaire covering a number of points salient to his interests. This would give him at least some of the breadth he wants, but with some economy in time – having covered everyone in small but significant measure he then can concentrate on fewer key people. Of course this option may have to be weighed against his promise not to make any or much work for his host. But didn't the chief want some answers to certain fundamental questions in line with the researcher's initial objectives?

Finally, he may secure assistance in the form of a *research team* if he has the requisite money – he may be able to buy time in order to do the job as he wishes. Or, he may be able to persuade some colleagues to join him, each taking a focus for himself although sharing data with all. A division of labor not only is time saving but can be productive conceptually, insofar as each can make an original contribution or simply function as a sounding board for another's ideas. Under team conditions, contributions tend to multiply rather than add up, and multiple researchers have the advantages of a built-in and rapid corrective to false ideas, which would take considerable time or at least more time to correct alone. Also, many blind operational alleys are avoided through mutual counsel. Yet, team work is not all positive. A lone researcher perhaps ought not to be dissuaded from pursuing an intriguing idea, or ought not to have to concern himself with compromises for the sake of "adjustment" to the personalities and hang-ups of colleagues. If the assistants are not "true" colleagues but have quite different conceptual frameworks, then considerable difficulty in cooperation is encountered. Likewise, if the assistants are not genuine equals but hired hands without much theoretical or methodological sophistication, then the chief researcher would need to train, monitor, and supervise them, and thereby do too little actual fieldwork for his own satisfaction.

All the above problems and options further depend on the researcher's degree of familiarity with the general activities and vocabularies of the scene or "world" that he is observing. When he is quite familiar with the scene, his observations and his interviews need not cover every aspect of activity or nuance of verbal meaning. He already has appreciable definition and conceptual grasp of the situation. We say this in the face of our own admonitions to students not to take meanings for granted, but to probe for them. However, the skilled and knowledgeable researcher will probe for nuance selectively, either because he doesn't yet understand something fully enough or is intent upon finding shades of difference among his respondents. To the extent that he knows reasonably well some of the major vocabulary of the persons in the particular world under study, he need not probe for the meanings of every term. But if the activities and vocabularies which structure the scene are new and perhaps strange, then the researcher has no recourse but to plumb their meanings. The option then to reduce the scope of study makes some sense. For those researchers who feel deeply that they must have a reasonably good grasp of the whole in order to research any part of it, the problem of encompassing the whole can be handled through highly selective interviews of a few key people coupled with selective observations. The mapping tour itself may be enough to provide sufficient context for whatever specific aspect or problem is being researched.

Of course, we are writing here in the light of possible "compromises" which may be required – given real limitations in time and other resources – yet a word is necessary bearing on the overall question of time in relation to "depth." In an older tradition of scholarship and thoroughness, particularly as developed in anthropology, the researcher set virtually no (or very long) time limits to his work in an effort to plumb the very depths of the culture under study. This length of time may be necessary for no other reason than that language systems have to be understood reasonably well before other aspects of culture can be understood. We do not need to follow this model in its purest form (nor do all social anthropologists). We can assume that our researcher has had some experiences – perhaps vicariously – with the phenomenon in question, some acquaintanceship with its special vocabulary, and above all probably the sense enough to know that he will not "get it all." (Again, we shall return to this topic in the chapter on analysis.)

Later we shall refer to a concept of "spinning off," wherein a researcher abstracts pieces of the whole over time, assuming that he wishes to go on and on as in a "lifetime" of work. For the most part, and realistically, researchers first will get a general picture and then focus on one or two special problems but only until their satisfactory completion. With some preplanning and especially with inclusion of such procedures as "casing" and "mapping," the researcher will know how much he can reasonably accomplish in any given period of time. We recall our having briefly visited and mapped eight semiautonomous treatment wards at a state hospital, and not having the time to study each to our satisfaction. What to do? Study everyone less thoroughly? Select three or four by strictly random number? But we had indeed visited them all and already knew enough about each to take a meaningful – that is, theoretically fruitful – sample. Since our foci of interests included treatment ideology as well as organization and operations, we developed a simple classificatory scheme which yielded four classes and one unique, nondescript case. One class offered three cases, of which we selected the ideological archetype; another class offered two cases of which we again selected the archetype. These selections, then, allowed us to screen out three questionably productive cases. Finally, we selected the nondescript case because, we felt, the uniqueness of its structure would yield data of theoretical importance to the understanding of the entire lot of wards. This is how we were able to conceptualize the whole and tailor it to the resources available to us.

Where Does One Start and When?

We have already indicated that when researching a social movement the observer begins his research with his first contact, wherever that may be, and makes his way from there by depending upon successive informants to guide or cue him to other persons and places. Initially, at least, there is little problem about when and where to start. If researching a new social movement, the researcher often has relatively few initial cues and leads, therefore works quite pragmatically and often depends primarily upon fortuitous circumstances. Eventually, through his effective interviewing, informants will offer him multiple opportunities for watching and listening. He will recognize that he is being offered options and will select them in sequence according to the requirements of any given stage of his research. Generally, he moves towards observing the ideological and organizational leadership and the larger and more stable clusterings of advocates.

In organizational research, where locations of activity and of groups are reasonably well laid out through the mapping process, care has to be given to where and when to "start." The decision concerning where to start has special importance, for it bears upon the relationships existing among organizational segments and their relative power and prestige – particularly between the formal administrative leadership and other echelons. Since the researcher has come through the front office, probably he will decide to start his research there for at least two good reasons.

First, he must eventually – the sooner the better – separate himself from the leadership by publicly establishing his independence in the research and in all his social relations on the job. Thus, if he is to study central administration at all he might well begin there. Then, either he leaves it and does not return until the end of his work, or visits there only intermittently, depending on his research purposes. In any event, the researcher must not appear to be reporting findings and may have to take special pains to prove that he is not. The researcher actually will tell people elsewhere about his independence and his respect for each and all groups; but he must demonstrate his honesty by actions as well as by assertion. It may take a bit of time before he earns trust.

The second reason for starting with the central administration is that it can provide a special overview of the entire operation, including its intended work, the rationale for it and its organization. Here, the researcher can get a history of the organization, and a "view from the top" bearing upon the present state and future plans of the organization – a view possibly neither fully shared with nor agreed upon by any other segment of the organization. Of course, this view, however apparently complete and "straight from the horse's mouth," is no more true or real than any other view; but it is one (or several depending upon the number of persons there) that provides a good working start for the researcher.

Following his observations and conversations with the leadership, the researcher returns to those people and places that he visited while mapping. His observational schedules reflect his current substantive interests, sampling plans, and estimates of personnel receptivity. If he has not already done so he will arrange, as he moves from one site to the next, to start there when most persons are present to hear him tell at least briefly of his work and of his independence. This is not at all difficult to arrange: in most service institutions the personnel meet frequently as teams.

In deciding to begin observing at any given sub-site, the researcher utilizes a number of tactics that takes into account the readiness of people to be observed. He has recognized *differences in receptivity* among the various people at the sub-sites, knowing that members at some sites require more time to get ready for him, or perhaps require time to hear that no untoward or threatening events have occurred as a consequence of his presence elsewhere. Once relatively good relations have been established, he will be a frequent visitor there, for he finds it advantageous to keep the relationship "warm." Indeed, his disappearance from any sub-site for too many days, sometimes even for hours, will cool relationships. Once people accept the researcher they want him to be present at their work – and expect him to be there. Many a researcher, though relatively saturated with data or concerned with planning his next steps, will visit a sub-site regularly not so much to observe as to maintain good relations until he can put a closure to a given set of observations. This tactic may not be necessary at later stages of the research when and if most people generally have accepted him, although if he expects to return again at all to the sub-site he may still have to plead being very busy pursuing his research interests elsewhere. However, his relatively continuous presence or at least occasional revisits will surely yield excellent results; once respondents take the researcher into account as a symbolic reference they will regularly tell him of things missed between his visits: "you should have been here this morning! ..."

All the above remarks apply to organizational research and also to research into social movements, whose sub-sites are spatially separate but not so distant that they cannot easily be visited. If the researcher is studying a social movement or an organization whose sub-sites are geographically dispersed (as in "branches"), then he may treat each as a kind of separate site which possesses its own sub-sites. There is an exception, however, and that is when the branches are so small as to constitute only a small group of people; seemingly then they have no sub-sites. Their absence may be more apparent than real, since even small groups usually have sub-groupings of persons who can be discovered meeting informally either in spatial areas of "the same place" or outside the organization's work place or the social movement's office or meeting place.

Suggested Reading

There is a paucity of good (or extensive) discussion on "getting started." However, in various monographs one can see the field worker in the early stages of the organization of his work. Listed below are a number of excellent monographs chosen both for their range of substantive focus and for their information (unfortunately sometimes too sparse) on starting and organizing processes.

Note

1. A search for boundaries – outer or inner – may prove elusive, for relationships and functions flow into and out of most social units. Yet the researcher will have to set some limits for very practical reasons. He will do so after he has established his main foci of interest.

Sociologists

Becker, Howard, Blanche Geer, and E. Hughes, *Making the Grade*. New York: John Wiley & Sons, 1968.

Becker, Howard, Blanche Geer, E. Hughes, and A. Strauss, *Men in White*. Chicago: University of Chicago Press, 1961.

Bott, Elizabeth, *Family and Social Network*. London: Tavistock Publishing Co., 1957.

Cavan, Sherry, *Liquor License.* Chicago: Aldine Publishing Co., 1966.

Cressey, Paul G., *The Taxi Dance Hall.* Chicago: University of Chicago Press, 1932.

Dalton, Melville, *Men Who Manage.* New York: John Wiley & Sons, 1959.

Dollard, John, *Caste and Class in a Southern Town.* New York: Doubleday & Co., 1937.

Fox, Renee, *Experiment Perilous.* New York: The Free Press, 1959.

Gans, Herbert, *The Levittowners.* New York: Pantheon Books, 1967.

Glaser, B., and A. Strauss, *Awareness of Dying.* Chicago: Aldine Publishing Co., 1965.

Hughes, Everett, *French Canada in Transition.* Chicago: University of Chicago Press, 1963.

Humphries, Laud, *Tearoom Trade.* Chicago: Aldine Publishing Co., 1970.

Lewis, Hyland, *Blackways of Kent.* Chapel Hill, N.C.: University of North Carolina Press, 1955.

Liebow, Elliot, *Tally's Corner.* Boston: Little, Brown and Co., 1967.

Lofland, John, *Doomsday Cult.* Englewood Cliffs, N.J.: Prentice-Hall, 1966.

Lynd, R., and D. Lynd, *Middletown.* New York: Harcourt Brace Jovanovich, 1929.

Olesen, Virginia, and E. Whittaker, *The Silent Dialogue.* San Francisco: Jossey-Bass, 1968.

Rainwater, Lee, et al., *Behind Ghetto Walls.* Chicago: Aldine Publishing Co., 1970.

Roth, Julius, *Timetables.* Indianapolis: Bobbs-Merrill, 1963.

Seeley, J., R. Sim, and E. Loosley, *Crestwood Heights.* New York: John Wiley & Sons, 1963.

Stanton, Alfred, and Morris Schwarts, *The Mental Hospital.* New York: Basic Books, 1954.

Strauss, A., L. Schatzman, R. Bucher, D. Erlich, and M. Sabshin, *Psychiatric Ideologies and Institutions.* New York: The Free Press, 1964.

Sudnow, David, *Passing On.* Englewood Cliffs, N.J.: Prentice-Hall, 1967.

Suttles, Gerald, *The Social Order of the Slum.* Chicago: University of Chicago Press, 1968.

Vidich, A., and J. Bensman, *Small Town in Mass Society.* New York: Doubleday & Co., 1960.

Vogel, Ezra, *Japan's New Middle Class.* Berkeley: University of California Press, 1967.

Whyte, William F., *Street Corner Society.* Chicago: University of Chicago Press, 1941. Revised edition, 1955.

Young, Michael, and Peter Willmott, *Family and Kinship in East London.* Baltimore: Penguin Books, 1962.

Anthropologists

Arensberg, Conrad, *The Irish Countryman.* New York: The Macmillan Company, 1942.

Beals, Alan, *Gopalur: A South Indian Village.* New York: Holt, Rinehart and Winston, 1970.

Berraman, Gerald, *Behind Many Masks: Ethnography and Impression Management in a Himalayan Village.* Ithaca, N.Y.: Sociological Applied Anthropology, Monograph #4, 1962.

Davis, Allis, et al., *Deep South.* Chicago: University of Chicago Press, 1941.

DuBois, Cora, *The People of Alor.* Minneapolis: University of Minnesota Press, 1944.

Evans-Pritchard, E., *Witchcraft, Oracles and Magic Among the Azande.* New York: Oxford University Press, 1937.

——, *The Nuer.* Oxford: Clarendon Press, 1940.

Firth, Raymond, *We, The Tikopia.* London: Allen and Unwin, 1936.

Fortes, Meyer, *The Web of Kinship Among the Tallensi.* London, New York: Published for the International African Institute by the Oxford University Press, 1949.

Gallagher, Arthur, *Plainville Fifteen Years After*. New York: Columbia University Press, 1961.

Geertz, Clifford, *Peddlers and Princes*. Chicago: University of Chicago Press, 1963.

Hitchcock, John, *The Magars of Banyan Hill*. New York: Holt, Rinehart and Winston, 1966.

Joseph, Alice, Rosamond Spicer, and Jane Chesky, *The Desert People: A Study of the Papago Indians*. Chicago: University of Chicago Press, 1949.

Kluckhohn, Clyde, and Dorothea Leighton, *The Navaho*. Cambridge, Mass.: Harvard University Press, 1961.

Leach, Edmund, *Political Systems of Highland Burma: A Study of Kachin Social Structure*. Cambridge, Mass.: Harvard University Press, 1954.

——, *Pul Eliya: A Village in Ceylon*. Cambridge, England: Cambridge University Press, 1961.

Lewis, Oscar, *Life in a Mexican Village*. Urbana, Ill.: University of Illinois Press, 1951.

Malinowski, B., *Argonauts of the Western Pacific*. New York: E. P. Dutton, 1961.

Phillips, H., *Thai Peasant Personality*. Berkeley: University of California Press, 1965.

Redfield, Robert, *The Folk Culture of Yucatan*. Chicago: University of Chicago Press, 1941.

Spiro, Melford E., *Kibbutz: Venture in Utopia*. Cambridge, Mass.: Harvard University Press, 1956.

Warner, W. Lloyd, *A Black Civilization*. New York: Harper & Row, 1937. Revised edition, 1958.

——, *The Social Life of a Modern Community*. New Haven, Conn.: Yale University Press, 1941.

18

In the Company of Teachers:
Key Informants and the Study of a
Comprehensive School

Robert G. Burgess

Ethnographic research is characterized by the intense nature of relationships that are established between researcher and researched. Accordingly, many of the basic sociological texts devoted to this style of social investigation discuss elements of the personal relationships involved in this work: establishing relationships, developing trust and the presentation of self (cf. Lofland, 1971; Schatzman and Strauss, 1973; Johnson, 1975). While such accounts touch the heart of ethnographic research that involves describing and understanding the lives of particular groups of people, they do, nevertheless, spend little time on key informants and their role within the ethnographic enterprise.

This omission is somewhat surprising on at least three counts. First, ethnography relies for its basic data on the testimony of individual informants (cf. Conklin, 1968). Secondly, some ethnographic accounts are focused upon the relationship between the researcher and a key informant. For example, the data that were collected in Whyte's classic study *Street Corner Society* (Whyte, 1981) and in Liebow's *Tally's Corner* (Liebow, 1967) relied heavily upon the key informants: Doc and Tally respectively. Indeed, it is the key informants who are synonymous with these studies.[1] Finally, if we turn to anthropological accounts of ethnographic work (cf. Agar, 1981) the informant and the informant's role is seen as a central part of ethnographic research. Indeed, Casagrande (1960) considers that the anthropologist who engages in fieldwork is involved in a collaborative enterprise with a group of informants, for he argues that

Source: Robert Burgess (ed.), *Strategies of Educational Research* (London: Falmer Press, 1985).

the successful outcome of field research depends not only on the anthropologist's own skills, but also on the capabilities and interests of those who teach him their ways. (Casagrande, 1960, p. x)

For Casagrande considers that the anthropologist-informant relationship will result in informants inviting the researcher to participate in their activities as well as teaching the researcher about events they feel will be of interest. It is in this way that the researcher becomes conversant with everything from routine activities to momentous events together with the role that gossip plays in the everyday lives of the people who are studied.

Nevertheless, when we turn to major educational studies that have utilized an ethnographic style of investigation we find that informants are not mentioned (cf. Hargreaves, 1967; Lacey, 1970). Even when they are discussed it is often in the context of other work, yet their role does appear to have had some significance. For example, Woods (1981) in discussing the role of talk in ethnographic work comments upon key informants. However, his remarks suggest that they played an important role in developing his methodology for he states:

I was fortunate in finding some key informants. They helped give perspective to the entire methodological front from the very beginning, for example by identifying the nature of other people's talk and behaviour. (Woods, 1981, p. 16)

Indeed, he points to the value of informants in providing knowledge on different social contexts, in providing explanations of situations that have been observed, and in giving the researcher some sense of the historical events in which observational work needs to be located.[2] Similarly, Ball (1984) commenting upon his study *Beachside Comprehensive* (Ball, 1981) indicates that teacher informants did play an important role. In particular, he discusses the role of five teachers who he argues could not be described as typical or untypical or representative of all teachers in the school. They were individuals who he got to know well and who could adopt a reflexive stance towards the school. They could also discuss and evaluate some of the situations that he had observed.[3]

Certainly, when I conducted an ethnographic study of a purpose built co-educational comprehensive school that I called Bishop McGregor (Burgess, 1983) I found that much of my fieldwork was done in collaboration with teacher and pupil informants (cf. Burgess, 1983, especially chapters 2, 4, 7 and 8). Yet when we turn to many methodological accounts of ethnographic work in educational settings we find little attention given to informants.[4] Accordingly, in an attempt to begin to fill this gap in our knowledge, this paper focuses upon a selection of teachers who became key informants in the course of my Bishop McGregor study. Among the issues that we shall address are: initial contacts, establishing and developing a group of informants, selection issues, informant roles and some ethical problems involved in the researcher–informant relationship.

Initial Contacts

As the authors of the celebrated anthropological guide to fieldwork, *Notes and Queries* (Royal Anthropological Institution, 1951) state, there is a sense in which every member of the group that is studied is a potential informant as all individuals may be observed in the course of an investigation. However, it is usual for the researcher to focus on particular individuals during the period of study but we might ask: are they purposely selected by the researcher? Do they select the researcher? Are they representative of broader groups that are studied?

My initial contact at Bishop McGregor School was the headmaster (Burgess, 1985a) but having agreed to allow me to conduct research within the school he passed me on down the staff hierarchy to a teacher called Sylvia Robinson who at that time was Head of Careers and in charge of the Newsom Department[5]; the department that I intended to study. It was Sylvia Robinson who was to become a key informant and who was to play a major role in my study.

Numerous anthropologists (cf. Williams, 1967; Harrell-Bond, 1976) have warned that some individuals who attach themselves to the researcher may well be marginal to the group or institution that is studied. At the time, I did not consider the extent to which Sylvia might or might not be representative of other teachers for she appeared to me to be an ideal guide for a research novice. She was willing to introduce me to a variety of teachers, to take me into groups to which she belonged and to facilitate my presence in various areas of the school. On the first day of term she made it her business to meet me in the early morning and to take me to the House to which I had been allocated where she introduced me to all the staff. Similarly, in terms of the department she busied herself introducing me to other teachers and to groups of pupils who I was to teach. Furthermore, during morning breaks she took me to the staff common room where I was introduced to the group with whom she regularly sat. This group consisted predominantly of Heads of House (the most senior teachers in the school). During my early days in the common room I kept a systematic record of the teachers who sat in this group and on this basis I found that not only was I marginal to this group in terms of status but so was Sylvia. Indeed, I later learned that it was widely rumoured that Sylvia Robinson sat with this group in an attempt to become involved in the day-to-day activities of those teachers who ran the school.

Sylvia Robinson was marginal to this informal group in the staff common room and to several groups in various departments (Newsom, biology and religious education) where she taught. However, she used her marginal position to engage individuals in conversation. She was a collector of gossip in the school and would relay whatever information she had acquired to other teachers. In this sense, she was widely regarded by teachers as the staff gossip-monger. Her role as collector and transmitter of gossip among the staff was of great value to me as a researcher as I acquired a working knowledge of different areas of the school, rapidly became acquainted with knowledge about members of the school (which needed subsequently to be checked with other informants) and was introduced to a wide variety of teachers.

However, it did not stop there. Sylvia was a fund of knowledge about individual pupils and could provide a potted history of their school lives, their misdemeanours and their relationships with other teachers. For just as she engaged staff in conversation so were many of her classes devoted to gossip with pupils, so much so that pupils regularly declared that 'Miss Robinson's been trying to find out all our business again'. Yet in research terms, it was gossip that provided a good start for my research as Sylvia gave me leads to follow, information that could subsequently be checked and ideas about documents that I should ask to see. Often when I wanted to hear about specific events in the past or to find out about a situation I had not witnessed or a meeting I had not attended, it was to Sylvia I turned as I could be sure that she would have a version of what had occurred or, if she did not, she would make it her business to find out what had transpired.

Sylvia Robinson worked with me throughout the whole period of my research and provided a constant supply of data about teachers, pupils, departments and various other areas of the school. Meanwhile, Maggie Rolls (a Head of House) provided guidance on the House system during my first term in the school. Maggie Rolls had joined the school as an assistant teacher when it had first opened four years before my research began. She had been a member of many of the initial planning meetings in departments and had been the first of several teachers to be promoted internally from the position of assistant teacher in a department to Head of House. However, among the Head of Houses she was the most junior in terms of chronological age and years of teaching experience. In the early days of my research she was willing to explain school routines, answer numerous questions and queries, dig out specific documents and pupil files which she thought would be of interest to me and give access to the whole filing system within her House that provided sets of minutes and logs of decisions on most activities that had been planned in the early development of the school.

In the case of this teacher I found her knowledge of the school and the background she could provide on the development of school routines invaluable. Indeed, many of her remarks could be followed up through the documents that were located in the detailed filing system she had established. Indeed, when documents were missing from her files she was able to indicate the kind of material that I should request from the school secretary. Just as Sylvia Robinson was a guide to the departmental system, so Maggie Rolls was a guide to the House system as she taught me what for her was involved in being a Head of House.

As far as Maggie Rolls was concerned, being a Head of House meant being the equivalent of a head of a small junior school. However, she did indicate that other House Heads saw the position in different terms. Furthermore, she indicated that for her, being a Head of House meant finding out about pupils' home backgrounds, following up situations when they were in trouble, handling court appearances and dealing out punishment in her House. She explained to me her policy on punishment and on corporal punishment which in some instances was different from other House Heads. For example, she indicated a number of offences, including truancy, for which she would always administer corporal punishment. By the time we discussed this matter I was already aware of the 'heavy' caning policy in her House as I often witnessed pupils waiting to be caned, heard caning taking place and saw corporal punishment being administered. However, when I asked if she entered each offence in the school punishment book she laughed and said that neither she nor her deputy could afford the time to enter everything in the book. Yet even in these circumstances I found that according to the records in the punishment book more pupils were caned in her House compared with other Houses and the offences as listed were different from those that were catalogued by other House Heads.

My initial contact with Maggie Rolls provided me with guidance on a different aspect of school organization to that provided by Sylvia Robinson. Maggie Rolls introduced me to the way in which she operated as a House Head. While it could not be claimed that her actions and activities were 'typical' of House Heads I did find that following her method of working gave me insights into this aspect of school organization, which helped me to orientate my questions on the House system and to make comparisons between her House and the other five Houses in the school. Certainly, when I moved to another House at the beginning of the next academic year I began to make comparisons between the rules and routines in the two Houses, to the ways in which the House Heads defined their activities and to the ways in which school routines were reinterpreted within the Houses. In this sense, this key informant not only helped to focus my data collection but also to orientate aspects of data analysis. However, at the beginning of the new academic year several new staff appointments were made, including some teachers who were to take Newsom classes for less able pupils that I had already been working with. It was this experience that helped me to establish a working relationship with some of these teachers and to broaden the group of individuals who were my key informants.

Establishing and Developing a Group of Informants

Among the teachers who were appointed to the staff in the autumn term 1973 were several probationary teachers, two of whom were required to teach their subjects to bottom sets in the fifth year that were heavily populated with

Newsom pupils. As these two teachers were allocated to the same House as I was in, we came into frequent contact with each other. They were eager to talk to me about the problems associated with teaching Newsom classes and for that matter about some of the routine difficulties that they encountered in their first few weeks of full time teaching. As a former teacher who was now doing research in the school and who was teaching Newsom classes it appeared that I could be used as a source of advice and support. Any admission of difficulty to me could be discussed without anything 'counting against them' in the formal assessment of probationary teachers, for although I was part of the school I was also an 'outsider'.

The two teachers belonged to the English and religious education departments. Of the two, I came to know Paul Klee in the English department best of all. He had recently completed a degree course in English and sociology and was acquainted with ethnographic research, having taken a special option on this subject in his final year at university. Without any prompting from me, he was able to ask searching questions about my research, my research focus, my methodology and the key aspects of my analysis. To begin with I found it somewhat unnerving to be confronted by someone who knew about participant observation. However, he was amused by what staff thought ethnographic research was about and what participant observation involved compared with what it *actually* involved. Without prompting from me, I found that he began to act as an honorary research assistant on my project.

For the purpose of research I was a part-time teacher in the school. Accordingly, I was only in the school for two days each week and could, as a lone researcher, only participate in a limited number of activities and meetings. Paul Klee would, therefore, spend time each day I was in the school updating me on the activities that had taken place in my absence. He was also willing to provide an eye witness account of meetings that he attended which gave me access to further dimensions of the school which could be checked out against my own observations. For example, he provided details of what occurred in the probationary teachers' meetings which gave me comparative data on the role of the head and heads of departments as well as data on activities that occurred in another sector of the school.

In turn, Paul Klee introduced me to members of the English department with the result that I used this department as a means of coming to terms with the 'academic' system in the school. Indeed, it was through Paul Klee that I became acquainted with the head of department and several English teachers, including those who taught Newsom classes. As well as introducing me to a wider range of teachers and helping to promote my work among them, Paul also talked about pupils and about classes. Indeed, it was Paul who would regularly update me on the latest round of activities that occurred in his English lessons and who informed me which pupils were absent and who was 'on form' on a particular day; a term that he reserved for pupils who were set on a course of maximum distraction and disruption in his lessons. Often Paul would join a group (including myself) in the staff common room where he would turn the conversation towards Newsom classes and Newsom pupils. This generated further material for me.

Of all the teachers with whom I worked, it was with Paul that I discussed my methodology in some depth. Indeed, it was on the basis of encouragement from Paul that I finally decided to invite teachers to keep diaries after which I conducted diary interviews with them (cf. Burgess, 1981; Burgess, 1984b, pp. 128–35). However, it was not merely at the level of talking about methods that Paul was helpful for he also assisted with data collection and analysis. On occasions when I indicated that I did not know the details about some activity, or that I did not know about an individual's involvement in a situation, Paul would agree to find out the information by entering into conversation with particular teachers. However, Paul was also eager to contribute to the way in which I might interpret my data and spent several evenings talking to me about his interpretation of situations and the sociological concepts that he would use in order to begin to organize the data and analyze it.

Paul Klee provided me with a new probationary teacher's perspective of the school and in turn fed me into a number of social networks to which he belonged in the English department and among young male teachers in the staff common room. In him I found that I had an informant who could provide a different perspective on the school and its members. However, I also appreciated that this junior teacher's perspective needed to be complemented by an account from a senior teacher. Here I was fortunate as in the spring term a new House Head was appointed to the House to which I belonged. The new House Head was a man called Ron Ward who had previously been a House Head in another Catholic comprehensive school. As a House Head Ron was responsible for discipline and order in the school and was a member of the House Heads' meeting which was part of the senior management team. On this basis, Ron was an ideal informant who complemented my other informants. His teaching duties included an assortment of subjects and some Newsom classes.

In common with other teachers Ron Ward found difficulty in teaching Newsom classes. Accordingly, he spent some considerable time talking to me about the Newsom pupils, the Newsom Department and the curriculum that was on offer. It was evident from Ron's remarks that he was not convinced by the approach that was being taken towards these pupils in Bishop McGregor School. He devoted some time with me trying to find out my ideas about Newsom teaching and about the way that Newsom teaching operated in the school, as well as testing out his ideas on me. Furthermore, he proceeded on several occasions to mount a critique of the way in which the school was organized and to offer suggestions about ways in which the headmaster's ideas about patterns of work and school routines could be redefined (cf. Burgess, 1983, pp. 52–83).

It was in these different ways that Ron provided me with a further perspective on the way in which the school operated. His remarks helped me to engage in further comparative analysis of the House system and the way in which it operated. However, he also gave me access to two other areas of school life. When I had negotiated access to the school I was given permission to examine all logs of decisions that came from the House Heads' meetings but I was not allowed to attend the meetings. Accordingly, much of my material on these meetings involved reconstruction of what had occurred on the basis of notes that were kept by the headmaster. Now with Ron's arrival I was given a participant's account as without prompting from me he was prepared to talk about the business that was transacted within the House Heads' meetings and the positions that were taken by individual House Heads over particular issues.

In the latter part of the spring term Ron indicated that he was finding particular difficulty with one of the Newsom groups that he taught. He suggested that because I was timetabled at the same time as he was and because I also had a small group we might combine our groups in order to engage in a team teaching activity. I considered this was a good opportunity not only to discover another teacher's conception of Newsom teaching but also to observe another teacher without having the label 'observer' attached to me. Accordingly, I agreed to co-operate in this activity as it provided further ethnographic data on teaching and on the relationships between teachers and pupils. In these terms, I used Ron's team teaching suggestion not only as a teaching venture but also as a further dimension to my research activities for it complemented the work that I had done with other teachers, and my own experience of teaching Newsom classes. On this basis it facilitated further comparative analysis. However, it might be argued that such activities were covert as far as my informant and his classes were concerned and that any researcher contemplating similar activities should consider whether the ends justify the means (Bulmer, 1982; Burgess, 1985a).

While Ron Ward gave me access to various dimensions of the school, the House system and the Newsom Department, he also, in common with many other teachers, indicated the importance of the headmaster in all the activities that were established in the school. It was evident from my research experience that the head should be one of my key informants yet there were few opportunities outside the formal school timetable when I could engage in conversation with him. All my contacts with the head on a one-to-one basis were fleeting encounters. I had an opportunity to meet him briefly when he came into the staff common room each morning break that he was in the school or during the course of many of his innumerable walks across the school site. On such occasions I found that, like other teachers, I would be the subject of a quick comment or question before he moved on to talk in a similar fashion to other teachers. While such encounters were the experience of many teachers they could not be used to provide detailed ethnographic material on the headteacher and on headship. Yet I also had further formal encounters with the head: when he took morning assembly, when he chaired meetings of the Newsom Department and when he chaired full staff meetings. In addition, much of the documentary material on routines and procedures in the school had been written by the head.

In these circumstances, I decided that I would need to conduct a series of informant interviews with him if I was to obtain his life history, his educational experience, his educational philosophy and details of the way in which his ideas were put into operation in Bishop McGregor School. Originally, I had planned for two sessions in which to interview the head, but we mutually agreed to a series of discussions that resulted in eight one-and-a-half-hour tape-recorded conversations. These interviews not only generated conversational data but also resulted in further documents being provided about the school and school activities. These eight encounters that took place over a three-month period were not merely 'interviews' but also chart the consolidation of a relationship. Here, I was tested with confidential information, used as a confidant, and as a 'sounding board' about further ideas for the school. Furthermore, just as I was attempting to get the head to talk about his conception of the school, so in turn he attempted (but in my view with relatively little success) to get me to talk about the views that particular teachers held of the school. At the end of this period of interviewing I negotiated permission to spend several days with him, rather in the style in which Wolcott (1973) had done with an elementary school principal in the United States. Accordingly, the study of the school has included a chapter on the headmaster where a detailed account could be provided about his activities and relationships with other teachers (cf. Burgess, 1983, pp. 26–51).

Finally, the head has, as a key informant, provided comments on all the materials that I have written about the school. All the material that he has read has always been in a pseudonymized form. Here, he has provided a check on the 'accuracy' of my material (at least from his perspective) and on occasion has provided alternative explanations to my accounts. Some of these I have not accepted as, for example, on one occasion when he indicated that a chapter was 'fine' apart from some repetition for which he gave me the page references and which he thought I could delete without further discussion. On checking I found that my 'repetition' included a critical passage on the head himself and I have, therefore, kept this material within the final study. However, there have been situations in which he has provided alternative explanations which I have entered in footnotes for the benefit of readers. In addition, he has also provided new perspectives on 'old' problems and generated further questions and further data that could be used for this study and subsequent projects. Accordingly, he has, for me, been an informant *par excellence*.

For the purpose of this discussion I have presented five people who I considered were key informants in my study. These informants included men and women, senior and junior teachers, teachers drawn from the pastoral, as well as the departmental side of the school and a range of people who although at different stages of their teaching careers all taught in the Newsom Department. As informants they provided different services for me and in turn introduced me to different dimensions of the school and raised different issues about key informants in ethnographic research to which we now turn.

Issues on Key Informants

(i) Selection Strategies

Many researchers have indicated that their encounters with individuals who became key informants occurred by 'chance' and/or that they were people who they got to know particularly well or with whom they became friends. While I would not deny that these are dimensions of my research encounters I would also argue that some account has to be taken of who becomes a key informant, their sex, status and role, if the researcher is to exercise some control over the collection of data. At Bishop McGregor School I kept a record of my informants and of my key informants in order that I could examine the pattern that emerged.

As Table 1 indicates there were twelve teachers who I regarded as regular informants, five of whom became key informants; that is teachers with whom I had a more intense relationship. All of these teachers provided a high level of co-operation with my research. However, I draw a distinction between informants and key informants on the basis of my contact with them, their commitment to my work and assistance with the project on a regular basis. It was the key informants whom I got to know best and who helped me to orientate my research questions, and my observations. In working with both informants and key informants I attempted to ensure that I had a cross-section of teaching staff in terms of age, sex, level of seniority, teaching experience, post of responsibility and areas of the school from which they were drawn. In these terms, I attempted to maintain some balance between the individuals with whom I worked. Furthermore, I tried to take into account the areas of the school to which they would give access. Of the informants with whom I worked there were individuals who represented academic subject departments, practical subjects and the Newsom Department. While I would argue that I obtained a cross-section of teachers on this basis, I think those teachers whom I got to know best tended to be concentrated more towards the arts subjects than the sciences. However, among these teachers I did have people with a range of teaching experiences which included probationary teachers, junior teachers, middle ranking teachers (who were deputy heads of departments) and a head of department. Meanwhile, beyond them in the teaching hierarchy my key informants included Heads of Houses and the headmaster.

On this basis I would argue that my informants, including key informants, constituted a cross-section of the teaching staff. Yet I cannot argue that they were purposely selected, for in some cases they included teachers who had attached themselves to me when I joined the school or when they joined the school. However, I monitored the kinds of people with whom I talked throughout the research period in order to take account of the different perspectives and different versions of the school to which I was exposed by my key informants.

Table 1: Key Informants and Informants at Bishop McGregor School

Name	Sex	Status/teaching experience	Post in school	House/department
Key Informants				
Sylvia Robinson	Female	Teacher of ten years experience with head of department status	Head of Careers in change of Newsom Scale III	Careers/Newsom
Maggie Rolls	Female	Head of House (a senior teacher but junior in terms of age)	Head of House Scale V	House
Paul Klee	Male	Probationer (new to the school)	Scale I	English
Ron Ward	Male	New Head of House	Head of House Scale V	House
Geoff Goddard	Male		Headmaster	A variety of teaching duties
Informants				
Jane Adams	Female	Deputy head of department	Scale III	English
George Jackson	Male	Head of department	Scale V	English
Keith Dryden	Male	Junior assistant teacher in departments	Scale II	Art/Newsom
Tony Davis	Male	Junior assistant teacher in departments	Scale II	Craft/Newsom
Terry Goodwin	Female	Junior assistant teacher in departments	Scale II	Home Economics/Newsom
Gerry Cochrane	Male	Probationer (new to the school)	Scale I	Religious Education
Michael O'Donoghue	Male	Assistant teacher in charge of a subject	Scale III	Science

Note: Teacher posts were graded one to five at the time of the study.

(ii) The Role of Key Informants

As with many aspects of ethnographic work and research involving participant observation, discussions about the roles played by key informants have
resulted in typologies (cf. Dean *et al,* 1967) consisting of informants who are
especially sensitive to the area of concern and informants who are willing
to discuss situations. While this may pinpoint the kind of person who is selected as an informant it does not highlight the role that an informant plays
in an investigation. For example, in my own study I found that key informants acted as guides, assistants, interpreters, providers of historical narrative,
and contributed to my preliminary data analysis. In particular I found individuals who fulfilled one or more of these aspects of the key informant role.
Indeed, on the basis of my five key informants I was able to distinguish four
major roles:

(a) The Guide

It is often assumed that key informants are guides to fields of study. However,
it is essential that researchers make some critical appraisal of the extent to
which informants provide only partial guidance to the institutions in which
they are located. Accordingly, in Bishop McGregor School some account had
to be taken of the areas to which individuals had access, the areas which they
wanted to advance or promote and those that they wanted to suppress. Furthermore, it was essential to consider those areas in which a key informant
was welcome and those areas which the individual was unable to penetrate
by virtue of his or her own social location within the school.

For example, of my key informants it was Sylvia Robinson who could provide me with access to the Newsom Department and to Newsom classes but
I had to compare her conception of Newsom work with conceptions that were
held by other teachers. Similarly, when she advanced a jaundiced view of the
House system and the Heads of Houses I had to consider this in relation to
the knowledge that she had on two occasions unsuccessfully attempted to gain
an appointment as a Head of House and was critical of many of their activities. However, her claim that there was a division between the Houses and
departments and especially between House Heads and heads of departments
resulted in me following up this line of enquiry which I found could be sub-
stantiated on the basis of the actions and activities of other teachers (cf. Burgess,
1983, especially pp. 52–119).

Among probationary teachers I found that Paul Klee alerted me to areas
of school organization that more senior teachers assumed were 'obvious' or
'self-evident'. Accordingly, Paul Klee pointed me towards examining the contradictions in the 'rules' that existed in different Houses and in different
departments. Furthermore, he was able to provide me with a portrait of the
activities at the probationary teachers' meeting to which my other key informants (apart from the head) did not have access.

(b) The Assistant

While informants may act as guides to the field of research they may also become informal or unpaid research assistants. Certainly, in my project Paul Klee performed this role. When I was not in the school Paul would collect any circulars that were issued to staff in order to ensure that I did not 'miss out' on any material that he considered important for my research. When meetings were held in my absence or when he attended meetings that I was unable to attend he relayed to me an account of the discussions and the positions that had been adoped by various members of the teaching staff. Finally, when activities occurred in which particular teachers were involved, Paul would make it his business to engage them in conversation in order to report back to me what had transpired.

While such a service by an informant is of great value to a researcher, it is essential to evaluate all the data that are provided. For the position of the key informant who takes on this role may result in only a selection of data about certain situations, events and activities being presented to the researcher.

(c) The Interpreter

In one sense, all key informants are interpreters as they sift and select the information that they relay to researchers and as they include and exclude areas on which the researcher might focus. However, some key informants provide interpretations of the words and the behaviour of other individuals. For example, Sylvia Robinson provided accounts of the behaviour of many of her Newsom pupils and gave her version of the reasons for their activities and actions with Newsom and non-Newsom teachers. Meanwhile, in the extensive interviews that I arranged with the headmaster I found that he spent some time not only reporting and interpreting the actions of members of his staff, but also providing a self-analysis by interpreting his own activities within the school. In these circumstances, the interpretations that were given by these key informants could subsequently be checked out with my own observations and the observations that were provided by other members of the teaching staff and by pupils. Such an approach highlights the importance of using multiple methods in an investigation and to cross checks occurring within a study (cf. Denzin, 1970; Burgess, 1982, pp. 163–99; Burgess, 1984b, pp. 143–65).

Another dimension to interpretation which I found came close to data analysis involved one informant who was prepared to offer suggestions about concepts that could be used to examine events and situations in which we had participated. Paul Klee spent some time with me trying out various sociological concepts that he considered would be appropriate to analyze particular aspects of school life. When I borrowed concepts from his analyses I have indicated where this occurs within the study. Furthermore, in situations where my analysis employs different concepts or differs from the analysis provided by Paul Klee I have discussed this within the notes and references provided in the study.

(d) The Historian

While the researcher who engages in ethnographic research may complement first-hand observations in the field with the analysis of historical documents (cf. Thernstrom, 1965, and 1968; Burgess, 1982, pp. 131–60), another way in which the historical context of a study can be established is by interviewing key informants.

Bishop McGregor School had opened four years before the beginning of my research; a period during which many school routines had been established. While many of these routines were discussed in various documents I also needed to obtain some first hand accounts about the ways in which these routines originated and how they were implemented and modified. By whom had they been formulated? How were they implemented? To what extent were they modified? Here, I relied particularly on two of my key informants the headmaster and Maggie Rolls to provide me with their versions of the ways in which school organization, rules and routines had been established. Both these teachers had been key participants but they had been involved from different perspectives. Accordingly, I obtained their accounts of situations which could be cross checked against each other and subsequently followed up with other teachers. In addition, these two teachers could not only provide data on the historical context, but they could also indicate further documents that I should consult and the areas in which I might locate this material.

On the basis of examining the roles which my key informants fulfilled I was able to identify four major roles which they performed. Not all these roles were played by each person, as different teachers provided a different range of services. In this sense, some of my informants played all these roles while others highlighted one or more of these dimensions to their role. Nevertheless, no matter which role or combination of roles that informants play, they do present a number of problems for the researcher to which we now turn.

Problems of Using Key Informants

Among the problems that I encountered while working with key informants I found that the majority focused on the ethical, political and moral dimensions of the research process to which we briefly turn.

(i) Manipulating the Researcher

Key informants are in a position of some considerable power as they can define those activities to which the researcher will have access or which they would like the researcher to have access. Furthermore, key informants are in a position to point the researcher towards certain areas of enquiry. Within my study I found that Sylvia Robinson in particular attempted to get me to talk about issues on which she required information. On several occasions she engaged me in conversation about the ways in which the headmaster used scale posts in the school. She enquired whether I knew if he had used all the points that the local education authority had allocated to him, as she found that whenever she went to see him to ask for promotion he always indicated that he had no further points to offer staff. At the time that she discussed this with me I had recently been given access to the head's confidential document on the distribution of points and posts within the school but I felt obliged not to divulge the contents of this document. Yet I did consider whether I should give her some idea about the contents of the document as she was providing me with a range of information and teacher contacts.

As well as attempting to seek information from me Sylvia also provided suggestions about what I might investigate and what I might say to the head. As she was critical of the basic organizational framework of the school she often suggested that I should communicate her views to the headmaster. Furthermore, she was also keen for me to suggest that she might play a more senior role in the school. However, I did not act on either of these suggestions as I thought this went well beyond my role as a researcher within the school.

(ii) Protecting Informants

As I have indicated, informants provided me with a range of services including giving me access to documentary evidence some of which was supposedly 'secret' and 'confidential'. On one occasion Ron Ward had shown me a 'secret document', that is a document which no Head of House was supposed to show to any assistant teachers. As a consequence I had asked the secretary for a copy of this document which was my usual practice when material was issued to teachers. However, when I asked the secretary for this document she refused to discuss it and went straight to report the fact that I knew about this material to the deputy head (cf. Burgess, 1983, pp. 101–14). While the deputy head explained that I could not have a copy of the document at that particular time, but that I could get a copy later, he did not enquire how I had come to know about this material. However, the school secretary had several questions: Who told you about this document? Who else has seen the document? While I told her how I had seen the document I was not prepared to let her know that Ron Ward had not only shown it to me but also to another teacher and had put the document in a place where other members of his House staff could consult it if they so wished

Just as I felt that I had a moral obligation to protect Ron Ward so I felt obliged to let Paul Klee know what had happened, for I had spent the whole of a 'free' lesson discussing the contents of the document with him and considering different ways in which it could be interpreted. Accordingly, I did not want to put him in a difficult position if he discussed the document in public. As a result I went to find him at the end of the lesson in which this situation had occurred in order to warn him about the circumstances surrounding the 'secret document'.

When my informants told me about the ways in which they worked I kept this confidential. Indeed, the headmaster claimed that he only discovered that pupils smoked in front of Newsom teachers when he read drafts of my study some six years after the fieldwork was completed and several years after the teachers concerned had taken up posts in other schools. He argued that I should have told him what had occurred within these classes as the pupils involved and those that had followed them in later years had gained very little from the experience. However, I maintained that it was my duty to use this material only for the purpose of sociological study rather than to act as an informer for the head. My research role and my obligations to the teachers outweighed my obligations to the head in this context.

(iii) Exploiting Key Informants

While conducting my study I got to know five teachers who became key informants. While I saw them as informants I never told them of their special role in my research. Indeed, for some who read this paper it might well come as a surprise to learn of the way in which I used them and the services which I consider they provided. In these circumstances one might ask: did I exploit them? Did these teachers expect to be written about in this way? Did they expect to become the principal subjects of my research?

At this point we might turn to some of the ethical problems that have been discussed by commentators such as Becker (1964) and Douglas (1976) on reporting field studies. I would argue that I did not deceive any of these teachers for the research was conducted openly and they were all informed that I was intending to write a study of their school. But here we come directly up against the meaning of 'informed consent' and whether these teachers really did not know what they were involved in when they agreed to co-operate with my investigation. Furthermore, it could be asked: what did they get for participating in my research? Unlike the informants used by social anthropologists no payment was involved but for some I provided assistance with Open University and higher degree courses, for others I loaned books and in one case I wrote a reference for the teacher to gain admission to a university. But was this just their equivalent of 'thirty pieces of silver' for their role in my research?

Conclusion

This paper has addressed an area that is relatively under-examined in ethnographic research on educational settings, namely the use of key informants.

In particular I have focused on five teachers with whom I became acquainted. They were not 'special teachers' but were merely individuals who I got to know during the course of my research at Bishop McGregor School and who influenced the collection and analysis of data. Certainly, we have come some distance from the time when the anthropologist's informants were summoned to the verandah of the local missionary or government official and questioned by the researcher, but have we yet thought through how we 'use' key informants and the ethical, social and political problems which that poses for them and for us in our attempts to understand social situations? It is to be hoped that researchers will, in future, consider the status of key informants in their studies and acknowledge the extent to which they play a major role in the collection and analysis of data.

Notes

1. For the use of key informants in British studies see, for example, Tim in Patrick (1973).
2. In this sense, informants, especially in work conducted from an interactionist perspective, may help to give an historical perspective which will benefit the studies (cf. Woods, 1983, p. 182 and Goodson in this volume, page 121).
3. For further accounts of informants in other settings who, while not representative, nevertheless help to shed light on patterns of social relations see Pons (1969) and Nichols and Beynon (1977, pp. 78–103).
4. See, for example, the papers in Simons (1980); Popkewitz and Tabachnick (1981); Spindler (1982); Hammersley (1983) and Burgess (1984a and 1985b).
5. The Newsom Department provided courses for pupils for whom the maximum expectation of success in public examinations seemed likely to be three CSE grade fives or less.

References

Agar, M. (1981) *The Professional Stranger*, New York, Academic Press.
Ball, S.J. (1981) *Beachside Comprehensive: A Case Study of Secondary Schooling*, Cambridge, Cambridge University Press.
Ball, S.J. (1984) 'Beachside reconsidered: reflections on a methodological apprenticeship', in Burgess, R.G. (Ed.) *The Research Process in Educational Settings: Ten Case Studies*, Lewes, Falmer Press.
Becker, H.S. (1964) Problems in the publication of field studies in Vidich, A.J., Bensman, J. and Stein, M. (Eds.) *Reflections on Community Studies*, New York, Harper and Row.
Bulmer, M. (Ed.) (1982) *Social Research Ethics*, London, Macmillan.
Burgess, R.G. (1981) 'Keeping a research diary', *Cambridge Journal of Education*, 11, 1, pp. 75–83.
—— (Ed.) (1982) *Field Research: A Sourcebook and Field Manual*, London, Allen and Unwin.

—— (1983) *Experiencing Comprehensive Education: A Study of Bishop McGregor School*, London, Methuen.

—— (Ed.) (1984a) *The Research Process in Educational Settings: Ten Case Studies*, Lewes, Falmer Press.

—— (1984b) *In the Field: An Introduction to Field Research*, London, Allen and Unwin.

—— (1985a) 'The whole truth? Some ethical problems in studying a comprehensive school' in Burgess, R.G. (Ed.) *Field Methods in the Study of Education*, Lewes, Falmer Press.

—— (Ed.) (1985b) *Field Methods in the Study of Education*, Lewes, Falmer Press.

Casagrande, J. (Ed.) (1960) *In the Company of Man*, New York, Harper and Row.

Conklin, H. (1968) 'Ethnography', in Sills, D.H. (Ed.) *International Encyclopaedia of the Social Sciences*, 5, New York, Free Press.

Dean, J.P., Eichorn, R.L. and Dean, L.R. (1967) 'Fruitful informants for intensive interviewing', in Doby, J.T. (Ed.) *An Introduction to Social Research*, (2nd edn), New York, Appleton-Century-Crofts.

Denzin, N. (1970) *The Research Act*, Chicago, Aldine (2nd edn published in 1978 by McGraw Hill).

Douglas, J. (1976) *Investigative Social Research*, Beverly Hills, CA, Sage.

Hammersley, M. (Ed.) (1983) *The Ethnography of Schooling*, Driffield, Nafferton.

Hargreaves, D.H. (1967) *Social Relations in a Secondary School*, London, Routledge and Kegan Paul.

Harrell-Bond, B. (1976) 'Studying elites: some special problems', in Rynkiewich, M.A. and Spradley, J.P. (Eds.) *Ethics and Anthropology: Dilemmas in Fieldwork*, New York, Wiley.

Johnson, J. (1975) *Doing Field Research*, New York, Free Press.

Lacey, C. (1970) *Hightown Grammar*, Manchester, Manchester University Press.

Liebow, E. (1967) *Tally's Corner*, Boston, Mass., Little Brown.

Lofland, J. (1971) *Analysing Social Settings*, New York, Wadsworth.

Nichols, T. and Beynon, H. (1977) *Living With Capitalism*, London, Routledge and Kegan Paul.

Patrick, J. (1973) *A Glasgow Gang Observed*, London, Eyre Methuen.

Pons, V. (1969) *Stanleyville: An African Urban Area Under Belgian Administration*, Oxford, OUP.

Popkewitz, T.S. and Tabachnick, B.R. (Eds.) (1981) *The Study of Schooling: Field Based Methodologies in Educational Research and Evaluation*, New York, Praeger.

Royal Anthropological Institution of Great Britain and Ireland (1951) *Notes and Queries in Anthropology* (6th edn), London, Routledge and Kegan Paul.

Schatzman, L. and Strauss, A.L. (1973) *Field Research: Strategies for a Natural Sociology*, Englewood Cliffs, N.J., Prentice Hall.

Simons, H. (Ed.) (1980) *Towards a Science of the Singular*, Norwich, Centre for Applied Research in Education, University of East Anglia.

Spindler, G. (Ed.) (1982) *Doing the Ethnography of Schooling*, New York, Holt, Rinehart and Winston.

Thernstrom, S. (1965) 'Yankee City revisited: the perils of historical naivete', *American Sociological Review*, 30, 2, pp. 234–42.

—— (1968) 'Quantitative methods in history: some notes', in Lipset, S.M. and Hofstadter, R. (Eds.) *Sociology and History: Methods*, New York, Basic Books, pp. 59–78.

Whyte, W.F. (1981) *Street Corner Society* (3rd edn), Chicago, University of Chicago Press.

Williams, T.R. (1967) *Field Methods in the Study of Culture*, New York, Holt, Rinehart and Winston.

Wolcott, H. (1973) *The Man in the Principal's Office*, New York, Holt, Rinehart and Winston.

Woods, P. (1981) 'Understanding through talk in Adelman', C. (Ed.) *Uttering Muttering: Collecting, Using and Reporting Talk for Social and Educational Research*, London, Grant McIntyre, pp. 13–26.

—— (1983) *Sociology and the School: An Interactionist Viewpoint*, London, Routledge and Kegan Paul.

19

Key Informant Interviews

Valerie J. Gilchrist

Introduction

The purpose of this chapter is to familiarize the reader with a research approach commonly used by ethnographers, which is useful in primary care research. This represents what Arthur Kleinman has called, "the translation of concepts from other fields into new ways of conceptualizing and analyzing health care problems" (Kleinman, 1983, p. 540). This method of qualitative data collection is another form of "research listening" as described by Miller and Crabtree (in press). This chapter developed from a literature review, my own research experience, and taped telephone interviews with experts in the field.

"Social science is a terminological jungle where many labels compete" (Lofland & Lofland, 1984, p. 3); therefore I will define terms as I use them (Field & Morse [1985], Kirk & Miller [1986], and Patton [1990] were helpful in clarifying terms). This chapter is titled "Key Informant Interviewing"; all three of those terms require clarification.

Informant is viewed by some social science researchers as both pejorative and inadequate to capture the relationship between the researcher and the individual providing information. Michael Agar, in a telephone interview, described the term in the following manner:

> I called the independent truckers I worked with in the last ethnography I wrote, "teachers." I decided that was really the proper term. It showed the kind of respect I feel for their knowledge. It showed the kind of role that they were really in, with reference to me, in terms of teaching me about independent trucking. But there's a lot of choices available.

Other terms that have been used are *consultant, friend, respondent, actor, participant, interviewee,* and *source.* I will use the term *informant* to mean "the

Source: Benjamin F. Crabtree & William L. Miller (eds), *Doing Qualitative Research* (Newbury Park, CA: Sage, 1992).

individual who provides information," simply because it still seems to be the most commonly used term in the literature.

An *interview* usually means some sort of formal discourse. In the present context, it describes the relationship between the ethnographic researcher and the key informant from which is negotiated an understanding of the culture. A key informant provides information through formal interviews and informal verbal interchanges or conversations. The informant may also provide the researcher with references – for example, a genogram, a picture, a map. The informant provides the researcher with introductions and interpretations. Finally, informants communicate with the researcher in a myriad of nonverbal ways – how they dress, when and how they speak, and the influence of context on their actions.

Key informants differ from other informants by the nature of their position in a culture and by their relationship to the researcher, which is generally one of longer duration, occurs in varied settings, and is more intimate.

After I was asked by Drs. Miller and Crabtree to prepare this chapter, the initial literature review left me with lots of material but only my own sense of what would be most useful for primary care clinician researchers. I felt it would be more helpful also to gather perspectives of ethnographic experts and other qualitative researchers in primary care. These interviews allowed me to sharpen the focus of the chapter. These "key informants" on key informants also allowed me to experience what I was writing about. They probably shaped this chapter in ways that at this time I do not yet appreciate.

Each interview began with the same six to eight general questions concerning the following: the individual's understanding of this method, how they personally had used key informants, the advantages and disadvantages of working with key informants, how it complemented other types of research, and any advice they might have for beginning primary care researchers. Each interviewee, at the conclusion, was asked for any texts or papers he or she might recommend and also for the names of other individuals whom I might wish to interview. As the interviews proceeded, they became more focused. The interviews took 20–45 minutes. All interviews were transcribed and transcriptions forwarded to the interviewees for review. I made the decision to seek no more interviews when no new information or references came to light during the interviews. Direct references to the interviews are cited by the informants' initials in the text.

I had met Drs. Helman, O'Toole, Bauer, and Lewis previously and already knew of their expertise. Dr. Cecil Helman (CH), a British anthropologist at University College and Middlesex School of Medicine, has written several books and papers in medical anthropology and in family medicine. Dr. Peter O'Toole (PO), a sociologist at Kent State University, had taught me a graduate course in qualitative methods. He has written extensively in medical sociology. Dr. Larry Bauer (LB), a social worker by training, now directs faculty development at Ohio State University. Dr. Barbara Lewis (BL) is a qualitative researcher in the Department of Family Medicine at the University of Colorado. I also asked Drs. Crabtree and Miller for their recommendations concerning experts in the field. They recommended CH and BL and also Drs. Bodgewic, Agar, Morse, and

Weller. Dr. Michael Agar (MA) is a professor of anthropology at the University of Maryland. He is probably the most well known of those I interviewed. His writings in ethnography are extensive and innovative. Dr. Janice Morse (JM), from the University of Alberta, has been a leader in qualitative health research. She not only writes extensively in the field but edits the journal *Qualitative Health Research*. Dr. Susan Weller (SW) is a medical anthropologist in the Department of Preventive Medicine and Community Health at the University of Texas Medical Branch, Galveston. She has written a methodology textbook and several articles pertinent to primary care. SW recommended Dr. Jeffrey Johnson (JJ). Dr. Johnson also had come to mind because of his book *Selecting Ethnographic Informants* (Johnson, 1990). He is an anthropologist at the University of East Carolina. Dr. Steve Bodgewic, the author of the previous chapter on participant observation, when approached for an interview, replied, "You don't want to talk to me. You want to talk to George. Why, he comes up with things I've never even thought of!" Dr. George Noblit (GN) is a professor of education at the University of North Carolina, Chapel Hill. He also has written extensively and has done several ethnographic studies in the school system.

The examples I use throughout this chapter come from the published articles in the family medicine literature, my interview experiences preparing this chapter, and two other examples that I hope are imagined easily by the clinician-researchers to whom this book is directed. The first example concerns one of my patients. Early in 1991 I was approached by the mother of a 15-year-old female in my practice who, according to this mother, had withdrawn from the family. "Susan" simply said these were "bad times" for her. Intrigued by Cecil Helman's (1991a) description of a "family's culture," I set out over the next few weeks and months to explore with Susan what she meant by "bad times." Armed with the ethnographers' approach of listening and learning from Susan, I tried to see her world from her perspective and later developed some translations with her as we discussed these "bad times." Another example of a study is a brief one that grew out of my department's need to develop plans for the future of one of our family practice centers. This center is 14 miles away from the hospital and the offices of our program. It serves both a small town and the surrounding rural area with a large Mennonite population. One of the receptionists in our office is Mennonite, and she became my key informant as I explored that culture in general but also more specifically with regard to how this Mennonite community used health care services.

Ethnography and "Key Informants"

Ethnography is what those of us who are not anthropologists think anthropologists do. The popular image is captured by the vision of Margaret Mead in her tent, taking notes from the natives. Although ethnography traditionally has entailed studying cultures to which the researcher is a stranger, this has changed (Patton, 1990). Agar (1980) describes ethnography as representing both content (usually a book) and process. It is the aspect of process with which this chapter is concerned. "Such work requires an intensive personal involvement, an abandonment of traditional scientific control, an improvisational style to meet situations not of the researcher's making, and an ability to learn from a long series of mistakes" (Agar, 1986, p. 12). Ethnography, according to Agar, is also crucially dependent on the researcher as an essential component of the research process. "Ethnography is neither subjective nor objective. It is interpretive, mediating two worlds through a third" (Agar, 1986, p. 19).

Ethnographers do not start with a hypothesis to test, but rather they attempt to discover a group's culture, or shared sense of reality. "Rather than studying people, ethnography means learning from people" (Spradley, 1979, p. 3). An essential element of the ethnographer's approach is that he or she takes the attitude of a student or child in relationship to the group being studied and attempts to find patterns, the implicit framework, within the culture. The ethnographer learns about the culture in basically three ways: (a) observation – what people actually do, as well as examination of artifacts of any sort, (b) discussion – what people say they think, believe, or do, and why, and (c) reflection – what the ethnographer infers or interprets (Helman, 1991b). Participant observation is described in chapter 3 (Crabtree & Miller, 1992b) by Steve Bodgewic. A large part of this chapter will deal with the "discussion" means of learning about a culture, recognizing that the separation of observation and interviews is artificial. For example, "the manner in which an informant discusses an issue, thus revealing patterns of personal choosing, is, for the ethnographer, just as important as the revelation of social patterns themselves" (Dobbert, 1982, p. 114). In the field the researcher or research team will learn by simultaneously observing multiple aspects of people and settings while talking to individuals and making interpretations. Ethnography is the context for key informant interviewing.

Who Is a Key Informant?

"Although almost anyone can become an informant, not everyone makes a good informant" (Spradley, 1979, p. 45). Historically the key informant was often the anthropological researcher's link to the tribe. He or she might have been the translator. It was often the individual with whom the researcher developed a special friendship. Rather than thinking of key informants as distinctly different from any other individual or informant, I think it is more helpful to view key informants as individuals who are able to teach the researcher. The teacher may vary according to the topic and the relationship between the individuals. There are often many teachers, or there could be one special teacher or mentor. As GN stated, "… a key informant for me may not be a key informant for you."

Key informants are individuals who possess special knowledge, status, or communication skills, who are willing to share their knowledge and skills with the researcher and who have access to perspectives or observations denied the researcher (Goetz & LeCompte, 1984). For example, in my study of our local Mennonite culture, my key informant was our receptionist. She possessed the special knowledge and the access to the culture which I did not have. Another example is when I requested interviews with ethnographers in preparing this chapter. All but one openly shared their information and perspectives. One, however, felt that I really should not conduct research in this manner and directed me to the library. This reaction acutely exemplified the fact that the researcher's relationship to the key informant has to be such that the informant is willing to share his or her knowledge and skills. During the investigation of the adolescent's family, she, my patient, was my key informant. Her mother was also a key informant. Clinicians will realize immediately the different perspectives key informants demonstrate, as well as the interpretation and subsequent negotiation that involves the clinician. Schein (1987) writes about the need for the clinician's approach in ethnographic research. I would echo Stein's (1990) call for an ethnographic perspective within clinical work.

The ideal key informant is described as "articulate and culturally sensitive" (Fetterman, 1989, p. 58). This cultural sensitivity may or may not be analytic. "Some informants use their language to describe events and actions with almost no analysis of their meaning or significance. Other informants offer insightful analysis and interpretation of events from the perspective of the native or folk theory. Both can make excellent informants" (Spradley, 1979, p. 52). The informant, however, needs to be thoroughly enculturated and currently active within his or her own culture in order to represent accurately that culture to the researcher. Ethnographic texts often include warnings about the translator or the first person to approach the researcher. These individuals, by their very ability and willingness to straddle two cultures, often do not represent the native culture (Lofland & Lofland, 1984; Patton, 1990; Pelto & Pelto, 1978; Spradley, 1979). *Articulateness* often refers to the ability to be a good storyteller or an everyday life philosopher. GN described one of his key informants in this manner.

> So he could take, kind of stand outside a little bit and look at it. He was also a real good storyteller and, so I could do things like say, "Tell me about someone who would say this." And then he would be able to render perspectives for me of different groups in the organization … but [he was] someone who is heavily vested, with some experience and a known role and connections with other people.

The Researcher/Informant Relationship

As stated previously, the key informant teaches the researcher. The researcher attempts to see reality as the informant sees it.

I want to understand the world from your point of view, I want to know what you know in the way you know it. I want to understand the meaning of your experience, to walk in your shoes, to feel things as you feel them, to explain things as you explain them. Will you become my teacher and help me understand? (Spradley, 1979, p. 34)

This is what the researcher asks of the key informant.

The researcher also represents a crucial component of the research process. Agar (1980) describes the understanding that evolves out of the relationship between the informant and researcher as a "joint construction of reality." Each person contributes a perspective. It is not that the informant simply describes what happens in his or her culture, but that the ethnographer's very questions, as well as subsequent interpretations, are within the context of his or her own cultural assumptions or traditions. "Having been socialized into culture means that the sensory clues we perceive from the external world and from within ourselves are filtered, selected, and interpreted according to meaningful patterns we have learned" (Burkett, 1991, p. 110).

This may present specific difficulties to those researchers who choose to investigate cultures with which they are at least somewhat familiar. Rather than questioning some aspect of a culture, an assumption is made that may not be correct. For example, I often have assumed that families act in a loving manner toward their members only to be reminded that it is not true in all cases. The kinds of ethnographic questions I will later describe are helpful in countering those assumptions. As BL said, " … good informants can actually be difficult to locate, but there's two sides to the equation. You have to not only have a good informant, but you also have to have a good interview." The point is that the researcher fashions the ethnographic account as much as the informant.

This relationship between the researcher and informant is not static. Like any relationship, it develops over time, founded on mutual trust. The informant may start as a respondent, answering questions; then may become an interpreter, explaining observations and expanding on questions; later may become more of a teacher asking questions; and finally may become a collaborator. Ethnographic accounts frequently are shared with key informants, "which serves both an ethical and a methodological function" (MA). PO described to me writing his account of a vocational rehabilitation program with his key informant, one of the rehabilitation counselors.

Why Use Key Informants?

One might appropriately ask, Why use key informants? Why not just interview everyone you possibly can and get all the different perspectives you possibly can without relying on the interpretations of just a few select individuals?

The simplest answer is the *pragmatic limits* that constrain the researcher. One generally cannot interview everyone or observe everyone. One cannot be in all places at all times. If one is going to use only a few key individuals, it is better to understand the limits of their information based on who they are and to develop a relationship with them to ensure the richness of that information. Efficiency also plays a role in the choice of key informants, especially in the face of limited resources. Gregor and Galazka's (1990) article in *Family Medicine* nicely describes how they used key informants to investigate the need for geriatric services in their community. Key informants provided them the information they needed in a cost-effective manner.

Key informants also can provide the researcher both *access* and *sponsorship*. This access may mean access to information that is unavailable except from the key informant – for example, a description by a senior faculty member of what the Family Practice Center (FPC) was like when it first started. Access also may be afforded individuals, based on the key informant's status within the community. I would be treated very differently if I simply walked into a Mennonite community meeting or Bible study rather than being introduced by my key informant. Likewise some aspects of the "adolescent culture," which my patient Susan described, are denied me because of my personal characteristics – in this case my age. Other common limiting personal characteristics include gender and race. An example of sponsorship in a medical setting is described by Bosk (1979) in his study of medical mistakes. When Bosk approached a senior surgeon, asking for his cooperation, the surgeon said his sponsorship would be "the kiss of death" and that Bosk had best obtain entrée through the house staff. He gave him the telephone number of the chief resident.

As discussed earlier, the key informant may become a *research collaborator*. This is another reason to use and treasure key informants. The key informant first answers questions and provides the explanations – what, when, who, why, and how (Schatzman & Strauss, 1973). As the researcher begins to formulate interpretations, it is the key informant who will expand, modify, and clarify these interpretations. The key informant will be able to help transform the researcher's translations of the native culture into something with meaning in the researcher's own culture. A key informant is a *translator* both literally and figuratively.

How Do You Select Key Informants?

In the past, little was written about how the researcher went about finding key informants, although anthropology is full of stories about how this relationship went awry (Wax, 1971). Good luck or personal contacts somehow magically lead to the perfect key informant who is "trustworthy, observant, reflective, articulate and a good storyteller"(Johnson, 1990, p. 30). Thankfully, more recent accounts describe who the key informants are, how they are selected, and how the relationship with the researcher evolves. What follows is largely abstracted from Johnson's book *Selecting Ethnographic Informants* (1990).

**Figure 1. Selection Criteria for Finding Key Informants
(Adapted from Johnson, 1990)**

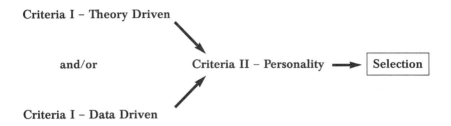

Criteria I – Theory Driven

and/or

Criteria II – Personality ⟶ Selection

Criteria I – Data Driven

Key informants are not selected randomly. Random sampling, as one type of probability sampling, assumes that the characteristic under study is represented equally in a study group. The knowledge or perspective the researcher is seeking, as well as the inclination and ability to share that with the researcher, is not equally distributed within a study group. Also the members of a culture are often not easily identified or defined as members of a study group. The selection of key informants represents nonprobability or information-rich sampling (see Chapter 2). The selection attempts to yield a small number of informants who provide representative pictures of aspects of information or knowledge distributed within the study population. This nonprobability sampling is also referred to as purposeful, strategic, or judgment sampling. "It is not opportunistic, but rather guided by the ethnographer's theoretical or experimentally informed judgments" (Johnson, 1990, p. 27).

Johnson describes two sets of selection criteria to be used sequentially in finding key informants (see Figure 1). The first set of selection criteria differ based on one's approach. One of these, referred to as "theory driven," results from "the use of prior theoretical knowledge in constructing a framework" (Johnson, 1990, p. 24). For example, an investigation of the FPC might include interviews with representative members of functional groups such as those in education or patient care, or professional groups such as physicians, nurses, secretaries, residents, or groups based on other characteristics such as length of employment in the FPC. One could assume reasonably that their perspectives of what life in the FPC is like would differ.

Johnson calls the second set of criteria "data driven" or exploratory, which results from "the emergent nature of the within-group and between-group comparisons, eventually leading to the discovery of categories that can help in developing grounded theory" (p. 24). For example, an investigation of the FPC might start with a survey of the various roles within the FPC. A factor analysis might then separate those who had different roles – education, patient care, research, administration – and the individuals who scored strongly in each of those directions could be interviewed.

Gregor and Galazka (1990) used a snowball method for identifying key informants from the researchers' initial contact with an individual known to staff members (emergent or data driven) and later specifically sought representation of the black community (theory driven). Johnson also gives examples representing compromises within these frameworks.

This first set of selection criteria, driven by theory and/or data, results in a pool of potential key informants. Within that pool the researcher seeks out those who are willing and able to work with the researcher – selection criteria II. Sometimes good key informants are acquired serendipitously, and thus only selection II criteria are considered. For example, I might have struck up a friendship with the Mennonite woman at the flea market with whom my children were playing, and she might have become an excellent key informant. I would have to discover, however, her position in her community and to document how she became a key informant.

Interviews

Clinicians are generally good interviewers. Some of us even teach the subject! The ethnographic interview differs from the medical interview, however, in its openness.

> Because the researcher's aim in using informants is to uncover patterns and not to get questions answered, the researcher cannot, like the interviewer, direct the conversation. Indeed, by directing the conversation, the researcher can only uncover patterns predicted in advance ... [W]ith an informant, the basic aim is to determine what patterns the informant sees and considers important enough to bring up. (Dobbert, 1982, p. 114)

The emphasis is on listening. "The question is not, how do you talk to an informant? But, how do you listen to an informant?" (Dobbert, 1982, p. 118). The astute clinician will recognize that these two features – following the direction of the informant and astute listening – characterize a good interview in primary care too. The doctor-directed, focused interview, concentrated on diagnosis, may characterize the interview of some areas of medicine, but the parallel between the descriptions of ethnographic interviews and "patient-centered interviews" in primary care is striking (McWhinney, 1989).

Just as in medicine we ask certain types of questions (Can you describe the pain? Where does it hurt? What makes it better? What makes it worse?) to better understand and develop a picture of a patient's pain, so does the ethnographer ask certain types of questions to help develop an understanding of that person's culture. Spradley (1979) identifies three different types of questions and principles that guide their use. Although the clinician-researcher may find the names unfamiliar that Spradley uses to categorize these questions, the types of questions will be recognized readily. I will use my own investigation of our local Mennonite community and of the life of my adolescent patient for examples.

Descriptive Questions

Descriptive questions, Spradley's first category of questions, are often introductory. The clinician-researcher would recognize them as very *broadly open-ended questions*. A *grand tour question*, a type of descriptive question, attempts to elicit a rich story that is completely directed by the informant. One may ask about a typical situation, such as, What's a typical day like for you? or be more specific, What happened yesterday? What happens on Mondays? The researcher may ask the informant to focus on an activity or task. When I was inquiring about the Mennonite community in our area, I asked my informant to locate the members of her community on a map. When I was trying to understand what were important activities in the life of my adolescent patient Susan, I asked her to describe her weekly school schedule.

Spradley describes *mini-tour questions*, which focus on a smaller unit of experience, for example, after-school work. As questions become more focused the researcher may ask for examples: Can you give me an example of something about which one might consult a community healer? Can you describe some situation that might result in an argument at home? The researcher also might ask the informant for any experience he or she may have had in a particular setting: Tell me about the last time you talked to a community healer; Tell me about the last argument you had at home. It is essential to be aware that you the researcher may not be using the same language or terms as your informant. What Susan described to me as "bad times" she described to her girlfriends as "bummers," "downers," "fights," "one of those times," as well as "bad times," depending on the situation.

Structural Questions

The ethnographer generally chooses to investigate some areas of a culture in more depth than others. Spradley's second category of questions, structural questions, function to focus further the researcher's inquiry. I think of these questions as *questions of inclusion*, expanding and enhancing the description of the particular area of research interest. In reference to the two examples that I am using, I asked questions in an attempt to develop an understanding of the structure of that aspect of the culture referred to in the Mennonite community as "health care" and of the times in Susan's life that she referred to as "bad times."

Spradley's *verification questions*, a type of structural question, seek to prove or disprove the researcher's understanding of what aspects are included within the area of interest. A domain verification question I posed to our receptionist was "Are there different kinds of health care within your community?" Other verification questions are used to discover whether specific terms that the researcher has heard are within the area of research interest. For example, a question I asked our receptionist was "Is 'manipulation' considered a kind of health care?"

One not only needs to know the terms within the area of interest but also their relationships. An example of this type of question is, Is a chiropractor a type of health care? or Do you go to a chiropractor for health care? Other structural questions described by Spradley include those that ask for examples of what is included within the area of study – both in general, What are the different kinds of health care in your community? and more specifically, What elements would your community elders think necessary to provide for optimal health care in your community?

In order to enhance the richness of the description of the area of interest, one may use what Spradley calls substitution frame questions, or one might use card sorting questions. *Substitution frame questions* remove one term and the informant is asked to replace it with another. For example, "When I feel ill I go to bed" is replaced with "When I feel ill I ____." *Card sorting questions* are a type of pile-sorting exercise. The researcher lists terms, each on separate cards, and asks the informant to separate them according to a category. For example, Which of these are health care providers – the health food store owner, family members, chiropractor, MD, public school nurse, urgent care center staff, midwives, community elders, neighbors? Writing terms on cards helps elicit, verify, and discuss various aspects of a particular area of interest. (For further discussion of pile sorts, see Weller & Romney, 1988.)

Other examples of structural questions that I used when I was trying to understand Susan's "bad times" are as follows: Are there different kinds of bad times? What kinds of bad times do you have? If it's a bad time when your folks are fighting, can you fill in the blank with some other examples such as, "It's a bad time when ____." Would you say that when you're quiet, that's a "bad time"? When you're angry? Sad? Is a "bummer" a kind of bad time?

In this example it was obvious that I had to verify constantly that the term I used for a situation was appropriate. One can confirm this by asking directly. For example, Is this how you would talk about "bad times" to your girlfriend? In other settings the limits of the language may not be as obvious but just as important.

Contrast Questions

Contrast questions further clarify the area of research interest. I think of these questions as those dealing with *criteria of exclusion*, rather than inclusion, or the multiple types of relationships within a given area. For example, the area of health care includes various treatments, practitioners, different patient ages, problems, and issues of decision making, to mention only a few. Susan's "bad times" varied by the precipitant, her effect at the time, and who was involved.

Once the researcher has a sense of the differences between various terms, he or she can present this to the informant for verification. I asked, "Am I correct in understanding that there's a difference between how a fever would be treated by your grandmother, the health food store owner, and a physician?" Contrast questions also require some knowledge on the part of the researcher. These questions begin with a known characteristic and ask about contrasts within that category. For example, I knew that within health care there were various practitioners – chiropractors, physicians, the health food store owner, knowledgeable community members, midwives. I could ask then, "You said you'd go to a chiropractor for a backache – can you go through other types of illness and tell me when you would and wouldn't go to a chiropractor?"

Comparisons and contrasts may be made using terms the researcher has verified as part of the area of study, the researcher asking the informant to identify differences between terms. For example, "What's the difference between a chiropractor and a physician?" Another example is the triadic contrast question, in which three terms are presented to the informant and she or he is asked, "Which are alike and which are different?" I asked Susan, "You have used different terms at times and I want to see if I understand. Are 'bummer' and 'bummed out' the same while 'burnt out' means something else?"

Another variation on pile sorts, called *contrast set sorting questions* by Spradley, differs from card sorting questions in that the terms are ones the researcher already has grouped in some manner. Terms relating to various treatments such as vitamins, antibiotics, salves, various herbs, and poultices can be resorted by your informant according to whatever parameters the informant thinks are important. My informant in this example chose cost, the practitioner's recommendation, and the age of the person likely to use it.

Finally it is helpful to use rating questions. These questions seek to discover the values placed by the informant within any categorization that the researcher is developing. Examples I used were "What is the best type of health care?" and "What is the worst time with your parents?"

Principles of Ethnographic Questioning

Clinicians will be able to imagine an abundance of questions to use in their research. The function of these ethnographic questions is to expand and then enrich the researcher's understanding of what the informant is describing. This requires, above all, *constant vigilance*. One cannot assume, without verification from the informant, that your understandings and assumptions are the same as the informant's. This is especially important for most clinician-researchers who will work within their own culture or one very similar. This brings to mind an example with which many physicians are familiar. Your 30-year-old obese patient says she's taking "the pill." The physician assumes this is the birth control pill, but the patient actually means her diabetes pill!

Spradley also outlines some principles surrounding the asking of ethnographic questions. All the different types of questions – descriptive, structural, and contrast – should be asked concurrently and repetitively. Ask the same questions at different times to elicit all the possible examples, similarities, and differences surrounding any event or construct. Explain why you are asking the question, and put it in context. Most researchers feel it is unethical to hide the primary focus of the research, although specific themes may be shared differently with different people. For example, to one individual in the Mennonite community I might say, "I'm interested in your community," while to another, "I'm interested in how you define health and keep healthy," and yet to another, "We're looking at how your community uses health care resources to see if we should increase our services here." It is also helpful to put the questions in a cultural, as well as personal, framework. For example, "You described using Union Salve for cuts and rashes. Are there any other times when you might use it? Would most people in your community use this for rashes?"

Language

A discussion of how the researcher tries to understand a culture by means of a verbal interchange with another individual is not complete without at least a brief discussion of language. "Language is a way of organizing the world" (Patton, 1990, p. 227). Spradley goes on to say that language functions "not only as a means of communication, it also functions to create and express cultural reality" (Spradley, 1979, p. 20). Consequently the researcher's questions will frame the respondent's answer. "[I]nterviewing assumes that questions and answers are separate elements in human thinking.... Ethnographic interviewing ... begins with the assumption that the question-answer sequence is a single element in human thinking. Questions always imply answers" (Spradley, 1979, p. 83). The researcher should attempt to phrase questions as they might be asked in the native culture.

"Every ethnographic description is a translation" (Spradley, 1979, p. 22). This quote not only reflects the fact that the researcher must translate from the native culture to the researcher's culture, but that the information also must be filtered by both the informant and the researcher. What each one of us sees and remembers from any setting depends very much on who we are. "As an exclusive or dominant method of ethnographic inquiry, the dialogic mode boxes the informant into an ethnographic present defined by Western, middle class discourse and alienates her or him from the historical, interpenetrating settings that informant and ethnographer may come to share" (Sanjek, 1990, p. 405).

Validity/Trustworthiness

What is a valid or truthful ethnographic account? Because qualitative ethnographic research is so much a reflection of the researcher as the research instrument, validity has been difficult to define. GN defines a valid ethnographic account as one in which "the second person finds the same story. My belief is that if I'm good enough, other people would find a story that resonates with mine. Not that it would necessarily be the same, but we would be able to understand the other person's story from our own. And that is as close as you get."

How does a researcher develop a trustworthy description of a setting or culture? How does a reader know when to believe what is written? Four criteria modified from Kuzel and Like (1991) provide a framework for evaluation. (See also Borman, LeCompte, & Goetz, 1986; Howe & Eisenhart, 1990; Kirk & Miller, 1986; Lather, 1986b; Sanjek, 1990).

Member Checks. This refers to the recycling of analysis back to key informants. This recycling should be documented in the study account, preferably with mention of the informant's comments. The research relationship may also change the key informant. Rather than not acknowledging this possibility, Lather describes including an assessment of what has changed, called *catalytic validity.* "My argument is premised not only on a recognition of the reality-altering impact of the research process itself, but also on the need to consciously channel this impact so that respondents gain self-understanding and, ideally, self-determination through the research participation" (Lather, 1986a, p. 67).

Searching for Disconfirming Evidence. "The job of validation is not to support an interpretation, but to find out what might be wrong with it. A proposition deserves some degree of trust only when it has survived serious attempts to falsify it." (Cronbach as quoted in Lather, 1986a, p. 67). Searching for disconfirming evidence involves both purposive sampling and prolonged engagement. Documentation of the selection process leading to key informants allows the researcher to seek accounts from other informants who may differ from the key informant in critical ways. This purposeful sampling of individuals and the inclusion of conflicting, as well as complementary, accounts strengthens an ethnographic description. The sampling and inclusion also allow consideration of potential biases due to informants' stakes in specific outcomes or due to their position in the organization. Prolonged engagement also allows the researcher to confront the conflicts any informant may exhibit. Do they do what they say they do? Informants will report more accurately on events that are usual, frequent, or patterned and less accurately on things that are not readily observed or are inferential (Johnson, 1990). Prolonged engagement allows the less readily observable aspects of the setting to become visible.

Triangulation. This is an essential check for the researcher. Triangulation refers to both the use of multiple data sources, for example multiple informants, and of multiple methods, such as participant observation and informant interviewing, as well as the use of various records. One informant may give highly reliable but invalid information. I would go beyond what one usually thinks of in terms of triangulation to include multiple theoretical perspectives. "Valid-rich ethnography must make explicit as many ... theoretical decision(s) ... as possible by reporting when and why judgments of significance are made" (Sanjek, 1990, p. 396). This quote implies, of course, a rejection of any one objective reality. "The attempt to produce value-neutral social science is increasingly being abandoned as at best unrealizable, and at worst self deceptive, and is being replaced by social sciences based on explicit ideologies" (Hess as quoted in Lather, 1986a, p. 67).

Thick Description. This is "a thorough description of the context or setting within which the inquiry took place and with which the inquiry was concerned ... [and] a thorough description of the transactions or processes observed in that context that are relevant to the problem, evaluand, or policy option" (Guba & Lincoln as quoted in Kuzel & Like, 1991, p. 153). This description should use "native language" and describe not only the final analysis of the study but also how that analysis was obtained. Also needed is "an accounting of the relationship between field notes and the ethnography based upon them...." (Sanjek, 1990, p. 401). This accounting starts with recognizing one's initial suppositions and assumptions. Lather calls for a "systematized reflexivity which gives some indication of how a priori theory has been changed by the logic of the data" (Lather, 1986a, p. 67).

Applications in Primary Care

Key informants have been used to plan for health services delivery in many different settings (Penayo, Jacobson, Caldera, & Burmann, 1988). It is also easy to see how an investigation of other issues within a more circumscribed culture, such as a hospital, might benefit from key informant interviewing. In our hospital we have a high turnover of ICU nurses. I suggest that, rather than distribute questionnaires, interviews with key informants are a more informative approach. Many of the problems we confront professionally have been illuminated by such ethnographic studies as Bosk's (1979) study of mistakes and Smith and Kleinman's (1989) study of management of one's emotions in medical training. What I find personally most exciting is the application of some of the methods of anthropology and the ethnographic approach to our everyday contact with patients. CH's view is that "every patient is an informant" and that the clinician's access to the culture of a particular family is through our patient or "key informant." Howard Stein (1990) characterizes an ethnographic approach to patient care as "quintessentially contextual and open-ended."

In conclusion, here are what I consider to be the critical features that ethnography and a discussion of key informants offer us for our research and for our patient care:

1. An abiding respect for context as influencing the clinician-researcher, the patient-informant, and their constructed reality.
2. A consideration of the clinician-researcher as part of that context. "Doing ethnography differs from many other kinds of research in that the ethnographer becomes a major research instrument" (Spradley, 1979, p. 76).
3. An awareness of the constraints imposed by language. This awareness includes an acknowledgement of the extent to which questions frame responses and the role of translation in constructing a joint reality. "For a consultation to be a success there must be consensus" (Helman, 1990, p. 118).
4. An understanding that a truthful account is obtained not by trying to eliminate bias but by comprehending it. "The ethnographic method is as much concerned with how and why we observe as with what we observe, for the former heavily influences the latter" (Stein, 1990, p. 206). (See also Crabtree & Miller, 1992a; Kuzel & Like, 1991.)

Readers of this chapter are not likely to become ethnographers. The long term relationships with our patients, however, can be thought of as relationships with key informants. Techniques from ethnography can enrich our research and our practice. "Naturalistic research is first and foremost emergent. Today's solutions may be tomorrow's problems" (Lofland & Lofland, 1984, p. 19). I urge the researcher to reject the "tyranny of methodology" and use whatever method best answers the question at hand and honestly report what is done.

Summary

What are your experiences? What are your patients' experiences? What are the dilemmas and puzzles in these experiences? What are the researchable questions embedded in these stories? This is where primary care research begins and to where it must always return. The authors of this book have shared their knowledge and experience of qualitative methods. These methods expand and enrich primary care investigators' ability to answer more of the questions that matter. A multimethod primary care research craft is now in the river. It is time to steer our craft with qualitative and quantitative oars. The qualitative methods presented here provide yet another view into the water. What makes this view special is that it not only shows us more of the river bottom, but it keeps us in the stream, and if the sun is before us, it reflects ourselves. Turn your global eye toward home, step down the ladder, and join in the dance. The questions and hopes of primary health care depend on seeing how like our patients we are.

References

Agar, M. H. (1980). *The professional stranger: An informal introduction to ethnography.* Orlando, FL: Academic Press.

—— (1986). *Speaking of ethnography.* Newbury Park, CA: Sage.

Borman, K. M., Lecompte, M. D., & Goetz, J. P. (1986). Ethnographic and qualitative research design and why it doesn't work. *American Behavioral Scientist,* 30, 42–57.

Bosk, C. L. (1979). *Forgive and remember: Managing medical failure.* Chicago: University of Chicago Press.

Crabtree, B. F., & Miller, W. L. (1992a). The analysis of narratives from a long interview. In M. Stewart, F. Tudiver, M. Bass, E. Dunn, & P. Norton (Eds.) *Tools for primary care research* (pp. 209–220). Newbury Park, CA: Sage.

—— (Eds.) (1992b). *Doing qualitative research.* Newbury Park, CA: Sage.

Dobbert, M. L. (1982). *Ethnographic research: Theory and application for modern schools and societies.* New York: Praeger.

Field, P. A., & Morse, J. M. (1985). *Nursing research: The application of qualitative approaches.* Rockville, MD: Aspen.

Helman, C. G. (1990). *Culture, health and illness.* Boston: Butterworth-Heinemann.

—— (1991a). The family culture: A useful concept for family medicine. *Family Medicine,* 23, 376–381.

Howe, K., & Eisenhart, M. (1990). Standards for qualitative (and quantitative) research: A prolegomenon. *Educational Researcher,* 5, 2–9.

Johnson, J. C. (1990). *Selecting ethnographic informants.* Newbury Park, CA: Sage.

Kirk, J., & Miller, M. (1986). *Reliability and validity in qualitative research.* Newbury Park, CA: Sage.

Kleinman, A. (1983). The cultural meanings and social uses of illness. *Journal of Family Practice,* 16, 539–545.

Kuzel, A. J. (1986). Naturalistic inquiry: An appropriate model for family medicine. *Family Medicine,* 18, 369–374.

Kuzel, A. J., & Like, R. C. (1991). Standards of trustworthiness for qualitative studies in primary care. In P. Norton, M. Stewart, F. Tudiver, M. Bass, & E. Dunn (Eds.), *Primary care research: Traditional and innovative approaches* (pp. 138–158). Newbury Park, CA: Sage.

Lather, P. (1986a). Research as praxis. *Harvard Educational Review,* 56(3), 257–277.

—— (1986b). Issues of validity in openly ideological research: Between a rock and a soft place. *Interchange,* 17, 63–84.

Lofland, J. G., & Lofland, L. H. (1984). *Analyzing social settings.* Belmont, CA: Wadsworth.

McWhinney, I. R. (1989). *A textbook of family medicine.* New York: Oxford University Press.

Patton, M. Q. (1990). *Qualitative evaluation and research methods* (2nd ed.). Newbury Park, CA: Sage.

Penayo, U., Jacobson, L., Caldera, T., & Burmann, G. (1988). Community attitudes and awareness of mental health disorders: A key informant study in two Nicaraguan towns. *ACTA Psychiatry Scandinavian,* 78, 561–566.

Sanjek, R. (Ed.). (1990). *Fieldnotes: The makings of anthropology.* Ithaca, NY: Cornell University Press.

Smith, A., & Kleinman, S. (1989). Managing emotions in medical school: Students' contacts with the living and the dead. *Social Psychology Quarterly,* 52, 56–69.

Spradley, J. P. (1979). *The ethnographic interview.* New York: Holt, Rinehart & Winston.

Stein, H. F. (1990). Bridging the gap via context: An ethnographic clinical-training model. In H. F. Stein & M. Apprey (Eds.), *Clinical stories and their translations* (pp. 149–175). Charlottesville: Altheide.

Weller, S. C., & Romney, K. A. (1988). *Systematic data collection.* Newbury Park, CA: Sage.

DATE DE RETOUR   L.-Brault